THE UNSEEN WAR

Published in cooperation with the RAND Corporation

THE  WAR

Allied Air Power and the
Takedown of Saddam Hussein

BENJAMIN S. LAMBETH

Foreword by Gen. T. Michael Moseley, USAF (Ret.)

Naval Institute Press
Annapolis, Maryland

Naval Institute Press
291 Wood Road
Annapolis, MD 21402

Library of Congress Cataloging-in-Publication Data
Lambeth, Benjamin S.
  The unseen war : allied air power and the takedown of Saddam Hussein / Benjamin S.
Lambeth.
     pages cm
  Includes bibliographical references and index.
  ISBN 978-1-61251-311-9 (pbk. : alk. paper) — ISBN 978-1-61251-312-6 (ebook) 1.
Iraq War, 2003–2011—Aerial operations, American. 2. Iraq War, 2003–2011—Campaigns.
3. United States. Central Command—History. 4. Air power—United States—Case
studies. I. Title.
  DS79.76.L347 2013
  956.7044'348—dc23

                                                                              2013017743

♾ Print editions meet the requirements of ANSI/NISO z39.48-1992 (Permanence of
Paper).
Printed in the United States of America.

21 20 19 18 17 16 15 14 13   9 8 7 6 5 4 3 2 1
First printing

CONTENTS

FIGURES, MAPS, AND CHARTS

FOREWORD

THE THREE-WEEK AIR OFFENSIVE THAT FIGURED CENTRALLY IN THE TOPPLING OF Saddam Hussein was a testament to air power's final maturation for the sort of high-intensity warfare that the major combat phase of Operation Iraqi Freedom represented. In both its independent strategic role and its enabling support to allied ground troops, that offensive reflected a culmination of all that the United States and its coalition partners had done by way of steady force improvement, doctrinal refinement, and realistic training since air power's breakthrough achievement during the first Persian Gulf War more than a decade earlier.

It was my special privilege to command and lead the many fine airmen who made possible that remarkable air power success story. Notwithstanding our unmatched combat systems and technology, it is our high-quality professionals at all levels whose devotion to mission and natural adaptability to overcome any challenge have rendered the American air weapon a unique asset to our nation. Those key shapers of events were backstopped in every way by the able contributions of the United Kingdom and Australia, whose respective air contingent commanders, then Air Vice-Marshal Glenn Torpy of the RAF and then Group Captain Geoff Brown of the RAAF, were my partners from the start of our planning to the final execution of the campaign. It speaks volumes for the uncommon reservoir of talent that they brought to the fight that both of these outstanding airmen later went on to head their respective air forces.

In the years since those eventful three weeks, the United States and its allies have been consumed by lower-intensity counterinsurgency operations in which kinetic air attacks have been largely overshadowed by ground combat—to a point where some observers suggest that the sort of cutting-edge applications of air power that were so pivotal in 2003 have since been superseded by a new form of warfare in which high-technology weapons have become irrelevant. That notion could not be further removed from the realities of today's world. The era of major wars entailing existential threats to the United States and its closest allies has not ended. Demands for the most lethal and survivable air capabilities that our nation can muster will arise again. And there is much in our experience gained from the air war over Iraq in 2003 that offers a preview of how such capabilities might be best exploited in the future.

This important book, begun under my sponsorship as the commander of U.S. Central Command (CENTCOM) Air Forces, reconstructs the campaign's air contribution in impressive depth of detail. Along the way, it weaves a gripping narrative of the air war at multiple levels of analysis, from the perspective of the coalition's most senior leaders all the way down to individual airmen as they watched the campaign play out from their cockpits in the heat of combat. One of the many notable aspects of the air offensive explored in the pages that follow concerns the trust relationships that were first forged within CENTCOM during Operation Enduring Freedom against Al Qaeda and its Taliban hosts in Afghanistan in late 2001 and 2002. Those close interpersonal ties were sustained among the same top leaders as we segued into the campaign against Iraq's Ba'athist regime the following year. They were indispensable in accounting for the campaign's all but seamless cross-service harmony.

This assessment also explores the many challenges that those at the center of preparations for Iraqi Freedom faced, including the possibility of an Iraqi chemical weapons attack on both allied forces and civilian populations in the theater, our felt need to ensure that the Iraqi air force would not generate a single combat sortie, our determination to ensure that our air support arrangements were in closest possible accord with the land component's anticipated maneuver needs, and our resolve to keep Iraq's western desert free of any means for Hussein's forces to fire missiles into Israel and Jordan.

The compression of the campaign's phases into a concurrent air-land push into Iraq compounded those concerns. That last-minute development saddled CENTCOM's air component with the daunting need to satisfy multiple mission demands simultaneously—establishing airspace control, finding and destroying hidden Iraqi Scud or other tactical missiles, targeting Iraq's key command and control centers to impose rapid paralysis on the regime, and supporting the conventional land advance and associated covert activities by allied special operations forces in both southern and northern Iraq.

Finally, this book spotlights the many unique achievements registered during the three-week air offensive, such as the close integration of our naval and Marine Corps air assets into the overall campaign plan, meeting the immense challenges of securing adequate fuel supplies and tanker support, assigning a senior airman to the land component as my personal representative, and securing for the air component the all-important prerogative of approving the nomination of enemy targets without my having to defer repeatedly to higher authority for permission. It also explains the many valuable lessons that were driven home by the campaign experience, such as the importance of *organizing* the air component's elements for maximum effectiveness, *training* those elements routinely in peacetime in a way that fully exercises the entire command and control system, and *equipping* our forces with the most effective and survivable aircraft and systems.

Ben Lambeth's assessment offers an exhaustive account of the Iraqi Freedom air war in its most essential details. His adept telling of that story is conveyed with a tone of authority that will resonate instantly among the airmen who were actually there in the fight. Yet at the same time, it is written with a clarity of expression that will render it equally accessible to a wider circle of readers. I commend it highly to all who have an interest in air power and its key role in our nation's defense, and most particularly to the successor generation of military professionals in all services who will gain much of lasting value from its many informed observations and insights.

> —*T. Michael "Buzz" Moseley*
> General, U.S. Air Force (Ret.)
> Commander, U.S. Central Command Air Forces (2001–2003) and Chief of Staff, U.S. Air Force (2005–2008)

PREFACE

SINCE EARLY 2004, UNDER THE SPONSORSHIP OF U.S. AIR FORCES CENTRAL (AFCENT), I have pursued an in-depth assessment of the American and allied air contribution to the three weeks of major combat in Operation Iraqi Freedom that ended the rule of Saddam Hussein. This research followed an earlier AFCENT-sponsored study to assess the war against Al Qaeda and its Taliban hosts in Afghanistan between early October 2001 and late March 2002 in response to the terrorist attacks against the United States on September 11, 2001. That earlier effort is reported in Benjamin S. Lambeth, *Air Power against Terror: America's Conduct of Operation Enduring Freedom.*[1] The present book offers a similar treatment of the shorter but more intense air war that occurred over Iraq a year later when American air assets, aided substantially by the contributions of the British Royal Air Force (RAF) and the Royal Australian Air Force (RAAF), played a pivotal role in securing the immediate campaign objectives of U.S. Central Command. This book aims to fill a persistent gap in the literature on Operation Iraqi Freedom by telling that story as fully and credibly as the available evidence will allow.

---

1 Santa Monica, Calif.: RAND Corporation, MG-166-1-CENTAF, 2005. The abbreviation CENTAF (for U.S. Central Command Air Forces) was changed to AFCENT (for U.S. Air Forces Central) on March 1, 2009, after the U.S. Air Force leadership redesignated some of the Air Force's numbered air forces as formal warfighting headquarters. I use the abbreviation CENTAF throughout this book because it was CENTAF that planned and fought the three-week Iraqi Freedom air war in 2003.

ACKNOWLEDGMENTS

FOR THE INDISPENSABLE SUPPORT HE OFFERED TOWARD MAKING THIS BOOK POSSIBLE, I am indebted, first and foremost, to Gen. T. Michael "Buzz" Moseley, former U.S. Air Force chief of staff and, before that, commander of U.S. Central Command Air Forces (CENTAF) during the planning and conduct of the major combat phase of Operation Iraqi Freedom. General Moseley consented unhesitatingly to underwrite the research reported here as a sequel to an earlier study I prepared for CENTAF, also under his sponsorship, on the largely air-centric war against the Taliban and Al Qaeda in Afghanistan in 2001 and 2002. I am also grateful to Lt. Gen. Robert Elder, then vice commander of CENTAF, who lent abiding support to me in late 2003 and early 2004 after General Moseley had moved on to become the Air Force vice chief of staff. My thanks go as well as to Kathi Jones, CENTAF's command historian, who oversaw this effort throughout its long gestation.

I also am indebted to Vice Adm. David Nichols, deputy air component commander under General Moseley throughout the major combat phase of Iraqi Freedom; to Gen. Gene Renuart, director of operations at CENTCOM during the planning and initial execution of Iraqi Freedom; and to Lt. Gen. Daniel Darnell, principal director of CENTAF's combined air operations center (CAOC) at Prince Sultan Air Base, Saudi Arabia, during the workups to and initial conduct of Iraqi Freedom, for generously sharing their time and recollections of those aspects of the air war that most bear remembering.

I am additionally indebted to Gen. Gary North, who as CENTAF's commander in 2007 sponsored an extension of this effort so that I could flesh out my initial draft by incorporating the many reader reactions that I had received and take advantage of some important additional documentation bearing on the Iraqi Freedom air war that I had since accumulated. In this regard I owe particular thanks to Col. Douglas Erlenbusch, at the time CENTAF's director of operations, and to Maj. Anthony Roberson, then chief of General North's commander's action group, for commenting in detail on my initial analysis and helping me to refine my plan for this more expanded and enriched final product.

In connection with my treatment of the contribution of the United Kingdom's Royal Air Force (RAF) to the major combat phase of Iraqi Freedom, I am pleased to acknowledge the generous support that I received from Air Chief Marshal Sir Jock Stirrup, then chief of the air staff. During a four-day visit to the United Kingdom on October 26–29, 2004, I was able to meet virtually all of the RAF players who were pivotal in the planning and conduct of the RAF's contribution to the British role in the campaign, code-named Operation Telic. These included Air Chief Marshal Stirrup and his personal staff officer, then Group Captain Stuart Atha; Air Commodore Andy Pulford, who commanded the UK Joint Helicopter Command during the air war; Sebastian Cox and Sebastian Ritchie of the RAF's Air Historical Branch; then Air Marshal Glenn Torpy, at the time chief of Joint Operations, who had served as the British air contingent commander during Operation Telic; Air Chief Marshal Sir Brian Burridge, commander in chief of RAF Strike Command and the British national contingent commander up to and throughout the major combat phase of Iraqi Freedom; Air Vice-Marshal Andy White, air officer commanding of Strike Command's No. 3 Group; Group Captain Mike Jenkins, station commander at RAF Wittering; Group Captain Chris Coulls, station commander, and a group of his subordinate unit commanders at RAF Waddington; and Air Commodore Chris Nickols, commander of the RAF's Air Warfare Centre at Waddington.

With respect to my similar treatment of the role played by the Royal Australian Air Force (RAAF), I thank former chief of the air staff Air Marshal Ray Funnell, RAAF (Ret.), and Alan Stephens, former chief historian of the RAAF, who brought my initial working draft to the attention of Group Captain Richard Keir, then director of the RAAF's Air Power Development Centre. Group Captain Keir provided me with copious documentation on the RAAF's role in the three-week campaign that allowed me to fill in that still-outstanding gap in my chapter on the allied air effort.

For their valued help in providing me additional documentation, for commenting on all or parts of my earlier draft, and for otherwise helping to enrich this assessment in various ways, I wish again to thank General Moseley for the generous amount of time he shared from his busy schedule, first as Air Force vice chief and then as chief of staff, during three lengthy sessions in which he offered his reflections on those aspects of the war that mattered most from his perspective as the air component commander; Gen. John Corley, commander of Air Combat Command; Lt. Gen. Allen Peck, then commander of the Air Force Doctrine Center at Maxwell AFB, Alabama, and numerous members of his staff, particularly Lt. Col. John Hunerwadel and Lt. Col. Robert Poyner; Lt. Gen. Michael Hamel, then commander of 14th Air Force at Vandenberg AFB,

California, and Maj. Mark Main, chief of his commander's action group; Lt. Gen. Richard Newton, then with AF/A3/5, Headquarters U.S. Air Force; Lt. Gen. William Rew, CENTAF's director of operations and co-director of the CAOC during the three-week air war; Maj. Gen. Eric Rosborg, commander of the 4th Fighter Wing's F-15E Strike Eagles during the campaign; Air Vice-Marshal Geoff Brown and Group Captain Keir of the RAAF; Dick Anderegg, director of the Office of Air Force History; Maj. Gen. David Fadok and Col. Scott Walker, Air Force Studies and Analysis Agency; and Brig. Gen. Mark Barrett, commander, 1st Fighter Wing, and former executive assistant to the USAF vice chief of staff.

For their helpful comments on various earlier iterations of this study, I thank Brig. Gen. Michael Longoria, commander of the 484th Air Expeditionary Wing, who oversaw air-ground integration on the CAOC's behalf during the campaign; Col. David Hathaway and Col. Mason Carpenter, key principals in the CAOC's strategy division during Iraqi Freedom; Col. Lynn Herndon, director of the ISR Division in the CAOC during the air campaign; Col. David Belote, former air liaison officer to the commander of the U.S. Army's III Corps at Fort Hood, Texas; Brig. Gen. Rob Givens, an F-16CG pilot with the 524th Fighter Squadron during the three-week air war; Col. Matt Neuenswander, commandant of the USAF's Air-Ground Operations School at Nellis AFB, Nevada, during the campaign; Col. Gregory Fontenot, the principal author of *On Point: The United States Army in Operation Iraqi Freedom* (Naval Institute Press, 2005); Col. Thomas Ehrhard; Col. Charles Westenhoff; Lt. Col. Mark Cline, head of the CAOC's master air attack planning cell during the major combat phase of Iraqi Freedom; Lt. Col. Chris Crawford, who served with CENTAF's air component coordinating element to the land component during the campaign; Lt. Col. John Andreas Olsen of the Royal Norwegian Air Force; Maj. Scott Campbell, A-10 Division, USAF Weapons School; Robert Jervis, professor of political science, Columbia University; Sebastian Ritchie, deputy director of the RAF's Air Historical Branch; and Thomas Rehome of the Air Force Historical Research Agency at Maxwell AFB, Alabama, for his helpful archival research.

For their informed suggestions regarding my treatment of U.S. Navy and Marine Corps air operations, I extend my thanks to Adm. Tim Keating, CENTCOM's maritime component commander during the major combat phase of Iraqi Freedom; Adm. John Nathman, then commander, Naval Air Force, U.S. Pacific Fleet; Vice Adm. Lou Crenshaw, then director, assessments division, OPNAV N81; Vice Adm. Marty Chanik, then director, programming division, OPNAV N81; Adm. Mark Fitzgerald and Vice Adm. Tom Kilcline, successive directors of air warfare, OPNAV N78; Vice Adm. Dick Gallagher, then commander, Carrier Group Four; Vice Adm. Jim Zortman, then commander, Naval Air Force, U.S. Atlantic Fleet; Adm. Sandy Winnefeld, then executive assistant to the vice chief of naval operations; Vice Adm. Mark Fox, then commander, Naval Strike and Air Warfare Center; Capt. Brick Nelson and Capt. Flex Galpin, OPNAV N3/5 (Deep Blue); Capt. Chuck Wright, then director for naval aviation systems, Office of the Secretary of Defense (Operational Test and Evaluation); Capt. Calvin Craig, then OPNAV N81; Capt. Ken Neubauer and Cdr. Nick Dienna, both former Navy executive fellows at RAND; and Capt. Andy Lewis, then executive assistant to the commander, Naval Air Force, U.S. Atlantic Fleet.

Although this book is primarily a product of research, it is also informed by opportunities I was privileged to have in direct support of it to fly in six aircraft types that took part in Operation Iraqi Freedom. These experiences included a close air support training sortie in a Block 40 F-16CG with the 510th Fighter Squadron at Aviano Air Base, Italy, on May 19, 2004; a strike mission orientation flight in a Tornado GR4 with 617 Squadron out of RAF Lossiemouth on October 27, 2004; a fifteen-hour night combat mission over Afghanistan in an E-3C AWACS out of Al Dhafra Air Base, United Arab Emirates, with then Lieutenant General North, CENTAF's commander, in April 2007; three F-16B Topgun sorties and an F/A-18F Super Hornet sortie with the Naval Strike and Air Warfare Center at Naval Air Station (NAS) Fallon, Nevada, on August 4–6, 2009; a U-2 high flight to more than 70,000 feet on a surveillance mission orientation sortie with the 1st Reconnaissance Squadron at Beale AFB, California, on September 3, 2009; and an air combat training sortie in an F/A-18 with No. 2 Operational Conversion Unit at RAAF Base Williamtown, Australia, on March 26, 2010, with an RAAF pilot who took part in the major combat phase of Operation Iraqi Freedom. For these opportunities to gain firsthand conversancy with many of the tactics, techniques, and procedures that figured centrally in the Iraqi Freedom air offensive described in the chapters that follow, I am grateful to Lt. Gen. Glen Moorhead (Ret.), former commander of 16th Air Force; and Maj. Gen. Mike Worden (Ret.), then commander of the 31st Fighter Wing, U.S. Air Forces in Europe; Air Chief Marshal Stirrup; General North; Vice Admiral Kilcline, then commander, Naval Air Forces; General Corley; and Air Marshal Mark Binskin, chief of air force, RAAF.

Finally, I thank Barry Watts at the Center for Strategic and Budgetary Assessments and my RAND colleagues Nora Bensahel, Paul Davis, James Dobbins, David Johnson, and Karl Mueller for their helpful suggestions regarding all or parts of an earlier version of this book. I am additionally indebted to Harun Dogo, a doctoral candidate at the Pardee RAND Graduate School of Public Policy, for his outstanding and well-targeted research support. Finally, I owe a special note of thanks to my able editor, Mindy Conner, for her keen eye and deft touch in improving my use of words at every chance. As always, any remaining errors of fact or interpretation, sins of omission, or other failings in the pages that follow are mine alone.

ACRONYMS AND ABBREVIATIONS

AAA	Antiaircraft Artillery
AAMDC	Army Air and Missile Defense Command
ABCCC	Airborne Battlefield Command and Control Center
ACA	Airspace Control Authority
ACCE	Air Component Coordination Element
A-day	Day of Commencement of Air Operations
ADF	Australian Defence Forces
AEF	Air Expeditionary Force
AFB	Air Force Base
AGM	Air-to-Ground Missile
AHR	Attack Helicopter Regiment
AIM	Air Intercept Missile
ALARM	Air-Launched Antiradiation Missile
ALO	Air Liaison Officer
AMC	Air Mobility Command
AMRAAM	Advanced Medium-Range Air-to-Air Missile
AOC	Air Operations Center
AOD	Air Operations Directive
AOR	Area of Responsibility
APC	Armored Personnel Carrier
ARG	Amphibious Ready Group
ASOC	Air Support Operations Center
ASOG	Air Support Operations Group
ATACMS	Army Tactical Missile System
ATF	Amphibious Task Force
ATFLIR	Advanced Technology Forward-Looking Infrared
ATO	Air Tasking Order
AWACS	Airborne Warning and Control System
BCD	Battlefield Coordination Detachment
BCL	Battlefield Coordination Line
BDA	Battle Damage Assessment
BFT	Blue Force Tracker
C2IPS	Command and Control Information Processing System
CALCM	Conventional Air-Launched Cruise Missile
CAOC	Combined Air Operations Center
CAP	Combat Air Patrol

CAS	Close Air Support
CBU	Cluster Bomb Unit
CEC	Cooperative Engagement Capability
CENTAF	U.S. Central Command Air Forces
CENTCOM	U.S. Central Command
CFACC	Combined Force Air Component Commander
CFLCC	Combined Force Land Component Commander
CJSOTF	Combined Joint Special Operations Task Force
CJTF	Combined Joint Task Force
CIA	Central Intelligence Agency
CNN	Cable News Network
COIN	Counterinsurgency
CRAF	Civil Reserve Air Fleet
CSAR	Combat Search and Rescue
CTCB	Combined Targeting Coordination Board
CVW	Carrier Air Wing
D-Day	Commencement of Major Combat Operations
DASC	Direct Air Support Center
DCI	Director of Central Intelligence
DEAD	Destruction of Enemy Air Defenses
DGS	Distributed Ground Station
DSB	Defense Science Board
DSP	Defense Support Program
EASOS	Expeditionary Air Support Operations Squadron
EGBU	Enhanced Guided Bomb Unit
EUCOM	U.S. European Command
FAC	Forward Air Controller
FAC-A	Airborne Forward Air Controller
FDL	Fighter Data Link
FLOT	Forward Line of Own Troops
FMC	Fully Mission-Capable
FROG	Free Rocket Over Ground
FSCL	Fire Support Coordination Line
FTI	Fighter Tactical Imagery
G-day	Commencement of Ground Combat Operations
GAT	Guidance, Apportionment, and Targeting
GBU	Guided Bomb Unit
GMTI	Ground Moving Target Indicator
GPS	Global Positioning System
HARM	High-Speed Antiradiation Missile
HMS	Her Majesty's Ship
HMAS	Her Majesty's Australian Ship

IADS	Integrated Air Defense System
ID	Infantry Division
IFF	Identification Friend or Foe
ISR	Intelligence, Surveillance, and Reconnaissance
JASSM	Joint Air-to-Surface Standoff Missile
JCS	Joint Chiefs of Staff
JDAM	Joint Direct Attack Munition
JFCOM	U.S. Joint Forces Command
JFC	Joint Force Commander
JFN	Joint Fires Network
JIPTL	Joint Integrated and Prioritized Target List
JSOTF	Joint Special Operations Task Force
JSOW	Joint Standoff Weapon
JSTARS	Joint Surveillance Target Attack Radar System
JTAC	Joint Terminal Attack Controller
JTL	Joint Target List
JWICS	Joint Worldwide Intelligence Communications System
KI	Kill-Box Interdiction
LANTIRN	Low-Altitude Navigation and Targeting Infrared for Night
LGB	Laser-Guided Bomb
MAAP	Master Air Attack Plan
MAGTF	Marine Air-Ground Task Force
MAW	Marine Aircraft Wing
MEF	Marine Expeditionary Force
MEZ	Missile Engagement Zone
MIDS	Multifunction Information Distribution System
MOAB	Massive Ordnance Air Blast
MoD	Ministry of Defense
NALE	Naval Air Liaison Element
NAS	Naval Air Station
NIMA	National Imagery and Mapping Agency
NOFORN	No Foreign Nationals
NSTL	No-Strike Target List
NVG	Night-Vision Goggles
OIF	Operation Iraqi Freedom
OPLAN	Operations Plan
PAC	Patriot Advanced Capability
PGM	Precision-Guided Munition
RAAF	Royal Australian Air Force
RAF	Royal Air Force
RAN	Royal Australian Navy
RAPTOR	Reconnaissance Airborne Pod for Tornado

ROE	Rules of Engagement
RPG	Rocket-Propelled Grenade
RTL	Restricted Target List
SAM	Surface-to-Air Missile
SAR	Synthetic Aperture Radar
SAS	Special Air Service
SASO	Stability and Support Operations
SCA	Space Coordination Authority
SCAR	Strike Coordination and Reconnaissance
SEAD	Suppression of Enemy Air Defenses
SEAL	Sea-Air-Land Commando
SIPRNet	Secure Internet Protocol Router Network
SLAM-ER	Standoff Land Attack Missile—Extended Range
SOF	Special Operations Forces
SOLE	Special Operations Liaison Element
SPIN	Special Instruction
TACC	Tactical Air Control Center
TACP	Tactical Air Control Party
TACS	Theater Air Control System
TAOC	Tactial Air Operations Center
TARPS	Tactical Air Recainnaissance Pod System
TBM	Theater Ballistic Missile
TBMCS	Theater Battle Management Core System
TES	Tactical Exploitation System
TF	Task Force
TIALD	Thermal-Imaging Airborne Laser Designator
TLAM	Tomahawk Land Attack Missile
TOT	Time on Target
TPFDD	Time-Phased Force and Deployment Data
UAV	Unmanned Aerial Vehicle
UEx	Unit of Employment "X"
UN	United Nations
UOR	Urgent Operational Requirements
USAF	United States Air Force
USAFE	U.S. Air Forces in Europe
USN	United States Navy
USS	United States Ship
VFA	Navy Fighter-Attack Squadron
VMFA	Marine Corps Fighter-Attack Squadron
WCMD	Wind-Corrected Munitions Dispenser
WMD	Weapons of Mass Destruction
WSO	Weapons System Officer

Introduction

The first Persian Gulf War of 1991 ended inconclusively for the United States. Although it succeeded in its overarching goal of driving Iraq's occupying forces from Kuwait, it left Saddam Hussein in control as Iraq's dictator and saddled the United States and the United Kingdom with the costly burden of enforcing the subsequent United Nations (UN)–imposed no-fly zones over Iraq through Operations Northern and Southern Watch.[1] Twelve years later, Operation Iraqi Freedom, again led by the United States in close concert with Great Britain and now Australia as well, finally closed out that unfinished business in just three weeks of air and ground combat by bringing down Hussein's regime once and for all.

America's second war against Iraq differed notably from the first. Operation Desert Storm in January and February 1991 was a limited and purely coercive effort by U.S. and coalition forces to drive out Iraqi troops who had seized and occupied neighboring Kuwait nearly six months before in August 1990. More than five weeks of around-the-clock allied air attacks against Iraq's forces in the Kuwaiti theater of operations, during which time the only significant and sustained ground combat activity involved allied special operations units, rendered Iraq's armed forces ineffective. An equally relentless and punishing four-day combined air and ground offensive completed the routing of Iraqi forces from Kuwait, consolidated the allied military victory, and secured the coalition's declared objectives.

In sharp contrast, the major combat phase of Operation Iraqi Freedom conducted in the spring of 2003 was a true joint and combined campaign by American, British, and Australian air, land, and maritime forces to bring about a decisive end to Hussein's regime.[2] President George W. Bush and his administration anticipated that the operation would lay a foundation for the eventual establishment of a post-Ba'athist democratic government in Iraq. Unlike the first Gulf War, the 2003 campaign featured a concurrent and synergistic rather than sequential application of air and ground power. During the course of this three-week campaign, U.S. and British ground forces pressed from Kuwait to the outskirts of Baghdad within just eight or nine days. Allied air power quickly neutralized the already heavily degraded Iraqi air defense system and established uncontested control of the air, while at the same time paving the way for the allied ground thrust toward Baghdad by defeating Iraq's Republican Guard divisions even as a raging three-day sandstorm reduced visibility on the ground to mere meters.

This war was plainly one of choice rather than necessity.[3] Senior members of the Bush administration did not regard Hussein's regime as presenting an imminent threat to U.S. security at the time the campaign commenced. Nevertheless, given President Bush's understanding of Iraq's involvement in the development of weapons of mass destruction (WMD) and his fears that the September 11 attacks portended even worse future horrors, he judged that timely and decisive U.S. action against Hussein was warranted, with or without the legitimizing support of the UN.[4] "If we waited for a danger to fully materialize," he wrote in his memoirs, "we would have waited too long."[5]

Some argued at the time that the nation should await a stronger casus belli. To such arguments the president replied that he could not afford to wait passively lest a nuclear mushroom cloud over an American city prove Hussein's intent to provide weapons to Al Qaeda. In an interview on April 6, 2002, almost a year before the war against Iraq commenced, President Bush asserted: "The worst thing that could happen would be to allow a nation like Iraq, run by Saddam Hussein, to develop weapons of mass destruction and then team up with terrorist organizations so they can blackmail the world. I'm not going to let that happen."[6]

Several weeks before the war began nearly a year later, in a joint press conference with Prime Minister Tony Blair of Great Britain, the president reaffirmed that determination when he commented: "After September 11, the doctrine of containment just doesn't hold any water as far as I'm concerned."[7] By that time, his decision to go to war had been made. The resultant campaign's quick success in toppling Hussein's regime attested not only to the underlying fragility of Hussein's despotic rule and the general incompetence of his military forces (to say nothing of Hussein's personal incompetence in deploying them), but also to the mature and robust combat capability that the United States and its allies had steadily developed since Desert Storm.

The subsequent revelations that Hussein and his Ba'athist regime neither possessed WMD stocks nor had any direct complicity with Al Qaeda thrust the

United States and much of the rest of the world into an acrimonious debate over the wisdom and propriety of the administration's decision to initiate the war. That debate grew all the more heated with the steady rise of American combat fatalities (nearly 4,300, with more than 30,000 additional troops wounded, many grievously, as of mid-2011) and the 111,000 Iraqi civilian fatalities incurred as a result of the festering insurgency and sectarian violence that ensued in Iraq after the three weeks of major combat ended in early April 2003.[8] That costly follow-on war appeared by 2007 to be nearing an end as the result of a shift in U.S. strategy from brute-force efforts to defeat the insurgency to a more sophisticated counterinsurgency (COIN) approach that has offered a real sense of personal security to the Iraqi rank and file.

The Iraq war and its steadily mounting costs and implications were by far the most inflammatory issues in the 2004 U.S. presidential election campaign. One scholarly assessment that appeared three years after the regime takedown observed that the expanding insurgency in Iraq a year later "heightened popular reservations in the United States about the original decision to go to war and cast a shadow on the president's bid for reelection."[9] A subsequent formal determination by the special adviser to the director of central intelligence (DCI), following a fruitless year-long weapons hunt by the government's Iraq Survey Group, that the U.S. intelligence community had failed completely to call the facts of Iraq's prewar WMD involvement correctly, helped to keep the war a burning issue in the United States for more than five years. The capture of Hussein in December 2003, the successful completion of long-awaited Iraqi free elections in January 2005, and the creation of a functioning, if shaky, post-Hussein Iraqi democratic government have done much to dispel the controversy.[10] These and other developments since Hussein's regime was toppled in 2003 have led a growing number of once-doubtful observers to suggest that history may yet vindicate President Bush's decision to go to war against Iraq.[11] Whether this happens or not, the three-week period of major combat that ended Hussein's rule has now become an almost forgotten footnote to that more recent and still-unsettled history. Nevertheless, the three weeks of major combat that ended Hussein's rule are a casebook example of successful joint and combined warfare at the operational and tactical levels (leaving aside the administration's colossal *strategic* error of failing to understand that providing sufficient forces to ensure a stable and secure postwar Iraq was an essential ingredient of any effective coalition campaign plan, a failure that led to manifold and cascading unanticipated consequences).[12]

This book seeks to cast instructive light on the crucial but still largely unexplored and unappreciated contributions of allied air power to the successful first phase of the political transformation of Iraq. The initial round of Operation Iraqi Freedom was the first major U.S. combat involvement in recent times in which virtually *all* of the nation's force elements other than nuclear weapons played a role. Unlike the operations that preceded it—Desert Storm, Deliberate Force, Allied Force, and Enduring Freedom—the second Gulf War was not primarily an air war, even though allied air power, including the critical supporting air- and space-based intelligence, surveillance, and reconnaissance (ISR) aspects of it, contributed significantly toward setting the conditions for its outcome.

Nor was the major combat phase of Operation Iraqi Freedom predominantly a *ground* combat affair, despite the fact that nearly everything written about it has focused almost exclusively on the land portion of the three-week campaign. Even the most widely cited campaign assessment to have appeared to date, which purported "not to offer up a slice of the war" but "to prepare a contemporary history of the entire conflict," focused all but entirely on the allied land offensive.[13] A more scholarly treatment that likewise presumed to address the campaign holistically and that attracted considerable attention in academic circles when it first appeared also spoke solely to ground operations, even going so far as to characterize the major combat phase of Iraqi Freedom as a "mechanized" campaign—a term commonly used to denote *land* encounters between opposed armored forces.[14]

In fact, again leaving aside its gross underresourcing by the Bush administration at the most crucial strategic level, the campaign that brought down Saddam Hussein was an all but flawless undertaking by joint and combined forces that included not just the land component of U.S. Central Command (CENT-COM) but also the indispensable involvement of virtually the entire spectrum of allied air, maritime, and space capabilities. Indeed, each allied force element played a crucial role in producing the campaign's unexpectedly rapid outcome. Just as the toppling of Hussein's regime could not have occurred without a substantial allied ground presence to seize and occupy Baghdad, the ground offensive could not have succeeded with such speed and such a relatively small loss of friendly life (only 108 American and 27 British military personnel during the campaign's 23 days of formal combat) without the contribution of allied air power toward establishing prompt air supremacy over Iraq and then beating down enemy ground forces to a point where they lost both their will and their capacity to continue organized fighting.

By the same token, allied ground forces could not have progressed from Kuwait to the heart of Baghdad in just three weeks without the contribution of the ISR portion of the air- and space-power equation in providing ground commanders the needed confidence that their exposed flanks were free of enemy threats. That unblinking ISR eye over the war zone gave allied ground commanders at the brigade level and above a high-fidelity picture of the entire Iraqi battlespace along their line of northward movement. As a well-researched operational assessment of the campaign from the Army's perspective summed up the point that matters most in this regard, within just days after the start of CENTCOM's combined-arms offensive, the air component "transitioned from its initial strategic air focus to concentrate on destroying Iraqi ground forces. With a level of air-ground integration not seen before, the [air component's] CAS [close air support] and interdiction operations destroyed threatening Iraqis and enabled ground maneuver."[15]

Coming as it did only a scant year after Operation Enduring Freedom against the Taliban and Al Qaeda in Afghanistan, the war against Hussein's Iraq featured many of the same tactics and equipment innovations that were battle-tested during that earlier campaign. In addition, Iraqi Freedom's major combat phase was planned and led largely by the same principals who were responsible for the success of Enduring Freedom: President Bush; Secretary of Defense Donald Rumsfeld; the chairman of the Joint Chiefs of Staff (JCS), Gen. Richard Myers; the commander of CENTCOM, Gen. Tommy Franks; and CENTCOM's air component commander, Lt. Gen. T. Michael Moseley. The Iraqi Freedom experience thus offers a rare opportunity for analysts to examine the procedural and operational errors made during the six-month war in Afghanistan that were systematically corrected in time for the subsequent campaign against Hussein. Such corrections included bringing General Franks and General Moseley within the same time zone; providing more efficient target approval procedures to meet the expected higher demands for quick-response target attacks; and assigning a two-star air component representative, Maj. Gen. Daniel Leaf, to CENTCOM's land component commander, Lt. Gen. David McKiernan, to help ensure closer and more harmonious air-ground coordination.[16]

An especially novel feature of Iraqi Freedom was CENTCOM's decision to embed some five hundred civilian reporters within many of the combat units that would conduct the war in the interest of fostering journalistic accounts informed by firsthand observation. Correspondents had been kept away from direct contact with combat operations in Afghanistan, and General Franks felt that the resulting reportage had been "error-ridden and mediocre." Although initially reluctant, Franks eventually decided that reporters who were permitted to accompany allied fighting units into battle would "experience war from the perspective of the soldier or Marine" and would at least "get their facts straight."[17]

Allied air operations over Iraq did not benefit from such firsthand reportage, in part because there was no ready way for journalists to fly routinely in allied combat aircraft on strike missions, but even more so because various host-nation sensitivities precluded the presence of foreign journalists in CENTCOM's combined air operations center (CAOC, pronounced "kay-ock") in Saudi Arabia and at most other pertinent locations throughout the region from which they could have observed the conduct of the air war. Of the roughly 500 embedded reporters who accompanied U.S. forces, some 150 were in Navy ships at sea and nearly all of the rest accompanied U.S. Army and Marine Corps ground units during their advance into the heart of Ba'athist Iraq. A mere 28 journalists, roughly 6 percent, were assigned to selected Air Force units that operated from four locations.

Because most of the media representatives were embedded within CENT-COM's *ground* units, the vast majority of the subsequent firsthand journalistic accounts of the war have naturally been exclusively ground-focused.[18] For their part, allied air operations and their effects were all but unseen by outside observers. Air power's pivotal role during Operation Desert Storm in 1991 received far more media coverage because for all but the last four days of that war, coalition operations had little else to report. Video clips of precision weapon attacks from the cockpit displays of coalition strike fighters did not have to compete on the evening news with reporters in Kevlar helmets racing across the Iraqi desert in armored fighting vehicles.[19] The Air Force's top public affairs officer during the campaign, Brig. Gen. Ronald Rand, summarized the air component's predicament in this respect as CENTCOM was completing its final preparations for combat: "The challenge for us is finding ways—through real-time transmission of information and imagery, use of websites, interviews and everything else we can think of while respecting the conditions of our host nations—to create virtual access to our bases and people."[20]

Even after the major combat phase of Iraqi Freedom reached peak intensity and allied air attacks moved from fixed targets to Hussein's fielded forces, the vast majority of reportage was provided through the eyes of journalists who were embedded with advancing allied ground units. Anyone who watched the three-week campaign unfold solely through the lenses of CNN or Fox News would inevitably have been left with the impression that the war had been fought and won by allied soldiers and Marines equipped with tanks, rifles, and other appurtenances of land warfare. As the initial coordinating draft of a major postcampaign "lessons-learned" assessment of the war experience produced by U.S. Joint Forces Command (JFCOM, pronounced "jif-com") rightly pointed out in this regard, although the embedding of reporters with combat forces represented "a public relations milestone" for the U.S. armed forces, it also "supported coverage of events and activities only within the view of the embedded reporter. Without a balance of coverage to provide context and perspective, embedded reporting could not always, in itself, provide comprehensive understanding of the overall effort."[21] That was an understatement when it came to the almost completely unrecognized contribution of CENTCOM's air component.

To be sure, televised video clips showed U.S. Navy and Marine Corps strike fighters being launched from aircraft carrier flight decks and Air Force aircraft operating from selected forward land bases. Those images, however, did not convey the full extent and accuracy of CENTCOM's bombing effort and its profound physical and psychological effects on Iraqi ground forces, which were overwhelming in their contribution to the course and outcome of the three-week campaign. Anthony Cordesman correctly pointed out that regardless of the "near-reversal" of media coverage from Desert Storm to Iraqi Freedom, it was CENTCOM's "ability to tailor new *joint* mixes of ground-air-sea power to the needs of a particular campaign that proved decisive."[22] Similarly reflecting on how the air war over Iraq in 2003 "received far less media attention than did the air effort in 1991," military historian Williamson Murray and Maj. Gen. Robert Scales commented that notwithstanding "the spectacular footage of the massive [allied air attacks] on the Iraq government's infrastructure, . . . the reporters and cameramen in Baghdad could offer little insight into the purpose and context of these missions." Moreover, they added, "the air campaign was competing with hundreds of TV and newsprint stories from reporters embedded in ground units. Yet the importance of the air campaign should not be underestimated."[23]

The chapters that follow begin with a review of the high-level planning that took place in Washington, D.C.; at CENTCOM's headquarters at MacDill Air Force Base (AFB), Florida; and at the headquarters of Central Command Air Forces (CENTAF) at Shaw AFB, South Carolina, to prepare for the campaign and the subsequent mobilization and deployment of allied forces. The book next turns to early kinetic and nonkinetic air operations undertaken to prepare the Iraqi battlespace for the impending war. This discussion is followed by a reconstruction of the air war in its most significant operational and strategic dimensions, with occasional vignettes of experiences at the tactical level to depict how the air war looked to those who fought it at the point of contact with the enemy.

The book concludes with a synopsis of the Iraqi Freedom campaign: what worked well; unanticipated problems; and identifiable shortcomings in execution that might be corrected (and, in some cases, already *have* been corrected) by improved training, tactics, command and control arrangements, and equipment capability and interoperability. The final chapter also addresses the interaction of the involved services in pursuit of areas of activity that could stand further improvement in the continuing maturation of joint and combined warfare.

The Road to War

America's second war against Saddam Hussein was all but foreordained even before the dust from Desert Storm had fully settled. The authors of the first book on Iraqi Freedom to appear in print attributed the second Gulf War, "on the simplest level," to "the failure of the United States' policy makers to seize the victory its armed forces had so decisively won in the winter of 1991."[1] The allies had indeed succeeded in evicting Iraqi forces from Kuwait in less than six weeks of fighting, but the campaign did not break the back of Hussein's Republican Guard. More important, it left the Iraqi dictator in power and allowed him to convince himself that he had actually "won" the war, thanks to the incompleteness of the allied coalition's victory. Emboldened by Iraq's ostensible "victory," Hussein and his senior subordinates taunted the United States and the UN throughout the 1990s by repeatedly violating UN-imposed disciplinary resolutions and then retreating only at the last minute when confronted with a credible show of U.S. force.

In the early aftermath of Desert Storm, many observers asked why the coalition's ground advance had ended after only four days of uninterrupted progress, just as allied air and land operations had moved into what is commonly called the exploitation phase of war, with Iraq's occupation forces in Kuwait not just in retreat but in uncontrolled flight. In response, the first Bush administration's leadership insisted that the intent of the campaign plan and of the crucial UN and congressional resolutions that had authorized and enabled it had never been to knock Iraq out of the regional security picture altogether, but merely to free Kuwait from Hussein's military occupation. President Bush and his most senior associates further insisted that had the United States pressed all the way to Baghdad in an effort to end Hussein's rule, America would have found itself bogged down in an Iraqi quagmire.[2] Secretary Rumsfeld recalled in his memoirs that "regime change in Baghdad had not been among the U.S. goals when the pledge to liberate Kuwait was first made. The [first Bush] administration felt it would not have full coalition support if it [had] decided to continue on to Baghdad."[3]

Yet a full-blown invasion of Iraq with a view toward driving out Hussein and his Ba'athist regime was not the only alternative to declaring a cease-fire just as the allied air and land offensive had moved into high gear. A less ambitious and problematic alternative might simply have been for the coalition to continue its ongoing air-land assault against the fleeing Iraqi forces for another twenty-four to forty-eight hours. Not only would such an alternative have remained within the spirit and letter of UN Resolution 678 authorizing the use of "all means necessary" to undo Hussein's conquest of Kuwait, it might also have broken the back of the Iraqi military and unleashed internal forces that might have brought down Hussein's regime on their own. Whether such an outcome would have ensued from the exercise of that alternative option will never be known. It remains, however, a telling fact of Desert Storm history that perhaps the war's single most memorable quotation—Gen. Colin Powell's confident assertion on the eve of the war, on being asked by a reporter what the allied strategy against Iraq's army would be, that "first, we're going to cut it off, and then we're going to kill it"—was only half correct.[4]

Hussein continued to pursue a confrontational policy toward the West throughout the decade that followed. He repeatedly violated the terms of the Desert Storm cease-fire arrangement and continued to pursue an active WMD

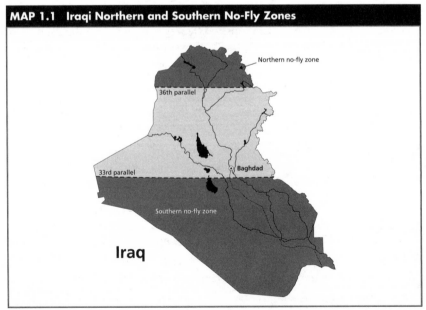

MAP 1.1 Iraqi Northern and Southern No-Fly Zones

Northern no-fly zone

36th parallel

33rd parallel

Baghdad

Southern no-fly zone

Iraq

Source: CENTAF

program, albeit ineffectively. Despite determined Iraqi obstructionism, UN inspectors uncovered evidence of a far-ranging effort to acquire chemical, biological, and nuclear weapons. Hussein's efforts to hamper the inspectors gave the clear impression that he had something to hide. Ultimately, he threw out the UN inspectors altogether. He also repeatedly challenged allied efforts to enforce the UN-approved no-fly zones over Iraq by firing on patrolling allied combat aircraft—some seven hundred times in 1999 and 2000, and more than one thousand times more by September 2002 (see map 1.1).[5] He even tried to have his Desert Storm nemesis, the first President Bush, assassinated in 1993 while the former president was on a personal visit to Kuwait.[6]

Throughout the eight years of the administration of President Bill Clinton, the United States pursued a series of measures that were more symbolic than determined either to force a change in Hussein's behavior or to terminate his transgressions once and for all. Those measures, which included cruise-missile attacks against unoccupied government buildings in the dead of night and the limited-objectives Operation Desert Fox air strikes that were conducted for four nights in 1998, served to reinforce Hussein's assessment of the United States as weak-willed and irresolute. In Secretary Rumsfeld's opinion, the Iraqi dictator "came to believe that the United States lacked the commitment to follow through on its rhetoric. He saw America as unwilling to take the risks necessary for an invasion of Iraq. As he would explain to his interrogators after his capture in December 2003, Saddam had concluded that America was a paper tiger. He interpreted the first Bush administration's decision not to march into Baghdad as proof that he had triumphed in what he called 'the mother of all battles' against the mightiest military power in history."[7]

Saddam Hussein was thus arguably fated for a decisive showdown with the United States. The terrorist attacks of September 11, 2001, almost certainly sealed Hussein's fate by fundamentally altering the Bush administration's assessment of the WMD threat, whether direct or indirect, posed by Ba'athist Iraq. The attacks also made it that much easier for the administration to persuade the American people of the merits of invading Iraq. The combination of the most consequential terrorist attack on U.S. soil in American history and Hussein's persistent defiance of UN resolutions prompted an ultimate conviction—right or wrong—among the administration's principals, most notably President Bush himself, that the Iraqi ruler had to be dealt with decisively before another event of the magnitude of September 11 occurred as a result of his malfeasance. As early as September 17, 2001, less than a week after the terrorist attacks, the president signed a memorandum directing the U.S. defense establishment to begin planning not only an offensive against the Taliban in Afghanistan, but one against Iraq as well.[8] As the Department of State under Colin Powell continued to pursue resolutions to enforce Iraq's compliance with the UN's edicts, the Department of Defense under Donald Rumsfeld began preparing for war.

Laying the Groundwork

Even before the first combat moves took place in Afghanistan in early October 2001, senior Bush administration officials already had their sights set on Hussein as a perceived problem to be dealt with at the earliest opportunity in the rapidly unfolding global war on terror. On the very afternoon of the September 11 attacks, Secretary of Defense Rumsfeld broached the idea of going after Iraq as an early possible response when he wrote a note to himself asking whether to "hit S.H. [Saddam Hussein] @ same time—not only UBL [Usama bin Laden]."[9] Immediately thereafter he directed Under Secretary of Defense Paul Wolfowitz to enlist the assistance of the Pentagon's legal staff in determining a possible Iraqi connection with bin Laden.

At a gathering of the president's emerging war cabinet the next day, Rumsfeld asked whether the terrorist attacks had presented an "opportunity" to go after Iraq.[10] Two months later, with Operation Enduring Freedom in full swing, President Bush followed up on that query. He pulled Rumsfeld aside after a National Security Council meeting on November 21 and asked him: "What kind of a war plan do you have for Iraq? How do you feel about the war plan for Iraq?"[11] He also asked Rumsfeld if a buildup for such a war could be initiated in a manner that would not be clearly apparent as such. With respect to this early attention to Iraq on the administration's part, Rumsfeld later attested to the almost instant crystallization of a sense among key administration leaders that the nation could no longer deal with terrorist threats from a defensive posture alone: "You can't defend at every place at every time against every technique.... You have to go after them. And you have to take it to them, and that means you have to preempt them."[12]

In his State of the Union address on January 29, 2002, Bush referred for the first time to what he called the "axis of evil" comprising Iraq, Iran, and North Korea (with the latter two reportedly included in part to make Hussein feel that he was not being singled out). The president added that the quest for WMD by these three countries and their known trafficking with terrorists had made for an intolerable convergence. Mindful of the September 11 precedent, he swore: "I will not wait on events while dangers gather."[13] Columnist Charles Krauthammer later characterized the speech as "just short of a declaration of war" on Iraq.[14]

On February 16, 2002, President Bush signed an intelligence order directing a regime change in Iraq and empowering the Central Intelligence Agency (CIA) to support the pursuit of that objective by granting the agency seven new tasks: to support Iraqi opposition groups, to conduct sabotage operations inside Iraq, to work with third countries, to conduct information operations, to run a disinformation campaign, to attack and disrupt regime revenues, and to disrupt the regime's illicit purchase of WMD-related materiel.[15] The following month, CIA director George Tenet met secretly with Massoud Barzani and Jalal Talabani, the leaders of the two main Kurdish groups in northern Iraq. The Kurds were still simmering over the failure by the previous Bush administration, in the early aftermath of Desert Storm, to follow through on its promise to support a Kurdish uprising, as a result of which Hussein's troops slaughtered thousands of Kurdish rebels. Tenet's message to the two Kurdish leaders was clear: this time the American president meant business. Saddam Hussein was definitely going down.[16]

While hosting British prime minister Tony Blair and his family at the Bush ranch in Crawford, Texas, on April 6, 2002, Bush declared to a reporter during a televised interview: "I made up my mind that Saddam needs to go. That's about all I'm willing to share with you." When pressed for further details, the president replied firmly: "That's what I just said. The policy of my government is that he goes." Bush added: "The worst thing that could happen would be to allow a nation like Iraq, run by Saddam Hussein, to develop weapons of mass destruction, and then team up with terrorist organizations so they can blackmail the world. I'm not going to let that happen." When asked how he intended to forestall such a dire development, Bush replied: "Wait and see."[17]

The major combat phase of Operation Enduring Freedom had barely ended in April 2002 before the administration began radiating indications that planning was under way for a major offensive against Iraq to begin sometime in early 2003. In his commencement address at West Point two months later President Bush declared: "If we wait for threats to fully materialize, we will have waited too long. We must take the battle to the enemy, disrupt his plans, and confront the worst threats before they emerge."[18] The president also unveiled his emerging idea of preemptive warfare, telling the assembled cadets: "The war on terror will not be won on the defensive."[19] Soon thereafter, Vice President Dick Cheney told the crew of the aircraft carrier USS *John C. Stennis* operating in the Arabian Sea: "The United States will not permit the forces of terror to gain the tools of genocide."[20]

On September 1, 2002, Bush told his national security principals that he wanted to secure a resolution by Congress to support military action against Iraq.

Toward that end, he invited eighteen key members of the Senate and House of Representatives to the White House on September 12 and reminded them that Congress had declared as far back as 1998, by an overwhelming majority, that a regime change in Iraq was essential. He further stressed that his administration had embraced that view with even greater conviction after September 11. He added: "Doing nothing is not an option."[21] Bush gave a speech to the UN General Assembly that same day emphasizing Iraq's repeated noncompliance with a succession of Security Council directives. While preparing for that speech he had told his speechwriter: "We're going to tell the UN that it's going to confront the [Iraq] problem or it's going to condemn itself to irrelevance."[22]

In a major speech on October 7, 2002, Bush declared that Iraq "gathers the most serious dangers of our age in one place." He added: "Facing clear evidence of peril, we cannot wait for the final proof, the smoking gun, that would come in the form of a mushroom cloud."[23] Two days thereafter, following two days of intensive debate, the House of Representatives passed a resolution empowering the president to use force in Iraq "as he deems to be necessary and appropriate." The resolution passed by a vote of 296 to 133, gaining 46 more votes than President George H. W. Bush had garnered in support of Operation Desert Storm in 1990. The following day the Senate approved the same resolution by a vote of 77 to 23.[24]

On November 8, 2002, the UN Security Council voted 15 to 0 in favor of UN Resolution 1441, which held Iraq in material breach of previous resolutions and ruled that if Hussein continued to violate his disarmament obligations he would face "serious consequences."[25] Such a resolution had been one of Prime Minister Blair's requirements before the United Kingdom would agree to participate in a war against Iraq, and he had already made that clear to Bush. Later, facing an imminent vote of confidence in Parliament, Blair urged Bush to seek a second UN resolution supporting action in Iran. In the end, the president elected not to do so, on the understandable ground that the 15-to-0 vote that had been registered for the first resolution would now be regarded as the expected bar, and that seemed unattainable a second time around.

In his third State of the Union address, on January 28, 2003, the president went further yet in putting the world on notice that the United States was determined to nip any assessed Iraqi threat in the bud: "Trusting in the sanity and restraint of Saddam Hussein is not a strategy, and it is not an option. . . . We will consult. But let there be no misunderstanding. If Saddam Hussein does not fully disarm, for the safety of our people and for the peace of the world, we will lead a coalition to disarm him."[26] The two most insistent charges presented by the Bush administration in justification of these threats were Iraq's alleged (and later discredited) ties to Osama bin Laden's Al Qaeda terrorist network and its suspected WMD program. In its Key Judgments section, a ninety-two-page National Intelligence Estimate flatly asserted that "Baghdad has chemical and biological weapons," even though the estimate's supporting text was reportedly more ambivalent.[27]

As the United States edged ever closer to war, palpable tensions arose among Bush's national security principals, with "Powell the moderate negotiator and Rumsfeld the hard-line activist."[28] *Washington Post* reporter Bob Woodward called Wolfowitz "the intellectual godfather and fiercest advocate" for a forceful end to Hussein's regime and portrayed Vice President Cheney as "a powerful, steamrolling force" throughout the lead-up to the war against Iraq.[29] Even before President-elect Bush was inaugurated—and nearly eight months before the September 11 attacks—Cheney had approached the outgoing secretary of defense, William Cohen, and indicated that he wanted to get Bush "briefed up on some things," to include a serious "discussion about Iraq and different options."[30]

Framing a Plan

In consonance with the administration's thinking in the early aftermath of the September 11 attacks, Secretary Rumsfeld directed that all regional combatant commanders review their contingency plans from the ground up, starting with the most basic assumptions. Rather than merely fine-tuning existing plans, he said, "we're going to start with assumptions and then we're going to establish priorities." At the same time planners were to make every effort to compress the planning cycle dramatically.[31]

In its planning for dealing decisively with Hussein, CENTCOM had the advantage of ten years of uninterrupted involvement in the region as a result of its mandate to enforce the southern no-fly zone. Effective intelligence preparation of the battlefield was thus less acute than it would have been had the command faced a totally new theater of operations, as had been the case for Afghanistan the year before. Because Iraq's main vulnerabilities and centers of gravity were well known and understood, discriminating and effective targeting could be conducted from the earliest moments of any campaign. On this point, the CIA had recently concluded that major military force would be required to topple Hussein's regime because any attempt to foment a coup by covert action from within would simply play to the regime's greatest strengths.[32]

While the major combat phase of Operation Enduring Freedom was still under way in Afghanistan, Rumsfeld called Franks on November 27, 2001, and told him that the president wanted the defense establishment to look at military options for Iraq. (Rumsfeld later recalled that the president had asked him on November 21 about the status of U.S. contingency options against Iraq. Rumsfeld had replied that there was already a plan in hand, but not one that the president would wish to implement."Get one," the president countered.)[33] Rumsfeld also asked Franks for the status of CENTCOM's planning in that regard. Franks replied that his command's existing Operations Plan (OPLAN) 1003-98 for Iraq was essentially just Desert Storm II and characterized it as "stale, conventional, predictable," and premised on a continuing U.S. policy of containment.[34]

The basic OPLAN 1003-98 was roughly two hundred pages long. More than twenty annexes on logistics, intelligence, and individual component operations added an additional six hundred pages.[35] The plan had last been updated after the conclusion of Operation Desert Fox in 1998, yet it remained troop-heavy and did not account for subsequent advances in precision attack and command and control capability. It outlined an assault on Iraq intended to overthrow Saddam Hussein by an invading force of 500,000 troops, including 6 Army and Marine Corps divisions, to be led by air attacks and followed by a surfeit of armor. Rumsfeld characterized the plan in his memoirs as essentially "Desert Storm on steroids."[36]

In response to Rumsfeld's incessant prodding for more imaginative alternatives, Franks developed a new approach that was dominated by a matrix of seven so-called lines of operations and nine "slices," the latter a concept that had been suggested earlier by Rumsfeld.[37] The lines of operations embraced various ways of influencing Iraqi behavior, either singly or in combination. The "slices" sought to define the assumed centers of gravity of Hussein's Ba'athist regime. The underlying idea of this new approach was to exploit not just military force but all elements of national power in going simultaneously after all identifiable regime vulnerabilities.

Franks' proposed seven lines of operations were intended to minimize the amount of brute force that would be needed to bring down the regime. They included kinetic operations consisting of precision attacks by both air- and surface-delivered firepower; unconventional warfare involving Special Operations Forces (SOF) activities throughout Iraq; operational maneuver by high-speed and high-mobility Army, Marine Corps, and British ground forces; influence operations involving information and psychological warfare; support for opposition groups, to include the Kurds and disaffected Shia groups; diplomacy, including civil operations after the major fighting was over; and humanitarian assistance to Iraqi civilians.

Franks described the nine slices of Iraqi vulnerabilities in his proposed concept of operations as "a series of pillars, a kind of Stonehenge that supported the weight of the Ba'athists and Saddam Hussein."[38] The slices entailed leadership, notably Saddam Hussein, his two sons, and his innermost circle; internal security, including Iraq's Special Security Organization, Fedayeen Saddam (Saddam's Martyrs), with a strength of between 20,000 and 40,000 fanatic paramilitary troops, the Iraqi intelligence service, the Directorate of General Security, and the command and control network; and finally Iraq's WMD infrastructure, Republican Guard forces, regular army, land and territory, civilian population, and commercial and economic infrastructure.

These two overlapping constructs—the lines of operation and the slices—produced a matrix of combat options and Iraqi vulnerabilities consisting of sixty-three intersections that ranged over the full spectrum of identified military, diplomatic, and economic instruments that the United States and any allied coalition could employ in an effort to topple Hussein's regime (see figure 1.1).

Franks further proposed three generic force employment options as a basis for a more detailed weighing of alternatives. His robust option assumed unrestricted combat and combat-support operations conducted from Turkey, Egypt, Saudi Arabia, Kuwait, and other Persian Gulf states. It further assumed freedom for CENTCOM to stage forces from forward operating locations in Central Asia, as well as from Hungary, Romania, and Bulgaria, and from U.S. aircraft

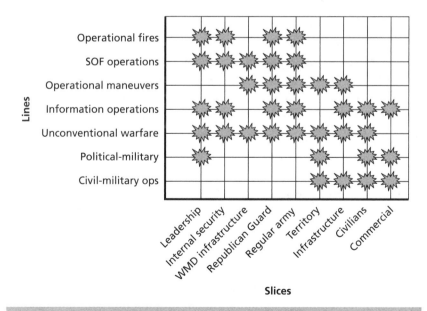

FIGURE 1.1 General Franks' Lines and Slices Matrix

Source: American Soldier

carriers operating in the Mediterranean Sea, Red Sea, and North Arabian Gulf. This option offered the advantage of simultaneous or near-simultaneous operations. As Franks put it to Rumsfeld: "Simultaneous operations, not separate air and ground campaigns, represent optimum mass."[39] Franks' second alternative, the reduced option, assumed participation by fewer supporting countries, reduced staging and support, a less concurrent introduction of forces, and a more conventional sequencing of force employment, with initial air attacks followed by a ground offensive. His third alternative was the unilateral option, which would rely solely on U.S. aircraft carriers and on bases in Kuwait. The pattern of force employment would be absolutely sequential, with ground forces introduced only gradually after a prolonged air-only offensive. The unilateral option was, said Franks, "not an option we would want to execute."[40] In all three cases Franks envisaged the required buildup of allied forces in the region as an ebb and flow of assets under the cover of Operations Northern Watch, Southern Watch, and Enduring Freedom, so as to minimize the likelihood that Iraqi intelligence would detect an undeniably threatening trend.

On December 4, 2001, a week after his initial tasking by Secretary Rumsfeld, Franks briefed Rumsfeld and General Myers via secure video teleconference on the first iteration of his commander's concept for a war against Iraq, with the main objectives being regime takedown and elimination of any Iraqi WMD. Franks subsequently briefed this approach to the president on December 28. During the course of that briefing he indicated that he could set a start date for a planned offensive as early as April to June 2002 if a number of preparatory measures were undertaken in a timely way. Those preparatory measures (a dozen in all) included establishing the requisite interagency intelligence capability, commencing influence operations, gaining needed host-nation support, forward-deploying CENTCOM's headquarters and needed equipment, forward-deploying the lead Army division, and creating a sustainable logistical line of communications. They also entailed preparing to use the secondary CAOC at Al Udeid Air Base in Qatar in case the primary one in Saudi Arabia should not be available, positioning the lead Marine Corps force, preparing for combat search-and-rescue (CSAR) operations, surging a third carrier battle group to the region, pre-positioning other Marine Corps equipment, and pre-positioning aircraft at selected hubs around the world so that an air bridge would be in place and ready to move forces and equipment when they were needed.[41]

After Franks concluded his briefing to the president, Rumsfeld directed him to come up with an executable war plan within ten days. Franks put his component commanders to work toward that end, with each commander assigned a separate security classification compartment. Only his director of operations, Maj. Gen. Gene Renuart, and a few others were allowed to see the entire picture, with Renuart pulling the overall plan together for Franks.[42] Rumsfeld and Franks both later characterized the close interpersonal relationship that evolved between them during this time as "an iterative process."[43]

On January 7, 2002, Franks informed his inner circle at CENTCOM that his commander's concept would be the basis for OPLAN 1003V, a major redesign of OPLAN 1003-98 in response to specific tasking from Secretary Rumsfeld.[44] The strategic goals for 1003V were to bring down and drive out the regime of Saddam Hussein; to identify, isolate, and eliminate Iraq's WMD; to capture or drive out terrorists who had found safe haven in Iraq; to collect intelligence on terrorist networks in Iraq and beyond; to secure Iraq's oil fields and other resources; to immediately deliver humanitarian relief; and to help the Iraqi people restore and rebuild their country.

The operations order for 1003V, as summarized by CENTCOM's deputy air component commander, stated that the campaign objectives would be to minimize the strategic exposure of the coalition by a "fast and final" application of overwhelming force that would attack simultaneously along multiple lines of operation, work inside Saddam Hussein's decision cycle, be prepared for the achievement of "catastrophic success," and attempt to set the necessary conditions for Iraq's reconstruction once the Ba'athist regime was driven out.[45] The Bush administration's leadership accepted General Franks' concept and timetable, and the revised OPLAN 1003V became the "Generated Start" plan. Its underlying premise was that all allied forces would be in place before major combat operations commenced. The plan's new timeline allowed 30 days for preparation of allied airfields and pre-positioning of equipment (what Franks called the "enablers"), followed by 60 days to deploy the force forward, 3 to 7 days of offensive air operations before the start of ground combat, and 135 days of joint and combined operations to bring down Hussein's regime. The final committed force would number 300,000 military personnel, a larger force than had been fielded for Desert Storm, but with its required deployment time halved from 180 to 90 days.[46]

For its contribution to Generated Start, CENTAF divided Hussein's regime into three broad target categories: leadership, security forces, and the command and control network. With respect to fielded enemy forces, CENTAF wanted to persuade Iraqi ground units to surrender or cease resisting before allied ground forces contacted them directly. Failing that, Iraqi ground units would be attacked from the air until they were neutralized or destroyed. The underlying presumption here was that a focused combined-arms assault would bring about an early collapse of the regime. The principal concern entailed the extent of risk that could be tolerated in any effort to establish the required conditions for such an early regime collapse, particularly considering that the near-concurrent onset of air and ground operations would offer little time to assess the effects of the air offensive before allied ground forces were committed to combat.[47]

In response to tasking from General Franks, General Moseley established eleven air component objectives for the buildup of forces in the forward area and the subsequent campaign: (1) neutralizing the regime's ability to command its forces and govern effectively; (2) suppressing Iraq's tactical ballistic missiles and other systems for delivering WMD; (3) gaining and maintaining air and space supremacy; (4) supporting the maritime component commander to enhance maritime superiority; (5) supporting the land component commander to compel the capitulation of Republican Guard and regular Iraqi army forces; (6) helping to prevent Iraqi paramilitary forces from impeding allied ground operations; (7) supporting the needs of the SOF component commander; (8) supporting efforts to neutralize and control Iraq's WMD infrastructure and to conduct sensitive site exploitation; (9) establishing and operating secured airfields within Iraq; (10) conducting timely staging, forward movement, and integration of follow-on and replacement force enhancements; and (11) supporting CENTCOM's quest for regional and international backing. The main challenges that General Moseley saw standing in the way of meeting these objectives included streamlining a suitable command structure for conducting major theater war, standing up the alternate CAOC at Al Udeid Air Base in Qatar, seeing to the needs of theaterwide force protection, securing host-nation basing approval, and meeting expeditionary combat support requirements. General Moseley also underscored the severely limited number of available tanker aircraft for in-flight refueling support, significant fuel sustainment requirements, and multiple host-nation airspace challenges.[48]

General Franks and his staff also began discussing a "Running Start" option, in which covert operations would commence before the start of major combat. This discussion focused on what Franks called "strategic dislocators," such as Iraq's firing of Scud missiles into Israel. The prevention of that occurrence, which might provoke Israel to enter the war, was a top priority for CENTCOM because Israeli leaders had put the Bush administration on clear notice that they would not refrain from retaliating against Iraq during this impending war as they had done when Israel had endured repeated Scud attacks during Operation Desert Storm in 1991.[49] One way of avoiding that undesirable turn of events would be for allied forces to seize control of all potential Scud launch boxes in western Iraq as soon as possible.[50]

On February 7, 2002, Franks briefed CENTCOM's refined Generated Start plan to President Bush. This was the first time the president had been shown a plan that CENTCOM's leaders believed could actually be implemented. The plan required 225 days for completion, in a breakdown that Franks labeled "90-45-90": 90 days for laying the groundwork and moving forces to CENTCOM's area of responsibility, 45 days of aerial bombardment and SOF activities to fix Iraqi forces while CENTCOM assembled its ground force, and then 90 days of joint and combined operations to bring down the Ba'athist regime. The plan envisaged an invasion force reaching 300,000 toward the end, with 2 armored and mechanized infantry corps attacking from the south and a third from the north, should the Turkish government ultimately consent to allow CENTCOM to conduct combat operations from Turkish territory.[51]

On February 28, 2002, in what Woodward described as taking the lines of operations and slices "from starbursts on paper to weapons keyed on buildings and people," Franks briefed Rumsfeld on some four thousand potential targets that CENTCOM planners had identified from the latest overhead imagery.[52] Those target candidates ranged from leadership, security, and military force concentrations to individual ground-force and air defense units and facilities. They also embraced paramilitary forces, including Hussein's Special Security Organization (consisting of about four thousand personnel) and Special Republican Guard; command and control nodes; and more than fifty of Hussein's palaces. Key concerns at CENTCOM included the possibility of Iraq mining waterways, firing Scud missiles into Israel, torching the country's oil fields, and using chemical weapons (referred to colloquially as "sliming"). The possibility of such disruptive actions forced CENTCOM to compress the so-called shaping phase to an absolute minimum. (On this point, General Moseley later indicated that he had been sufficiently concerned over the possibility of a large-scale Iraqi use of chemical weapons that he arranged for a ninety-day food supply at every CENTAF bed-down location within range of a potential Iraqi air or missile attack.)[53]

On March 22, 2002, almost a year to the day before the start of Operation Iraqi Freedom, Franks gathered all of his component commanders for his first joint force "huddle" at Ramstein Air Base, Germany. Using an old SOF expression indicating that he was convinced that war was coming and that the time had come for CENTCOM to get serious about it, he told them: "Guys, there is a burglar in the house."[54] He added that CENTCOM's planning activity was no longer an abstract endeavor and that each component now had to begin focus on its likely operational tasking. For the air component, this meant, first and foremost, precise determination of probable target sets and timing. Outlining his 7 lines and 9 slices and his "90-45-90" plan for a 225-day effort, Franks added: "Don't let yourself believe that this won't happen."[55]

Franks emphasized his determination to have "joint planning for joint execution," with "no time [allowed] for service parochialism."[56] Yet despite that injunction, and not surprisingly, in hindsight, a pronounced divergence in outlook regarding how the campaign should begin soon emerged between CENT-COM's air component commander, General Moseley, and the Army's land component commander at the time, Lt. Gen. Paul Mikolashek. General Moseley insisted that he needed a minimum of ten to fourteen days, preferably more than that, of air-only operations to disable Iraq's integrated air defense system (IADS) before allied ground forces commenced their offensive. He particularly stressed the importance of beating down what his planners had taken to calling the "Super MEZ" (missile engagement zone) around Baghdad, which had remained untouched by periodic allied air attacks against various Iraqi IADS nodes inside the northern and southern no-fly zones throughout the twelve years since Desert Storm. Mikolashek, however, wanted the ground component to make the first move, not only to ensure timely seizure and securing of the endangered Rumaila oilfields but also to catch the Iraqis—who would naturally be expecting the war to begin with an air-only offensive—by surprise.[57]

Franks was reportedly uncomfortable with both men's perspectives, feeling that Moseley's prolonged air-only phase exceeded his anticipated needs, but also that Mikolashek's alternative concept of operations would take too long to get allied ground forces to Baghdad. While he worked to come up with a better solution, he asked General Moseley to start thinking about how the air component might "adjust" (i.e., degrade) Iraq's air defenses by responding more "vigorously" to Iraqi violations in the no-fly zones.[58]

In addition, General Moseley unfolded his first cut at a concept of air and space operations for a joint and combined air-land offensive. He stressed that the air armada that would figure centrally in any such offensive was not the one that took part in Desert Storm, Deliberate Force, and Allied Force. CENTCOM's air component had sharpened its combat edge dramatically since then in four important areas: (1) its command and control and ISR capabilities, including the Global Positioning System (GPS) constellation of navigation satellites, the E-3 Airborne Warning and Control System (AWACS, pronounced "a-wax") and E-8 Joint Surveillance Target Attack Radar System (JSTARS, pronounced "jay-stars") aircraft, and the RQ/MQ-1 Predator and RQ-4 Global Hawk UAVs (unmanned aerial vehicles); (2) its improved precision all-weather target attack capabilities that would allow CENTAF to engage multiple aim points with a single aircraft rather than the other way around; (3) its improved efficiencies in effects-based operations through more scaled and selective target destruction; and (4) its greatly improved hard-target penetration capability.

To expand on the important third point noted above, effects-based operations tie tactical actions to desired strategic results. They are not about inputs, such as the number of bombs dropped or targets attacked, but rather about intended combat outcomes. At bottom, they ensure that military goals and operations in pursuit of them are relevant to a combatant commander's core strategic needs. As such, they are better thought of as an organizing device rather than as a more narrow approach to targeting. A classic example of "effects-based targeting" is selectively and methodically bombing enemy ground troops or surface-to-air missile (SAM) sites to induce paralysis or to inhibit their freedom of use rather than attacking them seriatim to achieve some predetermined level of desired attrition through physical destruction.[59]

General Moseley further noted that CENTAF's air assets slated for deployment to the war zone would allow attacks against roughly 1,000 Iraqi target aim points per day. In the first category he listed as anticipated targets some 300 enemy IADS facilities, 350 airfields, and 250 systems for the possible delivery of WMD. In the second category he highlighted 400 identified leadership targets, 400 national command and control targets, 400 enemy security and intelligence facilities, 100 key lines of communications, and more than 1,000 potential counterland targets.[60] Two days thereafter, the JCS initiated a related planning exercise called Prominent Hammer aimed at assessing the practicality of OPLAN 1003V in such areas as transportation, its impact on U.S. forces worldwide, and its effect on the war on terror and on homeland security. Remarkably, not a hint of this planning exercise ever leaked to the press.[61]

Franks earlier had decreed that once the war order was given he would need forty-five days to deploy the initial force forward, air operations for another forty-five days, after which offensive ground operations would commence at day 90. He later concluded that ninety days before starting the ground push was an unacceptable length of time and began working on his lines of operations to compress the allotted time, in the process accepting a modicum of risk at the operational level in order to mitigate risk at the strategic level.[62] This phase compression inescapably complicated General Moseley's force apportionment challenge because he was facing a need to conduct five concurrent air battles: the Scud hunt in western Iraq, the establishment of theater air superiority, strategic attack against leadership and command and control targets in Baghdad and elsewhere, support to land-component and SOF operations in southern Iraq, and the same in northern Iraq.[63]

On March 28 General Moseley convened the first "merge" meeting of planners and operators engaged in the conduct of Operations Northern Watch and Southern Watch to discuss differences in special instructions (SPINs) for aircrews, command and control arrangements, and rules of engagement governing combat operations in each of the two no-fly zones. Because Northern Watch was being conducted under the auspices of U.S. European Command (EUCOM) rather than CENTCOM, this initial meeting provided early insights into what would sometimes prove to be a frustrating relationship between CENTCOM and its sister combatant command in trying to fight a war from several countries that were not in CENTCOM's area of responsibility. Also during this first merge meeting, CENTAF planners developed a first cut at determining the air component's likely munitions requirements. Although these assessed requirements would later undergo numerous changes at the margins, this early estimate gave CENTAF's logistics planners a clear initial look at the problem. In addition, the initial anticipated airspace plan and prospective SPINs for coalition aircrews were drafted for a major air war against Iraq.[64]

CENTAF's main operations planners convened their first so-called Dream Team meeting on April 17, 2002, to lay the groundwork for assembling a world-class combat plans team. General Moseley personally met with this group and discussed command and control issues and desired arrangements with respect to Marine Corps involvement in the joint air war to come, as well as best ways of incorporating ongoing Northern Watch operations, combat air patrol (CAP) locations for the defensive counterair mission, and the use of the nation's global power-projection capabilities. CENTAF's planners concurrently forwarded their initial master air attack plan (MAAP, pronounced "map"), drafted the previous February, to the Air Staff's Project Checkmate and to the Air Force Studies and Analysis Agency in Washington so that those expert groups could provide feedback regarding the adequacy of the draft MAAP for anticipated opening-night campaign needs. The feedback that the two groups provided included initial consideration of possible enemy GPS jamming efforts, with Checkmate providing a detailed GPS-jamming study that greatly helped CENTAF planners working to negate any such possible threat.[65]

CENTCOM's initial campaign plan envisaged only a single front advancing into southern Iraq from Kuwait. Concerned over that plan's possible insufficiency to meet prospective worst-case challenges that might arise once the campaign was under way, General Franks sought to explore the possibility of a second front that would concurrently move into northern Iraq from Turkey. (During Operation Desert Storm, Turkey's Incirlik Air Base had provided an important springboard for strike operations into Iraq.) He summoned the commanders and principal planners from CENTAF and from the land and maritime components to CENTCOM's headquarters in Florida for a high-level meeting on May 8–10, with the goal of synchronizing emerging ideas in that and a number of other areas. During that three-day meeting, Franks directed his component commanders to begin developing plans for a second-front option into northern Iraq from Turkey. He had little confidence that Turkey would go along with such an option, but he wanted the essential preparations undertaken anyway for an initial U.S. footprint in Turkey of 25,000 to 30,000 personnel.

The assembled participants also addressed the land component's emerging ground scheme of maneuver and the likely support it would require from the air component, as well as various other notional courses of action. CENTAF's planners henceforth remained intimately involved in all subsequent land- and SOF-component planning sessions throughout the joint force buildup. That close involvement led to the development of deep trust relationships across component and service lines that would pay off handsomely once major combat began.

In a synopsis of all CENTCOM deliberations to date on May 10, 2002, Franks reviewed with Rumsfeld what the latter called the "known unknowns." The two also addressed a variety of "unknown unknowns," one of which was the possibility that Hussein might somehow force the hand of the Bush administration before the latter was ready to be committed. At that still-early stage in the preparations, the only response options available to CENTCOM would involve coalition forces already deployed in support of Operations Northern Watch and Southern Watch. Those forces included a carrier air wing with 70 aircraft and an additional 120 land-based aircraft, which together could enable what CENTCOM called the Blue Plan with 4 to 6 hours' notice. A more robust White Plan could be executed with about 450 aircraft that could be moved to the region within 7 days of an Iraqi provocation. Finally, a Red Plan involving 750 to 800 aircraft—half the number that had been deployed for Desert Storm—could be readied within about 2 additional weeks to conduct a gradually escalating series of attacks while allied ground forces were deployed to the region for an eventual combined air-land offensive.[66]

General Moseley's chief strategist later recalled that

> the Blue, White, and Red plans were not developed as separate plans. Rather, they were all part and parcel of a single concept of

operations. As the air component began to execute Operation Southern Focus [described in detail below] and to become more provocative in its reactive strike activities, CENTCOM asked the CAOC's combat plans division to develop a list of possible Iraqi actions and the recommended response to each by coalition aircraft conducting missions in Southern Watch. The Blue list was a roster of response actions that could be handled by in-place Southern Watch forces with a fairly typical Southern Focus strike. A second set of more aggressive possible Iraqi actions was represented in the White category. Such possible actions would be met by a more robust response that would require enough aircraft to execute the sort of response options that had been reflected in Operation Desert Fox. The last category was the Red list of possible Iraqi actions. These actions would require even more aircraft and would lead to the commencement of OPLAN 1003V. Of course, we also realized that any Iraqi actions that triggered a Blue or White response could escalate into a Red response, requiring coalition air power to contain the Iraqis until the required ground forces could be deployed.[67]

CENTAF staffers, assisted by planners from CENTCOM's maritime component and from U.S. Air Forces in Europe (USAFE) headquartered at Ramstein, developed for each option a strategy that included a three-day MAAP, daily air operations directives (AODs), and an ensuing joint integrated and prioritized target list (JIPTL, pronounced "ji-pittle") for each day. The MAAPs for each day in each of the three graduated options were detailed all the way down to individual target types, assigned weapons, scheduled times on target, and weapon aim-point placement.[68]

The following day, Franks traveled to Camp David for a lengthy planning session with President Bush and his senior advisers. CENTCOM's commander proposed five notional invasion fronts: a western front dominated by SOF and air operations devoted to Scud hunting, a southern front consisting of the main axis of attack from Kuwait, an information operations front, a vertical attack on Baghdad by CENTCOM's air component, and a northern front through Turkey if the Turkish government would permit it (see map 1.2).[69]

On June 3, 2002, Franks outlined the modified Running Start plan to Secretary Rumsfeld. This concept, which envisaged starting combat operations before all allied forces were in position, entailed using the Blue, White, or Red air employment options as might be needed to maintain pressure on Iraqi troops

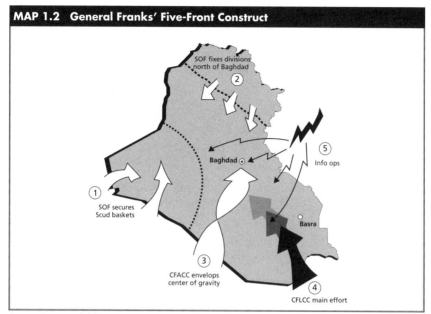

MAP 1.2   General Franks' Five-Front Construct

- ② SOF fixes divisions north of Baghdad
- ⑤ Info ops
- Baghdad ⊙
- ① SOF secures Scud baskets
- Basra
- ③ CFACC envelops center of gravity
- ④ CFLCC main effort

Source: American Soldier

while allied ground forces were flowing into the theater. Rumsfeld was intrigued by this concept and directed Franks to refine it further. Franks also presented what he called his "inside-out" notion for dealing with the possible scenario of having to confront a "Fortress Baghdad" at the end of the campaign. Its core idea was for CENTCOM to disable Iraq's command and control system and then to attack Republican Guard forces deployed nearest the capital first, to prevent them from concentrating in the center of Baghdad and hunkering down for a prolonged urban fight that would risk turning the city into a "Mesopotamian Stalingrad."[70] Attacks would then work from the center of the city outward to prevent any Republican Guard or Iraqi regular army troops from entering. (In connection with the inside-out approach, Franks noted that Republican Guard formations positioned within and around Baghdad would be vulnerable to precision air attacks.) Franks subsequently reconvened his component commanders at Ramstein on June 27–28 and directed them to shift their planning emphasis from Generated Start to Running Start.

The initial seeds of 1003V envisaged a multipronged air-land attack into southern Iraq from Kuwait and into northern Iraq from Turkey, with heavy covert SOF involvement to pave the way before the formal start of the war. CENTCOM's initial proposal called for about 250,000 ground troops, including 3 armored divisions. Under relentless prodding from Secretary Rumsfeld, however, that number was whittled down to 2 Army divisions and 1 Marine Expeditionary Force (MEF). The refined plan also placed greater reliance on precision bombing and close air-land coordination with both SOF and conventional ground forces.[71] The plan underwent more than two dozen revisions before it was finally accepted in turn by Secretary Rumsfeld and President Bush.[72] As attested by these progressively refined options, it was becoming clear that Franks was edging not toward a Desert Storm II–type force, but instead, in Woodward's words, "toward a lighter, quicker plan that was more complex, with lots of moving pieces."[73]

CENTAF's main effort in support of this process in July 2002 entailed integrating key personnel from the Royal Air Force (RAF) into the emerging air options planning effort, thus embedding the RAF professionals who would soon serve with the British air contingent in the CAOC intimately into CENTAF's planning staff at Shaw AFB. These allied staffers soon became completely enmeshed in the concurrent development of the joint air operations plan, the MAAP for the first three days of the campaign, and the JIPTL, as well as in associated planning for munitions requirements and for the bed-down of forces throughout CENTCOM's area of responsibility. The initial RAF cadre also joined actively in the further refinement of the target list. This early cooperative work led to the development of deep and enduring trust relationships that paid off well when these same personnel later assumed key positions in the CAOC during the final fine-tuning and execution of OPLAN 1003V (see Chapter 4). Staffers from the Air Force Doctrine Center at Maxwell AFB, Alabama, also took part in a concurrent effort by CENTAF planners to consider the emerging air operations plan from a doctrinal perspective, particularly with respect to cross-command relationships and possible jurisdictional issues that might arise between CENTCOM and EUCOM for any forces that would operate out of Turkey.

On August 5, 2002, Franks and Renuart briefed President Bush and the National Security Council on Generated Start, Running Start, and a new concept called Hybrid Start that combined key elements of the first two. Generated Start still envisaged a 90-45-90 timeline. Running Start was a variation on Generated Start that envisaged a 45-90-90 timeline, with a forward flow of allied ground forces and no-notice aerial bombardment commencing simultaneously, followed by 90 days of "decisive combat operations" and 90 days more for complete regime takedown. Hybrid Start embraced four successive phases. Phase I envisaged 5 days to establish an air bridge to the region, including the mobilization of the Civil Reserve Air Fleet (CRAF) if need be, followed by 11 additional days to move allied forces forward. Phase II would entail 16 days of offensive air and SOF operations. Phase III envisaged 125 days of joint and combined major combat operations aimed at bringing down Hussein's regime. Phase IV would entail postwar stability operations of an open-ended and unknowable duration.[74]

On August 6, 2002, Franks directed his component commanders to replace their focus on the Running Start concept with an emphasis on the faster Hybrid Start. Phase I of the latter plan entailed "preparation." Phase II was called "shaping the battlespace." Phase III was "decisive operations." Phase IV was "posthostility operations." Franks later recalled that he envisaged Phase IV as possibly lasting "years, not months," and thought it "might well prove to be more challenging than major combat operations," although those pronouncements came well after the postcampaign insurgency had already entered full swing.[75]

As General Franks continued to busy himself with these high-level coordination activities, General Moseley and his staff hosted a major warfighter conference at Nellis AFB, Nevada, during the week of August 5–9, 2002, that included representatives from CENTCOM, its subordinate components, the four services, and the United Kingdom. One agenda item entailed further refining CENTAF's anticipated munitions requirements for the looming campaign within the context of CENTCOM's recently evolved Hybrid concept of operations. Although the provision of munitions to joint warfighting commands is a service responsibility, CENTAF's planners worked closely with their counterpart service representatives to ensure that General Moseley would have the full spectrum of needed weaponry from all services. Toward that end they organized a separate gathering of concerned parties aimed at brokering an interservice "munitions trade" to ensure that the munitions required to meet the air component's needs would be on hand when the time came.[76] Also during this conference, General Moseley's counter-Scud working group, led by a team of experts from Air Combat Command headquarters at Langley AFB, Virginia, got down to work in earnest.[77] A senior CAOC staffer later recalled of this crucial meeting that "key concepts of operations were either developed or refined, and relationships between and among the involved staffs were further strengthened."[78]

CENTCOM planners identified December through February as the ideal time window within which to initiate the campaign's formal combat operations. Iraqi ground force training was least intensive during that period and was conducted at the individual unit level rather than in larger and more cohesive formations. The period from December through March was also deemed to offer the best weather window because high winds and sandstorms typically commenced in March and April, with summer heat following soon afterward. Franks assumed that his troops would be fighting in hot and uncomfortable sealed garments to protect themselves against chemical and biological weapons. Because fighting in summer temperatures that could reach as high as 130° Fahrenheit was to be avoided at all costs, ground operations had to start no later than April 1.

On August 14, 2002, the president's national security adviser, Condoleezza Rice, chaired a principals' meeting to discuss a new draft national security presidential directive titled "Iraq: Goals, Objectives and Strategy." This document stipulated that the overarching aim of the United States was to free Iraq from Ba'athist rule in order to eliminate its WMD and end threats by Iraq to its neighbors, utilizing all instruments of national power and with a coalition if possible, but alone if necessary. It stressed the need for any invasion plan to demonstrate that the American goal was to liberate rather than conquer Iraq and decreed that the underlying strategy must show that the United States "is prepared to play a sustaining role in the reconstruction of a post–Hussein Iraq."[79]

That same day, Franks and Renuart again met with Rumsfeld, this time to discuss targeting. Concern over the need to avoid collateral damage at every reasonable cost led to the development of more than 4,000 target folders before the war started. CENTCOM also issued collateral-damage mitigation charts to all air operations planners detailing how specific weapons types should be employed against different kinds of targets to minimize unintended damage to adjacent structures such as homes and religious sites.[80] That concern, the British national contingent commander, Air Marshal Brian Burridge, later recalled, "informed everything we did . . . from kinetic targeting through to the way in which we dealt with urban areas."[81] Out of those roughly 4,000 possible targets CENTCOM planners had identified 130 as entailing a high collateral-damage risk, defined as the likelihood that an attack would kill 30 or more Iraqi civilians. That number was expected to diminish after the application of collateral-damage mitigation measures by CENTCOM. Franks indicated that the proper servicing of 4,000 targets could require as many as 12,000 to 13,000 separate munitions for individual target aim points, because it could take from 4 to 12 munitions to achieve desired effects against some targets.[82]

The land component's overall scheme of maneuver envisaged a two-pronged ground assault, with the Army's V Corps pressing northwesterly from Kuwait through the Karbala gap and directly on to Baghdad, and the Marine Corps' First Marine Expeditionary Force (I MEF) also attacking northwesterly from Kuwait into the Mesopotamian plain that lay between the Tigris and Euphrates Rivers and ultimately joining up with the Army contingent as both simultaneously neared Baghdad. The plan was for both the Army and Marine

Corps combat elements to bypass any cities that lay directly in the path of their advance to Baghdad, neutralizing with air power and long-range indirect surface fire any Iraqi forces that might be capable of ranging the highways before those forces were engaged head-on.

At that point in the planning, Secretary Rumsfeld concluded that the time had come for him to enlist the support of the JCS. He convened a meeting of the service chiefs at which the president, but not General Franks, was present. The Air Force chief of staff, Gen. John Jumper, indicated that in his judgment, CENTCOM's emerging air plan was supportable and Iraq's IADS could be overcome, but he expressed concern over the possibility that Iraq could jam the signals from the space-based GPS constellation of twenty-eight satellites in semisynchronous orbit on which allied navigation and satellite-aided joint direct attack munition (JDAM, pronounced "jay-dam") weapon guidance depended. He warned that the Air Force's air mobility assets would be stretched thin but could nonetheless handle any likely tasking by CENTCOM. Both he and the chief of naval operations, Adm. Vern Clark, questioned whether the participating services would have sufficient stocks of precision munitions. Admiral Clark further voiced concern that continuing operations in Afghanistan would mean two concurrent wars, which could impose an unusually demanding stress on aircraft carrier availability. But he too concluded that all tasks that CENTCOM might levy on the Navy's carrier force could be accommodated.[83]

In September 2002 CENTAF planners visited each prospective air operating facility in CENTCOM's area of responsibility to present a detailed air operations plan and to elicit reactions from the wing commanders at each base with respect to the plan's supportability from their particular unit's perspective. Planners from the Royal Australian Air Force (RAAF) also were embedded with the CENTAF staff at Shaw AFB for the first time. In addition, on September 19, another "huddle" between General Franks and General Moseley and their respective staffs was convened to consider proper materiel flow to ensure that the required force would be in place and ready for combat on A-day, the first day of full-fledged offensive air operations.

General Moseley hosted a "quick frag" convocation at Shaw AFB during the week of October 7–11 that included key planners from the CAOC's strategy and combat plans divisions. The meeting also included representatives from CENTCOM's maritime component and aviators from the 3rd Marine Aircraft Wing who would take part in the campaign. A major aim of that gathering was to update the airspace plan and SPINs, develop workable identification friend or foe (IFF) arrangements and procedures, refine the air defense plan for

CENTCOM's area of responsibility, and begin fine-tuning the database that would be used to manage the daily air tasking process. A subsequent exercise of a similar nature organized by CENTAF at Shaw on October 15–25 included participation by representatives from USAFE, the maritime components of both CENTCOM and EUCOM, Project Checkmate on the Air Staff, the RAF, and the RAAF. Subject-matter experts on the conventional air-launched cruise missile carried by the B-52 were also there, as well as experts on the B-2 and F-117 stealth attack aircraft. From these two sets of discussions emerged refined AODs, JIPTLs, and MAAPs for the first three days of planned combat operations.[84]

By early November 2002 the essential elements of the final war plan were in place. A *Washington Post* account reported that "the broad outlines are now agreed upon within the administration," adding that several known aspects of the plan were being withheld from publication at the request of senior civilian and military officials in the Department of Defense. Those aspects included "the timing of certain military actions, the trigger points for other moves, some of the tactics being contemplated, and the units that would execute some of the tactics."[85] There were further reports that Kuwait had quietly sealed off a third of its territory for the use of American troops already deployed along the Iraqi border, that an effort was under way for U.S. aircraft to drop propaganda leaflets over Iraq urging Iraqi soldiers not to fight and to defect once the campaign began, that attacks against Iraqi IADS targets had been stepped up, and that CIA paramilitary units had already been inserted into northern Iraq to work with Kurdish resistance elements.[86] (Thanks to the successful prior efforts of Operation Provide Comfort and Operation Northern Watch to keep Iraqi forces from attacking the Kurds from the air, the Kurds had managed to establish an autonomous political sanctuary in northern Iraq.) Franks was cautiously optimistic about the likely cost of the impending invasion in friendly lives, telling some on the CENTCOM staff that he anticipated fewer than one thousand coalition casualties, and probably only several hundred.[87]

General Moseley summoned a Red Team of experts from Air Combat Command to Nellis during the first week of November so that the team could be briefed on all aspects of CENTAF's emerging air offensive plan.[88] In addition to personnel from Air Combat Command, the Red Team also included appropriate subject-matter experts from USAFE's 32nd Air Operations Group, the Navy's Deep Blue staff, the Air Staff's Project Checkmate, and other organizations. During the course of this meeting CAOC planners further fine-tuned the emerging MAAP for the first days of the impending air war. Because many of the Red Team invitees had by now been in-briefed on the emerging plan in full detail, General Moseley recruited them to join his battle staff.[89]

A related conference convened at Air Combat Command's Air-Ground Operations School (AGOS) at Nellis starting on November 2 focused on refining CENTAF's emerging concept of operations for kill-box interdiction and close air support (KI/CAS). Col. Matt Neuenswander, the AGOS commander at that time, later recalled that General Moseley directed the attendees to ensure that CENTAF's emerging KI/CAS plan was both workable and in close harmony with the Army's anticipated fire support needs. Among the main breakthroughs that emerged from this effort was a set of executable air-ground SPINs that enabled the fullest possible air-component support to engaged Army ground forces. Colonel Neuenswander later remarked that "General Moseley bent over backwards from the beginning to support the Army."[90] CENTAF's rear air operations center at Shaw concurrently underwent an expansion of its already numerous campaign management functions and was staffed by most of the air component's key planners and operators who would ultimately populate the forward CAOC at Prince Sultan Air Base. That effort provided yet another opportunity for the air component to dry-run the CAOC's anticipated battle rhythm while at the same time building working and trust relationships within the CAOC.[91]

The final campaign plan aimed at seizing key objectives as rapidly as possible, which inevitably dictated concurrent air and ground operations. The plan also sought to keep Iraq from using WMD against coalition forces, firing ballistic missiles at Israel, and sabotaging its own oil fields, while simultaneously discouraging the regular Iraqi army from fighting and also making every reasonable effort to keep Iraq's infrastructure intact. In Desert Storm such Iraqi infrastructure elements as electrical power generation, oil refineries and distribution and storage facilities, and transportation nodes—including bridges and rail junctions—had been attacked and destroyed on a substantial scale. CENTCOM was determined this time not to appear to be at war against the Iraqi people. The targeting of such infrastructure facilities during the first Gulf War had not achieved the intended goal of undermining Iraq's immediate warfighting potential. Such assets were also included on the no-strike list to spare the United States the burden of having to rebuild them after the war and because the expected rapid success of the ground offensive did not require their destruction.[92] Only command and control networks, regime security forces, select palaces, government ministries, command bunkers, counterair and countermaritime targets, and facilities associated with Iraq's ability to produce and deliver WMD were to be struck in the air component's initial "strategic" attacks.[93] Offensive air operations this time were to be studiously effects based, seeking desired outcomes and not just attacking targets for the sake of destroying them.

CENTAF's staff employed a strategy-to-tasks approach in accomodating these mission requirements. Targeting began with General Moseley's operational objectives, such as achieving and maintaining air and space supremacy. Operational objectives led to tactical-level objectives, such as neutralizing Iraq's IADS in order to mitigate its assessed threat potential. These tactical objectives drove such tactical tasks as destroying IADS command and control nodes by A+1 (the start of preplanned offensive air operations being A-day). The CENTAF staff assigned a desired effect to each tactical task (such as rendering the enemy's IADS unable to coordinate a coherent air defense throughout the campaign's major combat phase), a focus of effort (for example, on such key command and control enablers as the air defense operations centers, sector operations centers, and intercept operations centers), and a measure of physical achievement (for example, 100 percent of all targeted enablers destroyed). Each target aim point chosen was tied to a specific tactical task that could be traced back to General Moseley's operational-level objectives, which supported General Franks' operational objectives, which in turn supported the president's strategic objectives.[94]

CENTAF's planners spent most of 2002 and the initial months of 2003 studying Iraq first as a "system of systems," then looking at candidate targets, and finally drilling down to the aim-point placement level, consulting experts from a variety of concerned national agencies who worked closely with CENT-COM's intelligence and operations staffs. The Joint Warfare Analysis Center provided detailed targeting analysis of Iraq's airfields and communications nodes, as well as empirically substantiated recommendations as to how best to attack certain hardened targets using particular warheads, impact angles, and impact velocities.[95]

Lt. Col. Mark Cline, a key participant in this process, recalled that "CEN-TAF's planners and targeteers were figuratively tied at the hip for days at a time, producing several iterations of the first seventy-two hours of the air campaign from February 2002 all the way through the campaign's commencement on March 19, 2003." At a five-day conference in late January 2003, all of the concerned national agencies, CENTCOM's intelligence and operations staffers, and cruise-missile operations planners reviewed every aim point associated with the most significant targets. This process was then repeated in-theater at the CAOC. "Simply put," Cline said, "the placement of every aim point had a focused purpose."[96] In later characterizing this process in a press interview General Leaf observed: "We are working very hard to make the difficult intellectual leap to ask what it is we want to achieve instead of going right to the weapon, the platform, or the results in terms of rubble."[97]

CENTAF developed a strategy that envisaged six parallel and concurrent air offensive missions: strategic attack, to include strikes against leadership, regime security and support, command and control, WMD and associated delivery systems, and the Special Republican Guard; air and space supremacy, to include disabling Iraqi access to space support and neutralizing the Iraqi air force and IADS; operations to prevent Iraqi theater ballistic missile launches and to destroy any targeted missiles that might attack Israel or Jordan; counterland operations and providing support to the land component commander by interdicting and destroying Iraqi ground forces and providing on-call CAS; supporting the SOF component commander by means of airlift, ISR, and on-call strike operations; and supporting the maritime component commander and achieving maritime supremacy by neutralizing Iraqi weapons that might threaten allied vessels and lines of communication in the Persian Gulf.[98]

With respect to the prodigious amount of jet fuel that would be required to sustain such large-scale air operations, General Moseley's chief of strategy recalled:

> One of the huge constraints that was imposed on CENTAF's planners going into the initial workups for the air contribution to OPLAN 1003V was that we were not allowed to assume the availability of any provision of basing or fuel from Saudi Arabia. From the very beginning, we realized that this plan was not executable without Saudi basing and fuel, especially as the ever-evolving plan moved toward a near-simultaneous execution of air and ground operations. However, the Office of the Secretary of Defense kept this constraint on planning until the start of January 2003. Throughout the preceding months, CENTAF planners had continued to voice their concerns about the constraint until the Pentagon finally relented and gave General Moseley the go-ahead to seek basing and fuel from the Saudi government. The resultant short-notice permission granted by the Saudis for coalition basing in their country resulted in their having to contract thousands of fuel trucks to keep facilities such as Prince Sultan Air Base operating.[99]

As of January 2003, the overall campaign plan still envisaged 16 days of preparation (5 days to mobilize and establish an air bridge and 11 days to deploy the forces forward), followed by 16 days of shaping the battlespace (including continued SOF insertions and selective air-only attacks), leading into an anticipated 125 days of decisive offensive operations (including the start of major ground combat), and then a post-hostilities phase of unknowable duration.[100] The concept of operations for the opening round was simultaneity in an aerial onslaught that envisaged 80 percent or more of the target attacks being carried out with precision-guided munitions. An Air Force planner predicted that the air employment strategy would be "highly kinetic."[101] The plan entailed the delivery of some three thousand precision-guided bombs and cruise missiles within the first forty-eight hours—ten times the number used during the first two days of Desert Storm—directed against enemy air defenses, political and military headquarters facilities, communications nodes, and suspected WMD delivery systems, followed quickly thereafter by the start of the allied ground offensive. That prospect promised an anticipated air campaign that many in the media soon came to characterize by the term "shock and awe," an expression that had gained popular currency after Rumsfeld sent a note to General Franks in December 2002 suggesting that Franks and his planners at CENTCOM review a recent study bearing that title that maintained that precision weapons could neutralize an enemy's command and control and thereby achieve "rapid dominance" in major combat.[102]

On February 5, 2003, Secretary of State Powell briefed the UN Security Council on the Bush administration's many premises and assumptions regarding Iraq's presumed WMD efforts. With CIA director Tenet sitting behind him, Powell laid out a raft of raw intelligence facts and figures, recited Iraq's known UAV violations, alluded to indications of Iraqi links with Al Qaeda, and suggested that despite the contrasting religious fanaticism of Al Qaeda and secular nature of Saddam Hussein, "ambition and hatred are enough to bring Iraq and Al Qaeda together."[103] Powell argued for a UN resolution authorizing the use of "all necessary means" to prevent any such possibility from occurring. France and Russia, however, refused to endorse the stronger language. As always, Powell counseled caution. He later told President Bush privately that once Bush committed the nation to war, he would immediately become "the proud owner of 25 million people. You will own all their hopes, aspirations, and problems." (Powell and Under Secretary of State Richard Armitage characterized this cautionary injunction as the Pottery Barn rule—if you break it, you own it.)[104]

Flowing the Forces

On November 26, 2002, nearly a year to the day after the president had asked Secretary Rumsfeld to get started on a war plan for Iraq, General Franks sent a mobilization deployment order to Rumsfeld for his approval. This was the first concrete step taken by CENTCOM toward implementing the planning that had taken place throughout the preceding year. The order directed an incremental movement of forces, including two Navy carrier battle groups, and notified all tasked units to prepare to deploy their forces forward to the war-zone-to-be. Rumsfeld responded: "We're going to dribble this out slowly so that it's enough to keep the pressure on for the diplomacy but not so much as to discredit the diplomacy."[105] The issuance of this initial deployment order represented one aspect of a two-pronged approach, one part diplomatic and the other military.[106] The first deployment order approved by Rumsfeld was issued on December 6.

In January 2003, in one of the first major deployment moves for the impending invasion, Secretary Rumsfeld ordered the USS *Abraham Lincoln* carrier battle group to redeploy to the North Arabian Gulf from its holding area near Australia. The group was en route home from a six-month deployment in the Middle East but was directed to remain in CENTCOM's area of responsibility as a contingency measure. The USS *Theodore Roosevelt* battle group, just completing a predeployment workup in the Caribbean, received orders to move as quickly as possible to reinforce USS *Constellation*, already in the Gulf, and USS *Harry S. Truman* in the eastern Mediterranean for possible operations against Iraq. A fifth carrier battle group spearheaded by USS *Carl Vinson* moved into the Western Pacific to complement two dozen Air Force heavy bombers that had been forward-deployed to Guam. U.S. Air Force F-15E Strike Eagles were sent to Japan and Korea as backfills to cover Northeast Asia as USS *Kitty Hawk* moved from the Western Pacific to the North Arabian Gulf. The USS *Nimitz* carrier battle group got under way from San Diego in mid-January, wrapped up an already compressed three-week training exercise, and headed for the Western Pacific. Finally, the USS *George Washington* battle group, which had just returned home to the East Coast in December following a six-month deployment in support of Operation Southern Watch, was placed on ninety-six-hour standby alert.[107]

The six carrier battle groups that were committed to the impending campaign were the core of a larger U.S. naval presence comprising 3 amphibious ready groups (ARGs) and 2 amphibious task forces (ATFs) totaling nearly 180 U.S. and allied ships, 80,800 sailors, and 15,500 Marines. The carrier battle groups were all under the operational control of Vice Adm. Timothy Keating, 5th Fleet's commander and CENTCOM's maritime component commander. Admiral Keating wrote that "never before in history [had] one naval force projected such a concentrated amount of firepower and technology in such a small geographic area, and not since World War II [had] a larger logistics force been assembled."[108] In late February Secretary of the Navy Hansford Johnson and the chief of naval operations, Admiral Clark, testified before the House Armed Services Committee that the Navy's inventory of precision-guided munitions (PGMs) had been replenished since the drawdown that had resulted from major combat operations in Afghanistan and that the six forward-deployed carriers were adequately stocked for a possible conflict with Iraq. "Two years ago," Clark told the committee, "I could not have deployed the force structure I have out there and be in the green across the board."[109]

In yet another indication of ongoing preparations for major combat, the Air Force canceled its regularly scheduled bimonthly Red Flag large-force training exercise at Nellis AFB planned for the second week of January 2003 after its 4th Fighter Wing, an F-15E unit based at Seymour Johnson AFB, North Carolina, and the designated lead wing for that exercise, received deployment orders to CENTCOM's area of responsibility.[110] Two months later, the next scheduled Red Flag exercise was also canceled because at least 50 percent of the more than two thousand slated participants, many of whom were from the designated lead unit, the 48th Fighter Wing at RAF Lakenheath in the United Kingdom, could not marshal the assets needed for transportation to Nellis.[111] Throughput figures at Rhein-Main Air Base, Germany, for the months of January and February 2003 attest to the increased flow rate of U.S. military personnel being airlifted to Turkey, Qatar, and elsewhere in Southwest Asia. C-17 transports averaged 30 to 35 transits a day, two-thirds of which were bound for Turkey and Southwest Asia. The ramp activity at Rhein-Main, which one official there characterized as "staggering," saw upward of 32,000 passengers, or about 2,000 a day, in just the first half of February, up from a flow of only 10,000 passengers a month the previous November.[112]

The commander of the Air Force's Air Mobility Command (AMC) later called the airlift contribution to the buildup for Iraqi Freedom "one of the most challenging force deployments in recent memory."[113] AMC's tankers delivered 405 fighters and bombers and also supported 570 airlift and 80 ISR missions. The KC-135's multipoint refueling system and the KC-10's wing air refueling pods were indispensable force multipliers in supporting Navy, Marine Corps, and allied aircraft that used the probe-and-drogue in-flight refueling system. The deployment phase required 1,696 tanker sorties, with the tanker force offloading more than 245 million pounds of fuel and achieving a 92 percent effectiveness rate in 82 days of operations. At the peak of the deployment flow on March 6–7, 2003, AMC moved more than 180 aircraft, with more than 120 of those airborne simultaneously.[114] To support this effort, AMC used 222 KC-135s and 35

KC-10s that were deployed to 17 locations. This air mobility effort was conducted by a total-force team, with 51 percent of the deployed AMC force made up of active-duty personnel and 49 percent by Air National Guard and Air Force Reserve Command personnel during the peak periods of deployment operations.

On February 8, 2003, to support the deployment of U.S. military personnel who would take part in the campaign, Secretary Rumsfeld activated the CRAF Stage 1 long-range passenger segment, only the second CRAF activation in the program's fifty-one-year history (Operation Desert Storm having entailed the first). The American airline industry responded by providing forty-seven aircraft and aircrews to support AMC's aerial deployment and sustainment mission needs for the upcoming campaign. Because voluntary airline contributions exceeded Stage 1 levels, the long-range cargo segment of the CRAF was not needed. During the CRAF's time of activation, which lasted until June 18, 2003, civilian airliner contributions moved more than 250,000 U.S. troops into CENTCOM's area of responsibility.[115]

Moving coalition forces into the region quickly enough to deny the Iraqis sufficient time to react in an orderly way was not a trivial challenge for CENTCOM's planners. General Franks sought to pursue a calculated deception effort that had been proposed by General Moseley and General Renuart based on periodic deployment "spikes," with an expectation that initial media attention to those force increases would lapse once the deployment surge receded.[116] His intent was to accustom any observers with potentially unfriendly motivations to view such spikes as merely business as usual, at which point the spikes would begin to occur more often; as when the Navy moved in a second carrier battle group, had its air wing take part in Operation Southern Watch for a week or two, and then had it appear to depart the region. With respect to these periodic spikes, Franks proposed increasing the number of carriers on station in the region from one to three and then cycling them in and out to create a deceptive pattern. Similarly, he sought to portray U.S. troop increases in Kuwait as part of regional training exercises. His underlying intent was to acclimate Iraqi intelligence to "military expansion, then apparent contraction," with the flow of forces being managed as an apparent sine wave that no one would perceive as a buildup with warlike intent.[117]

General Moseley dispatched Major General Leaf along with an eleven-member air component coordination element (ACCE, pronounced "ace") to the land component's headquarters at Camp Doha, Kuwait, in early February 2003 to work closely with General McKiernan.[118] This move was meant to prevent the sort of near-debacle that had occurred a year earlier when the failure of the land component to communicate its intentions clearly to the CAOC had left the latter almost completely unprepared to supply urgently needed air support for Operation Anaconda in Afghanistan after the mission unexpectedly turned sour.[119]

Prompted by that near-miss experience, according to an A-10 pilot who was a key player in bringing effective CAS to embattled Army troops on the ground at the eleventh hour, General Moseley "directed a theater-wide CAS emergency conference where we took a hard look at command and control and discussed the very high target-approval levels and centralized execution that [had] posed restrictions on flight leaders in the air."[120] General Leaf's appointment as the head of the ACCE was one of the measures that ultimately emerged from that conference. Leaf was the first truly pivotal ACCE chief (the idea had been tested with the SOF community in Afghanistan after Anaconda), and he coordinated air-ground operations as General Moseley's senior representative to General McKiernan.[121] Seven ACCE teams were distributed throughout the various Army ground elements in the war zone, with General Leaf's being the largest.[122] The intent of this important liaison move, still unrecognized at that time in formal joint doctrine, was, in General Leaf's words, to provide an "extension of General Moseley" to the land component as a de jure emissary from the CAOC who knew the air component commander's intent, concepts, and priorities and who was authorized to speak for him without having to coordinate every decision when the exigencies of high-intensity combat warranted it. Leaf reported as the start of Iraqi Freedom neared: "I have been received as a team member—as a member of the tribe here—with open arms. And I've been very impressed with how diligently both the land component and the air component are working to understand the priorities, the intent [and] the requirements of the other." General McKiernan echoed this joint-minded spirit in noting that the ACCE presence at his headquarters "is indicative of the quality of the joint and coalition team assembled, and reflects the commitment of all the services to work together as one team to meet our objectives and desired effects on the battlefield."[123]

General McKiernan saw no need to reciprocate by creating a comparable two-star Army position in General Moseley's CAOC. An Army colonel served as the land component's battlefield coordination detachment (BCD) chief in the CAOC, but no senior Army counterpart to Leaf was assigned to the air component. The BCD had long since been battle-proven, and McKiernan deemed it sufficient. The commander of the 32nd Army Air and Missile Defense Command (AAMDC), Brig. Gen. Howard Bromburg, frequently visited the CAOC to meet with its leadership on theater air defense issues, but he was not considered a liaison officer.[124]

Allied flying units initially deployed with a 1.5 crew ratio, which was raised to 2 (that is, to 2 aircrews per aircraft) before the start of combat operations. CENTAF's planners had given all committed units advance warning of this requirement, recognizing that a crew ratio of 2 would be essential to support around-the-clock combat operations in a campaign of this one's expected duration.[125] The Air Force's Air Expeditionary Force (AEF) rotation experience amassed over the course of the preceding decade made that service's deployment of assets for the impending campaign easier because all of its committed players already had a running start. In anticipation of expected CSAR requirements, the Air Force identified forward operating locations near Iraq and positioned HH-60G helicopter detachments there to shorten the response time should an allied aircrew be downed.[126] In the end, Saudi Arabia approved CENTAF's request to use the CAOC at Prince Sultan Air Base and authorized the conduct of SOF reconnaissance and CSAR operations out of a small airfield at Arar near the Saudi border with Iraq's western desert.[127] Additional ramp space was also installed at Al Jaber Air Base and Ali Al Salem Air Base in Kuwait to accommodate anticipated strike operations and munitions storage requirements.[128]

The aircraft bed-down bases available to CENTAF by March 21, 2003 (the formal start of major combat operations) included Moron Air Base in Spain; RAF Fairford in the United Kingdom; Constanta, Romania; Sigonella, Italy; Souda Bay, Crete; Akrotiri, Cyprus; Cairo West, Egypt; Arar, Prince Sultan Air Base, and Tabuk in Saudi Arabia; Doha and Al Udeid in Qatar; Ali Al Salem and Al Jaber in Kuwait; Manama and Shaikh Isa in Bahrain; Al Dhafra and Minhad in the United Arab Emirates; Masirah, Seeb, and Thumrait in Oman; Diego Garcia in the Indian Ocean; and Sabiha Gokcen, Afyon, Diyarbakir, Corlu, and Incirlik in Turkey. Forces afloat included two U.S. Navy carrier battle groups in the eastern Mediterranean, three carrier battle groups in the North Arabian Gulf, and a Marine Corps ARG also in the North Arabian Gulf.[129] As a hedge against last-minute political contingencies involving Turkish support, General Moseley planned four alternative air tasking orders (ATOs) for A-day: the participation of the Mediterranean-based carrier air wings in the event of Turkish basing and overflight approval, Turkish tanker basing and Egyptian overflight approval, Egyptian basing and overflight approval, and an ATO that excluded the use of those two carrier air wings in the worst-case event of Turkey denying both basing and overflight into Iraq.

CENTCOM's worst fear in this respect came to pass on March 1, 2003, when the Turkish parliament rejected the Bush administration's request to stage

U.S. troops from Turkey into Iraq, denying General Franks the opportunity to use the Army's 4th Infantry Division (ID) to spearhead the opening of a northern front in Iraq. The rejection also meant the loss of two wings' worth of Air Force fighters and tankers based at Incirlik, as well as the loss of two additional Turkish bases that accommodated thirty-six KC-135R tankers. (An existing agreement between Turkey and the United States that allowed allied combat aircraft to operate out of Incirlik permitted only defensive operations in connection with the enforcement of the northern no-fly zone over Iraq.)[130] Were Turkey to deny overflight as well, that would mean the loss of the two Mediterranean-based carrier air wings for conducting attacks into the heart of Iraq and for supporting planned SOF operations in the north.[131] Despite these real and potential disappointments, however, General Franks felt that having the troops of the 4th ID deployed forward in twenty-seven ships in the eastern Mediterranean made for an effective deception option. Accordingly, those troops were left in position there. That decision had the salutary effect of keeping eleven regular Iraqi army divisions and two Republican Guard divisions tied down in northern Iraq.

The Air Force had already spent some $7 million to improve a number of Turkish air bases in preparation for a possible war against Iraq, and continued the improvements right down to the wire in the hope that so doing might help occasion a change in Turkish policy. Among the sites being built up was an air operations center (AOC) at Diyarbakir Air Base where the commander of USAFE's 16th Air Force, Lt. Gen. Glen Moorhead, would oversee allied air operations over northern Iraq in a supporting role under General Moseley. Diyarbakir was intended to serve as a mini-CAOC to support combat and airlift missions into the north and to be, in effect, a repeater node to General Moseley's master air operations center in Saudi Arabia. By the time combat operations began on March 19, however, only a small fraction of the needed bandwidth had been installed, and it would have taken hours for the mini-CAOC's computers to download the ATO. In addition, USAFE spent approximately $4 million on permanent improvements at Incirlik, where Operation Northern Watch had been headquartered since 1991.[132]

During his final meeting with the president and his national security principals in the White House on March 5, 2003, General Franks informed President Bush: "All key infrastructure improvements have been completed, and the required force is now in place in the theater."[133] Some 208,000 U.S. military personnel were in the region at that point, including a ground force of 137,000. Franks told the president and Secretary Rumsfeld that he could initiate the campaign any time the president was ready. Rumsfeld suggested that the president give Hussein an ultimatum to step down and leave Iraq with his two sons within forty-eight to seventy-two hours or be prepared to face a war that would end his rule. Franks concurred with Rumsfeld's proposal, noting that it would provide CENTCOM enough time to get all planned SOF assets across the border to secure the oil wells in the south and Scud launch boxes in the western desert. He also told the president that CENTCOM had identified twenty-four targets that would almost surely result in high collateral damage if attacked, and he explained CENTCOM's planned collateral-damage mitigation measures. Bush, however, refused to play a personal role in the selection of targets.[134]

By the end of the first week of March, *Theodore Roosevelt* and *Harry S. Truman* were on station in the eastern Mediterranean, and three more carriers—*Kitty Hawk, Constellation,* and *Abraham Lincoln*—were deployed in the North Arabian Gulf along with their embarked air wings, each of which included about fifty strike aircraft.[135] *Nimitz* was en route to the North Arabian Gulf to relieve *Abraham Lincoln,* which had been deployed for an almost unprecedented nine months.[136] The five carrier battle groups in position and ready for combat included upward of forty allied surface vessels and submarines armed with BQM-109 Tomahawk land-attack missiles (TLAMs, pronounced "T-lams"). In addition, Air Force F-15Es, F-16s, and F-117s were in place at Al Udeid Air Base in Qatar; tankers and various ISR platforms were forward-deployed to Prince Sultan Air Base; and more than two hundred additional aircraft, including F-16s and all of the Air Force's in-theater A-10s and land-based Marine Corps F/A-18s, were positioned at two bases in Kuwait, with still more in Oman, Turkey, and the United Arab Emirates, all ready to carry out a multidirectional attack. This fielded inventory of aircraft included fourteen B-52s operating out of RAF Fairford in the United Kingdom and B-1 and B-2 bombers deployed to the Gulf region and the British island protectorate of Diego Garcia in the Indian Ocean.[137] Four of the B-2s that would take part in the war were deployed on March 13 from Whiteman AFB, Missouri, to Diego Garcia.[138]

Marine Corps sea-based air assets in the North Arabian Gulf were concentrated in 2 amphibious task forces, ATF West and ATF East. The first consisted of the amphibious assault ships USS *Dubuque,* USS *Cleveland,* USS *Boxer,* and USS *Bonhomme Richard.* These 4 ships embarked a total of 24 AV-8B Harrier attack jets, 16 CH-53E heavy-lift helicopters, 18 AH-1W Cobra attack helicopters, and 9 UH-1N and 12 CH-46 helicopters with their aircrews and supporting equipment and personnel. ATF East consisted of the amphibious assault ships USS *Kearsarge,* USS *Bataan,* and USS *Saipan,* which carried roughly the same complement of aircraft as ATF West. Including its larger complement of land-based air assets, the 3rd Marine Aircraft Wing totaled 435 aircraft in-theater by the time it was fully in place, making it the largest air wing to deploy since Vietnam. All but 16 of the Harriers operated from *Bonhomme Richard* and *Bataan*.[139] Two squadrons of Marine Corps F/A-18Cs that did not fall under the command of the 3rd Marine Aircraft Wing were VMFA-323 and VMFA-115, which operated as a part of the air wings embarked in *Constellation* and *Harry S. Truman* respectively. Of the total F/A-18 contingent, 60 were Marine Corps Hornets attached to the 3rd Marine Aircraft Wing and were operating out of land bases in the region in anticipated support of Lt. Gen. James Conway's I MEF.[140] In all, allied aircraft committed to the impending Iraqi Freedom air offensive included 236 Navy and carrier-based Marine Corps F/A-18s, 56 F-14s, 35 EA-6Bs, 40 S-3Bs, and 20 E-2Cs. The Marine Corps also provided another 130 land-based strike aircraft and 22 KC-130 tankers. Those combined assets contributed to a coalition total of 1,801 aircraft, 863 of which were provided by the U.S. Air Force.[141]

The early force presentation planning that produced this massive deployment of American air assets was considerably more deliberate than had been the case in Operation Enduring Freedom, which entailed more of a crisis-response planning challenge because of the comparatively short notice that CENT-COM had been given after the September 11 attacks. During the course of this buildup, the Saudi government quietly approved CENTCOM's request to operate tanker aircraft from Saudi bases in support of allied strike operations (see chart 1.1 and map 1.3).[142]

As the start of combat operations neared, the commander of the *Constellation* battle group, Rear Adm. Barry Costello, indicated that planning to coordinate U.S. and allied air attacks had been completed and the battle group was "ready today if required to execute the mission."[143] The high-profile force buildup and such candid leadership statements denied the Bush administration any chance of achieving strategic surprise, but tactical surprise was still possible.

As the campaign's scheduled start drew closer, General Moseley listed as his chief planning and execution concerns the effective conduct of attacks on time-sensitive targets, high-value targets, and other targets designated for immediate strikes. He called for a strategic attack, decapitating the country's leadership while destroying the regime's command and control and security forces. One hundred percent Scud suppression and denial of WMD use were also essential. All of this required the prompt establishment of air and space supremacy. Other concerns included countermaritime operations against mines, coastal defenses,

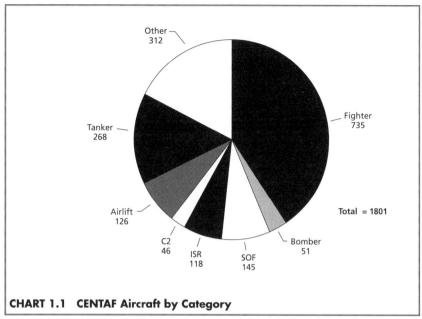

CHART 1.1 CENTAF Aircraft by Category

Source: CENTAF

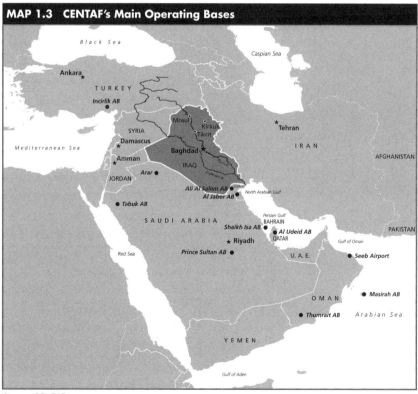

MAP 1.3 CENTAF's Main Operating Bases

Source: CENTAF

and Iraqi naval command and control. Counterland operations, including deep attack, CAS, and kill-box interdiction along with complete ISR coverage of Iraq and the surrounding area of operations were major parts of the plan. All of this would play a key role in establishing a forward tanker and high-value aircraft presence and a robust intratheater airlift capability while concurrently maintaining an effective theaterwide combat level of effort that extended to include continuing operations in Afghanistan and the Horn of Africa region.[144]

Throughout the course of CENTAF's planning for possible major combat operations, General Moseley and his key subordinates had tried to anticipate a number of "what if?" contingencies. These nightmare possibilities included a possible early salvo of Iraqi aircraft armed with a mix of conventional and WMD munitions on suicide missions against coalition forces; an early salvo of Iraqi civilian airliners loaded with conventional munitions, WMD, fuel, and perhaps hostages; an early salvo of Iraqi missiles carrying a mix of conventional and WMD munitions; an early salvo seeding of Iraqi mines into local waterways and the North Arabian Gulf; torching of the southern and northern oil fields and its possible impact on coalition air operations; an early WMD attack against CENTAF's airfields by SOF teams and other unconventional combatants; a more sustained attack on CENTAF's airfields by Al Qaeda and Iraqi internal security forces, particularly against leadership, fuel trains, personnel, food and water storage facilities, and key command and control nodes; and a D-day start later than March or April, which would expose troops and equipment to excessively high temperatures and affect the enthusiasm of host-nation support throughout CENTCOM's area of operations.[145]

Final Adjustments

Beginning in late 2002, the National Security Council, Office of the Secretary of Defense, and Agency for International Development all submitted nominations to CENTCOM for a no-strike list of potential targets to be avoided, based on solicited recommendations by various UN agencies and nongovernmental organizations.[146] The final no-strike list, which included such facilities as hospitals, water plants, and key nodes of Iraq's electrical power grid, eventually grew to include thousands of facilities that were duly incorporated into CENTCOM's target attack planning. The list was updated almost daily as the start of combat operations drew closer. CENTCOM also issued a collateral-damage-mitigation chart to inform target planners how destructive particular munition types would be against the cross-section of specific target types. Air operations planners divided metropolitan Baghdad into zones that were further subdivided into alphabetized sectors, with each building in each sector assigned a number.

In early December 2002 General Franks opened his forward headquarters in Qatar, where he conducted an Internal Look exercise like those convened by CENTCOM in 1990, 1996, and 2000. In preparation for it, General Moseley's "go-to-war" team first gathered at Shaw AFB to plan and "chair-fly" several ATOs against Iraq, in the process learning lessons that proved valuable when full-scale combat operations began the following March. The four-day exercise in Qatar involved the intimate participation of Franks and his subordinate component commanders and was publicly announced only in broad outline. It focused mainly on rehearsing the Hybrid plan for the first stages of what would become the major combat phase of Iraqi Freedom, homing in particularly on the exact requirements for troops and equipment as well as on the diplomatic clearances for basing and overflight that would be needed from key countries in the region.[147]

This Internal Look exercise also gave CENTAF an opportunity to hand-pick personnel for eventual CAOC assignments and to further cement early working ties with other important centers of air warfare expertise such as Project Checkmate on the Air Staff; the Navy's Deep Blue staff in the office of the chief of naval operations; the USAF Weapons School at Nellis AFB; the Naval Strike and Air Warfare Center at NAS Fallon, Nevada; and the Joint Warfare Analysis Center. In marked contrast to its earlier rushed experience of getting ready for Operation Enduring Freedom after the terrorist attacks of September 11, 2001, CENTAF had the opportunity to marshal the most expert and capable air warfare professionals available. In addition, CENTAF was able to take the first steps toward developing and testing the CAOC's proposed wartime processes, which provided an opportunity to train key personnel at all levels on new systems, to practice and refine CAOC procedures, and to form personal cross-service relationships that would pay handsome dividends once the campaign was finally under way. In many respects it was a "worthwhile dress rehearsal" for the entire CAOC staff in preparing for the challenges to come.[148]

The exercise entailed ensuring that the deployed tactical operations center at CENTCOM's forward headquarters in Doha had sufficient bandwidth to conduct combat operations and that it was adequately interoperable with CENTCOM's land, air, maritime, and SOF components.[149] The deployable joint tactical operations center, known in its prototype form as XC4I, was designed to provide command and control connectivity through commercially developed computer tools and common operating systems software, including near-real-time friendly force tracking.[150] Ultimately the center was deployed to provide a forward headquarters for General Franks and his staff.[151]

During the course of the Internal Look exercise, differences of view emerged between the air and land components over the planned sequencing of force employment during the campaign's opening round. General McKiernan, the land component commander, proposed that General Franks forgo the sixteen-day air-only offensive included in the Hybrid plan. As he had during the previous component commanders' meeting at Ramstein, General Moseley countered that the air component needed adequate time to weaken Iraqi air defenses and disable key leadership and command and control targets before any significant ground push could be safely undertaken.[152] Although it would ultimately be Secretary Rumsfeld's call, Franks split the difference between his two component commanders by ruling that the war would start with a determined SOF and air effort to secure western Iraq with the goal of preventing any Iraqi launch of theater ballistic missiles toward Israel, after which the air and ground offensives would commence almost simultaneously. This session convinced Franks that the Hybrid plan did not allow enough flexibility for adaptive planning.[153] Identified shortcomings, he later said, included "communications bandwidth problems, misinterpreted orders, timing-and-distance issues, [and] seams between elements of the joint force."[154] Allied commanders on the eve of Operation Iraqi Freedom reportedly had more than forty times the bandwidth that had been available during the 1991 Persian Gulf War, and that still proved insufficient to meet their anticipated needs.[155]

Air Marshal Glenn Torpy, the British air contingent commander, recalled that CENTCOM and the Bush administration had decided early on not to start the campaign with a preparatory air phase. The initial planning prior to that decision had followed the familiar template of Operation Desert Storm, with a discrete opening phase in which air attacks would shape the battlespace. But in early 2003, as the planning evolved and as operational-level intelligence continued to flow in from Iraq, the preparatory phase of air-only attacks was reduced from sixteen days to about five days. Torpy attributed the change to at least three considerations. First, CENTCOM's leaders realized the need to secure the oil fields in southern Iraq as quickly as possible; second, General Franks and the land component were concerned that a large ground force concentrated in a small area in Kuwait was vulnerable to Iraqi WMD; and finally, General Franks was convinced that close synchronization of the air and land components would offer the best chance of dislocating the Ba'athist regime and ending the campaign quickly.[156]

This reasoning eventually resulted in A-day and G-day (as the start of the air and ground offensives were respectively called) converging. The convergence entailed a risk in that it placed great pressure on General Moseley to undertake his five air-warfare tasks simultaneously and to prioritize his resources correctly in the process. Torpy noted that "the air component's nervousness in compressing the campaign was (1) would [General Moseley] have the resources to carry out those tasks, and (2) would he be able to execute, for instance, gaining air superiority in sufficient time for him to be able to do some of the other tasks?"[157] In the end, the near-simultaneous start of air and land combat would be enabled by the land component commander's willingness to rely on such organic platforms as his attack helicopters and Marine Corps fixed-wing strike fighters for the first few days, with the clear understanding that the air component would provide additional as-needed CAS should the coalition's ground offensive bog down, even if this might require diverting allied strike aircraft from regime, command and control, and WMD targets and a consequent major divergence from the initially planned air offensive.[158]

By late 2002, President Bush had privately decided that war with Iraq was all but inevitable, yet he continued with at least an appearance of diplomatic efforts. CENTCOM's deployment of forces was now under way at full speed, and the president asked Franks when the final go/no-go commitment point would be at hand. Franks replied that the president's point of no return would be when the first allied SOF teams were inserted on the ground in Iraq to commence offensive operations.[159]

At CENTCOM's request, General Moseley hosted a strategy conference at Shaw AFB on January 7–8, 2003, aimed at bringing all of the strategy team members up to speed with the permanent CAOC party. Later that month, instructors from the F-15C, F-15E, F-16, A-10, HH-60, and command and control divisions of the USAF Weapons School visited Shaw to offer quality-control checks on various aspects of the emerging air offensive plan in their specific areas of expertise. Many of these highly pedigreed subject-matter experts would later serve as tactical coordinators in the CAOC during Operation Iraqi Freedom.[160]

On January 11, 2003, Rumsfeld and the JCS chairman, General Myers, met with the president in the White House to brief the Saudi ambassador to the United States, Prince Bandar bin Sultan. General Myers gave Bandar an overview briefing on the war plan, outlining its anticipated start with an intensive bombing campaign aimed primarily at the Republican Guard, Hussein's security services, and command and control targets. After the briefing ended, Rumsfeld said to Bandar: "You can count on this. You can take that to the bank. This is going to happen."[161]

On January 20–24 CENTAF convened a targeting conference to produce an updated four-day MAAP to determine which target aim points had to be struck and in what order to achieve the desired effects. During this extremely labor-intensive planning session, representatives from CENTCOM, CENTAF, USAFE, the land and maritime components, I MEF, the CIA, the Defense Intelligence Agency, the National Security Agency, the National Imagery and Mapping Agency (NIMA), and the Joint Warfare Analysis Center examined each selected target and each individual weapon aim-point placement to ensure that General Franks' commander's intent would be met. A CENTAF participant later recalled: "This meeting was crucial, and although things would change, it provided the 95 percent targeting solution."[162]

CENTAF later convened another targeting conference focused expressly on U.S. air-launched cruise missiles, TLAMs, and the RAF's Storm Shadow missiles to ensure optimal targeting of those standoff-attack weapons. CENTAF planners deemed an early sorting-out of the many and varied intended targets for these weapons necessary in light of the large number of cruise missiles that would figure in the ultimate air offensive plan. Again, as participating CENTAF staffers later recalled, although new target information would inevitably occasion changes, "this conference provided the 90 percent solution and gave the cruise-missile planners ample lead time."[163]

The following month, CENTAF's core planning staff deployed forward en masse to the CAOC in Saudi Arabia to join up with their Internal Look teammates who were already in place there. On February 22–23, at General Moseley's direction, the planners convened yet another conference that was attended by the in-theater Air Force, Navy, and Marine Corps wing and squadron commanders and weapons officers whose flying units were slated to participate in the upcoming air war. In addition to getting updated on all aspects of the plan and on the latest SPINs, they all had an opportunity to "chair-fly" the A-day sequencing and deconfliction procedures that were crucial to enabling a serviceable ATO on the air war's opening day. A participating CENTAF planner later recalled of the convocation, "Given the complexity of operations, this conference paid large dividends in ensuring that the planners and executors were synchronized."[164]

Throughout February 2003 the CAOC staff undertook steps to ensure a smooth transition from Operation Southern Watch to OPLAN 1003V. The first step was to establish an around-the-clock rhythm of operations that would approximate the actual flow of a full-fledged air war. Second, the CAOC's standard operating procedures were amended to reflect CENTAF's new procedures that had been developed and refined in the most recent Internal Look exercise.

Third, and equally important, new systems such as the CAOC's MAAP toolkit were brought on line to give CAOC personnel training in their use. Finally, combat operations in connection with Operation Southern Focus (discussed in detail in Chapter 2) were gradually increased in both intensity and breadth of target coverage to generate more of a full-up air campaign tempo. A last-chance targeting and commanders' conference was held on March 2, 2003, to allow CENTCOM and CAOC planners their final major update with respect to planned target aim points, as well as to enable a final consensus between the CAOC's apportionment and targeting chiefs, on the one hand, and CENTCOM's operations and intelligence planners, on the other.[165]

Nearly all of the required weaponeering for CENTAF's planned operations had been attended to well in advance of the campaign's actual start. Yet CENTAF staffers would not have been able to complete this daunting process without marshaling the weaponeering talent of a variety of centers of excellence for such highly specialized work, such as Air Combat Command's 480th Intelligence Group and CENTCOM's maritime component, both of which provided indispensable targeting support.[166]

CENTAF staffers later recalled that the targeting information that had been available to them going into the war had been little short of "phenomenal." In their collective opinion, the ultimate success of the three-week air war was attributable largely to the extent of prewar collaboration that had taken place among CENTCOM, its subordinate warfighting components, and the national intelligence community. Proposed MAAPs for the first three days of the war were studied and reviewed down to the individual weapon aim-point placement level on at least three occasions at conferences attended by the national intelligence community's top experts on each target category. A final conference held at CENTCOM's forward headquarters in Qatar two weeks before the onset of major combat aimed at eliciting recommendations for final tweaks to the A-day MAAP capped off the effort. That individual target review and MAAP refinement was said to have been key to ensuring the successful execution of the A-day ATO and all that followed.[167]

Two weeks before the campaign's start, General Myers remarked to the press that were President Bush to decide to commit the nation to action, the ensuing war would unfold in a way "much, much different" than the forty-three-day Operation Desert Storm had in 1991. The JCS chair said that the goal this time would be a shorter war in order to minimize civilian casualties to the greatest extent possible. In fact, he said, the war might end before a battle for Baghdad was required. The best guarantee of a short war, he added, would be to impose "such a shock on the system that the Iraqi regime would have to assume early on [that] the end was inevitable."[168]

At roughly the same time, the director of the National Security Agency, Lt. Gen. Michael Hayden, decided, against all the inclinations of his community's tightly closed culture, to open up his agency's "national vaults" to American war-fighters at the tactical level, a move that would enable senior noncommissioned officers on the ground to tap directly into the most sensitive signals intelligence for gaining real-time awareness of ongoing Iraqi military activity of immediate tactical concern to them. This arrangement was reportedly provided by means of a computer chat room assigned the code name Zircon Chat. It offered CENT-COM unprecedented wherewithal for enabling combat operations informed by undeniably accurate real-time intelligence reporting at the tactical level.[169]

On March 4 General Franks arrived in Washington for final prewar brief-ings with the president and Secretary Rumsfeld. After a meeting of the Bush war cabinet on March 5, the last face-to-face encounter between the combatant commander and the administration's leadership in Washington, General Franks declared: "If the president of the United States decides to undertake action, we are in a position to provide a military option." Franks added: "There is no doubt we will prevail." He subsequently proceeded to his forward headquarters in Qatar, where he met with his land, maritime, and Marine Corps commanders, and then flew to Prince Sultan Air Base in Saudi Arabia for final consultations with Gen-eral Moseley. General Franks characterized what was about to unfold as "the most complex and fully integrated joint-service military operation in history."[170]

By March 17 it was clear that France would veto any attempted second UN resolution to empower the coalition against Iraq, and the president accordingly reaffirmed his determination to forgo any further effort at seeking such a reso-lution. White House press secretary Ari Fleischer told reporters: "The United Nations has failed to enforce its own demands that Iraq immediately disarm. As a result, the diplomatic window has now been closed."[171] Later that evening the president issued an ultimatum to Hussein and his two sons to leave Iraq within forty-eight hours. Should they fail to comply, Bush promised an attack "commenced at a time of our choosing [with the] full force and might" of the assembled coalition. The president also declared that "the United States of America has the sovereign authority to use force in assuring its own national security."[172] He added: "The United Nations Security Council has not lived up to its responsibilities. So we will rise to ours."[173] The wording of his warning left open the possibility that allied forces might attack in less than two days if Hus-sein openly refused to comply.

At that point during the final force buildup, the CIA reportedly had eighty-seven "Rockstars" agents at work inside Iraq communicating with their handlers via Thuraya satellite telephones, which the agency had determined that Iraqi intelligence could not intercept.[174] These agents provided updated and in some cases fresh intelligence on Iraqi SAM and antiaircraft artillery (AAA, pronounced "triple-A") positions, which CENTCOM subsequently geolocated by means of overhead imagery. Some agents reported that Iraqi unit commanders had said that they would refrain from fighting in the event of an allied attack. These announcements briefly raised hopes at CENTCOM for a possible capitulation strategy that would rely on surrendered Iraqi units for postwar stabilization efforts in Iraq.[175]

In a clear sign of Iraq's awareness that a major showdown was impending, Iraqi troops began moving military equipment into civilian areas and positioning combat aircraft, munitions, and communications equipment near warehouses, mosques, and schools. More than two hundred American, Canadian, Australian, and European peace activists flocked to Baghdad and elsewhere, including to the northern city of Kirkuk, to volunteer their services as human shields to protect Iraqi assets. More than half of those activists left in frustration shortly afterward when their Iraqi handlers insisted that they stay away from low-risk facilities like hospitals and instead cluster around such dual-use target candidates as electrical power plants, water pumping stations, and communications centers.[176] U.S. defense officials had identified Iraq's communications facilities as "extremely significant command and control targets."[177] A CENTCOM briefer warned obliquely that "if a government chooses to collocate those weapons with one of these protected sites, [the latter] lose their status under international law as a protected target."[178]

As the start of combat operations neared, General Leaf noted increasing concern on General Moseley's part that CENTCOM's air component might not be able to achieve, in a mere twenty-four hours, all of the strategic objectives that General Franks wanted completed before the start of the land offensive. General Moseley, Leaf recalled, was "especially concerned about having his support assets spread too thin."[179]

Assets in particularly short supply included aircraft for conducting suppression of enemy air defenses (SEAD, pronounced "seed") operations, ISR platforms, electronic jammer aircraft, and tankers. In particular, Moseley voiced concern that overtasking his air assets might jeopardize allied ground forces. He felt that if the planned attacks against potential Iraqi Scud capabilities and leadership targets could precede the ground push by at least a few days, he could then swing more assets to the south in support of coalition land operations when the time came. His concern grew even more pronounced when the Turkish parliament voted on March 1 to deny permission to the 4th ID's 16,000 troops to open a second front from the north, suggesting to some in the CAOC that a longer air-only offensive was now more than ever needed to offset the less-than-expected strength of allied ground forces. The land component's unit commanders, however, were determined to lose no time in commencing offensive ground operations because allied ground forces massed in place and waiting along the southern border of Iraq were highly vulnerable to enemy artillery and missile attacks. The land component also pressed to have the Iraqi artillery positions along the southern border within range of U.S. and British troops attacked and neutralized by Southern Focus sorties before the campaign got formally under way. CENTCOM elected to defer any such attacks until other operations were already in progress inside Iraq, believing that such precursor strikes would not fall within the broadened but still-limited mandate of Southern Focus and also would appear excessively provocative at a time when the command was still not ready to execute OPLAN 1003V.[180]

As the start of Iraqi Freedom neared, palpable tensions arose again between CENTCOM's air and land components, each of which was now tightly boresighted on its respective assigned tasks. Discussions at lower levels in each component took on a typically parochial tone, although both land and air commanders credited General Leaf and his ACCE staff with resolving major eleventh-hour differences between the two components. For example, during the back-and-forth between the components over the precise timing of G-day, General Leaf sought to ensure that ground commanders, in his words, "understood the risk and the airman's perspective" that would attend moving G-day up to precede the start of major air operations by twenty-four hours. The ensuing exchange provided the land component's unit commanders with "realistic expectations" of what the air component could provide them in the changed circumstances and thus "helped limit emotionalism." In a reflection on that important achievement, the land component's assistant chief of staff for operations, Maj. Gen. J. D. Thurman, recalled that General Moseley "told us before we started the war: 'If it was a [land component] target, it was [an air component] target.'"[181]

In the compromise arrangement that was ultimately worked out, General Moseley and General McKiernan shared the risk of compressed timing occasioned by CENTCOM's decision to start air and ground operations on the same day. General McKiernan further accepted that he would not have on call all of the dedicated CAS sorties that he might want during the first days of the ground offensive. General Moseley accepted a reduced length of time for establishing control of the air over Iraq and conducting attacks against Iraqi leadership and command and control targets. "The basic elements of the plan remained intact," General Leaf later said, but "the time lines changed. For example, given the need to support ground operations earlier in the war, it was expected to take longer to accomplish the destruction of regime [or] strategic targets." In the end, added Leaf, the tradeoffs that General Moseley had accepted in assigning targets in the midst of the competing priorities "turned out to be sufficient. The initial ground attack went very well, the Iraqi air force did not fly, and there weren't any other major surprises that further stretched air assets."[182]

Turkey's eleventh-hour refusal to allow coalition forces to use its airspace was a blow to planners. The Turkish parliament, mindful of the fact that Turkey had lost $100 billion after having supported allied combat operations in the 1991 Gulf War, also turned down a U.S. request to use Turkey as a launch point from which to insert some 62,000 U.S. troops into Iraq to open up a northern front.[183] The Bush administration promptly withdrew a promised $15 billion in aid to Turkey and continued to apply diplomatic pressure. In the meantime, thirty U.S. Navy cargo ships waiting to unload tanks and other heavy equipment of the Army's 4th ID stood by in the eastern Mediterranean.

Turkey's denial of access to its airspace promised to complicate the impending allied war effort greatly because the carrier-based aircrews in the eastern Mediterranean had planned to transit Turkish airspace en route to targets in northern Iraq, with Air Force tankers supporting them out of Incirlik. The Navy also had planned to fire TLAMs through Turkish airspace into Iraq. Without access to that airspace, one alternative would have been to reroute the carrier-based strike aircraft and TLAMs into Iraq from the west through Israeli and Jordanian airspace, which would be an even shorter route than transiting Turkey's airspace, and some administration officials pressed hard for the use of Israeli airspace if Turkey continued to balk on the issue. Secretary Rumsfeld, however, backed by his senior military advisers both in the Pentagon and at CENTCOM, concluded that attacking along a course that crossed Israel would be too politically risky because it would further inflame Arab anti-American passions.[184]

Alternatively, strike aircraft from the carriers *Theodore Roosevelt* and *Harry S. Truman* could fly over Egypt's Sinai Peninsula and then turn north into Jordan before entering Iraqi airspace.[185] Or the two carriers could redeploy from the eastern Mediterranean through the Suez Canal to the Red Sea, a move that would force them to launch their aircraft several hundred miles farther away from Iraq. The land-based tankers slated to support those aircraft would have to operate from even more distant shore bases. The Navy was not yet ready to relocate its carriers, however, because leaving them on station in the eastern Mediterranean would send Turkey a clear message of continued American determination. One Navy spokesman noted: "The minute you start to move the carriers, it will be seen as a sign that we have given up the Turkish option. We are not quite there yet."[186]

When Turkey remained firm in denying the use of its territory in support of allied combat operations, and acting on a decision made by General Franks on March 10, CENTCOM began moving some ships from the eastern Mediterranean to the Red Sea on March 16 so that they would be positioned to fire TLAMs at Iraq through Saudi airspace when the war commenced.[187] Franks also decided to hold *Theodore Roosevelt* and *Harry S. Truman* in the Mediterranean, where they were repositioned to a new operating location from which they could most effectively provide around-the-clock strike fighter coverage for the allied SOF troops who would soon be engaged in combat in northern Iraq. "One of the ways you make up for the difference in a light force," General Myers remarked, " . . . is with air power."[188] In a largely unnoted side development that, in hindsight, may have been a serendipitous stroke of good luck, the failure of the Turkey option to materialize had the effect of taking EUCOM out of the picture, because Turkey was in EUCOM's rather than CENTCOM's area of responsibility. One commentator observed later that "having both CENTCOM and EUCOM in the operations would have added an extra dimension, and an already complex situation would have been even more so."[189]

The initial goal of the first allied SOF teams slated to enter Iraq was to take down the visual observation posts along Iraq's western border. The SOF troops were to laser-designate the targeted structures for SOF AH-6 Little Bird and MH-60 armed helicopters and Air Force fixed-wing strike aircraft, which would attack them with Hellfire missiles and 500-pound laser-guided bombs (LGBs), in the process blinding the Iraqis as follow-on allied SOF teams fanned out into the night to seize Scud launch baskets and a number of airfields in Iraq's western desert.[190] Nine such towers facing Jordan were disabled first, followed by twenty-four more along the Saudi border several hours later. Those attacks on the night of March 19 marked the start of the war's preplanned kinetic phase.[191] They also featured the initial delivery of leaflets containing surrender instructions for Iraqi troops that were dropped into the western desert by Air Force SOF aircraft.[192]

CENTCOM planned to begin the move into southern Iraq on March 20 with allied SOF teams seizing the offshore gas and oil platforms and the main oil-loading terminal on the Al Faw Peninsula near the Iran-Iraq border. Concerned that the Iraqis were planning to torch the oilfields and the gas and oil platforms, General Franks asked the component commanders if they could execute OPLAN 1003V ahead of schedule. The CAOC's chief of strategy later recounted that "General Moseley asked the chief of the MAAP cell and me if we could move it up. We both replied that any dismantling and reassembling of the plan at that point on such short notice would sacrifice the intended impact of the planned A-day attacks on the Iraqi regime. We both felt that it would be better to leave the initial MAAP intact and execute it as planned, even if the land component and its SOF teams would start their opening moves early."[193]

The plan's initial timeline stipulated that G-day would begin at 0600 on March 21. A-day was scheduled to start at 2100 on March 21 with strikes from Navy aircraft carriers and from three Air Force land-based expeditionary air wings. In the end, G-day was advanced eight and a half hours to 2130 on March 20, or D+1. As a result, G-day would commence almost twenty-four hours before the initial wave of air strikes.[194] This change represented a major planning departure from CENTCOM's original concept of operations, which had envisaged sixteen days of air-only operations to shape the battlespace before the start of major ground combat. With this new sequencing of joint and combined offensive operations, allied tanks would already be deep into Iraq when the air component launched its initial air attacks.[195] In deciding on it, Franks calculated that moving G-day ahead of A-day at the last minute would allow U.S. and British SOF teams to secure the Rumaila oil field and, in the process, attain tactical surprise, because the Iraqis would be expecting an air offensive first.

On March 19, 2003, CENTCOM's evolved Hybrid plan was redesignated Operation Iraqi Freedom by President Bush as the CAOC, at 0300Z (Zulu, or Greenwich Mean Time), transitioned from Southern Watch to OPLAN 1003V airspace rules, thus instantly changing the routes, altitudes, and call signs for allied aircraft entering Iraqi airspace and also moving the location of airborne tanker tracks. At the same time, both V Corps and I MEF moved into their final attack positions as General Franks signed Fragmentary Order 09-009 directing the early start of G-day. At 1800Z the new SPINs for Operation Iraqi Freedom's opening ATO went into effect, substantially altering the rules of engagement from those that had governed CENTAF's air operations throughout the preceding twelve years of Operation Southern Watch.[196]

The final rules of engagement and SPINs for the impending campaign had already been disseminated to the wing commanders and weapons officers of those units slated to participate in the campaign in mid-February so that those key personnel could start familiarizing themselves with what was soon to come. The aircrews themselves, however, were not given access to those documents until the campaign was about to commence. Because the SPINs for Iraqi Freedom were written as full-up combat SPINs, General Moseley wanted to withhold their release to line aircrews as long as possible to preclude any potential confusion with the different SPINs that were still in effect for Southern Watch. In the end, the definitive combat SPINs for the first day of Iraqi Freedom were not approved and released by CENTCOM until seventy-two hours before the first combat mission was flown in OPLAN 1003V.[197]

CENTCOM's Air Offensive

The United States and the United Kingdom went into the second Persian Gulf War with three significant military advantages compared with the 1991 war. First, their own combat capability, particularly in the strike warfare arena, had improved substantially since the time of Operation Desert Storm. Both countries commanded unprecedented defense-suppression, all-weather precision attack, and battlespace awareness assets. Second, and more important, Iraq's military posture was only a shadow of what it had been when a much larger allied coalition mobilized forces to liberate Kuwait in 1991. Third, the coalition's air contribution to Operation Enduring Freedom in Afghanistan in 2001 and 2002 had taught valuable lessons that would apply directly to facilitating CENTCOM's air war against Iraq.

With respect to its land warfare potential, Iraq's ground order of battle had declined from more than a million men under arms in January 1991 to only some 350,000 over the decade since Desert Storm. The regular Iraqi army had fallen in strength from 68 to 23 divisions, from 6,000 to 2,660 tanks, from 4,800 to 1,780 armored personnel carriers, and from 4,000 to about 2,700 rocket launchers and artillery pieces. The once-elite Republican Guard had been reduced from ten divisions to six, only four of which were heavy divisions equipped with T-72 tanks.[1] That still, however, gave Iraq more than twice as many tanks and artillery pieces than the United States and the United Kingdom deployed for Iraqi Freedom (see map 2.1 for the disposition of those ground units on the eve of the campaign).

Iraq's ground order of battle included 11 regular army divisions and 2 Republican Guard divisions positioned in the north, with 5 regular army divisions and the remaining Republican Guard and Special Republican Guard divisions concentrated around Baghdad. The Iraqi navy had just 2 or 3 warships remaining in service, and the number of still-operational Iraqi radar-guided SAM sites was down from 100 to only slightly more than 60, consisting of 14

MAP 2.1 Iraqi Theater of Operations

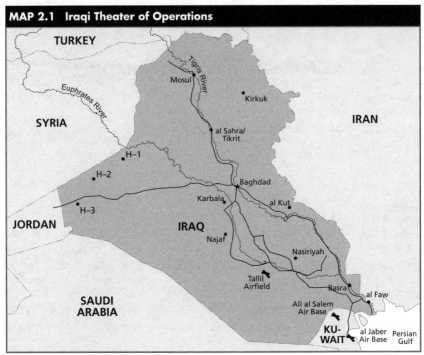

Source: Adaptation by Charles Grear based on CENTAF map

MSA-2, 10 SA-2, 24 SA-3, and 15 SA-6 sites.[2] Finally, Iraq's air order of battle had declined from 820 to fewer than 300 fighter and attack aircraft, including 29 Mirage F1s, 14 MiG-29s, 12 MiG-25s, 44 MiG-23s, 98 MiG-21s, 28 Su-25s, 1 Su-24, and 51 Su-17/20/22s.[3] Many of those aircraft, moreover, were thought to be unflyable because of an acute lack of periodic maintenance and spare parts. CENTCOM's main concern with respect to the Iraqi air threat was the possibility that Iraqi UAVs carrying chemical or biological agents might be used against coalition troop concentrations as a desperation measure. The UN Security Council had limited the permissible range of Iraqi UAVs to only 150 kilometers; however, one Iraqi UAV type being flown off the backs of trucks was demonstrating a range capability of 500 kilometers. CENTCOM also had a related concern that unmanned Iraqi L-29 jet trainers might be pressed into service as drones for delivering chemical or biological weapons.

Prewar Defense-Suppression Moves

To prepare the expected battlespace in ways that would give the coalition the greatest possible starting advantage once Operation Iraqi Freedom was formally under way, CENTCOM undertook a number of measures well before the commencement of overt hostilities to diminish Iraq's ability to resist the impending offensive. The most notable of these was a concentrated effort by CENTCOM's air component to begin systematically degrading Iraq's air defenses whenever and wherever opportunities to do so might present themselves.

During the briefing of the Generated Start option by Secretary Rumsfeld and General Franks to the president on February 7, 2002, a question had arisen concerning how CENTCOM might take advantage of Operation Southern Watch as a framework within which to increase the intensity of the bombing, with a view toward eliminating some critical Iraqi IADS nodes *before* the scheduled start of decisive combat operations.[4] Over the course of the preceding 10 years, allied aircrews had flown nearly 200,000 armed overwatch sorties into Iraq's northern and southern no-fly zones.[5] They had been fired on by Iraqi air defenses numerous times, albeit with no loss of any aircraft over Iraq. That was a remarkable accomplishment, considering that the normal peacetime accident rate for that number of sorties would have occasioned as many as a dozen or more aircraft lost to in-flight mechanical failures or pilot error. Since January 2002 alone, CENTCOM had flown more than 4,000 sorties over southern Iraq, during which time Iraq's IADS had targeted coalition aircraft at more than twice the rate registered throughout the preceding year.

Accordingly, on June 1, 2002, CENTAF initiated Operation Southern Focus, a determined effort to use Operation Southern Watch as a legitimate aegis under which to conduct intensified attacks against the Iraqi IADS in response to what General Moseley described as "more numerous and more threatening attacks" against allied combat aircraft patrolling the no-fly zones.[6] Three months earlier, Moseley had laid the essential groundwork for this new undertaking by initiating a systematic transition from Southern Watch, which was geared toward maintaining the status quo in the southern no-fly zone, toward an operation aimed at "mapping the south" (i.e., cataloguing the Iraqi IADS in southern Iraq) through what he called "intrusive ISR." That effort reflected his "desire to reseize the initiative and ensure air superiority in the southern no-fly zone and establish conditions for potential future operations to remove the Ba'athist Iraqi regime." He also wanted to "expand targets beyond 'self-defense' solely against identified Iraqi 'shooters' to new target systems that also embraced Iraq's IADS, regime command and control, and possible systems for the delivery of weapons of mass destruction."[7] What set this escalated concept of operations apart from the more straightforward tit-for-tat nature of Operation Southern Watch was the assumption by Southern Focus of the right to strike *any* IADS-related target in the southern no-fly zone in response to an Iraqi provocation, not merely the specific offending SAM or AAA site. An F-15E pilot, Capt. Randall Haskin, explained the logic: "This philosophy was basically that it was better to come back later with all of the appropriate assets on hand than it was to knee-jerk react to getting shot at and risk actually getting hit."[8]

In connection with Operation Southern Watch, CENTAF had long maintained five graduated standing response options from which to choose when Iraqi air defenses fired on an allied aircraft. Counterattacks were mandatory and automatic in all cases, with the most forceful response option entailing concurrent or sequential attacks against multiple targets outside the no-fly zone. Such preplanned counterattacks required higher-level approval, in some cases from the president himself. Operation Desert Badger, to be executed in case an allied aircraft was downed by Iraqi fire, aimed at disrupting Iraq's ability to capture the downed aircrew by attacking key command and control nodes in the heart of downtown Baghdad. Additional preplanned options were available in case an allied aircrew member was actually captured. Operation Desert Thunder was on tap in case of a Ba'athist assault against the Kurds in northern Iraq.[9]

Secretary Rumsfeld wielded an aggressive hand in seeking to bolster these anemic response options, which CENTCOM had inherited from the previous eight years of the Clinton administration. "Iraq's repeated efforts to shoot down our aircraft weighed heavily on my mind," he wrote in his memoirs. " . . . I was concerned, as were the CENTCOM commander and the Joint Chiefs, that one of our aircraft would soon be shot down and its crew killed or captured. . . . The plan code-named Desert Badger was seriously limited. Its goal was to rescue the crew of a downed aircraft—but it had no component to inflict any damage or to send any kind of message to Saddam Hussein that such provocations were unacceptable." Rumsfeld went on to recall: "Our friends in the region had criticized previous American responses to Iraqi aggression as weak and indecisive and had advised us that our enemies had taken comfort from America's timidity. The Desert Badger plan was clear evidence of that problem. . . . If an aircraft was downed, I wanted to be sure we had ideas for the president that would enable him to inflict a memorable cost. The new proposals I ordered included attacks on Iraq's air defense systems and their command and control facilities to enable us to cripple the regime's abilities to attack our planes."[10]

In a precursor to Operation Southern Focus, two dozen American and RAF aircraft had struck some twenty radar and command and control nodes throughout Iraq on February 16, 2001, some as close to the country's heartland as the suburbs of Baghdad, in prompt response to intelligence reports that Iraq's IADS was nearing a point of interconnecting some critical command and control sites with underground fiber-optic cables that were very difficult to locate. The intent of that attack, the most massive in two years, and conducted under the aegis of enforcing the southern no-fly zone, was to negate or at least hinder any such development before the installation could be completed.[11] This effort by Hussein's regime to enhance its IADS with a fiber-optic network was in part the result of an earlier loosening of economic sanctions against Iraq that had allowed French and Chinese commercial firms to provide Hussein with $133 million of telecommunications improvements, including fiber-optic cable installations and other digital enhancements to telecommunications that could be leveraged to increase the lethality of Iraq's radar-guided SAMs.[12]

Indeed, well before the terrorist attacks of September 11, 2001, CENTAF's commander at the time, then Lt. Gen. Charles Wald, had fought to gain approval for more appropriate coalition responses to increasingly aggressive attempts by Iraq's IADS to fire on coalition aircraft patrolling the no-fly zones in an apparent effort to shoot one down. With respect to his growing concern regarding the need for more forceful strike options, General Wald commented in an interview: "When I became the commander at CENTAF, I was not interested in just doing the status quo. My feeling was that we needed to do something different. . . . So we built a briefing and gave it to the CINC [commander in chief of CENT-COM] and the [Air Force] chief of staff, and in that briefing we recommended a change in how we did business—either we push it up, or we do the status quo, or we do hardly anything, we quit. We needed to get out of this middle road that was really dangerous . . . this cynical status quo approach to the no-fly zones and to Iraq. You can't do this tit-for-tat thing. Our recommendation was that we do something more aggressive."[13] Rather than risk coalition aircraft in such small-scale retaliations, General Wald sought to establish restricted operating zones and gun-engagement zones that coalition aircraft were to avoid due to the concentration of Iraqi defenses, a measure that, in effect, ceded parts of the southern no-fly zone back to the Iraqis.

All of that changed dramatically with the onset in June 2002 of Operation Southern Focus, a substantially escalated initiative that allowed the coalition to reclaim the entire southern no-fly zone while at the same time drawing down Iraq's command and control network in the southern half of the country by systematically going after enemy systems that allowed Iraq's IADS to acquire and threaten coalition aircraft. Lt. Col. David Hathaway, General Moseley's chief of strategy, explained how targets were chosen.

> After I pitched the Southern Focus plan at CENTCOM, General Franks asked all the other component commanders for their

proposed lists of desired Southern Focus targets. Both the land
and maritime component commanders proposed targets in the
vicinity of the Al Faw peninsula and the city of Basra, ranging
from long-range artillery to Seersucker missile, naval command
and control, and mine storage locations. Initially, those target
nominations were deemed by CENTCOM to be insufficiently
related to hostile Iraqi actions taken against coalition aircraft
operating in the southern no-fly zone. It was not until the execution of OPLAN 1003V drew closer that such targets were considered and ultimately approved by General Franks.[14]

A pair of B-1s, for example, attacked and destroyed a Soviet-built P-15 Flat Face
SAM acquisition radar near the H-3 airfield and an Italian-built Selena Pluto
low-altitude surveillance radar near the Saudi and Jordanian borders.[15]

In a follow-up to this initiative, staff planners at CENTAF, in conjunction
with those assigned to Joint Task Force Southwest Asia operating out of Saudi
Arabia, generated an "RO-4" response option aimed at systematically taking
down Iraq's increasingly interconnected IADS by attacking the static surveillance radar and fiber-optic cable nodes inside the southern no-fly zone that
had been providing enhanced early-warning information to Iraq's southern air
defenses. Iraq had directed AAA fire at allied aircraft at least fifty-one times since
January 1, 2001, and had launched SAMs with hostile intent fourteen times. In
light of this, General Franks, who had replaced Gen. Anthony Zinni as CENT-
COM's commander in chief in July 2000, approved sending the RO-4 option
on to the Joint Staff for approval by the new civilian leadership of the recently
inaugurated administration of President George W. Bush.[16]

A report of slightly more than one hundred Iraqi SAM launches against
U.S. and RAF aircraft between February 16 and May 9, 2001, that were characterized as "an unusually determined effort to shoot down an [allied] aircraft"
added incentive for the new administration to approve this ramped-up effort
against Iraq's air defenses.[17] Furthermore, there had been a significant spike in
recent incursions into the no-fly zones by Iraqi MiG-25 interceptors flying at
speeds of up to Mach 2.4 at times when patrolling allied aircraft were either
leaving the zones or were known to be low on fuel. By the summer of 2001
the Iraqi IADS had also begun targeting U.S. Navy E-2C Hawkeye surveillance
aircraft. One Hawkeye crew reported observing the smoke trail of what its pilot
thought at the time was an Iraqi SA-3 SAM that had been fired into Kuwaiti
airspace (where the Hawkeye was orbiting) in an attempt to shoot it down.[18]

It was in light of this increasingly aggressive Iraqi activity that General Franks suggested during his briefing to President Bush on December 28, 2001, that the no-fly zones might be leveraged as a convenient framework within which to conduct the initial preparation of the battlespace for any future allied campaign against Hussein's regime. Shortly thereafter, at the March 2002 CENTCOM component commanders' conference at Ramstein, General Moseley formally suggested that CENTAF's planners begin thinking about how they might take advantage of a stepped-up pace of operations in the no-fly zones to help shorten the time between A-day and G-day. By this time it had become clear that only Operation Southern Watch would be involved because the Turkish government was unlikely ever again to authorize an expanded Operation Northern Watch out of Incirlik to include major offensive strikes.[19]

Once this idea gained the blessing of CENTCOM and the Bush administration in principle, a more detailed concept of operations for the stepped-up patrolling of the southern no-fly zone was considered and refined at a meeting of air operations planners from CENTAF, USAFE, and Joint Task Force Southwest Asia at Camp Doha, Kuwait, on April 24, 2002. Those planners proposed that allied sorties return to patrolling north of the Tigris and Euphrates Rivers in aggressive pursuit of opportunities to impart real combat effectiveness to Southern Watch by using the operation as a means for both tactical intelligence collection and gradual kinetic preparation of the battlefield for what might eventually become a major offensive to liberate Iraq. CENTCOM's director of operations, Major General Renuart, recalled in an interview with respect to this changed planning focus: "If the Iraqis keep giving us ROE [rules-of-engagement] triggers, we'll keep degrading them."[20]

The standing ROE for Southern Watch were restructured to meet a new set of operational goals in an expanded effort, now formally code-named Operation Southern Focus, that was scheduled to get under way in June 2002. Those goals included gaining and maintaining air superiority, degrading Iraqi tactical communications, using information operations to achieve strategic and tactical surprise, and eliminating surface-to-surface and antiship missiles.[21] A comprehensive new target list was built at a meeting at CENTCOM headquarters in Florida between May 8 and May 10, 2002, characterized by Lieutenant Colonel Hathaway as a "systems approach to targeting" that concentrated on command and control targets associated with Iraq's IADS in the southern no-fly area. Hathaway noted that "the list was put together using nodal analysis, fused from two separate efforts, one done by the CENTAF information operations flight and the other built at [the Joint Warfare Analysis Center]. It aimed to achieve the most effect with the least damage. It also had 'revisit' windows built in, allowing restrikes to be regularly undertaken if our leaflets hadn't persuaded the Iraqis to desist from repairing the sites."[22]

Accordingly, with Operation Southern Focus now shaped by this new planning emphasis and slowly ramping up as the summer of 2002 approached, a de facto undeclared allied air war against Iraq was under way aimed at taking advantage of every opportunity to neutralize key components of Iraq's IADS and command and control network south of Baghdad piece by piece.[23] By that time, even American fighter pilots still at their home bases had begun memorizing mission-specific details of the Iraqi threat environment. One F-16 squadron operations officer recalled efforts by squadron pilots who were preparing to deploy forward in the coming months to "learn everything possible about Iraq's air defense structure and, more importantly, about their ground forces. Pilots would understand the Iraqi ground order of battle as well as be able to identify doctrinal Iraqi defensive formations from the air."[24] In connection with this expanded effort, General Franks indicated his determination to continue using CENTCOM's standing response options in prompt reaction to any and all Iraqi provocations, with a view toward rendering Iraq's IADS "as weak as possible."[25]

As the intensity of Southern Focus strike operations mounted, CENTAF planners placed some air-to-air fighters on "Apollo alert" to provide a quick-turn hedge in case the Iraqi air force tried to use the twice-daily Baghdad-to-Basra shuttle flown by an Iraqi Airlines Airbus A320 to mask the movement of its fighters southward into the no-fly zone.[26] Evidently undaunted by the escalated allied strikes, an Iraqi SA-2 crew on July 25, 2002, fired at a U-2 flying over southern Iraq at 70,000 feet. The missile's warhead detonated close enough for its shock wave to reach the aircraft.[27]

Operation Southern Focus reached full swing in September when General Moseley received approval from Secretary Rumsfeld to begin attacking Iraqi command and control targets routinely.[28] This escalated effort was spearheaded by a major strike on September 5, 2002, against the nerve center of Iraq's western air defenses, the sector operations center at the H-3 airfield in western Iraq. That attack represented the leading edge of a rolling minicampaign to grind down the Iraqi IADS. Not long thereafter, every other sector and interceptor operations center south of the 33rd parallel was successfully attacked and neutralized by precision hard-structure munitions. Concurrently with this expanded effort to chip away at Iraq's air defense communications network, CENTAF dropped more than four million propaganda leaflets instructing Iraqi IADS operators to refrain from firing on coalition aircraft and warning Iraqi civilians to remain clear of already destroyed IADS fiber-optic nodes.[29]

During the last week before the formal start of Iraqi Freedom, Southern Watch operations surged to nearly eight hundred sorties a day.[30] Halfway through February 2003, reflecting an evident change in the rules of engagement as the formal start of the campaign approached, CENTAF struck identified Iraqi SAM launchers in response to repeated Iraqi AAA firing at coalition aircraft, instances of which had totaled more than 170 since the beginning of 2003.[31] Two days before the commencement of the campaign, CENTAF also struck Iraqi long-range artillery positions along the Kuwaiti border and on the Al Faw Peninsula. Several days before that, allied aircraft had begun attacking Iraqi early-warning radars along the Kuwaiti and Jordanian borders, as well as the air traffic control radar at Basra airport, which CENTCOM had determined to be a dual-use facility but had hitherto kept on its no-strike list.[32]

Allied aircrews operating within the southern no-fly zone were instructed to keep meticulous track of observed enemy tanks, artillery, and other military assets. Some missions were devoted exclusively to such reconnaissance. These so-called nontraditional ISR sorties flown by allied strike aircraft using their Low-Altitude Navigation and Targeting Infrared for Night (LANTIRN) and Litening II targeting pods, radar, fighter data link, and ZSW-1 data link pods for intelligence collection were supplemented by high-flying U-2 reconnaissance aircraft to gather signals intelligence from central Iraq, as well as by a multitude of multispectral imaging satellites. The one RQ-4 Global Hawk high-altitude UAV that was dedicated to Iraqi Freedom began flying long-duration sorties to observe changing patterns in the Iraqi order of battle and monitor movements of Iraqi SAMs and surface-to-surface missiles.[33] Fine-grained mapping of the Iraqi early-warning radar system was one critical goal of these sorties. Another was scanning for any signs that Hussein and other top Ba'athist leaders might attempt a dash to political sanctuary in Syria.

Some F-16 pilots initially misunderstood this pioneering use of nontraditional ISR. Maj. Anthony Roberson, an F-16 weapons officer who had been recruited from USAFE's 32nd Air Operations Group, where he had been serving as head of the combat plans division, to join General Moseley's CAOC team during the workups for Iraqi Freedom, explained that the tactic required "a different mindset. For a Block 52 [the SEAD version of the F-16 called F-16CJ] guy to be told, 'I just want you to fly to this destination and take a picture of this, then come back and show it to me,' would seem to most fighter pilots as a total waste of time. They don't think it's an effect, and . . . the value of this mission was misunderstood."[34] Major Roberson went on to point out that such mission applications provided General Moseley with a much-needed picture of Iraq's most current electronic order of battle. He added: "It is critical for an F-16CJ to be able to swing to that role and use its array of pods to get our pre-strike reconnaissance, thus providing coherent change detection—something that was there yesterday is not there today. We needed to get that information back into the analysts' hands so that they could tell us what the adversary was doing. The Viper [its pilots' term of endearment for the F-16] is a good platform for this tasking."[35] The various collection platforms CENTAF employed toward this end revealed the Iraqis to be repositioning high-value military equipment nearly every day, but always in ones and twos or small groups, hoping to avoid the merciless gaze of the E-8 JSTARS.[36]

During the first week of March 2003, the number of allied CAPs flown over southern Iraq was doubled to give aircrews more experience at operating in a high-threat environment.[37] From March 1 until the start of major combat on March 19, allied aircrews flew four thousand sorties into the no-fly zones, in the process acquainting themselves with various procedures that had been established for the impending campaign and further familiarizing themselves with mission-related details of southern Iraq. Of this heightened operating tempo, a Pentagon spokesman noted that "we also want to establish different looks, different flight patterns, in order to preserve some element of tactical surprise."[38] The carrier air wings embarked in *Kitty Hawk, Constellation,* and *Abraham Lincoln* took turns participating in these patrols, with F-14s and F/A-18s armed with LGBs and supported by E-2Cs launching on combat sorties day and night. The heightened sortie rate in such a small and congested block of airspace made mission management particularly demanding.

The assistant director of operations of the 77th Expeditionary Fighter Squadron at the time, Lt. Col. Scott Manning, described a harrowing near-miss during the night of March 5, 2003, while he was leading the SEAD escort force in support of a U-2 as the latter skirted the Baghdad-area Super MEZ:

> During the second refueling between tanker operations and NVG [night-vision goggles] transition, I had a very close call with [my wingman,] Rowdy. We pulled off the tanker in a right-hand climbing turn, and it was pitch black. Rowdy rotated his light switch to "off." Having been watching him in the right turn, I could not see that he had stopped his turn. I, however, stayed in my right turn while perceiving him to still be in his. In retrospect, I should have rolled out and called for his lights. Instead, I stayed in the turn and reached up to pull my goggles down. I heard the blast of the mighty GE-129 [jet engine] pass right over

my canopy, at which point I looked up to the left (keep in mind I am still in my right turn) only to see Rowdy now out on my left side and only about 20 feet away. I was fortunate that Rowdy had looked at me during this and pulled back on his stick to let my aircraft pass underneath him.[39]

The minicampaign against the Iraqi IADS that unfolded under the aegis of Southern Watch during the months immediately preceding the war significantly degraded Iraq's air defense capabilities within the southern no-fly zone. That ramped-up effort had no effect in the least, however, against Iraqi IADS assets fielded in and around Baghdad, which General Leaf characterized as more robust than the defenses that had been in place there on the eve of Desert Storm more than a decade before. Iraq, Leaf said, had marshaled all of its assets for a vigorous defense of its capital city: "Countrywide, they are weaker. In Baghdad, they are stronger because they have brought everything in." Iraq's echeloned defenses around the capital included SA-2, SA-3, and SA-6 radar-guided SAMs; man-portable infrared SAMs; and AAA.[40] Furthermore, Iraqi air defense technicians had met with their Serbian counterparts after Operation Allied Force in 1999 and had carefully studied the unique tactics Serb air defenders had applied against NATO's combat aircraft.[41]

The Iraqi air force had continued to fly as many as a thousand training sorties a month in the airspace between the two no-fly zones right up to the eve of the campaign's start, and thus could not be completely discounted as a threat to allied forces.[42] Just a month before the campaign began, the Iraqis conducted a rare MiG-25 reconnaissance mission toward the west in an attempt to assess allied force dispositions.[43] Barely a month before that, on December 23, 2002, a MiG-25 had succeeded in downing an MQ-1 Predator that had been especially configured with a Stinger infrared missile.[44] General Moseley later explained that a special projects effort had been initiated to configure the Predator, which normally mounts AGM-114 Hellfire air-to-ground missiles, with the infrared-guided Stinger with the intent to lure the Iraqi air force to come up and engage it with a fighter. Although the Predator was shot down in the end, the bait worked and provided valuable updated intelligence on the MiG-25's radar performance parameters and the Iraqi command and control system.[45]

Within the context of Operation Southern Focus, the coalition responded to 651 incidents of Iraqi firing on allied aircraft by dropping 606 bombs on what General Moseley called a "wider set of air defense and related targets."[46] Under Southern Focus, allied aircrews were authorized to attack Iraqi IADS-related facilities that had not directly threatened allied aircraft but were associated with the air defense system. Fiber-optic cable repeaters were of particular interest. Because they are about the size of manhole covers, they called for especially precise munitions delivery. Allied aircrews attacked known fiber-optic nodes whenever possible in an attempt to force Iraqi air defenders to rely on their more vulnerable shorter-range acquisition and tracking radars, which could be more easily monitored and jammed. These expanded responses continued right up to the formal start of Operation Iraqi Freedom on the night of March 19.

Toward the end of Southern Focus, three defensive counterair CAP stations were established inside southern Iraq, with the western position moved forward to include the airspace above the 33rd parallel at the time initial SOF operations began on the ground on March 19 (see below). Although no Iraqi aircraft attempted to fly at any time during the three-week campaign, those CAP stations were established and maintained lest Iraqi pilots try desperation attacks against vulnerable allied aircraft like tankers and ISR platforms operating in rear areas.[47]

By March 18, 2003, CENTCOM's air component had flown 21,736 combat sorties into the southern no-fly zone under the aegis of Southern Focus and had destroyed or damaged 349 specific targets. The 651 known instances of Iraqi surface-to-air fire directed against CENTAF aircraft during this eight-month period were all ineffective.[48] After the campaign ended, General Moseley acknowledged that the heightened intensity of allied air operations may have elicited a more intense Iraqi response, giving allied aircrews more opportunities to attack ground targets of all types: "We became a little more aggressive based on them shooting more at us, which allowed us to respond more. Then the question is whether they were shooting at us because we were up there more. So there is a chicken-and-egg thing here."[49]

Viewed in hindsight, Southern Focus conferred an early advantage on CENTCOM's effort to gain total control of the air over a large portion of Iraq once the full-up campaign was ready to be launched. More important yet, it also was a key enabler of CENTCOM's ultimate decision to commence air and ground operations almost simultaneously because it allowed General Moseley, in effect, to start the air war more than eight months in advance of the formal execution of OPLAN 1003V. By that time, General Jumper observed, "we felt that [Iraq's air defenses] were pretty much out of business."[50] Former Air Force chief of staff Gen. Merrill McPeak later added that it was incorrect, strictly speaking, to suggest that there had been no independent preparatory air offensive prior to the unleashing of allied ground forces against Iraq from Kuwait, as had been the case for nearly six weeks during Operation Desert Storm in 1991. On the contrary, McPeak noted, because of the prior air preparation that had been made possible under the aegis of Southern Focus, "Iraq's air defenses stayed mostly silent, and our aircraft were able to begin reducing opposing ground forces immediately" once the major combat phase of Iraqi Freedom was under way.[51]

Preparatory Air-Supported SOF Operations

Precursor operations to pave the way for Iraqi Freedom also took place on the ground. Months before the campaign began, Army Special Forces A-teams (the nickname commonly used to denote numbered twelve-man Operational Detachments Alpha) were assigned individual provinces in Iraq and were directed to study their populations, terrain, infrastructure, and social setting.[52] As the onset of formal combat neared, allied SOF teams rehearsed activities planned for the western Iraqi desert in the Nellis AFB range complex in Nevada. They subsequently deployed to the war zone as an integrated and combat-ready force because they had already trained together as such.[53]

In a related move, on February 20, 2002, the first CIA team entered the Kurdish area of northern Iraq to lay the groundwork for a planned insertion of paramilitary teams that would comprise the CIA's northern Iraq liaison elements.[54] CIA operatives on the ground in Iraq soon began providing solid human intelligence reports on Iraqi air defenses hitherto unknown to CENT-COM.[55] CENTCOM asked the CIA to provide geographic coordinates for the reported sites, and once those coordinates were in hand, successfully struck the sites during Southern Focus operations. Woodward later reported that "the quantity and quality of [this] intelligence . . . was dwarfing everything else."[56]

As allied preparations for war continued toward the final countdown, CIA operatives reportedly recruited an active-duty Iraqi air force Mirage pilot and a MiG-29 mechanic. From those two sources the CIA learned that Iraq's air arm was in a state of near-collapse and was capable of performing only suicide missions, and that Iraqi pilots were feigning illness on scheduled flying days to avoid having to fly barely airworthy aircraft.[57]

On March 19 at 2100 local time, nine hours before the scheduled start of the ground war, more than fifty allied SOF units (including both Special Forces A-teams and similar British and Australian units) covertly entered Iraq's western desert and neutralized some fifty enemy observation posts along Iraq's borders with Jordan and Saudi Arabia. As those initial SOF operations began to unfold, RQ-1 Predator UAVs flying overhead streamed live video into the CAOC, showing the observation posts being systematically taken down in accordance with the plan. Additional SOF teams poured into the western desert and fought a series of fierce battles to secure the areas from which Iraq had launched Scud missiles against Israel in 1991. The principal aim of this operation was to give Israel every incentive to refrain from intervening militarily.[58] Allied SOF units also promptly isolated and captured the H-1, H-2, and H-3 military airfields in Iraq's western desert where chemical munitions and Scud missiles had been stored prior to Operation Desert Storm.

The SOF operations were backed up by airborne strike aircraft armed with PGMs, including thirty-six F-16C+ fighters of the Air National Guard and Air Force Reserve Command, eighteen A-10s, eight RAF Harrier GR7s, ten B-1s, four RAF Tornado GR4s on call if needed, and a variety of airborne and space-based ISR assets.[59] To support the counter-Scud mission and other SOF operations in the western desert, General Moseley had established the 410th Air Expeditionary Wing composed of aircraft from the RAF in addition to the Guard and Reserve. This was the first instance in which a SOF task force drew all of its apportioned CAS, as well as much of its air interdiction support, from a single wing that had been expressly task-organized for the purpose. In a major first in the annals of air-land operations, General Franks gave General Moseley control of the counter-Scud mission as the supported component commander. He also gave the subordinate commander of Combined Joint Special Operations Task Force (CJSOTF) West the responsibility for interdicting ground-based time-sensitive targets in support of that mission. Never before had the air component of a joint task force been given operational control of an extensive portion of enemy territory; nor had a SOF task force commander on the ground served in a supporting role to the air component commander.[60]

The vice director of operations on the Joint Staff at the time, Maj. Gen. Stanley McChrystal, noted later during the campaign that these SOF-dominated operations represented "probably the widest and most effective use of special operations forces in recent history."[61] In contrast to the five hundred or so coalition SOF troops who deployed for Operation Enduring Freedom, active SOF involvement in Iraqi Freedom soared to nearly ten thousand personnel from U.S. and allied services. During the counter-Scud operations in the Iraqi western desert, a commentator noted, allied SOF teams went "quail hunting" with harassing raids intended to flush out Iraqi military units, "which then became targets for U.S. air strikes. Indeed, air power proved to be the Special Forces' trump card."[62]

The B-1s used in these operations were essentially precision bomb-carrying trucks, each loaded with as many as twenty-four JDAMs. They also were equipped with a Ground Moving Target Indicator (GMTI) radar that could detect any Iraqi ground force movement.[63] (At a unit cost of less than $20,000, the JDAM tail-kit that was affixed to standard 2,000-pound and 1,000-pound general-purpose high-explosive bombs during the major combat phase of Iraqi Freedom in 2003 yielded a nominal 10-meter attack accuracy against mensurated target coordinates that had been further reduced to a 3-meter circular error probable, barely more than the length of the munition.)[64] New onboard jamming systems and ALE-50 towed decoys protected the B-1s in defended Iraqi airspace, with the decoy reportedly having performed "smashingly."[65]

Allied SOF teams operating in the western desert encountered unanticipated resistance from Iraqi ground units and required greater-than-expected air interdiction and CAS. The counter-Scud mission eventually evolved into three additional missions: maintaining an allied western presence, blocking attempted escape of Ba'athist leaders, and direct action against Iraqi ground forces. The SOF units, supported by the air assets noted above, quickly established fairly secure operating areas and were able to block both escape and incoming materiel reinforcements. In the process, all Iraqi forces in the region were destroyed or forced to surrender, obviating the need for allied conventional ground forces.[66] Commenting on this operation shortly after the campaign ended, a senior U.S. official noted that "there were a lot of dead bad guys left in that desert who were planning some really nasty things, from shooting Scuds at Israel to blowing up oil and air fields to messing with Jordan."[67] In fact, there was no indication after the campaign ended that any of the allied SOF teams encountered Iraqi Scuds.[68]

Allied SOF operations in northern Iraq followed a roughly similar pattern. Because the issue of Turkish basing and overflight had not yet been resolved, the SOF component started with only a small presence of forces on the ground, with B-1s providing support. The CAOC was unable to provide more significant air support because CENTAF could not use its strike aircraft based at Incirlik. As a result, air superiority over the area had not yet been established in a situation in which tankers had to be pushed into Iraq to refuel the fighters that were escorting the B-1s. Iraqi troops attempted some halfhearted attacks on Kurdish forces in the north, but they made no determined effort actually to penetrate Kurdish-controlled areas. Iraqi AAA positions did on one occasion fire on 6 MC-130s that were attempting to insert some 250 allied SOF personnel into a predesignated operating area, hitting one and forcing it to make an emergency landing at Incirlik on 3 engines.[69]

A typical tactical air control party (TACP) of Air Force joint terminal attack controllers (JTACs) operating in northern Iraq consisted of two SOF airmen paired up with a Kurdish Peshmerga militiaman and armed with a .50 caliber sniper rifle and a Viper laser target designator configured with a 50′ magnification telescope.[70] The fire support procedures involving kill boxes and the fire support coordination line (FSCL, pronounced "fissile") that predominated in kill-box interdiction and close air support (KI/CAS) operations in the south (see below) generally did not apply in northern Iraq because there was never a clear moving line of advance for allied forces.[71] In light of the largely guerilla-type war that Kurdish Peshmerga fighters were conducting in this part of the war zone, allied aircrews performing CAS missions could determine the precise location of friendly troops on the ground only by contacting them by radio during the final stages of preparation for an air-support attack.[72]

For the first two days of the war, the aircraft of Carrier Air Wing (CVW) 3 embarked in *Harry S. Truman* and those of Air Wing 8 in *Theodore Roosevelt* operating in the eastern Mediterranean could not support allied SOF operations in northern Iraq because they lacked permission to transit the airspace of any of the countries that lay between the carrier operating areas and their likely targets. After Turkish airspace was finally made available to the coalition by D+3, however, numerous carrier-based strike sorties were flown over Turkey and were pivotal in forcing the eventual surrender of Iraqi army units in the north. In the end, having sustained no combat fatalities as a result of enemy fire, a mere thousand SOF combatants enabled by allied air power effectively neutralized eleven Iraqi army divisions in the north, whose troops, by one account, "simply took off their uniforms and walked home."[73] This successful synchronization of allied SOF teams and air power was a direct result of the deep mutual trust relations between the two communities that had been cemented by their highly successful joint combat operations during Operation Enduring Freedom in Afghanistan.[74]

An Unplanned Start

As D-day neared, CENTCOM had settled on a plan that called for the allied air and ground offensives to kick off more or less concurrently, with a view toward undermining the cohesiveness of Iraq's highly centralized political and military establishment. A heavy opening round of air attacks would be closely followed by allied ground forces advancing in strength to secure such time-sensitive objectives as the oil fields in southern Iraq. This carefully arranged plan was abruptly preempted on the afternoon of March 19, 2003, however, by an eleventh-hour report from CIA director George Tenet that the intelligence community had learned of a "high probability" that Saddam Hussein and his two sons Qusay and Uday would be closeted with their advisers for several hours in a private residence in a part of southern Baghdad known as Dora Farms.[75] Tenet took this information directly to Secretary Rumsfeld, and both men went to President Bush with the news that a timely decapitation opportunity had arisen that might bring down the Ba'athist regime in a single stroke and perhaps make the full-scale allied offensive unnecessary.

Earlier that day, President Bush had held a final video teleconference with General Franks, who was in the CAOC at Prince Sultan Air Base with General Moseley, and CENTCOM's other component commanders. The president had polled the component commanders one by one, asking each in turn if he had what he needed to proceed comfortably with the planned campaign. General Moseley replied: "My command and control is all up. I've received and distributed the rules of engagement. I have no issues. I am in place and ready. I have everything we need to win." The other commanders replied in much the same way. Franks then reported to Bush: "The force is ready to go." Bush replied: "I hereby give the order to execute Operation Iraqi Freedom."[76] The plan called for forty-eight hours of covert operations to insert SOF teams into Iraq as the campaign's initial moves. At that point, thirty-one SOF teams quietly entered western and northern Iraq.

Up to that point, CENTCOM's campaign plan had called for A-day to commence two days later on March 21 at 2100 local time, nearly 24 hours *after* the scheduled start of the allied ground push. The tantalizing prospect of beginning—and ending—the campaign with a single surgical strike, however, was simply too good to pass up. President Bush approved the decapitation attempt. A CAOC staffer later observed that OPLAN 1003V in its initial planning stages had been aimed at Hussein principally in a figurative sense; now, the Iraqi dictator "would literally be in the crosshairs."[77]

General Myers immediately phoned General Franks and asked him if he could prepare the needed TLAMs within two hours to meet the required time-on-target. Franks replied that he could. General Myers subsequently reported intelligence indications that there was a hardened bunker within the target complex that TLAMs could not penetrate, thus necessitating the use of 2,000-pound penetrating EGBU-27 laser-guided and satellite-aided bombs that could be delivered only by F-117 stealth attack aircraft. Franks initially told Myers that he did not believe he could have an F-117 ready to launch in sufficient time, but then he checked with General Moseley in the CAOC.

The air component commander immediately summoned his subject-matter expert on the F-117, Maj. Clinton Hinote, and told him: "The answer I owe the president is, is this doable, and what is the risk?" Major Hinote pondered the question for a moment and replied: "Sir, it is doable, but the risk is high."[78] Hinote outlined various operational considerations that would figure in any such gamble, offered a couple of alternative strike options that might work, and listed support assets that would be needed to maximize the chance of mission success. Armed with Hinote's input, General Moseley informed Franks that a single F-117 could promise only a 50 percent chance of mission success and that it would take *two* of the stealth aircraft to ensure an effective target attack. Moseley added that the bombs could be salvoed in pairs, even though that delivery mode had never before been attempted.

As good operators would naturally be expected to do with a major offensive looming, mission planners in the 8th Fighter Squadron that operated the forward-deployed F-117s had already been "leaning forward" and had arranged to have one aircraft fully loaded with the penetrating munitions that would be required for any such short-notice mission. Intelligence experts in the CAOC, however, did not have accurate information regarding the precise location of the presumed bunker. CAOC weaponeers hypothesized that the bunker would most likely be buried beneath a field near the main house in the Dora Farms complex, and accordingly spread four weapon aim points across the field to maximize the likelihood that one bomb would penetrate the suspected bunker.[79] (Only after the campaign ended and U.S. forces were able to examine the site did it become certain that there was no underground bunker and no evidence that Saddam Hussein had been at Dora Farms at the time.)[80]

As soon as it was clear that the two F-117s could be made ready in sufficient time, General Franks told the president that he needed a committal decision from the White House by 1915 eastern standard time if the aircraft were to have any chance of safely exiting Iraqi airspace before dawn. The sun would rise over Baghdad the following morning at 0609 local time, with first light occurring about a half-hour earlier, rendering the F-117s visible and hence vulnerable to optically guided Iraqi AAA fire. President Bush gave the "go" order at 1912, three minutes before Franks' stipulated deadline.

The F-117s took off from Al Udeid Air Base at 0338 local time, less than ten minutes before the cutoff time of 0345 local. CAOC mission planners hastily scrambled to round up needed tanker support for the F-117s by diverting tankers that had been flying night missions near southern Iraq in connection with Southern Focus. The TLAMs in the scheduled strike package were then launched in sequence as planned, starting at 0439. They would arrive at their assigned aim points within minutes after the impact of the EGBU-27s as SOF operations concurrently unfolded in the west and south and on the Al Faw Peninsula. Immediately before the F-117s' scheduled time-on-target, four F-15E

Strike Eagles, in the one and only use of the GBU-28 hard-structure munition throughout the entire campaign, successfully neutralized the interceptor operations center at the H-3 airfield in the western Iraqi desert.[81] That was the last bomb dropped during a Southern Watch mission.

The aerial attack against the three-building Dora Farms complex was conducted just before sunrise at 0536 Baghdad time by the two F-117s, each of which dropped two EGBU-27s directly on their assigned aim points. Scant minutes after those four bombs detonated, a wave of conventional air-launched cruise missiles (CALCMs) from B-52s operating at safe standoff ranges struck the Dora Farms compound, followed by forty Navy TLAMs launched from the North Arabian Gulf and Red Sea by four surface warships (*Milius, Donald Cook, Bunker Hill,* and *Cowpens*) and two nuclear fast-attack submarines (*Montpelier* and *Cheyenne*), partly to help further suppress Iraqi radar-guided SAM defenses in the area.[82]

This was the first combat use of the EGBU-27, which featured both laser guidance for precision targeting and GPS guidance for all-weather use, a combination that greatly improved its combat versatility.[83] The F-117s were supported by Air Force F-16CJs that performed preemptive defense-suppression attacks against selected Iraqi SAM sites and by three Navy EA-6B Prowlers that were launched on short notice from *Constellation* to jam enemy IADS radars.[84] As the preplanned time for EGBU-27 weapon release neared, a partial cloud cover obscured the designated aim points within the target complex. A lucky break in the cover gave the F-117 pilots roughly six seconds to identify the target visually and drop their bombs. The pairs of munitions in each drop were clustered so closely together after release that they almost collided on their way to the target. The two pilots observed all four detonations, which occurred about ninety minutes after President Bush's deadline for Hussein and his two sons to leave Iraq had expired.

Capt. Paul Carlton III, an F-16CJ pilot who was airborne that night leading a two-ship element, later recalled the campaign's impromptu opening as he observed hints of its evolution from a distance:

> On March 19/20, we were flying on-call SEAD. . . . I was a night guy, flying only at night, and it was early in the morning. I had one more vul [vulnerability period] to cover before I went home. We were covering six-hour vul times, where we'd come away to get gas when we needed it and then go back in again. I came out of the [operating area], contacted the appropriate agency, and they said, "Copy. You're going to support Ram 01." That's all I

got. Who's Ram 01!? I had no idea what was going on. I asked, "Can you tell me who Ram 01 is, what their TOT [time-on-target] is and where they're going?" I got nothing back. . . . The [rules of engagement] at the time were that we couldn't shoot or drop anything unless we were given permission to do so. . . . So I sent [my wingman] off to get permission to fire our weapons if needed, and at the same time I start looking for Ram 01 on the radio. I had no idea what he was or what was going on. . . .

Ram 01 came up on the radio and told me roughly where he was and the coordinates of where he was going. He also gave me the coordinates of his IP [initial point] and his target, which I plugged into my jet so as to figure out where he was going and what his target was. His target plot fell into the little map of Baghdad. That clued me in to what he was about to do, and I knew that things were about to get much more exciting.

Having learned the TOT and seen where he was going, I knew all I needed to know. I knew what threats he was up against, and now I was thinking about how best I could support him. . . . Having devised a basic strategy, I flew back into the [area of operations], but chose not to go up near his target, even though we were now allowed to cross the no-fly zone. The F-16 is a radar-significant target, and I didn't want to trip anything off or stimulate the air defenses before they needed to be. I never heard anything else from Ram 01, which, thinking about it now, makes sense to me as the pilot always "cleans up" as they go to war [i.e., the F-117 retracts its communications antennas when entering defended airspace].[85]

Carlton and his wingman continued to watch the Super MEZ for about an hour. "Then," he said,

I hit Bingo fuel [the fuel level at which an aircraft must either initiate a return to base or depart the area to seek a tanker]. I've not seen anything happen or anything to suggest what's happened to Ram 01, so I told the controlling agency, "I'm Bingo and have to go home." I got handed off to different agencies and headed back to the tanker down south to get gas for the trip home. We were on the tanker when Ram 01 came over the radio and said, "Tanker 51, Ram 01 behind you and checking in for gas." As I came off the tanker with my wingman, I looked behind me and there's this Stinkbug [fighter-pilot slang for the F-117] taxiing up. That was the first clue that I had that we'd just helped start the war.[86]

Roughly two hours after the mission had been completed and all its aircraft had safely returned, President Bush announced to the nation and the world: "On my orders, coalition forces have begun striking selected targets of military importance to undermine Hussein's ability to wage war. These are the opening stages of what will be a broad and concerted campaign. . . . I assure you this will not be a campaign of half measures, and we will accept no outcome but victory."[87] Franks later recalled: "We did not want President Bush to speak in a way that sounded good to America and our allies, but inadvertently compromised our plan."[88] Shortly after the eleventh-hour decapitation attempt, the chairman of the JCS, General Myers, declared that "regime leadership command and control is a legitimate target in any conflict, and that was the target that was struck last night."[89] Early reports that Hussein had been killed or injured in the attack proved to be false.[90]

Iraq promptly responded to the attempted decapitation attack by launching five surface-to-surface missiles into Kuwait in a move that obliged allied troops and Kuwaiti civilians to don chemical warfare protective garb. One of those missiles, an Ababil 100 (an Iraqi variant of the Soviet FROG [free rocket over ground] missile), was fired from a launch basket south of Basra. USS *Higgins*, a Navy Aegis destroyer positioned in the North Arabian Gulf, detected the missile on radar within two seconds after its launch, determined its launch point, and generated a firing solution within fourteen seconds. An Army Patriot PAC-3 SAM from one of the twenty-seven Patriot batteries stationed in Kuwait, Bahrain, Qatar, and Saudi Arabia destroyed the Iraqi missile in flight.[91] Moments thereafter, a pair of airborne F-16s geolocated the two offending Iraqi mobile missile launchers and destroyed them.[92]

Technical evidence suggested that Patriot PAC-3 SAMs destroyed all of the intercepted Iraqi missiles, including the Ababil 100 and an Al Samoud 2 (an Iraqi modification of the Soviet SA-2 SAM with a maximum range of about 112 miles). One Iraqi missile that got through allied defenses was believed to have been a Chinese-made CSSC-3 Seersucker cruise missile that flew low over the water from the Al Faw Peninsula into Kuwait, beneath the field of regard of nearby Patriot radars that were scanning for higher-flying ballistic missiles.[93] Four of the incoming Iraqi missiles were intentionally not fired at because they posed no threat. Two landed in the water, one impacted in the empty desert, and the fourth exploded shortly after being launched.[94] Later that day, Franks reported to Rumsfeld that "we have air supremacy in the battlespace."[95]

The abrupt change in the initially planned timeline for Iraqi Freedom occasioned by the decapitation attempt had far-reaching consequences. Fearing a loss of tactical surprise, heightened vulnerability of exposed allied ground troops in Kuwait to missile and artillery attack, and an Iraqi move to torch the country's vital oil wells in a punitive response, CENTCOM unleashed the lead elements of deployed Army, Marine Corps, and British ground troops thirty-six hours ahead of the originally planned start of heavy air operations, essentially reversing the plan that had been so painstakingly developed during the preceding months.[96] That eleventh-hour reversal was rendered more palatable for CENTCOM because its air component had already established air superiority over southern Iraq by means of Operation Southern Focus, thereby freeing up the coalition's strike aircraft to concentrate almost entirely on supporting the allied ground units.

The most detailed of the postcampaign assessments of V Corps' land offensive noted that

> crossing the berm [into southern Iraq] was a major combat operation. Erected to defend the Kuwaiti border by delaying attacking Iraqi troops, the berm now had the same effect on coalition troops heading the other way. Breaching in the presence of Iraqi outposts required rapid action to deny the Iraqis the opportunity to attack vulnerable coalition units while they were constrained to advance slowly and in single file through the lanes in the berms. . . . Literally a line in the sand, the berm was a combination of massive tank ditches, concertina wire, electrified fencing, and, of course, berms of dirt. The breaching operation required four major tasks—reducing the berms, destroying the defending Iraqi forces along the border (mostly observation posts), establishing secure lanes through the berms, and then passing follow-on forces through to continue the attack into Iraq.[97]

In conjunction with this major movement into southern Iraq by V Corps, Navy sea-air-land commandos (SEALs) and British Special Air Service (SAS) troops conducted an air assault on an oil manifold and metering station on the tip of the peninsula and promptly secured that high-value objective. The start of the allied push into the Al Faw Peninsula was set for 2200 local time on the night of March 20, 2003. It was preceded by supporting JDAM attacks by carrier-based F/A-18s as well as by highly accurate optically directed cannon fire from AC-130 gunships that were orbiting nearby. Carrier-based jets also attacked command and control targets in southern Iraq and delivered leaflets containing capitulation instructions to Iraqi troops who might be inclined to surrender without a fight. Promptly on the heels of these preparatory air attacks, allied SOF and regular forces entered on the ground and secured the remainder of the objective.

A coalition SOF contingent crossed into Iraq from Arar in Saudi Arabia that same night, with a similar contingent launching from a more northward departure point to seize and hold the strategically vital H-2 and H-3 airfields in the Iraqi western desert and the equally important Haditha dam. This operation was backed by a strong air element of B-1s, F-15Es, and F-16s carrying LGBs and satellite-aided JDAMs. The SOF teams marked Iraqi vehicles and other targets with hand-held laser designators, and the strike aircraft destroyed or disabled seventeen ZSU-23/4 AAA guns and some twenty-three other Iraqi armored vehicles, as well as numerous trucks and barracks. Shortly thereafter, two C-17s that had flown nonstop from North Carolina landed on an unprepared strip in western Iraq, in the first direct combat insertion of a U.S. mechanized force.[98]

Allied strike and combat support aircraft were subsequently launched from carriers in the North Arabian Gulf and selected land bases throughout the theater to begin the air war in a measured fashion during the night of March 19–20. Although the ATO for that day (the carefully preplanned D-day for Operation Iraqi Freedom) generated 2,184 sorties in all, the initial round of air strikes was carefully meted out, as one defense official put it, to "see if we can try to tip things first."[99] Secretary Rumsfeld continued to urge Hussein's government to concede, saying, "We continue to feel that there's no need for a broader conflict if the Iraqi leaders act to save themselves."[100]

The initial strikes were directed mainly against Republican Guard headquarters and related targets with the goal of trying to separate the Iraqi rank and file from the regime. As one account later recalled in this respect, the allied coalition "did not attack with overwhelming force, and operations over the first 40 hours were characterized by judicious use of the minimum force necessary."[101] General Moseley's chief of strategy described the underlying nuances of the minimum-force approach as follows:

> While all planners, both air and ground, began with a desire to go in with overwhelming force (General Franks' initial Generated Start), the president and secretary of defense kept pushing us toward a leaner and more quickly moving force. This forced me to be more deliberate with effects-based planning. It is fairly easy

to get many of the desired effects when you have overwhelming force. In the end, with a more fine-tuned effects-based approach, we found ways (both kinetic and nonkinetic) to achieve the desired effects with our forces split against all of the planned major combat phase objectives at once.[102]

By the end of the campaign's first full day on March 20, the air component was well into the Scud hunt in the Iraqi western desert; allied SOF teams had begun infiltrating into the west, north, and south of Iraq and were in partial control of the western desert that constituted a quarter of Iraq's entire territory; and the land component's forces were fully poised in attack positions on the planned line of departure.[103] Remarking on CENTCOM's last-minute need to reset its plans, British defense analyst Michael Knights observed that "in contrast to the beginning of Operation Desert Storm, which had been a triumph of orchestration, the opening of Operation Iraqi Freedom would prove to be a triumph of improvisation."[104]

The initial hope that Hussein's regime might quickly implode led CENTCOM at the last minute to remove many high-value targets within the city limits of Baghdad from the initial target list (see below). A senior CAOC staffer later explained this sudden truncation of the initially planned ATO for that day: "There was a hope that there would be a complete and utter collapse of the regime early on. In order to let that come to fruition, [CENTCOM's leaders] initially held back on those targets."[105] As it turned out, however, many of the air component's planned A-day southern targets had been either already destroyed by earlier Southern Focus attacks or overrun by the advancing land component and SOF units during the first day.

The Full Campaign Begins

The actual start of preplanned offensive air operations, designated A-hour by CENTCOM, took place precisely on schedule at 2100 Baghdad time on the night of March 21 with large-scale air attacks that would total more than 1,700 sorties in all, including 700 strike sorties against roughly 1,000 target aim points and an additional 504 cruise-missile attacks in the opening round. This start sequence had been essentially set in stone almost from the outset of campaign planning because of the complex and inflexible orchestration of allied strike platform takeoff times required to enable those aircraft to achieve a simultaneous time-on-target in the Baghdad area from widely dispersed operating locations ranging from nearby Kuwait all the way to the United Kingdom and the continental United States.

The commander of Carrier Air Wing 2 in *Constellation*, who led the initial strike force, recalled that he deemed the potential for midair collisions both inside and outside Iraq

> one of the greatest risks we faced. . . . In concert with the CAOC planners and our CVW-14 teammates, we created simple procedural airspace deconfliction measures—three-dimensional "highways in the skies," complete with off-ramps, reporting points, and altitude splits that helped mitigate the midair hazard. Still, the prudent aviator always stayed on altitude, did belly checks, and kept his head on a swivel when joining the tanker. . . . The indispensable U.S. Navy and Marine Corps EA-6B Prowlers provided continuous multiple-axis jamming in support of approximately 70 aircraft attacking nearly 100 different targets throughout Baghdad.[106]

The target list for the opening-night attacks consisted of known or suspected leadership locations, regime security, communications nodes, airfields, IADS facilities, suspected WMD sites, and elements of Iraq's fielded forces. Regime security targets on the initial strike list, approximately 104 in all, included facilities of the Ba'ath Party, Fedayeen Saddam, Internal Intelligence Service, Special Security Organization, Directorate of General Security, Special Republican Guard, and the personal security units that were assigned to protect the regime's leaders. The roughly 112 communications targets that were attacked during the initial round consisted of cable and fiber-optic relays, repeater stations, exchanges, microwave cable vaults, radio and television transmitters, switch banks, satellite antennas, and satellite downlinks. Sea- and air-launched cruise missiles were the main weapons used in the initial wave, followed by a concentration of F-117 and B-2 stealth attack aircraft that were supported by fully integrated conventional strike and electronic warfare aircraft packages. During one of those attack segments, a B-2 dropped two 4,700-pound GBU-37 satellite-aided hard-structure penetrators on an Iraqi communications tower in Baghdad. (The B-2 can carry eight GBU-37s and is the only aircraft in the Air Force's inventory configured to deliver the munition.)[107]

Although it could not be immediately determined how many Ba'ath regime leaders, if any, were caught by surprise and killed in these attacks against headquarters buildings, command centers, and official residences—some fifty-nine buildings in all—the impact of the attacks was broadly reflected in the failure of the leadership to attempt to rally the Iraqi people, the limited scope and impact of Iraqi information operations, the slowness of the Iraqi army to react, the absence of any observed enemy ground maneuver above the battalion level, the slowness of Iraqi forces to reinforce Baghdad, and the complete failure of the Iraqi air force to defend Iraqi airspace. The general absence of hard and reliable intelligence on Iraqi WMD sites precluded a robust attempt against that target set, although such WMD delivery systems as surface-to-surface missiles, artillery, and UAVs were struck whenever they were located and positively identified. CENTCOM made a high-level decision not to focus attacks on WMD infrastructure unless there were indications of an imminent threat to coalition forces.[108]

Initial SEAD Operations

The defense-suppression portion of the A-hour offensive unleashed on the night of March 21 was led by a barrage of allied sea- and air-launched cruise missiles that were targeted against the eyes, ears, and lifeblood of Iraq's still-intact and highly distributed IADS. In this initial assault wave, more than one hundred TLAMs took down the ring of high-power, low-frequency acquisition and tracking radars that surrounded Baghdad. The capital city's main defense node was its air defense operations center, which fed threat information to subordinate sector operations centers that, in turn, fed that information to interceptor operations centers. All of these nodes were attacked, as were microwave landlines and fiber-optic cables that relayed air defense information and key long-range early-warning radars.[109]

These initial counter-IADS attacks struck the most critical fire control and communications nodes of the many SAM batteries aggregated in the Super MEZ around Baghdad and Tikrit, as well as leadership and other regime facilities in central Iraq. The Super MEZ, which appeared on aircrew navigational charts as a racetrack with extensions on the opposite sides of each end (see map 2.2), consisted of a profusion of SA-2, SA-3, and SA-6 missile launchers, as well as some French-made Roland SAMs and at least one American-produced I-Hawk SAM complex that had been captured when Iraq occupied Kuwait in late 1990 and early 1991. Each radar-guided SAM site was also accompanied by a profusion of AAA guns of calibers ranging up to 100 mm.[110] Many of these sites had never been precisely geolocated by U.S. intelligence.[111]

Concurrently, all major airfields of the Iraqi air force were rendered unusable by JDAM attacks that cratered the main runways and taxiways (see map 2.3). CENTAF planners had intended to use TLAMs against the SA-2 and SA-3 sites defending fighter airfields, but the absence of good real-time intelligence

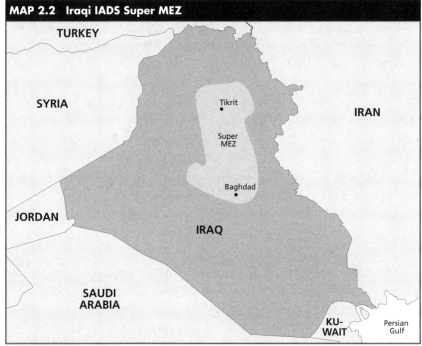

MAP 2.2   Iraqi IADS Super MEZ

TURKEY

SYRIA

IRAN

Tikrit

Super
MEZ

Baghdad

JORDAN

IRAQ

SAUDI
ARABIA

KU-
WAIT

Persian
Gulf

Source: Adaptation by Charles Grear based on CENTAF map

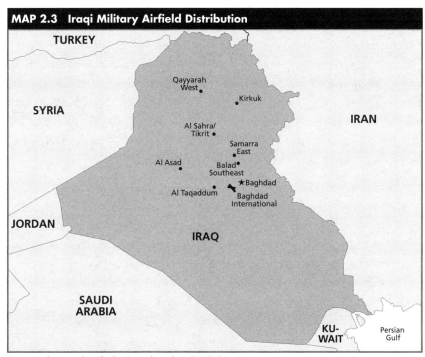

MAP 2.3   Iraqi Military Airfield Distribution

TURKEY

Qayyarah
West

Kirkuk

SYRIA

IRAN

Al Sahra/
Tikrit

Samarra
East

Al Asad

Balad
Southeast

★ Baghdad

Al Taqaddum

Baghdad
International

JORDAN

IRAQ

SAUDI
ARABIA

KU-
WAIT

Persian
Gulf

Source: Adaptation by Charles Grear based on CENTAF map

confirming their locations most likely precluded those attacks.[112] These cruise missile strikes were followed at 2146 by the first attacks by stealthy B-2s and F-117s. Eight of the twelve F-117s scheduled in this initial attack wave had to abort without expending their munitions because of their inability, in the confusion of the opening hours, to make their scheduled tanker connections. By 2300, nonstealthy Air Force and Navy strike aircraft had entered the fray in large numbers, bringing the total number of target aim points attacked to about a thousand by the end of the first night of air attacks. As a result of the assessed effectiveness of these attacks, General Moseley deemed it safe to push the first E-3 AWACS aircraft into Iraqi airspace to support joint and combined air and SOF operations in northern Iraq.[113] As a testament to the extent of air dominance achieved by the coalition at that point, B-1s operated in the heart of the most heavily defended Iraqi airspace, including night missions on the campaign's second day and daylight missions beginning on the third.[114]

During the course of these initial counter-IADS attacks, allied strike aircraft, supported by SEAD assets armed with AGM-88B/C high-speed antiradiation missiles (HARMs), used penetrating hard-structure munitions to attack underground command centers and overwhelm Iraq's IADS operators, who thereafter elected to launch all of their SAM shots ballistically (i.e., without radar guidance). The cutting edge of the air component's SEAD capability during these initial forays into still heavily defended Iraqi airspace was the Air Force's F-16CJ, which had been expressly configured to perform this demanding mission.[115]

The SEAD escort mission required the F-16CJs fly in close coordination with strike aircraft en route to their targets, remaining alert to Iraqi IADS radar activity and specific pop-up SAM threats, and firing HARMs periodically from standoff ranges in a preemptive effort to suppress the Iraqis' ability to engage the strikers with radar-guided SAMs. One account explained that this preplanned HARM operating mode, called preemptive targeting (PET),

> allows [the missile] to be fired at a suspected [SAM] site regardless of whether [the site] is emitting or not. Based on precise and thorough preflight planning, the timings are calculated so that the HARM will be in the air as the strikers are over the target, or at their most vulnerable point. If the threat radar comes on line during the missile's time of flight, the HARM's seeker will detect the radar energy and issue corresponding guidance commands to steer it toward the source. The main priority . . . was to get threat emitters off the air as soon as possible, or to dissuade them from coming on line at all.[116]

A related tasking for the F-16CJs came in the form of so-called lane SEAD, in which the aircraft patrolled the ingress and egress lanes used by coalition strike aircraft. Because seeking out enemy IADS targets of opportunity required flexibility, aircraft assigned to lane SEAD missions typically carried, in addition to their standard HARMs, GBU-31 JDAMs and CBU-103 wind-corrected munitions dispenser (or WCMD, pronounced "wick-mid") canisters for potential pop-up hard-kill opportunities. During the campaign's first five days, the HARM was used almost exclusively in its preemptive targeting mode because pilots flying the SEAD missions had no way of knowing what tactics the Iraqi SAM operators might attempt or which enemy threat systems might suddenly come up and start emitting—although, as one F-16CJ pilot noted, "the Iraqis knew for sure that if they came on the air, they were going to get a face full of HARM."[117] SEAD sorties typically lasted six to nine hours, with the longest ones continuing up to twelve hours, during which time the pilot could anticipate as many as nine tanker hookups.

Allied strike aircraft kept up the pressure on Iraq's IADS in the Super MEZ for three days. During that time General Moseley continued to limit offensive air operations to night missions flown solely by stealthy B-2s and F-117s (only twelve of the latter had deployed forward for the war) or to standoff missile attacks either from high altitude, such as conventional air-launched cruise missiles carried by B-52s, or from ship-launched TLAMs.[118] He directed a "staggering" of alternating waves of TLAM and manned aircraft attacks so that the enemy's air raid alarms would be going off constantly.[119] Only when Iraq's air defenses in the Baghdad area were assessed without question to be down for the count did the CAOC begin operating nonstealthy aircraft throughout Iraqi airspace during daylight hours.[120] It was only during the first week of the campaign that allied fighter aircrews operating in the relatively safe altitude regime above 20,000 feet repeatedly encountered heavy, if ineffective, Iraqi AAA fire.[121] The commander of CVW-14, who led the opening-night strike package, recalled that "the Iraqi defenses were spectacular but ineffective. None of the SAMs were guiding, no one had any indication of being illuminated by fire control or target track radars, and the vast majority of the fireworks were in front of and mostly below us. Still, co-altitude AAA bursts and SAM trajectories rising through our altitude kept our jets in constant maneuver and our eyes out of the cockpit for the entire attack."[122]

An F-16CJ pilot who was supporting a night F-117 strike near the heart of the Super MEZ recounted his tense experience while conducting such operations:

It was my first ride in country, and I had no idea. We had the Navy guys, who also wanted to go downtown, on our assigned tanker, and they wouldn't let us get gas. . . . We all had HARMs, eight in total, and we didn't know if the Iraqis were going to turn on their radars or not, so we were going to be firing preemptive shots. [W]e only got about 2,000 lb of gas each [from the tanker], meaning that our external tanks were still dry and that we had only our internal fuel to rely on. We turned off all our lights and pressed downtown in an offset container [box formation] in full afterburner. I was on NVGs, and all I could see were three big afterburner plumes racing downtown. Flying at 30,000 feet and Mach 1.2, I wanted to know what the guys in the AWACS must have been thinking. It was full on. I was a little light on gas, so I kept creeping up on everyone else, trying to find the right after-burner setting to keep in position. We got to about two minutes from Baghdad, and we knew that the F-117s should be just about to reach downtown. In plain English, we worked our target sort-ing—"I'll take this one, you take that one"—and I was ready to shoot. I didn't want to shoot first, though, as I wasn't keen to be the one who screwed everything up! I was waiting and waiting, and nothing happened. Then there was this *big* freakin' freight train of a missile whooshing right next to my canopy. You could smell the burnt powder of the rocket motor. What I didn't realize was that it wouldn't go high straight away. Instead, it was heading straight for [my flight leader and his wingman]. I was scared stiff until the missile eventually climbed and did its thing. . . .

We were still over the Mach [the speed of sound], and there was all this stuff coming up from the city. I was thinking to myself, "It's going to be the one you don't see that gets you." My head was now literally looking everywhere in the sky and on the ground. In fact, I don't think I was actually looking at anything, because my head was moving so fast. We finally shot our second missiles, and then we realized we had used up a lot of gas. We were right over the Super MEZ, and we turned around nice and slowly and went looking for a tanker. At this time, the tankers were still over Saudi Arabia, but we eventually found a guy who flew into Iraq with all his lights on, blinking away. Everyone else in Iraq must also have seen him, and then [my wingman] over-shot him! We asked if he'd make another turn north, and he told us that he'd do it, but that it would be better for him if he headed *south*, as he was already over Iraq! I [finally] hooked up with only 800 lb of gas remaining. That's about five minutes' flying time, and we were still about an hour away from [our home base].[123]

The four F-16CJs took turns taking fuel from the tanker until each had enough to make it home.

Also in connection with the counter-IADS effort, several BQM-34 Firebee drones equipped with chaff dispensers and launched from airborne DC-130s were used as decoys to draw Iraqi SAM and AAA fire. Two Predator UAVs at the end of their service life (characterized by their operators as "chum") were likewise pressed into service. These Predators, the oldest in the Air Force's inventory, were stripped of their sensors and weapons and launched on missions that lasted between twenty-four and thirty-six hours to try to provoke a response from Iraqi air defenses and expose any remaining pockets of potential threats. The fact that the Predators survived as long as they did in the still-defended Super MEZ before running out of fuel was yet another testament to the intimidation effect that the coalition's SEAD capabilities had on Iraq's SAM operators in the Baghdad region.[124]

Leadership and Other Strategic Attacks

Some strikes against leadership targets were largely symbolic, aimed at projecting a recognizable pattern of avoiding collateral damage within walled compounds and at targeting Hussein's regime rather than the Iraqi rank and file.[125] Others sought to achieve highly functional effects, making the most of fused imagery, human intelligence, and signals intelligence to attack specific nodes in or underneath government structures based on their actual known usage, such as forcing the regime to abandon the use of fiber-optic communications early on during the campaign.[126]

Just the day before this initial night of sustained air attacks, the Turkish parliament finally relented and voted to allow coalition aircraft to transit Turkish airspace en route to their operating areas in Iraq.[127] At the same time, however, Prime Minister Recep Tayyip Erdogan decided to forgo further efforts to seek parliamentary approval for the allied use of Turkish air bases as well, which meant that Air Force tankers initially slated to operate from those bases had to operate instead out of Bulgaria, some five hundred miles farther away. But the overflight approval did at least allow the carrier-based strike aircraft operating from the eastern Mediterranean to use an air transit corridor over Turkey rather than flying a far more circuitous route.[128]

At 0600 local time on March 21 (now both G-day and A-day), I MEF pressed northward from Kuwait into Iraq, followed shortly thereafter by the Army's 3rd ID to the west. On that first day, the 3rd ID advanced more than eighty miles into Iraq. In the face of this coordinated land onslaught, Iraqi army troops by the thousands simply took off their uniforms and melted away into the civilian population, with only scant individual or unit defections or surrenders.[129] At that point, President Bush informed Prime Minister Blair that coalition ground forces already had 85 percent of Iraq's oil fields and 40 percent of the entire country secured. Thanks to that prompt and coordinated ground offensive, only eight Iraqi oil wells were set on fire, and no other significant Iraqi oil infrastructure was destroyed.[130]

Both the Army's V Corps and the Marine Corps' I MEF were well into Iraq when CENTCOM's main air offensive finally began. An important subsidiary goal of the overall air effort was ensuring that the five main Iraqi military airfields remained incapable of supporting enemy air operations. That objective was achieved during the first night of Iraqi Freedom. Air Marshal Torpy, the United Kingdom's air contingent commander, later recalled that there also had been "a very robust defensive counterair plan, with fighters deployed 24 hours of the day to ensure that if an [enemy] aircraft did fly, we would be able to make sure it did not fly for very long."[131]

In a CENTCOM briefing to reporters on March 22, General Franks declared, "This will be a campaign unlike any other in history, a campaign characterized by shock, by surprise, by the employment of precise munitions on a scale never seen, and by the application of overwhelming force."[132] Yet despite that extravagant characterization, and for all the early media anticipation of an impending "shock and awe" air campaign, coalition attacks against Iraq once the full air offensive was under way were actually quite measured. CENTCOM removed hundreds of initially planned strikes from its target list in an effort to limit noncombatant casualties and unintended damage to Iraqi infrastructure.[133] Thanks in part to the unexpectedly rapid advance of the allied ground offensive, all leadership and command and control targets within the land component's battlespace (including 301 target aim points and 124 planned TLAM launches) were withdrawn from the ATO almost literally at the last minute as the CAOC re-roled many sorties initially scheduled against infrastructure targets to support the land component instead.[134] For example, allied aircraft struck none of the bridges across the Tigris and Euphrates Rivers that had been dropped during the Desert Storm air war, because such attacks would not serve any tactical objective that was tied to any of General Franks' broader operational goals. On the contrary, CENTCOM intended to use those bridges to move allied ground troops who would be advancing northward toward Baghdad. As Michael Knights later observed, "although the opening strike had a sense of occasion, it could never match the suspense of the initial strikes of Desert Storm. The opening of air operations in 1991 had been a thunderclap, the first shots in anger between the United States and Iraq, but the commencement of the strategic air campaign in Operation Iraqi Freedom felt like an afterthought, coming days after the beginning of hostilities when coalition ground forces were lodged scores, even hundreds of kilometers in Iraq."[135] To be sure, the actual damage inflicted on Baghdad during the first three weeks of Iraqi Freedom far exceeded that of the earlier Desert Storm campaign because of the extensive use of GPS-aided munitions that did not require clear weather for conducting precision target attacks. To this extent, the loss of the anticipated "thunderclap" in no way diminished the well-thought-out, highly accurate, and effective strikes that occurred. One air campaign planner recalled that "the original first strike was very, very thorough. There wasn't a target we hadn't accounted for."[136] At the heart of the planned operation lay the innermost elements of the Ba'ath regime's security apparatus, including government command and control facilities, the Republican Guard, the Special Republican Guard, and Hussein's family and bodyguards. To support this targeting plan, CENTCOM and its national intelligence providers had spent the last nine months of 2002 profiling the Iraqi military and civilian communications network, during the course of which the Joint Warfare Analysis Center singled out thirty-five critical nodes that would be exceptionally lucrative targets.[137]

At the same time, CENTCOM's planners bent every effort to minimize unintended civilian fatalities. An informed report noted that "of the 4,000 targets and 11,000 [more specific target aim points] the military reviewed at the start of Operation Iraqi Freedom, advanced weaponeering and tactical solutions (including axis and angle, timing variation, fusing and size-of-weapon tweaks) were able to reduce the collateral damage risk until merely 24 carried a collateral damage estimate of 30 or more probable civilian deaths."[138] CENTCOM compiled a no-target list of several thousand clearly identified civilian entities that was, according to Maj. Gen. Glenn Shaffer, a senior Air Force intelligence official, many times longer than the target list itself: "We had people looking at Iraq every day of every year, constantly generating new no-strike locations that they had identified as cultural, religious, or archaeological sites, schools or hospitals, or foreign embassies and nongovernmental organizations."[139]

Col. Gary Crowder, the chief of the strategy and plans division at Air Combat Command, described CENTCOM's plan to eliminate the government: We "wanted to kill the guys in those offices. Detailed analysis was undertaken showing when those guys were in the building. It showed that after a leisurely breakfast, they tended to be at the offices around nine in the morning, so that was when the time on target was set for. If [the attack] had been undertaken simultaneously with the beginning of ground operations, it would have gutted the regime's loyal manpower."[140] In yet another eleventh-hour change to the initially planned A-day air offensive, however, CENTCOM abandoned the 0900 time-on-target for the opening strikes against leadership targets. Some observers speculated that advocates of using the stealthy F-117 and B-2 had prevailed over those who had espoused a massive TLAM opening strike to breach the Baghdad-area Super MEZ during daylight hours. As Michael Knights reported in this regard, based on postcampaign interviews with some CAOC planners, "by changing the time of the assault, the only chance of effectively targeting regime forces was lost because only a daylight surprise strike could catch meaningful numbers of intelligence and security officers at key installations."[141]

The CAOC's chief strategist later explained the actual underlying facts behind this change in plan:

> We discussed the day versus night issue with General Moseley. Although a night strike would indeed allow us the use of our stealth aircraft, a daylight offensive using a large number of TLAMS in the Baghdad area was more in keeping with the effects-based decapitation strategy that we were pursuing. At the outset, we were hoping to catch as many as possible of the regime's leaders at work in their offices. Yet as we moved ever closer to execution and as the likelihood of our achieving operational and tactical surprise waned ever more, intelligence reporting indicated that many of the key regime officials had by that time either relocated or just stopped coming to work. Once our initial hope of achieving the desired decapitation effect began to dissipate, the stealth option at night made greater sense. Ultimately, therefore, we amended our A-day operations plan to start at night.[142]

Twenty-four targets with an assigned high collateral damage expectancy were deleted from the list of targets in the Baghdad area scheduled to be attacked at the slated A-hour of 2100 on March 21. A CAOC planner recalled that "due to the presumed success of the decapitation strike, General Franks placed a call to Moseley and told him that they didn't want to appear to be piling on. At the four-star and political level, they hoped it was enough and that we had proved our offensive capability was way beyond the regime's ability to protect themselves. At that point, the fear in Washington was that we would launch our main blow just as the Iraqis surrendered. . . . Within six hours, we had removed 300 [weapon aim points] from the target list—it felt like we had stripped out half the ATO."[143] Three years after the campaign's major combat phase ended, General Moseley frankly admitted that he had been "concerned" at the time that this decision to gut the opening-night ATO was "not right." On further reflection he concluded that it had been "a mistake."[144]

General Franks' decision to begin the ground offensive early left General Moseley with difficult choices. He could not reschedule CENTAF's attack to begin any earlier, because the five B-2 stealth bombers committed to the opening wave required fifteen hours of flight time to their targets from their launch point at Whiteman AFB, Missouri. That meant that CENTAF's long-awaited major air offensive would not begin until twenty-eight hours *after* the first wave of U.S. Army, U.S. Marine Corps, and British Army ground forces had advanced northward from Kuwait into Iraq and Iraq's leaders understood that they were facing a full-scale allied invasion. It was, as Michael Knights aptly remarked in this regard, "the complete opposite of tactical surprise."[145]

Many of the air component's scheduled targets now lay inside the land component's FSCL, an area of Iraqi terrain that extended roughly eighty-four miles in front of the advancing ground forces. These were deleted from the ATO because they had been overrun during the fifteen hours that now separated the start of the ground offensive and the scheduled start of major air operations. In the end, only 39 percent of the leadership, command and control, and regime security targets that had been initially slated for attack were actually struck by coalition air forces during the three-week campaign.

Of this toned-down opening air offensive, one F-15E crewmember recalled: "What we all saw was a scaled-back version of the original plan. When we were briefed on the original plan, everyone was shocked and awed. When we were then shown the follow-on plan, which outlined how quickly the Army and Marines were going to move when the first bombs fell, we thought that the whole situation on the ground and in the air was going to get pretty bad." Another F-15E crewmember added: "We jokingly started to call it 'shock and awwww-sh★t!' when it looked like the ground troops were spread too thin and got bogged down in An Nasiriyah and the like."[146]

till concerned that Iraq might launch Scud missiles against Israel, General Moseley persuaded his land component counterparts to make an exception to CENTCOM's general rule against key infrastructure target attacks so that he could target a dozen bridges in western Iraq that might enable Hussein's forces to move hidden Scuds from their storage facilities to launch areas. Although CAOC staffers knew that dropping these bridges might impede postcampaign food relief into Iraq from Jordan, they regarded the Scud risk as a more pressing priority. Accordingly, the coalition target coordination board, headed by CENTCOM's director of operations, General Renuart, acceded to Moseley's bid to attack the twelve requested bridges, ten of which were ultimately either destroyed or damaged from the air, leaving more than one hundred more in the area untouched. The bridges were all in the vicinity of previously known or suspected Scud launch areas in desolate locations, and all spanned smaller streams or dry washes in unpopulated parts of western Iraq. Encountering resistance from his political-military assistant, who sought to have the board's approval for the attacks reversed, General McKiernan replied that he trusted General Moseley's judgment on the issue.[147]

The widespread use of the term "shock and awe" by the media was badly misleading, in that it implied a visual spectacle that was never an intended part of the air attack plan. Air Chief Marshal Burridge dismissed the term as "a sound bite which got rather regenerated in Washington" that fundamentally missed what the air war was about and "was not very helpful elsewhere, frankly."[148] On the contrary, the initial goal of allied air strikes was to degrade IADS facilities around Baghdad, Basra, and Mosul and to destroy key command and control nodes.[149] Limited air strikes were also conducted against Iraqi artillery and surface-to-surface missile positions in southern Iraq.[150] Less than a week before the campaign started, Anthony Cordesman had presciently suggested that eleventh-hour news reporting was tending "to exaggerate the [likely] impact of the precision bombing plan in the first two nights." He even more presciently predicted that "events will increasingly dictate targeting from Day One on."[151] Indeed, by D+1 on March 20, Navy SEALs had seized the offshore gas and oil platforms and main oil tanker loading platform at Al Faw; by early the following morning, the Jalibah and Tallil airfields had been captured and the regular Iraqi army's 51st Mechanized Division had surrendered; and by the end of D+3 on March 22, the Rumaila oilfields and Umm Qasr in the Al Faw Peninsula had been secured.[152] Also on March 22, some seventy TLAMs were launched against bases of the Ansar Al Islam, an insurgent group that was thought to have ties with Al Qaeda.[153]

Regarding the opening-night spectacle, Knights observed that "the [Bush] administration and the military had played it safe, and the result was underwhelming to friend and foe alike. There would be no major collateral damage incidents directly attributable to the air campaign—a notable first for the post–Cold War U.S. military—nor would there be an appreciable effect on the enemy war effort."[154] The damage was extensive all the same, however, and it must have seemed overwhelming to those Iraqis who were on the receiving end of the bombs. President Bush later aptly characterized the opening round of A-hour attacks that began on the night of March 21 as "one of the most precise air raids in history."[155]

Air-Land Warfare Unfolds

After several days of preplanned attacks against government buildings and other fixed targets, allied air strikes shifted, as planned, to concentrate on Iraqi fielded forces, including the six Republican Guard divisions that were deployed in and around Baghdad. The principal focus of the initial air effort against Iraqi ground forces was on the command and control, armor, and artillery assets of the units positioned between Kuwait and Baghdad and on the Republican Guard divisions that were positioned to defend Baghdad. Coalition air attacks against the southernmost enemy ground formations were directed against, in order of priority, the Iraqi 3rd Corps, 51st Mechanized Division, 11th ID, and 6th Armored Division.[156]

Allied air attacks also now focused increasingly on "tank plinking" in designated kill boxes. This mission presented a major targeting challenge to allied aircrews because the Iraqis, having learned from the Serb experience four years earlier in Operation Allied Force, did not array the tanks of the Republican Guard divisions in battle formation, but instead dispersed them under trees and in the farming villages of the Euphrates River Valley.[157] Duly qualified allied fighter aircrews often performed as airborne forward air controllers (FAC-As) while searching for targets of opportunity during strike coordination and reconnaissance (SCAR) missions so they could direct other fighters and bombers to find and attack them.[158] This function complemented the work done by JTACs and SOF teams in locating Iraqi units and laser-designating them for airborne strikers. The mandatory altitude floor of ten thousand feet in the vicinity of Baghdad that General Moseley had imposed on allied aircrews made it hard for fighter pilots and their backseaters to discern targets, even with the aid of their infrared and electro-optical targeting pods, when JTACs on the ground tried to talk their eyes onto those targets.

Some FAC-As were initially underutilized in the air war. For example, in certain instances involving I MEF ground operations, F-14 pilots and radar inter- cept officers who were certified to perform FAC-A functions were held back in CAS stacks while fighters flown by more trusted Marine aviators were pushed forward to work directly with Marine JTACs on the ground. Once FAC-As were finally allowed to work in close concert with ground-based JTACs, partic- ularly during night hours, they substantially reduced the required time between aircraft check-in and bombs on target. When they were not operating directly with JTACs, FAC-As were often best used to conduct reconnaissance in closed kill boxes inside the FSCL. FAC-As and SCAR aircrews operating in concert with division- and brigade-level JTACs were often able to locate and engage previously undiscovered enemy force concentrations.[159]

CAOC staffers later characterized the use of SCAR operations in this man- ner as "the most effective method for maximizing combat effects within open kill boxes."[160] General Moseley used a few dedicated SCAR assets to find and identify moving targets and then either to attack them or to direct other aircraft to attack them. CAOC planners recalled that "SCAR jets typically took off with ATO-assigned kill boxes as their initial work areas, but they could be eas- ily retasked as the battlefield situation might require. Their inherent flexibility further enhanced kill-box interdiction in Iraq."[161]

The air component's sorties dedicated to supporting the land component were intended to undermine or eliminate Iraqi ground force resistance and thereby enable General McKiernan to maneuver his forces with no need to pause in response to enemy actions. General Moseley colorfully explained this intent before the start of combat operations: "I don't want [General McKiernan] to have to stop unless he decides to pull into the local 7-11 for a chili cheese dog and a cherry limeade."[162] Toward that end, using as a starting point the "push- CAS" kill-box approach that was first employed during Desert Storm and fur- ther refined during Enduring Freedom, the CAOC developed sophisticated and flexible KI/CAS procedures that provided a better means of identifying and promptly attacking Iraqi targets on the battlefield.[163] Each kill box in a larger common grid reference system overlaid on the battlefield was a thirty-minute by thirty-minute block of terrain, which translated into an area thirty nauti- cal miles long and slightly less in width depending on latitude.[164] Such blocks were further divided into nine "keypads" that allowed for additional target-area deconfliction, plus the ability to concentrate more strike sorties within a given block of airspace over the combat zone. Each row of kill boxes was assigned a numerical designator, such as 84, and each specific kill box was assigned a two-letter designator, such as AW. Then each individual key was given a number (see figure 2.1).[165]

The CAOC and the staff of its subordinate air support operations center (ASOC) assigned to support V Corps planned to use the kill-box system to ensure dedicated command and control procedures and a constant presence of FAC-As and JTACs within the battlespace. Controllers would assign allied pilots to specific kill boxes, both inside and beyond the FSCL, that were opened and closed for finite windows of time as might be required to ensure proper deconfliction of aircraft and artillery and to minimize the chances of friendly fire incidents. V Corps and I MEF were to control the kill boxes within the FSCL, and the CAOC would control those beyond it. The land component commander could open kill boxes within the FSCL to strike aircraft and close them at appropriate times to preclude any possibility of fratricidal fire from allied aircraft. In practice, however, the Army commander initially refused to open kill boxes inside the FSCL or to allow FAC-As to control kill boxes inside the FSCL in accordance with the KI/CAS plan (see figure 2.2), resulting in frustration for the air component and a resultant systemic inefficiency in the actual execution of the CAOC's KI/CAS plan. Only after the "strategic pause" (see below) was the KI/CAS plan executed as it had been initially envisioned.[166]

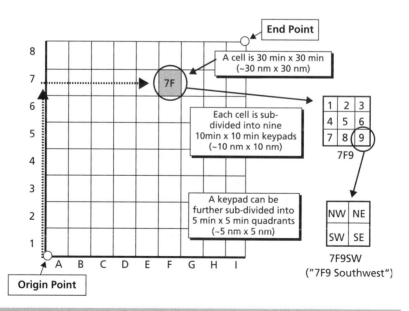

FIGURE 2.1   Common Grid Reference System

Source: Special Warfare

The kill-box arrangement was the result of a command and control construct that first saw widespread use during Operation Desert Storm. Subsequent improvements had made it a very effective measure for controlling battlefield interdiction and CAS sorties. General McKiernan or his designated subordinate could close entire kill boxes or merely portions of a keypad, either permanently or temporarily, to allow friendly ground operations in that particular piece of battlespace. A former Marine Corps fighter pilot explained that "airborne FACs [forward air controllers] could direct supporting aircraft to proceed to a given key on the keypad and await further instructions, or could use the system to help describe a target: 'A pair of T-72s just north of the road intersection in the northwest corner of 84AW-9.'"[167] Another informed account of this mission added: "The correct term for these dual-role sorties was KI/CAS, which inevitably became known as 'kick-ass.'"[168]

As the land component advanced relentlessly on Baghdad, kill boxes were opened and closed, on a minute-by-minute basis at times, "as ground troops

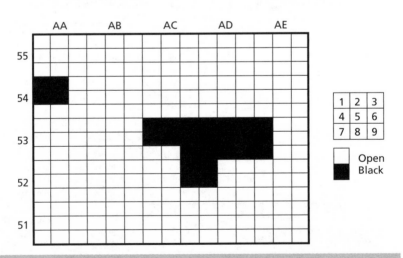

FIGURE 2.2 Kill-Box Status Change Request Format

Source: Special Warfare

neared them, artillery fired through them, or attack helicopters needed to service targets."[169] General McKiernan applied an atypically deep FSCL at the start of the ground offensive to prevent allied ground forces from overrunning the FSCL during their rapid advance, outstripping their supporting joint fires, and running the risk of sustaining Blue-on-Blue attacks by allied aircraft. This deep FSCL often worked at cross-purposes with the best interests of the land component, however, because it prevented the conduct of often urgently needed interdiction and CAS by allied fixed-wing air power (see Chapter 5 for a more detailed discussion).

In northern Iraq, the American and coalition teams assigned to JSOTF (Joint Special Operations Task Force) North were mainly charged with keeping the Republican Guard divisions positioned in that region from falling back toward Baghdad and impeding allied combat operations in the south. Air component support for those northern SOF units was severely limited until Turkey granted the coalition the use of its airfields and airspace. To make matters worse, JSOTF North had been assigned a lower priority than the SOF operations in Iraq's western desert and the main conventional ground force that served the land component working south of Baghdad. The CAOC found it impossible to provide a continuous air presence over northern Iraq by aircraft operating from bases south of Iraq because of the substantial distances involved. Accordingly, JSOTF North did not receive preplanned air support until Turkey finally granted overflight permission for Navy and Marine Corps strike fighters operating from the two carriers on station in the eastern Mediterranean. That Turkish approval came on March 24, five days into the war, and the first Navy sorties began flowing into northern Iraq two days later, on March 26. Eventually, CAS support was essentially constant.[170]

Ground forces ignored the importance of fixed-wing air support at their peril. In an attempt to use Army air power in direct support of the land offensive, for example, the commander of V Corps, Lt. Gen. William Wallace, elected late in the afternoon of March 23 to launch thirty-one AH-64 Apache attack helicopters in a deep assault against forward elements of the Republican Guard's Medina Division near An Najaf without prior preparation of the battlespace by the air component's fixed-wing assets. During the course of that operation, which an assessment of the Army's campaign performance later characterized frankly as "unsuccessful," nearly all of the Apaches were badly damaged by Iraqi AAA and other heavy-weapons fire, and one was forced down and its two-man crew captured.[171] An early account of this endeavor attributed the near-disaster to "hasty preparation, inadequate intelligence, a forewarned enemy, and an unfortunate selection of attack routes."[172] There was considerably more to the story, however, than that incomplete characterization suggested (see Chapter 5 for a more detailed discussion).

A more effective air power performance associated with the fighting near An Najaf occurred when orbiting UAVs and an E-8 JSTARS detected a formation of Iraqi T-72 tanks and other vehicles moving into position to attack U.S. forces. A well-aimed barrage of JDAMs delivered by fixed-wing aircraft destroyed some thirty of the armored vehicles and broke up the formation before it could get under way.[173] At this point in the land offensive, the forward line of allied troops had moved so far northward into Iraq that single-cycle carrier operations from the North Arabian Gulf (see below) could no longer reach the fight without refueling, prompting the Navy to press a number of tanker-configured F/A-18E/F Super Hornets into an organic tanking role. Concurrently, CENTAF moved two tanker tracks into Iraqi airspace, declared the captured Jalibah airfield operational for allied forces, and began kill-box operations in the land component's battlespace as approved transit of Turkish airspace by allied tankers and strike fighters finally began to ramp up.[174] "Throughout it all," the most thorough reconstruction of the Army's performance in the campaign noted, CENTCOM's air component "continued to degrade the regime's ability to command and control its forces and provided exceptional CAS to the coalition ground forces in contact. Coalition air forces roamed the skies over Iraq at will, providing CAS, interdicting enemy forces, and striking strategic targets across all of Iraq. Coalition ground forces maneuvered with impunity, knowing that the coalition determined what flew. Coalition air attacks were responsive, accurate, and precise."[175]

The forces of nature came to the forefront on March 24 when a massive sandstorm, or *shamal* (derived from the Arabic word for "north"), slowed the northward pace of allied ground units, which had advanced beyond An Najaf and had begun to encounter increased resistance. It was not, as General Renuart remarked at the time, "a terribly comfortable day on the battlefield."[176] The sudden storm was triggered by the passage of a strong, synoptically driven cold front through CENTCOM's area of operations. Such storms, which typically last three to five days, are common in Southwest Asia during the winter, spring, and summer months and represent the most hazardous weather condition associated with the region. They can stir up tremendous amounts of dust as they sweep across the Arabian Peninsula, Iraq, and Kuwait, often resulting in surface winds of greater than fifty knots and producing ten- to thirteen-foot sea swells throughout the North Arabian Gulf. The strongest storms can reduce visibilities to zero within hours, as occurred in this case.

Fortunately, CENTAF's weather experts predicted this *shamal* some five days before its onset, after a pass by a NOAA-17 polar orbiting satellite showed indications of surface winds activating the dust-source regions in northern Saudi Arabia. The commander of the 28th Operational Weather Squadron, the main Air Force entity responsible for Middle East weather forecasting, later remarked, "It's one thing to say there's going to be a big storm, but another thing to say where and when [and if] it's going to be sand or a thunderstorm and where there'll be cloud cover and rain. We hit this one pretty darn well."[177] That forecast gave mission planners in the CAOC ample time to front-load ATOs scheduled for execution during the sandstorm's estimated course with an extra allotment of sorties, as well as to make appropriate changes to previously planned weapons loads in favor of GPS-aided munitions over LGBs, which were more likely to be adversely affected by the sandstorm. By March 24, with the predicted storm rapidly approaching, CAOC weaponeers began calling for JDAM-only loadouts in an effort to minimize the anticipated effects of the upcoming storm on overall mission effectiveness.[178]

The sandstorm effectively grounded Army and Marine Corps attack helicopters, rendering fixed-wing aircraft the only platforms that could deliver needed direct and indirect fire support to allied ground troops who were sometimes surrounded by enemy troops in close proximity. One unit of the U.S. Army's 3rd ID was trapped for two days on the enemy side of the Euphrates River, surrounded by Iraqi forces who were equally blinded by the storm. The Air Force JTAC attached to the unit called in hundreds of JDAM strikes all around the unit, killing Iraqi troops on all sides.

A postcampaign assessment from the Army's perspective praised the air component's contribution to the joint and combined battle:

> Although hampered by severe sandstorms, coalition aircraft continued to attack air defense, command and control, and intelligence facilities in the Baghdad area. Coalition aircraft continued to achieve high sortie rates despite the weather. The focus of strike missions began to shift to the Republican Guard divisions in the vicinity of Baghdad. Control of the air allowed the employment of slow-moving intelligence-gathering aircraft such as the E-8C . . . and the RC-135 Rivet Joint. . . . The majority of the effort was against discrete targets designed to achieve specific effects against the regime, to interdict enemy movement, or in close support of ground forces. Even during the sandstorm, surveillance aircraft continued to provide data that enabled the coalition

to target Iraqi units over an area of several hundred square miles during weather the Iraqis thought would shield them from air attack. . . . Coalition air forces operated against strategic, operational, and tactical targets, demonstrating both the efficacy and flexibility of air power.[179]

Lieutenant Colonel Carlton, again leading a two-ship element of F-16CJs, launched from Prince Sultan Air Base into the teeth of the storm. Having been told that there were no suitable alternate landing fields in the entire theater, Carlton and his wingman headed for a tanker. "We made our way to the tanker, passing through a thunderstorm. . . . When we got to the tanker tracks, there should have been about 25 to choose from, but there were only three or four that had made it out there in the weather. I found my tanker on the radar and then broke out of the weather about two miles in trail. As we got our gas, I looked north and there was a wall of cloud as far as the eye could see from west to east, going up to 36,000 feet."[180] At that point Carlton heard a request for help over Guard channel: "Anybody with JDAM contact me on this frequency." The request for emergency air support had come from the U.S. Army's 3rd Squadron 7th Cavalry (3-7 Cav), which was hunkered down just south of An Najaf waiting out the *shamal*. Carlton described the reported situation on the ground: "The Iraqi Fedayeen are starting to suicide-bomb them with cars and are shooting at them. They've got a couple of ground FACs with them, and they can't see more than 10 to 15 meters at best, and there are no [other remaining] air-to-ground guys nearby to help them out because they've gone."[181] While Carlton and his wingman made their way toward An Najaf as fast as they could without using full afterburner, the Air Force JTAC (call sign Vance 47) supporting the embattled Army unit directed his TACP team to determine the perimeter of the friendly troops on the ground.

"We got there and start talking to Vance 47," Carlton said, "and we worked out our coordination to drop. One of my WCMDs failed, and I didn't drop it because the problem was with the guidance system, but the other one went straight through the weather and hit the target. . . . The feedback from the ground was very direct. They [the TACP operators supporting the Army unit] immediately came up on the radio and told us that they were no longer being shot at."[182]

Although the combination of the sandstorm and the concurrent (and completely unexpected) harassment efforts by the Ba'ath regime's paramilitary Fedayeen Saddam brought the allied ground advance to a temporary halt, neither of those fleeting impediments materially affected the tempo or intensity of allied air operations.[183] A series of smaller-unit allied ground attacks and feints allowed very effective air strikes against Iraqi ground forces. However, CENTCOM's initial hope of persuading large elements of the Iraqi armed forces to surrender at the outset rather than fight proved ill founded. The morale of Iraq's combatants appeared better than anticipated, and paramilitary forces of the Fedayeen Saddam and Special Security Organization fought tenaciously.[184]

Fedayeen Saddam documents seized and exploited by JFCOM after the regime collapsed on April 9 explained the tenacity of these typically dismounted, exposed, and lightly armed paramilitary combatants. The documents declared that the organization's main mission was to protect Iraq "from any threats inside and outside." In 1998 the organization's secretariat had promulgated "regulations for an execution order against the commanders of the various Fedayeen" should they fail in that duty: any section commander would be executed if his section was defeated, any platoon commander would be executed if two of his sections were defeated, any company commander would be executed if two of his platoons were defeated, any regiment commander would be executed if two of his companies were defeated, and any area commander would be executed if his governate was defeated. JFCOM's subsequent assessment remarked, "No wonder that the Fedayeen Saddam often proved the most fanatical fighters among the various Iraqi forces during Operation Iraqi Freedom," even though they were "totally unprepared for the kind of war they were asked to fight, dying by the thousands."[185]

The defending Iraqi ground units had been positioned and dispersed to allow for the greatest possible survival against air attack. Once directly threatened by the advancing allied forces, however, they were forced to move into more concentrated defensive positions, thereby rendering themselves more vulnerable to attack from the air.[186] As columns of Republican Guard vehicles attempted to move under what their commanders wrongly presumed would be the protective cover of the *shamal*, allied air strikes disabled a convoy of several hundred vehicles that were believed to be ferrying troops of the Medina Division toward forward elements of the 3rd ID encamped near Karbala, about fifty miles south of Baghdad. Air Force and Navy aircrews mainly used satellite-aided JDAMs for these attacks because LGBs, while still usable, did not perform quite as well in reduced-visibility weather conditions.[187] Although the JDAMs were unusable against moving vehicles, they were precisely what was needed when delivered through the weather against fixed targets with known coordinates. Recalling this experience, General Leaf later spoke of "our pause that wasn't a pause," since the air component never slackened its high tempo of operations throughout the *shamal*. General Moseley also later noted that 650–700 strike sorties had been directed against the Republican Guard over the three-day course of the *shamal*. Both he and General McKiernan agreed that allied air attacks against fixed leadership targets should be matched by concurrent attacks against the Medina and Hammurabi Divisions of the Republican Guard, which were expected to present the greatest threat to advancing allied ground forces.[188]

A CAOC planner said that when the *shamal* made classic CAS unworkable, "we went straight to the battlefield coordination detachment [the Army representatives in the CAOC] and said, 'Give us all the targets you want to hit in the next few days,' and they handed over 3,000 [target aim points]. They were the coordinates of every known revetment, every defensive area, every ammo storage dump. We didn't have any imagery to validate them by, so we just grabbed the Global Hawk [UAV] liaison community and sent them all 3,000 DMPIs [desired mean points of impact]. We said 'image these.' This broke all the rules regarding tasking of ISR, but it worked."[189] Other synthetic aperture radar (SAR) imaging for what CAOC planners called the "smackdown" effort against Iraqi ground forces included JSTARS, U-2s, and various satellites on orbit, as the single Global Hawk dedicated to the campaign remained airborne for twenty-six-hour sorties every other day, imaging 200 to 300 objects of interest to CAOC targeteers per sortie. With the coalition's ground advance virtually at a halt and the location of all friendly forces well known and confirmed via Blue Force Tracker, mission planners did not require fine-grained situation awareness.[190] "All they needed to know," Knights wrote, "was whether a revetment or a tactical assembly area was empty or full. Anything that resembled a threat was going to get bombed."[191] As the battle for Baghdad took shape, what Knights called "a synergistic combination of ground- and air-combat power . . . shared the battlespace as never before."[192]

Although CENTCOM's most senior commanders insisted that there was never a real "pause" during the *shamal*, because heavy air attacks continued, the commander of I MEF's 1st Marine Division, Maj. Gen. James Mattis, stressed that his Marines had been told to hold their offensive toward Baghdad just as they were becoming vulnerable to an Iraqi counterattack. "I didn't want the pause," Mattis said. "Nothing was holding us up. The toughest order I had to give [throughout] the whole campaign was to call back the assault units when the pause happened." Mattis added that Lieutenant General Conway, the commander of I MEF, and Maj. Gen. Buford Blount, the commander of the Army 3rd ID, had shared his desire to continue pressing the ground advance.[193]

General Leaf, the head of the ACCE at General McKiernan's headquarters, insisted that the pace of the defeat of the Iraqi armed forces . . . accelerated—it didn't slow. That didn't mean that the pace of advance didn't slow. But in that environment, the pace of destruction of Iraqi fielded forces accelerated. They were moving to contact, they moved to contact, they got killed. It was that simple. . . . If you can find an Iraqi field commander who says he thinks he got a break for a couple of days, I'd like to meet that guy. . . . An example of this supposed pause, one troop from 3-7 Cav was surrounded at night in a dust storm. . . . At the end of the engagement, the Iraqi force and a reinforcing element were destroyed with, I think, about 150 prisoners from the reinforcing element that surrendered before ever making contact because of a B-52 strike. And the particular troop, Charlie 3-7 Cav, suffered zero wounded, zero killed. That's when everybody thought things were grinding to a halt. As I said, the Iraqis were being ground up.[194]

TSgt. Michael Keehan, an Air Force JTAC assigned to a team of controllers from the 15th Expeditionary Air Support Operations Squadron, offered a riveting recollection of how things looked from the ground as the Army's 7th Cavalry Regiment was moving toward Baghdad during the battle of As Samawah, just as the three-day *shamal* had begun to develop. The regiment was crossing the Euphrates River at about 2230, well after nightfall.

Both sides of the road were taking fire. I had two A-10s overhead and used my IR [infrared] pointer to get their eyes on the target east of us. They strafed the entire area with 30 mm, which illuminated the area with brilliant white light. Enemy activity ceased to exist. Then I worked the west side of the road with eight 500-lb bombs and white phosphorous rockets. We were about 700 meters away when the bombs hit, and everyone felt the shock waves in their bodies. I think that last strike, so near the convoy, brought us new-found respect. I think the Army hadn't any idea of what we do. This display of sheer brute power was proof.[195]

At about 0100 or 0200, after crossing the river, Keehan's unit ran into another ambush—the third within eight hours.

I had called the ASOC and told them of our situation and to keep sending us aircraft. I had two A-10s overhead in a matter of minutes with a full load of eight 500-lb bombs, full guns and rockets—standard load. The enemy positions hit us from both sides of the road [with] small arms and mortars. Most of the left-flank enemy positions were neutralized by Bradley [armored fighting vehicle] fire, so I concentrated CAS on the right side of the road near a long line of palm trees that lined the adjacent river. . . . I had the aircraft first strafe the area along the riverbank, making sure they had the right area that I was illuminating with my IR pointer. . . . The winds were picking up off to the northwest, the first telltale sign of a sandstorm brewing. . . . We were down to 50 feet or less of visibility. We still had to take the bridge near An Najaf, the bridge across the Euphrates River. We would be the first unit to cross it, the first unit right of the river.[196]

As they neared the bridge, "Staff Sergeant Schrop [Michael Shropshire] took over the controlling, as he was closer to the bridge and could better coordinate the friendly posture as we laid down steel close to their positions. . . . We both worked all night over maps and tons of coordinates. I believe by this time we were in almost catatonic states of mind. How long had we been up now? Who knows? That night, Staff Sergeant Shropshire controlled more missions, and we made sure no friendlies were harmed. That was the main thing."[197] During that engagement Sergeant Keehan called in a dozen 2,000-pound JDAMs, another dozen 1,000-pound JDAMs, 2 500-pound JDAMs, and 1,200 rounds of 30-mm A-10 cannon fire. He also got 4 personal kills with his .50-caliber machine gun and M4 carbine. The repeated CAS attacks that he and Sergeant Shropshire called in destroyed some 30 Iraqi tanks and killed more than 100 enemy troops. In the midst of these events, a feint by other elements of the 3rd ID forced the opposing Iraqi Medina Division to begin repositioning its forces in an effort to block the American advance between the Tigris and Euphrates. After an E-8 JSTARS detected the ensuing movement of enemy armor and artillery on transporter trucks with its SAR and GMTI radars through the dust storm, CENTAF's now-alerted air component began, in General Wallace's words, "whacking the hell out of the Medina [Division]."[198]

During the combined-arms battle at Objective Montgomery, closer to Baghdad, the *shamal* hit Sergeant Keehan's unit with full force.

The sandstorm was just an eerie catalyst of what was to come our way. Since the first three ambushes thus far this night, there was worse to come. I remembered a jumbled quote from Abe Lincoln that goes something like "thank God the future only comes one day at a time." We were living hour to hour, kilometer to kilometer, and battle to battle. There was not a moment when I had time to think more than five minutes into the future, and that was more than likely terrain study up the road or looking off into the distant brush and rooftops for enemy soldiers. We were going into a populated area. That meant more places to hide, more ambushes, snipers, suicide-car bombers, and just plain fanatics. . . . I was the focal point for coordination and execution of CAS sorties. Thus far, I had controlled all the missions for 3-7 Cav's defense. . . . The daylight had turned into an almost indescribable orange hue. This was something none of us had ever experienced, something you might read in a Ray Bradbury book or see in a sci-fi movie. Visibility was 50 feet at best with heavy winds, everything was orange, and there were enemy soldiers out there set up to kill us as we drove through their city. The OK Corral on Mars. . . . Huge explosions rocked off our left flanks, we had no idea what they were or how close. But it was close enough for me. . . .

The weather continued to be horrible that night, and to top it off, it started to rain mud. No kidding, mud. . . . When the ASOC was looking for an area weather update, rather than a normal weather code for certain patterns, I had to say, "it's raining mud, over." There is no existing weather code for that, and I told them I was not kidding. . . . Any TACP, now or retired, will read this and think the possibility of doing CAS, given the circumstances we were in, would say it was close to impossible. Well, that night we did just that. . . . I would receive timely reports via JSTARS on military vehicles moving into our zones, so I was more than happy to be there and to help plan this mission. . . . I also had a lot of [intelligence] on enemy forces coming south into our northern and eastern flanks. They were coming at us from all directions, it seemed. . . . Without the courageous efforts of Staff Sergeant Shropshire, [Senior Airman Jonathan] Hardee, and myself using CAS in that area that night, I have no doubt in my mind that American lives would have been lost. . . .

It was [now] around midnight, and it was still raining mud. I had been tasked with Pinup flight, a B-1 bomber fully loaded with 28 2,000-lb GPS-guided bombs. I had permission to attack the enemy T-72s that were pushing down the highway. . . . I mapped out several coordinates along the highway to create a stick length for a string of bombs that was three kilometers in length.... I tasked Pinup to release half of their bomb load on the stick length prescribed.... I cleared them hot and heard the radio call back—"Advance 51, this is Pinup, one minute to impact." ... JSTARS confirmed that [enemy forces] had pooled in a low area just south of the city.... I retargeted [the B-1] and they made two more bomb runs, eight released, then the final six. By now, the ASOC let us have free rein of the [radio] net, thanks to them.[199]

The next mission took Keehan's unit through the Karbala Gap and northward to secure the western flanks.

I received two F-14s with four LGBs aboard, and I targeted two more T-72s hiding in the canal zone just seven kilometers from us. We devised a great plan using artillery, CAS, and tanks to engage the enemy. A picture-perfect combined-arms battle. ... The lead tanks stopped two kilometers short of the enemy positions.... I had Kiki flight of A-10s with their standard load of eight 500-lb bombs and full guns. They released their loads on the target area, and as soon as they were off and Winchester [out of bombs and ammunition], I had another flight of RAF [Tornado] GR4s with four GBU-16s. We bombed the same area, as they were hiding in the palm groves, well-camouflaged. I could not get accurate BDA [battle damage assessment], as the entire area was dust and smoke.... I was still controlling F/A-18s. They dropped another 18 500-lb bombs as we retreated back out of artillery range. ... Once back in the safe zone, I continued to call in CAS throughout the night, requesting aircraft with FLIR [forward-looking infrared sensors] to pick out the target by the heat source. I had another flight of F/A-18s that picked out ten tanks on the south side of the canal, warm and running. They dropped LGBs on them, shack [bull's-eye] again. I continued to work as many as four flights [four-plane formations of aircraft] in my airspace, each of us talking and confirming new targets and old ones. Cappy flight of two more F/A-18s acquired two more tanks and destroyed them as well. On their heels, I had two more RAF Tornados that also destroyed an additional two tanks trying to hide under bridge passes.

The results of this last action were twenty-five confirmed enemy tank kills, ten confirmed technical vehicles, some six hundred to one thousand enemy troops killed, numerous artillery pieces taken out, and an "unknown amount of enemy vehicles vaporized."[200]

The Army subsequently awarded Keehan and Shropshire the Silver Star for their exceptional gallantry under fire, making them two of the seven Air Force JTACs who earned that high accolade for similar acts of heroism during the course of campaign.[201] Sergeant Keehan's citation noted that his unit encountered heavy resistance in the defended city of As Samawah. While riding in a soft-skinned vehicle, he began receiving heavy fire and promptly called in CAS as artillery shells began exploding two hundred meters all around his position. Keehan directed air support against enemy positions along the riverbank and roads, which destroyed those forces with bombing and strafing runs, often within six hundred meters of friendly positions. Days later, his unit again faced a waiting enemy. After seizing the bridge at Sbu Sakhayr, the unit drove through a gauntlet of small-arms fire.

"In what was to be the decisive battle of the war," the citation continued, "enemy . . . forces surrounded his unit in the midst of the sandstorm." As the only available communications link for his unit, and "surrounded at night and blinded by sand and raining mud, [Keehan] orchestrated an almost impossible air support mission [against] approaching enemy armored formations." As his unit continued along on the main axis into Baghdad and was again met by heavy fire, "Sergeant Keehan continued to call in CAS under heavy direct and indirect fire from T-72 tanks and artillery. The CAS attacks destroyed the enemy forces without the loss of a single American life."[202] The citation for Shropshire, who also coordinated CAS operations during those battles, outlined a similar story of exceptional bravery:

> While securing a key Euphrates River bridge crossing, his unit was surrounded by enemy . . . forces and began receiving heavy small arms and RPG [rocket-propelled grenade] fire. Under a hail of gunfire in the midst of the sandstorm, he coordinated CAS while continually switching from his radio handset to his rifle, killing three enemy soldiers at close range. After receiving E-8 JSTARS cueing, and with complete disregard for his own safety, he left the APC [armored personnel carrier] during the sandstorm to confirm enemy armor locations and then directed a strike by 10 JDAMS that destroyed 10 T-72 tanks and the dismounted enemy forces who were about to overrun his unit's position. He hastily repaired his bullet-ridden satellite antenna

and quickly coordinated another air strike, destroying additional approaching enemy armor.[203]

Although General Mattis was plainly unhappy about having to halt the advance of his 1st Marine Division, General McKiernan had ordered the pause so that the land component could consolidate its gains and secure its lines of communication.[204] "If nothing else," a former Marine Corps fighter pilot observed,

> the pause was a great opportunity to methodically shape the battlefield rather than trying to keep up with the lightning-quick pace the ground forces had set in their race to Baghdad. . . . Coalition aircraft kept up around-the-clock attacks all throughout the pause and until the fall of Baghdad. Saddam's divisions were smote from above—almost literally out of existence. In the process, they demonstrated the breakthrough capability of an air component that was now able to destroy the military effectiveness of an enemy ground force in conditions that rendered that force not only incapable of maneuver but even of defending itself. There were no massive armor-on-armor battles or earthshaking artillery exchanges because none of the Iraqi armies survived [the constant pounding from the air].[205]

Military-affairs commentator Max Boot noted that this constant pounding "took place out of sight of the international news media, and so the devastating effectiveness of these strikes did not become clear until later."[206]

When the *shamal* abated and the allied ground advance resumed, the rate of allied air attacks increased commensurately to meet the renewed need for kill-box interdiction and CAS.[207] More than half of the attacks (480 out of 800 on one day) were directed against Republican Guard units.[208] By this time Iraqi ground force commanders had concluded, erroneously, that the only time they could successfully move and survive was at night. One commentator observed that "this made for good, clean hunting for the coalition aircrews. It was good hunting because it was the time the enemy chose to leave his hiding places. It was clean hunting because there was very little civilian traffic late at night."[209]

Capt. Russ Penniman, a Navy fighter pilot who was serving as co-director of the CAOC's combat plans division, observed that the video images televised back in the United States that presumed to portray the bombing of Baghdad gave no hint of the actual scope and magnitude of the ongoing attacks: "You have no idea of the vastness of that attack. Looking out of the window of a hotel [in which network video crews were positioned] is like looking through a soda straw."[210] Prior to the ground advance into Baghdad, these allied air strikes had crushed two of the six Republican Guard divisions and severely damaged two others, thereby clearing the way for the advance. Republican Guard lines were being shredded from the air, and the enemy was completely unable to hit back with any significant strength. Secretary Rumsfeld said: "They're being attacked from the air, they're pressured from the ground, and in good time they won't be there."[211]

Other Air Applications

On March 26 a fifteen-plane formation of Air Force C-17 intertheater airlifters departed Aviano Air Base, Italy, on a mission to air-drop elements of the Army's 173rd Airborne Brigade into Bashur airfield north of Tikrit, the final move toward completing the opening of CENTCOM's northern front in Iraq. The unopposed combat airdrop of 954 paratroopers and their equipment was the largest since the combat drop into Panama in 1989 during the hunt for dictator Manuel Noriega. It also was the first-ever combat airdrop of paratroopers by a C-17. The first five aircraft unloaded heavy equipment, and the remaining ten dropped paratroopers. The most authoritative reconstruction of U.S. Army operations in the campaign described this evolution: "The C-17s entered Iraqi airspace at 30,000 feet but descended to 1,000 feet for the actual jump. To reduce exposure to Iraqi air defenses, the aircraft literally dove down, with the paratroopers momentarily experiencing negative g-forces.... Colonel William Mayville, commanding the 173rd, followed the heavy drop as the first paratrooper out the door at 2010. 953 soldiers followed in 58 seconds."[212] Over the next four nights, C-17s delivered the full brigade into Bashur, landing in no-light conditions. In all, the operation entailed more than 60 C-17 sorties that carried more than 2,000 troops, 3,000 short tons of cargo, and more than 400 vehicles.[213]

Allied air strikes intensified toward the end of March, broadening their focus to include telephone exchanges, television and radio transmitters, and government media offices.[214] Baghdad television was continuing to pump out a stream of propaganda portraying the Ba'ath regime as holding firmly against the allied offensive, thereby encouraging Iraqi fighters by suggesting that the regime's command and control network was still intact and functioning—and, more to the point, that defending Iraqi forces were not doomed to defeat. President Bush, Secretary Rumsfeld, and General Franks began leaning hard on CENTCOM's planners to come up with an effective way of terminating the broadcasts.

Up to that point in the campaign, high-level concerns about the need to avoid collateral damage and an associated desire to preserve Iraqi infrastructure for postwar reconstruction had allowed Iraqi television to remain on the air. The head of targeting intelligence on the Joint Staff recalled:

> The main factor restraining us was the collateral damage issue— most of these places were downtown and not surrounded by walled compounds like the other regime targets were. After the first few strikes, they stayed on the air, and frustration was growing. This guy [Iraq's minister of information, Mohammed Said Al-Sahhaf, dubbed "Comical Ali" by some in the Western media] was still talking, and all the low-collateral-damage targets had been hit. What we needed to do, in a network-attack situation like this, was to attack all the nodes simultaneously instead of piecemeal. . . . There were three options—direct attack on the stations, taking out the power, and attacks on their transmission capabilities—the broadcasting antennae.[215]

The antennae were chosen as the most attractive targets, and MQ-1 Predator UAVs armed with Hellfire missiles eliminated the antennae on the roof of the Ministry of Information without causing other damage. TLAMs armed with submunitions were used to scrape aerials and satellite dishes off the roofs of other buildings, and one Predator used a Hellfire to disable the transmission dish of the Arabic-language Al Jazeera network in Baghdad to prevent the station from transmitting propaganda that worked to the regime's advantage. That particular strike kept the offending station off the air for only about six hours, however, because Al Jazeera had redundant broadcast systems.[216]

Viewed in hindsight, the failed decapitation attempt against Hussein and his two sons on March 19 initially appeared actually to stiffen the regime's resolve because the men were able to transmit an uninterrupted flow of propaganda through television and radio outlets that had been placed on CENTCOM's no-strike list. Only when administration leaders finally agreed to have the offending transmission facilities taken off the air did the coalition's effort to capture Iraqi "hearts and minds" begin to show signs of promise—aided in considerable part by a two-pronged psychological operations stratagem involving propaganda leaflets and the direct piping of counter-regime radio broadcasts into Iraq. This psychological-warfare effort entailed the dropping of more than 40 million leaflets containing 81 separate messages both before and during the major combat phase of Iraqi Freedom. In addition, EC-130 Commando Solo aircraft transmitted more than 300 hours of radio and television messages to Iraq's leadership, fielded forces, and rank and file. [217]

As the battle for Baghdad drew closer, the Republican Guard positioned their tanks under cover and in traditional revetments around the city. Coalition strike aircraft, including heavy bombers, struck the tanks with consistently lethal effect. Moving vehicles were engaged by LGBs or strafed by A-10s with 30-mm cannon fire. An F-15E weapons systems officer (WSO) explained how to bomb moving targets with LGBs:

> Hitting a moving target with a 500-lb GBU-12 was not dissimilar in theory to clay-pigeon shooting with a shotgun. The WSO would gauge the relative motion and direction of the vehicle and then point his laser a set distance ahead of it. By generating this lead, the bomb would be released with enough energy to strike the target as it continued to travel. With the bomb in flight, the laser would be fired some eight to ten seconds before impact and the weapon would guide onto the laser spot. If the WSO had been too generous with the lead, he could massage the laser spot back toward the vehicle, causing the LGB to sharpen its trajectory. Conversely, the bomb could be dragged further by adding lead to the vehicle. With the TIMPACT [time to impact] counter in the jet counting down, the WSO could gradually bring the laser spot onto the vehicle itself. With any luck, the bomb would score a direct hit.[218]

CENTAF's strike aircraft also attacked enemy tanks, artillery batteries, AAA emplacements, and Republican Guard barracks that were arrayed around the outskirts of Baghdad.[219] The intent was to bomb those units into submission before they could be pulled back into the city, with the specific goal of drawing down their combat capability by at least 50 percent.[220] At the height of this nonstop air offensive, some 150 allied aircraft were continuously in orbits over Iraq, waiting to conduct on-call attacks against targeted Republican Guard units. The complete intimidation of Iraq's air defenses countrywide had by that time emboldened General Moseley to operate his JSTARS aircraft deep within enemy airspace in a continuous search for both fixed and mobile Republican Guard vehicles with their SAR and GMTI radars.[221] It was a remarkably complex force employment choreography.

The Bush administration continued to place heavy emphasis on avoiding collateral damage, so planners at CENTCOM accordingly turned to the latest computer models and software in pursuit of measures to minimize it. Allied aircrews, intelligence analysts, lawyers, and public affairs officers were pulled into collateral damage mitigation teams to respond to specific incidents and false allegations. Every preplanned target underwent a rigorous review, which included assessment of the likely blast propagation for a given munition and matching of the bomb's size, fusing, and angle of impact, and the time of day of the attack—all with a view toward minimizing noncombatant casualties. A senior official observed, however, that "ultimately, if it's a high enough value target, you accept a higher risk of casualties."[222]

Every effort was made as well to avoid the destruction of infrastructure that would be essential to postwar reconstruction. For example, CENTAF's air operations planners sought to negate the capability and effectiveness of Iraq's IADS without destroying the electrical power–generation sources that sustained it. "There are other ways of taking down the integrated air defenses rather than just pulling the plug on the electricity," the maritime component commander, Vice Admiral Keating, noted. "You can disable the radars by striking them. You can take down the facility itself by putting a bomb in the roof. Or you can disable the means of communicating the information drawn by the radars and observers to higher headquarters."[223] Iraq's communications system was a particularly difficult target because it consisted of extensive backup networks connected by mobile dishes and deeply buried fiber-optic lines.[224] The Iraqi military computer net was so commingled with the civilian computer network that attacking it likewise presented a risk of collateral damage.[225]

Fighter Losses to Friendly Fire

Three particularly disturbing incidents of surface-to-air fratricide against allied aircraft (the second barely averted) occurred during the three-week campaign. The first took place on March 23 when an Army Patriot PAC-3 SAM crew accidentally shot down an RAF Tornado GR4 (call sign Yahoo 76), killing its two crewmembers, as the aircraft was returning to its base in Kuwait after a strike mission near Baghdad. Early speculation attributed the incident to either a failure of the Tornado crew to identify their aircraft properly to allied acquisition and tracking radar controllers or a failure of the Patriot battery operators to interpret correctly the Tornado's IFF signal.[226] The Patriot system is designed to classify a target based on its speed, trajectory, altitude, and IFF response, as well as its character as a fixed- or rotary-wing aircraft, antiradiation missile, or ballistic missile.[227] By one unofficial account, Army air defense logs showed that the offending battery manually fired a single missile at the aircraft after the battery's radar symbology indicated an incoming antiradiation missile 9 miles downrange at 18,300 feet with an airspeed of 511 knots, an improbably slow speed for an antiradiation missile.[228] Whatever the case, the aircraft, having just initiated it descent and not yet having established radio contact with air traffic controllers in Kuwait, was plainly misidentified as something other than a friendly fighter, and the Patriot battery fired in self-defense.[229] A subsequent British military investigation determined that the Tornado's IFF system had not been working properly.[230]

A second Blue-on-Blue surface-to-air incident occurred south of An Najaf nearly twenty-four hours later when another Patriot battery locked onto an Air Force F-16CJ with its fire control radar.[231] Remarkably, the F-16CJ's HARM targeting system was not programmed to recognize and identify the Patriot's radar signature, and the aircraft's radar warning receiver displayed it as an "unknown" threat. The F-16 pilot responded accordingly by firing a HARM into the Patriot's radar dish, effectively disabling it. Fortunately, no one was hurt in this incident.[232] After this near miss, another F-16 pilot remarked unapologet-ically: "We had no idea where the Patriots were, and those guys were locking us up on a regular basis. No one was hurt when the Patriot was hit, thank God, but from our perspective they're now down one radar. That's one radar they can't target us with any more."[233] Regardless of that angry remark, the Army's Patriots in-theater were an indispensable—and frequently utilized—defense against a very real Iraqi theater ballistic missile (TBM) arsenal that threatened exposed troops marshaled in Kuwait as the allied land offensive was in its final stages of preparing to push northward.

Nevertheless, many allied pilots believed that the Patriot posed a greater threat to them than did any SAM in Iraq's inventory. Among the main problems associated with the Patriot batteries was their failure to remain linked into the overall air picture as they moved forward along with the ground forces' advance. An Air Force analyst noted that "in many cases they would set up and go opera-tional before linking back into the air picture—or even notify the CAOC of their new location. This is why the Viper [F-16] drivers and others 'never knew where the Patriots were.' It also contributed to fratricide potential, in that dis-connected but operating Patriots could not use the common air picture to help identify radar targets as friendlies."[234]

The third Blue-on-Blue surface-to-air incident involved a Navy F/A-18C from the carrier *Kitty Hawk* that was downed by a Patriot over southern Iraq on April 2 while conducting a strike mission over Karbala. The pilot was killed. Both he and his wingman, who observed the entire evolution, had taken evasive action to avoid the incoming SAM.[235] The Navy leadership was understandably distressed that the Patriot battery had failed to distinguish the F/A-18 from a faster-moving enemy missile, and that it was even scanning for aircraft targets at all, considering that the Iraqi air force had not generated a single sortie since the invasion began.

The three Patriot-related incidents prompted the former director of the Defense Department's operational testing and evaluation, Philip Coyle, to ask pointedly why the Army's SAM batteries had been paying attention to fixed-wing aircraft in the first place: "We ruled the skies in Iraq, so almost by defini-tion any aircraft up there was either ours or British."[236] After an initial inquiry by CENTCOM, General Moseley insisted that the Patriot crews stop using the automatic target engagement mode. "Although it might take a little longer for a Patriot battery to get a defensive shot off in manual mode," Moseley's chief strategist later noted, "that risk was clearly better than the alternative of continu-ing to take friendly losses, all the more so since we had attained unquestioned air supremacy over all of Iraq except the immediate Baghdad area."[237]

The third instance of friendly fire described above begot another when two Air Force F-15Es were vectored to search for the F/A-18's crash site and look for signs that the pilot had survived the attack. The F-15E crews were not informed that the F/A-18 had likely been lost to a Blue-on-Blue engagement. Consequently, when they saw flashes on the ground near the estimated impact point, they evidently concluded that they had been targeted by the same Iraqi SAM battery that had shot down the F/A-18. They attempted to establish con-tact with V Corps, which was coordinating air operations behind the FSCL in that area. That failing, they contacted the nearest E-3 AWACS, whose controller for the area cleared an attack on the suspected SAM site after gaining approval from the CAOC. In fact, the source of the flashes was a V Corps artillery battery, which the F-15Es targeted and attacked with GBU-12 LGBs. That error, which resulted in three Army soldiers killed and six wounded, was later attributed in part to the CAOC's decision not to inform the F-15E aircrews that they were responding to a suspected fratricidal surface-to-air incident.[238]

The director of the Missile Defense Agency, Lt. Gen. Ronald Kadish, later told a Senate investigating committee that these Blue-on-Blue incidents could have resulted from both mechanical and human errors. A subsequent report indicated that the downed Tornado GR4 had failed to reenter Kuwait through one of the air corridors that had been cleared for that purpose. "You have to remember that this is a very complicated business," General Moseley said of that incident. "So when things like this happen, you do step back and begin to inves-tigate the process, the procedures, the tactics, and the techniques, and you begin to look and see if we have hardware issues or people issues."[239]

Whatever the explanation, the Patriot quickly became the main concern of coalition aircrews operating over and in the vicinity of U.S. Army troop positions in Iraq. To ensure that Army operators manning Patriot batteries could clearly identify CENTAF's aircraft, the CAOC advised pilots to use not only their encrypted Mode 4 military IFF transponders but their civilian Mode 2 systems as well. Although the latter measure made them less likely to be inadvertently targeted by Patriot operators, it also provided Iraq's SAM operators with an added means of tracking their movements.[240]

With regard to the Patriot incidents discussed above, an experienced F-16 pilot later said: "I think that the responsibility for the weapon's use falls squarely with the Army. The whole thing about losing a British jet and a Hornet to the Patriot is the ROE that goes into it. When is the Army allowed to put the system into automatic mode? When can they pull the trigger? If the ROE is stringent, then you don't have a problem, but if it's too free or loose, then you open the door up for decisions to be made that have tragic consequences."[241]

Another Air Force pilot fingered the absence of adequate communications standards between the Army and Air Force as one explanation for the F-16CJ's HARM self-defense shot against the Patriot site:

> The Army was not coordinating with us to tell us where they were, who they were, and what was going on. In my opinion, we didn't have a good enough picture of what the Army had. And it's not just what's located on the ground—it's what emitters do they have, what radars and what electrons are they throwing out into the air? Our airplane is mechanized to sense all of these things and adapt accordingly. We have to know what both the good guys and the bad guys are throwing out electronically so that we can distinguish between them. If we don't know, we can't program the software to do that.[242]

This pilot almost surely was alluding to the fact that the F-16CJ was not programmed to recognize the signature of the friendly Patriot's radar, thus forcing the aircraft's radar warning receiver to display the offending Patriot radar as an "unknown" SAM (see Chapter 5 for more on friendly fire).

From SEAD to DEAD

The intense Iraqi IADS activity that planners had expected in response to the allies' opening-night air operations never occurred. On the contrary, Iraqi acquisition and tracking radars did not emit even once over the course of nearly a month of virtually nonstop air attacks, and allied aircraft encountered no radar-guided SAM or AAA fire from Iraq's air defenses. The initial allied SEAD effort concentrated on enemy sector operations centers, early-warning radars, and associated communications nodes. Subsequent attacks went after SAM radars and launchers. Iraq's radar-guided SAMs were not initially struck on a massive scale because they were hard to locate; the Iraqis repositioned them every eight to twelve hours and withheld radar emissions. That tactic increased the survivability of Iraq's SAMs even as it all but negated their operational effectiveness.[243] The SAM and AAA fire that did occur was invariably unguided, although these barrages came increasingly closer to the targeted aircraft, sometimes within a mile or less. Nevertheless, this sporadic fire, most of which occurred after allied bombs had already hit their targets, had thus far failed to down a single coalition aircraft. This was no doubt due in part to the four thousand sorties flown over the nearly nine months of Operation Southern Focus.[244] The CAOC had put considerable effort into piecemeal attacks against Iraqi SAMs and radars, as well as toward breaking open fiber-optic vaults to complicate enemy command and control arrangements.[245]

F-16CJ pilots nevertheless earned their flight pay on these often harrowing forays into Iraq's still heavily defended airspace. Capt. Gene Sherer had a hair-raising experience on one such foray.

> I was SEAD mission commander, call-sign Vouch 61, and we were flying in the Super MEZ in the southwest corner of Baghdad. We were a four-ship supporting a B-1B, with some EA-6B Prowlers doing some jamming and some F-16CGs, F/A-18s and F-14s bombing targets. . . . We had one vul [period of vulnerability] time that was supposed to be 25 minutes. . . . Flying on station, the next thing I know, [my wingman] calls for a break turn. In the break, I look and see a missile go straight past him, and I think, "Oh, sh★t!" We started to get a heartbeat going, and we're using the [electronic jamming] pod trying to do our stuff. Well, I ended up seeing another three missiles unguided, and at least two more that guide [optically] on me and my wingman, who was a mile and a half to the east in line-abreast formation. All of it was unguided, but I later saw on my HARM tape that an SA-3 came on line. I didn't see it at the time because we had AAA all over the place and my wingman was defensively maneuvering. It was squirrelly [and] the most incredible thing I've done. We all shot HARMs that day except [one member of the four-ship flight]. We were in the MEZ for 45 to 50 minutes.[246]

"After the first three days," General Moseley noted as the three-week campaign was reaching endgame,

> we switched from a suppression campaign to a destruction campaign, and we've been literally hunting them down one by one and killing multiples of them every day. We use our F-16CJs and the F/A-18s with the munitions they carry, and our Rivet Joint and the Global Hawk and the F-15E ... and we have a ... specific mission to go hunt them down and kill them. Kill the antennas, kill the launchers, kill the support vans, the comm vans, break up their command and control, and force them to move. And as they're moving, they're not setting up and plugging in and getting their systems up. And every time they move one of those things, they have a tendency to break something on them, and by forcing them up and by individually hunting them down and keeping them on the run, you begin to be able to control the airspace. That's exactly how we've been able to transition from the starting condition of air superiority now to air supremacy.[247]

SEAD escort and on-call SEAD operations were highly successful in that Iraqi SAM operators were simply not emitting with their radars. As one Air Force pilot later summarized it concisely, "Iraqi radar was a no-show."[248] Virtually all of the observed AAA fire and SAM launches were unguided. Accordingly, CAOC planners decided to take a more a proactive approach toward dealing with Iraq's IADS. Major Roberson explained:

> The strategy that the Iraqis elected to follow meant that they did not come up and actively engage our aircraft, which presented a big challenge for us. So long as the threat is emitting, we have the sensor suite to detect it across a large frequency range, but because they chose not to emit and overtly target our aircraft, it made it very challenging to locate those threats. One can argue that because they chose to do that, that was suppression in and of itself. The very presence of the CJ meant that we [had] achieved SEAD. But that wasn't enough. We still had to execute an air campaign, so we needed to go to downtown into Baghdad and downtown into Tikrit with LGBs and JDAM and hit some very important targets, and we had to get close to do that.[249]

In this move from SEAD to the actual physical destruction of enemy air defenses (DEAD, pronounced "deed") on the campaign's third day, Air Force

F-16CJ pilots went after Iraqi SAM and AAA sites with mixed munitions loads that included the satellite-aided GBU-31 JDAM and the CBU-103 WCMD, as well as the infrared-imaging AGM-65 Maverick air-to-ground missile, giving them both SEAD and DEAD capability. Navy and Marine Corps EA-6Bs provided vital electronic jamming support. This transition was not part of any coordinated shift to a preplanned DEAD campaign. It occurred because the situation no longer required each CJ to carry two HARMs per aircraft. The resultant hard-target capability added much greater mission flexibility to CEN-TAF's SEAD assets.

A more comprehensive and coordinated DEAD effort began six days later, on D+9. As allied ground forces pushed ever closer to Baghdad and Iraq's IADS remained silent, CAOC planners realized that a determined DEAD effort would be required. The majority of Iraq's SAM inventory remained intact and operationally usable. Accordingly, a concentrated effort began on March 28 to draw down Iraq's SAM capability in the Baghdad area. The U-2 and the Global Hawk were enlisted to find and geolocate SAM targets. The DEAD strike force consisted mainly of Air Force F-16CJs armed with GBU-31s, CBU-103s, and Maverick missiles, and Navy and Marine Corps F/A-18Cs carrying joint standoff weapons (JSOWs). These aircraft, supported by EA-6B Prowlers and further augmented by B-2s, maintained around-the-clock DEAD CAPs over Baghdad. Lt. Col. Scott Manning, a CJ pilot with the 20th Fighter Wing, recalled, "DEAD wasn't so much a coordinated mission against specific objectives, but more a case of 'if you find it and you can get permission to strike it, then go ahead and kill it.'"[250] The move from SEAD to DEAD entailed "a scary decision" for General Moseley, but, he explained, "we needed to kill those SAMs."[251] In the end, the DEAD effort succeeded in considerable part because effective ISR platforms were used directly in a focused operation that commanded both an abundance of appropriately loaded attack assets and the required command and control backup to link the sensors to the shooters.

The Counterair Effort

The Iraqi air force did not launch even one fighter sortie during the allied campaign. Nor, in a welcome surprise, did Iraq launch any cruise missiles at allied naval forces. Nevertheless, allied offensive counterair missions continued throughout the war because the Iraqi air force had been generating as many as 150 sorties a day before the war started on March 19. That earlier flight activity had occasioned legitimate concern in the CAOC that enemy aircraft might deliver biological or chemical weapons with little or no warning in suicide attacks against allied forces. Enemy airfields were heavily targeted to prevent Iraqi fighters from taking off on such missions.

General Moseley assured General Franks during the final countdown to war: "I will make it my life's work that the Iraqi air force will not fly."[252] Toward that end, he instructed Lieutenant Colonel Hathaway to deny the enemy even a remote chance of getting an aircraft airborne by marking target aim points on every runway and other flyable surface on and immediately adjacent to all of the active Iraqi fighter airfields and cratering them during the first night, as well as locating and destroying all identifiable squadron buildings, fuel storage facilities, and command and control sites. Should any evidence be detected of attempted enemy runway repair efforts, those airfields were to be promptly reattacked as a top priority. Because civilian airliners were the only long-range aircraft at Hussein's disposal, General Moseley ordered their destruction as a hedge against their use as suicide weapons. (Evidently anticipating this, the Iraqis removed the engine nacelles from their airliners before the campaign's start, providing observable confirmation of their inability to fly. That had the effect of getting them removed from the CAOC's target list at the last minute.)[253]

The initial attacks against Iraq's fighter airfields focused on runways and aircraft parked in the open, with the first bombs fused to detonate about fifteen minutes after the initial time-on-target for the A-hour strategic strikes throughout the country. Follow-up attacks were visited on all airfields on which the Iraqis made attempts to repair runway damage. Not only did the Iraqi air force make no attempt to fly during the war, many fighter aircraft were actually moved away from their bases and buried. One intelligence report indicated that Saddam Hussein did not trust his air force and had ordered pilots to remain on the ground.[254] Subsequent allied interviews with senior Iraqi leaders who had surrendered or were captured after the campaign amply validated this assessment. Interviews with dozens of Iraqi military and political leaders as well as literally hundreds of thousands of captured Iraqi documents indicated that Hussein had so little confidence in the combat capability of his air force that he elected to husband what remained of it as a hedge against possible future needs. The commander of Iraq's air force and air defense force admitted to coalition interrogators that Hussein had decided two months before the start of the war that the air force would not participate.[255] Instead, Hussein decided to move the combat aircraft away from their bases and conceal them from coalition ISR assets so he might later dig them out and return them to service—yet another testament to his refusal to believe that allied ground forces would ever reach the Iraqi heartland. Once it became clear that Iraq's fighter pilots would not be a factor in the war, sorties originally dedicated to offensive counterair missions were re-roled to support advancing allied ground forces.[256]

Nonkinetic Operations

As the air attacks continued, CENTCOM employed propaganda leaflets, radio broadcasts, and loudspeakers in an effort to induce enemy troops to surrender, spreading the message that were they to refuse, the Al Nida Division would suffer the same fate as did the Baghdad Division.[257] Major Roberson, a CAOC planner who helped orchestrate the air component's contribution to CENT-COM's psychological warfare effort, recalled one circumstance in which a leaflet mission appeared to have been particularly effective. The land component's planners wanted to neutralize the Iraqi 34th Armor Brigade on one flank of V Corps' advance and accordingly targeted it for leaflet deliveries. "Two consecutive days of leaflets told them, 'Hey! Your time's coming. Capitulate and lay down your arms, because if you don't, then we're going to attack you.' Since we had that capability and [also] air superiority, that's what happened. After the [initial bombing] attack, we came back and dropped more leaflets that said, 'We told you we'd do it. So, any of you guys who are left, go home!'"[258] The targeted Iraqi armor brigade never showed up on the battlefield.[259]

CENTAF distributed more than 40 million leaflets between October 2002 and the end of the three-week campaign. They included warnings against employing WMD, conducting air operations, backing the Ba'ath Party, destroying oil fields, and mining Iraqi waterways. They also provided frequencies for coalition radio broadcasts urging civilian noninterference with allied operations and, toward the campaign's end, providing instructions on how Iraqi military units should surrender or desert. Radio broadcasts from EC-130E/J Commando Solo aircraft and radio network intrusions conducted by EA-6B Prowlers and EC-130H Compass Call aircraft transmitted similar instructions.[260]

The Compass Call aircraft were called on to play an especially important part in helping allied SOF teams gain control of important parts of the Iraqi infrastructure during the opening days of Iraqi Freedom, including a number of Iraqi airfields and a group of key oil installations on the Al Faw Peninsula. It was thought at the time—incorrectly, as it turned out—that Iraqi troops stationed at the oil rigs were awaiting orders to detonate explosives at some of the installations and that the ability of the EC-130H to block orders from Iraqi commanders had been instrumental in preventing that calamity. The aircraft likewise supported the SOF seizures of the important H-2 and H-3 airfields in Iraq's western desert, and EC-130s were on station during two successful prisonerof-war rescue operations. Indeed, SOF commanders commonly regarded the EC-130 as a "go/no-go" asset.[261]

Although much effort went into preparing for and implementing psychological warfare operations, however, there is no substantial evidence attesting to their overall impact on the course and outcome of the three-week campaign, even though there were indeed isolated cases that suggested the achievement of a clear desired battlefield effect.[262]

Key Air Component Achievements

As allied ground forces advanced northward toward Baghdad, a recurrent media refrain suggested that CENTCOM was using air strikes to "soften up" the Iraqi ground troops positioned in and around the city, after which the land component would send in "raiding parties of armored units, special forces, and light infantry to finish off their targets."[263] To that suggestion, General Moseley was finally moved to comment tersely: "Our sensors show that the preponderance of the Republican Guard divisions that were outside of Baghdad are now dead. We've laid on these people. I find it interesting when folks say we're 'softening them up.' We're not softening them up. We're killing them."[264] An Australian analyst writing as the major combat phase of Iraqi Freedom was nearing its end noted that "the coalition air fleet has, to date, accounted for most of the heavy damage to the Iraqi land force. Often the ground force only mops up remnants left after sustained battlefield air strikes." This writer went on to portray the plains of the Tigris and Euphrates Rivers south of Baghdad as "an enormous kill zone for an ongoing aerial turkey shoot unseen since 1991."[265]

Throughout the three-week campaign, the majority of the air component's strike assets were expressly apportioned to support the land component, with CAS being the single most numerous mission type flown by all combat aircraft, including B-52s.[266] One account aptly summarized the impact of the air offensive on Iraq's ground forces: "The much-vaunted Republican Guard did not put up any coordinated resistance along the Karbala–Al Kut line after a week of pounding from the air. Most of the Republican Guard units in frontline areas had been debilitated by desertions, and when the 3rd Infantry and 1st Marine Divisions advanced, they found many positions abandoned, along with hundreds of tanks and armored vehicles. When the 3rd ID arrived in the vicinity of Baghdad's main airport, it met only sporadic counterattacks from Special Republican Guard units."[267]

Air assets operated by the SOF component also played a significant, and at times heroic, role in facilitating SOF operations throughout the three-week campaign. An especially notable instance of valorous air support unfolded shortly after midnight on April 2 during a covert raid by American SOF units on the Thar Thar Palace near Baghdad, a known residence of Hussein and his two sons. The raid yielded no regime leaders, but it netted a trove of documents of considerable intelligence value.[268] Three Air Force Special Operations Command MC-130E Combat Talon pilots who took part in that raid, Lt. Col. Kenneth Ray, Maj. Bruce Taylor, and Maj. James Winsmann, were subsequently awarded the Silver Star for their actions during the operation. Their aircraft had been tasked to provide low-altitude in-flight refueling during both ingress and egress for a formation of SOF helicopters that were infiltrating a Navy SEAL team, Army Special Forces troopers, and a CIA unit into the palace. As the MC-130s neared their assigned target area with their lights out and with their pilots wearing NVGs, they and their accompanying ten-ship package of helicopters triggered a hail of heavy enemy surface-to-air fire. Iraqi SAMs engaged them three times during their initial ingress refueling evolution. The MC-130 pilots executed prompt and aggressive defensive countermaneuvers, taking their aircraft down to less than 100 feet above ground level in one instance while dispensing defensive countermeasures against enemy surface-to-air fire. They successfully negated the enemy threat, with one MC-130 avoiding a missile hit by less than 50 feet. The aircraft then pressed to a second aerial refueling point that still lay within the enemy's surface-to-air threat envelope. The MC-130s conducted 6 in-flight refuelings and transferred more than 30,000 pounds of fuel to 10 fuel-critical helicopters deep inside enemy-controlled territory at night and in blowing dust, accomplishing their mission with no losses.[269]

Air support for the 1st Marine Division was provided by the F/A-18 Hornets, AV-8B Harriers, and AH-1W Cobra attack helicopters of the 3rd Marine Aircraft Wing (MAW) in conformance with the well-honed Marine Air-Ground Task Force (MAGTF, pronounced "mag-taf") concept of operations. General Moseley gave the wing considerable latitude to underwrite the immediate and often rapidly changing needs of the engaged Marine ground commander. A subsequent report explained this informal contract:

> As [Gen. Charles] Horner had done in Desert Storm, Moseley conceded that they would use their aircraft primarily to shape the battlefield in their area. In fall of 2002, he had prepared for this by convening a conference with top Marine generals to work out the [command and control] of Marine air power. Without any formal written agreements, the generals worked out an arrangement that allowed the Marine air commander to tell the

air component how many sorties [I MEF] needed. The planners in the CAOC then allocated these sorties, arranged all the support for them, and sent that information back out in the ATO. To make this plan work, Moseley insisted the Marines provide some of their best officers to serve as liaison officers, one of whom became the CAS planner for the entire theater. It was another example of working out relationships prior to the conflict to make the electronic collaboration run more smoothly during the conflict.[270]

The official Marine Corps after-action assessment of I MEF's contribution to the campaign noted that "the agreement among the generals was to 'nest' Marine command and control under [the] CFACC [combined force air component commander, pronounced "see-fack"]. There would be a Marine ATO within the CFACC ATO; the primary mission for Marine air would be to support the MEF scheme of maneuver; excess sorties would be made available to the CFACC—and there would be provisions for the reverse to occur as well."[271] The 3rd MAW's commander, Maj. Gen. James F. "Tamer" Amos, "found General Moseley to be a commander who readily understood the utility of the MAW as a part of the MAGTF while asserting his own rights to the airspace over the battlefield."[272] In the ensuing scheme of Marine air employment, the Cobras were typically used to suppress and draw down the Iraqi troops that were most directly arrayed against advancing Marine formations while the Hornets and Harriers worked farther north of the line of friendly advance in preemptive kill-box interdiction of enemy ground force movements.

Three variants of CAS performed in joint and combined combat are recognized. The most permissive of these is Type III CAS. Once a pilot is sure of the enemy's position and the positions of all nearby friendly forces, he can be cleared by a JTAC to engage a validated target with no further approval needed. Type II CAS occurs when either visual acquisition of the attacking aircraft by a JTAC on the ground or visual acquisition of the target by the attacking pilot before weapon release is not possible. Type I CAS, the most exacting, requires the JTAC or FAC-A to visually acquire and positively identify both the attacking aircraft *and* the target being attacked. JTACs may use either Type I or Type II CAS with the approval of the fire support coordination center. Type III CAS is used only when there is a low to nonexistent danger of fratricide, in which case the appropriate ground commander can authorize unrestricted weapon release.[273]

To facilitate the closest possible integration of Marine Corps air and ground assets, the 3rd MAW assigned selected pilots not only to the company level to serve as JTACs, but also to each battalion of the 1st Marine Division as an extra support measure to ensure that the unit's CAS needs would be properly met.[274] By the time the Marines rolled into Numaniyah, well into their northward convergence on Baghdad, what had been expected to be a hard-fought showdown with a brigade from the Republican Guard's Baghdad Division had yielded only sporadic small arms fire that was quickly and effectively suppressed. By all indications, the previous week of aerial and artillery bombardment had driven the enemy unit's personnel from their positions.[275] Once the Marines finally contacted the remaining remnants of the Baghdad Division, allied intelligence estimated that the division retained only 6,000 of its 11,000 troops and less than 25 percent of its artillery. Many enemy troops simply deserted their positions.[276]

Similarly, when the Army's 3rd ID came into contact with the remnants of the Republican Guard forces on the outskirts of Baghdad, only about a dozen enemy tanks came out to fight. They were quickly destroyed in one of the few direct tank-on-tank engagements of the entire war.[277] CENTCOM estimated that even before they had been engaged frontally by allied ground forces, the Republican Guard units fielded around Baghdad had already lost more than 1,000 of Iraq's total inventory of 2,500 tanks to air attacks.[278] Of the more than 8,000 munitions that had been dropped since March 19, as many as 3,000 were expended in the last 3 days of March, mostly against Republican Guard units south of Baghdad.[279] The Medina Division received particularly intense strikes, as a result of which it and the Baghdad Division were estimated to have been drawn down by 50 percent before allied ground forces moved to contact. The Hammurabi and Nebuchadnezzar Divisions that were trying to reinforce those two had also been pummeled and were lacking leadership at higher levels.[280] "After a week of sustained aerial bombardment of the opposing Medina and Baghdad Divisions," one analyst wrote, "the [coalition's] 'Panzers' rolled through the remnants with little resistance."[281]

The exact amount of Iraqi ground force equipment destroyed by these air strikes may never be known, but the strikes handily achieved CENTCOM's desired effect of preventing the Republican Guard divisions from mounting a cohesive defense of Baghdad. When allied ground units finally moved within range of enemy ground forces on D+12, they encountered only what one observer called "small determined pockets of Iraqi regime loyalists."[282] By April 2 the Medina Division was officially deemed by CENTCOM to be "combat-ineffective."[283]

General Jumper's precampaign concern that the Iraqis might try to jam the GPS signals on which allied JDAMs and navigational systems depended proved unfounded, although American ground troops raiding a targeted residence in Al Qaim discovered a stash of Russian-made GPS jammers with an address label on the shipping container showing that it had been delivered to the Iraqi embassy in Moscow in January 2003.[284] Allied forces experienced ineffectual enemy attempts at GPS jamming, but no jamming of communications. Ironically, allied strike aircraft destroyed enemy GPS jammers with GPS-aided JDAMs.[285] That fact bore out a comment made by General Leaf two months before the war started when he was still the director of operational requirements on the Air Staff: "If a potential adversary . . . is betting their future on GPS jamming, it's going to be a serious miscalculation. I'm very confident of our ability to operate effectively in that environment."[286] His prediction was validated during the first week of the air war when the Joint Staff's vice director for operations, Major General McChrystal, declared: "We have been aware for some time of the possibility of GPS jammers being fielded, and what we've found is through testing and through actual practice now, that they are not having a negative effect on the air campaign at this point."[287] In fact, GPS jammers had essentially *no* effect on the air component's munitions delivery operations. Under Secretary of the Air Force Peter Teets acknowledged, however, that GPS was indeed susceptible to jamming attempts and noted that the Air Force was taking appropriate steps "to make it much more jam-resistant on the satellite side, on the control-element side, and on the user-equipment side."[288]

In effect, the nonstop precision aerial bombardment from the night of March 21 onward so resoundingly paved the way for allied ground forces that the entrance of the latter into Baghdad was a virtual fait accompli. The allied air contribution to the major combat phase of Iraqi Freedom reconfirmed a lesson from Afghanistan that air power can effectively substitute for artillery if fully exploited toward that end. After just a week of allied bombing, Iraq's ground troops were so disorganized and disoriented that they were unable or unwilling to fall back to a secondary line of defense; instead, they simply walked away. Much of the impact of the bombing was psychological rather than physical; the destruction of a mere ten or so enemy vehicles, for example, might have the secondary effect of convincing several hundred Iraqi troops to give up the fight and go home. Those troops who remained in place were so heavily outmatched that they were put to rout even before they could see their approaching American opponents.

In the end, thanks in substantial part to the enabling contributions of CENTCOM's air component, advancing allied ground forces covered a distance through defended enemy territory equal to that from the Mexican border to San Francisco within less than three weeks.[289] Moreover, the worst-case fear of an Iraqi military retreat en masse into Baghdad and the urban fighting and widespread collateral damage to civilian structures that inevitably would have accompanied it were never realized. Using its previously developed urban CAS plan in which most buildings inside Baghdad had their own individual designation, the CAOC succeeded in precisely directing those munitions that were delivered into the city in a way that minimized unintended damage to civilian infrastructure.[290] A last-ditch Iraqi attempt to torch oil trenches in the Baghdad area with the goal of obscuring prospective targets with heavy smoke did little but foul the air for the civilian population and create video images for attempted propaganda exploitation. The SAR sensors of the E-8 JSTARS could image targets right through the smoke, and satellite-aided munitions could guide themselves completely unhindered to their assigned aim points. An analyst remarked with respect to this vain Iraqi attempt that while the obscuration "might impair some optical reconnaissance tools, it was largely irrelevant in slowing the bombardment."[291]

To a considerable degree, directives handed down by Saddam Hussein were responsible for the thorough drubbing Iraqi ground forces sustained in the allied combined-arms offensive. The Republican Guard had been fielded primarily in a peacetime watchdog role to block any attempted mutiny by regular Iraqi army units and to ensure that the latters' commanders stayed in line. Yet, Hussein did not allow his Republican Guard units to deploy in strength in central Baghdad. Instead, he chose to defend the city by positioning the Hammurabi Division to the southwest, the Al Nida Division to the southeast, and the Nebuchadnezzar Division spread out in positions to the north and southwest.[292]

In fact, the integrity of Iraq's command and control network failed so badly under the weight of the allied air offensive that at one point an Iraqi two-star general drove directly into an American military checkpoint, unaware that allied forces were even in his vicinity.[293] As late as April 5, when U.S. troops were knocking on Baghdad's front door and the regime was just four days from collapse, an Iraqi colonel who had been taken into custody that morning said that his commanders had told him that American forces were still a hundred miles away.[294] In the immediate aftermath of the war, CENTCOM remained unsure how many Iraqi armored vehicles had been destroyed, but the number was clearly in the high hundreds, if not more. General McPeak remarked that the asymmetric application of precision long-range air power against an enemy whose only strength lay in short-range ground power left the Republican Guard with only two options: they could "either hunker down outside Baghdad and die slowly or maneuver and die quickly."[295]

A widely acclaimed account of the allied invasion of Iraq concluded that "declining morale and an abiding fear of U.S. air power had clearly taken their toll on what was supposed to be one of the premier Republican Guard divisions."[296] Intelligence gathered by U.S. occupation forces after the regime fell plainly attested that

> the Al Nida [division] was nowhere near full strength when [American Marines] smashed into it. The commander of the unit later told his interrogators that the leaflets dropped on his troops telling them to depart the area or be bombed by U.S. warplanes had had a tremendous effect. The soldiers became demoralized when they realized that allied aircraft could fly over their positions with virtual impunity and that the leaflets could just as easily have been bombs. Originally a division of 13,000 soldiers and 500 vehicles, it had been reduced to 2,000 troops and 50 vehicles of all sorts by the time the Marines closed on the Iraqi capital. . . . Like the Medina Division, the Al Nida was just a shell of itself when it was attacked by U.S. troops.[297]

This account tellingly concluded, "The Iraqis' fear of U.S. air power was as crippling as the air strikes themselves. . . . In the final days, it was impossible to tell from the air which Iraqi tanks were operational and which had been abandoned, so Moseley instructed his aircrews to 'keep killing it all.'"[298] The CAOC even used inert cement-filled GBU-12 500-pound LGBs (redesignated BDU-50s) during the urban CAS endgame of Iraqi Freedom, essentially "bombing with concrete" to disable Iraqi tanks and other armored vehicles through the munition's kinetic-energy effect alone rather than risk inflicting collateral damage on surrounding buildings and killing noncombatants.[299]

Carrier-Based Operations

Like all of the allied air assets that took part in the three-week campaign, the five carrier air wings that were committed to Iraqi Freedom operated around the clock, with *Theodore Roosevelt* taking the night shift in the eastern Mediterranean and *Constellation* taking the night shift in the North Arabian Gulf.[300] The average flight operations day was sixteen hours during the first twenty-three days of the war, after which it ramped down to thirteen to fourteen hours.[301] Each air wing averaged fifty to sixty sorties a day, perhaps an unimpressive number until one considers that all were staggered multicycle missions lasting six or more hours and often entailing four or more in-flight refuelings. Carrier flight decks were manned twenty-four hours a day for long stretches because strike aircraft and tankers frequently recovered later than planned as a result of repeated requests for on-call CAS. Sea-based strike aircraft were airborne twenty-four hours a day, seven days a week. As had been the case in Operation Enduring Freedom, alert strike packages were also launched every day as previously undiscovered targets of interest were identified. Also as in Enduring Freedom, carrier-based aircraft relied heavily on land-based U.S. Air Force and RAF tankers. That access allowed mission lengths to be extended from one to three or more launch-and-recovery cycles, which in turn eased carrier deck loading and increased the flexibility of the air wings.

These references to aircraft launch-and-recovery cycles speak to a fundamental aspect of carrier air operations that warrants further explanation. Every minute a carrier is headed into the wind during ongoing flight operations, it is committed to a predictable course that opponents can detect and track. Fleet tactics thus dictate that launches and recoveries take place as rapidly as possible while allowing for the routine problems that inevitably arise in the course of such operations, such as a temporarily fouled deck and occasional bolters.[302] Cyclic operations offer the best way to deal with these requirements.

In such operations, a 1+0 cycle is one that lasts an hour from an aircraft's launch to its recovery. A 1+15 cycle lasts an hour and fifteen minutes. In the instance of a notional 1+15 cycle, while one wave of aircraft is being launched, the preceding wave that was launched an hour and fifteen minutes earlier will be holding overhead, its pilots watching their constantly dwindling fuel levels and, as may be required, refueling in flight from recovery tankers near the carrier as they await the signal to extend their tailhooks and commence their approach to the carrier in sequence. Twenty to thirty aircraft can be kept airborne at any given time using such an approach to operations, while the extra space thus freed up on the flight deck can be exploited for respotting aircraft to prepare for the next launch. During these gaps in flight operations, aircraft can also be moved back and forth to the hangar bay as may be required by the flight schedule or maintenance needs.[303]

A continuous cycle of launches followed by immediate recovery of the preceding wave of aircraft reduces the time the carrier needs to remain on a predictable course into the wind. It also gives the flight deck crews sufficient time to ready the deck for the next cycle. A *Nimitz*-class carrier's two bow catapults and two waist catapults can launch twenty aircraft in approximately ten minutes. In ideal conditions, the carrier can recover twenty aircraft on its angled deck in as little as fifteen minutes. A total of twenty-five minutes on a predictable course is ideal for a twenty-aircraft cycle and is generally achieved when the embarked air wing and the carrier's crew work harmoniously together.

Within the span of a single deck cycle, whatever its duration, an air wing's aircraft are launched, recovered, dearmed, spotted, repaired, exchanged with hangar-deck aircraft, serviced, fueled, reconfigured with ordnance, and made ready for the next cycle. Managing the flight deck and respotting aircraft during such an intense operations flow involves an exquisitely complex choreography in which the manipulation of assets and proper timing are crucial. After the last cycle during a day of flight operations has been concluded, as many as forty aircraft may be parked on the flight deck, each carefully spotted to take up the least amount of deck space while allowing a clear path to at least one of the carrier's catapults for the next cycle's initial launch. Aircraft parked on the flight deck are often only inches apart, with their landing gear sometimes perilously close to the flight deck's edge. The carrier's air department monitors all this activity from flight deck control, where a tabletop representation of the flight deck indicates each aircraft's location on the deck and is updated whenever aircraft are respotted. Any disruption of this complex and carefully managed choreography can foul the landing area and force aircraft on final approach to be waved off, consuming more fuel as a result and, at worst, creating gridlock.

During the three weeks of major combat in Iraqi Freedom, E-2C Hawkeye early-warning and battle management aircraft played an indispensable role in getting carrier-based strikers to the right kill boxes. They frequently served as communications links between the carriers, the CAOC, and ground tactical commanders. EA-6B Prowlers also played a pivotal part in the air war. The availability of support jamming was an ironclad go/no-go criterion for all strike missions, including those that involved B-2 and F-117 stealth aircraft. Throughout the three-week campaign, the Navy continued its practice of assigning four EA-6Bs to each embarked squadron. With five air wings participating, along with additional land-based Prowlers, mission planners in the air wings and the CAOC were satisfied that sufficient support jammers were available.[304]

U.S. Naval Reserve squadrons also played an important part in carrier-based strike operations, as perhaps best represented by VFA (Navy Fighter-Attack Squadron)-201, home-stationed at Joint Reserve Base Fort Worth, Texas. That unit was administratively attached to CVW-8 embarked in *Theodore Roosevelt*, making it the first Naval Reserve squadron to deploy for combat since the Korean War. The squadron had only recently converted to the F/A-18+ and joined the air wing during the final phases of the latter's predeployment workups at NAS Fallon. It offered a uniformly high experience level and integrated well with the wing's active-duty squadrons. Unlike a normal fleet squadron, which typically features a younger and less seasoned aircrew complement, VFA-201's pilots averaged 35 years of age, 350 arrested carrier landings, and 2,700 flight hours. Moreover, fourteen of the eighteen were graduates of Navy Fighter Weapons School (Topgun). The executive officer of VFA-15, the fleet squadron that mentored the pilots as they joined CVW-8 for this precedent-setting deployment for a reserve unit, recalled: "The biggest problem they faced was the fact that they had operated almost exclusively as adversary pilots [in the air-to-air training role] for so long. This meant that they did not routinely practice 'Blue air,' or offensive [strike] mission tactics. However, being very high-time Hornet pilots, they quickly ironed out these tactical wrinkles."[305]

Adequate stocks of LGBs and JDAMs allowed the deployed air wings to play a significant role in seeking out and attacking enemy theater ballistic missile launchers. The two wings operating out of the eastern Mediterranean focused on suppressing Scud launches into Israel from Iraq's western desert. The three Gulf-based wings concentrated on potential missile launches from southern Iraq against Kuwait, Saudi Arabia, and other neighboring Gulf states. Each carrier possessed about forty magazines for munitions storage, with row after row of GBU-12 and GBU-16 LGBs stacked up for use. Ten or so crewmembers needed roughly ten to twelve minutes to build up a bomb ready for use.[306] Because the CAOC could not always guarantee targets that could be positively identified and attacked without an unacceptable risk of collateral damage, Navy strike fighters sometimes recovered with unexpended ordnance. A maximum of two thousand pounds of allowable bring-back ordnance was eventually dictated for most carrier-based fighters by the circumstances of the ground advance.[307]

Carrier aircraft losses were almost nil. In one such case, an S-3B tanker veered off the flight deck of *Constellation* and into the water following a suspected runaway throttle or brake failure. The two crewmembers ejected safely and were promptly recovered. Also, an F-14 went down over Iraq due to a mechanical failure involving the aircraft's fuel system.[308] The pilot and radar intercept officer likewise ejected safely and were recovered shortly thereafter. A Marine AV-8B Harrier crashed during a night mission from the assault ship *Nassau*. The pilot ejected and was recovered from the North Arabian Gulf.[309]

The sandstorm that essentially halted the allied ground advance for three days also affected carrier operations in the North Arabian Gulf. At times, the *shamal* generated sustained winds of twenty-five knots gusting to fifty and visibility that was often less than three hundred feet. Desert dust penetrated aircraft inlets and orifices, caused damage to canopies and engines, and occasioned some harrowing aircraft recoveries. Carrier landings into whiteouts occurred more than a few times, with cockpit sensor display videotapes showing eye-watering arrested landings that were performed flawlessly in visibilities of less than half a mile. Landing signal officers would talk each aircraft down the centerline of the carrier's recovery area, sometimes with the aircraft becoming visible only seconds before it trapped.

Throughout the *shamal*, air wing tanker squadrons flew twice their normal number of sorties to refuel fighters that were orbiting above the carrier and waiting for openings through which they could penetrate and trap.[310] Tankers transferred fuel to strike fighters and to EA-6Bs, typically in heavy turbulence and at altitudes as high as 30,000 feet, where in-flight refueling evolutions would not normally take place. Six launch and recovery cycles on the three carriers in the North Arabian Gulf had to be canceled because of persistent airborne grit, lightning, and wind shear. Despite these challenging conditions, the Navy did not dramatically reduce its overall sortie rate during the sandstorm, and the coalition continued to fly as many as two thousand ATO sorties daily. CVW-5 launched one hundred strike sorties a day and also conducted organic tanking, with its eight S-3B tankers flying thirty or more refueling sorties a day.

The F/A-18E Super Hornet had entered squadron service only nine months before the start of Iraqi Freedom with VFA-115 of CVW-14 embarked in *Abraham Lincoln*. In November 2002, shortly after its maiden deployment, the F/A-18E saw its first exposure to combat in Operation Southern Watch, dropping GPS-aided JDAMs on targets in southern Iraq. This combat first for the aircraft also marked the first successful operational use of the GBU-35, a 1,000-pound JDAM variant that the Navy prefers over the original 2,000-pound version because it is a lighter load to bring back to the carrier in the event the munition is not dropped during the sortie. (The Boeing Company had delivered an initial batch of 434 of the weapons to the Navy the previous March.)[311]

At the start of Iraqi Freedom, VFA-115 had been averaging about fifteen maintenance man-hours per flight hour with the F/A-18E, as compared with twenty for the older F/A-18C and sixty for the F-14. The electronic technical publications (about 80 percent of the required documentation) supplied to the squadron and the F/A-18E's ability to upload technical updates added to the ease of maintenance, as did the fact that the aircraft were the newest in the Navy's inventory, some having come straight to the squadron off the production line. Initially, the F/A-18E was assigned missions in Iraqi Freedom that did not utilize its increased endurance or greater load-carrying capability. That practice was later changed as pilots gained more combat experience with the aircraft. The Super Hornet's increased payload capability over that of the earlier F/A-18C meant the same number of targets (or more) could be attacked while exposing fewer aircraft to danger.

During VFA-115's initial workups, the F/A-18E had been used extensively as a mission tanker to refuel combat-configured Super Hornets and other air wing aircraft. In Iraqi Freedom, one F/A-18E out of the squadron's dozen was fully dedicated to tanking, although the wing's S-3Bs retained the recovery tanking role. Because the Super Hornet, unlike the S-3B, has a self-protection capability with its AIM-9M and AIM-120 air-to-air missiles and an electronic warfare suite for protection against surface-to-air threats, it can accompany strikers into enemy airspace in its tanker role and can escort damaged aircraft back to friendly airspace. The aircraft also was equipped with the ALQ-165 advanced self-protection jammer and the ALE-50 towed decoy—the first pairing of such a decoy with a Navy aircraft. In all, Super Hornet tankers transferred more than 3.5 million pounds of fuel to receiver aircraft.

On March 31 an embarked squadron of 12 F/A-18F two-seat Super Hornets arrived in-theater in CVW-11 on board *Nimitz*, the first carrier to deploy with the new aircraft, en route to the North Arabian Gulf to relieve *Abraham Lincoln*. Two E-models from VFA-14 and two F-models from VFA-41 were flown four thousand miles from *Nimitz* in the Strait of Malacca to *Abraham Lincoln* to augment CVW-14 and to give the two-seat F model an early first exposure to combat. The addition of those extra four Super Hornets gave CVW-14 a more flexible mix of strike and tanker capability as well as additional FAC-A support. (*Nimitz* herself was expected to arrive on station in the Gulf in early April.) As with VFA-115 embarked in *Abraham Lincoln*, the Super Hornets in *Nimitz* had deployed without all of their equipment, most notably the shared reconnaissance pod, fully tested. Although the pod, called SHARP, had no data-link capability and was equipped only with a medium-altitude sensor package, it performed adequately. (Data-link capability and a high-altitude digital camera were to be added later.)

The F/A-18F was the first Navy aircraft to be equipped with the advanced technology forward-looking infrared (ATFLIR) pod, which by the start of Iraqi Freedom was in full-rate production.[312] Problems with the initial ATFLIR pods in *Abraham Lincoln* were overcome with the successor generation of pods provided to another F/A-18E squadron and to the first F/A-18F squadron embarked in *Nimitz*. Four Super Hornets in the deployed F/A-18E/F squadrons were configured for use primarily as tankers. As the campaign unfolded, some in the F/A-18E/F community pressed for an early integration of the extended-range standoff land attack missile (SLAM-ER), as well as a 500-pound LGB and eventually the 500-pound JDAM. At the time, the smallest precision weapon the aircraft could carry was a 1,000-pound LGB, which was too large for some CAS mission requirements.[313] The aircraft also lacked a long-range standoff weapon as it awaited provision of the U.S. Air Force–developed joint air-to-surface standoff missile (JASSM).

Even with the recent introduction of the Super Hornet into fleet service, the F-14 remained a viable platform because it offered greater range than the Super Hornet and its LANTIRN targeting pod was available in greater numbers than the F/A-18E's new ATFLIR pod. Tactics and operating procedures for the F-14 focused on hunting down mobile targets. Because friendly ground forces did not have the technical wherewithal to generate mensurated target coordinates, the F-14's full-capability tactical air reconnaissance pod system (TARPS) and fighter tactical imagery (FTI) suite enabled real-time imagery transfers whereby SOF teams on the ground could cue F-14s to locate and attack moving targets with LGBs.[314] The F-14's sensor and targeting systems were also being provided to the F/A-18F, whose aircrews could thus acquire, view, send, and receive electro-optical imagery in near-real time, along with text messages that might be sent either as attachments or as stand-alone transmissions. Receivers of such transmissions could include other aircraft as well as land combatants ranging from senior commanders to SOF teams in the field using laptop computers as downlinks.[315] Spare parts for the F-14Ds turned out to be the parent air wing's single greatest challenge, although it was never so acute as to prevent the wing from meeting its goal of having seven of its ten F-14Ds operational at all times.[316]

Combat operations conducted by the two Mediterranean-based carrier air wings differed markedly from those flown by the three air wings that operated in the congested waters of the North Arabian Gulf. The former had initially been tasked with supporting the planned invasion by U.S. Army ground forces from Turkey. After the Turkish government ruled out that option, the Mediterranean-based air wings were re-roled to support the allied SOF teams operating in northern Iraq and the western desert. When the war began, however, the Turkish government was also denying its airspace to allied strike operations against Iraq, a measure that threatened to keep the two air wings in Carrier Task Force 60 out of the fight altogether as the three carriers in the North Arabian Gulf made their contribution to the war effort from the south. Fortunately for CENTCOM, that changed on March 20 when Saudi Arabia relented under U.S. diplomatic pressure and granted transit approval for allied combat aircraft to pass through its previously restricted airspace. The commanding officer of VFA-105, embarked in *Harry S. Truman*, recalled his relief: "We had a way in! The new route was going to be long. From a position just off the Nile Delta, CVW-3 aircraft flew down the Sinai Peninsula, around the southern tip of Israel and Jordan and worked their way across the Saudi desert to refuel from Air Force tankers just short of the Iraqi border. Once topped off, F/A-18s and F-14s, supported by EA-6Bs, would strike at targets located west and northwest of Baghdad."[317]

As the campaign entered its third and final week, that sea-based capability allowed General Moseley to report that "the Navy is carrying a large, large load up there [in northern Iraq] operating out of the eastern Mediterranean and flying across Turkey. . . . With two aircraft carriers in the eastern Med and with our tankers, we're able to provide near-continuous pressure."[318] More to the point, those sea-based strike fighters, along with Air Force B-52s operating out of RAF Fairford in the United Kingdom, made some things possible in northern Iraq that could not have been accomplished otherwise. Because of range-payload limitations and tanker-related operating restrictions, the CAOC could not range land-based U.S. Air Force and RAF strike fighters, even the exceptionally long-legged RAF Tornado GR4s based in Qatar and Kuwait, very far north of Baghdad. Moreover, during the three-day *shamal*, Navy strike fighters from the carrier operating areas in the eastern Mediterranean and the North Arabian Gulf were the only allied fighters that could play in the air effort against Republican Guard and other Iraqi ground forces, because Al Udeid and Al Jaber Air Bases in Qatar and Kuwait were both completely weathered in. The senior CAOC director recalled that Navy aircrews were "absolute heroes" during that critical time window, saving a lot of Army lives when a convoy of Iraqi vehicles began heading south toward their positions. More than one aircraft returned to its carrier with severe hail damage and even radomes ripped off as a result of the storm.[319]

Cdr. Andy Lewis, the commanding officer of VFA-15 in CVW-8 on board *Theodore Roosevelt*, implemented a pilot management plan that proved to be a perceptible force multiplier: "One thing that we did in our squadron that I think paid big dividends when [Iraqi Freedom] started was to create a tactical organization, or, in other words, assign permanent lead-wingman combinations. We took the most experienced pilots and paired them with the least experienced. After that, pilots were assigned by tactical pairs as strike sorties were given to the squadron. As a result, my young guys were never without guidance either before or during the war, and this allowed even the most junior 'nugget' to fly strikes starting from Day One regardless of their overall experience."[320]

The five carrier air wings that took part in the campaign were better integrated into the ATO process than ever before, with each wing having representatives in the CAOC where the daily ATO was assembled to ensure that the wings were assigned appropriate missions. Lessons learned during Enduring Freedom carried over into the now much-improved joint force planning for Iraqi Freedom, with CENTAF staffers at all levels coordinating seamlessly with their counterparts in the maritime component and with at least one Navy Fighter Weapons School graduate eventually embedded full time in the CENTAF planning staff.

The Navy's carrier air wings also had ready access to software that automatically searched the complex ATO for Navy-specific sections, eliminating the need for air wing mission planners and aircrews to sort through the entire immense document. Closer cooperation in recent years between their weapons schools yielded still further dividends in improved joint Air Force–Navy interoperability. By all accounts, the Navy and the Air Force worked together unprecedentedly well in integrating their respective air operations. Almost all strike packages were joint operations, with Air Force F-16CJs and Navy EA-6B Prowlers routinely embedded together to enable the most robust possible defense suppression capability.[321]

Of the 41,404 combat and combat support sorties flown during the three weeks of major combat in Iraqi Freedom, Navy and Marine Corps aircraft flying from carriers and large-deck amphibious ships flew nearly 14,000. Of those, 5,568 were fighter sorties, 2,058 were tanker sorties, 442 were E-2C sorties, and 357 were ISR sorties. Of the roughly 5,300 bombs dropped by Navy and Marine Corps strike aircraft, fewer than 230 were unguided. More than 75 percent of the precision weapons delivered by Navy strike aircraft were JDAMs. In addition, Navy F/A-18Cs flew 24 of the 158 propaganda leaflet delivery missions. Most of the Navy's fighter sorties were dedicated to providing CAS.[322] Fully mission-capable (FMC) rates for carrier-based aircraft throughout the campaign were significantly higher than the normal peacetime rates for deployed air wings. The FMC rate was 89 percent for the F-14A, 98 percent for the F-14B, 78 percent for the F-14D, 80 percent for the F/A-18A, 87 percent for the F/A-18C, 90 percent for the F/A-18E, 91 percent for the F/A-18F, 80 percent for the EA-6B, 89 percent for the S-3B, and 79 percent for the E-2C.[323]

The End of the Ba'athist Regime

By April 4, 85 percent of the allied air effort was concentrated on drawing down the Medina, Hammurabi, and Baghdad Divisions of the Republican Guard that were defending the approaches to Baghdad. Army intelligence reported that day that allied air attacks had degraded the Hammurabi Division to 44 percent of its assessed full-up effectiveness and the Medina Division to 18 percent.[324] That same day saw the first deployment of allied fixed-wing combat aircraft into Iraq when Air Force A-10s began operating out of the Iraqi air force's Tallil airfield after Marine Corps and RAF Harriers had established a forward arming and refueling point one hundred miles inside Iraq. That forward move eliminated some of the burden on the coalition's heavily taxed tanker force.

General Moseley reported during a press conference on April 5 that Iraq's military airfields "for the most part, are not flyable. This morning we had only a handful of landing surfaces that could be used, and as we go through the day we will crater those again, as we do every day to attempt to minimize the opportunity to fly. . . . That does not mean that he [Saddam Hussein] won't be able to get an airplane airborne somewhere, . . . [but if] he does get something airborne, it will not have a strategic dislocating impact on us." As to why the Iraqi air force had remained out of the fight throughout the campaign, General Moseley replied: "I believe that he has not flown because in their mind they've made calculation that they will not survive."[325]

On April 6 Major General McChrystal reported: "Coalition air forces have established air supremacy over the entire country, which means the enemy is incapable of effective interference with coalition air operations."[326] Iraq's air defenses had not yet been completely neutralized, however. Lt. Col. Raymond Strasburger was leading an element of A-10s that same day in support of Advance 33, an Air Force JTAC team attached to the Army's Task Force 2/69 Armor, when he observed enemy tanks and armored fighting vehicles engaging the force's lead company from the east end of a bridge spanning the Tigris River. In an ensuing sequence of events for which he was awarded the Silver Star, Lieutenant Colonel Strasburger led his element through heavy AAA fire despite severely reduced visibility and conducted an initial reconnaissance run against the target.

> Relinquishing the element of surprise to Iraqi AAA gunners, he used the same attack heading to protect friendly forces and repeatedly attacked a battalion-sized enemy armor element that was dug in on the east side of the bridge. For 33 minutes, he continued with his wingman to press the attack in the face of heavy AAA fire, demobilizing three T-72 tanks, six APCs, and multiple utility vehicles that were within striking distance of the friendly ground force. His effort ultimately allowed TF 2/69

Armor to press their northward attack with minimal combat losses, linking up with adjoining coalition forces and completing the 360-degree encirclement of Baghdad.[327]

On April 7 General Moseley reported that the CAOC was running out of worthwhile targets.[328] That same day, however, allied intelligence sensors reportedly intercepted a telephone conversation that suggested that Saddam Hussein and his two sons were in downtown Baghdad's Al Mansoor district. A signals intelligence cut from the intercepted cell phone exchange provided exact GPS coordinates for the location. The crew of a B-1 bomber orbiting nearby was given mensurated target coordinates by the CAOC and dropped two deep-penetrating and two delay-fused GBU-31 2,000-pound JDAMs on the target within twelve minutes after the CAOC had received the raw target coordinates from an E-3 AWACS.[329] The entire sequence between the identification of the target and the attack reportedly took less than an hour.[330] Once again, Hussein was not at the site, but the attack nevertheless confirmed that CENTCOM was continuing to exert every effort to hunt him down and kill him.

On April 8, thanks mainly to the unrelenting precision air attacks throughout the preceding three weeks, CENTCOM intelligence reported that only 19 of the roughly 850 tanks of the Republican Guard divisions defending Baghdad at the beginning of the campaign remained intact, and that only 40 of the Iraqis' 550 artillery pieces were still serviceable.[331] In effect, the Republican Guard had lost nearly all of its tanks and artillery to allied air attacks. When the 3rd ID was ordered to send its 2nd Brigade on a raid into central Baghdad to capture the presidential district, the brigade penetrated to its objective opposed only by dismounted paramilitary harassment. Iraqi resistance was highly fragmented and confused, and seemed unable to organize.[332] The most thorough review of the U.S. Army's contribution to the three-week campaign noted that the advancing armored task force's encounter with exclusively dismounted resistance "would become *de rigueur* all the way to Baghdad. . . . The enemy used innocent men, women, and children as human shields. Iraqi forces also used trucks, taxis, and ambulances to transport fighters onto the battlefield. . . . This pattern of operation became routine as the war wore on."[333]

A former Marine Corps F/A-18 pilot later wrote that "the Iraqi army was notable during the campaign for the incredible fact that it never really showed up. . . . American air power vaporized a great number of Iraqi formations before they could even start toward the fighting, while some enemy units just chose not to do battle and never left their garrisons."[334] This observer went on to note that the continuous air strikes well in front of advancing coalition ground forces were "an undeniable factor, indeed, perhaps the most important factor, in the success of the ground effort. . . . Quite simply put, the Iraqis were never able to mass in units large enough to slow the American advance. This fact was sometimes lost on ground commanders whose awareness of the battlefield was often no more than what they could see from the road."[335] RAND analyst David Johnson echoed this assessment in noting that "the importance of 'shaping' the battlefield with air power, enabled through high levels of operational situational awareness, was that it created a tactical condition whereby coalition ground forces never faced large Iraqi formations 'eyeball-to-eyeball.'"[336] On the contrary, the ground component mainly confronted fanatically tenacious but disorganized and suicidal dismounted Iraqi paramilitary fighters in repeated skirmishes in which "after the AK-47 [rifle], the RPG was the most ubiquitous weapon of the war."[337]

After allied ground forces had enveloped Baghdad, the CAOC began shifting its kinetic effort toward Tikrit and Mosul farther north. Already, B-52s and Navy strike fighters had been conducting armed overwatch operations in that area in support of JSOTF North. On April 9, A-10s and RAF Harrier GR7s were folded into that effort to increase the pressure on enemy units in the area and accelerate their surrender. Saddam Hussein's regime finally collapsed that same day. The U.S. troops that drove through the streets of Baghdad encountered only scattered resistance as thousands of residents poured into the streets to celebrate the regime's defeat. By this time, U.S. and British forces were in control of at least two-thirds of the country and all of its main centers south of Baghdad. Hussein, his family, his ministers, and other key members of the ruling Revolutionary Command Council still remained at large.[338] The noose on most of those holdouts, however, tightened relentlessly.[339]

By mid-April, allied combat and combat support sorties were down to about seven hundred a day, only a third of the peak rate that had been sustained through the previous three weeks. The *Kitty Hawk* and *Constellation* carrier battle groups and their embarked air wings were sent home from the North Arabian Gulf on the war's twenty-seventh day, leaving one carrier remaining in the Gulf and two in the eastern Mediterranean within range of Iraq should CENTCOM need their services. By D+31 the Navy's carrier presence in the region had ramped down to a single battle group headed by *Nimitz* with CVW-11 on board.[340] The Air Force's four B-2s on Diego Garcia and forward-deployed F-117s at Al Udeid also returned to their home bases in the United States. At that point the U.S. Defense Department's public affairs chief, Victoria Clarke, declared that "the [Hussein] regime is at its end, and its leaders are either dead, surrendered, or on the run."[341] President Bush later added an important qualifying note: "Our victory in Iraq is certain, but it is not complete." He emphasized that a final allied victory over Iraq would not be declared until General Franks had determined that all allied military objectives had been obtained.[342]

In the end, it was the combination of allied air power as an effective shaper of events and the speed of the ground advance that got allied forces to Baghdad before the enemy could mount a viable defense, a process greatly aided by the ineptitude of the Iraqi armed forces. As a senior military official put it, "we executed faster than they could react." The Iraqi troops that were rushed to the field found themselves on a killing ground for allied air power, in what CENTCOM staffers called "reinforcing failure."[343] Vice President Cheney quoted historian Victor Davis Hansen in assessing the coalition's unexpectedly rapid success: "By any fair standard of even the most dazzling charges in military history, . . . the present race to Baghdad is unprecedented in its speed and daring and in the lightness of its casualties."[344]

Although the "shock and awe" blitz the media anticipated against enemy urban targets never materialized, the CAOC nonetheless succeeded in hitting what its planners had wanted to hit in Baghdad during the first night of the air war. It also excelled uniformly in providing a measured and steady concentration of allied air power against the Republican Guard. Col. Michael Longoria, the commander of the Air Force's 484th Air Expeditionary Wing, described the effects of the air war on the coalition's ground effort: "It's just awesome the number of tanks, APCs, tracked vehicles and enemy positions that were attacked. . . . I don't know if we are going to understand how significant this effort was until we do more analysis. But when you can destroy over three divisions worth of heavy armor in a period of about a week and reduce each of these Iraqi divisions down to even 15, 20 percent of their strength, it's going to have an effect."[345] The coalition lost only twenty manned aircraft in achieving this effect, including six helicopters and one A-10 that were downed by enemy fire.

A report in the British press suggested that an F-15E that went down on April 7 during the war's last days may have been hit by a Stinger missile that had been abandoned by British special forces during their retreat from an ambush, but CENTCOM immediately discounted that suggestion as pure hearsay with no evidentiary basis whatever. A senior British Special Boat Service source likewise greeted the dubious report with skepticism, saying: "You would rather leave a man behind than equipment like that."[346] The aircraft had been bombing enemy positions near the northern town of Tikrit. The pilot, Capt. Eric Das, and his weapons systems officer, Maj. William Watkins, did not attempt to eject and were killed. A closer inquiry ruled out radar-guided SAMs or AAA, and the cause of the loss was never determined.[347]

As for the joint and combined campaign's bottom-line results at the strategic level, the Republican Guard and Special Republican Guard had been crushed, Iraqi mines and coastal cruise missiles had been neutralized, the southern and northern oil fields had been secured, and the Iraqi air force had been grounded. The three-week campaign brought a decisive end to Operations Northern Watch and Southern Watch. The former ran for 4,365 days (just 2 weeks short of 12 years) and generated 106,170 armed overwatch and combat support sorties out of Turkey; the latter lasted 3,857 days (10.5 years) and generated almost 3 time as many sorties—285,681—out of bases in Saudi Arabia and from carrier air wings operating in the North Arabian Gulf.[348] In planning the campaign, General Franks had mitigated strategic-level risk by accepting risk at the operational level, and that operational-level risk had been mitigated by audacity, speed of movement, combined arms lethality, and tactical-level acumen, with more than a little help from Iraq's military incompetence. In all, the twenty-one-day experience showed that overwhelming force is not just about numbers and that jointness can be a true force multiplier when pursued and applied with commitment and conviction by all players from the most senior echelons on down.[349]

To be sure, the campaign's planning and conduct had its share of critics on the American domestic front who complained for a time that the ground offensive, with only one Army division and one MEF attacking from the south with unprotected flanks on both sides, represented a needlessly risky gamble by the Bush administration and by CENTCOM.[350] Those critics, however, failed to recognize the effectiveness of the transformed allied air capability against fielded enemy ground forces that had evolved since the first Persian Gulf War in 1991. Gen. Charles Horner, the air component commander during Desert Storm, explained that improvements in air-delivered precision target attack had "made it possible [in Iraqi Freedom] to destroy a very large number of Iraqi ground forces in a short period of time. Moreover, the attacks were made from medium or higher altitudes, which eliminated exposure to short-range air defenses. And, from these altitudes, Iraqi soldiers had little or no warning time to disperse and take cover." Horner added: "Iraqi units were being targeted with precision air attacks before they could pose a threat to advancing U.S. land forces or were within range of the cameras of embedded news media."[351] He further noted the psychological effects of constant exposure to such attacks, which are almost never taken into account in the archaic attrition warfare models that continue to be used in official war games.[352]

Maj. Gen. Robert Scales, the lead author of the Army's after-action account of Desert Storm and no air power enthusiast, succinctly summed up this newly emergent fact of modern military life when he remarked that "the American way of war substitutes firepower for manpower. We expose as few troops as possible to close contact with the enemy. We do that by killing as many enemy as we can with precision weapons."[353] Air Chief Marshal Burridge echoed that assessment during his postcampaign testimony before the British House of Commons: "Von Clausewitz always told us that if you are going to invade somebody's country, go at three to one. . . . We did it the other way around, but von Clausewitz did not have the understanding of air power. Air power was decisive in the maneuver battle."[354]

Critical to allied air power's decisiveness in the campaign's ground maneuver battle was its remarkable effectiveness against Iraqi armored forces. After the campaign ended, an assessment by the U.S. Department of Defense determined that all but two dozen Republican Guard tanks had been either destroyed or abandoned. There was no indication, however, that many crewmembers had been killed inside them. A group of *Time* magazine reporters who later visited a number of the most notable land battlefields discovered that most Iraqi soldiers had survived by staying away from their tanks as the latter were being destroyed with unerring precision by allied air power. Those troops simply fled as allied ground forces moved northward. This may help explain why those Iraqi units defending Baghdad put up virtually no resistance to CENTCOM's prompt capture of the city. The Baghdad, Medina, Nebuchadnezzar, and Hammurabi Divisions of the Republican Guard had been deployed in two defensive arcs south of the capital, an outer arc about one hundred miles long and an inner arc spanning some thirty miles from Yusifiyah to Suwayrah. All of these troop positions had reportedly been undermanned. Each division had a strength of about 10,000 troops on paper, but the Department of Defense later estimated that the Iraqi troops who had been positioned against attacking allied forces actually numbered only between 16,000 and 24,000 in all. For the most part, those troop positions were attacked by allied air forces, with JSTARS, Predator, and Global Hawk geolocating enemy tanks and allied strike aircraft then being called in to engage and destroy them.[355]

In telling testimony to the accuracy of those attacks, five Iraqi tanks in an open marketplace in Mahmudiyah were struck from the air while they were sequestered in alleyways so cramped that the turrets of the tanks could not be turned. Some storefront windows just a few feet away from the tanks were blown out, but no harm was done otherwise to the surrounding buildings. Iraqi troops sometimes parked tanks and other vehicles beneath overpasses to prevent detection from above, only to have them destroyed or disabled by LGBs that entered from the side and left the bridges overhead intact. More than a few tanks that were hidden under trees were also destroyed because the Iraqi unit commanders and soldiers who placed them there failed to realize that the palm fronds offered no sanctuary from modern thermal imaging technology.[356]

In yet another testament to the consistent precision of allied air attacks, the battlefields south of Baghdad featured few of the sorts of craters that carpet-bombing attacks would have produced. Instead, combat effects assessors found blown-out Iraqi tanks and other vehicle hulks standing alone in ones and twos, most having been destroyed from the air before advancing U.S. ground forces arrived within weapons range. A Republican Guard colonel on the Iraqi General Staff later told his allied interrogators that "the . . . divisions were essentially destroyed by air strikes when they were still about 30 miles from their destination. . . . The Iraqi will to fight was broken outside Baghdad." This colonel added: "Defeat was in large part due to our inability to move troops and equipment because of the devastating U.S. air power." Similarly, a Republican Guard captain said of his recollections of the *shamal* experience: "It was night and in the middle of a severe sandstorm. The troops and vehicles were hidden under trees. The soldiers thought they were safe, but two enormous bombs and a load of cluster munitions found their targets. Some soldiers left their positions and ran away. When the big bombs hit their targets, the vehicles just melted away."[357]

Allied psychological warfare operations in the form of leaflets dropped on Iraqi positions and e-mail messages sent directly to Iraqi commanders may have helped considerably in eliminating the Iraqis' will to fight. Iraqi military survivors who subsequently spoke with *Time* reporters were anything but belligerent. The survival of so many Iraqi troops did not concern U.S. commanders, because their intent was not to kill large numbers of Iraqis but to break down their resistance. As further evidence that little significant ground combat took place, earthwork bunkers, trenches, and sandbagged enemy gun emplacements facing southward showed few traces of the shell casings, cartridges, and scorch marks that are the normal residue of ground warfare.[358]

Iraqi soldiers interrogated both during and after the campaign freely admitted that their morale had quickly collapsed when their armored vehicles began exploding all around them in the midst of the blinding three-day sandstorm (see Chapter 4 for more on the views of Iraqi commanders). In those circumstances Iraqi troops simply had no place to hide. As CENTCOM's deputy commander, Lieutenant General DeLong, pointed out, "after fourteen days of bombing,

Baghdad's Republican Guard troops were down to minimum capacity, numerous key leadership targets were taken out, and Iraqi military communications were in disarray."[359] Offering his own perspective on this achievement in subsequent testimony to a defense committee of the British Parliament, Air Chief Marshal Burridge similarly remarked: "I suspect that we disrupted his command and control very early on, and I think they simply lost the ability to mount any sort of coherent defense. They were also surprised by the speed of advance, particularly from the Karbala gap up to Baghdad airport. . . . I think they were incapable of responding."[360]

Overall, CENTCOM achieved tactical surprise at the outset and, with the singular exception of the unsuccessful Apache deep-attack attempt on March 24, retained its offensive momentum throughout the major combat phase of Iraqi Freedom. Iraqi forces were never able to mount a coherent counter to the allied offensive. Saddam Hussein never stopped believing that an attack would come through the north from Turkey and Jordan. As a result, he kept eleven Iraqi army divisions tied down there as insurance against a second front, which was never a possibility after Turkey refused to grant CENTCOM the use of its territory. In the end, noted one assessment, "rather than the Grozny-like carnage and destruction predicted—and feared, Baghdad fell and the regime fell after only three days of hard [localized] fighting. . . . With soldiers and Marines able to move at will throughout the city, the regime evaporated."[361]

Postcampaign interrogations of Iraqi political and military leaders revealed that right up to the start of the campaign, Hussein believed that the United States would not invade Iraq because timely French and Russian intervention would prevent it. He also was said to have believed that in the event the United States did invade, it would quickly yield to international pressure to halt the war; that no coalition forces would ever reach Baghdad; and that the Bush administration would be content to settle for an outcome that fell short of regime change.[362]

Looking back over the campaign experience, the deputy air component commander, Admiral Nichols, remarked, "We were much more successful than even the most optimistic among us had predicted. We moved farther and faster than projected, and our combined arms fires set new standards for persistence, volume, and lethality, day and night in all-weather conditions. The Iraqi military tried but could not react to the tempo we set on the battlefield. By the time they made a decision to do something, we had foreclosed that option."[363] An assessment of the U.S. Army's contribution to the campaign aptly noted that "the essential lesson of these urban fights was that integrating combined arms, heavy and light forces, armored raids, and a liberal application of precision air power applied in each case. . . . Coalition airmen delivered responsive and highly accurate close air support, turning the tide of battle in ground tactical engagements on more than one occasion in the final assault on Baghdad."[364] CENTCOM's leaders would not know until the Ba'athist regime had been toppled and its former principals could be interrogated, however, that Hussein had been mainly concerned with the threat from within and accordingly had configured and fielded his forces to address that concern above all else.[365]

The Allies' Contribution

As in the first Persian Gulf War in 1991, Washington's main partner in Operation Iraqi Freedom was the United Kingdom. By every measure that matters, especially given its small size and limited resources, the United Kingdom was a coequal player with the United States when it came to the quality of its equipment, military leadership, concepts of operations, and combat prowess. Such close involvement was hardly surprising; the United States and Great Britain have had a long-standing special relationship dating back to the early twentieth century. The United Kingdom was a similarly pivotal participant in Operation Desert Storm, as well as a close partner of the United States in a succession of subsequent UN-approved military contingency responses, including Operation Deliberate Force and Operation Allied Force over the Balkans during the 1990s, and the decade-long enforcement of the UN-mandated no-fly zones over post–Desert Storm Iraq through Operations Northern Watch and Southern Watch (the British portions of which were code-named Operation Resinate).[1]

In addition, the RAF had routinely trained with the U.S. Air Force in realistic large-force exercises such as Red Flag at Nellis AFB, Nevada, and similar training evolutions elsewhere around the world. Perhaps most important of all, ever since the terrorist attacks of September 11, 2001, the British Ministry of Defence (MoD) had maintained an embedded senior leadership and staff presence at CENTCOM's headquarters at MacDill AFB, Florida, in connection with Operation Enduring Freedom, to which the RAF contributed notably in the support role by providing VC-10 and Tristar tankers, E-3D Sentry AWACS and Canberra PR9 reconnaissance aircraft, and intratheater airlifters, as well as basing provisions at the British island base of Diego Garcia that were crucial for supporting U.S. bomber operations.[2]

Yet the United Kingdom's participation in the second Gulf War was by no means a foregone conclusion. On the contrary, Britain's close involvement in the planning for the campaign from its earliest months continued, almost up to the beginning of combat operations, against a backdrop of persistent uncertainty as to whether British forces would actually take part in those operations.[3] Prime Minister Tony Blair faced substantial opposition in that regard both within the Labour Party and among the British public. Barely a day before the first bombs fell, he was subjected by his own party to what was, in effect, a vote of confidence in Parliament. The vote passed by a comfortable margin of 396 to 217, largely on the strength of Blair's compelling performance in laying out the case for war.[4] After that, the British government secured parliamentary approval to use "all means necessary" in the conduct of the impending campaign, albeit with the backing of only about a third of British public opinion.[5]

In the end, however, all of the required pieces fell into place in time for the United Kingdom's combat involvement, code-named Operation Telic, to commence at the war's opening moments. There was, moreover, a closer alignment of American and British campaign objectives for Iraqi Freedom than had been the case for enforcing the no-fly zones over northern and southern Iraq. That allowed the campaign to be conducted at the optimum tempo and with minimum political friction. On March 20, just as the campaign was getting under way, Britain's secretary of state for defence declared the campaign's objectives in Parliament as being to disarm Iraq of WMD and to secure key elements of Iraq's economic infrastructure from sabotage and willful destruction by the Ba'athist regime of Saddam Hussein. After the campaign ended, the initial after-action report by the MoD affirmed that the nation's "overriding political objective [had been] to disarm Saddam of his weapons of mass destruction."[6] A subsequent report by Britain's comptroller and auditor general further affirmed that a second key task had been the elimination of Hussein's regime.[7]

Toward both ends the United Kingdom contributed, among other assets, some 46,000 military personnel, 19 warships, 115 fixed-wing aircraft, and nearly 100 helicopters.[8] That contribution made Operation Telic Great Britain's largest force deployment for combat since Operation Granby, its contribution to the first Gulf War, in late 1990 and early 1991. The deployment entailed moving a highly capable force some 3,400 miles in just 10 weeks, less than half the time that had been required to deploy a roughly similar-sized force to take part in the 1991 war. It occurred against a backdrop of concurrent British operations in the Balkans, Sierra Leone, Afghanistan, and Northern Ireland and at a time when the RAF was already overflying northern and southern Iraq as a part of the twelve-year UN effort to enforce the no-fly zones.[9]

Australia likewise offered a spirited and substantial military contribution to Operation Iraqi Freedom that reflected a deep and politically courageous national commitment. Under the successive code names Operation Bastille and Operation Falconer, the Australian government provided twenty-two aircraft— nineteen from the Royal Australian Air Force (RAAF) and three from the Australian Army—and upward of two thousand military personnel to the coalition effort. That contribution included a national headquarters similar to but smaller than that of the British contingent that was collocated with CENTCOM's forward headquarters at Camp As Saliyah in Qatar.[10] In addition to the RAAF contingent, the Australians committed HMAS (Her Majesty's Australian Ship) *Kanimbla*, an amphibious landing ship with three Sea King helicopters; HMAS *Darwin*, an Oliver Hazard Perry–class guided missile frigate (FFG) with two S-70B-2 Sea Hawk helicopters; HMAS *ANZAC*, a light frigate (FFH) with one S-70B-2 Sea Hawk helicopter; a clearance diving team from the Royal Navy; thirty Australians on exchange assignment with deployed U.S. and UK units; and an Army Special Operations Task Group (SOTG) built around a Special Air Service Regiment (SASR) squadron supported by a reinforced commando platoon as a quick-reaction force. The Australian Army also provided three CH-47D Chinook helicopters to support the SOTG.[11]

Australia's contribution to Iraqi Freedom likewise stemmed from a long history of close bilateral ties with the United States, in this case going back to the Australian government's decision in 1941 to align itself formally with Washington in the security arena, an agreement that was subsequently ratified in the ANZUS (Australia–New Zealand–United States) Treaty of 1951 and that has been sustained ever since by an extensive and continuing series of bilateral service-to-service relationships in such areas as joint training (the RAAF, like the RAF, had participated for years in the USAF's recurrent Red Flag exercises), contingency planning, intelligence sharing, and, in the cases of Korea and Vietnam, actual combat as partners in arms.

Australia's input consisted first of Operation Bastille, the forward deployment of Australian forces to CENTCOM's area of responsibility and initial area orientation and in-theater training, followed thereafter by Operation Falconer, the actual participation of Australian forces in combined coalition combat to help disarm Hussein's regime. This contribution, moreover, came at a time when the Australian Defence Forces (ADF) were heavily engaged in other forward-deployed military commitments, including Operation Citadel, Australia's involvement in UN peacekeeping operations in East Timor; Operation Relex, the protection of Australia's northern borders against illegal immigration; and Operation Slipper, the ADF's involvement in the U.S.-led Operation Enduring Freedom against the Taliban and Al Qaeda in Afghanistan that commenced immediately after the terrorist attacks of September 11, 2001.[12]

As in Great Britain, popular opinion in Australia ran against involvement in Iraqi Freedom. The leader of the opposition Australian Labor Party, Simon Crean, vocally declined to support Prime Minister John Howard's effort to make Australia part of the coalition. The minister for defence and the government's leader in the Australian Senate, Robert Hill, responded to Crean in a press interview as Operation Bastille's initial force deployment was getting under way: "I'd like to think that the Australian Labor Party . . . are nevertheless totally behind the forces as they are deployed. And I think that's the case. Again, the Australian way is that once forces are deployed, the community does come together and back them 100 percent." Senator Hill added: "The alliance is a strong and important alliance. It's not the primary reason why we are predeploying these forces. We're predeploying these forces in our own national interest. But the alliance is very important as our ultimate form of national security."[13]

Although the RAAF's initial involvement in CENTAF's early planning workups began in late summer 2002, it was not until January 10, 2003, that the Australian government formally announced that it would deploy ADF units to the Middle East in case such a commitment should become necessary to help implement UN Security Council resolutions calling for a disarmament of Iraq—by means of force should matters come to that.[14] Three weeks later, on February 1, the government declared that the ADF would commit a squadron of fourteen F/A-18 Hornet strike fighters, as well as three C-130s (two C-130Hs and a C-130J), two AP-3C maritime patrol and surveillance aircraft, and three Australian Army CH-47D Chinook helicopters, along with a forward air command element that, according to an ADF spokesman, would reside in the CAOC and be "responsible for coordinating air operations with coalition partners and providing national control of Royal Australian Air Force assets."[15]

Also in February 2003, in clear acknowledgment of its support in principle for the Bush administration's determination to deal definitively with Iraq, the Australian government released its latest strategic review declaring that "the prospect that Saddam Hussein might threaten to use WMD against his enemies in the region or supply WMD to terrorists reinforces the international community's efforts to ensure Iraq is disarmed."[16] At roughly the same time, the Australian government assigned responsibility for Iraqi matters to a new Iraq Coordinating Group chaired by the Department of the Prime Minister and Cabinet and consisting of key government representatives, notably including from the Department of Defence, as ADF planners continued to refine possible Australian force contribution options. On March 18, the day President Bush delivered his ultimatum to Saddam Hussein and his two sons to leave Iraq within forty-eight hours or face the full force of coalition operations to drive them out of power, Prime Minister Howard advised the Australian parliament that his government had authorized the ADF to join in force employment by the coalition once the campaign was under way. The ADF commenced Operation Falconer immediately afterward, with Australian air, naval, and special forces initiating combat operations with the CENTCOM force components with which they had planned and trained over the preceding months.[17]

Command Arrangements

The British military contingent that had been embedded at CENTCOM headquarters since Operation Enduring Freedom began getting indications as early as May 2002 that the command was increasingly engaged in NOFORN (no foreign nationals) planning, with a likely Iraq contingency in mind. The British representatives interpreted those indications as clear evidence that something unusual was gearing up, because normally, in the words of Lt. Gen. John Reith of the British Army, the eventual chief of joint operations for Iraqi Freedom, they had "very, very good access on everything."[18] The RAF in particular had embedded staff officers at all echelons both at CENTCOM's headquarters in Florida and at CENTAF's headquarters at Shaw AFB, South Carolina, as well as in the latter's forward-deployed CAOC at Prince Sultan Air Base, Saudi Arabia. That early embedding of key personnel at all levels ensured visibility, credibility, and the development of a deep trust relationship between the British team and its American counterparts.

Once it became clear that British involvement in such a contingency might eventually take place, the MoD established a contingency operations group comprising representatives from the MoD's Defence Crisis Management Organization and its Permanent Joint Headquarters at Northwood on the outskirts of London. It further established a current commitments team to manage all preparations that would require ministerial direction. For its part, Permanent Joint Headquarters formed a contingency planning team to plan the eventual British military contribution, should the British government approve it. The chief of the defence staff then issued a planning directive to Permanent Joint Headquarters that the contingency planning team used to formulate the plan. As for the RAF's prospective involvement, headquarters Strike Command convened a contingency action group to plan the air portion of the chosen course of action, employing cell members who were overseen by the contingency plans division at Strike Command.

Roughly concurrently, the chief of the defence staff in autumn 2002 appointed the Northwood-based commander of Permanent Joint Headquarters, General Reith, as joint commander for all British military involvement in the impending campaign. Within the United Kingdom, the MoD and Permanent Joint Headquarters collectively constituted the Defence Crisis Management Organization for the impending British participation in Iraqi Freedom. As the designated chief of joint operations, Reith exercised operational command over all participating British forces through Permanent Joint Headquarters and would be responsible to the chief of the defence staff for the conduct of operations. He delegated operational control of British forces committed to Operation Telic to the three-star national contingent commander, Air Marshal Brian Burridge, who was to be forward-deployed in the theater and would report daily to the chief of joint operations.[19]

In this chain-of-command arrangement, Air Marshal Burridge was the senior MoD representative to CENTCOM's commander, General Franks, with whom he would have close daily contact throughout the campaign. He later acknowledged that Franks' forward deployment to CENTCOM's area of responsibility constituted a major improvement in command efficiency over the Operation Enduring Freedom experience.[20] Burridge reported through the chief of joint operations to the defense staff in the MoD, with General Reith serving as a welcome buffer between Burridge and London. This arrangement closely followed the pattern first established by the British in Operation Desert Storm. During that earlier combined campaign, however, Permanent Joint Headquarters had not yet been formed, so the chief of the defence staff instead chose an existing four-star headquarters—RAF Strike Command—and designated its commander in chief, Air Chief Marshal Sir Patrick Hine, as the overall UK-based joint commander, with Lieutenant General Sir Peter de la Billiere of the British Army as the national contingent commander deployed forward in the theater.

Reith further delegated tactical command of all RAF forces through Air Marshal Burridge to the two-star British air contingent commander, then Air Vice-Marshal Glenn Torpy.[21] Torpy's initial responsibility was to establish the force in-theater; then, during the execution phase, to ensure that British forces were used as effectively and efficiently as possible, and that operations were conducted as safely as possible in light of combat conditions within the constraints of British policy; and finally, after the period of major combat was over, to bring the forces home. Like his counterpart British land and maritime contingent commanders who worked alongside their respective CENTCOM three-star component commanders, Torpy delegated operational and tactical control of all British air assets to the air component commander, General Moseley. This was consistent with years of British-American military interaction within NATO and in connection with Operations Northern Watch and Southern Watch. With respect to the differences between operational command, operational control, tactical command, and tactical control, Burridge noted that "it actually takes longer to describe than it does to use in practice."[22]

Air Vice-Marshal Torpy's air contingent headquarters staff at Prince Sultan Air Base numbered about two hundred personnel, some of whom were embedded in various CAOC staff positions. Air Commodore Chris Nickols headed the contingent's staff and also was one of three rotating one-star CAOC directors each day who oversaw the day-to-day execution of the ATO for General Moseley. That arrangement gave the RAF both visibility and influence within the CAOC organization. It also preserved British direction of British forces and ensured that those forces would only undertake specific operations that had been approved by British commanders. In this post–Desert Storm arrangement, the United Kingdom built on the structure that it had developed a decade before in connection with its involvement with CENTCOM in enforcing the no-fly zones over Iraq.

In subsequent testimony before the Defence Committee of the House of Commons, Burridge noted that as the British national contingent commander, his role had focused specifically on three areas: first, supporting the three British military contingents (air, land, and maritime); second, informing the senior government leadership in London of details they needed to know for conducting responsible political and military decision making; and third, influencing CENTCOM's planning and execution of the campaign to the extent possible and appropriate. General Reith explained in similar testimony that Burridge "was controlling the operation as the man in theater dealing with the detail."[23] The chief of joint operations assigned different British forces to different CENTCOM missions. Burridge, as the designated wielder of operational control, was assigned forces and tasks by the chief of joint operations and, in his words, "just had to match them up with the American plan."[24] Reith, he said, "was looking at the London end and some of the international aspects away from the theater," whereas he, as the national contingent commander deployed forward, "was looking horizontally at the region of the theater and downwards."[25] Burridge attributed the resultant smoothness of fit and flow among the various players to the key personalities involved, a fact on which the American system heavily depended.

The American arrangement was less structured and more personalized than was the more formal British approach, with General Franks and Secretary of Defense Rumsfeld in daily direct contact and with the American service chiefs often making direct calls to CENTCOM's component commanders. Moreover, the interface between the senior U.S. military leadership and the political authorities in Washington was far more direct, from the president through the secretary of defense to General Franks. In contrast, Burridge made a point of noting that he was "happy" with the United Kingdom's command arrangement because it shielded him from direct dealings with London and further allowed him to be "very much left to get on with things."[26]

Air Chief Marshal Burridge also pointed out that many on General Franks' CENTCOM staff "would regard us as their conscience because we see things through different eyes."[27] He attributed this good relationship to the many years of close RAF involvement with CENTCOM going back to Desert Storm and the subsequent enforcement of the no-fly zones, as well as to the fact that Franks and his principal deputies recognized the quality of the thinking that the embedded British staff brought to CENTCOM's policy and strategy deliberations. That broad-based acceptance enabled the British contingent, as appropriate, to influence CENTCOM's decision making from the bottom up.

With respect to Australia's involvement in CENTCOM's command and control arrangements, Prime Minister Howard announced on March 18 that the Australian government had authorized the chief of the defence force, General Peter Cosgrove, to offer already deployed ADF forces as a contribution to any U.S.-led coalition that might commit to combat operations in accordance with existing UN resolutions authorizing the use of force against Iraq.[28] Throughout Operations Bastille and Falconer, General Cosgrove retained full command of all Australian forces. Operational and tactical control, as in the case of British forces committed to the campaign, was seconded to CENTCOM's component commanders as appropriate, but national command of those forces remained with the commander of the Australian national headquarters for Middle East operations, Brigadier Maurie McNarn. The Australian Department of Defence's after-action report explained that "this arrangement let coalition commanders assign specific tasks to ADF forces while they remained under their Australian commanding officers at the unit level." In addition, "although ADF force elements worked toward the overall coalition combat plan, there were processes in place to ensure that Australian forces were always employed in accordance with Australian government policies."[29]

Early Planning Involvement

The British were the first allies to be brought into CENTCOM's planning for Iraqi Freedom. They were invited by the U.S. government to join in the process in June–July 2002, well in advance of Australia and at a time when U.S. forces were still reconstituting after having just completed the major combat portion of Operation Enduring Freedom in Afghanistan. After Britain's secretary of state for defence announced in September 2002 that the United Kingdom was involved in contingency planning for a possible Iraq scenario, key RAF station and squadron commanders were drawn into the planning process. Even at that early stage of preparations, a significant portion of the RAF's high-readiness forces were already deployed and flying operational missions in CENTCOM's area of responsibility as part of Northern Watch and Southern Watch. Regarding this early involvement, Air Chief Marshal Burridge later recalled that although no timetable had been announced or even determined at that point, "it was put to me that if the [United Kingdom] was at any stage likely to participate, then best we at least understand the planning and influence the planning for the better."[30] Air Marshal Torpy similarly recalled that the United States was "absolutely clear that there was no commitment on Britain's behalf at that stage to commit forces to any sort of operation."[31]

Most of the equipment that was procured expressly for Operation Telic was obtained through the MoD's well-established urgent operational requirements (UOR) process. The MoD's after-action report explained that the UOR process, announced in Parliament on November 25, 2002, was created to "provide a cost-effective solution to specific capability shortfalls related to a particular operation."[32] The associated establishment of the Defence Logistics Organization's logistics operations center ensured that needed equipment was delivered to CENTCOM's area of responsibility in accordance with the priorities of Permanent Joint Headquarters. UORs also helped to increase the number of RAF aircraft configured to deliver precision-guided munitions and to provide for additional stocks of precision munitions and other weapons. Thirty-three percent of the UORs that were issued in support of the war effort accelerated existing programs, with another 20 percent introducing new and previously unprogrammed capabilities, 30 percent topping off holdings already in the inventory, and 17 percent modifying existing equipment or infrastructure.[33]

The MoD moved in mid-December to encourage the shipping market to tender for the timely provision of possible needed surface transportation vessels, as well as to begin specific unit training and to reduce the notice time to move for some units.[34] The British contingent was a fully invested participant in CENTCOM's Internal Look planning exercise in December 2002, during which CENTAF's force requirements and the RAF's contribution to the impending campaign, were it to participate, were finally nailed down.[35] The RAF also participated in multiple CENTAF "chair-fly" exercises, as well as in actual large-force strike and other mission rehearsals at Nellis AFB and elsewhere. The RAF's E-3D Sentry AWACS community conducted tactical employment seminars, did spin-up training to include getting needed U.S. combat information release and access, and conducted briefings and simulations prior to final mission certification.[36]

Shortly before the 2002 holiday season, the British contingent conducted an exercise that determined that the command structure in place was, in Air Chief Marshal Burridge's words, "pretty much 95 percent right."[37] In the course of that exercise the contingent identified potential friction points, and liaison officers were installed at those points. That timely evolution bore out the value of mission rehearsals. The British government did not, however, make its final decisions regarding the composition and deployment of British assets until early 2003.

Australia joined in CENTCOM's planning for possible contingency operations against Iraq not long afterward. On June 18, 2002, the minister for defence had declared that the government of Australia was ready to consider supporting additional U.S.-led coalitions beyond Operation Enduring Freedom in Afghanistan. In addition, in response to the obvious resolve of the Bush administration to address the challenge posed by Iraq, the government further directed Australian defense planners to initiate contingency planning for an Australian contribution to any U.S.-led coalition in case diplomacy should fail. In return, in August 2002, the U.S. government invited initial Australian participation in CENTCOM's planning workups in Tampa, Florida, albeit with no firm military commitment sought by either side. The well-developed personal ties and trust relationships established within CENTCOM throughout the course of Australia's earlier contributions via Operation Slipper made it clear to all that the initial groundwork was now in place should Australia be included in a U.S.-led combat coalition against Iraq.[38]

By August 2002 the ADF's joint planning staff had gained a fairly thorough understanding of CENTCOM's evolving contingency plans for Iraq and began developing appropriate options for the Australian government to consider should the latter ultimately decide that Australia would participate in coalition operations against Iraq. Later in November, Prime Minister Howard declared that the ADF had "made appropriate contingency arrangements," including moving the Australian national headquarters for Middle East operations forward to be collocated with CENTCOM's deployed headquarters in Qatar.[39] The following month the government directed the ADF to begin training for combat operations in case Iraq failed to comply with the weapons inspection regime stipulated in UN Resolution 1441. Finally, on January 10, 2003, as the start of its initial deployment of forces to CENTCOM's area of responsibility neared under the aegis of Operation Bastille, the government formally declared that it would commit ADF forces to the allied coalition and would begin preparing them for possible combat operations soon to come. The ADF's deployment itself finally began on January 23, 2003, with the departure of the amphibious transport ship *Kanimbla* from Sydney to the North Arabian Gulf and other Australian force elements concurrently moving forward by air.[40]

The Allied Force Component

In a force buildup code-named Operation Warrior, the United Kingdom committed to Operation Iraqi Freedom the largest composite military force that it had deployed since its contribution to Operation Desert Storm twelve years before. RAF Strike Command was the designated force provider for all British air assets presented for the impending campaign. In response to requests submitted by CENTCOM and CENTAF, and working closely with Permanent Joint Headquarters, Strike Command identified RAF force requirements and volunteered options, including the new Storm Shadow standoff hard-target munition and Tornado F3 interceptors, to help with the anticipated defensive counterair effort.[41]

Even before the start of focused planning for the impending campaign, the RAF already had in place a well-functioning presence of some 25 aircraft and associated personnel in the Gulf region. On February 6, 2003, Britain's secretary of state for defence disclosed that the RAF's contribution to Iraqi contingency response needs would be increased to 100 fixed-wing aircraft manned and supported by an additional 7,000 uniformed British personnel. This increased force contingent included E-3D Sentry AWACS and Nimrod and Canberra PR9 reconnaissance aircraft, VC-10 and Tristar tankers, Tornado F3 counterair fighters, Tornado GR4 and Harrier GR7 strike aircraft (with Storm Shadow missiles fitted to the GR4), and C-130 Hercules intratheater transports. The United Kingdom fielded 46,150 service personnel, 8,100 of whom were to support the impending RAF air operations. The deployment reinforcement provided 115 fixed-wing RAF aircraft and about 100 helicopters, including 27 RAF Pumas and Chinooks that were fielded by Joint Helicopter Command. Among the numerous RAF ground support assets were Rapier SAMs, force protection units, and explosive ordnance disposal and expeditionary airfield units.[42]

The roster of committed British equipment included a third of all of the tanks that were available to CENTCOM's land component. It featured a force of Challenger 2 tanks, Warrior infantry fighting vehicles, AS90 self-propelled guns, and some 28,000 personnel drawn from British Army units in the United Kingdom and Germany. For maritime operations, Naval Task Group 2003 was led by the aircraft carrier HMS (Her Majesty's Ship) *Ark Royal* and accompanied by the helicopter carrier HMS *Ocean*, which operated Royal Navy Sea King and Royal Marine Gazelle and Lynx helicopters.[43] It further included two nuclear fast-attack submarines (HMS *Splendid* and HMS *Turbulent*) armed with TLAMs. In all, the United Kingdom's contribution of military personnel came to about 10 percent of the coalition total of roughly 467,000. This deployment into CENTCOM's area of responsibility began in January 2003 and was accomplished with 670 airlifter sorties and 62 ship moves. During the course of the deployment, the RAF's four C-17s and other mobility aircraft transported roughly half of the personnel and equipment that needed to be moved by air.[44]

A potential spanner in the works that complicated this deployment evolution for planners at Strike Command entailed keeping the time-phased force and deployment data (TPFDD, pronounced "tip-fid") on track in the presence of continued uncertainty, right up to the very eve of combat operations, as to whether Turkey would support the coalition's impending campaign. Some senior RAF officers felt that CENTCOM's leaders had taken Turkey's prospective support more for granted than they should have, possibly in part because Turkey was in EUCOM's area of responsibility rather than CENTCOM's, and accordingly was not an object of daily attention and concern on CENTCOM's part. After the Turkish government declined at the last minute to support the coalition, the United Kingdom's TPFDD essentially went out the window as ships that had been dispatched to the eastern Mediterranean in anticipation of offloading their troops and equipment in Turkey were rerouted instead to the North Arabian Gulf and Kuwait via the Suez Canal.[45] (The initial planning for Operation Telic had envisaged significant British air and land forces operating out of Kuwait in the south and from the north through Turkey. As a hedge against the possibility of Turkish noncooperation, however, alternate plans were developed for a British air contribution solely from the south. That hedge turned out well in the end, because the ability of Hussein's Ba'athist regime to resist in the north proved to be extremely limited.)

RAF Strike Command also looked at first for additional bed-down space to the south of Iraq for its Jaguar GR3A attack aircraft that were flying reconnaissance missions out of Turkey in support of Operation Northern Watch. In the end, Air Marshal Burridge concluded that such a move would have been both impossible and unnecessary given the existing tactical reconnaissance capability already present in the RAPTOR (for "reconnaissance airborne pod for Tornado") kits that had been fielded for the Tornado just the year before, to say nothing of additional U.S. Air Force and Navy reconnaissance assets. Ultimately, as the three-week phase of major combat began winding down in early April 2003, the joint reconnaissance pods that had been attached to the Jaguars were removed and refitted to the RAF's Harriers that were operating out of Al Jaber Air Base in Kuwait.

Australia committed more than two thousand ADF servicemen and -women to the impending campaign against Iraq. The principal equipment contribution consisted of fourteen F/A-18 Hornet multirole fighters from 75 Squadron of the RAAF's 81 Wing that deployed to Al Udeid Air Base via Diego Garcia from RAAF Base Tindal in Australia's Northern Territory. The Hornet's multirole capability made it a clearly preferred choice over the RAAF's only other combat aircraft alternative, namely, its single-mission F-111C long-range maritime strike aircraft. In addition, the profusion of U.S. Navy and Marine Corps F/A-18s that were also committed to the campaign offered the added advantage of commonality with respect to munitions, spare parts, and overall mission capability.[46]

The F/A-18s that the RAAF contributed to the campaign were all Hornet Upgrade (HUG) 2.1 jets that had recently been provided with improved APG-73 radars, APX-11 combined interrogator transponders, and an ASN-172 GPS provision embedded within the aircraft's inertial navigation system. Because the upgrade program was still in an early phase at that time and only HUG variants were to be sent forward to Al Udeid, HUG aircraft had to be marshaled from all three of the RAAF's combat-coded F/A-18 squadrons.[47] Six aircraft came from 75 Squadron at Tindal, and four each were drawn from 3 and 77 Squadrons based at Williamtown. A select group of twenty-two experienced pilots was also gathered from the RAAF's three operational Hornet squadrons.[48]

Group Captain Bill Henman, the commander of the RAAF's air combat wing deployed for Operation Falconer, later explained that the twenty-two pilots

> were selected from across the wing so that we could have a suitable residual capability, continued training, and preparation for rotation back in Australia. This was part of my challenge as the commander of 81 Wing at the time, because there were obviously

going to be some fairly disappointed people not going in the first tranche, [so we accordingly] avoided any reference to an A-Team or a B-Team. . . . We wanted a balanced force in Australia preparing and ready to deploy on rotation, and therefore the first group that went over was not in any way seen or judged to be better than those people who remained behind. . . . If Iraq had put up stiffer resistance [and] we got into a prolonged campaign, it was hard for us to see, as planners, that we should plan only for three months and then not consider a rotation. So our eye was always on a sustainable rotation through to at least six months, rotating at the three-month period, and that's what we considered.[49]

En route to Diego Garcia from Tindal, the F/A-18s conducted seven in-flight refuelings from a U.S. Air Force KC-10, which itself had been topped off by a U.S. Air Force KC-135 tanker. After spending two nights on Diego Garcia, the pilots pressed ahead to their final destination at Al Udeid, again accompanied by a KC-10 tanker escort and a support element of some 250 RAAF personnel. This detachment represented the largest deployment of RAAF fighters for combat since the Korean War. On arrival, 75 Squadron was embedded in the U.S. Air Force's 379th Expeditionary Air Wing, which had also deployed to Al Udeid. In addition, the RAAF contributed two C-130Hs from 36 Squadron and one C-130J from 37 Squadron of the RAAF's 86 Wing headquartered at RAAF Base Richmond, New South Wales; and two AP-3Cs from 92 Wing headquartered at RAAF Base Edinburgh, South Australia, each with appropriate combat support personnel. (The AP-3C, which had just entered line service in the RAAF the year before, is a much-upgraded Orion configured with a variety of sensors that include a digital multimode radar; electronic support measures; and electro-optical, acoustic, and magnetic detection equipment.)

Finally, the RAAF provided an air forward command element consisting of 42 of its best air warfare experts to further augment CENTAF's overall CAOC staff of around 1,700 U.S. and allied personnel at Prince Sultan Air Base. That liaison element was responsible for coordinating RAAF air operations with the other two coalition partners and providing national control of all RAAF assets that had been seconded to the coalition. Elements of an expeditionary combat support squadron were also deployed forward to fulfill security, logistics support, airfield engineering, administrative, medical, communications, and other essential support functions. Of this group, 79 servicemen and -women drawn from RAAF units around Australia supported the F/A-18s, 75 supported the AP-3Cs, and 66 supported the C-130s.

Target Approval Provisions

The British contingent was directly involved in CENTCOM's early selection of more than nine hundred target areas of potential interest throughout Iraq. The target approval machinery for the British portion of Operation Iraqi Freedom was developed in close consultation between the MoD, Permanent Joint Headquarters, and the in-theater national contingent commander, who worked together to create the most expeditious approval arrangement possible. That machinery was developed and put into place to head off the sorts of target approval delays involving coalition partners that had afflicted NATO's Operation Allied Force in 1999 and Operation Enduring Freedom two years later, when British government approval was required before CENTCOM could attack emerging targets with American aircraft that operated out of Diego Garcia or had just taken on fuel from RAF tankers. (The Australian target approval process was very similar to the United Kingdom's process.)

Target approval in the southern no-fly zone had proceeded at a relatively slow pace, and decisions were routinely referred back to Permanent Joint Headquarters and the MoD.[50] The anticipated rapid tempo of Operation Telic, however, would not allow that luxury. Target approval decision making would have to go from "sedate" to "fast and furious," in Air Chief Marshal Burridge's formulation.[51] That requirement, in turn, dictated significant delegation of target approval authority to Burridge and his targeting board. As was the case for the U.S. side within CENTCOM's chain of command, powers delegated to the in-theater British national contingent included the authority to attack emerging targets quickly as actionable intelligence on them became available. Air Chief Marshal Burridge later summed up his role in this respect succinctly: if a target was to be attacked with a British platform, either he or someone in the British contingent to whom he had delegated authority had to approve it. The same applied in the case of a U.S. heavy bomber operating out of a British facility such as Diego Garcia or RAF Fairford.[52]

Target nominations that required approval at the highest levels were submitted through Permanent Joint Headquarters to the MoD's targeting organization, whose principals would present the target requests to the appropriate ministers for approval. Such ministerial involvement with target approval was kept to an absolute minimum in the campaign. The secretary of state for defence laid out the broad parameters of what was acceptable and what was not, and reserved beforehand certain target categories that only minister-level authority could approve; those categories, however, were very few. As one minister put it, "the military men were given maximum flexibility within those parameters to go about their task."[53] Air Marshal Torpy could not recall a single situation in which the British contingent's need to seek political clearance conflicted with immediate campaign operational requirements, because so many contingencies had been anticipated and planned for in advance.[54] The only targets within the United Kingdom's cognizance that really needed London's approval were command and control targets that could result in a significant amount of collateral damage.

Consistent with the laws of armed conflict, target nominations stipulated that no target attack would be carried out if any anticipated loss of noncombatant life, injury, or other harm were deemed excessive in relation to the direct and material military advantage anticipated from the attack. Air Vice-Marshal Torpy was the designated "red card" holder should any suggested target over which the United Kingdom had veto power prove unacceptable for any reason. Furthermore, with strong British concurrence, CENTCOM planned effects-based operations and selected all targets with a view toward achieving a particular military effect. Air Chief Marshal Burridge observed in that vein that "there are other ways of doing shock and awe than by breaking things."[55]

British command elements did sometimes influence the selection of targets over which the United Kingdom did not wield veto power, as well as some targets that lay outside its formal purview altogether. In such cases the American side freely accepted proffered British advice, even when not required to do so. Air Chief Marshal Burridge later explained that the British contingent felt that it provided valuable input "in saying yes, okay, this is an American target, American platform, no British involvement, but actually let me just say how this might be viewed in Paris, Berlin, or wherever."[56] In its after-action report, the MoD noted that there had been no instances in which such proffered British advice had not been accepted. It further noted that the targeting authority that was delegated to British commanders was "significant" and allowed for flexible and responsive operations.[57]

As in the case of the United Kingdom's involvement in coalition planning and decision making, RAAF and Australian SOF legal officers were also assigned to the CAOC to ensure that targets assigned to 75 Squadron were "appropriate and lawful."[58] The combined targeting coordination board (CTCB) was chaired by Major General Renuart, CENTCOM's director of operations, with the United Kingdom and Australia represented, respectively, by Burridge and McNairn. As did Burridge, Brigadier McNairn provided senior military campaign advice to the CTCB as he deemed useful and appropriate. ADF commanders also had service lawyers at their side who vetted targets on CENTCOM-developed strike lists that were assigned to 75 Squadron and assessed them in accordance with Australian legal obligations. Several target categories were subject to ministerial approval, and, as was the case with all other coalition aircrews, Australian pilots could, and did, abort attacks when there was concern for collateral damage or if the assigned target could not be identified and validated from the air.[59] In a belated but ultimately helpful additional contribution to this effort, the Australian Department of Defence announced on March 31 that it was sending six RAAF imagery analyst officers and airmen to support U.S. Air Force U-2 operations to help assess wet-film target images taken over Iraq, select targets, and assess strike results. In addition, a four-person RAAF battle damage assessment team was embedded within CENTCOM's headquarters at MacDill AFB, Florida.

Reflecting on the instant trust relationship that he established with General Moseley on arriving in the CAOC, the Australian air contingent commander, then Group Captain Geoff Brown, commented:

> I think we lucked in with the fact that he was in charge of CEN-TAF at the time, because my first day there, he sort of grabbed me, there was an RAF air commodore and I'm [just] a group captain and he's the three-star general, and he took me under his wing and bang, sat me down at the table with him at the first [video teleconference] he was having. . . . It was interesting the way he treated me . . . he let the rest of his colonels know that I had direct access to him. At the time, I didn't realize the value of that. . . . But the reality was that they were incredibly inclusive of us in the planning side. . . . [We weren't even sure yet that we would get the F/A-18s there at all], but they allowed us to have a look at the plan, where we wanted to go, how we wanted to operate, they pretty much allowed us to do what we wanted to do. . . . [General Moseley] was just happy to have us there.[60]

Punctuating this point, the commander of the RAAF's 75 Squadron later remarked in his own postcampaign reflections: "If you ever have to go to war, go to war with the Americans. They set things up very well."[61]

Overall Combat Performance

The second Persian Gulf War was a genuinely combined operation when it came to British and Australian involvement, with RAF and RAAF sorties wholly integrated into the CAOC's daily air tasking flow. For the RAF these included offensive strike, defensive counterair, surveillance and reconnaissance, tanking, intratheater lift, and aeromedical sorties. Offensive strike missions included firing a number of air-launched antiradiation missiles (ALARMs) at Iraqi SAM radars.[62] In all, the RAF flew 2,519 sorties, approximately 6 percent of the coalition total of 41,000.[63] RAF tankers dispensed some 19 million pounds of fuel, more than 40 percent of which was transferred to U.S. Navy and Marine Corps strike fighters.[64] (RAF tankers, with their drogue refueling system, are compatible with probe-equipped U.S. Navy and Marine Corps aircraft, whereas many U.S. Air Force tankers, which mainly employ the boom refueling system, are not.)

One clear lesson the RAF had learned from its experience in Operation Allied Force was the need to improve its all-weather strike capability. After the Kosovo campaign the RAF stepped out smartly to acquire antiarmor Maverick missiles and enhanced Paveway LGBs equipped with additional GPS guidance, thus building on its existing Paveway LGB capability. (The enhanced Paveway II and Paveway III have a dual-mode laser seeker and GPS guidance kit and can be delivered both by laser spot tracking, if accurate target coordinates are not available, and by GPS guidance should weather or other factors prevent target designation.) The RAF also increased the number of Tornado GR4s and Harrier GR7s that were capable of delivering such munitions.

The RAF in Operation Iraqi Freedom operated out of eight forward locations in various countries throughout the region.[65] It employed fewer aircraft than it had in Desert Storm, but its greatly expanded use of precision munitions allowed those aircraft to produce substantially greater combat effects than before. RAF aircraft released 919 of the 29,200 munitions expended by the coalition, with roughly 85 percent of the 919 being precision-guided. Weapons released on RAF sorties included Storm Shadow, Paveway II, enhanced Paveway II, enhanced Paveway III, Maverick, ALARM, and unguided general-purpose bombs. The 138 unguided bombs included 70 cluster bombs that were used against enemy troops and armor in the open, primarily in the vicinity of Baghdad. The RAF also delivered a number of precision-guided inert 1,000-pound bombs in an effort to minimize collateral damage, but these concrete-filled shapes, which relied on kinetic energy, often did not produce the desired effect when they hit their designated aim point.

Operation Iraqi Freedom saw the first combat use of the RAF's Storm Shadow precision standoff ground-attack cruise missile. This weapon, designed to penetrate and disable hardened structures, is powered by a turbojet engine, cruises at Mach 0.8, and has a range of more than 130 miles.[66] It is guided by GPS and digital terrain profile matching, with a terminal seeker for maximum accuracy and collateral damage avoidance, and was delivered by Tornado GR4s against such exceptionally fortified enemy installations as communications bunkers. It was used both day and night and in all weather conditions to attack a variety of high-value targets. The missile was almost invariably accurate, offering what the MoD's initial after-action look called the promise of a "step change" in the RAF's precision standoff attack capability.[67] On March 21, 2003, for example, four GR4s each armed with two Storm Shadow missiles launched from their base in Kuwait against Iraqi IADS command and control centers housed within bunkers at Taji and Tikrit. Battle damage assessment the following day showed that all four targets had been successfully struck.

Storm Shadow was one of a number of weapons and other systems that were made available for Operation Telic under the UOR arrangement. The missile had only just begun coming off the production line, so the RAF had a limited supply. It proved adequate, however, for the targets that General Moseley designated. Indeed, apart from the B-2 stealth bomber armed with GBU-37 hard-structure munitions, Storm Shadow provided General Moseley with the only significant deep-penetration target attack capability available to CENTAF. Twenty-seven Storm Shadow missiles were fired during the course of the campaign, mostly during the first few days against especially hardened enemy command and control facilities. Storm Shadow was able to disable four such key targets in the opening seconds of the air war. Its hard-target penetration features made it uniquely qualified to fill a critical niche.[68] The MoD's after-action synopsis reported that Storm Shadow had been the most effective weapon in the coalition's inventory to penetrate these hardened targets. Storm Shadow was attractive to CENTCOM's weaponeers because it offered a better hard-target penetration capability than anything in the American standoff munitions inventory.

The tactical reconnaissance capability offered by the RAF's Tornados, Harriers, and Jaguars was likewise in short supply among U.S. forces; only the Navy's F-14s configured with TARPS offered a similar capability. Tornado GR4s equipped with RAPTOR imaging pods and Canberra PR9s provided high-quality, near-real-time imagery in the tactical reconnaissance role. The Nimrod MR2, normally employed as a maritime surveillance platform, supported coalition operations in the Iraqi western desert, providing both surveillance and reconnaissance support and also serving as an airborne radio relay platform. RAF Harriers and Tornados had thirty thermal imaging airborne laser designator (TIALD) pods on hand and used some of them in a nontraditional way as a surveillance and reconnaissance asset for monitoring enemy tank positions and potential Scud launching sites. That novel use prompted subsequent efforts to determine the utility and practicality of data-linking TIALD imagery to ground stations and other airborne aircraft.

The RAF had just completed a major midlife upgrade of its Tornados to GR4 standard, adding a wide-field-of-view head-up display, new avionics and forward-looking infrared systems, GPS navigation, cockpit lighting modifications to allow the use of NVGs, and additional modifications that enabled the aircraft to carry the new Storm Shadow missile and the RAPTOR reconnaissance pod, first employed in Operation Resinate. Operating the RAPTOR system required the Tornado pilot to fly straight and level for a significant period of time to record target images, which made for a predictable flight path. Accordingly, Tornado GR4s conducting reconnaissance missions were typically escorted by U.S. Air Force Block 50 F-16CJs armed with HARMs.[69] Although successfully used in the CAS role, the Tornado GR4 was not the best-suited aircraft for that mission because of its limited maneuvering performance at high altitude. Target-area searches often require a bank angle of 30 degrees or more at 20,000 feet, while the GR4 was designed for high-speed, low-level operations. Offsetting this liability in some mission profiles, however, was the GR4's range capability, which exceeded even that of the USAF's F-15E. A CAOC planner recalled that the GR4 "was the only aircraft that could make it up to Kirkuk on Night One."[70]

In another important contribution, the RAF deployed four E-3D Sentries to provide continuous coverage of one of the four AWACS tracks that were constantly manned adjacent to and, eventually, over Iraq. In Operation Veritas in the Afghan air war, RAF E-3Ds had flown 473 missions between October 9, 2001, and January 29, 2002, with 97 percent mission accomplishment. In Operation Telic they flew 127 missions from March 12 through May 27, 2003, with a 100 percent mission success rate.[71] Initially, nine crews were made available for the four aircraft, but available billeting at Prince Sultan Air Base, from which the aircraft operated, could accommodate only six AWACS crews. Each crew flew a twelve-hour mission every other day to maintain three daily eight-hour on-station periods with only a fraction of the equipment and spare parts that would normally be available at the aircraft's home station of RAF Waddington.[72] Because the E-3D can refuel with both probe-and-drogue and boom systems, it was refueled by U.S. Air Force and Air National Guard KC-135s and U.S. Air Force KC-10s in addition to RAF Tristar and VC-10 tankers. (By the end of major combat, the 6 VC-10s deployed from RAF Brize Norton to Prince Sultan Air Base had flown 223 missions, with an average sortie length of 4.5 hours, no mission aborts, and a consequent operational success rate of 100 percent. A quarter of the 3,700 tons of fuel they offloaded were transferred to U.S. combat aircraft.)[73]

Although the United Kingdom's Phoenix UAV offered less capability than the U.S. Air Force's RQ-1 Predator, it nonetheless played a key role in supporting coalition land forces, primarily by geolocating ground targets. Initially, it was used around the clock. As the campaign progressed, however, it flew mostly at night to extract the greatest resolution from its thermal-imaging sensor. In all, Phoenix UAVs flew 138 sorties; 23 ended with the platform being lost or damaged beyond repair, and another 13 sustained repairable damage. Most of the losses were due to technical difficulties associated with operating in Iraq's unforgiving spring weather.

Helicopters from the United Kingdom's Joint Helicopter Command provided combat support to ground forces from land and sea bases. At the time, the British armed forces did not possess a full-fledged attack helicopter, although the AH-64 Apache was on order. Royal Navy Lynx and Gazelle helicopters, however, fired forty-nine TOW (tube-launched, optically tracked, wire-guided) missiles in successful attacks against enemy tanks, APCs, and bunkers.

The RAF Tornado and Harrier squadrons that were a part of General Moseley's air order of battle maintained a crew ratio of two to one throughout the three-week campaign. The only notable limiting factor associated with personnel tempo that caused even momentary concern had to do with the E-3D, since the four deployed AWACS aircraft were constantly operated at an exceptionally high utilization rate. At one point the British contingent's leadership considered bringing more AWACS aircrew members into the theater to relieve the heavy workload.

Allied air involvement over the Iraqi western desert in support of Scud missile hunting and related SOF activities on the ground were later portrayed by an RAF Harrier GR7 squadron commander who took part in them as having been "possibly the best-integrated air-land operation since World War II" and "a good role model for future operations involving SOF and air." He further noted that the associated tactics, techniques, and procedures had all been carefully rehearsed by all participants; that they were aided by ample support assets and suffered no shortage of needed communications; that the troops on the ground were some of the best soldiers in the world and they fully understood how to make the most of modern air power; and that the operations resulted in a persistent air presence that effectively countered outdated criticisms alleging the impermanence of air power.[74]

The United Kingdom's contribution to Operation Iraqi Freedom bore out the vision of the nation's 1998 Strategic Defence Review that the British armed forces should develop an expeditionary-based strategy aimed at maximizing maneuver warfare and seeking decisive effects. The RAF's accomplishments showed the extent to which it had embraced and captured the new expeditionary

culture. Much of that success was the result of more than a decade of close operational proximity to U.S. forces. As a measure of the effectiveness of the overall
British contribution to the campaign, as of April 19, 2003, of some 46,000 British
military participants, only 27 were killed in action and 55 were wounded, with
the majority of the fatalities having resulted from noncombat-related accidents.[75]

In reflecting on the many reasons that accounted for the RAF's strong
showing in the three-week campaign, Air Chief Marshal Burridge noted that
the technology gap between American and British air power had for years been
quite small, and was narrowed further by the RAF's experience at working
almost in lockstep with U.S. forces in enforcing the northern and southern no-
fly zones over Iraq and in training together with American combat air forces in
joint and combined exercises such as Red Flag.[76] An informed and thoughtful
RAF observer remarked that the various challenges the British encountered
during the lead-up to and execution of Operation Iraqi Freedom were overcome by a combination of mutual dependence, good fortune (in everyone's
having had the comparative luxury of a fairly unrushed planning period); ready
willingness by both sides to engage in burden sharing; deep mutual trust at all
levels, especially deep and strong interpersonal relations at the most senior levels;
and "a motivation to find common ground and to engineer solutions to any
problems that threatened the coalition's integrity."[77]

From the very start of CENTCOM's planning for Operation Iraqi Freedom, the British contingent was brought into the division of labor between
the two main coalition partners in a way aimed at leveraging British assets that
might best complement and enhance American forces. "We very definitely were
not there for the ride," Air Chief Marshal Burridge recalled. "On the air side,
we flew [only] seven percent of the sorties, but we provided a larger proportion of precision-guided munitions than did the Americans," as well as "niche
capabilities . . . that the U.S. was lacking in, particularly tactical reconnaissance."[78]
After the period of major combat ended, both Burridge and Torpy confirmed
that in contrast to the experience of Operation Allied Force in 1999, final target
approval delegations in Iraqi Freedom had been far more flexible. An informed
account noted that use of Britain's red card "was avoided, on more than one
occasion, because the trust that existed at all levels of command allowed informal dialogue to preempt any potential formal action. This approach was absolutely pivotal in minimizing friction."[79] In a related vein, Air Marshal Torpy later
indicated that the British national contingent never felt that only RAF assets
should support British land forces, because "that would be an inefficient use
of air power. Inevitably, we would not have sufficient [British] assets to provide

cover, for instance, to a [British] land component 24 hours a day."[80] The use of air power, Torpy added, has to be planned and prioritized centrally, with execution decentralized, for efficient employment of air resources.[81] At bottom, the British contingent benefited from close commonality with its American counterparts in equipment, communications, and operational mindset, as well as from close personal relationships from the four-star level all the way down to aircrews working conjointly and harmoniously at the tactical level.

Australia's contribution to the three-week air war began almost as soon as the RAAF's 75 Squadron arrived in-theater and was declared operationally ready. The squadron sought to gain an early combat edge by joining the RAF in Operation Southern Watch so that Australian pilots could be exposed to the CAOC's mode of operations in managing the airspace over southern Iraq, but the Australian high command refused to grant permission. A U.S. Marine Corps exchange pilot with the squadron later reported, "Although the coalition wanted Australians to fly [Southern Watch] missions, the federal government in Canberra had sent us . . . [only] to support 'offensive operations' against Iraq. In the government's eyes, [Southern Watch] didn't warrant our participation. As termed by the commander of Australian forces, that would have been 'mission creep.'"[82] In fairness to the Australian government's position in this regard, enforcement of the no-fly zone under the UN mandate was never one of the reasons for which the ADF had been deployed to the Persian Gulf region.[83]

The RAAF's Hornets were initially assigned to provide defensive counterair protection for such high-value coalition aircraft as the E-3 AWACS, E-8 JSTARS, RC-135 Rivet Joint, and allied tankers operating near and over southern Iraq, with 75 Squadron typically generating twelve sorties a day toward that end. These defensive counterair missions typically lasted between five and six hours, with the F/A-18s conducting three or four in-flight refueling evolutions from allied tankers in the process. Because of the considerable distance between Al Udeid and their assigned area of operations in southern Iraq, the Hornets were always configured with three 330-gallon external fuel tanks in addition to their normal air-to-air and ground attack weapons loadouts. A 75 Squadron pilot later described these initial sorties: "We'd fly out of our host nation and then we'd refuel up in the Gulf region around Kuwait. You would pretty much cross over into Iraq with full tanks. Although most sorties lasted six hours, some of those I was involved with turned out to be nine-hour marathons. That meant you were strapped into the jet for up to ten and a half hours from the time you started up until finally shutting down at mission end. . . . It was like being strapped to a kitchen chair and put into a phone booth for ten and a half hours."[84]

With respect to the Australian contingent's confidence level going into the RAAF's first shooting war since Vietnam, the commanding officer of 75 Squadron, Wing Commander Mel Hupfeld, later reflected on the question candidly and at considerable length.

> The Americans had been fighting there for 12 years, so they knew what Iraq had. That was shared well with us as Australians, so we had a good idea of the threats, and we pretty much trained to what we thought the worst case would be. . . . Our basic level of training was right where we needed it, so it was quite a simple process to actually then focus it more on the threats that we expected in the Iraqi theater. . . . I was very comfortable that our aircrews knew what was required, and there was a broad range of skills that we needed. . . . [Yet] I was very comfortable with our level of skill at that stage and comfortable with the capabilities of the aircraft. There were some limitations with the aircraft, but we knew what they were, and we could mitigate against those and operate in an appropriate manner not to have those affect us. . . . Before the major conflict started, [there were naturally] a few nerves, but once we actually got across the border and started doing what we were doing, it was business as usual. And with the training that we'd been doing, it was all second nature.[85]

At the outset, when 75 Squadron's fighters were principally assigned to defensive counterair CAPs (with the option to be re-roled as necessary for strikes against emerging ground targets), the typical weapons loadout for each aircraft consisted of two wingtip-mounted AIM-9M Sidewinder infrared air-to-air missiles, three AIM-120 advanced medium-range air-to-air missiles (AMRAAMs), and a single 500-pound GBU-12 LGB. Just a day into the campaign, however, the CAOC asked a 75 Squadron Hornet escorting a high-value coalition aircraft to strike a designated ground target that had just emerged and been validated. After confirming that the requested attack was consistent with the laws of armed conflict and standing rules of engagement, the Australian air contingent commander, Group Captain Brown, approved the attack. One of his F/A-18s promptly dropped the first Australian bomb released in anger since a 2 Squadron Canberra light bomber last did so during the Vietnam War. The entire request and approval sequence took less than thirty minutes, with an initial bomb damage assessment provided to the ADF's forward headquarters ten minutes thereafter.[86] Within forty-eight hours of the campaign's commencement, the CAOC switched 75 Squadron to a "swing mission" configuration, swapping out one of the three AMRAAMs for an additional GBU-12 or 2,000-pound GBU-10.

On March 24 the RAAF's chief, Air Marshal Angus Houston, reported that 75 Squadron's Hornets were being assigned strike missions against selected fixed targets in Iraq, even as they continued to fly defensive counterair sorties as required by the CAOC. In the strike role, RAAF fighters flew as autonomous formations within a larger coordinated package of coalition aircraft, with one such early strike featuring an RAAF Hornet pilot serving in the role of mission commander.[87] As the campaign moved closer to its endgame and the squadron found itself performing almost exclusively CAS missions, smaller 500-pound GBU-12s replaced the GBU-10s.

The RAAF's air contingent commander, by then Air Commodore Brown, recalled that "in the initial planning, the USAF wanted to have about four CAPs [provided by 75 Squadron's fighters], but we were tanker-limited, so we ended up just having the three CAPs. . . . We normally had a counter-rotating CAP of two aircraft and [another] two aircraft would be on the tanker at any one particular time. Just to maintain that over an eight-hour period—which we did— took 12 of our 14 aircraft. So over [the first] nine days, we had to keep 12 of the 14 F/A-18s serviceable. That was a challenge, as the logistic system did not work quite as well as I would have liked."[88] Nevertheless, the RAAF's F/A-18s managed to maintain a better than 90 percent FMC rate throughout the campaign. It was fortunate, Air Commodore Brown added, that the Australian government had deployed the Hornet detachment more than a month before the campaign got started, because "it took us probably about two weeks to make sure we had communications links and everything working properly."[89]

Once it became apparent to CAOC planners after about nine days of combat that the Iraqi air force was likely to remain out of the fight, the RAAF's Hornets were swung almost exclusively to ground attack operations. The first preplanned strike mission took place even before that determination when a four-ship flight of 75 Squadron F/A-18s was integrated into a strike package that also included American and British strike and electronic warfare aircraft in an attack against Republican Guard units near Al Kut. In addition, as the allied land offensive reached full swing, RAAF Hornets contributed to KI/ CAS operations in support of both V Corps and I MEF. Because the RAAF's F/A-18s were not configured to carry JDAMs, they dropped either the GBU-10 2,000-pound LGB or the GBU-12 500-pound LGB, depending on target weapon requirements; these two precision munitions types accounted for all of the bombs delivered by RAAF fighters during the campaign.[90]

By March 29, 75 Squadron's Hornets had flown defensive counterair, strike, and CAS missions, with CAS sorties typically being diverted from initially assigned defensive counterair missions. At that point in the campaign, the fourteen aircraft were totaling about ninety flight hours a day, five times their normal peacetime operating rate. The ADF's air contingent commander credited his support staff: "The maintenance guys did an outstanding job. We had to have 12 of those 14 aircraft serviceable. Most of the time they had 13, often 14, serviceable and we never missed a mission."[91] During the campaign's final days, when kinetic attacks became increasingly infrequent, the RAAF's Hornets would join other coalition strike fighters on request from ground commanders to provide so-called shows of force by making low-altitude, high-speed passes over concentrations of Iraqi civilians to break up gathering crowds that were causing problems for allied occupation forces. By the deployment's end, the 14 RAAF Hornets had flown 1,800 hours and more than 670 sorties, with more than 350 of those having been combat sorties, and had dropped 122 LGBs on assigned enemy targets, all to useful combat effect.[92]

RAAF C-130s also supported allied operations in southern Iraq, their first mission having been to airlift ground refueling trucks into the recently captured Tallil Air Base near An Nasiriyah on March 30 so that coalition aircraft could use the base as a forward operating facility. On April 13, after the major combat phase had ended, RAAF C-130s flew their first mission into the newly named Baghdad International Airport as part of the coalition's Operation Baghdad Assist. Although the three C-130s provided by the RAAF represented only 3 percent of the total coalition Hercules force, they lifted 16 percent of the coalition's total cargo delivered by C-130s into CENTCOM's area of operations.

Finally, the RAAF also operated one of its two deployed AP-3C Orions in various time windows over the North Arabian Gulf, using the aircraft's onboard sensors to detect and identify vessels in or near Iraqi waters, with special interest in any such vessels that might threaten coalition and civilian maritime operations by means of mine-laying or suicide attacks. By April 11, two days after the Ba'athist regime collapsed, the RAAF's Orions had maintained a near-perfect FMC rate of 98 percent.[93]

ADF Special Air Service (SAS) troopers joined with other coalition SOF teams in scouring the Iraqi western desert for concealed ballistic missiles that might be fired against Israel or other countries. During these ground sweeps, allied combat aircraft performed armed overwatch missions in constant readiness to provide any immediate on-call CAS that might be required. The previous February and early March, before the campaign's start, these forces had conducted full mission profile exercises day and night with other coalition SOF teams, including the involvement of on-call CAS by U.S. and RAF combat aircraft. Beginning on the night of March 19, the Australian SAS teams were flown deep into Iraq by low-flying American SOF helicopters, often through heavy enemy air defenses.

On April 11, two days after allied forces took Baghdad and the Ba'athist regime collapsed, an entire Australian SAS squadron, at CENTCOM's request, captured Al Asad Air Base some 120 miles west of Baghdad, with RAAF F/A-18s providing top cover. In the course of securing the base, the squadron discovered more than fifty concealed MiG-21 and MiG-25 fighters. The task force then cleared and repaired Al Asad's runways using captured Iraqi equipment so that allied fixed-wing aircraft could operate out of the base, with the first arriving aircraft being an RAAF C-130 from 36 Squadron.

Not only was 75 Squadron's involvement in Operation Iraqi Freedom the first time an Australian aircraft of any type had seen combat since Vietnam, it also represented the RAAF's first fighter combat operation since 77 Squadron's P-51 Mustangs and, later, Meteor jets joined U.S. forces in Korea a half-century before. By the time the Ba'ath regime fell, 36 Squadron's C-130Hs and 37 Squadron's C-130J had exceeded 2 million pounds of cargo and more than 700 passengers delivered since the start of the deployment. In a message issued five days before the fall of Baghdad, Air Marshal Houston quoted the chairman of the American JCS, General Myers, who had declared that "the contributions from the Australian force have been tremendous. . . . They have been absolutely superb, and we appreciate it."[94] For their exceptional performance throughout the campaign, 75 Squadron earned a meritorious unit citation from the Australian government. The squadron's commanding officer, Wing Commander Hupfeld, was one of only three participating ADF officers (and the only RAAF officer) in Operation Falconer to be awarded Australia's Distinguished Service Cross.[95] The RAAF's air contingent commander, Group Captain Brown, was also awarded the U.S. Legion of Merit by General Moseley, as was the RAF's air contingent commander, Air Marshal Torpy.

Afterward, Group Captain Brown reported that there had been no major interoperability issues with the F/A-18s, C-130s, or P-3s. He added:

> If you ask any of the guys who flew in the missions over Iraq, they were pretty happy with the [rules of engagement] that they had, and they were pretty happy with the targeting directives. I believe that that was a very mature approach by everybody who was involved in the chain. In the CAOC, I also had exactly the

same sort of collateral damage criteria as [General Moseley did] and, again, that made it easier to operate [in a coalition context]. . . . The fact that we fitted into the operation seamlessly, I think, had a lot to do with the training regimes that we have had over the last 50 years.[96]

Among the operating issues that 75 Squadron encountered, Brown singled out the Nighthawk targeting pod (the same as the one carried by U.S. Navy and Marine Corps F/A-18s before the advent of ATFLIR) as "the one that gave me the most heartache over the five weeks" because it "was unreliable and . . . did not have enough magnification capability." He also mentioned the RAAF's lack of NVGs, an inadequate electronic warfare suite, and a lack of all-weather stand-off precision munitions such as the satellite-aided JDAM series. (The RAAF has since acquired both JDAMs and the Litening II pod for its strike fighters, as well as NVGs and a new electronic warfare capability for their F/A-18s.)[97] As for the many positives, he concluded:

> The coalition with whom we worked, and the USAF in particu-lar, were incredibly accommodating. The USAF allowed us to do pretty much what we asked them. I do not think I was ever knocked back on any particular request. . . . If you are going to work with anybody, you cannot pick a better partner. We also had the RAF there and, again, they were incredibly generous to us. I did not have a communications aircraft to get from where I was to the other bases, but the two-star there [then Air Vice-Marshal Torpy] gave me a pretty free rein in his HS 125. So great coop-eration . . . really made the difference.[98]

One minor problem experienced by the RAAF's Hornet pilots, and often, no doubt, by U.S. Navy and Marine Corps and RAF pilots, whose aircraft were similarly configured with the probe-and-drogue in-flight refueling system, had to do with refueling from the U.S. Air Force's KC-135 tanker, which normally uses the boom refueling system but also is equipped to provide probe-and-drogue refueling for non–USAF aircraft. One RAAF F/A-18 pilot frankly recalled:

> Tanking was comfortable from the KC-10, as it had a large and forgiving basket. The KC-135, on the other hand, was a night-mare to refuel from. Although it was easy actually to plug in, stay-ing in the basket and getting gas was challenging, to say the least. You had about four feet in which to move around before you

got sprayed with fuel or fell out of the basket, with no formation cues to use. The basket was made of hard metal and was attached to the solid boom by about six feet of hose—crazy design. We nicknamed it "the wrecking ball," and one of our pilots trashed a probe soon after we arrived in theater.[99]

Another reported source of frustration for 75 Squadron's pilots, and one that was encountered at times by *all* coalition combat aircrews, entailed the inefficient apportionment of KI/CAS targets by the U.S. Air Force ASOC that supported V Corps due to the V Corps commander's insistence on close control of kill-box operations on his side of the FSCL (see Chapter 5). Like the other allied strike pilots, those in 75 Squadron soon eagerly sought assignment to the far more efficient Marine Corps direct air support center (DASC) that supported I MEF so that they might have greater opportunities to employ their GBU-12s to useful effect rather than returning to Al Udeid with unexpended munitions. At first, the ADF's air contingent commander and the commander of Australian forces denied the request because it smacked of "mission creep." Eventually, however, as the U.S. Marine Corps' exchange pilot with 75 Squadron recalled, "after figuring out that Warhawk [the ASOC's call sign] was not a good organization to work for, the Aussies asked to get into I MEF's [area of responsibility] and were accepted—as any jet carrying bombs was."[100]

Looking ahead, the MoD's after-action report on Operation Telic recognized that "the implications of maintaining congruence with an accelerating U.S. technological and doctrinal dominance [will] need to be assessed and taken into account in future policy and planning assumptions."[101] The most senior British military leaders also recognized the importance of planning for future combined contingency responses with the United States, especially those that might entail policy dimensions and implications less than fully congruent with British national interests. On this point, Air Chief Marshal Burridge underscored the fact that the current American style of military decision making, going at least as far back as Operation Desert Storm, depends largely on the personalities of the most senior principals involved. He added that were UK participation in future combat with the United States to become "more the norm than the exception," Britain should approach with care the question of whether "we need a different sort of command and control structure which fits a bit more easily with that direct line that the Americans are currently using." Noting the personality-driven aspects of the U.S. approach, he suggested that "you cannot always say that their doctrine looks like this and that is what they will do. If we modify, we may find that the next time it does not work quite so well."[102] In a similar vein, the Defence Committee of the House of Commons acknowledged that the British officers embedded at all levels of CENTCOM's command hierarchy gave the United Kingdom welcome influence over CENTCOM planning. However, it went on to raise a cautionary note about the "parallel dangers of being locked into American policy where that planning leads to military action."[103]

Perhaps most important from an operational perspective was the serious and legitimate concern within the British defense establishment, and particularly within the RAF, that the close commonality of operational styles and the trust relationships established between British and American airmen through their combined involvement in enforcing the no-fly zones over Iraq would disappear once Northern Watch and Southern Watch were no longer needed. In this regard, RAF officers from the chief of the air staff on down acknowledged a pressing need to replace that former real-world marriage of forces with surrogate peacetime mutual training opportunities that are regularly exercised either in the United States or wherever else the airspace and required training infrastructure might allow. Addressing an important facet of this concern, an RAF group captain noted that since "it is most unlikely that the [United Kingdom] will ever fight another major campaign of the nature of Operation Iraqi Freedom except as a coalition partner of the United States, . . . we need to develop an understanding, particularly in our middle-ranking officers, of our shared concepts for the employment of air power to enable them to understand the context of any combined operations and headquarters in which they may find themselves involved."[104]

RAF operators further identified an ever-growing need for joint and combined air-ground training for close air support that regularly exercises the entire command and control system from the CAOC through the ASOC to JTACS and FAC-As.[105] General Moseley emphasized the same point in his postcampaign reflections, insisting that all services, both U.S. and allied, must devise ways of jointly exercising such crucial command and control assets as the theater battle management core system (TBMCS) and area deep-operations coordination system in a dynamic peacetime training setting.[106] On this important point, some CENTAF planners declared that "counterland is, arguably, the most difficult mission that the air component performs. The size, diversity, and mobile nature of the counterland target set, in combination with the extensive real-time coordination that is required, challenges both aircrews and command and control unlike any other air-component mission." In the face of this challenge, these planners added, both the U.S. Air Force and the U.S. Army still lack any realistic means for rehearsing the joint counterland mission in peace-time training. Lacking in particular are significant opportunities to exercise and refine critical force employment processes through extended, large-scale, live-fly execution of the KI/CAS functions that proved so critical time and again throughout Iraqi Freedom.[107]

To head off or ameliorate this mounting concern, the U.S. Air Force and the RAF in 2005 implemented a new engagement initiative aimed at sustaining close ties between the two services to help ensure that their long-standing interoperability efforts and joint training and dialogue would continue to flourish. An early testament to this continued commitment was the successful conduct of the first Coalition Flag exercise involving U.S., RAF, and RAAF aircrews held at Nellis AFB in January 2006. More important yet, ever since the period of major combat in Iraqi Freedom ended, RAF and RAAF officers have continued to serve in key positions in CENTCOM's CAOC at Al Udeid Air Base, with air commodores performing rotational duties both as British and Australian air contingent commanders and as CAOC director. RAF aircrews have continued to contribute to the counterinsurgency air operations over Iraq and Afghanistan that have ensued at varying levels of intensity in each country since 2003, although that commitment ended in Iraq in May 2009 at the behest of the elected Iraqi government in compliance with the agreed timetable for the gradual withdrawal of coalition forces from that country.[108]

Key Accomplishments

Unlike the first Persian Gulf War, the major combat phase of Operation Iraqi Freedom did not begin with a sudden attack from a standing start after a gradual buildup of forces in the region. It was the culmination of a sustained pattern of force employment that exploited infrastructure laid down during the early aftermath of Desert Storm and that entailed continual offensive air operations throughout the twelve-year course of Operations Northern Watch and Southern Watch.[1] Good adaptive planning on CENTCOM's part, unprecedented joint force integration, and a thorough melding of special operations forces with allied air power were only three of the many factors that accounted for the campaign's rapid success in bringing down Hussein's regime.

In the crucial air portion of the three-week offensive, roughly 1,800 allied aircraft were committed to the campaign, more than 850 of which were provided by the U.S. Air Force and nearly 800 more of which were operated by the Navy and Marine Corps from carrier flight decks and shore bases in the region. These aircraft operated from more than 30 bed-down locations in various countries surrounding Iraq, ranging from nearby Kuwait, Bahrain, Oman, and the United Arab Emirates to locations as far away as Spain, Diego Garcia, the United Kingdom, and the United States. Allied aircraft flew 41,404 combat and combat-support missions during the major combat phase of Iraqi Freedom, roughly half of which were fighter sorties and nearly a quarter of which were supporting tanker missions (see chart 4.1). Of the nearly 20,000 strike sorties, more than 15,000 performed kill-box interdiction and CAS in direct support of the land component (see charts 4.2. and 4.3).[2]

Precision target attacks reached an unprecedented high in both number and intensity during the three-week campaign. All told, CENTAF strike sorties delivered 29,155 munitions to 24,898 designated target aim points, with precision-guided weapons accounting for almost 70 percent of all munitions expended, in contrast with only 8 percent in Operation Desert Storm.

As an added reflection of the extent of allied air support to ground operations, 328,448 rounds of cannon ammunition were shot during strafing attacks against enemy surface targets during the campaign, the vast majority from the

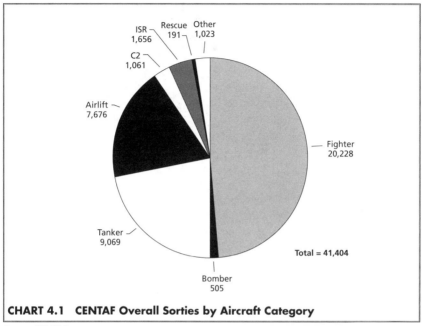

CHART 4.1   CENTAF Overall Sorties by Aircraft Category

Source: CENTAF

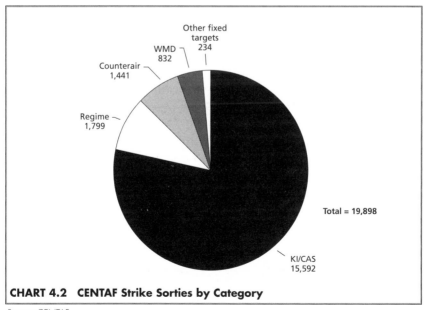

CHART 4.2   CENTAF Strike Sorties by Category

Source: CENTAF

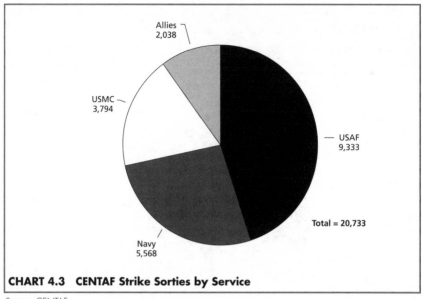

CHART 4.3 CENTAF Strike Sorties by Service

Source: CENTAF

GAU-8 30-mm antitank gun carried by the A-10.[3] In connection with the information operations effort, more than 40 million propaganda leaflets were dropped and more than 600 hours of radio broadcasts were made to various targeted Iraqi audiences. Only 108 U.S. and 27 British military personnel lost their lives during the 3 weeks of fighting that led to the regime's collapse, with another 339 Americans wounded, compared with 148 killed and 467 wounded during the 6 weeks of fighting in Operation Desert Storm. Estimates of casualties incurred on the Iraqi side ranged from 5,000 to 20,000 military fatalities and no fewer than 4,000—and most likely more—civilian fatalities.[4]

As indicated above, precision attack was a dominant feature of CENT-COM's air war. Thanks to increased weapons accuracy and a far greater number of available PGMs, allied aircraft expended fewer than 30,000 munitions against all Iraqi targets in three weeks, compared with about 250,000 during the five-week air portion of Operation Desert Storm. In addition, 850 TLAMs were fired from U.S. and British ships operating in the North Arabian Gulf, with 350 launched during a single night in the opening round of the campaign.[5] A number of CALCMs fired by Air Force B-52s also figured in the cruise missile contribution to the overall air campaign.

The satellite-aided GBU-31 JDAM, which made its combat debut during NATO's air war for Kosovo in 1999 and saw extensive use during Operation Enduring Freedom in 2001, truly came into its own during the major combat phase of Iraqi Freedom. Although the Air Force's B-1B heavy bombers flew only 2 percent of all recorded sorties, they dropped roughly a third of all of the JDAMs (some 2,100 in all) that were expended during the campaign.[6] This widespread availability of GPS-aided munitions, observed a former Marine Corps F/A-18 pilot, "meant that rather than putting his aircraft at a precise point in space, at an exact airspeed, altitude, attitude, and heading, a pilot could simply fly to the vicinity of a known set of target coordinates, release a bomb, and reliably expect that the bomb would guide directly to the target. He could do this without ever seeing what he was attacking—day, night, or in poor weather."[7] Amplifying on this, he added: "One of the chief advantages of JDAM weapons is that the pilot . . . can release the bomb once his aircraft enters a pie-shaped envelope that is calculated by the onboard mission computer and depicted on the navigation display. Once the bomb leaves the airplane, its tailfins adjust its trajectory and guide it to the preprogrammed coordinates. In essence, the JDAM is a launch-and-leave bomb that guides itself to the target."[8] An Air Force F-16 pilot explained it more candidly: "Dropping JDAM was so easy even a monkey could do it. You put in your north, south, east, and west coordinates, input your altitude, and then drive to the target. The jet tells you when the bomb's in range and when it is at minimum range, and you can select the impact angle you want, and what route you want the bomb to take, if applicable. And that's about it."[9]

The Iraqi Freedom campaign saw a number of new air power "firsts." For example, the campaign featured the first concurrent use of B-52, B-1B, and B-2 heavy bombers in a single package to attack multiple targets simultaneously. Related concepts of operations that were first tested over Afghanistan, such as loading bombers with precision munitions, putting them into holding orbits and stacking them, and using them for providing on-call CAS, finally matured in Iraqi Freedom. The Iraq war also saw the first combat use of the CBU-97 sensor-fused weapon. This munition, dropped from an altitude of 20,000 feet or more, dispenses 10 heat-seeking BLU-108 submunitions, each containing 4 armor-penetrating projectiles with infrared sensors, that descend by parachute to sniff for individual tanks and then attack those tanks with bomblets designed to penetrate the tops of their turrets.[10] On one occasion, a B-52 delivered 6 CBU-97s against a concentration of Iraqi tanks. In addition, the campaign saw the first air delivery of a combat-loaded M1A1 Abrams main battle tank directly into conflicted battlespace for immediate combat use when the 362nd Air Expeditionary Group operating out of Rhein-Main Air Base in Germany flew five Abrams tanks, five M2 Bradley armored fighting vehicles, and fifteen M113 APCs from Ramstein, Germany, to Bashur, Iraq, in early April 2003. Less

Bad description [handwritten marginal note]

than two weeks before, Air Force C-17s had conducted their first low-altitude combat airdrop of a large Army unit, the 173rd Airborne Brigade, which parachuted into northern Iraq.[11]

The three-week campaign also featured a number of firsts for American carrier-based air power as old platforms racked up new combat accomplishments. To begin with, the war saw the first delivery of a JDAM by an F-14D strike fighter—ironically enough as that jet was nearing the last days of its storied thirty-five-year service life. Earlier models of the F-14 had already been upgraded to carry JDAMs and had dropped them during Operation Enduring Freedom, but with three deployed F-14D squadrons operating near Iraq, CENTCOM and 5th Fleet planners wanted the latter aircraft to have JDAM capability as well. Accordingly, immediately before the campaign got under way, the Navy upgraded its F-14Ds to carry and deliver JDAMs, with the modification performed afloat by squadron maintenance technicians assisted by a Naval Air Systems Command team that had embarked with the squadrons, but with no direct support from depots or contractors in the United States. The campaign also saw the first use of an F/A-18E Super Hornet in an in-flight refueling role, the first use of the EA-6B in a psychological operations role, and an AGM-65 laser-guided Maverick missile fired for the first time by an S-3B at a target designated for it by an F/A-18C.

ISR milestones achieved during the Iraqi Freedom campaign included

- the first employment of the RQ-4A Global Hawk UAV as a SCAR asset, geolocating 50 SAM launchers, 10 or more SAM batteries, and roughly 70 missile transport vehicles;

- the first full integration of information operations into an ATO following the pioneering steps in that regard taken during Enduring Freedom;

- the fielding of a cryptological cell to work directly with the CAOC in retasking signals intelligence sensors to address urgent tactical needs, generating some 2,500 cues derived from signals intelligence;

- the use of the Navy's upgraded E-2C Hawkeye 2000 to direct allied air strikes during adverse weather;

- the use of pairs of RC-135 Rivet Joint aircraft to geolocate such moving targets as short-range theater ballistic missiles and mobile SAM launchers;

- the use of the E-8 JSTARS to provide dynamic surveillance and targeting during brownout conditions occasioned by the *shamal*;

- the first employment of the B-1 radar's GMTI capability in an ISR role;

- the wide-scale use of electro-optical and laser pods for both targeting and BDA;

- the use of the E-3 AWACS as a dynamic tasking tool, leveraging the Joint Tactical Information Distribution System carried by some F-15Es and other data modems to direct and redirect allied strike platforms;

- the use of a Navy Aegis anti–air warfare cruiser as a tactical ballistic missile early-warning system;

- the use of fused ISR to enable single platforms to attack multiple targets with precision munitions during a single mission;

- the use of Defense Support Program (DSP) satellites on orbit as a part of the tactical sensor network, detecting 26 missile launches, 1,493 static infrared events, and 186 high-explosive events;

- the targeting of Iraqi media facilities as a focused part of an information-operations campaign;

- and the simultaneous use of multiple ISR assets, including the concurrent use of 4 Predator UAVs during a single mission and the first ATO to include 6 simultaneous high-altitude U-2 sorties.[12]

Although the allied force buildup in the region began in November 2002, the Air Force's Air Mobility Command (AMC) did not start keeping track of its support contributions until January 1, 2003. From that date through mid-April, AMC's airlifters and additional chartered transport aircraft carried more than 214 million pounds of cargo and nearly 276,000 personnel in support of the campaign. Most of the American and allied troops were flown to the war zone in chartered jets. Nonmilitary chartered aircraft carried 224,047 military personnel to various forward operating locations in 4,542 sorties, with the next highest total (25,151) being transported on board C-5s. Together, C-5s and C-17s flew 11,400 sorties during the force buildup alone, with the C-5 averaging 53.8 tons per sortie and the C-17 averaging 33.1 tons per sortie. C-5s flew 99 fewer sorties than the C-17 but hauled 11,500 more tons and 5,300 more personnel.[13]

The Air Force reached beyond its normal CRAF assets on tap to charter some Soviet-made An-124 heavy airlifters for especially high volume cargo missions in support of Iraqi Freedom, contracting for these aircraft with Volga Dnepr Airlines on an as-needed basis. They performed seventy-nine lift missions for CENTCOM at a cost of $28.9 million. The Air Force also chartered fifty-three flights of Il-76 medium airlifters from Ukrainian Cargo Airways in March and April 2003. Beyond those, no other foreign carriers were contracted by the United States to support the campaign.[14]

The C-17 was the more reliable of AMC's two strategic airlifters. Having entered service only in the mid-1990s, it averaged an 88 percent in-commission rate, compared with the C-5's 67.5 percent rate, over the four months from the start of January to the end of April 2003. (The mission-capable rate for the C-5 rose from 62.1 percent in January to 71.6 percent in April.) The air mobility portion of CENTCOM's deployment of assets for Iraqi Freedom proved to be almost accident-free, with C-17s experiencing seven minor mishaps and the C-5 recording four incidents, but with no aircraft losses or aircraft damage totaling more than $1 million.[15]

With respect to logistic support, the British contingent was similarly pleased with the overall aircraft serviceability and spares support that it received, which worked smoothly thanks to resupply procedures that had been developed and perfected during the twelve years the United Kingdom was involved with enforcing the no-fly zones and operating in a desert environment. Although the British contingent's leaders allowed afterward that they could always have asked for more, they indicated that what they received was more than adequate to support the level of tasking to which the RAF was committed on the ATO. Air Chief Marshal Burridge did single out one important shortfall in logistics: "We are not yet fully invested in a logistic tracking system which tells us, in the same way as a global logistic company would know where every bit of kit is in transit, we have not yet got that system embedded."[16] Of the benefits in hedging against anticipated support needs he observed: "If you adopt a just-in-time concept against planning assumptions, then you are introducing risk."[17]

There also were notable contrasts between the major combat phase of Iraqi Freedom and the six-week Persian Gulf War of 1991. For one thing, the speed of deployment of needed forces was very rapid in the latter campaign—only three months compared with the seven months required for Operation Desert Storm. For another, all allied strike aircraft could now drop LGBs, whereas only one in five could do so in Desert Storm. In addition, TLAMs during Desert Storm had only a five-hundred-plus-mile range and required two to three days for the target to be programmed into their terrain-following guidance systems, whereas TLAM range in Iraqi Freedom exceeded one thousand miles and each missile could be programmed within hours of a target being geolocated. Also in Iraqi Freedom, it took only minutes rather than up to two days for commanders at all levels to receive target imagery and coordinates from space-based sensors and UAVs. Only one type of UAV was available to coalition forces in Desert Storm, as opposed to ten types in Iraqi Freedom that ranged from a small, hand-launched drone to Global Hawk. Moreover, whereas in Desert Storm a hard copy of the ATO had to be delivered daily to each aircraft carrier, in Iraqi Freedom it went out simultaneously in electronic format to all units via the secure Internet protocol router network (SIPRNet). Finally, secure communications in Desert Storm were limited to the STU III secure telephone unit, whereas in Iraqi Freedom, communications via secure video teleconferencing were possible all the way down the chain of command to the tactical level of a small ground unit commander sitting in a Humvee.[18]

Even before the dust from the campaign had fully settled, the four services were eager to begin compiling service-specific accounts of how each had leveraged the various technological, tactical, and doctrinal improvements that it had instituted over the course of the preceding decade. Secretary of Defense Rumsfeld, however, had determined even before the campaign started that JFCOM would instead undertake a single collaborative effort to report key combat lessons learned by all of the services. "This was not a war fought by the Army or the Navy or the Air Force or the Marines," he reiterated soon after the Ba'athist regime collapsed. "It's a war that's been fought by joint forces."[19] CENTCOM's director of operations at the time, Major General Renuart, observed that it had been deemed "important to consolidate the process, to make it as simple as we could for the warfighters, and give the services and other agencies the access they needed to provide a meaningful product. That has turned out to be a very, very positive relationship."[20] In hindsight, having JFCOM conduct this initial assessment on behalf of all the services was well advised. Apart from the enduring fact that instant history is usually bad history, any such efforts right out of the blocks by the individual uniformed services would almost certainly have been flawed by service parochialism. General Moseley remarked on this point shortly after the collapse of the Ba'athist regime: "Lessons-learned briefs are dangerous because the people who listen to your brief stop listening as soon as they hear the one or two items that foster their particular agenda."[21]

Nevertheless, during his subsequent postcampaign briefing at a conference attended by air war participants at all levels who had gathered at Nellis AFB in July 2003 to review, assess, and document the air war's main events, General Moseley recited a long checklist of items and areas of activity that he personally deemed effective and useful campaign developments. These included:

■ General Franks' integrated war plan and the generally effective jointness among CENTCOM's subordinate warfighting components;

- General Franks' designation of General Moseley, in his capacity as the air component commander, as CENTCOM's space coordination authority;

- integration and partnership better than experienced previously in coalition warfare;

- the aggressive and well-orchestrated theater engagement effort all of the coalition partners;

- a command relationship between the air component commander and his subordinate commander of Air Force forces forward-deployed to the theater (COMAFFOR) that was consistent with good doctrine;

- a CAOC organizational construct, manning level, and composition that were consistent with established doctrine;

- the ACCE assigned to the land component;

- the presence of other component-commander liaison officers in the CAOC;

- and the similar presence of host-nation liaison officers in the CAOC.

With respect to highlights of the air component's actual combat operations, Moseley's roster included:

- the highly effective use of precision-guided munitions;

- the early transition from SEAD to DEAD operations on D+3;

- the early deployment of tankers, sensor aircraft, and UAVs forward into Iraqi airspace;

- a markedly reduced sensor-to-shooter cycle time;

- the KI/CAS concept of operations and its execution;

- the air component's urban CAS concept of operations and its execution;

- and improved interaction between the air component and supporting national intelligence agencies.[22]

JFCOM's initial look at the campaign concluded that the major combat phase of Iraqi Freedom attested to the dominance of "overmatching power" over "overwhelming force," with the latter construct being fixated mainly on numbers "as befits a traditional, attrition-based campaign," whereas the former looks beyond numbers to focus "on harnessing all the capabilities that [the U.S.] services and special operations forces bring to the battlespace in a coherently joint way."[23] Among the many positive accomplishments of CENTCOM's conduct of air operations during the campaign, this chapter emphasizes improvements in air-ground coordination since Operation Anaconda in Afghanistan in early 2002; improvements in force connectivity across service lines; increased targeting efficiency on CENTCOM's and the CAOC's part in comparison to the initial days of Operation Enduring Freedom; improvements in the effectiveness of the CAOC as a budding weapons system in its own right; advances in the combat support performance of such key enablers as space, UAVs, JSTARS, and information operations; and new munitions and technologies that saw their first combat application during the major combat phase of Operation Iraqi Freedom. The overall combat effects and battlespace achievements racked up by CENTCOM's air component during the three weeks of major combat are also treated below.

Improvements in Air-Ground Coordination

Operation Anaconda, a U.S. Army–led effort to bottle up and capture or kill Al Qaeda holdouts in the Shah-i-Kot Valley of eastern Afghanistan in March 2002, demonstrated the dangers of faulty air-ground coordination. The failure of Combined Joint Task Force (CJTF) Mountain (which had been tasked with planning and executing the mission) and CENTCOM's land component more generally to plan for the involvement of the air component nearly resulted in a disaster for the operation when CJTF Mountain's attempted insertion of allied ground troops met unexpectedly fierce Al Qaeda opposition and left those troops for a time without adequate on-call air support. Prompted by a heated Army–Air Force argument that ensued in the early aftermath of that near debacle, when CJTF Mountain's commander wrongly accused the Air Force of having failed to provide his embattled troops with adequate CAS in a timely manner, the Air Force's chief of staff, General Jumper, initiated a four-star dialogue with his Army counterpart, Gen. Eric Shinseki. Their discourse did much to itemize the many misunderstandings on all sides associated with Anaconda and to implement appropriate measures to ensure that such a failure to communicate would never again hamper the effective integration of U.S. land and air forces in joint warfare.[24]

A direct outgrowth of that high-level interservice dialogue was General Moseley's establishment of an ACCE physically collocated at the headquarters of the land component commander, Lieutenant General McKiernan, in ample time for the start of Operation Iraqi Freedom. As briefly explained in Chapter 1, General Leaf's responsibility as ACCE was to represent the air component as General Moseley's personal ambassador and spokesman, and not merely to serve as an air liaison officer between the air and land component commanders.

General Leaf's two-star status put him on an equal footing with General McKiernan's principal deputies for operations, intelligence, and other combat functions, thus ensuring that General Moseley's perspective as the air compo-nent commander would be accorded due attention during land component staff meetings and briefings. In comments after the major combat phase of Iraqi Freedom was over, General Leaf said that the campaign experience had strongly validated the ACCE concept as a means of better facilitating air-land integra-tion. McKiernan's deputy for operations, Maj. Gen. William Webster, echoed Leaf's views:

> I think the access to joint fires, especially close air support and interdiction, was unprecedented. The ability to shoot things with access to Navy, Marine [Corps], and Air Force air was unprec-edented. A lot of it had to do with the [air component com-mander] placing General Leaf there with me, side by side. He and I made an agreement up front that whether we disagreed personally at any point in time, we would not let that get in the way of anything. . . . And there were times when we didn't agree on something. But as we train and fight together, we will get better over time.[25]

To further enhance the integration of air and land component operations, General Moseley established the 484th Air Expeditionary Wing as an overarch-ing theater air control system (TACS) headquartered in Qatar. Col. Michael Longoria, the unit's commander, observed that the timely initiative reflected "the realization [of] General Moseley's vision [to have] one person, one com-mander . . . to go to [and] address any issues [with] how that system is working."[26] The TACS organization extended the reach of the CAOC down to the lowest tactical level of allied ground forces operating in Iraqi battlespace. It also pro-vided the TACPs that supported V Corps' ground units throughout Iraq by con-ducting terminal attack control for on-call CAS sorties. One of the wing's sub-ordinate groups, the 4th Air Support Operations Group (ASOG), ran the ASOC (call sign Warhawk), which vectored airborne aircraft into the fight and put their aircrews in contact with TACPs on the ground who were assigned to the 4th ASOG's 15th Expeditionary Air Support Operations Squadron (EASOS).[27] An informed account later explained that the ASOC at first was basically "a traffic cop pushing V Corps sorties to forward air controllers. To improve fires between the Air Force and Army, the ASOC was redesigned to not only provide timely air support to the [Army] divisions, but also to allow the corps commander to shape the battlespace. The ASOC would continue its traditional role of providing CAS to the divisions, but it would also direct kill-box interdiction in open ground space that became known as *corps shaping*. . . . All these improvements would have a dramatic effect on the upcoming conflict in Iraq."[28]

The ASOC coordinated with V Corps' plans and operations functions and integrated its own operations with the fires and effects coordination cell and Army airspace command and control at the corps level. During the three-week campaign, the ASOC's battle managers made a determined effort to assign additional JTACs to the 3rd ID during the latter's advance toward Baghdad. A much-improved communications link between the ASOC and the CAOC since Operation Enduring Freedom allowed both entities to make the most of TBMCS, a latest-generation CAOC mission-planning tool (see below).

Problems encountered in Enduring Freedom accounted almost entirely for CENTAF's determination to assign a full-up ASOC to General Wallace's V Corps. The initially flawed execution of Operation Anaconda by CJTF Mountain starkly highlighted the need for a properly equipped, staffed, and functioning ASOC collocated with key ground combat headquarters to enable more responsive and effective air support to counterland operations. During their workups for Anaconda, the commanders of CJTF Mountain, and of CENTCOM's land component more generally, did not bring the CAOC into their mission planning. As a result, once the operation was under way and on the point of coming unglued in the face of unexpected heavy fire from the defending Al Qaeda force, supporting JTACs in need of urgent air support put their requests either directly to the CAOC or to an airborne E-3 AWACS that was operating in the area. This hastily arranged procedure permitted neither coordination nor prioritization of those air support requests.

In addition, the absence of a common operating picture throughout Anaconda left fighting units on the ground unaware of the presence and location of other friendly units in their immediate area of operations, not only conventional ground combat units but also covert SOF and CIA teams. This untenable situation led to the subsequent establishment of an ASOC at Bagram Air Base, which in turn became the precursor to the joint air control element that was eventually created for Iraqi Freedom. Although the relationship between V Corps' ASOC and the CAOC once Iraqi Freedom got under way sometimes became strained (see Chapter 5), it can be said without qualification, as CENTAF staffers later recalled, "that the close working relationship between the ASOC and V Corps' fires and effects coordination cell increased the level of trust between the land and air component commanders."[29]

As the planning workups for Operation Iraqi Freedom neared execution, a close trust relationship was also forged between the air component and I MEF with respect to the apportionment and combat use of Marine Corps aviation. General Moseley, in accordance with accepted joint doctrine and in his capacity as the overall air component commander, retained ultimate authority (*operational* control) over the allocation of Marine fixed-wing aircraft for all long-range strike, tactical air reconnaissance, and defensive counterair mission needs. Also in accordance with joint doctrine, however, based on the authority granted to him as CENTCOM's airspace control authority (ACA) by General Franks, he delegated to the Marine ground commander *tactical* control over all Marine Corps air assets deemed necessary for direct support of Marine combat operations on the ground, with the proviso that on the rare occasion that those air assets might be needed to help underwrite broader theater air component needs, the Marine commander would cede unemployed Marine air assets back to the CAOC for the length of time required to help meet broader theater combat requirements.[30]

General Moseley further promised to provide the Marines any additional air component–controlled air support that they might require from Air Force and Navy strike assets in order to meet their direct support needs of the moment.[31] This trust relationship was facilitated by I MEF's provision of a Marine aviator, Col. Ron McFarland, to General Moseley's CAOC staff. McFarland helped educate Air Force airmen regarding Marine Corps operational requirements and potential contributions to the joint and combined air war.[32] An especially notable success story that emerged from this close relationship entailed integrating I MEF and its associated command and control system into the air component's overall KI/CAS operation without, as CAOC planners later put it, "creating an airspace bubble within a bubble."[33] General Moseley held several conferences with members of the Marine aviation community before the start of Iraqi Freedom aimed at integrating all airspace requests and control measures into a single structure. His success is evident in the fact that no significant Marine-associated airspace management problems occurred during the war.

Yet another such issue that had a happy ending entailed ensuring that the Marine Corps' direct support ATO was fused into the air component's overall ATO and the ensuing joint and combined air offensive. Toward that end, KI/CAS planners in the CAOC worked closely with I MEF's direct support ATO planners to ensure an overall unity of effort. I MEF agreed to release its direct support F/A-18C sorties to General Moseley on an as-needed basis to support deep-attack operations in exchange for CAOC-controlled A-10 sorties.

As a result, CAOC and I MEF planners succeeded in overcoming the daunting challenge of providing needed air support to friendly ground forces operating deep inside central Iraq with the limited tanker assets that were available at the time. CENTAF staffers later recalled, however, that overcoming these distances required the KI/CAS planners "to perform a day-to-day balancing act."[34]

The air component's arrangement for providing as-needed CAS to I MEF worked differently and more efficiently than did the V Corps/ASOC system (see Chapter 5). Throughout the major combat phase of Iraqi Freedom, I MEF preferred to follow established Marine Corps doctrine, which normally places the FSCL approximately eighteen nautical miles in front of the forward line of troops (FLOT). Because a MEF is essentially a division-sized combat element that lacks both long-range artillery and a corps-level force element for conducting battlespace shaping at the forward edge of its area of operations, the Marines typically position their FSCL closer to their FLOT and use their organic direct support air assets to conduct shaping beyond it. Whenever the Army's FSCL was placed deeper than eighteen nautical miles beyond the FLOT, I MEF units operating within it used a fire support coordination measure called the battlefield coordination line (BCL). All battlespace shaping beyond the BCL was conducted by fixed-wing air assets. In addition, I MEF opened all kill boxes beyond its BCL to enable air interdiction even when those kill boxes were inside the FSCL. This resulted in a more efficient use of the air component's KI/CAS assets than did V Corps' more restrictive arrangement.[35] On this score, General Moseley later wrote in his candid foreword to a book on Marine aviation's contribution to Iraqi Freedom: "As the fight began, planning work and execution responsibility were taken and shared so effectively that lines between the services faded over the battlefield. . . . What matters is having the right weapon at the right place at the right time."[36]

The ACCE position that proved so pivotal in Iraqi Freedom has since been formally codified in U.S. joint doctrine. What has yet to be put into joint doctrine, however, is the notion that an ACCE can be supplied to a joint task force commander in lieu of a full-up air component commander and AOC, even though such a simpler arrangement might be the more efficient and effective way to use joint air power. As for the likely composition of future ACCEs, General Leaf suggested that the team should be structured to allow the ACCE director to function as a senior representative of the air component commander around the clock, requiring varied air and space operations expertise, intelligence support, and a limited staff. At most, such a team would not exceed eighteen officers. For Iraqi Freedom, Leaf chose to augment his twelve-member Air

Force team with a Marine Corps pilot, a naval aviator, and three RAF officers who had already been forward-deployed for the impending campaign.[37]

One problem reported with the ACCE construct was the seam it created in the otherwise smooth interface in command relations between the ACCE and the air component commander, on the one hand, and the ASOC and CAOC director, on the other. Current joint doctrine states that the ASOC is an extension of the CAOC and accordingly reports to the CAOC director. Yet the plan worked out by the 4th ASOG that was assigned to support V Corps stressed that the ASOC should be regarded as the sole controlling agency for all aerial weapons delivery *inside* the FSCL, recognizing both the ASOC's better awareness and appreciation of the local state of play on the ground compared with that of the more remote CAOC, and its close integration with V Corps' intelligence staff and its fires and effects coordination cell. The ASOC staff's main frustration concerned the center's inability to make the best use of the large number of aircraft that had been allocated to it by the CAOC because the V Corps commander insisted on complete control of all kill boxes inside the FSCL. He opened the kill boxes only when munitions delivery into them could be disciplined by the most stringent Type I CAS control, even though incoming requests for air support by engaged Army units were generally for situations that neither entailed close proximity of V Corps troops to enemy forces nor required the detailed integration of air support with the fire and movement of friendly ground troops that is mandated by Type I CAS procedures. Air planners and operators later concluded that the relationships between the ACCE, the ASOC, and the CAOC need to be better defined.[38]

Nevertheless, the air component's delivery of CAS throughout the major combat phase of Iraqi Freedom earned high marks from both Army and Marine Corps consumers of the service. The commander of V Corps, Lieutenant General Wallace, later recalled: "We've gotten more close air support and more availability of CAS and more access to CAS than I can remember."[39] The most thorough review to date of Army operations in the three-week campaign enthusiastically agreed:

> The air component's units moved and fought at the strategic, operational, and tactical levels and performed brilliantly at all levels. Rapid and precise attacks on time-sensitive targets at all three levels demonstrated the inherent flexibility of the air arm. Air interdiction and CAS had been a bone of contention between the Army and the Air Force, in particular. In this campaign, thanks in part to personal efforts on the part of senior leaders,

but also as a consequence of the maturation of joint doctrine and joint operations, that seam practically disappeared. . . . CAS proved decisive in assuring tactical victory and, on more than one occasion, decisive in preventing tactical defeat. Perhaps just as important, CAS provided a strong boost to troops on the ground, who were profoundly grateful to the airmen who flew those missions. What had [once] been a source of irritation has become a source of satisfaction and admiration.[40]

The 3rd ID's after-action assessment of the division's experiences during the three-week campaign likewise spoke warmly of the air component's contributions to the success of the land offensive: "Throughout [Operation Iraqi Freedom], air support had a major impact on the battlefield. Air support proved highly successful both in shaping operations [and] in the close fight. The division utilized air support for a number of different missions, including shaping, armed [reconnaissance], counterfire, and CAS. Responsiveness, lethality, and integration into maneuver contributed to the success of CAS on the battlefield."[41] Characterizing CAS as "a great combat multiplier," the assessment reported that "a total of 925 CAS sorties were flown in support of 3 ID (M), resulting in 656 enemy combat systems destroyed and 89 enemy facilities destroyed. Corps shaping accounted for an additional 3,324 sorties destroying an estimated 2,400 enemy targets."[42] With respect to the combat performance of fixed-wing air power in facilitating the ground advance, the assessment further noted that "division ALOs [air liaison officers] positioned CAS stacks to facilitate quick response based on the ground commander's scheme of maneuver. . . . As a result, CAS requests for troops-in-contact situations were available in 5–10 minutes. In fact, CAS was so responsive [that] at times the [ASOC] held CAS in waiting for division clearance. For all other requests, responsiveness ranged from 5–30 minutes. These delays were due to higher-priority division requests being filled, as well as gaps within the [ATO]. There were very rare occasions when weather increased the CAS responsiveness to 45 minutes to an hour."[43]

Effective provision of CAS by allied fixed-wing aircraft required the use of a nine-line attack briefing format, a standard procedure in joint air support practice going back to well before Desert Storm in 1991, that contained all the information an attacking pilot needed in order to approach his assigned target area, conduct his attack safely, and egress expeditiously. The nine-line briefing consists of the following components:

1. Initial point—the point from which the CAS platform commences its attack run

2. Bearing/offset—the heading from the initial point to target and offset direction (left or right)

3. Distance—in nautical miles from the initial point to the target

4. Elevation—of the target in feet above mean sea level

5. Target description (as brief, concise, and complete as may be needed)

6. Target location—geographic coordinates for the target

7. Mark—type of visual or laser mark that the JTAC will put on the intended target aim point

8. Friendlies—heading and distance from the target to the nearest friendly unit

9. Egress—heading and initial point for the CAS aircraft to fly to clear the target area after weapon release

An informed account explained the practical application of this procedure:

> Additional information was provided after the nine-line brief, including the expected time on target (time when [the] CAS aircraft's bombs must hit the target) and final attack heading/cone (either a heading or an arc of headings that the CAS aircraft must fly down when delivering weapons onto the target). This information would be relayed to the pilot via a radio frequency unique to this particular FAC team, the latter having literally a phonebook of frequencies they could choose from....The pilots, in turn, had a notebook-sized frequency "smart pack" that they would leaf through in order to ascertain the correct channel to dial into their radios to allow them to communicate with their FAC....The pilot would physically write down the FAC's nine-line brief onto his kneeboard, and he would then read back the coordinates to check that he had copied them correctly. The FAC would then confirm with a simple "yes" or a mike click. Once he had received this, the pilot would then start to punch the target coordinates into the bomb guidance system.... Once the release parameters had been met, the pilot would tell the FAC that he was set up for his run to the target, giving him the "wings-level" call, which would prompt [the FAC's] reply of "cleared hot." The pilot now had the FAC's authority to release his ordnance—the former could not do so without the latter's approval....The final call on whether to release the ordnance or not was ultimately [the FAC's] to make. A pilot would never question his decision.[44]

One F/A-18 pilot recalled with respect to the application of this procedure: "Communication between the pilot and the FAC could be difficult at times, especially if the frequencies weren't quite right or the SOF guy had a weak radio or low battery power. On some occasions, you could only hear him when you were right on top of him."[45] It was by no means unusual for pilots to come off a tanker, establish radio contact with a FAC, and then use up their entire load of just-replenished fuel trying to determine exactly what the FAC was talking about. Sometimes pilots would have to make more than one return trip to the tanker to top off their fuel before they were sure what targets their FAC wanted to have attacked.

Despite such occasional friction at the margins, the provision of CAS was typically smooth throughout the major combat phase of Iraqi Freedom, regardless of the color of the uniform that delivered it. During his briefing to the media on April 5, 2003, General Moseley remarked: "If you check into the CAS stack, you may be working with a Marine in an F/A-18 or a Navy crew in an F-14 or an Air Force pilot in an A-10. You won't know the difference. You'll just know the call sign and the location. So I think that's another wonderful testimony to joint training, joint doctrine, joint CAS, and being able to work the command and control to get the airplanes up there."[46]

As for the overriding importance of simply getting the job done correctly rather than seeking credit for having done it, Moseley added: "As the air component commander, I'm not sure I care how we kill the [enemy] tank. I just want the tank to die so my Army captain doesn't have to face it. . . . There will be someone somewhere along the way [who] will want an accounting scheme of who killed what vehicle, but right now that's not important to us and it's not important to that lieutenant or captain." He further noted that the lion's share of recognition for having fostered the tone for this joint-minded approach belonged to General Franks, who "from the very beginning has conducted [the campaign] in the absolute finest traditions of jointness and coalition and combined operations, and each of us, the component commanders, have been involved from the very beginning on the development at the strategic and operational level. There's been nothing that we've asked for that we haven't got. . . . We're in absolute harmony with each other on being able to complement and supplement each other's capabilities and, in some cases, limitations."[47] A CAOC staffer later added, "At times, air power enabled the land forces by attriting the enemy. At others, the maneuver forces enabled air power by forcing the enemy out of concealment and causing them to mass. The FSCL placement lost its importance because the corps commander could open kill boxes through the

ASOC to facilitate fires. With this new paradigm, the Army received air power fires where and when it wanted."[48]

The KI/CAS concept accepted in principle by all participants used a common grid reference system for CENTCOM's area of operations that allowed both airmen and ground combatants to operate and communicate within a common frame of reference. The lessons learned from the effective integration of air power and SOF teams during Enduring Freedom were folded into General Franks' concept of operations for Iraqi Freedom, thereby increasing the combat effectiveness of a far larger air and ground team that had previously experienced virtually *no* significant interaction. As a former U.S. Army officer later expressed this key point: "Air and ground forces, which had fought essentially separate wars in Operation Desert Storm in 1991, were now integrated to a higher degree than ever before. By relying on precision air strikes, CENTCOM was able to slim down the U.S. ground force element to a single heavy division, one light division, and two light brigades.... Even before U.S. ground troops came into contact with Republican Guard units, these elite Iraqi formations were subjected to punishing attacks by Air Force, Marine, and Navy aircraft, just as they had been in 1991."[49] A V Corps after-action assessment likewise gave the air component high marks for having provided more than adequate support: "It was not merely the parallel functioning of two armed services; it was the almost flawless operation of a thoroughly integrated combined-arms team. Army officers of the V Corps staff described the results in superlatives. It was the best, most efficient, most effective, and most responsive air support the Air Force has ever provided to any U.S. Army unit."[50]

The after-action assessment of the Army's 3rd ID reflected a similar satisfaction with the performance of the air-land interface, noting that "the teamwork of key leaders and supporting arms was vital. We avoided 'rice bowl' protection and 'gave way together' to get the job done.... The effort of our [ALOs and JTACs] demonstrated 'gauntness' in action—with no concern for 'who gets credit' for mission success—one team, one fight, one successful mission. The commendable end result was directly attributable to the months of tough training and close personal relationships that only true professional organizations produce and sustain." In particular, "the working relationship between the fire support element (FSE) and [ALO] at the division tactical command post ... was exemplary, resulting in a dynamic fires team. Together, they labored to provide a permissive environment for massing fires."[51]

The Department of Defense later attributed the campaign's rapid success largely to this unprecedented level of joint force integration among CENTCOM's principal warfighting components. Adm. Edmund Giambastiani, the commander of JFCOM at the time, noted that arriving at such insights as the importance of joint integration, adaptive planning, and speed in staying ahead of the enemy's decision cycle "was actually not all that easy. They had to be proven in conflict" and required "a significant change in U.S. service culture to accept the message that the power of the joint force is far greater than that of any individual service." Giambastiani added: "The key to harnessing the full power of jointness begins at [the level of] command and control. It is at this level—the level of the combatant commander; the joint task force commander; [and] the air, land, and sea commanders—where the real work of seamlessly integrating service capabilities into ... what we call the coherently joint and combined force takes place."[52]

Advances in Force Connectivity

Throughout the duration of major combat in Iraqi Freedom, CENTCOM had more than forty times the amount of bandwidth on tap than had been available for the conduct of Operation Desert Storm. The bandwidth capacity of the command's joint operations center in Qatar alone was said to have been roughly equal to that of a large American city. This greatly expanded capability allowed for network-enabled operations unprecedented in their comprehensiveness and connectivity. A subsequent Air Combat Command briefing on the air war reported that "bandwidth and information connectivity resulted in a high degree of interoperability between the components," aided by a "seamless integration of service component efforts in the CAOC." Demand for bandwidth nevertheless exceeded the available supply as "frequency and bandwidth became an important ... commodity that corps- and divisional-level staff fought over throughout the war."[53]

The centerpiece of the situation display capability in CENTCOM's joint operations center was a Blue Force Tracker (BFT) system that was enabled by GPS transponders mounted on selected surface vehicles in each ground combat unit. The BFTs transmitted the geographic coordinates, direction, and speed of those platforms at any given moment as they moved about the battlespace. An early draft of JFCOM's after-action assessment of the campaign described the complexities of this new aid to battlespace situation awareness: "Ground forces provided to CENTCOM arrived in theater with seven different, noninteroperable BFT systems. Each had different hardware, software, and transmission paths; operated on different frequencies; and flowed information through different ground stations. CENTCOM had to integrate these systems to obtain a common operating picture of [friendly] ground force dispositions."[54]

Hundreds of allied SOF combatants were likewise issued two-pound GPS transmitters the size of a cigarette pack that provided their geographic coordinates to senior commanders, sometimes located thousands of miles away, via airborne and satellite uplinks. The signals from these miniature transmitters were captured by National Reconnaissance Office satellites and relayed to command centers worldwide via the SIPRNet from Air Force Space Command in Colorado Springs. The transmitters interconnected roughly a quarter of the entire allied SOF contingent in Iraq as they searched for Scud missiles in Iraq's western desert, attacked enemy command posts, and sought to track down fleeing Iraqi leaders. Their locations within the battlespace, along with those of other ground forces and airborne support aircraft, were depicted as icons on digital displays at the joint operations center, in the CAOC in Saudi Arabia, and at CENTCOM headquarters in Florida. Every key node that figured in this network-enabled campaign enjoyed plasma displays that showed the precise location of all friendly forces at any moment. The system allowed ground commanders from the brigade level on up to monitor on laptop computer screens the movement of each friendly vehicle as it advanced across Iraqi terrain.[55] "It allowed them to be tracked throughout the battlefield so we knew where our forces were," noted Lt. Gen. Joseph Cosumano, commander of the Army Space and Missile Command, "and it allowed them to work better with conventional forces."[56]

CENTCOM also maintained a Red Force tracking capability that marshaled the best intelligence from overhead multispectral sensors and signals intelligence. By one account, it "swept up enemy radio and radar transmissions, cell- and satellite-phone conversations, land-line communications and data transmissions—even the Iraqis' military e-mail system." Although the Red Force picture was less up-to-date and complete than that provided by Blue Force Tracker, because it was only as good as its intelligence inputs and necessarily required more processing time, General Franks characterized it as "the best any commander had ever had in wartime."[57]

The ISR network for Iraqi Freedom, controlled centrally by CENTCOM's directorate of intelligence, represented an unprecedented fusion of military and national sensor platforms, starting with three dozen daily passes by imaging satellites and supported by eighty dedicated ISR aircraft that provided continuous multispectral imaging, thermal imaging, signals intelligence monitoring, and other surveillance of Iraq.[58] These dedicated platforms were further backstopped by a wide spectrum of strike aircraft whose onboard sensors, such as ground-mapping radars and electro-optical and infrared-imaging targeting pods, were also used for the first time in a systematic and organized way for ISR monitoring through the integration of information gathered by their various targeting systems through Link 16 and the many other data-link capabilities that produced the common operating picture that was available to everyone at levels ranging from the Pentagon and CENTCOM's forward headquarters down to operating units in the field.

CENTCOM made particularly effective use of an arrangement involving an extended tether network through which satellite-derived information could be vectored directly to Beale AFB, California, for subsequent cueing of U-2s orbiting high over Iraq. The Air Force deployed an unprecedented fifteen of its thirty-four U-2s to the war zone to support the campaign, attesting to the continuing advantages offered by this vintage but still uniquely capable aircraft in ISR.[59] Configured with multiple imagery systems and a unique signals intelligence collection capability for an air-breathing platform, the U-2 carried a substantially bigger payload than any UAV. With as many as 6 of the aircraft concurrently airborne on the same ATO—a combat first—U-2s flew 169 sorties averaging 8 hours' duration each, for a total of some 1,400 combined flight hours.[60]

In addition, airborne RQ-1 Predator UAVs forwarded real-time imagery to downlinks in the United States via satellites, as did the single RQ-4 Global Hawk high-altitude UAV that was deployed forward to support the campaign. That platform, which also forwarded target area information to Beale for real-time processing, flew only 3 percent of CENTCOM's high-altitude ISR missions in support of combat operations (357 hours total), yet it provided about 55 percent of the required time-sensitive target information to General Moseley's staff in the CAOC.[61] Offering three times the persistence of manned ISR platforms, Global Hawk helped significantly in shortening CENTCOM's "kill chain" (the sequence of events ranging from initial target acquisition and identification through committing the most appropriate weapon against it and receipt of clearance to fire to the target's destruction). At any given moment, there were three or more U-2s and as many as six Predator UAVs overhead in direct support of allied combat operations.

"Reachback" (i.e., forward-deployed combat operations centers tasking rear-area facilities as far back as the home front for information support) was another key enabler of allied force employment, as exemplified by the case of a B-52 crew that experienced a radio failure after taking off from RAF Fairford in the United Kingdom but was able to salvage its mission by falling back on MILSTAR satellite communications with the help of ground-based space support facilities in the United States. Reachback allowed more tactical intelligence than ever before to be pushed down to wing-level staff personnel. The new fighter data-link (FDL) system represented yet another boon for force connectivity. It enabled the prompt transfer of target coordinates and related information among the RC-135 Rivet Joint, the E-8 JSTARS, the E-3 AWACS, and F-15Cs and Es and a few F-16C+s as soon as any of those platforms detected and geolocated a new target of interest.[62] That capability enabled more efficient and effective time-critical targeting by allowing strike fighters to locate assigned targets almost immediately and to hook their radars and infrared weapons guidance systems directly onto targets generated by FDL.[63]

The stringent visual target identification requirements that CENTCOM levied on all of its subordinate components created an unusually great demand for real-time tactical imagery.[64] The fusion of real-time information from FAC-As, ground observers, UAVs, and JSTARS helped substantially to meet those requirements. In general, the networking tools that were available to the CAOC for Iraqi Freedom were better than those that enabled the earlier Afghan campaign in that they allowed heightened reliance on "decision-quality" information and reduced the reaction time for time-sensitive targets down to almost single-digit minutes, as attested by the twelve-minute information cycle time for the B-1 that was targeted against a location where Saddam Hussein was thought to have been present. Networking also enabled the concept of "swarming" a target with multiple attack platforms either simultaneously or in sequence.[65]

U.S. naval forces that participated in the opening round of Iraqi Freedom were also fully integrated into the digital data stream. For example, the aircraft carrier *Abraham Lincoln* featured a joint fires network (JFN) and cooperative engagement capability (CEC) that allowed its battle-group participants to share radar information and to fire missiles based on information provided by other ships. The arrival of *Nimitz* and the first E-2C Hawkeyes that were equipped with the system expanded that capability. The JFN, a Navy adaptation of the sensor fusion mechanism that enables the Army's tactical exploitation system (TES), allows deployed aircraft carriers to receive imagery from airborne platforms and signals intelligence from the Air Force's RC-135 Rivet Joint aircraft. When the campaign began, the Navy was still considering whether to invest more money in its version of the Army's system or to try to make do with a cheaper and somewhat less robust remote terminal capability. The Navy's version showed considerable potential, but some of its capabilities remained to be validated.[66]

The multifunction information distribution system (MIDS), a nodeless and secure Link 16–based jam-resistant tactical data link, also made a major difference in enhancing interoperability with other joint and allied platforms equipped with that capability. Now in the U.S. fleet and with more than a thousand Link 16 terminals in the four services, it was a major contributor toward the continuing transition from analog to digital warfighting, and it paved the way for the next step in network-enabled combat operations.[67] The Navy's subsequent pursuit of such capabilities as Link 16 and JFN to move target information into the cockpit faster reflects its determination to become a fully linked force.[68] Notwithstanding the substantial shortening of the target approval process, it still took time for the CAOC to pass along a clearance to fire to an airborne controller, who would relay the target coordinates to a strike crew, who then had to identify the target positively before expending ordnance against it.

Although senior commanders had up-to-date information about the position and movement of Iraqi ground forces, that information could not usually be passed down in sufficient time to the friendly ground units that were nearing actual contact with Iraqi forces. The rate of advance of allied ground troops was often so fast that CENTCOM had difficulty providing real-time intelligence to their short-range and line-of-sight-limited voice and data communications. As Michael Knights observed, those units were on the wrong side of the digital divide where "the slope got a lot steeper at the brigade level and below" and where tactical-level subordinate units "lay at the base of a veritable digital cliff." For them, real-time situational awareness of the presence and location of enemy ground forces was all too often "earned the hard way: by meeting the enemy at close hand."[69] Another account expressed the same point, noting that "many U.S. troops got their first clue about enemy resistance when they bumped into their foe."[70] Although CENTCOM's operational-level commanders generally had sufficient situation awareness to meet their needs, tactical commanders approaching the point of contact with enemy ground troops needed a more refined degree of detail that was rarely available to them. Two RAND analysts likewise observed that allied ground forces faced the "constant danger of encountering the enemy without warning." They compensated with "a high degree of passive protection and overwhelming firepower."[71]

The Iraqi Freedom experience highlighted the persistent shortfall in wideband data-link capacity as a major limiting factor in infrastructure effectiveness. A key challenge in this regard entails acquiring more and bigger data transfer "pipes" while continuing efforts to better manage the bandwidth capacity that already exists.[72] Another challenge entails improved knowledge management, with a view toward determining what information is in greatest need of being moved rather than trying to move more information on the net. Yet a third challenge entails a persistent stovepipe problem in the relationship between operations and intelligence.

The services are still in the process of going from "technology push" to "technology pull" by moving away from an operating framework in which forces "kind of send the information to the shooter and let him shoot," as described by then Rear Adm. Mark Fitzgerald, to one in which "the shooter pulls the information he needs from an enormous network of information." Fitzgerald added, "We're still in the push area. The Navy does a little pull, but it's manual pull. It is very rudimentary, but it's a start [to] where we need to get to."[73]

The inability of strike aircrews to obtain refined target coordinates in a timely manner was another impediment to more effective operations that continues to beg for attention. One possible solution might lie in a methodology that would allow faster weapon and target pairing. The war experience also suggested that a mission-specific rather than a platform-centric focus in future force management would better enable combatant commanders to receive the air support they need.

After the major combat phase of Iraqi Freedom was over, Lt. Gen. Ronald Keys, at that time the Air Force's deputy chief of staff for air and space operations, characterized ISR connectivity as having made possible a "war of neighborhood nets." He suggested further interconnecting these nets and integrating them into "citywide nets" with a view toward "a global, commercial internet-type of capability. No matter where I am or in what platform, I should be able to log onto this net. We must discipline ourselves to adopt a common architecture that really enables the plug-and-play approach," devoting special attention to broadening "machine-to-machine language cross-cueing" such that "we get our machines, our sensors, our weapons to talk to each other, to automatically exchange and share information." Keys stressed the need to bring coalition partners into this net to make them more effective players.[74]

The absolute requirement for all fighter, bomber, attack, combat support, and command and control aircraft to be equipped with common link systems that can receive real-time data and imagery directly into the cockpit also came to the fore during Iraqi Freedom. The CAOC, which routinely uses these capabilities, will always oversee joint and combined air operations, and it must be able to transmit common data messages and mission-essential imagery to all participating aerial platforms, which must likewise be able to report back to CAOC command and control entities via the same link with real-time in-flight tactical information.

Officials from the Air Force's command and control constellation and the Navy's FORCENet initiatives teamed up after the campaign to work toward developing a common architecture for network-enabled operations aimed at merging their current service-specific nets into something that can be used by all four services and eventually can be turned over to an appropriate program office. Similar cross-service efforts were initiated in such related areas as ISR management, target aim-point generation, tactical data links, and joint tactical radios. The Air Force's constellation network connects such sensor platforms as Global Hawk, AWACS, and Predator UAVs. Its ultimate intent is to provide uniform information to all activities in the kill chain. This linking of network-enabling capabilities has been rendered easier because Air Force and Navy strike warfare operations have become increasingly similar since Operation Desert Storm.[75]

Greater Targeting Efficiency

The delays in securing timely target approvals from higher headquarters that had repeatedly plagued the CAOC's effectiveness in prosecuting time-critical targets in Afghanistan had been largely eliminated by the time Iraqi Freedom commenced. In a fundamental departure from the Enduring Freedom experience, General Franks elected to delegate to General Moseley and his planners in the CAOC full control over the daily process of preparing the joint integrated and prioritized target list, or JIPTL, for the major combat portion of Iraqi Freedom. Throughout the months that had spanned the end of major combat operations in Afghanistan and the start of initial planning for Iraqi Freedom, the air component, under General Moseley's leadership, had made major improvements in its working relations with CENTCOM.[76] After months of negotiations, General Franks ceded to General Moseley not only control over the daily JIPTL development process, but also the authority and tools required to conduct collateral damage estimation and casualty estimation for targets in Iraq, activities over which CENTCOM had retained close control throughout the war in Afghanistan. The only consent authority that remained at a higher level than the CAOC, either with Franks or with Secretary Rumsfeld, entailed requests to attack politically sensitive targets having to do with leadership, WMD, or high collateral damage expectations.[77] A study of the U.S. experience in this arena summed up the essence of this changed arrangement: "The resulting process called for the air component to run the joint guidance, apportionment, and targeting (JGAT) process that assembled all target requests and made recommendations to Franks. . . . CENTCOM still held a [daily] targeting VTC [video teleconference] . . . but, unlike in Afghanistan, it was an approval authority now—not a target development authority. . . . Authority for most of the important emerging targets was pushed down to the air component. . . . Moseley had forcefully argued for this change, so he had to organize and plan to handle it."[78]

General Moseley later amplified with respect to the dissatisfying Afghan experience: "When I took over [from then Lieutenant General Wald] in November [2001] and began to plug in some of the big pieces of Afghanistan after the fixed targets were hit . . . [General Franks] and I agreed that we needed to look at a different way of striking this Taliban and Al Qaeda target set and we needed to look at something much more akin to time-sensitive targets and dynamic targets. That is how we began to work this prior to the fall of Mazar-i-Sharif."[79] Before that realization set in, staffers in the CAOC's time-sensitive target cell routinely had to seek target attack approval from their counterpart cell at CENTCOM headquarters in Florida.[80]

It was principally because he recognized the much higher target-servicing demands that Iraqi Freedom would entail that General Franks decided to delegate most of the approval authority for attacking fleeting targets to General Moseley. Moseley later recalled in connection with this decision:

> I think as we came through the Operations Northern Watch and Southern Watch habit pattern of 10- or 11-plus years of doing this, [we took on] the notion of a time-sensitive target being a reaction to being fired upon in the no-fly zone, which means you have to go back and go through an approval process. But when you get into [the war against the Taliban and Al Qaeda], we find that we need to go faster. We don't have the luxury of time to go back and go through all of that. We learned lessons from November and December and January of 2001 and 2002 of how to streamline that process and how, effectively, to formalize these processes and delegate as much of it as possible to the [air] component.

Once CENTCOM made the necessary procedural changes to avoid a replay of that earlier war's initial errors, Moseley added, its efficiency in attacking time-sensitive targets went up from 50 to 100 percent in Iraqi Freedom.[81]

A key CAOC planner for both Afghanistan and Iraq later recalled that

> there was a *huge* difference between Operations Enduring Freedom and Iraqi Freedom when it came to operational-level execution. Throughout the major combat portion of Enduring Freedom, the JIPTL was closely controlled by CENTCOM for a number of reasons, distrust of the air component and the limited scope of the conflict being only two. During the initial planning stages of Operation Iraqi Freedom, General Moseley and

his closest subordinate air operations planners stressed repeatedly to CENTCOM's operations staff that CENTAF would *have* to be granted control of the JIPTL by General Franks if it was to be expected to conduct and effectively manage a major theater air offensive on the scale and at the pace of execution that were anticipated. Throughout the two years in which OPLAN 1003V gradually evolved and came together, CENTCOM's leaders steadily acquired the essential trust in CENTAF's planners that would be required if they were to relinquish control of the JIPTL to the latter. In the end, the CAOC became a truly joint enterprise, with representatives of each of CENTCOM's subordinate warfighting components shaping the JIPTL each day in support of the collective campaign.[82]

General Moseley's arrangements for time-sensitive targeting in Iraqi Freedom represented what CAOC planners called "a quantum leap" over the experience in Enduring Freedom.[83] The experience acquired in Afghanistan and in subsequent joint training exercises was encapsulated in new techniques and procedures aimed at better codifying the overall targeting process. In the end, the CAOC's time-sensitive targeting cell and its offensive operations duty officers effectively worked more than 3,000 targets and tasked 2,100 of those for attack during the 3 weeks of major combat.

Maj. Gen. Daniel Darnell, the senior CAOC director who ran the most mission-intensive night air operations shift, recalled:

> The joint target coordinating board met every evening at CENT-COM, and I always had the distinct pleasure (in the middle of the night) of trying to balance the target list they came up with (supposedly sanctioned by General Franks) and what I knew were General Moseley's priorities. . . . I discussed with General Moseley the targeting issues and centralization they dealt with in Operation Enduring Freedom. He didn't want a repeat in Iraqi Freedom. . . . The sheer enormity and pace of the effort (over 2,000 sorties a day) did not allow micromanaging of the targeting effort. We had a parallel conflict (war of simultaneity, I often call it) going on across the entire country. We were supporting SOF operations in all quadrants of the country, offensive counterair missions against airfields and suspected WMD storage sites and SAM sites, strategic strikes on leadership locations, defensive

counterair, CSAR, KI/CAS in support of the 3rd ID and I MEF, tactical and strategic airlift, ISR . . . and aerial refueling. Lots of fog of war involved. Not to mention . . . a couple of nightly calls from Washington concerned that we were going to whack one of their covert personnel during a time-sensitive targeting event. These types of things occurred at about 0200–0300 every night. We did not have the time . . . to micromanage anything.

Remarkably, as General Darnell affirmed, top-down micromanagement of tactical-level events was largely avoided:

The only time we reached down to the tactical level (one time) was during a Predator Hellfire shot on a SATCOM [satellite communications] antenna behind the ministry of information (again at 0300). . . . We made a decision that the potential for collateral damage was way too high. . . . I gave my consent to launch when ready. . . . The obvious question is why did I get involved at my level? It was a very high-priority mission. The regime was using the antenna for propaganda purposes to embolden the population and Iraqi military to continue fighting, and the secretary of defense and the president wanted the propaganda to stop. . . . Fortunately, all went perfectly. The Predator was never detected on ingress, the crew immediately identified the correct target, I concurred, and they shacked it with a direct hit.[84]

The after-action study of Iraqi Freedom's major combat phase commissioned by Secretary Rumsfeld and conducted by JFCOM attributed the remarkable improvement in CENTCOM's ability to service emerging targets in a timely manner to the use of a single, common process for time-sensitive target coordination and execution; the use of common coordination and collaboration tools; the disciplined use of a focused, high-priority target set; and extensive training and realistic battle drills.[85] In large measure, this achievement was a direct result of lessons learned from initial errors made at the command level in Operation Enduring Freedom. As the first air component commander for the Afghan campaign (then Lieutenant General Wald) flatly declared in retrospect, "without the educational experience of Enduring Freedom as a basis for planning the Iraq War, CENTCOM would never have succeeded in getting its approach to emerging targets right."[86]

The practice of having military lawyers routinely inserted as essential advisers in CENTCOM's daily target vetting and approval process finally gained general air-component approval in Iraqi Freedom. Air Chief Marshal Burridge summed up the consensus of the senior CAOC leadership when he declared without hesitation: "I feel extremely comfortable with the construct we use embracing legal advice, because it protects me and it protects the person who is delivering the weapon....We train our lawyers as operational lawyers, so they do get lots of practice with how to deal with targets.... I am very happy and most of us operators are very happy about having a lawyer alongside."[87]

The CAOC's Contributions

Having been duly seasoned by the Enduring Freedom experience of 2001 and 2002, CENTCOM's CAOC at Prince Sultan Air Base was primed and ready for the more concentrated air operations of Iraqi Freedom. Most of the CAOC's team for the latter campaign was in place about a month before the start of major combat, by which time Operation Southern Focus against the Iraqi IADS had become a full-time force employment activity. The CAOC organization itself was headed by General Moseley as the overall air component commander; below him were his principal deputy, then Rear Adm. David Nichols of the U.S. Navy, three alternating day and night one-star CAOC directors, and five major divisions with varied combat planning and mission management responsibilities. The CAOC's staff of nearly two thousand personnel included representatives from all four of the U.S. services as well as other U.S. government agencies, the RAF, and the RAAF.[88]

To support the daily air tasking cycle, targeteers were assigned to work in all five of the CAOC's divisions: strategy, combat plans, combat operations, ISR, and assessments. The series of steps that were involved in generating the daily ATO passed from the CAOC's strategy division to the combat plans and then combat operations divisions for promulgation and execution, finally returning again full circle to the strategy division for execution assessment. General Moseley's chief strategist explained the ATO cycle as the means by which the air component commander seeks to provide the most efficient and effective employment of coalition air capabilities:

> The cycle begins with joint force commander [JFC] and component commander guidance. The CAOC strategy division then determines the tasks to be accomplished in the next cycle. This, in turn, is developed into targets that are vetted through a joint and coalition selection and approval process. This prioritized list then goes to the master air attack plan (MAAP) team that assigns air assets to the targets. The ATO production team then builds

the ATO and sends it out to the various units for execution. After execution, the results flow back into the CAOC, where the assessment team determines the outcome and the combat effects achieved. This feedback then flows back to the JFC, the component commanders, and the strategy division, where the cycle starts all over [see figure 4.1].[89]

The combat plans division comprised four subordinate cells: guidance, apportionment, and targeting (GAT); master air attack planning (MAAP); ATO production; and command and control planning. The MAAP cell consisted of fifty-three highly qualified professionals from all services and coalition partner-nations who normally worked in two twelve-hour shifts. That cell was responsible for producing the daily MAAP in two phases, the first from thirty-six to twenty-four hours before ATO execution, and the second from twenty-four to twelve hours before execution. The MAAP cell was further divided into subcells that included force allocation, force enhancement, defensive counterair, force application, KI/CAS, and air refueling. The force allocation group was responsible for coordinating all participating flying units, including the U.S. Navy's five carrier air wings and all RAF and RAAF aircraft, as well as for developing sortie flows and aircraft turn schemes at each operating facility. Force enhancement was tasked with planning all command and control and ISR employment, as well as with managing the many changes in individual force package commitments that were generated by the air component's theater air control system (TACS) that supported the land component.[90] The defensive counterair group determined

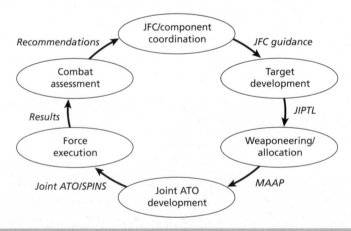

FIGURE 4.1 Air Tasking Order Processing Cycle

Source: CENTAF

CAP compositions and locations and recommended changes to General Moseley as counterair requirements evolved over the course of the campaign.

The force allocation group within the MAAP cell was responsible for
matching up available strike assets against fixed targets on the JIPTL and for
ensuring that those assets were assigned adequate SEAD protection. The KI/
CAS team saw to pairing combat assets against mobile target nominations and to
fulfilling incoming air support requests from both the Army's BCD and the SOF
component's special operations liaison element (SOLE) in the CAOC. Finally,
the air refueling group was responsible for all in-flight refueling operations other
than the organic tanking that the Navy provided for its carrier-based aircraft.

The MAAP cell chief's responsibilities included chairing a pre-MAAP
meeting that occurred thirty-six hours prior to every ATO execution at which
he presented the AOD, the JIPTL, tentative aircraft flows, and appropriate notices
to airmen (or NOTAMs) for that day. The Army, Navy, Marine Corps, SOF, and
air mobility team chiefs would then present their intended schemes of maneuver
and air support requests. After this initial planning process the team prepared the
MAAP decision brief, which was in turn briefed to General Moseley or, in his
absence, to Admiral Nichols for approval.

The workload associated with this fast-paced flow of activity was onerous.
Although the daily shifts in the MAAP cell were nominally slated to last twelve
hours, the constantly changing nature of the air war frequently drove MAAP
team members to work fifteen to eighteen hours or longer. Unlike Afghanistan
operations, when the daily sortie rate was typically rather modest and easily
manageable, the pace of both air and land operations during the major combat
phase of Iraqi Freedom required significant and often rapid changes every day
inside the ATO cycle, which often necessitated last-minute changes in force
commitments.

It was not at all unusual for an AOD generated within the strategy division
and approved by General Moseley sixty hours before its scheduled execution to
be overtaken by events before it reached the MAAP cell twenty-four hours later.
Even after the MAAP had been approved and moved along to ATO production,
significant changes sometimes had to be entered, often resulting in late dissemination of the ATO to the flying units.

The last 12 hours before an ATO's execution were the most challenging
part of the ATO cycle. The time-sensitive targeting cell, for instance, planned
and executed more than 840 emerging targets over the course of the three-week
campaign. Most of the officers involved in this demanding process had been
handpicked, and some had worked in that capacity during Operation Enduring

Freedom. A CENTAF staffer who served in the CAOC during the three-week air war recalled that "these officers were, by and large, experts with can-do attitudes who paid superb attention to detail."[91]

At the heart of the CAOC, known more formally as the AN/USQ-163 Falconer in its standard Air Force configuration, were some eighty unique command and control capabilities, the "engine" for which was the TBMCS (Theater Battle Management Core System) that provided General Moseley an integrated set of software that enabled him to control all theater air operations and to coordinate them with the land and maritime components. A CAOC staffer later noted in this regard that "transmission of the [air component commander's] intent to those executing the ATO is arguably the most critical part of the ATO process. TBMCS is the means by which that intent was passed."[92]

The head of the combat plans division during the major combat phase of Iraqi Freedom recalled that

> the MAAP cell was never initially intended to be a twenty-four-hour operation. They would begin coordinating on the next ATO once they pushed the MAAP to the ATO "thumpers" who hammered out the actual air tasking plan in TBMCS some twelve hours before execution. What drove us to a twenty-four-hour MAAP process was the ensuing speed of operations. Normally, any changes required for an ATO, once pushed, would take place on the combat operations floor. But the "replanning" cell was not sufficiently robust to handle that. So we had our MAAP staff on call twenty-four hours a day to re-MAAP targets inside twelve hours from execution as necessary, even after the ATO had been pushed. What was good about this was that it proved that our ATO cycle was flexible. I have heard over the years from multiple complainants that our ATO cycle was too long and not flexible. I believe we proved that charge to be false.[93]

At bottom, TBMCS was the means by which the ATO and each of its subsections were transmitted each day to all operating units assigned to the air component. It also was the central command, control, communications, computers, and intelligence core for both of CENTAF's CAOCs—the primary one at Prince Sultan and the backup one at Al Udeid. The CAOC at Prince Sultan, which had been declared fully operational in August 2001 just before the start of initial planning for Operation Enduring Freedom, had been configured with the initial Block 10 baseline software, which included TBMCS V1.0.1. As a result of the substantially increased tempo of air operations that ensued throughout Southwest Asia after the terrorist attacks of September 11, 2001, however, CENTAF did not succeed in upgrading its baseline software for TBMCS until December 2002, more than a year later. At that time the system was upgraded to the Block 10+ configuration and subsequently to V1.1.1, the latest version then available.

TBMCS brought together three legacy systems—the contingency theater air planning system (CTAPS, pronounced "see-taps"), the combat intelligence system, and the wing command and control system—into a single, integrated system with common databases and software tools. In contrast to the three older systems that it superseded, TBMCS could generate ATOs containing three times the amount of information regarding scheduled combat sorties and could assign targets in half the time and with a third fewer planners. It also pulled together imagery and other pertinent tactical information to build a common operating picture in the subordinate AOCs and ASOCs that supported allied ground forces. At the wing and squadron level, it offered the tools necessary for enabling aircrews to conduct detailed final mission planning. By early 2003 TBMCS had been installed in twenty American AOCs worldwide, as well as in more than three hundred additional command and control centers all the way down to Air Force wings and squadrons and on board four Navy command ships and all twelve Navy aircraft carriers. By the start of Iraqi Freedom, it was the system of record for the conduct of air operations by air component commanders.[94]

During the Iraqi Freedom air offensive, TBMCS provided the tools required for managing CENTAF's air operations, including airspace management, electronic warfare support, airborne battle management and surveillance, and airlift and tanker operations. It enabled the planning of each daily ATO beginning two days in advance. It also included a retasking capability that allowed CAOC operators to reassign aircraft in real time to attack suddenly emerging targets. In addition, TBMCS gathered incoming information from all intelligence sensors and translated that information into usable data for developing targeting concepts and matching aircraft to targets. The CAOC received actionable target intelligence within single-digit minutes, with target-area imagery typically being provided within fifteen minutes. It also generated the assigned SPINs to aircrews each day, which were issued as an attachment to the ATO and which, in effect, represented the CAOC's daily guidebook for conducting all air operations. The daily SPINs could run to hundreds of pages, covering everything from assigned call signs and radio frequencies for individual allied aircraft to General Moseley's guidance as air component commander and CENTCOM's rules of engagement. Finally, it generated the campaign's airspace control plan in the form of the airspace control order, which, like the ATO, changed every day and could be changed even within a day.[95]

TBMCS offered the first-ever opportunity for integrated and automated command and control, and it successfully managed some 47,000 sorties during the three-week campaign. In the process it proved to be much faster than the more primitive planning tools that had existed to support the Desert Storm air war. It took the CAOC staff about fourteen hours to plan and execute three thousand sorties during Desert Storm; by March 2003 TBMCS had reduced that time to five or six hours.[96] On a typical day during the major combat phase, the CAOC's targeting cell gathered operationally relevant information on some three hundred targets that might have entailed anywhere from one thousand to two thousand individual weapon aim points.

Indeed, TBMCS proved to be a major mission management facilitator for CENTCOM's air component throughout the offensive. It pulled together into a single consolidated network what had formerly been handled by a wide variety of disjointed command and control systems, and it allowed CAOC operators to monitor constantly the flow of both strike sorties and support assets. It also fed an extension of its capability into the 4th ASOG's ASOC that supported V Corps to allow for closer coordination of Army target-servicing requests. TBMCS users were also distributed in twenty subordinate air operations centers and Navy ships.

The CAOC's director of combat plans during Iraqi Freedom recalled, however, that "TBMCS was *not* the cure-all. We had significant problems with the database when we arrived at the CAOC in February 2003. Contractors had to construct a 'patch' to the software to allow us to push the large sortie count."[97] The system was designed to support the planning and conduct of 1,500 sorties a day. Yet during the first three weeks of Iraqi Freedom, TBMCS supported operations that sometimes exceeded 2,500 sorties a day. CAOC staffers later noted that "exceeding the design limits of the system [sometimes] prevented operations until a patch could be installed.... Nevertheless, the system proved stable and reliable."[98] At the same time, although TBMCS was indeed a major force multiplier throughout the campaign, it required continuous human intervention and effort to ensure that its automated processes worked reliably and provided CAOC planners with the mission management support they needed to sustain an effective around-the-clock air tasking process. And despite the automated mission-planning tools that were available in the CAOC, MAAP planners still had to do manual quality-control checks on the final ATO product going into TBMCS.

To note one example, because the automated targeting tools available in the CAOC varied so widely in the formats they used and the extent of their compatibility, there often were awkward and problematic transfers of targeting data, as well as a continuing need for manpower-intensive manual data entry. General Moseley needed constant support from information technology and TBMCS database administrators to manage target-list transfers satisfactorily because there was no easy means for tracking a target's status in the ATO cycle.

Whenever a dynamic or time-sensitive target was discovered, a process for weapon aim-point mensuration using an automated system called RainDrop immediately began. If the required attack asset was available and if the threat level in the target area was sufficiently permissive, an airborne aircraft with a targeting pod would be sent to investigate, target, or actually engage and destroy the object in question. According to CAOC planners, RainDrop, the digital imagery workstation suite, and the precision targeting work station were the only systems in use that were certified by NIMA to provide geographic coordinates and elevations sufficiently accurate to enable the targeting of satellite-aided JDAMs. Those planners concluded during their after-action review of the air war at Nellis AFB in July 2003 that coordinate mensuration must become even more automated: "In today's environment, with mounting collateral damage concerns and ever greater reliance on coordinate-seeking weapons, target coordinate mensuration has become a necessary evil. RainDrop is the only Air Force accredited mensuration tool, and while accurate, it involves a lengthy process and requires highly skilled operators."[99]

While TBMCS was not perfect, however, CAOC operators agreed that it provided "an unprecedented level of data visibility across all CAOC functional areas. In addition, it provided interoperability between CENTCOM's subordinate components and other joint and coalition services to an exponentially greater degree than that achieved during Operation Desert Storm." Fortunately, CENTCOM's other warfighting components came to Iraqi Freedom configured and ready to interoperate fully with the CAOC's mission management systems. CENTAF experts later remarked that "both the Navy and Marine Corps were equipped with TBMCS, and the Army and Air Force had worked together to develop a stable and reliable interface between TBMCS and Army systems. Joint standards were used to bring these component systems together. This resulted in an unprecedented capability to conduct distributed air battle planning across the components."[100]

Operation Iraqi Freedom also represented the first air campaign in which an AOD was developed for each day's ATO. On the one hand, that arrangement offered a notable improvement over the process that had been in effect for

Afghanistan, in that the AOD was a single, coherent document that succinctly reflected General Moseley's strategy and guidance for each ATO. On the other hand, Moseley approved each AOD sixty hours before its execution, and there was no easy way in which his or higher-level guidance could be updated after that point. That being the case, there were times when late-breaking events occurring after the AOD's approval would render that day's AOD less applicable, or even inappropriate altogether, to the demands of the moment. "In most cases," a CENTAF staffer recalled on this count, "the MAAP cell either had to delay its process until appropriate guidance was received or else build the MAAP without the necessary guidance, hoping to receive approval after the fact."[101]

Despite the improvements in flexibility noted above, most CAOC planners later agreed that long-established air tasking practices remained "too slow."[102] A senior CAOC staffer remarked in this respect that "the air component's ability to . . . prosecute mass volumes of targets outpaced its ability to track and assess its progress toward achieving operational objectives. An overarching challenge of mastering digital combat at the operational level of war is to develop new processes that lend more speed and flexibility to operations without sacrificing the coherence and purpose that the established strategy-to-task methodology provides."[103] CAOC planners further concluded that the ATO cycle running from strategy to GAT to MAAP and ATO production was simply "too long, given the mobility of critical targets and the dynamics of the battlespace in a combined-arms environment."[104] They added that the CAOC director, who oversees this process, needs to be able to introduce high-payoff targets into the ATO *during* its execution.

The British MoD's after-action report similarly complained that CENTAF's seventy-two-hour air tasking cycle could bear further compression and noted the need for more flexibility in tasking.[105] It should not be forgotten, however, that the ATO planning cycle was premised throughout Iraqi Freedom, and remains premised today, on the fact that the air component commander's preeminent concern is with the *operational*—that is to say, theaterwide—level of war. Compressing the ATO cycle *too* much entails the danger that the ATO will become constructed instead in knee-jerk response to immediate tactical events. Some pressures to compress the ATO, such as that voiced in the MoD's report and repeatedly heard from many American land combatants as well, reflect shortsighted tactical thinking that loses sight of the effects-based and strategy-driven approach to air employment.[106]

Only 43 percent of the personnel assigned to the CAOC during the major combat phase of Iraqi Freedom had received formal AOC training. Nevertheless, this staff successfully prosecuted 156 time-sensitive targets (mostly in southern

Iraq) and 686 dynamic targets (highly mobile or otherwise important targets) that were struck by aircraft that had been re-roled from other mission taskings. Of these 686, the majority were located in western Iraq and were related to suspected WMD facilities and mobile missile units. (At the height of the air war, the CAOC staff had risen from its previous level of 672 to 1,966 assigned personnel.)[107]

Notably, Operation Iraqi Freedom was the first conflict in which ISR operations (including collection management and the determination and assignment of aerial platform locations) were brought under the purview of the CAOC's strategy division. In earlier air wars that function was typically executed by the combat plans division, whose staff tended to view and use ISR assets in support of the combined force commander's and air component commander's declared intent rather than as input into the actual shaping of the resultant strategy. In yet another command and control "first" during Iraqi Freedom, an expeditionary intelligence group was established at Langley AFB, Virginia, to coordinate a broad spectrum of intelligence units worldwide to provide as-needed reachback support to the CAOC. This ad hoc group coordinated and directed the nation's combat intelligence architecture; eliminated bureaucratic bottlenecks and system breakdowns; and enabled a smooth, continuous, and rapid flow of actionable intelligence into the CAOC.[108]

In a related Iraqi Freedom ISR first, the distributed ground station (DGS) at Beale AFB, California, supported three concurrent U-2 missions over western, southern, and northern Iraq that were exploited at three different ground stations on two continents, with all of the flow going through the distributed processing, exploitation, and dissemination operations center at Langley AFB. In addition, an amalgamation of twelve libraries on SIPRNet and eight on the joint worldwide intelligence communications system (JWICS, pronounced "jay-wicks") enabled the prompt and uninterrupted provision of imagery products and other pertinent information for every flying unit and component commander in CENTCOM's area of responsibility entirely by means of e-mail, video teleconferencing, and telephone communications. The overarching ISR campaign plan that leveraged these diverse assets and capabilities allowed for predictive battlespace awareness so that CAOC staffers could anticipate and predict enemy actions such as the movement of mobile SAMs and theater ballistic missiles. In turn, as the head of the CAOC's strategy division later recalled, "predictive assessments on threat locations, detailed collection planning to find threats, dynamic cross-cueing between multiple sensors to locate them precisely, and synchronization with strike packages resulted in increased strike effectiveness." He called the entire process an "intelligence success story that should serve as a benchmark for future intelligence reachback."[109]

The Iraq war also set a new record for close Navy involvement in the high-level planning and command of joint air operations. By its own free admission the Navy was more than adequately represented in the CAOC throughout the major combat phase. As noted earlier, Rear Admiral Nichols, the commander of the Naval Strike and Air Warfare Center at NAS Fallon, served as General Moseley's deputy air component commander. Capt. William Gortney was the naval air liaison coordinator. Alternating with Col. Douglas Erlenbusch, Capt. Russ Penniman was the co-director of the combat plans division, which, among other functions, did all of the target analysis and weaponeering.[110] Other key leadership positions in the CAOC filled by naval officers included deputy chief of the strategy division, chief of combat operations, and deputy chief of the ISR division. In all, 158 Navy personnel (95 active duty and 63 Naval Reserve) were included in the CAOC's staff, filling a total of 20 percent of the CAOC's 695 principal operator billets.[111]

The Navy Reservists assigned to the CAOC had the added advantage of coming from the 2nd and 3rd Fleet staffs and being both formally trained and well versed in the processes of the CAOC. Vice Admiral Keating, the maritime component commander, noted that detailed and coordinated planning had taken place during the buildup for the campaign between the Navy's 5th Fleet and CENTAF in determining which personnel the Navy would send to the CAOC and what their qualifications needed to be. If a qualification requirement had not been met, selected individuals received rush schooling in the needed skills to enable them to augment the CAOC staff. Thanks to that timely effort, Admiral Nichols had an augmentation team of 101 Navy personnel, about half of whom were reservists; the rest were drawn from the weapons schools, the Naval Strike and Air Warfare Center, and fleet units.

Integrated air-land operations suffered from at least one significant command and control shortfall. Allied aircrews and ground commanders alike felt the absence of the EC-130E airborne battlefield command and control center (ABCCC, pronounced "A-B-triple-C") from CENTAF's roster of fielded assets. During its heyday, the ABCCC was an Air Force asset dedicated to meeting the communications needs of ground commanders and providing them needed confidence in the air service's ability to deliver timely CAS. In this respect, as one expert observer has pointed out, the ABCCC "was more than a flying radio relay platform or long-loiter forward air controller; it was a forward command element engaging in maneuver warfare."[112]

President George W. Bush flanked by Secretary of Defense Donald Rumsfeld and Under Secretary of Defense Paul Wolfowitz at the Pentagon on March 25, 2003, as he announces a $74.7 billion supplemental budget request to pay the campaign costs for Operation Iraqi Freedom.

Department of Defense photo by R. D. Ward

CENTCOM commander Gen. Tommy Franks (second from left) holds a video teleconference with the president, joined by his air commander, Lt. Gen. Michael Moseley; the British air commander, Air Vice-Marshal Glenn Torpy (far right); and the Australian air commander, Group Captain Geoff Brown (far left), March 19, 2003.

Courtesy of Air Marshal Geoff Brown, RAAF

Main operations floor of the backup CAOC at Al Udeid Air Base in Qatar, with multiple large-screen displays and more than one hundred high-speed T-1 Internet lines.

U.S. Air Force photo by TSgt. Demetrius Lester

The aircraft carrier *Theodore Roosevelt*, March 20, 2003, having just arrived in its assigned operating area in the eastern Mediterranean.

U.S. Navy photo by Photographer's Mate Airman Todd M. Flint

F/A-18F Super Hornet pilots and weapons systems officers of Strike Fighter Squadron 2 in *Constellation* in the North Arabian Gulf are briefed on mission details and threats they can expect to encounter during their periods of vulnerability inside enemy airspace. Shown prominently at the map's center is the Super MEZ.
U.S. Navy photo by Photographer's Mate 2nd Class Felix Garza Jr.

The deputy commander of Carrier Air Wing 3 in *Harry S. Truman* (second from left), an F/A-18 pilot, receives inputs from air wing F-14 pilots (right) and a member of SEAL Team 8 (far left) as he prepares on March 19 to lead a strike package from the eastern Mediterranean into the heart of Iraq during the air campaign's opening attacks.
U.S. Navy photo by Photographer's Mate 1st Class Michael W. Pendergrass

An array of 2,000-pound general-purpose bombs fitted with satellite-aided GBU-31 JDAM kits and other air-delivered munitions lie on the hangar bay floor of *Abraham Lincoln* awaiting transfer to the flight deck for loading on board strike fighters assigned to Carrier Air Wing 14. An F/A-18C and F-14 in the background are also being readied for early flight operations.

U.S. Navy photo by Photographer's Mate Airman Jason Frost

An F-14D assigned to Fighter Squadron 213 of Carrier Air Wing 8 in position on one of *Theodore Roosevelt*'s four steam-driven catapults, with its engines at full power and its crew of two ready for action on March 21. The catapult will accelerate the Tomcat from a standing start to a speed of 140 knots in just two seconds.

U.S. Navy photo by Photographer's Mate 2nd Class James K. McNeil

A B-2 stealth bomber, returning to its forward operating base on Diego Garcia after a night mission into the Super MEZ, moves forward from a stabilized precontact position to take on JP-8 fuel from a KC-135 tanker over the Indian Ocean.

U.S. Air Force photo by SSgt. Cherie A. Thurlby

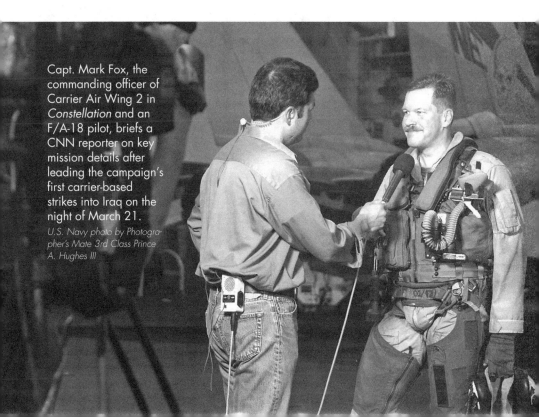

Capt. Mark Fox, the commanding officer of Carrier Air Wing 2 in *Constellation* and an F/A-18 pilot, briefs a CNN reporter on key mission details after leading the campaign's first carrier-based strikes into Iraq on the night of March 21.

U.S. Navy photo by Photographer's Mate 3rd Class Prince A. Hughes III

Ground maintenance technicians prepare two pallets of GBU-31s for loading into the three weapons bays of a B-1 being readied for a combat mission into Iraq.

U.S. Air Force photo

A sea-based AV-8B Harrier, still carrying two unexpended LGBs, approaches its hover for landing on *Bonhomme Richard* as another Harrier holds short for takeoff.

U.S. Navy photo by Photographer's Mate 3rd Class Chris Reynolds

Ground technicians lift an AIM-9M infrared-guided air-to-air missile from its rack before mounting it on an underwing pylon of the F-16CJ in the background.

U.S. Air Force photo by MSgt. Terry L. Blevins

Armed and ready F-16CJs assigned to the USAF's 379th Air Expeditionary Wing hunker down at their forward operating base near Iraq as the *shamal* rages around them.

U.S. Air Force photo by MSgt. Terry L. Blevins

A C-17 departs its forward base in Romania as part of a sustained air bridge to CENTCOM's AOR.

U.S. Air Force photo by Senior Airman Lakisha Croley

An F/A-18C assigned to Strike Fighter Squadron 105 in *Harry S. Truman* stands poised for launch at full power on the carrier's right bow catapult. The Hornet shown here is configured with wingtip-mounted AIM-9M Sidewinders and fuselage-mounted AIM-120 AMRAAMs for a defensive counterair sweep.

U.S. Navy photo by Photographer's Mate 1st Class Michael W. Pendergrass

Paratroopers of the U.S. Army's 173rd Airborne Brigade get a final safety inspection of their parachutes at Aviano Air Base, Italy, before boarding a C-17 for an unopposed night combat jump into the Bashur airfield near Tikrit on March 26.

U.S. Air Force photo by TSgt. Stephen Faulisi

An F-15C, having just refueled, turns away from the tanker and prepares to resume its offensive sweep aimed at keeping Iraqi aircraft on the ground.

U.S. Air Force photo by MSgt. Mark Bucher

The E-8C JSTARS, with multi-mode side-looking radar, was the only allied airborne platform capable of maintaining real-time surveillance of both stationary and moving enemy vehicles over a corps-sized area of the battlefield.

U.S Air Force photo

A Pave Hawk takes on fuel in flight from a tanker-configured C-130 before entering hostile airspace on a combat search-and-rescue mission on April 6.

U.S. Air Force photo by SSgt. Shane A. Cuomo

An A-10, armed with two AGM-65 Maverick missiles and four unguided 500-pound bombs in addition to its GAU-8 30-mm antitank gun, undergoes final checks in the arming area before taking off.

U.S. Air Force photo by SSgt. Shane A. Cuomo

A stealthy F-117 holds at the pre-contact position behind a KC-135 tanker, with two F-15Es at the inboard wing positions, two F-16CJs at the middle wing positions, and an RAF Tornado GR4 on the far right and an RAAF F/A-18 on the far left.

U.S. Air Force photo by MSgt. Ron Przysucha

Capt. Jeremy Quatacker, an F-16CG pilot assigned to the 524th Expeditionary Fighter Squadron, looks over the inescapable forms that require final checks before launching on any mission.

U.S. Air Force photo by MSgt. Stefan Alford

One of the twelve F-117 stealth attack aircraft used in the campaign at Langley AFB, Virginia, its pilot is greeted by the commander of the 1st Fighter Wing there before the craft departs on the last leg of its return to Holloman AFB, New Mexico.
U.S. Air Force photo by SSgt. Travis Aston

Ground crew members refuel a U-2 surveillance and reconnaissance aircraft following its return from an eight-hour mission over Iraq that took it to an altitude of more than 70,000 feet.
U.S. Air Force photo by SSgt. Matthew Hannen

A member of CENTAF's Combined Weapons Effectiveness Assessment Team examines the results of a 5,000-pound bomb dropped on the dome of one of Saddam Hussein's palaces.
U.S. Air Force photo by MSgt. Carla Kippes

The aircraft had finally been retired from the Air Force inventory in 2002 after three decades of continuous service going as far back as Vietnam, however, and other elements of the Air Force's TACS, notably the E-3 AWACS and E-8 JSTARS, were obliged to fill the gap. Both aircraft periodically assumed many of the ABCCC's former functions as CAS requests would be funneled to one or another, whose crew in turn would direct airborne fighters or bombers to JTACs on the ground in need of help. The Navy's E-2C Hawkeye surveillance aircraft was sometimes used in a similar way.

The E-3, E-8, and E-2C have other main missions, however, and are not really configured for the ABCCC role. The new tasking placed an added burden on already overworked aircrews, who often were unable to cope with the high volume of voice communications traffic.[113] Moreover, employing aircraft fielded to fulfill higher-end missions as mere communications relay platforms was arguably to misuse a low-density/high-demand asset that was already overburdened in its primary role. General Moseley's successor as CENTCOM's air component commander, Lt. Gen. Walter Buchanan III, spoke directly to this concern three years after the end of major combat in Iraqi Freedom when he commented that "we have people in Iraq who are very comfortable using the JSTARS as a radio relay platform. That is a very inefficient way to use [this] tremendously capable system . . . that I would much rather use monitoring the border and the open desert regions for which its radar is ideally suited."[114] Although the JSTARS either possesses or can be given all the tools needed to serve in a de facto ABCCC (and, in effect, airborne ASOC-extension) capacity, an informed account noted the "inherent conflict between command and control missions, ISR missions, and the ABCCC mission aboard one aircraft. . . . ISR missions require the E-8 radar to look at a specific area on the ground and to maintain digital and voice link with the units that need the intelligence. ABCCC missions [in contrast] require mission crew augmentation and detailed knowledge of ground operations."[115]

An experienced U.S. Army consumer of the E-8's ABCCC support function suggested that properly prioritizing the mission responsibilities for each given sortie and having the mission commander ensure that the entire crew understands these priorities might defuse that conflict. All the same, this writer concluded, because the E-8 (and, by the same token, the E-2 and E-3), unlike the single-mission EC-130 ABCCC, was acquired and fielded to serve many masters, "conflicts in priority do arise during a flight."[116] Such conflicts will persist, moreover, so long as the capability shortfall that was created by the retirement of the EC-130 is not rectified. ASOC staffers at V Corps headquarters often found themselves out of communications range of strike aircraft operating over the Baghdad area, an issue General Leaf frankly described as "worth looking into."[117]

After the major combat phase of Iraqi Freedom ended, and Operation Southern Watch along with it, the Department of Defense announced its intention to vacate the CAOC at Prince Sultan Air Base and switch over to its recently completed alternate CAOC (which had cost $40 million to build from scratch) at Al Udeid Air Base in Qatar. The Air Force now regards its Falconer Block 10X air operations center as a full-fledged weapon system on a par with combat aircraft. So oriented, the Air Force now maintains a requirements board for AOC standardization, just as it does for aircraft, and is working toward a standardized program for AOC staff training as well. Gen. Ron Keys, the former Air Force deputy chief of staff for air and space operations and later commander of Air Combat Command, remarked on this increasingly mature capability that a nation's military air assets without an AOC would amount to little more than an expensive flying club.[118]

To conclude on this theme, among the main factors that accounted for the CAOC's overwhelmingly successful performance was the uniformly high caliber of staffers at all levels assigned to the various divisions and cells. Between 5 and 10 percent of the CAOC staff were graduates of the elite USAF Weapons School, Navy Fighter Weapons School (Topgun), and Marine Aviation Weapons and Tactics Squadron One (MAWTS 1) who served in key leadership positions throughout the CAOC. In addition, as noted earlier, the Navy provided a substantial number of reservists with years of prior CAOC experience. Others on the CAOC staff had also gained previous seasoning by performing CAOC duties during Operations Northern Watch, Southern Watch, and Enduring Freedom. In all, about 90 percent of all targeting personnel assigned to the CAOC for Iraqi Freedom had been hand-picked by the air component's leadership before the start of the campaign. Most had convened at Shaw AFB in October 2002 to take part in the weeklong MAAP workshop described earlier that exercised and ultimately validated the targeting process. In addition, CENTAF had begun to work closely with both CENTCOM and the national intelligence agencies during the final months before G-day and A-day to conduct an aim-point-level review of every target on the joint target list.

Exercises conducted by team members from the strategy division and the target development, GAT, and MAAP cells before the campaign's start were also central to ensuring the success of the targeting process throughout the three weeks of major combat. Critical to this team-building process was bringing together all of CENTAF's operations and intelligence personnel, other CENT-COM headquarters and component players, and key coalition representatives during the October 2002 MAAP exercise. Without that prior training, such assets as TLAM, CALCM, stealth aircraft, and the RAF's Storm Shadow missile would not have been used to their greatest effectiveness. In this case as well, personal relationships were cemented that allowed all players to function more efficiently once the war was on and geographic separation did not permit face-to-face interaction.

The main players at CENTCOM headquarters, in the CAOC, and in the other warfighting components all understood CENTAF's targeting process. CENTAF analysts later reported that "training was the key to successful time-sensitive target execution" and that "situation awareness on the CAOC operations floor was never greater than that resident in the time-sensitive targeting cell during Operation Iraqi Freedom." To be sure, the CAOC's intelligence analysts and time-sensitive targeting cell staffers were sometimes overwhelmed with targets. Yet the process was highly efficient and successful. Part of that success stemmed from a realization that the most effective use of Global Hawk and comparable capabilities required placing support to a specific *mission* above requirements to support a specific *component*. Iraqi Freedom confirmed that synchronizing ISR to support a specific combat operation can succeed only when there is close coordination between the CAOC's and CENTCOM's operations and intelligence principals. As CENTAF planners later stressed, "it is a joint responsibility."[119]

Yet another major factor behind the CAOC's pivotal role in the planning and conduct of the air offensive was the unique composition of its strategy division. Its director during the final lead-up to the campaign later recalled that "never before had a strategy division of this magnitude been assembled. We had nearly 60 personnel in all, including 15 graduates of the Air Force's School of Advanced Air and Space Studies and the Army's counterpart School for Advanced Military Studies, as well as uniformly well-qualified targeteers and operational assessment experts."[120] This assemblage of uncommonly qualified airmen was responsible for developing the overarching air strategy for the campaign as well as needed branch points and sequels as the campaign plan evolved. Its experts also developed the daily AOD that transmitted General Moseley's commander's intent and priorities for ATO execution to both CAOC and wing-level personnel. In addition, they provided the needed apportionment of forces to specific campaign objectives, thus ensuring that the right weight of effort was applied toward achieving General Moseley's declared priorities. The large number of time-sensitive and emerging targets that routinely popped up within each ATO cycle produced ever-present temptations for those on the CAOC operations floor to hijack the ATO, in effect, and thereby lose sight of the larger desired effects and weight of effort. After about day 2 of major air operations in support of OPLAN 1003V, the daily AOD was amended to include priority assets that could not be re-roled or would have to be replaced with other, lower-priority assets. That amendment allowed the CAOC's operations floor to pull certain assets as needed to handle emerging high-value targets without compromising the overall synergy of the ATO.[121] All the same, as an experienced practitioner of modern air warfare made a point to insist, "the CAOC did not win the air war. On the contrary, it was the airmen in the jets and on the ground—with great leadership—who made it happen."[122]

Inputs from Assets on Orbit

Space-based assets represented an indispensable part of the ISR equation in Iraqi Freedom. CENTCOM exploited inputs from space in a fully integrated way in pursuing its campaign objectives. The constellation of infrared-sensing DSP satellites in geosynchronous orbit provided prompt indication of every Iraqi missile launch throughout the campaign, with the singular exception of the low-flying Seersucker cruise missile (which has a low infrared signature) that struck a shopping mall in Kuwait. It also offered CENTCOM's commanders timely battlespace characterization by providing near-real-time information on infrared events occurring in the war zone. In all, the DSP system detected 26 missile launches, 186 high-explosive events, and 1,493 static infrared events.[123]

The GPS array of 28 satellites distributed in semisynchronous orbit around the Earth provided constant on-call navigational support to allied ground forces, with each 9-person Army squad equipped with a GPS receiver, as compared with only 1 per company of 180 personnel during Operation Desert Storm.[124] The GPS system further provided enhanced around-the-clock target coordinates for the more than 5,600 JDAMs and TLAMs that relied on GPS signals for their accuracy. More than 1,500 GPS uploads allowed allied forces to enhance the accuracy of their GPS-aided weapons to less than 4 meters spherical error probable, the three-dimensional measurement of circular error probable.[125]

The MILSTAR satellite system, with its medium-rate data transmission capability, was pivotal in allowing Navy ships to send updated steering information to TLAMs en route to their targets. It also enabled the rapid movement of SOF combatants who had access to MILSTAR communications. Weather satellites were crucial in detecting and geolocating oil fires and in tracking the movement of the three-day sandstorm. American satellite assets also helped to take the "search" out of combat search and rescue. In the case of the F-14 that went down in Iraq as a result of a mechanical failure, space-based sensors geolocated the impact area and provided refined coordinates for those who rescued the two crewmembers, with space officers in the CAOC working to get the pilot and radar intercept officer safely recovered within a couple of hours.[126]

Commercial space imaging also played a significant role in providing enhanced situation awareness for campaign participants at all levels. Such imagery was a particular boon for Iraqi Freedom because it is not classified and could thus be shared with all coalition partners.[127] To cite but one example of the quality of information it offers to today's combined force commanders, Space Imaging had recently acquired a license approved by the National Oceanic and Atmospheric Administration to build and launch a satellite imaging system with a resolution of 0.4 meter.[128] Finally, communications satellites linked everything together, with the CAOC tasking the various Air Force space organizations that controlled the on-orbit assets. The military space community provided space surveillance, command and control of GPS and communications satellites, satellite communications network control, ballistic missile launch detection and warning, satellite tasking for ISR, space control, and other essential combat support functions.

General Moseley intended to use this diverse menu of space support options to provide precise navigation and timing capabilities to all of CENTCOM's warfighting components, as well as to enable accurate weapons employment, provide immediate missile launch warning and secure and dependable communications, and characterize real-time battlespace.[129] Accordingly, Air Force space planners and operators embedded space support teams both in the primary CAOC at Prince Sultan Air Base and in the backup CAOC that was being established at Al Udeid. The members of the primary space team, led and staffed by graduates of the USAF Weapons School, were the most experienced and combat-ready space professionals who had ever populated an air component's battle staff during wartime. The space contingent consisted of a space operations cell on the CAOC operations floor as well as space strategy and plans personnel. These experts were assigned throughout the CAOC's many operating entities, serving in the strategy and combat operations divisions as well as in the MAAP, GAT, and special technical operations cells.

The day before Iraqi Freedom was set to kick off, General Franks, for the first time ever in a U.S. joint operation, ceded control of the space coordination authority (SCA) to his air component commander, General Moseley, for the duration of the campaign. This move, intended to extract the greatest possible leverage from the nation's space assets, initially generated considerable pushback from some quarters. Many in the other services felt that Franks, as the overall joint force commander, should retain that responsibility in the best interest of all of the warfighting components. Although unprecedented in practice, however, the delegation was fully consistent with agreed joint doctrine, which stipulates that the combatant commander can either exercise space coordination authority or delegate it to a component commander. The measure increased tremendously the speed, lethality, and efficiency of the coalition's air operations that were soon to follow.[130]

Under this new arrangement, career space planners and operators were embedded in each CAOC division to provide not only GPS support but also assured theater missile attack warning, space-based infrared battlespace characterization, offensive and defensive counterspace measures, and real-time information on combat survivor location. General Moseley also gained the ability to integrate space activities for all components, uniformed services, and intelligence agencies associated with the impending campaign. As the in-theater space coordination authority, he was charged with integrating Department of Defense space activities for all of the uniformed services. Pursuant to that tasking, he implemented processes and procedures aimed at ensuring the coordination of both Air Force and national space capabilities throughout the theater.

To minimize potential interservice seams with respect to the efficiency of space systems exploitation, General Moseley established an Air Force director of space forces in the CAOC, with an Army deputy, to ensure the closest possible linkage of space assets to ground as well as air operations. Col. Larry James, the senior space authority in the CAOC reporting to General Moseley, recalled with respect to this arrangement: "This was not without a lot of blood and sweat. There were quite a few folks who thought that authority should be retained at the CENTCOM level. . . . We [in the air component] believed that the Air Force had the preponderance of space forces, had the ability to command and control those forces, and therefore General Moseley should have the authority to coordinate space efforts throughout the theater."[131] James added that once the Air Force succeeds in producing CAOC directors and air component commanders who are fully "space smart," the need for this delegated position in future conflicts may go away; until then, however, it should be preserved and institutionalized in the interest of efficiency in the operational exploitation of space assets.[132]

Among other benefits, the vesting of SCA powers in General Moseley "allowed the air component to synchronize the ATO with a space tasking order

(STO). The ATO told the space operators in the CAOC when the critical times were for GPS accuracy, and the STO specified how to tweak the constellation to achieve greater accuracy. For critical periods, the 28-satellite GPS constellation was configured to reduce the normal 3.08-meter accuracy to 2.2 meters."[133]

The Role of Unmanned Aerial Vehicles

A wide variety of UAVs supported CENTCOM's operations during the Iraqi Freedom campaign. More than a hundred UAVs of ten different types took part in the offensive, from the high-flying RQ-4 Global Hawk all the way down to the Marine Corps' Dragon Eye battlefield surveillance minidrone carried on an individual Marine's backpack. This array of unmanned platforms helped to create a fully fused intelligence picture.[134]

The primary UAV workhorse in Iraqi Freedom was the Air Force's Predator. Seven RQ-1 reconnaissance variants and nine MQ-1 armed versions participated in the campaign, operating first out of nearby host-nation locations and later directly from the captured Iraqi H-2 and H-3 airfields.[135] These sixteen platforms represented roughly a third of the Air Force's entire inventory of Predators. The CAOC relied especially heavily on the RQ-1 version to seek out, identify, and geolocate mobile Iraqi SAMs. In this mission application, one Predator detected a Roland SAM launcher north of Baghdad early in the campaign and laser-designated it for an A-10 pilot, who then destroyed the launcher with an LGB. That particular Predator was piloted from its squadron's home base at Creech AFB, Nevada, more than seven thousand miles away, the result of an Air Force decision in May 2002 to approve "remote split operations" whereby half of the Predators in the war zone could be operated from the United States. Also for the first time in a combat setting, four Predators, some flown remotely from Creech, were concurrently committed to a single joint operation. As during Operation Enduring Freedom, live-streaming Predator video imagery was directly linked to AC-130 gunships on numerous occasions to enable real-time targeting of their highly accurate onboard cannons. Armed MQ-1 Predators also fired AGM-114 Hellfire missiles at selected Iraqi targets. In an early instance of this application, an MQ-1 on March 22 located and destroyed an Iraqi ZSU-23/4 mobile radar-directed AAA gun near Al Amarah.[136]

The single RQ-4 Global Hawk that was committed to the campaign played a central role in enabling precision air attacks against Republican Guard forces by transmitting real-time imagery of enemy tanks and artillery emplacements to the CAOC, which relayed their geographic coordinates to fighters and bombers orbiting overhead. It also tracked enemy ground forces, even throughout the three-day *shamal*, with its synthetic aperture radar from an altitude of 60,000 feet or higher as adverse weather conditions grounded all other allied reconnaissance aircraft.[137] In one novel application, Global Hawk was used to pass real-time targeting information to a fighter cockpit, albeit indirectly through a ground control station. In that instance, the UAV used its synthetic aperture radar to cue its electro-optical and infrared sensors onto an Iraqi missile launcher that was partially hidden under a bridge. It then overlaid the target location on the resultant imagery and cross-referenced it with additional target information from its electronic surveillance system. The combined information was relayed via satellite uplink to a ground station in Kuwait for analysis and compression before being passed on to a Navy F/A-18 pilot, who used the information to destroy the partially obscured Iraqi missile system without damaging the bridge. The total reported length of time from initial sensor detection until the target's destruction was roughly twenty minutes, with most of that time taken up by man-in-the-loop target analysis.[138]

The Global Hawk ultimately flew 357 hours over the course of 60 missions in support of roughly half of all the time-sensitive target attacks conducted throughout the three-week campaign, in the process producing imagery that led to the destruction of some 300 Iraqi tanks, 50 SAM batteries, 300 SAM canisters, 70 SAM transporters, and 15 SAM launchers. During all that time it was remotely controlled from Beale AFB, California.[139] A later assessment credited the RQ-4 with shortening the time required for CENTCOM to defeat the Republican Guard by at least several days.[140] It typically took less than an hour from the time Global Hawk identified a target to the moment when munitions were released against it.[141] The UAV experience in Iraqi Freedom revealed that America's force posture remains more weapons-rich than sensor-rich. In addition, the coordination of information flowing from UAVs to tactical-level users was sometimes inadequate, with little or no provision made for integrated direct data receipt.

JSTARS as a Force Multiplier

The Air Force's E-8 JSTARS aircraft took part in Iraqi Freedom for the first time as a mature operating system. Two E-8A JSTARS aircraft that were still in initial development had been deployed to participate in Operation Desert Storm, and an improved E-8C developmental variant was committed to Operation Enduring Freedom in 2001 very late in the game. In the case of Iraqi Freedom, however, no fewer than nine of the fifteen JSTARS in Air Combat Command's E-8C inventory flew in the campaign from two locations. At times, two or more E-8s were concurrently airborne and operating, and one JSTARS mission lasted twenty-three hours with multiple in-flight refuelings. One E-8 crew remained on station for three hours providing ISR and command and control support to Marine Corps units moving into Tikrit after having lost one of the aircraft's four engines, an incident that normally would warrant a mandatory mission abort.[142]

The GMTI radar carried by the E-8 was one of the principal technology innovations that gave allied forces ISR dominance throughout the campaign. In Enduring Freedom in Afghanistan, the E-8 arrived too late to the fight and in insufficient numbers to provide persistent target-area coverage; by the time it was on-scene and at the disposal of the CAOC, most of the vehicular movement that had been the mainstay of Taliban and Al Qaeda operations during the earlier weeks of major fighting had either subsided or ceased altogether. In the case of Iraqi Freedom, however, the deployment of nine JSTARS aircraft to the war zone allowed for target-area coverage by three E-8 orbits, one of which was continuously manned. That capability satisfied the GMTI coverage requirement for a substantial portion of CENTCOM's area of major interest.

The JSTARS contingent also arrived in-theater early enough to collect baseline information on Iraqi ground force dispositions *before* the onset of major combat operations. That early arrival further helped to ensure that allied commanders and their staffs would be sufficiently familiar with the capabilities and limitations of JSTARS to use the aircraft intelligently once the campaign got under way. From that point on, the primary mission of the E-8 was to support allied air and ground forces by providing near-real-time information on both enemy and friendly ground movements. (JSTARS sensors cannot distinguish between civilian and military vehicles, but they can discriminate between tracked and wheeled vehicles. They also can track an entire convoy as well as a single vehicle, although the aircraft's crew cannot determine whether its contacts are friendly or hostile until they cross-cue their own radar imagery with other battlespace information.)

Learning how to use the E-8 as a real-time ISR asset was said to have been a significant challenge for JSTARS operators. The commander of the system's parent unit, Air Combat Command's 116th Air Control Wing based at Robins AFB, Georgia, later remarked that the aircraft's limited use during Operation Enduring Freedom, when it had performed for the first time exclusively in a dedicated ISR role, had provided valuable lessons. "The bulk of the learning curve was not in the employment of the system per se, but in more efficiently integrating JSTARS into the ISR and [time-sensitive targeting] process." The campaign provided the first occasion when JSTARS crews had large friendly force concentrations to monitor and track at the same time they were looking for large enemy troop formations. The wing commander admitted that although the goal for JSTARS was to go "from imagery to iron" as quickly as possible, the aircraft's persistent lack of a positive target identification capability "presented problems at times."[143] He added that divorcing JSTARS operators from their Cold War mindset of gathering information and taking days to analyze it and reorienting their thinking toward going after immediately actionable intelligence in support of attacking emerging targets was a continuing challenge.

Nevertheless, thanks largely to the contributions of JSTARS, Iraqi ground troops on the move were regularly detected by GMTI radar and subsequently attacked by allied fixed-wing aircraft, artillery, or attack helicopters whenever they moved. Enemy ground forces that dispersed or remained hunkered down instead were either bypassed by advancing allied ground units or destroyed by allied air attacks. JSTARS crews also coordinated various joint force activities through voice and data-link contacts with more than thirty ground control stations throughout the region. In particular, a new level of synergy was achieved in command and control and ISR through the interaction and mutual support of what one JSTARS operator called the "iron triad" of the E-8, the RC-135 Rivet Joint, and E-3 AWACS airborne control platforms.[144] Through its ability to cue both other ISR platforms and sensors and armed strike aircraft directly, JSTARS enhanced the efficiency of the entire ISR constellation and greatly facilitated true joint and combined operations by providing a common operating picture to all combatants, while helping to minimize fratricide and inadvertent attacks on innocent Iraqi bystanders.

Timely GMTI information proved to be an especially important enabler of rapid allied ground force maneuver by allowing ground commanders to advance confidently without concern for their flanks and supply lines, even though both were unsecured. Ground commanders could thus accept an element of risk and conduct high-speed operations with smaller and faster forces that relied on superior situation awareness to outflank, outmaneuver, and outsmart the enemy and to stay ahead of his ability to absorb and process information at all times. For example, during its final sprint toward Baghdad, the Army's 3rd ID had no protective forces on either side for hundreds of miles. At one point during that advance the Republican Guard's Medina Division nearly had the U.S. division's cavalry squadron surrounded as the latter was proceeding northward through the sandstorm. Thanks to the high-confidence ISR provided by JSTARS, the Iraqi maneuver was detected and the Medina Division's combat effectiveness was reduced to an estimated 20 percent by ensuing precision standoff attacks of all sorts, mostly by allied fixed-wing air power.[145]

An Air Force JTAC who had supported the 3rd Squadron of the 7th Cavalry (3-7 Cav) graphically described how JSTARS had provided nearly instantaneous actionable target information at the lowest tactical level:

> JSTARS saved our ass a couple of times! At one point we had a troop of the Cav with a [JTAC] holding an intersection near An Najaf. It was during the horrible sandstorm, and you couldn't see 50 yards in daylight, let alone anything at night. The [Iraqis] kept trying to drive fuel trucks into the intersection trying to blow up the Bradleys [armored fighting vehicles]. JSTARS was able to pick the vehicles up, relay that to the [JTAC] we had at the intersection, and he was able to call in JDAMs on all the roads and vehicles leading to their position. Middle of the night in a blinding sandstorm and we still nailed them with CAS.[146]

Similar JSTARS-aided air attacks destroyed dozens of Iraqi vehicles and killed hundreds of troops even at the height of the blinding *shamal*.

The commander of the 101st Airborne Division, Maj. Gen. David Petraeus, later reported that such JSTARS cueing had enabled his Apache crews to destroy "very significant targets on a number of occasions." (Among the new JSTARS capabilities successfully employed during the campaign was a direct data link with Army AH-64D Apache Longbow attack helicopters. In one notable application of this capability, E-8 crews were able to cue both Apaches and Air Force F-15Es onto enemy vehicular targets directly; all other allied strike aircraft received such cueing indirectly via the CAOC.) General Jumper similarly described the performance of JSTARS during the three-day sandstorm as "a major turning point," adding: "The Iraqis, who thought we couldn't see them any better than they could see us, boldly struck out on roads to try to reinforce [their units], especially the Medina Division." Having thus unwittingly exposed themselves, they "essentially got torn apart and, as a result, walked away from their equipment."[147]

In addition, General Moseley suggested that JSTARS may have played a role in helping to prevent Iraqi Scud missile launches against Israel or other friendly countries in the region. "I believe [Saddam Hussein] has not shot one because we've been out there," he declared on April 5. "We've been out there on the ground, we've been out there in the air, we've been out there with sensors, we've been out there with special ops, with conventional forces.... We've worked this problem very hard. . . . I'll tell you that we're closing down on the opportunities for him to get one of those things out and shoot it without us finding it."[148] (In the end, of course, no Scuds were ever found in Iraq's western desert.) This seemed to validate a comment by the former commander of U.S. Strategic Command, Adm. James Ellis Jr., that a major desired end state of the Department of Defense's ongoing "transformation" enterprise at the time was to develop and maintain an ISR capability so effective that it is a deterrent in and of itself. As the Air Force's *Transformation Flight Plan* issued in 2004 noted, such a capability forces an enemy to "fight blind, deaf, and dumb."[149]

To be sure, allied situation awareness was less fine-grained when friendly convoys were attacked by dismounted Iraqi troops or by Fedayeen Saddam paramilitary fighters on foot.[150] Otherwise, however, coalition forces were able to respond to enemy ground threats of any significant size by repositioning and by countering those threats with timely air attacks, even at the height of the three-day *shamal*. Although Iraqi ground forces outnumbered coalition forces, they never achieved tactical surprise or were able to mask their movements. With its broad and persistent target area coverage, JSTARS also was a critical enabler of time-sensitive targeting, directing strike aircraft onto targets of opportunity and cueing other allied ISR platforms onto emerging targets.[151] This capability allowed CENTCOM's ground commanders to substitute information, precision, and speed for mass and firepower. In the words of three JSTARS experts, the combination of near-real-time dynamic GMTI targeting information and satellite-aided JDAMs "redefined both close air support and battlefield air interdiction, air power's two major ground-support functions." By allowing these functions to be performed effectively irrespective of weather and visibility conditions by high-altitude strike platforms armed with large munitions loads, "GMTI and JDAMs [opened up] major opportunities for joint campaign planners to rewrite the book on integrating aerial fires with ground maneuver."[152]

Information Operations

CENTCOM undertook perhaps the most determined U.S. effort ever mounted to conduct information operations against key elements of the Ba'athist regime. At their core, such operations essentially entail measures aimed at influencing the perceptions of the enemy's leadership and rank and file, with the goal of producing a military advantage for the side that conducts them. Defined in that way, information warfare played a significant part in the major combat phase of Iraqi Freedom. CENTCOM's director of operations, Major General Renuart, later recalled that "perceptions had a big part to play in the power of the regime, and we [in CENTCOM's senior leadership] felt that those perceptions could have an important part to play as we began and conducted combat operations."[153]

One information warfare stratagem that CENTCOM applied from the campaign's very start was the generally successful effort to persuade regular Iraqi army troops to remain in their barracks or to desert once the pressure ramped up so that allied forces might concentrate on the Republican Guard and other regime targets. This effort began some nineteen days before the formal start of the campaign with a concentration of measures against what General Renuart called those in Iraq "who were smart enough to understand that the regime was going to come to an end." Regular army troops were targeted for this effort because they were deemed most likely to choose not to fight.[154]

Another part of the information war entailed keeping the U.S. Army's 4th ID afloat off the Turkish coast long after it had become clear that the Turkish government would not allow those troops to use Turkey as a springboard for offensive operations. This diversionary measure was meant to persuade the Iraqi leadership that the 4th ID's combat assets remained a vital part of CENTCOM's campaign strategy. Another such effort entailed CENTCOM's attempt to minimize incentives for destroying Iraq's oilfields. With respect to those equities and to Iraq's dams, both of which would be essential to underwrite postwar reconstruction, General Renuart recalled that "we felt like there was no good kinetic way to prevent bad things from happening. We either had to go occupy them or we had to convince the people occupying them not to destroy them."[155] As evidence that the effort worked, he cited instances in which explosives planted in Iraqi oilfields had been deliberately set incorrectly so that they would cause no damage and explosives that had been planted but never connected. Iraqi detainees later told their interrogators that they had been persuaded to undertake these measures by CENTCOM's targeted radio transmissions.

Propaganda leaflets were another of CENTCOM's successful information warfare stratagems. On March 19, the first day of scheduled operations involving the insertion of allied SOF units, CENTCOM's leaders were encouraged to learn that Iraqi formations that had left their garrisons after President Bush's March 17 ultimatum had assumed only defensive battle positions. Based on that determination, CENTCOM directed Air Force A-10 pilots to drop the first "capitulation" leaflets over enemy troops fielded in southern Iraq. The leaflets urged Iraqi troops who wished to avoid being killed by allied air and ground attacks to park all military vehicles in public squares, stow artillery and AAA pieces in travel configuration, display white flags on vehicles, show no visible man-portable air defense weapons, gather in groups at least a kilometer away from their vehicles, disarm (other than officers, who could retain their sidearms), avoid approaching coalition forces, and await further instructions. The correct timing of this stratagem was critical. One planner noted: "The main reason we haven't dropped capitulation leaflets before is that we did not want to invite Iraqi soldiers to surrender before there was anyone there to surrender to."[156]

The operation was not without problems. On one occasion the land component requested specific messages to be delivered with only a day's prior notice, and the air component could not comply. Leaflet delivery required special canisters loaded with the right combinations of leaflet messages and flight plans that took due account of wind speed and direction at the scheduled time of drop. For their part, ground commanders could rarely predict four days in advance when the battlefield situation might be right for specific messages to be delivered. The challenge, General Leaf observed, was "the lead time required not just to produce the products, but also to ensure [that] the message [was] clear, accurate, and properly translated into local languages and dialects." Another officer later reported that the "nonkinetic targeting process was still undergoing major refinements well into the conflict" and that the air and land component headquarters "were never able to develop a process that appropriately reflected the needs of both components. . . . There's a very narrow window to try to get capitulation leaflets [dropped] in, to be effective. . . . You don't want them to get there too early. You don't want them to get there too late, obviously, either." More to the point, added General Leaf: "While the risk is different than dropping a bomb on the wrong target, mistargeted information operations 'weapons' like leaflets could have just as negative an effect on military operations." Leaflet "BDA" was also problematic. For example, although Iraq's forces did not, as initially anticipated, set many oil wells afire, there was no way of determining the extent to which leaflets were responsible for that.[157]

In contrast to the aerial leaflet drops, which reportedly were relatively well planned before the start of the campaign, CENTCOM had not prepared adequately for nonkinetic information warfare attacks against, for example, the Ba'athist regime's computer networks. Most such operations were conceived and cobbled together on the run.[158] General Renuart indicated that computer network attack represented only a small part of the overall information campaign, largely because there were only some 15,000 computers in Iraq with access to the Internet and access was closely controlled by Hussein's regime. However, computer network operations were conducted to send messages directly to key Iraqi commanders, as well as to try to judge the effectiveness of CENTCOM's larger perceptions management effort against specific targets.[159]

On balance, CENTCOM did not do as well as its leaders would have liked at manipulating Iraqi and international perceptions during the three-week campaign and its early aftermath. Nevertheless, General Moseley established a combat information cell in the CAOC whose primary responsibility was to gather information quickly on all reported instances of collateral damage with a view toward developing information release strategies aimed at heading off and correcting any misstatements of the facts that appeared in both friendly and hostile media.[160] As for key information-related "lessons" from this collective experience, General Renuart cited the need "to step forward to create information operations units and to create tools that are agile, mobile, and are technically a step beyond Commando Solo [the EC-130]," as well as the need for a government-wide group to oversee information operations at a national and strategic level rather than the current profusion of niche capabilities in each service. A persistent problem in this respect, he added, was the absence of a common and accepted definition among the various concerned agencies as to what information warfare is and involves.[161]

New Munitions and Technologies

The air portion of the three-week campaign was largely a JDAM and LGB war, with various versions of those two precision-guided munitions making up about two-thirds of the total number of bombs dropped. The JDAM was a particularly welcome addition to CENTAF's munitions lineup not only because of its consistently high accuracy (generally landing within a bomb's length of the designated target aim point), but also because it could be released from level flight at high altitude even above a solid cloud cover, thereby allowing the delivery aircraft to remain outside the lethal envelope of most of the Iraqi SAM and AAA threats. Depending on the altitude and airspeed of the dispensing aircraft, a JDAM can be released as far away as fifteen miles from its target in ideal conditions.[162]

The greater availability of precision-guided weapons and the heightened imperatives of collateral damage avoidance also drove a progressive trend toward the use of smaller munitions in Iraqi Freedom. Lt. Gen. James Cartwright, USMC, at the time the Joint Staff's director for force structure, resources, and assessments, commented on that score, "We are still early in this game, but it appears that we moved off of the 2,000-pound [bomb] area down into the 500-pound area."[163] The ground attack munition of choice for the Air Force's F-15E Strike Eagle, for example, was the 500-pound GBU-12 LGB. With each aircraft able to carry nine of these, a two-ship flight of F-15Es could engage as many as eighteen target aim points on a single mission.

The expanded availability of advanced infrared navigation and targeting pods greatly increased the types of allied aircraft that could carry LGBs and self-designate targets for them. For example, B-52H heavy bombers dropped LGBs for the first time in combat using the AN/AAQ-28 Litening II targeting pod. This new system, configured with a laser spot tracker and an optical sensor in addition to an upgrade of its LANTIRN predecessor's forward-looking infrared sensor, had been integrated into the aircraft by mid-February 2003, with initial work on system compatibility having begun in October 2002. The Litening II pod allowed the aircraft's bombardier to visually identify and confirm the target under his display cursor from an altitude of 35,000 feet, a capability that the B-52 had not previously possessed.[164] Twelve B-52s were slated for conversion to this capability, but only two were available for use during the three-week campaign. The pod was useful not only for guiding LGBs, but also for marking targets for other strike aircraft and for providing irrefutable videotaped bomb hit assessments. Litening II pods were also carried by the A-10 and by all versions of the F-16C.[165] They were described as easy to use, easy to maintain, and reliable.

In addition, for the first time, a B-52 dropped six CBU-105 sensor fused weapons on a column of enemy military vehicles. The CBU-105 is a WCMD-equipped version of the CBU-97 dispenser, which carries ten BLU-108 sub-munition packages, each of which contains four "skeet" warheads with side-mounted, dual-mode infrared and active laser seekers to initiate the warhead charge and then fire a shaped projectile into an armored target. The munition was developed during the 1980s as a part of the Assault Breaker program directed against massed Warsaw Pact tank formations in Central Europe. (WCMD-equipped cluster munitions first saw combat use in Afghanistan in 2001 when WCMD-aided CBU-87s were employed against Al Qaeda and Taliban troop concentrations.)[166]

Other ground attack munitions available to CENTCOM included the AGM-154A joint standoff weapon (JSOW), a gliding submunition dispenser carried exclusively by the F/A-18 that was inertially guided and GPS aided, and could, under ideal conditions, be released twenty miles away from the target. It was effective during the initial days of the campaign, particularly against Iraqi IADS-related targets in the north.[167] Preproduction versions of the joint air-to-surface standoff missile (JASSM) were delivered to the 2nd Bomb Wing, a B-52 unit based at Barksdale AFB, Louisiana, for possible use during the air offensive, but were not employed.

Finally, the Air Force introduced the CBU-107 passive attack weapon, which it used at least once against an unspecified target. That munition was designed to disable nonhardened targets such as storage facilities while minimizing unwanted collateral damage. The thousands of steel and tungsten penetrating rods it released were designed to disable whatever might be inside without actually taking down the targeted building. The Air Force fielded this 1,000-pound-class munition through a $40 million quick-reaction initiative that was funded by the Office of the Secretary of Defense. The development program for the munition commenced in September 2002, and the first units were reported ready for the B-52, F-15E, and F-16 within just 98 days. Developed at the Air Force Armaments Center at Eglin AFB, Florida, the CBU-107 consists of a tactical munition dispenser that contains 3,700 penetrating rods and includes a WCMD tail guidance kit. Its destructive core consists of 340 14-inch-long tungsten rods that are ejected during the munition's descent, followed by 1,000 medium-sized (7-inch-long) tungsten rods and then by 2,400 2-inch-long steel rods that are the last to leave the unit. The larger rods are intended to breach the harder aspects of a target, such as fairly thick steel; the others damage softer elements within the targeted structure. The weapon, which appears capable of neutralizing large stores of chemical or biological agents (or at least denying the enemy access to such facilities), emerged from a multiyear Air Force study of alternatives for implementing a targeting concept called "agent defeat."[168] The weapon was first publicly described during a subcommittee hearing of the House Armed Services Committee on April 3, 2003, by the Air Force's chief acquisition official, Marvin Sambur, who testified that production had been completed on time and under budget and with 15 percent more munitions delivered than had been originally proposed.[169]

Some of Secretary Rumsfeld's deputies reportedly had pressed CENT-COM to use a 21,700-pound monstrosity called the massive ordnance air blast (MOAB) bomb, more colloquially known as the "mother of all bombs," which was designed to produce a tremendous explosion that would terrorize an enemy into submission. Although the Air Force chief of staff, General Jumper, was "not excited" about that suggestion, General Franks yielded to pressure from above and directed General Moseley to have two sent to the war zone "so we can help the designers do their work."[170] CAOC planners were hard put to come up with a suitable target for the bomb, especially given the Bush administration's insistence on avoiding collateral damage, because it was dropped from medium altitude from a C-130 to descend by parachute at the mercy of the wind. General Moseley remained unenthusiastic as well, stating that "unless we have a different mindset, dropping them in a city with a [circular error probable] of about 3,000 feet does not make much sense." "To the relief of the Air Force," authors Gordon and Trainor reported, "the war ended before the bomb was used."[171]

In contrast to the outsized MOAB, whose practical utility to combatant commanders has yet to be persuasively demonstrated, a real deficiency in strike warfare capability unmasked by the campaign experience was at the opposite end of the weapon-size spectrum. There is an increasingly pressing need for smaller munitions in the 250-pound category that will allow engagement of more target aim points during a single strike mission while being less likely to cause unwanted collateral damage. Both needs can now be met by the unprecedented accuracy of modern munitions. So-called small-diameter bombs (SDBs) in the 250-pound class with GPS and laser guidance and with extendable vanes enabling greater standoff capability have been introduced into the line inventories of the Air Force, Navy, and Marine Corps. These versatile new munitions have been used to consistently great effect toward both precision target attack and collateral damage mitigation in danger-close conditions in the nation's continuing counterinsurgency operations since the end of major combat in Iraq.

Overall Effects Achieved

Throughout the course of its campaign planning in 2002 and early 2003, CENTCOM sought multiple concurrent ways to get at the heart of Hussein's regime. First, it sought to attack key Iraqi leaders directly. Second, allied forces struck Iraqi command centers and communications infrastructure at virtually every significant node. Third, those same forces sought to fragment the regime with inducements aimed at subordinate leaders and with associated psychological warfare efforts to drive a wedge between the regime and its fielded forces. Finally, through focused information operations to impair the Iraqi dictator's assessment of the battlefield situation, CENTCOM worked hard to mislead Hussein regarding coalition activities.[172] The command's overall approach to leadership attack was, as one subsequent assessment put it, "comprehensive. It had physical and psychological components; it aimed at Saddam, his sons, their subordinate commanders, and the general population; and it employed both kinetic and nonkinetic means [that] included attacking command centers from the national level down to corps and division level."[173] The campaign further sought more directly, through the sustained application of kinetic measures by every asset at CENTCOM's disposal, to beat down Iraq's fielded forces to a point where they would be incapable of meaningful collective action.

CENTCOM achieved its most immediate and pressing goal of regime takedown, but it is worth considering each of its other campaign goals with the benefit of hindsight: those which were *not* achieved, those which *were* achieved, and the most plausible explanations for the failure or success in each case. On the first count, the campaign ultimately proved unable to kill any of Iraq's most notorious leaders by means of air attacks. An after-action assessment concluded that two factors, "or, more specifically, one factor with two facets," principally accounted for this failure. First, "Iraqi leaders adopted extreme protective measures to evade coalition attacks. These measures included strict secrecy and continual movement." Second, "the coalition was unable to attain actionable intelligence on the location of Iraqi leaders."[174] The air component's determined effort to locate and destroy Hussein's presumed stocks of theater ballistic missiles and WMD likewise failed, for the simple reason that those commodities were, by all subsequent indications, no longer in Hussein's arsenal by the time the campaign began.

When it came to the equally important matter of beating down Iraq's fielded forces, however, CENTCOM's final campaign plan more than handily met its objective. Furthermore, firsthand insights and supporting evidence gathered by coalition forces after Hussein's regime was toppled established incontestably that the air component had done the bulk of the heavy lifting in that regard. That said, one must acknowledge that the air component's banner performance did not by itself account for the campaign's singular achievements in that regard. No less important was the stunning incompetence of Saddam Hussein with regard to the planning and provisions for the defense and security of his regime.

Indeed, it was apparent even before the smoke from the campaign had cleared that Hussein's forces had not come remotely close to being a match for those pitted against them by the coalition. To cite an especially notable testament to that fact, the commander of Army V Corps, Lieutenant General Wallace, remarked not long after the campaign ended: "It continually took the Iraqi forces a long time—somewhere on the order of 24 hours—to react to anything we did. By the time the enemy realized what we were doing, got word to his commanders, and they actually did something as a result, we had already moved on to do something quite different. For a commander, that's a pretty good thing—fighting an enemy that can't react to you."[175] An early assessment of the campaign acknowledged that "American military prowess is a function not only of the capabilities stemming from its enormous advantages in resources, but also its relative effectiveness against the capabilities brought to bear by its enemies. Simply put, is the U.S. military that good, or was the Iraqi military that bad? The answer to both questions seems, at this early juncture, to be 'yes.' While the U.S. military's performance was striking in many respects, it may have been surpassed by the stunning ineptitude of its Iraqi adversary."[176]

Much of that ineptitude was the direct result of Hussein's own meddling and paranoia. Extensive interviews of former Iraqi military leaders in the early aftermath of the Ba'athist regime's collapse soon made it clear to JFCOM's team of analysts that CENTCOM's campaign planners had underestimated the psychological impact that precision bombing attacks would have on Iraq's ground combat units. In a pathbreaking synopsis of their findings, JFCOM's analysts concluded that "the largest contributing factor [accounting for] the complete defeat of Iraq's military forces was the continued interference by Saddam." His conviction that the real invasion threat was coming from the northwest, spearheaded by American troops moving in from Jordan, and his repositioning of forces to meet that perceived threat simply put more targets in the way of coalition aircraft.[177]

JFCOM's after-action canvass of former Ba'ath regime leaders further confirmed that Hussein's pattern of deploying his forces around Baghdad had been motivated chiefly by his pathological fear of a coup. Accordingly, he fielded his troops in concentric rings around the city, with the least trustworthy elements kept on the outside and the more trusted Republican Guard units nearer to the city's center. Even the Republican Guard, however, was not allowed to enter Baghdad proper. Only the most carefully screened and trusted Special Republican Guard units were permitted to position themselves that close to the regime's center of power. Moreover, senior officers in the Special Republican Guard were forbidden to communicate and coordinate with other Iraqi forces, or even to possess maps of Baghdad. The JFCOM study observed that "in Saddam's eyes, the only possible reason general officers would ever want to talk to each other was to plan a coup."[178]

Although coalition planners had long understood many aspects of Hussein's approach to command and leadership, they did not fully appreciate, as one CAOC staffer later explained, "just how dysfunctional the Iraqi leader and his government were. . . . The side effects of Hussein's coup-proofing . . . were catastrophic for Iraq. . . . Hussein had neither the information nor the disposition necessary to learn or adapt. . . . As coalition planners considered applying strategies of leadership attack to Saddam Hussein's regime, they did not realize that the Iraqi dictator had already done much of their job for them."[179]

First and foremost, Hussein refused to allow his military units to coordinate with one another. His abiding fear of a coup was plainly reflected in the flawed plan that he imposed on his commanders for a succession of defensive rings around Baghdad, the main purpose of which was to keep the Republican Guard *out* of the city, irrespective of the fact that a robust urban defense could have placed major obstacles in the path of any attacking coalition force. The above-noted assessment succinctly concluded, "Saddam's rule was a disaster for Iraq."[180]

In fact, Hussein's dysfunctional defense plan created an all but perfect target array for CENTCOM's air component when it came time to unleash the campaign to bring down his regime. Firsthand testimony from numerous Iraqi ground commanders bears that out. For example, the commander of the Republican Guard's I Corps, Lieutenant General Majid Husayn Ali Ibraham Al Dulaymi, recalled his shock when he visited the Republican Guard's Adnan Division shortly after a successive barrage of air attacks had obliterated one of its battalions that had moved into an exposed position: "The level of precision of those attacks put real fear into the soldiers of the rest of the division. The Americans were able to induce fear throughout the army by using precision air power."[181]

Although the Republican Guard's Al Nida Division experienced no significant direct contact with allied ground forces, it likewise felt the shock effect of coalition air power. One of its leaders later remarked that CENTAF's precision air attacks had made virtually every soldier feel as if he was in "a sniper's sight."[182] The division commander told JFCOM's interviewers:

> The air attacks were the most effective message. The soldiers who did see the leaflets and then saw the air attacks knew the leaflets were true. . . . Overall, [the air attacks] had a terrible effect on us. I started the war with 13,000 soldiers. By the time we had orders to pull back to Baghdad, I had less than 2,000; by the time we were in position in Baghdad, I had less than 1,000. . . . When my division pulled back across the Diyala bridge, of the more than 500 armored vehicles assigned to me before the war, I was able to get fifty or so across the bridge. Most were destroyed or abandoned on the east side of the Diyala River.

JFCOM's analysts concluded from their interviews with Al Nida Division troops that "precision air power and the fear it engendered made an entire division of the Republican Guard combat-ineffective. In this case, it was not so much destroyed as dissolved."[183]

Perhaps the most unimpeachable source of firsthand testimony regarding the effects of the coalition's unrelenting air attacks was Lieutenant General Ra'ad al Hamdani, the commander of the Republican Guard's II Corps and one of the few truly competent officers near the top whom Hussein seemed to trust implicitly. He was particularly well placed during the campaign to offer an informed view of how the allied air war looked from the receiving end because his corps was responsible for defending the southern approaches to Baghdad along which V Corps and I MEF advanced in their parallel offensives. JFCOM's study team was impressed by his rare perceptivity, candor, and honesty. Hamdani told his interviewers, for example, that when he tried to establish a defensive line west of Latifiya around March 30 after having fallen back in the face of the relentless allied advance, "American jets attacked our force as we moved down the road. We were hit by many missiles. Most of the Medina Division's staff were killed. My corps communication staff was also killed. When we reached the area near the bridge where the special forces battalion had set up a headquarters, we immediately came under heavy fire. Based on the volume of fire, I estimated at least 60 armored vehicles [destroyed by the air attacks]."[184]

With respect to the initial waves of air attacks during the campaign's open- ing days, the Al Nida Division's commander said: "The early air attacks hit only empty headquarters and barracks buildings. It did affect our communication switches which were still based in those buildings. . . . But the accuracy and lethality of those attacks left an indelible impression on those Iraqi soldiers who either observed them directly or saw the damage afterwards."[185] Another allied air attack against the Al Nida Division during the campaign's first week struck particularly hard against its 153rd Artillery Battalion located in the 41st Brigade area. The division commander told JFCOM interviewers that the unit had hid- den its artillery pieces in an orchard, its soldiers in a second hiding position, and its ammunition in still a third place that was separated from the first two. He recounted his shock when "the air attack hit all three locations at the same time and annihilated the artillery battalion." JFCOM interviewers noted that "such experiences became commonplace as coalition air power chewed up Iraqi ground forces that attracted the attention of satellites or aerial reconnaissance."[186]

Thanks in large measure to the coalition's air contribution, a CENTCOM ground contingent consisting of just two U.S. Army divisions and one Marine Corps division (plus smaller allied forces) was able to attack into the face of more than twenty enemy divisions and prevail handily—and at little cost. One subsequent land-centric assessment suggested that there had been "significant close combat" throughout the three weeks of major fighting, but it ultimately acknowledged the more important point that the "Iraqi paramilitaries and [Spe- cial Republican Guard] infantry [did not present] a serious threat to halt the coalition advance."[187] That assessment further conceded that "much of the close combat [that did occur] took the form of Iraqi paramilitaries charging coali- tion armored vehicles on the outskirts of Iraqi cities using unarmored civilian vehicles."[188] Although the allied ground contribution to the campaign entailed more than a few hair-raising skirmishes with defending Iraqi forces and was pivotal in toppling Hussein's regime, the land component did not encounter the sort of close-combat opposition for which it was so well configured and trained. On the contrary, as Andrew Krepinevich observed, the Fedayeen Saddam in the end "proved little more than a nuisance to coalition forces."[189]

Col. Matt Neuenswander well captured the point that matters most in this regard when he remarked that the allied air contribution to CENTCOM's counterland effort "truly validated General Moseley's air interdiction campaign and our efforts independent of the land component."[190] Commenting on that performance even as the campaign was still in its final throes, an Australian analyst reported:

> The Iraqi defenders could not disperse their armored and mechanized elements for fear of being engaged by raiding M1A1 Abrams tanks and AH-64 Apache helicopters. . . . Yet the very concentration of force they required to protect themselves against the [coalition's] armor and helicopter elements is what made them into lucrative targets for orbiting strike aircraft above. . . . With coalition air and information dominance, the latter provided by E-8C JSTARS, RQ-1/MQ-1 Predators, RQ-4 Global Hawks, RC-135 Rivet Joint and other assets, the Iraqi ground force became like the proverbial fish in a giant barrel, pinned in the Karbala-Baghdad–Al Kut triangle.[191]

All in all, as Krepinevich later concluded, "air superiority enabled the services to provide the level of close air support strikes [that were] needed by a relatively small but fast-moving ground force."[192] As to the practical effects on Iraq's ground forces achieved by these KI/CAS attacks from the air, the chairman of the JCS, General Myers, reported just before the Ba'athist regime was finally toppled that of the eight hundred–plus tanks that the Republican Guard had fielded at the start of the war, "all but a couple of dozen" had been destroyed by air strikes or abandoned by the campaign's third week.[193] A substantial portion of those were destroyed during the three-day *shamal*. Thanks largely to the sustained contribution by the fixed-wing air assets provided by the U.S. Air Force, Navy, Marine Corps, RAF, and RAAF, noted Krepinevich, "by the time the 3rd Infantry Division reached the outskirts of Baghdad, only about a dozen Iraqi tanks opposed it. They were quickly dispatched in what may have been the only traditional tank encounter of the war."[194]

In the end, the major combat phase of Operation Iraqi Freedom illustrated the fundamental reversal that has taken place in the traditional roles of land and air power in high-intensity warfare, starting with the precedent-setting experience of Operation Desert Storm in 1991, in which allied ground troops did the fixing and CENTCOM's air component did the majority of the killing of enemy ground forces rather than the other way around, as had hitherto been the norm for joint warfare against mechanized opponents. As I wrote in this regard in 2000, harking back to the example of the first Persian Gulf War,

> One can argue that the air power assets of *all* the U.S. services now have the potential to carry the bulk of responsibility for beating down an enemy's military forces of all kinds, thus enabling other friendly force elements to achieve their goals with a minimum of pain, effort, and cost. . . . More important than that, one can argue that air power . . . has fundamentally altered the way the United States might best fight any major wars over the next two decades through its ability to carry out functions traditionally performed at greater cost and risk by other force elements. . . . This, in turn, suggests that the primary role of U.S. land forces [in major combat] may now be increasingly to *secure* a win rather than to achieve it. . . . In this respect, there is growing ground for maintaining that a fundamental change has begun to take place in the long-familiar relationship between air and land forces when it comes to [combating] enemy armored and mechanized units.[195]

The three weeks of major combat in Operation Iraqi Freedom further bore out that changed relationship between the nation's air and land forces in high-intensity warfare. What largely accounted for the reversal in roles between those two force elements, even more in Iraqi Freedom than in Desert Storm, was that fixed-wing air power in *all* services had become "markedly more effective in creating the conditions for rapid success than [had been] existing ground systems."[196] This reversal did not entail the classic image of the "hammer" of friendly air power smashing enemy forces against the "anvil" of friendly ground power, to use David Johnson's words. Instead, it was "more a case of ground power flushing the enemy, allowing air power to maul his forces, with ground power finishing the fight against the remnants and controlling the ground dimension in the aftermath of combat. . . . The operational level of warfighting against large conventional enemy forces was dominated by flexible, all-weather, precision strike air power, enabled by ISR," whereas "the tactical level of war and the exploitation of the operational effects of air power were the primary domains of [allied] ground power."[197]

To cite the most telling factual testimony to that change, during the three weeks of major combat in Iraqi Freedom, V Corps launched only two deep-attack operations using a force of fewer than eighty AH-64 attack helicopters. The first combat foray nearly ended in disaster for the attacking force, and the second achieved only modest mission success. By the same token, Army field artillery units expended only 414 of their longest-range Army Tactical Missile System (ATACMS) missiles, principally because of the indiscriminate wide-area destructive effects of that weapon and its consequent inability to meet CENT-COM's stringent rules of engagement for collateral damage avoidance. In contrast, CENTCOM's air component during the same three weeks generated 20,733 combat and combat support sorties, which included the repeated use of 735 strike fighters and 51 heavy bombers and successfully struck more than 15,592 target aim points in support of the allied counterland campaign.[198]

Problems Encountered

All in all, CENTCOM committed remarkably few major errors during its campaign to topple the Ba'athist regime of Saddam Hussein. To be sure, as a subsequent review of postcampaign detainee operations in Iraq led by two former secretaries of defense, James Schlesinger and Harold Brown, harshly concluded, the Bush administration's overall strategy wrongly "presupposed that relatively benign stability and security operations would precede a handover to Iraqi authorities." The administration also failed utterly to "plan for a major insurgency" and "to quickly and adequately adapt to the insurgency that followed after major combat operations."[1] To infer from that stern judgment, as *Washington Post* military reporter Thomas Ricks later did, that the initial invasion and takedown of the Ba'athist regime was based on "perhaps the worst war plan in American history," however, was a considerable overreach.[2] Such a blanket dismissal of CENTCOM's chosen approach for defeating Hussein's forces was tantamount to throwing out the baby with the bathwater. A more discerning perspective was that offered by former secretary of state Colin Powell, who candidly remarked that what really went wrong with Iraqi Freedom was *not* the three-week major combat phase of the campaign, which was "brilliantly fought," but rather the transition afterward to "nation-building." In his well-informed opinion, there had been "enough troops for war but not enough for peace, for establishing order."[3]

Regardless of the wisdom of the Bush administration's decision to invade Iraq in the first place, there seems to be no question that the invasion was badly underresourced for the many needs of postwar stabilization and transition to democratic rule, about which senior administration leaders had been more than amply warned before the invasion by a multitude of credible advisers both in and out of government. This book, however, focuses on the strategic and operational use of air power in pursuit of CENTCOM's more immediate combat objectives during the three-week regime-removal phase of the campaign. By that more narrow measure, it is fair to conclude that those who conducted the campaign at all levels turned in a performance that was both exemplary and rich with useful lessons for the next major conflict the United States may face. Vice Adm. Joseph Dyer, the commander of Naval Air Systems Command, observed afterward in that respect, "Almost all of our thinking is proactive and looking toward future developments and amazingly little of it in terms of correcting deficiencies that were in evidence in this conflict."[4] CENTCOM's deputy air component commander, Rear Admiral Nichols, made the same point even more directly in stating that instead of thinking in terms of revealed problems in need of fixing, U.S. and allied airmen should be reflecting on "what we validated."[5] During the course of a two-week Iraqi Freedom "lessons learned" symposium conducted by CENTAF at Nellis AFB in July 2003, numerous air component representatives in attendance who had been personally involved in the planning and conduct of the campaign at all levels suggested that unlike previous air wars from Desert Storm through Enduring Freedom, this one celebrated air power's successes and would offer relatively few suggested equipment and procedural improvements for future campaigns. The collective sense of the participants was that few findings from the symposium would challenge prevailing service trends that had been established and validated in previous wars.[6]

Nevertheless, although the campaign to topple Hussein set new records for air power achievement and broader joint force effectiveness, its execution was not without certain areas of combat performance that, in the words of JFCOM's commander at the time, Admiral Giambastiani, "fell short of expectations."[7] General Moseley, also in attendance at the after-action review symposium, denoted seven areas of activity that, in his view, "worked less well" during the campaign: (1) insufficiently timely BDA, especially with respect to strategic targets and KI/CAS; (2) inadequate information transfer between the CAOC and shooter aircraft; (3) inadequate battlespace deconfliction; (4) totally unsatisfactory Army Patriot missile deconfliction and firing logic; (5) inadequate prioritization of theaterwide information operations; (6) a relatively poor performance by the ASOC supporting V Corps in comparison with the ASOC's more professionally manned and more efficient Marine Corps DASC counterpart; (7) and speed, range, maximum service ceiling, and defensive system inadequacies with respect to CSAR platforms.[8] The most notable air-related problems identified during the review were a succession of friendly fire incidents, continuing friction points in the air-ground interface, insufficiently timely provision of battle damage assessment, inefficiencies in the management of in-flight refueling support, and inadequate arrangements for the timely sharing of sensitive information with the nation's coalition partners.[9]

Incidents of Fratricide

The coalition's combat fratricide rate was lower during the three-week campaign to topple Hussein than it was during Operation Desert Storm, when
35 of the 148 U.S. fatalities (24 percent) and an even higher proportion of the
British casualties incurred resulted from friendly fire. All the same, a postcampaign report by the Center for Army Lessons Learned identified 17 friendly-fire
incidents during the major combat phase of Iraqi Freedom.[10]

The three episodes of Blue-on-Blue surface-to-air fire that occurred
involved the Army's Patriot SAM system and allied combat aircraft. In the first, a
Patriot PAC-2 missile struck an RAF Tornado GR4 on March 23 as the aircraft
was returning to its base in Kuwait, instantly killing the crew, Flight Lieutenant
Kevin Barry Main and Flight Lieutenant David Rhys Williams. The next day, a
U.S. Air Force F-16 pilot whose aircraft had been locked up by a Patriot acquisition and tracking radar about thirty miles south of An Najaf fired an AGM-88
HARM at the offending radar in presumed self-defense, destroying the radar
but remarkably causing no friendly injuries or loss of life. And on April 2, near
Karbala, a Patriot PAC-3 missile struck a U.S. Navy F/A-18C operating from
Kitty Hawk and killed the pilot, Lt. Nathan White.[11] Neither of the two downed
allied fighters in these Blue-on-Blue incidents appeared on the Patriot's threat
display as an aircraft.

Investigators who reviewed the details of the three incidents considered the
possibility that the Patriot system's tracking radars had generated false targets
and the Patriot operators had believed they were engaging enemy missiles rather
than aircraft. Because aircraft and missiles have such different radar profiles, the
investigators further considered the possibility of electromagnetic interference
caused by the close proximity of the offending Patriot batteries to such other
friendly radio frequency emitters as ground-based artillery radars, airborne surveillance sensors, and electronic jammers. In this regard the chief of Army air
defenses, Brig. General Howard B. Bromberg, commented, "This is the densest
battlefield we've seen. I believe there could be something there." The Patriot
batteries were clustered together looking northward toward Iraq from Kuwait,
with PAC-2 and PAC-3 radars reflecting back on one another. General Bromberg added: "You have three incidents like that—they've all got to have some
interrelationship. I'm convinced they did."[12]

Other early speculation pointed to a possible failure by the downed Tornado
crew to transmit the proper IFF code, as well as to a possible use of improper
settings by the offending Patriot crew to identify tracked targets accurately by
correlating their speed, altitude, trajectory, and other flight characteristics. A

board of inquiry convened by CENTCOM ultimately exonerated the Patriot battery crew who downed the GR4 during the latter's approach to landing at Ali Al Salem Air Base in Kuwait, reportedly concluding that the crew "mistook the aircraft for an antiradiation missile based on its high-speed descent and lack of a functioning IFF."[13] The British MoD refused at first to comment on that finding, although RAF sources insisted that IFF is a go/no-go checklist item. Informed sources initially deemed it unlikely that the aircraft's IFF could have failed in flight without the pilot noticing the failure and promptly alerting ground controllers. AWACS operators monitoring the airspace over southern Iraq likewise should have noticed immediately had the aircraft's IFF suite not been functioning.

A subsequent investigation revealed that although the Tornado crew believed that they were properly squawking in all assigned IFF modes, the aircraft's IFF system had indeed failed completely. The investigation further determined that the Patriot crew had been undertrained and should not have assumed that the Tornado was hostile simply because it was not squawking IFF Mode 4—or, for that matter, any other transponder mode.[14] An early assessment by a long-established specialist in Patriot performance at the Massachusetts Institute of Technology, based on careful examination of a 32nd AAMDC briefing released shortly after the campaign ended, determined that a large number of Patriot radars were operating in close proximity to one another in the immediate war zone; that those multiple, independently operating radars were often in line of sight and tracking the same aircraft; that their target contacts could be displayed as spurious ballistic missile tracks; that the Patriot unit would automatically engage the false target; and that Patriot operators could have intervened to stop the engagement, but only if they acted within a time window of less than a minute. He further reported that Patriot operators "were not trained to deal with this scenario, and this scenario was not incorporated in engagement training software embedded in deployed Patriot units. . . . Thus the combination of lack of timely information from other air defense surveillance assets, timelines of tens of seconds or less to fire on the believed target, and no software support or training to recognize and deal with such situations put the Patriot crews in an impossible situation."[15]

In early 2004 a television reporter who had been embedded with a Patriot battery during the campaign uncovered evidence that friendly aircraft had been showing up on Patriot radars as incoming enemy missiles and that this problem had first surfaced with a forward-deployed Patriot unit a month before the campaign's start. The reporter discovered that the Army had not alerted other Patriot operators or coalition aircrews to the problem. The deployed Patriot batteries had been operating in "weapons free" mode at the time of the two fratricide incidents, meaning that the launch crews could fire the missiles without first seeking higher approval. The account also reported that the battery that downed the Tornado GR4 was showing the incoming fighter as an enemy cruise missile, and that the one that subsequently downed the Navy F/A-18 had displayed its target "as a highly credible enemy ballistic missile symbol that did not resemble any false missile track that had been seen before."[16]

Whatever the explanation, allied aircrews soon developed a deep distrust of the Patriot system and made every effort to remain a healthy distance from its threat envelopes in their mission planning. One F-16 flight leader recalled what that effort entailed for his four-ship flight launching with no notice against an emerging target complex in the heart of Baghdad on March 30: "We . . . got airborne heading straight for the targets. Normally, we would have taken a westerly course in order to stay behind the northwest/southeast running line of our ground advance. The main reason for this was to stay behind the two Patriot batteries that had already been involved in two friendly fire incidents. To put it bluntly, the Patriots scared the hell out of us."[17]

The assessed threat to friendly aircraft presented by the Patriot SAM system had at least two undesirable consequences. First, it obliged allied aircrews to squawk secondary and unencrypted civilian Mode 2 IFF codes with their transponders, which could be tracked by Patriot but also by some Iraqi SAM systems. Second, allied aircrews experienced a notable spike in their stress levels whenever they operated within a Patriot threat envelope. More than a few who were locked up by a Patriot radar had been forced to drop chaff, engage in aggressive countermaneuvering, and make frantic radio calls to the AWACS to get the offending Patriot to break its lock.[18]

Starting in August 2003 and continuing into June of the following year, a Defense Science Board (DSB) task force on Patriot system performance examined the Patriot's operating experience during the campaign looking for lessons that might be incorporated into the continued development of Patriot and its planned follow-on system, the medium extended air defense system (MEADS). One of the key issue areas the DSB explored was the blend of causal factors that most likely accounted for the two Patriot-related fratricide incidents. The DSB's findings, issued in January 2005, noted that the Patriot's role in the campaign had been defense against enemy tactical ballistic missiles, with a secondary self-defense role against enemy antiradiation missiles, and that the system had no assigned air defense role. The board adjudged the Patriot's service in its primary combat role a "substantial success." The system had engaged all nine Iraqi TBMs that were fired against coalition forces; eight of those intercepts were confirmed kills, and the ninth engagement was deemed a probable kill. Given the reality of the Iraqi TBM threat and these manifest accomplishments against it, there was no question that the substantial deployment of Patriots, entailing up to forty U.S. Army fire units and twenty-two more from four coalition countries, was an essential ingredient of CENTCOM's overall force mix.[19]

With respect to the two surface-to-air fratricide incidents, the DSB cited "a complex chain of events and failures," noting that there was "insufficient data to pin down the exact causes of failure" that occasioned the two inadvertent downings of coalition aircraft. Among the known shortfalls in CENTCOM's capabilities and operating modes that might have been contributing factors, however, were consistently poor performance of the combat identification capability embodied in the Mode 4 IFF systems carried on allied aircraft; an absence of adequate situational awareness in CENTCOM's combined air defense system; and the Patriot system's "operating philosophy, protocols, displays, and software, which seemed to be a poor match to the conditions of [Operation Iraqi Freedom]." The report added that the Patriot's operating protocol "was largely automatic, and the operators were trained to trust the system's software," which was designed to accommodate the possibility of "heavy missile attacks." The task force further noted that with the "enormous" number of coalition aircraft sorties flown during the campaign (some 41,000) and the large deployment of Patriot fire units in-theater (62 in all), "the possible Patriot friendly aircraft observations were in the millions, and even very low-probability failures could result in regrettable fratricide incidents."[20]

With respect to minimizing the likelihood of future surface-to-air fratricide incidents, the DSB's report concluded that the Department of Defense needed to "find and fix the Mode 4 IFF problem" and "improve the situational awareness of [the U.S. defense establishment's] air defense systems." As for the Patriot system in particular, the DSB further spotlighted a need "to shift its operation and control philosophy to deal with the complex environments of today's and future conflicts," especially conflicts that "will likely be more stressing than [Iraqi Freedom] and [will] involve Patriot in simultaneous missile and air defense engagements." Key to such a system improvement, the DSB concluded, will be "a protocol that allows more operator oversight and control of major system actions."[21]

Despite such efforts to get to the bottom of the fratricide incidents and correct their causes, however, General Moseley concluded more than three years after the campaign ended that the Patriot problem "is still not fixed."[22] For its part, the Army would say for public consumption only that "application of lessons learned . . . has already improved upon Patriot's performance and the system will be continuously refined. . . . Some changes include the integration of satellite radio technology at the battalion information coordination center which provides improved situational awareness through voice and data connectivity with higher headquarters identification and engagement authority, as well as enhanced command and control and software improvements that enable better identification, classification, and correlation of airborne objects."[23]

The Army's Patriot operators were not the only ones culpable in inadvertent friendly fire occurrences. Air-to-*ground* fratricide was also significant during the three weeks of major combat. An especially notable incident took place on March 23 when a two-ship element of Air Force A-10s was targeted against a group of what turned out to be friendlies by a Marine Corps ground FAC and subsequently fired on those troops near An Nasiriyah, disabling tanks, APCs, and Humvees and killing an undetermined number of Marines. In what the official history of I MEF's contribution to the campaign later characterized as "arguably . . . the most notorious friendly fire incident of the war," that A-10 formation (call sign Gyrate 73) responded to a call for immediate CAS from the commander of Bravo Company of the 2nd Marine Regiment's 1st Battalion, which had been assigned the mission of securing two bridges on Highway 8 over the Euphrates River (the southern bridge) and Saddam Canal (the northern bridge) in An Nasiriyah. The account noted that the A-10 was "usually a welcome sight on the battlefield and had already done good work on March 23 against other targets. But now it was bearing down on friendlies."[24]

A postmortem report on the incident issued by a CENTAF investigating board two months later noted that "witness statements and testimony indicate that the majority of [friendly] casualties were most likely caused by friendly fire." The report went on to say, however: "Considering information made available upon reconvening, this is no longer the board's opinion. . . . Of those 18 Marines [killed during the encounter], it is the opinion of the board that enemy fire killed 8 Marines. Due to the mixture of intense enemy fire, combined with friendly fire from Gyrate 73 flight, the board is unable to determine, by clear and convincing evidence, which type of fire killed the remaining 10 Marines." In a cover memorandum forwarding the report to General Franks, General Moseley noted that "the investigating board concluded that the primary cause of the incident was a lack of coordination regarding the location of friendly forces due to a number of contributing factors."[25]

A subsequent CENTCOM assessment of the incident issued on March 6, 2004, reported that the battalion's Charlie Company "began taking heavy enemy fire from artillery, rocket-propelled grenades (RPGs), mortar and small-arms fire. At approximately the same time, the air officer, located with the forward command post, called the Bravo Company forward air controller (FAC) ... requesting CAS to combat enemy forces attacking their location. . . . The A-10s targeted what turned out to be Charlie Company assets, making multiple passes against them. Eventually, the A-10s were told to cease fire, which they did."[26]

The CENTCOM assessment reconstructed the incident as follows:

> The Bravo Company commander, collocated with the FAC, directed the FAC to engage the targets north of the canal. The A-10s spotted a burning vehicle (thought to be an enemy vehicle, but turned out to be a damaged Charlie Company vehicle) north of the bridge and reported it to the FAC, who could see the smoke and verified that it was in the target area. . . . The FAC was not able to see the A-10s or a specific target. Therefore, he confirmed the target location with the A-10s and attempted to verify the location of the lead element with the Bravo Company commander. . . . Based on the information he possessed concerning the [unit's] scheme of maneuver [and] believing that only enemy forces were ahead, [the Bravo Company commander] cleared the target for fire. No additional authorization was sought. The FAC informed the A-10s that there were no friendly forces north of the bridge and they were cleared to engage.[27]

In his cover memorandum forwarding the assessment, CENTCOM's commander at the time, Gen. John Abizaid, recommended "a reexamination of joint doctrine as it relates to Type III CAS control." He also recommended that the Marine Corps consider "appropriate administrative or disciplinary action against the Bravo Company FAC" who called in the A-10s.[28] With respect to the latter recommendation, a press account that appeared several weeks after the incident reported that the A-10 pilots had been repeatedly cleared to engage what were thought to be paramilitary Fedayeen Saddam fighters by a "disoriented" Marine Corps ground FAC who was located behind the Marine company's position.[29] Essentially bearing out that early report, a Marine Corps publication issued in September 2009 confirmed that CENTCOM's incident investigation "logically concluded that the cause of the incident was the [FAC's] violation of a standing order not to use Type III [the least stringent form of CAS] without approval from higher headquarters. If he had contacted the battalion commander, he would have known that friendly forces were north of the Saddam Canal. Even if he failed to make contact with the battalion commander but still adhered to the standing order, the incident would not have occurred."[30] (The incident, it bears noting, erupted after a group of Iraqi troops had begun firing on the Marines after having first pretended to surrender.)[31]

On March 27 an A-10 mistakenly strafed another group of Marines, a regimental combat team that had become caught up in a firefight and had requested immediate fire support. The A-10 pilot was given an incorrect grid zone designator that had the Marine combat team right in the middle of it. Thus improperly cued, the A-10 pilot misidentified the friendly unit as hostile and was cleared to engage it with his 30-mm cannon. This time, remarkably, no one was hurt.[32]

A week after the fratricidal Tornado GR4 downing, an A-10 attacked two British Army Scimitar armored reconnaissance vehicles, killing one British soldier. In another fratricide incident involving British forces, an A-10 on March 28, 2003, mistook reconnaissance elements from D Squadron of the British Army's Household Cavalry for Iraqi forces and in two consecutive engagements with them left one British trooper dead and three wounded.[33] In a similar incident, an American SOF team aiding Kurdish forces called in two fighters to attack an Iraqi tank that was firing at them from a mile away. Instead, one of the fighters mistakenly dropped a bomb on the Kurdish convoy, killing eighteen Kurds and injuring three American soldiers.

Finally, three U.S. Army soldiers were killed and six were wounded near Baghdad International Airport on April 2 when an F-15E inadvertently struck their position in a quick-reaction attack against what its crew thought was an active Iraqi SAM site. The 3rd ID's after-action assessment assigned responsibility to an uncoordinated and improper attempt by the CAOC to engage targets inside the FSCL: "Much to their credit, [V] Corps was able to stop a total of 14 of these attempts. However, an F-15E under CFACC control was successful in one attempt. The F-15E misidentified an MLRS [multiple-launch rocket system] as a [SAM] launcher approximately 15 miles from his position. The pilot found 14 vehicles in that area and asked permission from [AWACS] to engage those targets. . . . The end state was fratricide—3 killed in action, 6 wounded in action, and 3 vehicles destroyed. This is unacceptable."[34]

The Army report cited combat identification errors; fatal navigation errors; a loss of fire control; errors in reporting, battle tracking, and clearance to fire; ineffective maneuver control; and either weapons errors or failures in troop discipline as the primary causes of the fratricide incidents. The report concluded that the likelihood of future air-to-ground fratricide incidents could best be reduced through such means as standardized tactical air controller training and equipment across all U.S. forces. The use of standardized geographic designation systems, cross-checking battlespace information, and ensuring that all friendly aircraft remain within assigned boundaries through proper preparation and detailed intelligence was also crucial. Proper maintenance of situation awareness and understanding at the lowest level along with the marking and positive identification of targets, both day and night, was also essential. As for ways of minimizing the likelihood of surface-to-air incidents, the report emphasized proper IFF procedures, the development and standardization of battlefield identification systems, and positive identification of targets.[35]

In his assessment of the Tornado episode and other instances of fratricide over the three-week course of the campaign, Air Marshal Torpy conceded that occasional fratricide in warfare is simply "one of the facts of life. It is our job to make sure that those tragic incidents are reduced to the absolute minimum."[36] Although the GR4's downing temporarily strained the trust relationship between the British and American contingents, General Franks later echoed the ultimate British sentiment on the matter when he commented: "When there are friendly fire incidents across coalition boundaries, it brings allies closer together."[37] After the incident, the British contingent made appropriate adjustments to the rules of engagement and the manner in which the U.S. Army's Patriot was employed.

The Failed Apache Deep-Attack Attempt

Although air-land integration within CENTCOM had significantly improved prior to Iraqi Freedom, the long-standing discontinuity between Air Force and Army cultures with respect to how best to draw down and neutralize an enemy's ground forces nonetheless resurfaced during the campaign's initial days. Air Force proponents in the CAOC argued in favor of using fixed-wing air power to degrade enemy force capability to the greatest extent possible *before* allied ground units moved to direct contact, while their Army counterparts insisted that early close ground force engagement with the enemy was the ideal mode of operations. Such thinking clearly underlay the Army's abortive attempt to conduct an independent deep attack against a concentration of Republican Guard forces by a formation of AH-64 Apaches without prior preparation of the battlespace by fixed-wing air power.

In a move that appears to have been completely uncoordinated with CENTCOM's air component, the V Corps commander, Lieutenant General Wallace, approved a staff request to launch a deep attack mission that would send

AH-64 Apache attack helicopters from the 11th Attack Helicopter Regiment (AHR) to engage three brigades and the organic artillery of the Republican Guard's Medina Division deployed northeast of Karbala and south of Baghdad. The Apache community had been itching to get a piece of the action from the campaign's very start. A postcampaign review of Army operations noted that "some pilots had compared this attack to the 101st Aviation Brigade's legendary deep attack operation in Operation Desert Storm; they too were going to be heroes. Their frustration continued to build, adding to the 11th [AHR's] collective desire to get into the fight."[38]

The attack was plagued by a host of miscalculations from the very outset of mission planning. First, because the corridor near An Najaf through which the Apache crews would penetrate to their assigned targets was lightly populated, planners elected to forgo the normal precursor suppressive fire, principally by artillery. Second, the regiment lacked adequate situation awareness of the target area because the *shamal* had grounded the UAVs that would have provided the Apache crews with refined target coordinates. Because of spotty and incomplete intelligence reporting on the disposition of Iraqi forces in the area where the attack was to be concentrated, the regiment's pilots lacked specific grid locations for their targets and had only rough approximations, within a kilometer or so, of Iraqi company positions. Essentially, they would have to grope about in a calculated way to find the enemy forces.[39]

In addition, the speed of the 3rd ID's northward advance during the preceding two days made it necessary to move the Apache attack up twenty-four hours. Although nine potential ingress routes had been initially considered and proposed by the 11th AHR, only three southern routes were ultimately approved by V Corps due to concern at headquarters that use of the western approach options would encroach on airspace that had been allocated to the 101st Airborne Division. To make matters worse, friendly convoys bearing fuel and ammunition had been delayed by traffic jams, and inadequate fuel supplies at the planned point of departure necessitated dropping one of the three squadrons of Apaches from the attack plan. (Sixty AH-64s had been flown into a staging area at Objective Rams to marshal for the planned attack.)[40]

The lack of close coordination with the air component resulted in several problems. First, no prior dedicated fixed-wing defense suppression was requested or provided. On top of that, allied aircraft overhead in CAS stacks and supporting friendly artillery units were not notified of a two-hour delay in the planned launch of the attack, and thirty-one ATACMS missiles were fired on a preplanned schedule into the intended target area before the Apaches had even left their marshalling area at Objective Rams, a miscue that warned the enemy of an impending attack. By the time the Apaches reached the target area, allied fixed-wing strike aircraft that had been holding in CAS stacks overhead had departed as a result of low fuel states, leaving the Apache crews without available CAS in case it should be needed.[41]

In the end, at 0115 local time on March 24, only thirty of the initial planned contingent of sixty Apaches got safely airborne, one of the AH-64s having crashed during takeoff after its crew became disoriented by swirling dust. Once aloft and in their prebriefed ingress formation, the thirty Apaches proceeded along the fifty-mile route to the designated target area, flying one hundred feet above the ground and maintaining a nose-to-tail separation of fifteen rotor lengths. Few of the Apaches ever got close enough for their crews to engage the enemy. As their final attack run was under way, the power grid in the An Najaf area went black for a few seconds, most likely as a signal to Iraqi gunners that the Apaches were en route to their objective. When the lead element of the Apache formation neared the target area, the defending Iraqi forces opened fire. Aware that the Apaches would have to ascend to two hundred feet to clear the power lines, Iraqi gunners aimed their streams of fire above the power lines, and the helicopters flew into a fusillade of enemy fire. One Apache was downed and its two-man crew captured.[42]

Enemy gunfire damaged all but one of the Apaches. On average, each sustained sixteen to twenty bullet holes. Sixteen helicopters suffered damage to main rotor blades, six to tail blades, six to engines, and five to engine driveshafts. During their hasty withdrawal from the target area, two of the Apaches barely avoided a midair collision. For their efforts, the 11th AHR successfully attacked a dozen Iraqi vehicles. A month would go by before the regiment was fully ready for combat again. The land component staff subsequently came to believe that the Apaches' assembly areas in the Iraqi desert had been under surveillance. General Wallace also subsequently told reporters that an Iraqi major general in An Najaf had used a cellular telephone to warn the Iraqi defenders that a wave of AH-64s was heading toward their position near Karbala.[43] Wallace freely granted that the attempted operation "did not meet the objectives that [he] had set for that attack" and concluded that "deep operations with Apaches, unless there's a very, very, very clear need to do it, are probably not a good idea."[44]

In the immediate wake of the failed attack, the 101st Airborne Division's attack aviation units shifted their mission focus from nighttime deep attack operations to armed reconnaissance, and the planning for a second Apache foray against Karbala on March 28 clearly incorporated lessons learned from the many mistakes made during the lead-up to the first.[45] For a time, a later report noted, V Corps leadership "debated whether to attempt the mission at all," but eventually they gave the green light.[46] Precursor defense suppression attacks and on-call CAS from allied fixed-wing air power were better coordinated for this attack, and the Apache crews now had their flanks protected by F/A-18s and other fixed-wing aircraft. This time, the 101st Aviation Brigade "relied heavily on its air liaison officer, who in turn requested an airborne forward air controller . . . on the mission to ensure [that] CAS would be coordinated directly between fixed- and rotary-wing aircraft."[47] Also, the raid was preceded by four minutes of preparatory artillery fire to pin down any Iraqi gunners who might have been lying in wait for the attackers, and the Apache crews expressly avoided any built-up areas from which concealed man-portable infrared SAMs and small arms fire might emanate.

Moreover, the Apaches were led this time by Kiowa Warrior scout helicopters that were sent in to validate targets first. The Apaches destroyed seven Iraqi AAA positions, three artillery positions, five radars, and twenty-five vehicles, with no Apache losses, but this second performance still left much to be desired in terms of the ultimate payoff achieved for the effort and risk that went into it. After that, V Corps abandoned any further pursuit of deep attack air operations, and its use of Apaches was generally limited to providing organic armed reconnaissance and close-in CAS for Army ground units.

As for the good-news part of this story, the unsuccessful deep attack attempt on March 24 was the *only* major Army setback during the entire three-week campaign. And it resulted in significantly improved air-ground coordination. After that failed effort, the Army's vice chief of staff, Gen. John Keane, pointedly asked: "Does our doctrine still make sense?" General Keane admitted that the Apache formation "ran into an organization that was much more spread out" than had been expected. As a result, he said, "we are taking a look at aviation doctrine and how to use Apaches at long distances." Subsequently, the land component routinely requested Air Force A-10s to suppress enemy ground fire before planned Apache operations. "In other words," said General Keane, "we had air power with them as well."[48] General Wallace later reported that once this arrangement was in place, "the U.S. Air Force had a heyday against those repositioning Iraqi forces."[49]

The Army's postcampaign assessment candidly admitted that the Apache experience "will affect how the Army trains and equips units for years to come."[50] The assessment noted that the incident "placed in question the efficacy and utility of attack helicopters in Army doctrine" and attributed its shortcomings to the centrality of "the human ego in war" and "the indomitable warrior spirit to get into the fight."[51] In a remarkably unflinching display of frank institutional introspection, the assessment concluded that "the Army will need to consider under what conditions flying attack helicopters deep will produce the kind of benefits that warrant the potential risk."[52]

Most Air Force airmen would readily agree with this judgment. Without question, the flawed and ultimately abortive deep-attack attempt by the 11th AHR showed yet again the limited ability of even the best attack helicopters to cover extended areas of terrain and to conduct precision attacks in heavily defended airspace when compared with far more versatile fixed-wing fighter aircraft. At more than $30 million a copy in today's dollars, an Army AH-64 costs roughly the same as an Air Force F-16, yet it lacks the F-16's range, persistence, striking power, and survivability. Mindful of that comparative performance limitation, former Air Force chief of staff Gen. Merrill McPeak suggested in a post-campaign comment that the Army should limit its use of the Apache to CAS or, "if it must go deep, hand it over [to the air component] for joint tasking."[53]

Inefficiencies in Controlling Joint Battlespace by V Corps

Doctrinally imposed limitations on the joint delivery of fire support, especially with respect to the placement and use of the FSCL, were a continuing bone of contention between the air and land components that many airmen felt needlessly inhibited the most effective application of joint fires in support of V Corps. David Johnson called differences regarding the management of battlespace "the single greatest issue between the Army and the Air Force" and put "Army deep attack concepts and the placement of the FSCL . . . at the heart of the matter."[54] Michael Knights expressed the same line of thought in his apt observation that "battlespace is a jealously hoarded commodity in modern warfare."[55]

The FSCL was the primary fire support mechanism for dividing CENT-COM's battlespace between the land and air components. Any enemy terrain on the *far* side of the FSCL was essentially a free-fire zone for the air component because there could be no possibility of friendly troops coming into contact with enemy ground forces in that portion of the battlespace. All kill boxes on that side of the FSCL were open to attacks from the air. The terrain on the *near* side of the FSCL was the land component's battlespace. Kill boxes that lay within that terrain were closed to attack from the air unless the land component commander expressly opened them for a finite window of time to permit air attacks under the control of properly trained and certified FAC-As or ground-based JTACs who were tasked by the ASOC supporting V Corps.

During the initial allied ground advance into Iraq, General McKiernan, with General Franks' concurrence, extended the FSCL to eighty-four miles ahead of the line of advancing coalition ground forces. (The one exception was the transitory opening of kill boxes by V Corps during the "operational pause" prompted by the three-day *shamal*.) The extended FSCL put an additional strain on the tankers supporting CENTAF's strike fighters because the latter had to fly farther north in order to provide effective interdiction and CAS. General McKiernan similarly moved the FSCL forward dozens of miles in front of coalition forces to facilitate the Apache assault planned for March 24. That decision, observed General Leaf, "cost us [the air component] . . . a full night of fixed-target strikes inside the FSCL. We—the entire coalition team—had not hit our stride in achieving the command and control required to operate in volume effectively inside the fire support coordination line."[56]

This problem could have been easily anticipated and headed off had V Corps' most senior planners harked back to very similar situations that had arisen during Operation Desert Storm. In his presentation to the Commission on Roles and Missions in September 1994, then Air Force chief of staff General McPeak noted Army commanders' decision, on the third day of the ground offensive, to fix the FSCL well beyond their ability to affect the close battle with their own organic artillery and attack helicopters. In doing so, the XVIII Airborne Corps commander prevented the air component from interdicting the main resupply line connecting Baghdad and Kuwait for seventeen hours. General McPeak mentioned a similar extension of the FSCL inside the Kuwaiti theater of operations by the VII Corps commander that had essentially created a sanctuary for Republican Guard units, whose commanders took advantage of the opportunity to escape to Basra. Although the overall joint force commander, Gen. H. Norman Schwarzkopf, had expressly directed the air component commander, Lt. Gen. Charles Horner, to engage and destroy those forces, Schwarzkopf's ground commanders, according to McPeak, "unilaterally placed boundaries that effectively contradicted [Schwarzkopf's] theater priorities." That, said McPeak, showed clearly "what can happen when boundaries are set by people who do not have full authority over military operations on both sides of the seam."[57] An Air Force pilot who served as an ALO with the 101st Airborne Division during Desert Storm pointed out that a big part of the problem was an outdated conception of "close air support." As this pilot bluntly put it, "what we really have is either air power applied in close proximity to troops or air power applied *not* in close proximity to troops. Definitions and lines on maps that don't allow the flexibility required by nonlinear battle plans should be scrapped."[58]

In the case of air component KI/CAS planning on behalf of V Corps in Iraqi Freedom, the coordination in ATO preparation was conducted through the Army's BCD in the CAOC. V Corps positioned FSCLs farther ahead of the forward line of friendly troops than usual because of an anticipated rapid rate of advance. An assistant to General Leaf recalled on this point: "Every day, General Leaf would arrange for the FSCL to be pulled a little back, but every night the Army majors would throw it far out again."[59] The land component would then request ground support sorties from the CAOC through the normal process. Within the V Corps area of operations, General McKiernan opened and closed kill boxes for interdiction attacks as he deemed appropriate, and the Air Force ASOC attached to V Corps provided terminal attack control for CAS strikes.

There was on occasion a pronounced disconnect between the CAOC and the Air Force's battlefield airmen who staffed the ASOC supporting V Corps with respect to the proper roles and responsibilities of an ASOC, with each entity harboring a different understanding of how land combat operations between a division's line of advance and the FSCL should be conducted.[60] Indeed, as one CAOC planner later recalled, "the single greatest issue that arose during Iraqi Freedom concerned the prosecution of counterland targets in the V Corps area."[61] Much of the difficulty alluded to here emerged from contrasting perspectives *within* the air component as to how best to employ fixed-wing air power in support of counterland operations. The CAOC planners who had developed CENTAF's KI/CAS concept of operations insisted that unless friendly forces were present in a way that absolutely required detailed air-land integration, the kill boxes in that particular area should be opened for unrestricted air operations as targets of opportunity presented themselves. For its part, the ASOC sought instead to extract the most from the air component assets that were available to it by means of a procedure called "corps CAS."

V Corps used the term "corps CAS" to refer to its intended use of CAOC-supplied air power to prosecute or shape targets in its assigned area of operations. Yet from the CAOC's perspective, certain aspects of that concept needlessly hampered the shaping effort. For example, V Corps and its supporting ASOC considered the aerial engagement of *any* target on their side of the FSCL to be CAS, which, by definition, requires rigorous and time-consuming communications and command and control procedures. Yet in the view of those in the CAOC, those complicated CAS procedures were not required because the "corps shaping" in question was not conducted in even remote proximity to friendly ground troops.

Indeed, from the CAOC's perspective, "corps CAS" was not CAS at all. It was de facto interdiction, which, according to accepted joint doctrine, lies beyond the roles and responsibilities of an ASOC. CAOC planners recalled that "the V Corps area of operations began at the division's forward boundary, approximately fifteen nautical miles ahead of the forward line of own troops (FLOT), and extended to the FSCL. . . . Unfortunately, the ASOC was unable to conduct corps CAS at a rate commensurate with the number of air assets that were allocated to it."[62] As one might expect, friction ensued when the ASOC requested air support and then used it to conduct what were essentially battlefield interdiction operations. The ASOC also encountered problems in exercising the required degree of command and control throughout its assigned battlespace because the rapid forward movement of coalition ground troops typically exceeded the ASOC's ability to communicate with CAS aircraft. As a result, there were often times when a large percentage of the aircraft sent by the CAOC to an airborne CAS stack in V Corps' area of operations at the request of the ASOC were not used and had to return to their bases with unexpended ordnance. This inefficient force management exasperated aircrews. One F-16 pilot complained:

> We'd take off without a target, fly for eight hours trying to get someone on the ground to give us something to drop on, and then we'd come home with our bombs on board. It was frustrating for guys who wanted to feel like they'd contributed to the mission. [So a friend of mine who was a CAOC planner] sent us an e-mail saying, "Okay, I hear you guys. We're going to start Operation Home Depot, and we're going to go out in the desert and build you some targets so you can drop your bombs!" That made us laugh, but what he was really saying to us was that we'd still done our jobs, even if we came home with all our bombs.[63]

To be sure, such recurrent "no-drop" incidents were by no means invariably the fault of the ASOC's close control of open kill boxes in its battlespace at the insistence of V Corps. Some instances involving aircraft that had been holding overhead in CAS stacks to support V Corps rightly suggested a basic force utilization deficiency within the system.[64] Yet in other cases, weapons bring-back did not necessarily indicate a misutilization problem so much as the natural inefficiency that is part and parcel of CAS operations. Factors that affected the weapons bring-back rate ranged from an absence of assigned targets to communications problems, a lack of available tankers, and a less than ideal allocation of CAS assets by the ASOC.

The CAOC did indeed use bring-back rate as one measure of the efficiency of air support to the land component. Without more specific facts that might account for the number of prospective targets that went unserviced, however, weapons bring-back numbers did not, in and of themselves, provide a reliable measure of mission effectiveness. Simple communications deficiencies occasioned an appreciable number of combat aircraft returning to their bases without their pilots' having even established radio contact with the ASOC. Added to that, the initial shortage of available tankers and the considerable distances that orbiting strike aircraft had to travel to return to their bases sometimes meant that those aircraft could not deliver their munitions within the scant on-station time they were allowed.[65]

But the main problem lay in the fact that the common geographic reference system based on kill boxes and keypads had never been formally ratified in joint doctrine. Accordingly, Army operators did not naturally accept that system in their own tactical contingency planning. Although the kill-box approach had been amply validated as an effective alternative to the FSCL in Desert Storm and had since been refined in a succession of combat-related SPINs, the FSCL for its Army benefactors continued to be a more familiar and comfortable artifact signifying Army ownership and control of joint battlespace.

The senior CAOC director later reported that the Army's principals in the land component had agreed before the start of Iraqi Freedom to accede to the kill-box method but had reverted to the classic FSCL approach once the fight was under way.[66] CENTAF had offered training on kill-box operations to V Corps prior to the campaign, but the latter "chose instead to concentrate on other phases of their spin-up training. As a result, when the war started, their staff was not familiar with kill-box operations or the KI/CAS concept of operations, having never practiced it. So they fell back on more traditional methods that were less appropriate for the rapidly advancing ground situation."[67]

Viewed in hindsight, CENTAF was itself largely to blame for the situation. The commander of the USAF Air Ground Operations School at Nellis AFB at the time the Army's spin-up training for the looming campaign was in full swing recalled that "the big lesson I learned—and have continued to learn since 2003—is that the 'good idea cutoff point' for a major Army event is the mission rehearsal exercise (MRX). The final [CENTAF] KI/CAS planning occurred while V Corps was doing its MRX in Poland. Like it or not, the Air Force missed the opportunity to get kill-box operations integrated into the Army's planning for the event. When we went in after the fact and attempted to change peoples' minds or add a new way to do business, we failed."[68]

The Air Force ASOC that was supporting V Corps was organized, trained, and equipped to prosecute CAS missions with an FSCL positioned only some eighteen to twenty-two miles forward of the FLOT. Extending the FSCL out-ward to eighty-four miles allowed General McKiernan and his subordinate com-manders to control a larger portion of the battlespace in front of their advancing units, an entirely appropriate fires management measure for a linear engagement against massed enemy ground forces in open terrain. Yet Operation Iraqi Free-dom was envisaged and planned to include nonlinear engagements in or near congested urban areas.[69] By pushing the FSCL some sixty miles farther out than normal, V Corps' commander extended the battlespace beyond his force's abil-ity to deliver usable combat effects. As one airman pithily put it, "Although the Army has some organic assets that can reach out to targets that far away from the FLOT (i.e., ATACMS), for the most part, most organic fires for the Army can only affect targets at a range of 32 kilometers, or about 20 miles. From 20 miles to the 84-mile FSCL is essentially a sanctuary for the enemy."[70]

Indeed, some Air Force airmen viewed V Corps' unusual extension of the FSCL as directly contravening the guidance promulgated in Joint Publication 3–0, *Doctrine for Joint Operations*, which stipulates that "placement of the FSCL should strike a balance so as not to unduly inhibit operational tempo while maximizing the effectiveness of organic and joint force interdiction assets."[71] In a similar spirit, Joint Publication 3–09, *Doctrine for Joint Fire Support*, stipulates that "the decision on where to place or even whether to use an FSCL requires care-ful consideration. If used, its location is based on estimates of the situation and [concepts of operations]. Location of enemy forces, anticipated rates of move-ment, the concept and tempo of the operation, organic weapon capabilities, and other factors are all considered by the commander. . . . Placing the FSCL at greater depths will typically require support from higher organic [headquarters] and other supporting commanders."[72] For its part, Air Force Doctrine Docu-ment 2–1.3, *Counterland Operations*, specifies that "the optimum placement of the FSCL varies with specific battlefield circumstances, but typically it should be placed where the preponderance of effects on the battlefield shifts from the ground component to the air component. In this way, the FSCL placement maximizes the overall effectiveness of the joint force, and each component will suffer only a small reduction in efficiency."[73] During at least portions of the three-week campaign, V Corps clearly failed to honor these accepted stipula-tions of joint doctrine.

In fairness to General Wallace and his preferred approach to managing the battlespace on his side of the FSCL, however, a subsequent assessment of issues in command and control in air warfare rightly noted that the air component's inability to track the effects of its operations figured prominently in justifying the V Corps commander's determination to maintain close control over deep operations in his immediate area of regard. According to this account,

> Army officers who worked for the BCD in the CAOC . . . pointed out that the inability of the air component to determine and communicate the effects of air power was the biggest source of friction between the air and land components. As the ground troops made their way through the sandstorms, they needed to know how big an effect the [air] attacks were having on the Iraqi Republican Guard units. When the storms were finished, even General McKiernan, the CFLCC [combined force land component commander, pronounced "see-flick"], was unable to pinpoint weaknesses in the enemy toward which he could have directed offensive actions to fracture them. . . . The air component's practice of satisfying many of the land component's air support requests (ASRs) with kill-box interdiction did not give land commanders visibility into the results. . . . These were missions sent to a patch of airspace, not to a target, so the land component was unable to tell whether its requests were being serviced by the air component.[74]

The assessment concluded on this point that "the components had good relationships at the top, and they had worked out a joint strategy. Nonetheless, they had different and somewhat incompatible local systems for developing and tracking target data."[75] In explaining this disconnect, the assessment noted that Wallace viewed corps shaping as more effective than KI: "His data showed that enemy strength did not decrease appreciably after KI, but did after his Corps shaping."[76] In a postcampaign interview that further helped explain his preference for corps shaping over kill-box interdiction, Wallace recalled that every advance by V Corps troops at the platoon through brigade levels during the three-week land offensive ultimately became a "movement to contact" because his command had been consistently unable to acquire a clear picture of enemy force dispositions.[77]

More telling yet, Wallace observed that from his vantage point, the corps-shaping sorties that had serviced targets beyond the 3rd ID's forward boundary "were 270 percent more effective [in terms of targets destroyed per sortie] than kill box interdiction in V Corps' [area of operations.]" He freely conceded that with respect to the contentious issue of the FSCL versus KI as the preferred battlespace management tool, "both control measures are commonly used," the use

of both entails "a continuous debate across the services," and "doctrinal definitions and [the] use of both are not consistent across the services."[78]

After acknowledging the need for the Army and the Air Force to reconcile
these unsettled issues, Wallace addressed complaints that V Corps had "pushed
the FSCL too deep during [the campaign] and made attack short of the FSCL
difficult." He countered by noting that it was CENTCOM (with inputs from
the CFLCC), not V Corps or its ASOC, that determined FSCL placement; that
the FSCL was usually no more than thirty nautical miles from the FLOT during the three-week campaign; that the FSCL was more than fifty nautical miles
deep for only eight hours (less than 2 percent) during the campaign, and was
more than twenty nautical miles deep for only three days (less than 15 percent
of the campaign).[79]

Wallace's recollections provide an important backdrop against which to
examine the practical import of the assessed inefficiencies in joint battlespace
management. Clearly, the CAOC, on the one hand, and the CAOC's subordinate
ASOC that was channeling air support to V Corps, on the other, had contrasting
views with respect to the relative effectiveness of corps shaping versus kill-box
interdiction. In this regard, the lead author of the most thorough account of
Army operations during the three-week campaign was on solid ground in noting that "the CAOC versus ASOC differences [reflected] an internecine argument within the Air Force and not between the Air Force and Army."[80] From
the perspective of V Corps, however, the ASOC clearly met the command's
tactical- and operational-level needs throughout the land offensive. In all, 2,117
CAS missions were assigned to the ASOC, with 625 of those missions retasked
to other agencies. The ASOC itself thus controlled 1,492 missions, 886 of which
were so-called corps-shaping missions. Of all the corps-shaping missions, 525
(or 62 percent) ultimately dropped ordnance. In the case of division CAS, 307
of 606 missions (51 percent) dropped ordnance against valid targets. As one
authoritative assessment of this performance later reported, "combining those
two mission areas [corps shaping and division CAS], 55 percent of the missions
executed by the ASOC and its subordinate TACPs dropped munitions on valid
targets. That percentage is by far the highest ever seen in major combat."[81]

General Wallace carefully avoided taking sides in the intra–Air Force and
cross-service disagreements over the relative merits of ASOC-controlled corps
shaping versus CAOC-controlled KI/CAS. Instead, he offered an equitable
solution by concluding that achieving desired effects against enemy force dispositions as expeditiously as possible is what matters most in the air-ground
interface. Toward that end, he added, "the FSCL, if retained, must be modified

to facilitate rapid joint attack short of the FSCL" and "kill boxes, if used, must be more precise" because "joint effects in complex terrain demands it."[82] Of greatest importance by far with respect to the proclaimed inefficiencies in air apportionment discussed above is that the V Corps commander himself, the ultimate Army consumer of the air component's contribution to the land battle, was, by all indications, more than content with the CAS that he and his troops received throughout the three weeks of major fighting.[83]

A Marine Corps Approach That Arguably Worked Better

In marked contrast to the issues that divided the CAOC and ASOC with respect to battlespace management in V Corps' area of operations, General Moseley so trusted the MAGTF approach to air-land combat, and the Marines who were implementing it, that he delegated authority to I MEF to control the airspace above its immediate area of operations. As a result, I MEF created its own direct support ATO for execution by the 3rd Marine Aircraft Wing, and the Marine tactical air operations center and tactical air control center (TAOC and TACC respectively) opened and closed kill boxes for deep interdiction operations. For close interdiction inside the FSCL, the Marine direct air support center (DASC) provided terminal attack control.

Key to the greater efficiency of I MEF's unique arrangement for integrating CAS assets into the land battle was its willingness to open kill boxes *inside* the FSCL when its battle staff were confident that no friendly forces were present, something V Corps would generally not do. Opening kill boxes inside the FSCL allowed coalition aircraft to attack Iraqi forces without detailed coordination with the DASC and the resulting bottleneck that tended to create. The principal differences between the practices of the DASC and the ASOC supporting V Corps were that the ASOC was aligned at the corps level, was responsible for integrating air power for a multidivision fight, and accepted decentralized execution of allocated air assets, whereas the DASC was aligned at the division level, was responsible for integrating *all* organic Marine Corps firepower, and envisaged centralized combined arms execution in support of the MEF commander.

The DASC, assigned the radio call sign Blacklist, was configured much like the TACC but on a smaller scale. It coordinated with the fire support coordination center that was organic to the 1st Marine Division. Its operations staff, the "Dascateers," also handled emerging target requests that came in from outside normal Marine Corps channels. When Marine air operations ranged more deeply into Iraq beyond the normal radio range of the ground-based DASC, it was augmented by an airborne DASC (the DASC-A), with the assigned call sign

Sky Chief, on board a Marine Corps KC-130 to provide better communications connectivity across the entire span of the battlespace.[84]

By almost all accounts, the DASC supporting I MEF was able to integrate more fires into the Marines' battlespace for CAS and interdiction than was the ASOC assigned to V Corps. Particularly during the initial days of combined air-land operations, the ASOC was able to integrate an average of six combat sorties into the fight per hour, whereas the DASC was able to integrate twice that amount of air support in a smaller area in the same amount of time. An informed Air Force airman later noted that the well-trained DASC controllers' ability to make effective use of excess air component strike sorties in their zone "got to the point where Air Force KI/CAS pilots all wanted to go to the Marine sector where they knew they'd have a better chance of putting bombs on a meaningful target."[85] (Eventually, as joint air-ground operations hit their stride, the ASOC too became able to integrate CAS sorties more efficiently in closer keeping with I MEF's well-honed approach. Once that occurred, General Leaf noted, FSCL placement became less an issue as the air and land components succeeded in improving the coordination of their operations within kill boxes.)[86]

Even so, I MEF's fire support coordination measures in combination with its command and control arrangement generally allowed CENTAF aircraft supplying on-call CAS to provide more responsive fire support than did V Corps, whose less permissive arrangement created inefficiencies. In V Corps' area of operations, the ASOC was frequently overburdened by the land component's requirement for terminal attack control between the forward line of friendly troops and the FSCL for any open kill boxes. As a result, the ASOC was forced to turn away sorties that could have been effectively used to shape the battlefield. I MEF avoided this problem by dividing the area between the forward line of friendly troops and the FSCL with a battlefield coordination line (BCL) and by using *two* agencies—the DASC for terminal attack control between the forward line of friendly troops and the TAOC for tactical control between the BCL and FSCL.

As the campaign unfolded, short-range aircraft such as the Marine Corps' AV-8B Harriers and AH-1W Cobra attack helicopters and the Air Force's A-10s were generally used in the CAS role, while the longer-range Marine Corps F/A-18s supported I MEF kill-box interdiction requirements and the air component's deeper–strike mission needs. As the FSCL moved ever closer to Baghdad, the Marine Corps used a combination of forward basing, organic refueling, and nonorganic refueling from Air Force and RAF tankers to support Marine air operations.[87] With respect to the efficiency of this arrangement, Air Chief Marshal Burridge testified before the British Parliament: "The U.S. Marine

Corps are configured as relatively light forces, and they do not have indigenous deep fires, that is, a lot of artillery. They have very little artillery. Their equivalent of artillery is the Marine Air Wing F/A-18s. They live together very intimately, and their ability to do close air support, both the ground forces' ability to control it and the air's ability to integrate with it, is very impressive, very impressive indeed."[88]

A RAND assessment of persistent air-ground integration issues aptly attested to the contrast in operational styles between the two services in noting that "the Army and Marine Corps commanders largely fought independent campaigns [in Iraqi Freedom], with air power employed as each of these components deemed appropriate."[89] A well-informed survey of command issues ranging from Operation Desert Storm to the major combat phase of Operation Iraqi Freedom summed up the stylistic contrast as follows:

> The Army handled all missions short of the FSCL as CAS and required them to be controlled by the ASOC or a TACP designated by the ASOC. The Marines, on the other hand, chose to create another line . . . [the BCL] . . . which was closer to the ground troops than the FSCL. The Marine DASC opened up kill boxes further out than this BCL—so as a result, air support going into the Marines' sector had a greater chance of being sent to an open kill box than that going to the Army sector. To the aircrew, the difference in flexibility was so stark that pilots regularly requested to be sent to work with the DASC rather than with the ASOC. . . . The difference [was] in the degree of coupling the two services saw in these operations. To the Marines, beyond the BCL, the efforts of the ground and air forces were not tightly coupled and did not need to be closely managed. . . . To the Army, the efforts of the ground and air forces were tightly coupled all the way out to the FSCL. . . . Aircrews were more closely managed, so [V Corps commander General] Wallace had more visibility into the targeting, but the aircrews related it took longer to perform a mission in the Army's sector than in the Marines' sector.[90]

The 3rd ID's after-action assessment of the campaign took note of the superior efficiency offered by the Marine Corps' BCL in managing fixed-wing air assets in air-land warfare and expressly acknowledged that it "facilitates the expeditious attack of surface targets of opportunity between [the BCL and the FSCL]." Calling the BCL "clearly the most permissive measure, but also one that requires a thorough understanding of our doctrine and its use," the assessment concluded that "this measure would give Corps the battlespace they desire for air assets at their disposal" and recommended outright that "U.S. Army doctrine must be changed to incorporate the BCL as [a fire support coordination measure]."[91]

When the land component's northward movement all but ground to a halt during the three-day *shamal* and General McKiernan pulled in the FSCL to just beyond the Euphrates River, the Marine Corps' approach to managing air and ground fire support in common battlespace seemed validated. The shortened FSCL opened up numerous previously forbidden kill boxes for the air component to work. A true air-ground joint concept of operations emerged at that point, producing, as Michael Knights commented, "something akin to the arrangement that had been in place in the MEF sector throughout the war. The MAGTF concept underpinned the difference, allowing U.S. Marines (and their subordinate British division) to fight as a true air-land partnership rather than as a ground and air component trying to get out of each other's way."[92]

The Continuing Need for Closer Joint Force Integration

Among the cross-service problem areas spotlighted by the Iraqi Freedom experience were the acknowledged deficiencies in the Air Force's approach to organizing and manning its ASOCs. The Air Force staffs its ASOCs with officers from assorted operational flying backgrounds and with enlisted personnel from similarly diverse service career fields rather than assigning personnel specifically trained for ASOC operations. This means that there are very few expert Air Force ASOC operators, a situation that naturally perpetuates a general absence of ASOC proficiency and continuity. Further, the service had until recently given its ASOCs less than top billing in its rank ordering of attention and priorities. A senior staffer in the ASOC attached to V Corps during the campaign recalled with brutal frankness in this regard: "The CAOC is a significant piece of the CFACC's planning, command, and control capability, but it is not the entire structure. The CFACC's [ASOC] and subordinate [TACPs] are another significant piece" of that capability. "Unfortunately, prior to [Operation Iraqi Freedom], these [latter] organizations did not enjoy the same USAF focus and resources . . . [and] the USAF had no published [concept] for ASOC operations and [for the ASOC's] subordinate TACPs assigned to the supported land maneuver forces." To make matters worse from a training perspective, until the very start of the campaign, "the ASOC in the 4th ASOG had never exercised with the CAOC. . . . The first time the [V Corps] ASOC actually controlled a strike against a target in the ground commander's [area of operations and] the first time the CAS cell at the CAOC had ever directly worked with ASOC operations was the first day of combat operations." Identified shortfalls in the ASOC at that time "included radio limitations, a lack of a target coordinate generation system, and a lack of interconnectivity with Army targeting systems."[93]

In marked contrast, the Marine Corps has long followed a substantially different approach in its MAGTF organization, which, from top to bottom, is a well-trained and appropriately manned command and control system for closely integrated air-land combat operations. Each MAGTF, wherever it may be deployed worldwide, brings together a TAOC, a DASC, a DASC-A, and a DASC-forward into a coherent arrangement for conducting air-to-ground mission sets in support of a ground combat element commander. Furthermore, MAGTFs are routinely exercised in realistic peacetime training evolutions, and their capabilities and limitations are well determined and understood before the time arrives for them to have to visit fire and steel on enemy targets. CENTAF planners concluded after the major combat phase of Iraqi Freedom that the Marine Corps' approach to command and control in counterland operations would be well worth considering for future contingencies that might entail an ASOC as a subsidiary component of the CAOC.[94]

For their part, Army assessors eventually came to realize the opportunity cost of their traditional practice in situations in which the land component lacked the needed situational awareness and weapons reach to conduct deep attacks inside the FSCL with its own organic assets. The 3rd ID's after-action report freely admitted that "the U.S. Army must redefine the battlespace based on our ability to influence it."[95] The report went on to note that

> the FSCL was 100 kilometers beyond the range of standard munitions from our M109A6s and M270s. This created a dead space between the area that the Army could influence and the area shaped by the [air component]. The placement of the FSCL was so far in front of the forward edge of the battle area that neither divisional nor corps assets could effectively manage the battlespace. . . . The argument seems to be that [the air component] would not adequately address V Corps targeting requirements; 3 ID (M) [3rd Infantry Division, Mechanized] violently disagrees. [The CAOC is] manned and equipped to effectively manage this battlespace forward of the FSCL; V Corps is not and has demonstrated their inability to manage said battlespace. 3 ID (M) believes that [the air component] is better prepared to engage targets to effectively shape the battlefield versus V Corps' use of CAS.[96]

To be sure, cross-service misunderstandings of important service-related specifics did occur. For example, General Franks once asked General Moseley for eight Global Hawks—more than the Air Force had in its entire RQ-4 inventory. Misuse of terminology also sometimes led to misunderstandings between elements of different components in resource allocation, options planning, and execution. And there were at least three reported instances in which U.S. ground units failed to coordinate with the CAOC with respect to long-range ATACMS missiles that were fired into CAOC-controlled airspace. Fortunately, no fratricide incidents resulted from these three communications failures, all of which were attributed to V Corps.[97] An Air Force airman who had commanded an A-10 squadron that was mainly employed in support of SOF operations in Iraqi Freedom summed up the situation: "The air-ground coordination was . . . far from perfect and in many cases didn't exist. Just like Desert Storm, we made it work to support the guys on the ground."[98]

Despite recurrent problems, however, the mutually supporting application of air and land power in common battlespace in Iraqi Freedom represented a major breakthrough in the conduct of joint warfare. General Leaf observed that the campaign experience represented the first time that the American armed forces had conducted a large-scale combat operation with the air and land components working side by side "as equals." The air and land component commanders "achieved conceptual interoperability. . . . This was not [only] communications and software. We really had concepts linked. The real key was the collaborative planning at a senior level." Leaf added: "We used methodology [that was] most appropriate. Sometimes ground preponderance, other times the air, other times in the middle. . . . My staff worked to ensure [that] timing and methodology worked together. For example, airmen usually use latitude and longitude to mark the FSCL, and ground commanders use geographical features. At times when the advance was rapid, airmen used latitude and longitude. At other times, it was necessary to use geographical features. Sometimes a combination was used to set the FSCL. The level of collaboration gave us flexibility, we did it collaboratively."[99] In resounding testimony to the ultimate success of the arrangement, General Wallace declared proudly after the campaign was over that he did not lose a single soldier to an enemy weapon that could have been struck by coalition air power.[100] Throughout the three weeks of major combat in Iraqi Freedom, on-call CAS was overhead and available whenever the land component needed it.

The postcampaign recollections of the participating land and air combatants differ substantially, however, regarding the efficacy of the ASOC arrangement that had been put in place with V Corps in the wake of the near-disaster during Operation Anaconda in Afghanistan. General Wallace later said that he "never heard any of my commanders complain about the availability, responsiveness, or effectiveness of CAS—it was unprecedented."[101] General Moseley, however, in his capacity as the air component commander, described the ASOC arrangement as one of several areas of joint operations that had "worked less well" in meeting General Franks' theater campaign needs and one that definitely warranted a closer "joint look."[102]

General Jumper expressed similar sentiments when he said: "There is a whole lot more we can do better." He added that the services needed to keep talking to one another with respect to better air-ground integration to avoid continued misunderstandings in future conflicts. To cite one telling example, throughout the three weeks of major combat, the land component frequently wanted the air component's CAS providers to fly low, still not realizing that more effective CAS delivery can be provided from as high as 39,000 feet. "Close air support to many can [still] only be defined as airplanes 50 feet above the ground that are releasing something like napalm and creating a lot of heat and a lot of smoke and a lot of noise," General Jumper said. "What you really want," General Jumper argued, "is those bad guys dead."[103]

While both services recognize the need for more realistic joint peacetime training, however, the Air Force and Army have yet to develop and implement approaches to it that would prepare both tactical forces and their operational staffs truly adequately for major counterland warfare. In particular, the tactical-level air-ground exercises that are typically conducted at the Army's National Training Center at Fort Irwin, California, and in the Air Force's associated Air Warrior program conducted out of Nellis AFB, Nevada, have characteristically suffered because the respective training and evaluation objectives of the two services have been so widely inconsistent. The Army—naturally enough—wants to initiate its tactical training engagements at Fort Irwin with a close fight immediately at hand so that its company-grade officers can learn how to understand and conduct high-intensity tank-on-tank warfare. For its part, the Air Force has unsuccessfully sought to start such exercises instead with the ground troops *not* in close contact with the enemy to demonstrate the full potential of air power in air-land warfare.[104] An early draft of JFCOM's postcampaign "lessons learned" assessment was right on target when it insisted that in order to "duplicate the CENTCOM experience" in future major combat operations along the lines of the second Persian Gulf War, "a system that replicates joint operational-level warfare is required."[105]

Finally, in consonance with their U.S. Air Force compatriots, the RAF participants in Iraqi Freedom also found the integration of CAS with land component operations frequently inefficient, especially in the case of integration with British ground units, because of inadequate prior joint training between the RAF and the British Army over the preceding ten years.[106] The RAF's CAS effort was further hampered at times by the inability of airborne aircrews to secure sufficiently refined coordinates for attacking mobile targets. Because ground forces typically plot positions on maps rather than by using GPS, the targeting information provided by those forces often became rapidly outdated, creating a resultant need for aircrews to visually identify mobile targets before attacking them.

The failure of British ground commanders to recognize that CAS aircrews sometimes had go through the appropriate approval channels to clear specific target requests was another point of contention. In general, the MoD's after-action report found that in the area of air-land integration, "operational and tactical doctrine does not yet fully reflect the demands of high-tempo, time-sensitive or network-enabled operations."[107] It further noted that a "lack of experience in requesting, coordinating, and delivering CAS missions . . . was apparent."[108] This was all the more disconcerting given the prevalence of CAS delivery needs in Iraqi Freedom. The report noted that as many as a third of all KI/CAS missions had to be aborted because of problems in the air-land interface (more specifically because V Corps and I MEF were not able to provide tasking for aircraft conducting KI/CAS missions before those aircraft reached bingo fuel state and had to return home).[109]

In explaining why this had occurred, the MoD report observed that Operation Desert Storm had featured an extended and highly focused allied air campaign against fielded Iraqi forces followed by a very brief land offensive in which integrated air-land operations were seldom needed. Operation Enduring Freedom had entailed a closer integration between air and land forces, but the second Persian Gulf War, Air Marshal Torpy observed, was the first military operation in many years "where we have seen such close linkage between the air and land components. . . . We have forgotten some of the things that we were quite good at during the Cold War. . . . We have probably neglected the exercising of those over the years."[110] Now that CAS is an integral part of high-tempo warfare for producing immediate strategic effects, Air Chief Marshal Burridge concluded, "the relationship between air and land is now much, much more important."[111] The MoD report spotlighted identified shortcomings in joint RAF–British Army training for CAS and suggested reassessing the number of

JTACs and FAC-As maintained in service as well as the adequacy of the equipment provided for FAC-As, such as targeting pods with their inherent limits on range and resolution. It also called for using these assets more frequently in the joint training arena.

The many problems with U.S. air-land integration explored in the preceding two sections were expressly recognized in a postwar undertaking in the United Kingdom called Project Coningham-Keyes, a joint initiative between the British Army's Land Command and RAF Strike Command to identify and address current capability shortfalls, with special emphasis on tactical-level execution. That initiative led to high-level joint doctrine for CAS being improved in an October 2003 document called *Joint Air Operations*. Coningham-Keyes focused on training for JTACs and TACPs, with a view toward realigning exercises between the two commands to improve training opportunities. It also examined staff organizations within the land and air component headquarters and considered their interactions. The inquiry determined that there were too few people dealing with the air-land interface and identified an insufficiency of ALOs in ground units. Shortfalls identified by Coningham-Keyes were expected to lead to a virtual doubling of the numbers of certified JTACs and TACPs available to British Army units.[112]

Delays in Battle Damage Assessment

The flaws in CENTCOM's means for conducting and delivering timely, effects-based battle damage assessment (BDA) had been identified as far back as Desert Storm. In an effort to help meet this important progress-tracking need, General Moseley set up an operational assessment team within the CAOC's strategy division to provide a running account of the effects that both kinetic and non-kinetic air operations were having on the Iraqi leadership and armed forces. This assessment process entailed a continuing effort, and its results were folded into a readjustment of targets as needed for the next ATO cycle. In connection with this systematic strategy-to-tasks planning process, the assessment team developed measures of effectiveness for the overall air effort. The CAOC's assessment division likewise contributed to the effort.

Sources of information that went into this process included initial radioed assessments of mission performance by combat aircrews during their return to base, followed by more formal written reports that were then forwarded to the CAOC. Such reporting provided the best immediate insights regarding the results of missions flown against other than preplanned targets, such as on-call CAS attacks. ISR inputs from aircraft targeting pods, cockpit weapons system video, UAV imagery, and satellites went into the reports as well. Obvious indicators of strike effectiveness would be visible signs of destruction due to a successful weapon impact. Second-order indicators might include a sudden absence of electronic emissions or vehicle traffic. Most measures of effectiveness went well beyond simply assessing physical bomb damage.

This process worked reasonably well for fairly slow-paced target attacks such as those conducted throughout Operations Southern Watch and Enduring Freedom. General Moseley's chief strategist, Lieutenant Colonel Hathaway, frankly conceded, however, that in the frenetic atmosphere of Iraqi Freedom, with two thousand sorties a day or more, "there was no way to keep pace with execution."[113] Fortunately, he noted, the initial phases of the air war went essentially as planned, with few significant last-minute adjustments required. But it soon became apparent to Colonel Hathaway and others at CENTCOM that the overall picture of combat achievements "would be neither timely nor complete."[114] CENTCOM's production of BDA was simply unable to keep pace with the speed of air and land operations, a deficiency that in turn undermined munitions effectiveness assessment (MEA) and target reattack recommendations. During CENTAF's lessons learned conference at Nellis AFB in July 2003, General Moseley underscored his own concern regarding this deficiency when he declared emphatically: "Two wars without [a real assessment process] are enough. . . . I never received adequate, timely feedback. I basically had to wait for CENTCOM to produce the official BDA to have any idea of what happened."[115] One account observed that "official BDA" was simply "not timely enough to adjust the ongoing operations. When Moseley told Hathaway to close the loop, Hathaway [and others] . . . worked . . . to figure out what targets had been attacked, based on the mission reports. Then they made some assumptions based on the type of weapons used—precision munitions were given a high probability of hitting the target. It was a 'Band-Aid' on a broken process, but it was the best they could do."[116] As David Johnson described it, "effects-based operations in [Operation Iraqi Freedom] remained more art than science."[117]

Operational-level assessment of combat performance likewise suffered because it depends on reliable BDA and MEA to provide a foundation for further effects-based assessment of strike operations. Because of the rapid advance of allied ground units toward Baghdad after the line of departure was crossed, the CAOC necessarily focused the bulk of its collection efforts on *finding* targets and delegated BDA collection to the bottom of the priorities list. A CENTAF staffer later commented in this respect, "Probably the biggest lesson *not* learned [after the three-week campaign] entailed data collection during mission execution."[118] I MEF's commanding general likewise complained that "target tracking and assessment was extremely difficult. . . . There was no reliable and responsive process or means to determine whether air interdiction (AI) targets on the PTL [priority target list] were serviced and successfully attacked during and after ATO execution. The impact was that targeting personnel/LNOs [liaison officers] could not consistently and reliably provide the necessary feedback to MSC [major subordinate command] commanders that their AI target nominations were being serviced or not."[119]

A major undesirable result of its flawed BDA process was that *all* of CENTCOM's warfighting components, not just the air component, often found themselves short of badly needed real-time situation awareness. To cite one case in point, Colonel Hathaway recalled that

> during the sandstorms on or about the ninth day of execution, the [land component commander], General McKiernan, called General Moseley with concern that the CAOC was hoarding ISR and BDA. General Moseley assured General McKiernan that he [General Moseley] was just as much in the dark with respect to BDA. This lack of timely assessment limited the ability of the [land component] to determine the strength and movement of Iraqi ground forces. That uncertainty forced McKiernan to change his strategy to "maneuver to contact." This was a much less efficient form of offensive maneuver, but it was [nonetheless] necessary due to the unknowns.[120]

Indeed, CENTCOM's BDA process has long been widely regarded, at least among participating airmen at all levels, as unsatisfactory to the point of being useless. Colonel Hathaway observed on this point that the scale and rapidity of the air war "emphasized the weaknesses in the assessment chain, weaknesses that might have resulted in significant fog and friction had the plan not been so well thought out or the enemy more competent."[121] Lack of adequate manning and communications confined the BDA team in the CAOC to collecting and conveying in-flight reports, mission reports, and the fully executed ATO to CENTCOM's forward headquarters so that staffers there could then conduct more detailed assessments of all assigned targets that had been attacked. A CENTAF planner later noted, "Both BDA and combat assessment failed to meet expectations due to the dynamic nature of the ground war, numerous ATO changes, problems with CENTCOM's federated processes, the lack of realistic training and exercise of the BDA cycle, and the initial lack of a centralized tracking tool in the combat operations division."[122]

A big part of the BDA problem in that respect was—and remains—the persistence of reliance on destruction- and attrition-based rather than effects-based feedback. Regarding this important issue area, an Air Combat Command after-action briefing on the campaign flatly concluded: "We perform force application better than we can assess its effects."[123] The satellite-aided JDAMs were so accurate and reliable that MAAP planners in the CAOC were generally content to conclude that a designated aim point had been adequately "serviced" if a valid JDAM release had been assessed.[124] In their considered view, poststrike target imagery was essential only for particularly high-priority and high-value targets. This perspective inclined planners to conclude that a major change was warranted in the way BDA was conducted, at least with respect to targets attacked by JDAMs. Because any JDAM that had been released within proper parameters could be instantly deemed adequate for most targets, "the lightning speed with which the air component can destroy volumes of aim points demand[ed] a move away from the archaic, analog system that requires an electro-optical picture showing damage in order to categorize a target as dead."[125] More to the point, they concluded that senior leaders should cease insisting on visual assessments of attacked targets and instead settle for accurate reporting of the combat *effects* achieved by aerial strikes. On numerous occasions during the period of major combat, targets located and identified by overhead imagery, particularly IADS-related targets, were repeatedly renominated for inclusion on the ATO, even though those targets had already been struck on multiple occasions and no electronic emissions had since been detected from their radars. In light of that experience, there seems every reason for CENTCOM's leaders in future engagements to settle for effects-based BDA rather than continuing to rely on "mere observations of physical damage and bean-counting."[126]

BDA throughout the major combat phase of Iraqi Freedom typically lagged behind strike operations by as much as several days, and CENTCOM staffers made little effort to assess combat effects as a high-priority concern.[127] The senior CAOC director during the campaign later characterized CENTCOM's BDA process throughout the three weeks of major combat as "broken." He cited as just one of many examples the last-minute re-roling of a B-2 that occurred when CAOC operators determined from overhead sensors that a critical target against which the aircraft had been tasked had already been destroyed.[128]

In a conclusion that clearly emerged from the CAOC's experience with BDA throughout the three-week air war, Colonel Hathaway suggested that planners in future contingencies will need to formalize the assumptions they use in assessing weapons-delivery effectiveness so that the entire warfighting command understands the premises on which BDA can be provided on short notice. Further, high-value targets "must get a higher priority within the ISR collection deck," he said, "because not all targets are created equal."[129]

A widely cited early draft of JFCOM's after-action study reported that "collecting, analyzing, and assessing information became the bottleneck in the decision-making cycle. Once information was available and commanders made their assessments, coalition forces took rapid advantage, striking with lethality and effect." However, the study added, "when the speed of execution exceeded the capability to analyze and assess how those actions were changing the Iraqi system, operations reverted from an effects focus to an attrition focus. . . . Thus, while espousing an [effects-based operations] philosophy, ultimately the coalition moved toward an attrition-based assessment approach. . . . On the whole, coalition forces reverted to counting specific numbers of targets destroyed to determine combat progress rather than evaluating the effects created on the enemy." The study noted that the coalition "did not have a sufficiently sophisticated and mature approach to rapidly assess the enemy from a system-of-systems perspective. Better cultural understanding and 'red teaming' are needed to break the trap of 'mirror-imaging' that can miss important indicators." The study further observed that CENTCOM lacked an adequate approach to assessing non-kinetic effects and a methodology for providing "the subtle synthesis of direct and nondirect indicators needed to evaluate effectiveness."[130]

To offer an illustration of how this problem played out in practice, CENT-COM's senior commanders were frequently concerned that allied ground forces might encounter stronger than expected enemy forces or be forced to fight from unanticipated positions. General Leaf noted that the problem was not simply BDA per se, but rather "really understanding . . . [whether] we've achieved the [desired] effects."[131] With allied ground forces having already advanced two hundred miles into Iraq within the first five days of the campaign, there was bound to be a time lag in determining what combat effects had already been achieved by allied air attacks. The challenge in that situation was not really getting "damage" assessment so much as a timely and accurate assessment of achieved *effects*. In previous conflicts, said General Leaf, "there was a fairly stodgy pace to conducting assessment—go bomb a target and then collect information on what has been bombed, and then do some analysis and decide what the effects were."[132] This slow and impacted assessment process adversely affected virtually all of CENTCOM's warfighting components.

While allied interdiction and CAS sorties were shredding Republican Guard units for four straight days and nights, for example, the land component's headquarters continued to portray the assessed strength of those units as high as 85 percent because empirical evidence to the contrary was lacking. Some commanders actually slowed their rate of advance commensurately until they could be certain what they were up against. General Leaf recalled that the targeting cycle would typically begin with meetings of the coalition's daily effects board to focus the targeting process on desired results rather than on such instrumentalities as aircraft and munitions. General McKiernan's list of target-servicing nominations and priorities was then passed along to General Moseley, whose battle staff would build a single target list and seek optimum ways of meeting those priorities by achieving desired combat effects, ultimately culminating in a daily ATO. In the view of many in both the air and land components, the assessment process in support of this effort could have been speeded up significantly had strike assessors had access even to rough, unanalyzed imagery.

CENTCOM also experienced difficulty in promptly determining the collateral damage consequences of *land* component operations. A briefing by Air Combat Command on the air war clearly pointed out that "in air operations, we have developed, by necessity, a series of tools and operational procedures to accurately assess and mitigate collateral damage. No such tools exist for surface-centric operations, especially small-unit organic fires."[133] Nearly 1,500 cluster bombs had been dropped on Iraq throughout the three-week offensive, and only 26 of them had been targeted within 1,500 feet of civilian neighborhoods. Those munitions reportedly caused only one known Iraqi civilian casualty. The Air Force had learned its lesson well in Afghanistan, where 1,228 cluster munitions had reportedly killed as many as 127 Afghan civilians. Allied ground forces, however, lacking familiarity with the collateral-damage mitigation tools and procedures that are routinely employed by Western air arms, reportedly expended cluster munitions (in artillery shells and ATACMS warheads) with less discipline during the major combat phase of Iraqi Freedom.[134]

One long-term solution for the BDA deficiency described above would be for the services to develop and field weapons data links that are capable of providing auto-BDA by, for example, putting a red "X" over a just-attacked target symbol on a CAOC situation display to help reduce the need for unnecessary reattacks. Strike assessors must also develop and apply a new effects-based combat assessment methodology.[135]

Problems in Meeting Tanker Requirements

General Moseley later described tanker support as "*the* single-point failure factor" in the air portion of CENTCOM's joint and combined operations plan. He added that a failure by the air component to marshal and sustain a tanker flow sufficient to meet the in-flight refueling needs of the plan's daily ATO could easily have been a "showstopper."[136] As it was, the shortage of tankers created serious complications in both the planning and execution of the campaign. The challenge was further exacerbated by the need to distribute the fewer than 200 available U.S. Air Force and RAF tankers over 15 bases, in contrast to the Desert Storm precedent, when 350 tankers had operated out of only 5 regional bases. Three bases in Saudi Arabia—King Khalid Military City, Jeddah, and Dhahran—had the needed ramp space and fuel throughput to support tanker operations, but the Saudi government disallowed their use for supporting strike missions. Operating locations as far away as Moron Air Base in Spain, Akrotiri on Cyprus, Diego Garcia in the Indian Ocean, and Cairo West were used instead.

The tanker problem was further aggravated by Turkey's refusal to allow the coalition to use its bases, as well as—for a time—its denial of overflight permission. Turkish bases had constituted some 25 percent of the bases that CENTCOM had earmarked as forward operating locations for its 149 KC-135s, 33 KC-10s, 4 RAF Tristars, and 8 RAF VC-10s. Their unavailability required operating tankers for the first time from bases in Crete and Bulgaria. Because of these and related complications, CENTCOM had 51 fewer KC-135s available for tanker support than it had for Desert Storm.[137] Moreover, in order for the carrier-based fighters operating from the eastern Mediterranean to participate in the initial attack waves, the expeditionary air wing in Egypt and tankers based in Bulgaria had to provide fuel to other tankers that had no alternative but to fly around Israel and over Saudi Arabia to support allied strike aircraft flying into northern Iraq.[138] The last-minute loss of basing rights in Turkey and the limited tanker basing in Saudi Arabia created aerial force employment distances and sortie durations throughout Iraqi Freedom that, in many cases, matched those routinely flown into land-locked Afghanistan throughout Enduring Freedom.

Only the three bases in Kuwait that had been made available to allied strike aircraft were close enough to Iraq's southern border to allow strikers to reach deep into Iraq without refueling. Strike aircraft from all other bases within reasonable range of Baghdad required in-flight refueling during both ingress and egress. With hundreds of allied strike aircraft airborne at any given moment, queues of fighters behind tankers sometimes became so long that pilots had to abort their missions because they lacked sufficient fuel to hold for a preplanned tanker rendezvous. A related concern entailed positioning tankers far enough forward and timing scheduled tanker connections in a way best guaranteed to prevent strike aircraft from having to queue up in the first place and become inviting targets for enemy air defenses. Yet another complicating factor was the number of aircraft that were executing sustained holding and combat operations over Baghdad. During Operation Desert Storm, fuel-consuming CAS and SEAD loitering operations over Baghdad and other parts of Iraq in which ground combat operations were under way were uncommon.[139]

The war's initial days brought recurrent complaints about missed tanker connections from Gulf-based Navy strike pilots who could not get to the fight without refueling after the battle lines had moved more than two hundred miles north of Kuwait. Tanker apportionment planners in the CAOC countered that the complainers failed to appreciate the complexities involved. A canceled tanker rendezvous, for example, did not necessarily mean that the assigned tanker had not been on station. With the allied ground advance moving northward toward Baghdad with such dispatch, target sets sometimes shifted so rapidly that airborne strike sorties were deleted from the ATO after the aircraft were airborne because they were no longer needed to service targets, not because a needed tanker was not available. Vice Admiral Keating confirmed that during the war's first days, various tanker management challenges resulted in some carrier-based aircraft not prosecuting their targets and others having to divert into one of the Kuwaiti bases to top off before returning to their ships.[140] As the campaign progressed, tanker management became less of a problem. Capt. David Rogers, Admiral Nichols' special assistant, observed at the time, "If you ask somebody whether the tanking situation is better or worse than when we kicked things off, you would get a resounding change in opinion from what they would have told you earlier. Basically, we're getting fuel closer to the target."[141]

Inadequate fuel lines at tanker bed-down sites that necessitated trucking in jet fuel from the outside added to the tanker-related problems. This dependence on local fuel trucks increased tanker turnaround times and reduced tanker availability for strike operations into northern Iraq from the two carriers in the eastern Mediterranean. Captain Rogers called the situation "a more complex shell game than in Desert Storm."[142] Further, the ground offensive's rapid northward advance—before the CAOC had time to establish the desired margin of air superiority over the battlefield—soon outranged some of CENTAF's fighters. The difficulty was further compounded when General McKiernan moved the FSCL well forward of his own forces, leaving some allied aircraft assigned to provide on-call CAS with only minutes of available loiter time. More than a few had to recover with unexpended ordnance because the ASOC could not assign targets to them quickly enough. To compensate for this, the CAOC pushed some tanker tracks forward and also assigned shorter-range aircraft like the AV-8B and A-10 to support operations solely in the southernmost portions of the battlespace.

The problem was ameliorated when coalition ground units took Tallil Air Base and A-10s began flying CAS missions directly out of that forward location.[143] Col. James Dobbins, the commander of the 392nd Air Expeditionary Group that moved into Tallil, explained that the A-10s now had "more time over target [because they] . . . did not have to fly as far to get to the fight." In addition to enabling forward-based A-10 operations, Tallil also supported some airlift and CSAR missions. Although lacking such other critical needs as power grids, communications facilities, and water distribution systems, the base offered an adequate fuel capability for supporting initial U.S. flight operations so that A-10s could land, refuel, upload fresh ordnance, and get promptly back in the air.[144]

With more in-flight refueling occurring closer to the war zone as the campaign progressed, the distribution and placement of tanker orbits necessarily became more complicated. In view of the continuing enemy IADS threat, it was not feasible for the CAOC to maintain predictable tanker tracks each day with large stacks of aircraft waiting to take on fuel. That required more airborne tanker stations and often occasioned greater difficulty for strike aircrews in finding and rendezvousing with their assigned tanker. Furthermore, a tanker pilot might be more likely to break off a refueling if he felt that his aircraft was in imminent danger of being fired on. Unlike the coalition's strike aircraft, the tankers were not equipped with radar warning receivers or chaff and flares to provide threat situation awareness and active countermeasures against radar- and infrared-guided SAMs.

After CENTAF's defense suppression operations had reduced the assessed threat potential of Iraq's IADS to a sufficiently low level of risk, General Moseley moved tanker orbits and command and control and manned ISR aircraft, such as the E-3 AWACS, E-8 JSTARS, RC-135 Rivet Joint, and U-2, forward into Iraqi airspace in support of the advancing land forces. Indeed, OPLAN 1003V had *always* presumed that tanker tracks would be moved into Iraq just as soon as the assessed threat environment would permit it, because there was no other way for CENTAF to support a major allied land offensive in the vicinity of Baghdad. That long-standing plan, however, had presumed that G-day would begin three days *after* A-day. The FLOT had moved so far north from the line of departure in Kuwait after just the first day of combat operations that Navy and Marine Corps strike fighters operating from carriers in the North Arabian Gulf could no longer reach the fight on the ground without refueling in flight at least once.

As soon as CAOC planners opened the first tanker tracks inside Iraqi airspace, the Navy began using its S-3Bs and F/A-18E/F Super Hornets to provide organic tanking for some carrier-based sorties that were tasked to support the land component. These were the first of many measures the CAOC undertook to overcome the ever-widening distances to allied ground units advancing toward Baghdad. The assessed urgency of moving tankers into defended Iraqi airspace as soon as possible left little time to address possible IADS threats, and tanker planners were understandably reluctant at first to conduct in-flight refueling over southern Iraq, particularly at the lower altitudes that the A-10s required.[145] Yet another attempted palliative to address the tanker and fuel shortage entailed tasking A-10s to support I MEF in southeastern Iraq while Marine Corps strike fighters from Al Jaber and carrier air wings in the North Arabian Gulf operated farther north to support the parallel advance by V Corps. In this arrangement, General Moseley, in effect, traded a squadron of air component–controlled A-10s to I MEF to meet General Conway's CAS needs in return for a squadron of Marine Corps F/A-18Cs that the CAOC could use in meeting its deep-attack requirements farther north.

The two carriers that had been on station in the North Arabian Gulf for the longest time, *Abraham Lincoln* and *Constellation*, were selected to receive the greatest possible Air Force tanking support. The air wing embarked in the last carrier to arrive on station, *Kitty Hawk*, was given a predominantly CAS role in support of V Corps and I MEF in southern Iraq and was tasked to fulfill that role autonomously, which burdened the carrier's organic tanking capability to its limit. For the first time since Operation Desert Storm, strike aircraft in CVW-5 embarked in *Kitty Hawk* were allowed to return to the carrier with minimum fuel, and carrier cyclic and flex-deck operations ran at a maximum.[146] Marshaling these capabilities for an anticipated five-day surge option, CVW-5 proved itself able both to meet its CAS tasking and to provide strike packages for attacks against fixed targets in Baghdad. The S-3B tankers of CVW-5 were crucial in making that flexible employment possible.

The other two carrier air wings followed similar plans to enhance their capabilities. It turned out that S-3Bs in the Gulf-based air wings were sufficient in number and capability to permit the release of some Air Force tankers allocated to *Abraham Lincoln* and *Constellation* to support other strike sorties emerging from the Gulf region, including from *Kitty Hawk*, as well as Air Force heavy bombers arriving from Diego Garcia and elsewhere. This concept had been tested and validated during the final days of Operation Southern Watch, during which frontside and backside organic tanking (that is, in-flight refueling of fighters both on the outbound leg to their assigned target area and near or over the carrier shortly before their recovery) allowed F/A-18s to fly one-and-a-half-hour cycles with little difficulty, with S-3Bs launching and recovering immediately before and after the refueling evolutions. It also allowed an increase in on-station time for carrier-based strike fighters conducting CAS missions in southern Iraq around Basra and Nasiriya, and it showed that a five-day surge capability could be sustained on an open-ended basis throughout the days to come. By one informed account, the concept worked "flawlessly" throughout the three-week campaign.[147] In the end, the five participating carrier air wings transferred about half a million pounds of fuel a day from organic S-3Bs and Super Hornets in addition to the five million pounds a day they received from U.S. Air Force and RAF tankers.

Coalition pilots recalled that some of their most harrowing moments during the three-week air war resulted from their inability to find a tanker at the end of a mission when their fuel supply was critically low. Said one pilot: "We'd call for our tanker, ask AWACS where he was, and be told, 'he's gone home already.'"[148] At first, tanker tracks inside Iraqi airspace were too few to provide adequate support to the land component's KI/CAS needs, so alternative measures had to be undertaken. Defensive counterair operations were reduced by half; Air Force A-10s began launching combat sorties out of Tallil airfield; and F-15Es that had initially been operating out of Al Udeid in Qatar began generating combat sorties out of Al Jaber Air Base in Kuwait, which was closer to the Iraqi border. These measures allowed aircraft assigned to KI/CAS missions longer times on station without the need for in-flight refueling.[149]

There were several days during the march toward Baghdad when in-flight refueling requests from airborne strike aircraft conducting CAS operations went unmet due to conflicting interpretations of General Moseley's guidance regarding tanker track placement inside still-defended Iraqi airspace and risk mitigation. In particular, the period between day 4 and the regime collapse on April 9 saw some fuel requests for A-10 and other coalition CAS aircraft, as well as for A-10 support to the SOF component's Task Force 20 in Iraq's western desert, going unsatisfied. Dealing decisively with this issue required General Moseley's personal adjudication. CAOC planners later explained that "increased tanker risk acceptance by air refueling track placement into Iraq's southern plain was necessary to support ground operations, but the doctrinally inspired organizational structure caused resolution of such conflicts to occur at the [air component commander] level. Resolution couldn't always occur in a timely manner because of the multiple layers of leadership that existed between the MAAP chief and [General Moseley]."[150]

Planners in all components had tended to assume going into Iraqi Freedom that Southwest Asia's enormous fuel reserves would make fuel shortages nonexistent. Yet as CAOC operators later pointed out, "walls of [defensive counterair], robust global power, numerous land component target nominations, and 24-hour command and control and ISR coverage all constituted examples of legitimate needs that also happen to be very expensive in terms of fuel.... [P]lanners must not assume all the gas will be there to fulfill their wish lists. Tankers mustn't be an afterthought in wartime planning—they should be the first thought."[151]

Obstacles in Coalition Information Sharing

A final source of frustration in the day-to-day conduct of the major combat phase of Iraqi Freedom had to do with the sharing of sensitive information among the American and allied contingents. Although openness and candor between the allies were far better in this war than in any preceding instance because of the few coalition partners that were involved and their exceptional closeness, there was nonetheless difficulty at times with what one RAF officer described as "translating the trust engendered at the highest levels into sensible information sharing at lower levels."[152] The British and Australian contingents had full access to the American STU III secure telephone system and also could receive the product of TBMCS indirectly by means of read-only compact discs. Beyond that, however, the allies had more than a few problems getting timely access to U.S.-controlled information.

In particular, many of CENTCOM's most important command and control processes were based on SIPRNet (secure Internet protocol router network), a U.S. eyes-only system that could not be directly accessed by foreign nationals.[153] Accordingly, allied personnel in the CAOC were not allowed to work directly with such crucial SIPR-based U.S.-only planning mechanisms as TBMCS. As an attempted work-around solution, CENTCOM provided the allied contingents with the wherewithal to create a mirror image of SIPRNet called Xnet, which allowed them to use a separate TBMCS system that was not SIPR-based and accordingly was not linked to TBMCS. That makeshift arrangement allowed coalition planners to build their mission plans in a separate TBMCS "shell" that ATO production staffers would then merge into the overall ATO. Yet the MAAP cell's principal means for building mission sets used a MAAP toolkit rather than TBMCS. Because the MAAP toolkit was also SIPR-based, coalition staff were not allowed access to it either. Moreover, although the air component's daily SPINs were, of clear necessity, approved for release to the coalition partners and were routinely laden with specific coalition-partner information and guidance, the allies' lack of direct access to both TBMCS and SIPRNet forced CAOC staffers to burn a compact disc every day and hand-deliver it to RAF and RAAF mission planners, which created an additional source of self-inflicted friction.

In other ways as well, the coalition representatives' American counterparts were obliged to pick up the slack created by the stringent security measures, leading to heavier workloads and longer timelines for assembling attack packages. For example, before options planning for OPLAN 1003V began in earnest, standard U.S. intelligence management procedures dictated classifying most of the targeting information generated by CENTCOM and by the broader U.S. national intelligence community at the Secret/NOFORN level. Once actual combat operations neared, however, both CENTCOM and the broader intelligence community found themselves faced with the massive task of sanitizing large amounts of NOFORN targeting information so as to render it releasable to CENTCOM's coalition partners. The arrangement for sharing vital planning data that resulted was described by an RAF officer as "slow and cumbersome rather than responsive and agile."[154]

The CAOC staffers who produced CENTAF's after-action review of the campaign experience described the allies' lack of access to key mission-planning systems as "the single greatest frustration for what was otherwise an outstanding relationship" among the coalition partners. One key planner recalled pointedly that "the impact of this issue was felt throughout the CAOC."[155] Senior RAF officers who took part in Iraqi Freedom at both command and execution levels were likewise all but unanimous in spotlighting the NOFORN caveat that blocked ready allied access to SIPRNet, Intellink, and other U.S.-only information systems as a persistent and systemic impediment to fuller interoperability with U.S. forces.[156] They further singled out this problem as one that senior leaders in all three countries needed urgently to address in order to find a mutually agreeable "better way" that might allow less-fettered dialogue between special partners in the midst of high-intensity coalition warfare.[157]

Air Chief Marshal Burridge later remarked that the challenge presented by the access issue had not been prohibitively imposing in the case of Iraqi Freedom because the coalition partners of major note were solely the United Kingdom and Australia, both of which were close allies of the United States accustomed for years to operating "inside a known agreement for sharing intelligence." Because the process was manual rather than automatic, however, it required the American participants to find time in the midst of continuous high-tempo combat to decide on and carry out the transfer of information to the allied contingents as it was needed. This inherent impediment to smoother planning and execution was generally overcome through exceptionally close interpersonal and trust relations among the three contingents, but not without recurrent friction and inefficiency. Burridge further pointed out that the efficacy of such a system would be limited, perhaps even to the breaking point, in future contingency responses by a larger coalition that included partners "with whom we would not normally consider sharing high-grade intelligence."[158] Many CENTAF staffers recognized the necessity for both CENTCOM and the broader American national intelligence community to adopt a fundamentally different mindset aimed at facilitating allied combat options planning for future contingencies. Simply adding a caveat indicating "releasable to Great Britain, Australia, and Canada" would obviate the last-minute scrambling to sanitize targeting information that plagued Iraqi Freedom.

On the positive side, there was a clear contrast between the air tasking process employed throughout Iraqi Freedom and the one used during Operation Allied Force against Serbia in 1999, when the air component developed two separate ATOs each day as a result of EUCOM's determination to keep sorties using NATO assets and approved through NATO channels separate and deconflicted from the more sensitive use of U.S.-only assets, such as B-2 and F-117 stealth aircraft.[159] From the very beginning, CENTAF's planners maintained a "seamless integration" of U.S.-only stealth assets with other American and allied conventional aircraft. Previously, planners had thought that the stealthy F-117 and B-2 demanded special compartmentalization in any air operation involving allied participation to protect their most sensitive operational and performance details. During the buildup for and conduct of Operation Iraqi Freedom, however, stealth platforms were woven into the CAOC's conventional planning process from the very start, making the integration of stealth aircraft with conventional assets much more efficient and effective.[160]

As was the case with participating units from the RAF, the RAAF units and personnel seconded to CENTAF for the duration of the three-week campaign encountered few problems in the realm of force interoperability. A subsequent bilateral review of interoperability issues between the ADF and the U.S. armed forces conducted in 2004 at Victoria Barracks in Sydney, Australia, however, concluded that "not all interoperability achieved was the result of systematic planning and training. Shortfalls arose, and the high degree of operational-level interoperability achieved during the conflicts [both] in Afghanistan and Iraq often reflected the use of workarounds and ad hoc solutions." One of three broad categories of identified interoperability shortcomings concerned "information exchange issues, including the use of computer networks to plan, execute, and monitor operations and the extent to which national information policy architectures could respond to coalition information needs."[161]

An initial problem faced by the ADF that was *not* shared by the British contingent, owing to the latter's previous intimate involvement in Operations Northern Watch and Southern Watch, was near-total unfamiliarity with CENTCOM and its mode of operations. CENTCOM likewise had limited knowledge and appreciation of the ADF's breadth of capabilities. By the time the final countdown for Operation Iraqi Freedom began in early 2003, however, that issue had largely been resolved as a result of the ADF's contribution to CENTCOM operations in Afghanistan since October 2001 through Operation Slipper, the air portion of which consisted of the provision of four RAAF F/A-18s to provide local air defense of Diego Garcia and two Boeing 707 tankers operating out of Ganci Air Base near Manas, Kyrgyzstan, with two RAAF P-3 long-range maritime patrol aircraft being added in 2003.

Nevertheless, the Australians still faced an initial disadvantage when compared with their RAF compatriots. The air wing commander for the RAAF F/A-18s that deployed to Al Udeid recalled: "I never knew what an air expeditionary wing was, or what they did prior to getting there. Very few people [in the RAAF] had any idea of what a CAOC was and how it conducted operations and how the [United States] did its business. If you had asked me in November prior to being briefed in how we would conduct business with the [United States], I'd be at a loss to tell you."[162] The chief of intelligence and targeting within the Australian CAOC contingent under Group Captain Brown similarly remarked in his after-action observations: "Working with the U.S. Air Force at Shaw was definitely a highlight. They were extremely professional guys and had been doing Operation Southern Watch for quite some time, so what they didn't know about Iraq wasn't worth knowing. [Yet] this was an out-of-area operation for us, so there was a lot to learn and not a lot of time. It wasn't like being in the comfort zone of the Southwest Pacific or Southeast Asia, and even knowing the lay of the land, you had to learn pretty much everything from scratch."[163]

With respect to the sharing of sensitive U.S.-controlled information, however, the RAAF contingent embedded in CENTAF's CAOC reported very much the same experience as did the RAF contingent, namely, a U.S.-imposed firewall that blocked their direct access to needed mission planning information transmitted via SIPRNet and the necessity for jury-rigged workarounds. To be sure, that was not the case during the initial planning for prospective coalition air operations that took place at Shaw AFB in late 2002. The RAAF's chief of intelligence and targeting experienced outright astonishment at the remarkable openness of CENTAF's willingness to share sensitive intelligence information: "I walked in and I got a pass that let me in anywhere. It was quite amazing, actually. I didn't expect that. And I actually always felt a bit embarrassed letting myself into their [intelligence] area without knocking and saying 'I'm here' before I took a few steps. I can't recall any situation where I felt they weren't telling you something.'"[164]

Once the war was on, however, that openness changed. A senior air planner attached to the Australian contingent in the CAOC recalled in a postcampaign interview:

> General Moseley . . . and his deputy, Brigadier General [Robert] Elder, were both excellent. [General Moseley] just directed that whatever the Australians want, give it to them. . . . The biggest problem we had, [however], was plugging into their secure information technology systems and their communications, because that was a national sensitivity issue. The Brits had the same problem. . . . The TBMCS ran on SIPRNet, the secure system. That was where all the reporting occurred and where all the air tasking was issued. . . . They couldn't give us access to it, and there was a huge problem with that. . . . It was eventually resolved, and I'm not clear how it exactly was resolved, but I know General Moseley had a major hand in it, and it went extremely high in their [the American] system. I heard a report . . . [that] it went as high as the president to get approval to give the United Kingdom and Australia access to SIPRNet. Until we got that, we could not operate. We couldn't access the ATO, and all the command and control structure ran on that.[165]

The U.S.-Australian bilateral review committee's postcampaign assessment of interoperability issues between the two countries concluded that the impromptu informal workarounds that eventually triumphed over the ingrained obstructions to information sharing, albeit successful in the end, involved "departures from established, approved operating procedures"; were "usually based on a personal, trusted relationship"; and had "the net ongoing operational-level effect of . . . [degrading] the ability of Australian and U.S. forces" to interact seamlessly when it came to the most efficient planning and conduct of combat operations in a fast-paced and high-intensity coalition campaign context.[166] The review team singled out as the main culprits the American SIPRNet system at the Secret level and the JWICS at the Top Secret level. Both "by definition and design, [those pivotal planning systems] cannot be used for campaigns involving meaningful contributions from other countries."[167] Fortunately, however, such workarounds as the provision of relevant country-specific sections extracted from the ATO via a SIPRNet terminal either in hard copy or on a compact disc for the British and Australian contingents "were developed [and employed in a way] that allowed allies access to mission-critical information that was essential for their effective and safe participation" in the campaign. Nevertheless, the team added, such workarounds "are a poor solution to problems with information sharing among coalition members." Furthermore, consistent with the overarching stumbling block with regard to intracoalition interoperability that the British contingent repeatedly spotlighted in its postcampaign assessments, the U.S.-Australian review team also pointedly cited a statement by General Franks in testimony before the Senate Armed Services Committee on July 9, 2003, that identified "coalition information sharing in [Operation Iraqi Freedom] as an area that must be improved at all levels."[168]

Toward a New Era of Warfare

Operation Iraqi Freedom began as a preventive war in that the United States attacked another country because of an assessed future threat rather than in response to a blatantly hostile act or to preempt an imminent danger that the targeted country represented. As such, it was the first (and, with the advent of a successor U.S. administration in 2009, only) exercise of the then-emergent George W. Bush doctrine, which was distinguished by a willingness on the part of the administration to use force to protect the nation's avowed interests without an immediate provocation and without the support of a formal alliance.

During the final countdown that preceded the start of full-scale combat operations, Jessica Tuchman Matthews, the president of the Carnegie Endowment for International Peace, rightly characterized the impending campaign as an "optional war."[1] Vice President Dick Cheney justified Operation Iraqi Freedom somewhat differently as a proactive rather than reactive response to the terrorist attacks of September 11, 2001: "We had certain strategies and policies and institutions that were built to deal with the conflicts of the 20th century. They may not be the right strategies and policies and institutions to deal with the kind of threat we now face."[2] Explaining this shift in strategy from deterring enemies to forcefully eliminating their ability to inflict direct harm on the United States, Cheney added that the September 11 attacks had changed the preexisting rules: "If we simply sit back and operate by 20th-century standards, we say wait until we're hit by an identifiable attack from Iraq. The consequences could be devastating."[3] He later observed that the Bush administration's dominant concern after the September 11 attacks was that the next threat to American security would not be box-cutters but nuclear weapons, that the nation's leaders could accordingly no longer fail to connect the dots as they had done before the terrorist attacks, and that no responsible American president could have ignored the potential for an Al Qaeda–WMD connection in Iraq.[4]

Allied air operations against the enemy's ground forces were uniquely effective throughout the major combat phase of Iraqi Freedom. Yet in marked contrast to the first Persian Gulf War of 1991, they took a backseat to the ground effort not only in their sequencing in the joint campaign but also in the amount of information that was publicly released about them. In point of fact, the bombing attacks in downtown Baghdad during the air war's first two nights were the *only* visible parts of that effort to most observers who were watching the war unfold on their home television sets. What remained unseen was the constant pounding that allied air attacks were delivering elsewhere throughout the country with unremitting accuracy against Iraqi tanks, artillery emplacements, and IADS facilities. While those on the home front were riveted to television reportage of friendly ground troops tied down by the sandstorm and engaged by Fedayeen Saddam hit-and-run attacks, allied strike aircraft were shredding Republican Guard units wholesale by means of JDAM attacks into the gloom, thanks to Global Hawk and other ISR assets that could geolocate those enemy assets unerringly through the weather. As the Air Force chief of staff, General Jumper, later put it, "We killed a lot of those guys, that equipment, during the sandstorm when those people assumed that because they couldn't see ten feet in front of their face, neither could we."[5]

As if to reinforce this assessment, the most authoritative review of the U.S. Army's contribution to the campaign noted: "It is difficult to overstate the importance of air operations in the context of [Operation Iraqi Freedom]. By dominating the air over Iraq, coalition air forces shaped the fight to allow for rapid dominance on the ground. Air power decisively turned the tide in tactical operations on the ground on several occasions. . . . Integration of precision munitions with ground operations, supported by a largely space-based command and control network, enabled combat operations to occur in ways only imagined a decade ago."[6] The study cited "lethal combinations of A–10s, F–15s, F–16s, F/A–18s, B–1s, B–52s and a host of other aircraft" as being "absolutely essential to the ground campaign's success. The Air Force's investment of air liaison officers and enlisted terminal attack controllers embedded into the maneuver units paid off in spades." The only complaint voiced by Army commanders—one universally shared by Air Force airmen as well—was that "the clearance-of-fires process was sometimes unwieldy."[7]

CENTCOM enjoyed complete control of the air over Iraq essentially from the opening moments of formal combat. The earlier Desert Storm experience had started out with thirty-eight days of air-only operations that were obliged to focus on suppressing the Iraqi air force and Iraq's ground-based IADS before the campaign could proceed to attack Hussein's occupying forces in the Kuwaiti theater of operations. In contrast, this war, in Anthony Cordesman's words, "began with air superiority and moved swiftly to air dominance" thanks to more than a decade of prior Northern Watch and Southern Watch operations plus seven months of escalated Southern Focus attacks to further degrade the Iraqi IADS and prepare the battlespace for the impending second campaign.[8]

The immediate goals of the campaign were the neutralization of Iraq's armed forces and the expeditious takedown of Hussein's regime with minimal collateral damage by achieving tactical surprise, getting inside the regime's decision loop, severing its command and control links, and undermining its capacity for collective action. "Violating virtually all of the traditional wisdom about how to prepare for a campaign of this scope," the Army assessment noted, "the V Corps and I MEF forces appear to have achieved operational and tactical surprise when they started their attack before all of the 'necessary' forces had arrived and without a lengthy air effort. . . . The running start appears to have thrown the Iraqis off their defensive plan, and they were never able to regain their footing."[9] As coalition operations moved ever closer to direct contact with Iraqi troop positions, allied air power and light but high-impact SOF forces working in combination stayed ahead of the enemy at every step, often achieving specific mission objectives either before or independently of direct engagement by the main opposing forces on the ground. An American reporter captured the essence of the campaign when he described CENTCOM's strategy as "premised on the synergy of disorienting air power, faster-moving ground forces, information dominance of the digital battlefield, and greater reliance on special forces."[10]

Yet the war was more than just a preventive exercise in regime takedown. It also turned out to be a live battle laboratory for refining some novel approaches to joint and combined warfare that had first been conceptualized and applied during Operation Enduring Freedom in Afghanistan in 2001. To begin with, a major improvement during the preceding year in the trust relationship between President Bush and General Franks, as well as between General Franks and General Moseley, gave the latter essentially full autonomy in approving target nominations as well as allowing an autodelegation arrangement from CENTCOM to the CAOC for nearly all target categories. The senior CAOC director for the major combat phase of Iraqi Freedom recalled that the number of "Mother may I's" from the CAOC staff to him or to General Moseley, let alone from General Moseley to General Franks or to higher authority, could almost be counted on one hand, and none of those rare instances, in contrast to the Enduring Freedom experience, resulted in lost opportunities.[11]

Indeed, improved working relations both within and across CENTCOM's components proved indispensable in enabling the successful prosecution of Iraqi Freedom. In particular, CENTAF intelligence experts and operations planners brought together many outside individuals who had worked together just a year before in Operation Enduring Freedom. For example, the principal command and control planners for Enduring Freedom were reconvened to lead the Iraqi Freedom force enhancement and force application cells in the CAOC's MAAP team. Equally important, strong trust relationships between CENTAF and CENTCOM that were painstakingly developed by General Moseley and his key subordinates during the latter months and early aftermath of the major combat portion of Enduring Freedom went far toward eliminating previous tensions and ill will among CENTCOM's warfighting components and services. Many members of the CAOC's special operations liaison element in Enduring Freedom were likewise retained as primary planners for Iraqi Freedom. By the same token, operations planners in CENTAF's CAOC developed close and harmonious working ties with their counterparts at CENTCOM. "The daily contact with our CENTCOM counterparts during Operation Enduring Freedom continued throughout the buildup to Iraqi Freedom," a senior CENTAF planner recalled. "While the key players on each side did not always see things the same way, there was never distrust or secrets."[12]

As for bottom-line conclusions aimed at capturing the war's most memorable achievements from his personal perspective, General Moseley put at the top of his list General Franks' decisive "fast and final" plan, which was distinguished by an unprecedented level of jointness and coalition cooperation. He further noted the willing acceptance of risk across all components at the operational level, the integration of all theater air assets into a single focus, the close integration of air and SOF operations, and the air component's ability to operate deep inside defended Iraqi airspace right up to the edge of Baghdad from the campaign's opening moments. General Moseley also spotlighted as major campaign accomplishments the land component's march to Baghdad, which was the fastest mechanized ground advance in the history of modern warfare; CENTCOM's complete crushing of the Iraqi air force, navy, Republican Guard, Special Republican Guard, and Special Security Organization as coherent and functioning entities; and the offensive's all but complete dismantling of Iraq's command and control network. The Iraqi air force launched no sorties, and there were no attacks by other means against CENTAF's airfields, the U.S. Navy's carrier battle groups, constantly incoming sustainment trains of fuel trucks, or any other coalition facilities. Finally, with respect to the air component's carefully disciplined targeting and force employment, he pointed out that the air offensive had caused no catastrophic environmental effects, strategically dislocating collateral damage, or significant deleterious effects on Iraq's civilian and economic infrastructure, transportation infrastructure, key southern and northern oil fields, or associated petroleum, oil, and lubricants infrastructure.[13]

In particular, General Moseley valued the trust relationship between General Franks and himself (and between CENTCOM and its air component more generally) that had gradually evolved since the start of Operation Enduring Freedom in Afghanistan nearly two years before. Indeed, so great was Moseley's autonomy as Franks' air component commander that as the opening night of full-scale air operations against Iraq was unfolding, CENTCOM's director of operations, Major General Renuart, plaintively pressed him for an air component update, asking: "Will you tell us what you're bombing when you get a chance?" With regard to this significant improvement in the CAOC's freedom of action in setting the pace and focus of strike operations compared with the first halting weeks of Enduring Freedom, General Moseley frankly characterized the earlier air war over Afghanistan as "the JV [junior varsity] scrimmage" for Iraqi Freedom. Of the substantial improvement in joint force performance that the latter experience reflected, he noted that "you learn to fight by fighting."[14]

In this important regard, the Iraqi Freedom experience clearly highlighted the need for regular and recurrent large-force peacetime training evolutions among the participating warfighting components to exercise the joint command and control system from top to bottom. For example, kill-box management in the counterland war would most likely have been far more efficient and effective in execution if all involved command and control entities had been given a prior opportunity to rehearse tactics, manage kill boxes, and flow combat aircraft into areas in which immediate responsive CAS was needed. CENTAF analysts later concluded that Marine Corps expeditionary forces and Army corps elements *must* be included in such exercises to practice and refine the target nomination and prioritization process.[15] With continuing planned improvements to the Air Force's training CAOC at Nellis AFB, the entire joint force command and control and combat forces complex should have ample opportunities to gain access to such training in future Red Flag operations.

Based on the campaign experience, CENTAF staffers stressed the obligation of the U.S. Air Force's Air Combat Command and the U.S. Army's Forces Command to pursue increased opportunities for full-scale and joint live-fly training exercises, to include full-up AOCs and ASOCs in such exercises, and to recognize the value of training for future joint high-intensity warfare as it is most likely to be fought.[16] A knowledgeable airman aptly described the main problem with the present status of joint air-ground training, observing that air power has typically been

> handcuffed to operate in unrealistic ways. First, aircraft [in even recent past joint training exercises] were directed to fly low and in nontactical ways so the Army could "see" air power. Second, using air power realistically would have been so devastating to the OPFOR [opposing force] that it would have reduced the difficulty of the tactical problem for the brigade commander. Third, air power's effects were accordingly reduced to allow the brigade commanders to achieve the desired learning objectives. Fourth, the E-8 JSTARS was directed not to provide the full picture to the ground, since this would provide too much situational awareness to the brigade commander. JSTARS was not allowed to transmit the marshaling OPFOR's positions to the ground forces undergoing training. Finally, the participants did not practice conducting joint deep fires, since [the Army's National Training Center] was designed to test the close battle.[17]

In a comprehensive overview of the areas of combat performance that mattered most at the campaign's operational and strategic levels, an after-action assessment conducted at Air Combat Command concluded that new levels of achievement demonstrated by allied air forces while pursuing CENTCOM's initial goals in Operation Iraqi Freedom included early establishment of uncontested control of the air, the dominance of mass precision, unprecedented rapidity of action, unprecedented connectivity and integration of ISR and command and control, unprecedented efficacy of joint warfare, and unprecedented service flexibility in rapid adaptation.[18] On the first count just noted, the British MoD's after-action report observed that CENTCOM's plan for allied ground combat was "facilitated throughout by an air campaign which achieved significant attrition of the enemy's combat power and involved unprecedented accuracy and lethality based on the widespread, though not exclusive, use of precision munitions and linked sensors and data streams."[19] The air component's achievement of air dominance in the skies over Iraq enabled all else that followed with respect to harmonious joint force integration in conducting offensive operations with virtual impunity.

As for the tangible results that were made possible by this application of allied air power, the Air Combat Command review concluded that "the coordinated use of coalition air power quickly created the conditions that allowed land forces to achieve high rates of maneuver and tempo in response to enemy activity."[20] It further observed: "Captured senior Iraqi General Staff officers reported that the fighting effectiveness of the Republican Guard divisions had been largely destroyed by air strikes."[21] Essentially confirming this observation, Col. William Grimsley, commander of the 1st Brigade of the U.S. Army's 3rd ID, recalled: "We never really found any cohesive unit of any brigade, of any Republican Guard division."[22]

The air portion of CENTCOM's campaign to topple the Ba'athist regime actually began in the summer of 2002 when U.S. and British aircraft patrolling the southern no-fly zone began systematically picking apart the Iraqi IADS by attacking fiber-optic cable nodes that connected its command centers, radars, and weapons. When full-scale combat operations began in earnest on March 20, 2003, the rapid collapse of forward-deployed Iraqi ground units in the south freed up allied aircraft to concentrate on the Republican Guard almost from the very start. Lieutenant Colonel Hathaway, General Moseley's chief strategist, observed that the overarching objective of that effort was to ensure that the Republican Guard's forces would be so physically and psychologically incapacitated that they would be unable to mount any significant resistance when allied ground forces moved into contact with them.[23] Toward that end, the CAOC moved tankers and airborne ISR aircraft deep into Iraqi airspace and cleared allied aircrews to drop at will against any Republican Guard targets of opportunity in designated kill boxes. Aircraft returning to base with unexpended ordnance from missions against prebriefed fixed targets were often redirected to engage detected Republican Guard tanks and artillery emplacements, both static and moving, as their assigned "dump" targets.

The three-week air war was also distinguished by the application of mass precision for the first time. Although the total number of precision-guided munitions used during the major combat phase of Iraqi Freedom was about the same as that used in Desert Storm, that number represented an order of magnitude increase overall because only about 7 percent of the munitions employed in Desert Storm were precision-guided, whereas in Iraqi Freedom the number was close to 70 percent. CENTCOM's deputy commander, Lieutenant General DeLong, called Operation Iraqi Freedom "one of the most surgical and precise bombing and ground campaigns in the history of warfare."[24] Since all allied strike aircraft participating in the major combat phase were capable of delivering precision-guided munitions, the ratio of aircraft to targets attacked was unprecedentedly low. In contrast to the five-week air offensive portion of Operation Desert Storm in 1991, which saw 126,645 sorties flown, for a daily average of

2,945, the major combat phase of Operation Iraqi Freedom generated only about 41,000 sorties, for a daily average of only 1,576, while producing the desired combat effects.[25] During the campaign's first twenty-four hours, literally *every* allied air-delivered weapon directed against an Iraqi target was precision-guided. Even by March 24, well into the war's first week, 80 percent of the air-delivered munitions were precision-guided.

More important than CENTCOM's increased reliance on precision munitions per se was the addition of inertially aided munitions, which offered four distinct advantages over their laser-guided counterparts. First, they can be delivered accurately against fixed targets regardless of weather conditions. Second, the aim points do not need to be deconflicted with respect to their proximity to one another. In the case of laser-guided munitions, combat pilots must ensure that the infrared "bloom" of another weapon detonation nearby does not affect the effectiveness of their own bombs. Inertially aided munitions, in contrast, permit attack on a target complex en masse. Third, they can enable fighter aircraft to attack two or more aim points during a single weapons delivery pass. Finally, they allowed coalition aircrews to achieve the greatest possible standoff from defended targets because they could release their weapons and immediately depart the area without having to continue to mark their intended aim point with a laser spot on which an LGB could guide until impact. A senior CAOC planner pointed out in this regard, "These factors allowed us to achieve mass that had not been possible before on a large scale. Indeed, the only combat aircraft that did not carry inertially aided munitions during the first night's attacks were F-15Es, because they had not yet been loaded with the requisite software."[26]

This pathbreaking application of mass precision was for the first time accompanied by a prevalence of effects-based thinking; that is, allied air operations were driven by specific desired results rather than the achievement of arbitrary levels of target destruction per se. Col. Mason Carpenter, the head of the CAOC's strategy division, subsequently wrote in this regard:

> The air and space effort was measured in effects, not numbers.
> Numbers were only interesting insofar as they helped determine
> effects. It did not really matter how many armored vehicles were
> destroyed. The real measure was how hard and well did the Iraqi
> armored divisions fight. When an Iraqi tank crew took off their
> uniforms and deserted, their tank was almost as good as destroyed.
> . . . Many of the surface forces failed to fight; the Iraqi air force
> failed to fly; and the Iraqi leadership failed to command. Effects
> are the bottom line.[27]

Carpenter added that this important net effect "cannot be captured or appreciated by traditional measures, such as the percentage of vehicles destroyed, numbers of sorties flown, or the percentage of munitions expended."[28]

With respect to rapidity of action, Air Chief Marshal Burridge described the campaign as "the first operation that [he] would characterize as postmodern warfare," in that "the degree and speed of maneuver and the tempo that was achieved was startling."[29] The speed of the coalition forces' advance clearly impressed the Iraqi military leadership as well. During postcampaign interrogations conducted by JFCOM, numerous senior Iraqi officers and other operational-level commanders cited the speed and unpredictability of allied offensive operations as the main factors that led to the early collapse of their own forces.[30]

To be sure, the allied ground advance was slowed for a time by the unanticipated resistance from Fedayeen Saddam, the three-day *shamal*, logistics concerns, and the absence of prompt feedback on the progress of the land offensive. The air portion of the campaign, however, sustained its high pace of operations without interruption throughout the three weeks of major fighting. In the end, coalition forces made it to Baghdad from a standing start in just twenty-one days. It is hard to imagine how the ground advance could have gone much faster even had everything worked flawlessly. One assessment of the major combat phase of Iraqi Freedom credited its success to "massive, precise, and responsive air power and a ground force that attacked over unprecedented distances with previously unseen speed."[31] Colonel Carpenter later concluded in a similar vein: "Never in the history of warfare has this much precision air power been applied in such a compressed period of time."[32] A Marine Corps reconnaissance platoon commander who was at the leading edge of I MEF's final push toward Baghdad offered this succinct portrayal of what that accomplishment meant in practice: "For the next hundred miles, all the way to the gates of Baghdad, every palm grove hid Iraqi armor, every field an artillery battery, and every alley an antiaircraft gun or surface-to-air missile launcher. But we never fired a shot. We saw the full effect of American air power: every one of these fearsome weapons was a blackened hulk."[33]

This last testament underscores tellingly how the major combat phase of Iraqi Freedom showcased the manner in which counterland air attack has increasingly begun to move doctrinally beyond solely the classic supporting roles of CAS (direct support) and air interdiction (indirect support) toward missions that are not intended just to support the friendly ground force, but rather to destroy the enemy's army directly and independently as the overall main weight of effort. An Air Force doctrine expert commented in this regard, "In the last update to Air Force Doctrine Document (AFDD) 2–1.3, *Counterland Operations*, we added a short section describing the generic term 'attack' as applying to those counterland missions that do not fall under the traditional mission rubrics of CAS or air interdiction. . . . I think it will be a while before we get this into joint doctrine, but the momentum is there."[34]

In addition, owing again to the successful precedent established in Afghanistan, the Iraq war featured a more closely linked force than ever before. As one CENTCOM staffer put it: "Everything that had a sensor was connected."[35] Persistent ISR provided by airborne and space-based sensors coupled with a precision-strike capability by all participating combat aircraft allowed General Moseley to deliver discriminant effects throughout the battlespace virtually on demand. This cross-service synergy was greatly aided by the extraordinary collegiality that General Franks fostered all the way from the campaign's earliest planning workups to the conclusion of major combat. During a strategy review session in the Pentagon with all four service chiefs on March 29, 2002, almost a year before the start of combat operations, Franks stated categorically: "At the end of the day, combatants, and that's either me or the boss I work for [Secretary Rumsfeld], are going to put together a joint and combined operation here, and it is not going to scratch the itch of any one of the services."[36] The most comprehensive and thorough assessment of U.S. Army operations during the campaign characterized the unprecedented level of harmonious cooperation among the components as "arguably . . . the first 'jointly' coherent campaign since the Korean War," as well as also "arguably the first campaign in which the initiatives inherent in the Goldwater-Nichols legislation bore full fruit."[37] Much the same can be said for the integration of space, mobility, and information in General Moseley's planning and execution of allied air and space operations. One account characterized him as "the quarterback of the [air] operation, calling audibles in response to changing circumstances."[38]

This unprecedented efficacy of joint force employment was a significant force multiplier in and of itself. There was a minimum of preoccupation with who was "supported" and who was "supporting." On the contrary, the inter-component relationships were fluid and dynamic. In sharp contrast to the initially flawed execution of Operation Anaconda in Afghanistan, in which CJTF Mountain's two-star Army commander sought at first to go it alone rather than seek the active involvement of fixed-wing air power, the integration of the air component into the planning and execution of joint operations in Iraqi Freedom was generally done properly and was essential in producing the resultant joint-force synergy. Indeed, seemingly anticipating the harmonious interaction at the operational and tactical levels, Vice Adm. Arthur Cebrowski, at that time the head of the Pentagon's Office of Force Transformation, observed several months *before* the campaign's start that "a new air-ground system has come into existence where you no longer talk in terms of one being supported and the other being supporting. That would be like asking if the lungs are in support of the heart or if the heart is in support of the lungs. It's a single system."[39]

This pattern of performance, moreover, was light-years removed from so-called Little League rules of joint warfare, in which all force elements are treated as coequal and each gets its fair-share chance to play a part. Instead, the component commanders pooled their combined combat assets into a "job jar" from which they selectively drew and matched the right combination of forces for any given situation. The result was an unprecedented mutual-support relationship between allied air and ground forces working in full concert. "The Iraqi land forces were forced to expose themselves by the speed of land operations and then hit hard from the air," one author noted, "which, in turn, sharply reduced the Iraqi threat to U.S. and British land forces. Jointness took on a new practical meaning."[40]

Allied air and ground operations were almost seamlessly integrated, with target information flowing with unprecedented rapidity and ease from SOF troops to aircrews and vice versa. Thanks to what senior leaders in the CAOC described as a "ruthless, staring constellation [of surveillance assets] looking at Baghdad," allied SOF units could spot targets and pass that information to an ISR system that got it promptly transmitted to strike aircraft orbiting overhead.[41] General DeLong later commended the U.S. military for "successfully transforming itself from being service-based to being joint-based."[42] The war saw air and space operations integrated into "a combined and joint campaign in the truest sense of the words. . . . No single component held the key to success—it required the full team effort for the coalition to succeed quickly."[43]

With respect to that observation, Admiral Cebrowski spoke of a "new sweet spot" highlighted by the Iraqi Freedom experience in the traditionally conflicted relationship between land forces and air power: "My sense is that the comfort level in regard to all indirect fires is going up," suggesting that ground commanders may now be increasingly inclined to rely on precision air-delivered CAS rather than on organic artillery and mortar fire.[44] He added: "I think, when the lessons learned come out, one of the things we are probably going to see is a new air-land dynamic."[45] Indeed, as another account noted, the plan for Iraqi Freedom "so effectively integrated the different types of joint fires that the phrase 'air campaign' may have become anachronistic."[46] Thanks to the effectiveness of the combined allied air and ground offensives and to the fragility of Iraq's air and ground defenses, the major combat phase of Iraqi Freedom was successfully prosecuted in less than half the time, with fewer than a third the total number of strike sorties, and with only a tenth the number of bombs that were dropped during Operation Desert Storm. Furthermore, the studiously discriminating nature of the bombing left Iraq's infrastructure largely intact, and a potential ecological and economic disaster was averted by timely allied action on the ground in securing the country's oil fields.

Of this synergy, one senior officer, discounting talk of CENTCOM's reportedly "brilliant" plan, noted that there are two kinds of plans: "The plan that might work, and the plan that won't work. This was a plan that might work. It had lots of options in it. It was well rehearsed. All the leaders understood the plan. And when it came time to execute, I think we seized every opportunity to exploit success. So when you combine the effects of very devastating air power, special operations, and then . . . a fairly bold ground attack, all of that caused any regime defensive plans to crumble."[47] General Leaf agreed, saying, "There will be silly arguments about which component achieved victory. It was a combination."[48]

Admiral Giambastiani subsequently testified before the House Armed Services Committee that CENTCOM benefited not only from precision munitions but also from "precision decisions to direct our smart weapons" made possible by such recent improvements as the synergistic interaction of SOF and conventional forces. He attributed the campaign's success to the "overmatching power," with far fewer ground troops than would otherwise have been required, that was enabled by the leveraging of the "key dimensions of the modern battlespace—knowledge, speed, precision, and lethality."[49] That characterization, he added, spoke not only of an American style of warfare moving beyond the organizing construct of "overwhelming force" that had been the hallmark of Operation Desert Storm, but also of "a remarkable shift . . . in the way joint forces operate today," culminating in what he called "a new joint way of war."[50] Expanding further on this point, Admiral Giambastiani's director for joint requirements and integration at JFCOM added that the success of the joint and combined effort was substantially the result of "advances in technologies, coupled with innovative warfighting concepts joined together by a new joint culture," which collectively enabled "a level of coherent military operations that we have not been able to achieve before."[51]

Finally, with respect to flexibility in execution, the war featured a simultaneous conduct of offensive air and ground operations in which the use of various force elements by CENTCOM's component commanders was mutually supporting and synergistic in the operational results it achieved. In a postcampaign briefing at the Naval War College, the chairman of the JCS, General Myers, contrasted this approach with the "sequenced, sectored, and segregated campaign" of Operation Desert Storm in 1991, adding that what made the major combat phase of Iraqi Freedom distinct and unique was the essentially simultaneous start of the air and ground offensives. Myers characterized the latter approach as a "more flexible, adaptable, and agile campaign."[52] Although Iraqi leaders from Hussein on down thought that they could hunker down and endure any allied bombing campaign, the concurrent air and ground offensives were more than they anticipated. Ultimately, the intensity and effectiveness of nonstop allied air operations led some Iraqi units to expend as much as 80 percent of their effort merely on surviving by separating their ordnance, equipment, and personnel. Even then, Iraqi commanders conceded that allied forces managed to attack all three of those Iraqi equities concurrently and successfully.[53]

Allied air power was crucial in setting the conditions for the rapid conclusion of major combat on the ground. An RAF Harrier GR7 squadron commander who took part in the western desert operation called the performance nothing less than "awesome," a crucial point that, he added, tended to be overshadowed by the postcampaign insurgency and sectarian violence that festered after the successful toppling of Hussein's regime.[54]

Characteristic of the feedback that allied aircrews at the unit level received from their leaders after the three weeks of fighting were over was the praise from the commander of the Air Force's 524th Fighter Squadron, Lt. Col. Tom Berghoff, for his F-16 pilots:

> I am extremely proud of the squadron's accomplishments. We had a lot of guys who were young—without much experience out on the wing—who did just great. They did really well because my flight leads did what they were supposed to. They led the flights, made the right decisions, and took their wingmen and got them in and out of Iraq, and the end result was a 100 percent mission success rate. All the targets were positively [identified] as military, and there were no collateral damage issues—there was no fratricide by the squadron. Pilots made the right decisions, threat-reacted to survive, [and had] no battle damage. We flew a lot of sorties and worked hard. We didn't miss one of our [time-sensitive target] taskings, and a lot of that was quick reaction, quick thinking. When things happen fast, there is a tendency

to make mistakes, but they didn't. We blew up a lot of high-value targets and supported the Army's push to Baghdad. And we brought everybody home.[55]

Colonel Carpenter, who headed the CAOC's strategy division throughout the campaign, later observed that the three weeks of major combat made the most of "a disabling strategy intended to ensure the swift collapse of the regime by applying rapid, deliberate, disciplined, proportional, and precise force within fast decision cycles to dislocate and disrupt the regime at the strategic level." He further noted that it employed "selective disruption at the operational level, used enabling operations to empower the Kurds in the north, and used preventive operations in the west to preclude the Iraqis from employing WMD and/or conventional theater ballistic missiles that would trigger political involvement from Israel."[56] The last of those operations saw a uniquely heavy SOF involvement. Allied SOF teams scoured the western Iraqi desert for Scud missiles and launchers to prevent any such missiles that might have been in Iraqi hands from being fired at Israel. They also performed as ground FACs for allied air power on a far greater scale than they had in Afghanistan.

The integration of allied SOF teams and air assets in Iraqi Freedom was both a successful force multiplier and a template for future joint and combined operations. That successful integration emerged from seeds that were planted during an impromptu SOF and CAOC training exercise that had been held even before the start of Operation Enduring Freedom. The nation's earlier combat experience in Afghanistan made a perfect live-fire training environment for the CAOC's special operations subdivision, whose staff learned a great deal very quickly about the problems and virtues of working closely with joint and combined fixed-wing air power. The Afghan experience also gave airmen in the CAOC a valuable opportunity to learn how to interact with and maximize air support for SOF operations.

In a subsequent attempt to capture the essence of allied air operations throughout the major combat phase of Iraqi Freedom, University of Chicago political scientist Robert Pape alleged that the campaign had succeeded in toppling Hussein's regime only after allied air power "shifted from attacking leadership targets to bombing Iraq's Republican Guard and other regular military units." That flawed assessment was based on the mistaken premise that "the war began with an effort to shock and awe the Iraqi leadership into capitulating without a fight, but this quickly failed," as a result of which allied air power was instead "turned against Iraq's forces in the field."[57] In fact, *both* elements of the air campaign were carefully planned as sequential undertakings and were anticipated as such by CENTCOM's most senior leaders. CENTCOM's air component attacked Republican Guard targets from day one onward, but its main weight of effort, by careful design from the very start, moved progressively from the inside (i.e., those security and leadership protection forces closest to Saddam Hussein) to the outside (i.e., those forces farther away from Hussein—the Republican Guard).

In sum, the major combat phase of Iraqi Freedom was a true joint and combined effort in which all force elements played influential roles and in which, as two historians writing an early synopsis of the campaign aptly noted, there was "little of the petty parochialism that too often marks interservice relations within the [Washington] Beltway."[58] The CFLCC, General McKiernan, later spoke directly to that cooperative spirit when he reflected during an after-action interview: "The big strength in this campaign was the personalities of the various component commanders. . . . You can say a lot of that [interservice cooperation was possible] because of developments in joint doctrine and training. . . . But a lot of it [was] . . . also in the chemistry between . . . the leaders."[59] Such harmony was especially notable during the challenging and complex urban air-ground combat that occurred during the days immediately preceding the fall of Baghdad. Of that experience, General Moseley's representative to the land component, General Leaf, commented, "The key to adapting to that environment has been open communications and dedicated teamwork between the air and land components. Cooperation between ground and air forces in this conflict has been extraordinary, and our operations in urban Baghdad are an extension of that."[60] General Franks likewise observed on the eve of the regime's collapse, "The fact is that if you have a whole bucket of air force and a whole bucket of ground force and the rest, it's a fool who decides ahead of time which application against this pot you describe is the thing that reaches what I call the tipping point."[61]

General Myers added that the close integration of all force elements was "a huge lesson here."[62] His successor as JCS chairman, Gen. Peter Pace of the Marine Corps, echoed the same judgment when he said: "History is going to show that this war is the first time that U.S. forces operated . . . the way those who crafted Goldwater-Nichols envisaged."[63] Speaking as the maritime component commander, Vice Admiral Keating characterized the operational payoff as "joint warfighting at the highest form of the art I'd ever seen. . . . There was understanding, friendship, familiarity, and trust among all the services and special forces working for General Franks. He did, in my view, a remarkable job of engendering that friendship, camaraderie, and trust. In fact, he insisted on it. . . . There was no service equity infighting—zero."[64]

Indeed, the three weeks of major combat in Iraqi Freedom clearly vin-
dicated the Goldwater-Nichols Defense Reorganization Act of 1986, which
directed the gradual evolution of a true joint culture of mutual trust and coop-
erativeness in American joint force operations. As an early draft of JFCOM's
postcampaign lessons-learned assessment emphatically put this point, CENT-
COM pulled together for the second Persian Gulf War "what was arguably the
most coherently joint force the United States has ever fielded. . . . [It] developed
and matured a climate of jointness that, while deemphasizing various service
cultures, led to the components learning to trust each other, working together
to achieve unified action. The resulting joint environment and supporting joint
networks enabled CENTCOM to overcome obstacles and eliminate many of
the gaps that challenge cohesion in an ad hoc joint force."[65] In particular, the
campaign experience saw major improvements in the development of greater
harmony in the relationships between the Air Force and naval aviation (along
with the latter's important Marine Corps component).[66] That process materially
helped CENTCOM's air component to overcome persistent barriers that had
once impeded the fullest possible exploitation of American air power and its
integration with other force elements in a joint and combined context.

It would be premature, however, to conclude that the American armed services have reached the end of the long road from service *interoperability* to service
interdependence as a result of their Iraqi Freedom experience. As David Johnson
pointed out in this regard in 2006, "despite all the self-congratulatory talk of
. . . 'seamless joint operations' emerging from [the second Persian Gulf War], the
reality remains that within their [areas of operations], component commanders
called the shots, perhaps at the cost of overall joint effectiveness. . . . At the heart
of the issue [here] is the persistent reality that the services do not feel confident
that they can rely absolutely on each other when the chips are down. Thus they
maintain redundant capabilities and develop service warfighting concepts that
are largely self-reliant."[67]

Continuing in this vein, Johnson added:

> As it stands now, joint doctrine frequently reflects a consensus view
> of what the services will tolerate, rather than a truly integrated
> joint perspective. . . . A signal example of this reality is the FSCL, as
> employed by the Army in both Gulf Wars, which is permissive to
> ground component commanders . . . but restrictive to the employ-
> ment of air power. The FSCL, however, is merely symptomatic
> of the Army's desire to control a large [area of operations]—
> and all the resources of the other services entering that [area of

operations]—to execute its operational doctrine. This limits the employment and effectiveness of fixed-wing air power—which is more effective than organic Army systems for deep operations— in operations short of the FSCL but forward of the range of divisional indirect fire systems. . . . [Many] of the purported lessons learned about the relative roles of air and ground power since the end of the Cold War have been interpreted within service perspectives—perspectives shaped by experience and culture— and this has the effect of sustaining the status quo. Much work remains to attain a truly joint American warfighting system.[68]

The lead author of the most thorough assessment of U.S. Army operations throughout the major combat phase of Iraqi Freedom wrote more directly in that regard that notwithstanding much "chest-thumping" over the alleged achievement of unprecedented cross-service harmony, the persistent friction that bedeviled the relations between CENTCOM's land and air components over the ownership and control of joint battlespace throughout much of the three-week offensive "drove home the point that we really still don't fight joint campaigns."[69] Perhaps this conclusion may be safely regarded as the main downside lesson from the Iraqi Freedom experience.[70]

On the plus side, however, the air component in the campaign against Hussein's regime had everything to do with allied ground forces' freedom *from* attack and freedom *to* attack. In fulfilling its roster of combat tasks in the campaign, allied air power did not just "support" the land component by "softening up" enemy forces. More often than not, it conducted wholesale destruction of Iraqi ground forces prior to and independently of allied ground action. On other occasions, it both supported allied ground actions and was supported by them in shaping enemy force dispositions for more effective attack from the air.

The Iraqi Freedom experience further demonstrated that the air assets in all services are at the brink of a major transformation from analog to digital approaches to warfighting. Because virtually every combat aircraft that participated in Iraqi Freedom was capable of delivering GPS- and inertially aided munitions, the air component quickly exhausted its preplanned target list. With respect to target attack flexibility, air component strike missions throughout the three weeks of major combat called for a variety of weapons guidance mechanisms (both GPS and laser), fuzing options (instantaneous, delayed, or airburst), and warhead sizes (500-pound, 1,000-pound, and 2,000-pound). At least eighteen munition and fuzing combinations were available to CAOC weaponeers for the conduct of Iraqi Freedom.

The RQ/MQ-1 Predator and RQ-4 Global Hawk UAV platforms, which had operated together for the first time so effectively in Afghanistan, gave CAOC planners every incentive to leverage the diverse capabilities of these aircraft even more effectively during the three-week war in Iraq. Global Hawk was used to detect and geolocate such mobile targets as tanks, SAMs, and early-warning radars and then to forward this information in real time to airborne strike aircraft that were best positioned to engage those pop-up targets of opportunity. Just as the Predators had been major winners during Enduring Freedom, the Global Hawk truly came into its own in support of subsequent combat operations in Iraqi Freedom. As CAOC operators later reported, "Global Hawk's ability to gather information on troops, equipment, SAMs, and AAA, send that information to intelligence analysts, and finally deliver it to the CAOC floor for execution reflected a process and concept that need to continue."[71]

One informed account described the "critical role" played by the array of CENTAF's air assets "in every aspect of fighting during Iraqi Freedom, from high-intensity maneuver to low-intensity convoy security and urban or rural anti-guerilla operations. . . . At the outermost tier, beyond the FSCL, air assets shaped the battlefield by preventing operational movement by major Iraqi forces, keeping formations bottled up in Al Amarah, and preventing Republican Guard units from retreating into urban areas. Within the FSCL, air assets maintained a constant grinding action, wearing down Iraqi units well ahead of coalition ground forces. . . . This integration set aside many of the interservice disputes," yielding a "sophisticated synergy of [ISR] sensors, command and control processors, and precision-guided munitions—a nexus that advocates of air power feel was exploited in a mature form for the first time."[72] Allied air operations were intended to facilitate the quickest possible capture of Baghdad without any major head-to-head land battles between allied and Iraqi ground forces.[73] With respect to the interservice disagreements that recurred from time to time at the margins of the campaign's conduct, the lead author of the most thorough assessment of U.S. Army operations rightly concluded that "most of the issues we quibble over, while important, are not as important as the [more] fundamental truth—it was a joint fight with problems solved by men of good will who understood the stakes. . . . At the end of the day, I have nothing but admiration for the work the air component did in Iraqi Freedom."[74]

Unfortunately, the remarkable advances that were steadily made in American air warfare capability after the first Gulf War of 1991 and were so amply demonstrated in early 2003 have since been almost completely overshadowed by the subsequent insurgency and sectarian violence that prevailed in Iraq for four years after the three weeks of major combat that brought down Hussein's regime.[75] Only in 2007 did Gen. David Petraeus develop and implement a new approach stressing long-proven principles of counterinsurgency warfare aimed at providing genuine security to the Iraqi people to supplant the counterproductive brute-force approach that a succession of previous U.S. joint force commanders had used throughout the preceding four years of the allied occupation of Iraq. The steadily mounting political, economic, and human costs of that deadly turmoil tended, for a disturbingly long time, to render the initial three-week campaign in March and April 2003 an all but forgotten (and, to many, even irrelevant) achievement. The persistence of that civil strife led former secretary of defense Melvin Laird to offer a sober reminder to observers of all persuasions that "getting out of a war is still dicier than getting into one."[76] It also bore discomfiting witness to the "initial miscalculations, misdirected planning, and inadequate preparation" of the second Bush administration's leading national security principals that lay at the root of the ensuing devolution of events.[77]

Certainly, credible witnesses had warned of just such a festering predicament. Among numerous others, William Lind of the Free Congress Foundation wrote presciently: "When American forces capture Baghdad and take down Saddam Hussein, the real war will not end but begin. It will be fought in Iraq, in part, as an array of nonstate elements begin to fight America and each other. . . . This kind of war, fourth-generation war, is something American and other state armed forces do not know how to fight."[78] Ever since postcampaign developments in Iraq first began to turn sour, a legion of respected commentators have dissected and documented the hastily improvised, underresourced, and ineffectual attempts at stabilization in Iraq undertaken at the outset by the Bush administration.[79] *Washington Post* reporter Rick Atkinson observed on this score: "None of the people in Washington who had led the nation into a preemptive attack by a small invasion force nearly bereft of allies wanted to believe that the conflict could drag on for months, perhaps tying up most of the Army's ten divisions and bleeding the nation of money and manpower."[80]

All the same, in testimony before the Senate Armed Services Committee three months after the coalition took down the Ba'athist regime and well into the steadily intensifying postcampaign insurgency, Secretary Rumsfeld continued to appear either unmindful of or indifferent to the need for a sufficient allied presence on the ground to ensure the prompt social and political stabilization of Iraq and to provide adequate security for the Iraqi rank and file. Expressing the contrary view, Rumsfeld declared: "In the 21st century, mass may no longer be the best measure of power in a conflict. After all, when Baghdad fell, there were just over 100,000 American forces on the ground. General Franks overwhelmed the enemy not with the typical three-to-one advantage in mass, but by over-matching the enemy with advanced capabilities and using those capabilities in innovative and unexpected ways."[81] The error that both Franks and his superiors in the administration made, however, was to assume—against more than ample prior expert advice to the contrary—that a parsimonious commitment of allied ground troops to meet the immediate needs of regime change would also suffice to end the war satisfactorily and to achieve the coalition's broader goal of bringing a functioning democracy to Iraq.

Whether or not one believes that going to war against Hussein's Iraq was in the best interests of U.S. and international security, the overwhelming consensus today among informed commentators with the benefit of hindsight is that CENTCOM's campaign plan, encouraged and approved by the Bush administration, failed both completely and unpardonably to anticipate and address the needs of postcampaign stabilization and attempted democratization that have continued to demand American and allied attention ever since the end of major combat in 2003. That manifold failure, as well as such subsequent sins of commission on the administration's part as the ill-advised wholesale dismantling of the Iraqi army and police force and the forced displacement of all Iraqi civil servants with any senior Ba'ath Party connections into the ranks of the unemployed, overlooked the most fundamental tenet of democratic nation-building theory, namely, that an indispensable precondition of successful political modernization must be the establishment and growth of effective state institutions of governance.[82] Indeed, it would not be a reach to say that the first edicts of the Coalition Provisional Authority that were put into place in Iraq by the Bush administration under Ambassador Paul Bremer in the immediate aftermath of the Ba'athist regime's collapse had the direct and intended effect of doing precisely the opposite.

Today, in large part because of those misguided rulings and, even more so, of CENTCOM's and the administration's shared failure to see to the needs of ensuring public security in the immediate aftermath of the regime's collapse, most would concur with Thomas Friedman's judgment that the war "was not preordained to fail but was never given a proper chance to succeed."[83] Thomas Ricks put the same point in a different way in his postmortem on the American-led invasion: "Speed didn't kill the enemy—it bypassed him. It won the campaign, but it didn't win the war, because the war plan was built on the mistaken strategic goal of capturing Baghdad, and it confused removing Iraq's regime with the far more difficult task of changing the entire country."[84]

To be sure, the United States and its allies brought to an end not only the iron rule of a dictator who had brutalized his people for more than thirty years, but also the continuing regional security challenge from Ba'athist Iraq that had occasioned a costly American and British military presence in Southwest Asia ever since the conclusion of Operation Desert Storm. The flawed and incomplete way in which that laudable objective was pursued, however, points up most uncompromisingly the crucial importance of never forgetting the abiding rule that no plan, however elegant, survives initial contact with the enemy. It also provides a sobering reminder that any exhaustive plan for a complete regime takedown must anticipate and duly invest against the most likely political consequences in addition to planning the campaign's course and outcome through the major phase of combat operations. Johns Hopkins University strategist Eliot Cohen interjected perhaps the most incisive judgment yet rendered on this account when he wrote at the end of 2006: "From the outset of the Iraq war, much of our difficulty has stemmed not so much from failures to find the right strategy as from an astounding and depressing inability to implement the strategic and operational choices we have nominally made. . . . We have not come to the brink of failure because we did not know how important it is to employ young Iraqi men or keep detained insurgents out of circulation or to prevent militia penetration of the security forces by vetting the commander of those forces. We have known these things—but we have not done these things."[85]

On that point, a thoughtful treatise by Frederick Kagan that appeared in 2006 spotlighted "the primacy of destruction over planning for political outcomes" that had predominated up to that time in American military thought since Desert Storm. That focus, Kagan wrote, had occasioned a counterproductive situation in which the nation's military transformation efforts to date had entailed "a continuous movement away from the political objective of war toward a focus on [merely] killing and destroying things." Such misplaced emphasis, he suggested, was quintessentially reflected in the revealing label "Phase IV" (the then-envisaged follow-on to the major combat phase, or "Phase III," of Iraqi Freedom), which treated postwar stabilization and consolidation operations almost as an afterthought to the "decisive combat operations" that American military planners viewed as the "main mission."

Such an approach sufficed handily for Operations Desert Storm, Deliberate Force, and Allied Force during the 1990s, but those were limited undertakings aimed at coercing desired enemy behavior, not at the more demanding task of removing one government and replacing it with another. However, Kagan argued, if the nation's military engagements in its ongoing war against Islamist extremism are going to continue to be wars of regime change, as was clearly the case in both Operations Enduring Freedom and Iraqi Freedom, then the first concern in operations planning "should be determining what the political end state should look like in as much detail as possible," because "military victory over the incumbent government is . . . only the prelude to the operations that will actually determine the outcome of the effort." Accordingly, Kagan insisted, "Phase IV," or whatever the regime replacement activity is to be called, is "not subordinate to or even equal with 'decisive combat operations.' . . . It must predominate."[86]

Andrew Krepinevich offered a comparable observation even earlier, while the dust from Phase III was still settling, when he wrote that "the U.S. military's preference to do what it does best—defeat enemy forces in the field and then quickly depart—must be overcome. The practice of crafting quick exit strategies must yield to a willingness to develop a comprehensive strategy for winning both the war and the post-conflict period that follows." Krepinevich also was among the first to suggest candidly after the initial flush of allied self-congratulation had worn off and the new reality of post-Hussein Iraq had begun settling in that "as can be seen in the wake of the coalition's victory in Iraq, those who practice regime change incur consequences as well as certain moral and political responsibilities."[87] Finally, he rightly noted that the campaign experience had pointed up the criticality of continued U.S. access to overseas basing options, a luxury often taken for granted that had begun to appear in growing jeopardy since the end of the Cold War in 1991. As a case in point, he observed, CENTCOM's unexpected loss of the use of Turkish territory at the last minute sidelined some one hundred American aircraft that had been slated to take part in the campaign and disrupted planned U.S. tanker operations to support the Navy's carrier air wings deployed in the eastern Mediterranean. Rebasing those tankers in Bulgaria, said Krepinevich, "provided an acceptable, if not entirely satisfactory, solution."[88]

The successful conduct of Iraqi Freedom's major combat phase presaged a new era of warfare for the United States in two ways. At the same time that the experience heralded the nation's final mastery of high-intensity conventional warfare, it also brought Americans face to face for the first time since Vietnam with a refined mode of fourth-generation asymmetric warfare that is likely to be the defining feature of conflict in at least the world's most unstable and ideologically riven arenas for the indeterminate future. This newly emergent challenge, against which the United States remains inadequately configured in most respects despite steady improvement since 2003, is distinguished by nonstate and transnational actors and associations, loosely knit cells of self-generating action groups, dispersed and nonlinear operations without fronts, concurrent attacks on all elements of friendly governments and economies, sheer violence and disruption as its proximate goals, and terror as its primary instrument of choice.[89] As one of the best assessments of this burgeoning form of post–Cold War conflict put it, fourth-generation warfare "uses all available networks—political, economic, social, and military—to convince the enemy's political decision makers that their strategic goals are either unachievable or too costly for the perceived benefit. . . . It does not attempt to win by defeating the enemy's forces. Instead, via the networks, it directly attacks the minds of enemy decision makers to destroy the enemy's political will."[90]

Whatever errors the Bush administration's most senior leaders may have made by failing to insure adequately against the most likely needs of the end-game, however, there can be no denying that the allied combatants in all services who prosecuted the campaign at the operational and tactical levels, thanks in considerable part to the enabling contributions of CENTCOM's air component as described in the preceding chapters, performed in an exemplary way when it came to the execution of Iraqi Freedom's major combat phase in March and April 2003. A former Marine Corps F/A-18 pilot wrote of that experience that none of what ensued afterward "should detract from what was done and learned during [the three weeks of major combat in] Operation Iraqi Freedom. The successes were spectacular in a way that was unlike anything seen before."[91]

The air component's contribution toward that outcome bore powerful witness not only to the many investments that the U.S. Air Force, Navy, and Marine Corps, along with their RAF and RAAF counterparts, had made in the hardware ingredients of their combat repertoires since Desert Storm, but also to such crucial intangibles as the cutting-edge aircrew training at the postgraduate level provided by the USAF Weapons School at Nellis AFB, Nevada; the Naval Strike and Air Warfare Center with its integral Topgun program at NAS Fallon, Nevada; and Marine Aviation Weapons and Tactics Squadron One at MCAS Yuma, Arizona. The air component's banner performance further resulted from the repetitive case-hardening of allied aircrews and their commanders at all levels that had been inculcated over the course of the preceding decade through recurrent, realistic large-force training exercises, exacting operational readiness inspections and tactical evaluations at regular intervals in between, unrelenting frankness in training mission debriefings, and continuous joint and combined enforcement of the northern and southern no-fly zones over Iraq. All of that finally culminated in an opportunity for CENTAF to exercise those investments in high-intensity combat under the leadership of an able and aggressive air component commander and with the help of the most experienced CAOC staff in the history of air warfare.

Against that positive and gratifying backdrop, however, must be juxtaposed the exceptionally costly and arguably avoidable sectarian violence and sustained insurgency that the United States and its coalition partners were subsequently forced to contend with for more than six painful years as a result of the Bush administration's ill-considered going-in plan for achieving an orderly regime change in Iraq. If there is any enduring lesson to be drawn here with respect to the role and utility of air power in modern warfare in light of that subsequent bitter experience, it surely must be that even the most capable air weapon imaginable can never be more effective than the strategy it is intended to underwrite.

As Colin Gray insightfully noted in this regard in 2007, for air power's inherent advantage "to secure strategic results of value, it must serve a national and . . . overall military strategy that is feasible, coherent, and politically sensible. If these basic requirements are not met, [then] air power, no matter how impeccably applied tactically and operationally, will be employed as a waste of life, taxes, and, frankly, trust between the sharp end of [a nation's] spear and its shaft." More to the point, Gray went on to insist, a nation's overall campaign strategy can be so dysfunctional that it "cannot be rescued from defeat by a dominant air power, no matter how that air power is employed."[92] By all signs from the continuing unease that so many around the world have felt since 2003 as a result of the nation's still-undecided gamble in Iraq, this dictum remains no less pertinent to the challenges that the United States and its leaders face across the conflict spectrum today and for the foreseeable future. Those challenges entail not only our continuing counterinsurgency preoccupations of the moment, but also the all but certain prospect of higher-intensity showdowns against more able opponents who can be counted on to test us for higher stakes in years to come.

NOTES

Introduction

1. Those two operations were initiated to protect Shiite populations in the south of Iraq and the Kurdish peoples in the north by prohibiting, among other things, Iraqi fixed-wing aircraft operations south of the 32nd parallel (and, after 1996, the 33rd) and north of the 36th parallel. Southern Watch operations were conducted mainly from bases in Saudi Arabia and Kuwait; Northern Watch sorties flew mainly out of Incirlik Air Base in Turkey. The two combined operations denied the Iraqi air force the use of two-thirds of Iraq's airspace. From their inception in 1991 until the start of Operation Iraqi Freedom twelve years later, American and British (and, until December 1998, French) forces flew more than 200,000 armed overwatch and combat support sorties to police the two no-fly zones.

2. The term "joint" refers to the cooperative involvement of two or more U.S. armed services in a combat, peacekeeping, or humanitarian operation. "Joint and combined" refers to both multiservice U.S. and allied participation in such operations.

3. For a fuller development of this point, see Richard N. Haass, *War of Necessity, War of Choice: A Memoir of Two Iraq Wars* (New York: Simon and Schuster, 2009), especially 233–278.

4. A wide-ranging exploration of the many strategy and policy issues raised by this new thrust of American security planning in the wake of the September 11 attacks may be found in Karl P. Mueller and others, *Striking First: Preemptive and Preventive Attack in U.S. National Security Policy* (Santa Monica, Calif.: RAND Corporation, MG-403-AF, 2006).

5. George W. Bush, *Decision Points* (New York: Crown Publishers, 2010), 229.

6. Bob Woodward, *Plan of Attack* (New York: Simon and Schuster, 2004), 120.

7. Todd S. Purdum, *A Time of Our Choosing: America's War in Iraq* (New York: Times Books, 2003), 4.

8. For the U.S. figures, see "U.S. Casualties in Iraq," at http://www.global security.org/military/ops/iraq_casualties.htm. The number of Iraqi civilian fatalities due directly to combat and insurgency-related operations is highly disputed. One of the more reliable sources, the Iraq Body Count Project, an independent UK/U.S. group, put the number at around 111,000 in mid-

August 2011. See Iraq Body Count Project, at http://www.iraqbodycount .org.

9. Andrew Flibbert, "The Road to Baghdad: Ideas and Intellectuals in Explanations of the Iraq War," *Security Studies*, April–June 2006, 317.

10. See Charles Duelfer and others, *Comprehensive Report of the Special Adviser to the DCI on Iraq's WMD* (Washington, D.C.: Iraq Survey Group for the Central Intelligence Agency, September 30, 2004). Both President Bush and his closest White House counselor during the planning and conduct of the campaign have been frank in acknowledging their collective error in this regard. In his memoirs Bush freely admitted that "the reality was that I had sent American troops into combat based in large part on intelligence that proved false. That was a massive blow to our credibility—my credibility— that would shake the confidence of the American people" (Bush, *Decision Points*, 262). Bush's most senior political adviser, Karl Rove, later conceded in his own memoirs: "I am under no illusions—the failure to find stockpiles of WMD did great damage to the administration's credibility" (Karl Rove, *Courage and Consequence: My Life as a Conservative in the Fight* [New York: Simon and Schuster, 2010], 342).

11. The respected British newsweekly *The Economist* reported in late October 2011 that "the verdict of Americans at large is bleaker. . . . Even among those who fought in Iraq or Afghanistan, . . . only 44 percent now think the war was worth fighting, according to recent polling by the Pew Research Center; and an even smaller proportion of the general public, 36 percent, agrees with the veterans" ("No Satisfaction, No Resignation," *The Economist*, October 29, 2011, 42).

12. I am grateful to my colleague Nora Bensahel for urging me to highlight this important qualification to the otherwise impressive success story of the three-week major combat phase of Operation Iraqi Freedom.

13. Michael R. Gordon and Bernard E. Trainor, *Cobra II: The Inside Story of the Invasion and Occupation of Iraq* (New York: Pantheon Books, 2006), xxxi. The ground-centric emphasis of this otherwise superb account is telegraphed by its title, which was the code name adopted for the *land* component of Operation Iraqi Freedom, referring to the offensive launched by Lt. Gen. Omar Bradley's First Army eight weeks after the D-day landings during the Normandy campaign of World War II.

14. Stephen Biddle and others, *Toppling Saddam: Iraq and American Military Transformation* (Carlisle, Pa.: Strategic Studies Institute, U.S. Army War College, April 2004), 1. See also Stephen Biddle, "Speed Kills? Reassessing the Role

of Speed, Precision, and Situation Awareness in the Fall of Saddam," *Journal of Strategic Studies*, February 2007.

15. Col. Gregory Fontenot, USA (Ret.); Lt. Col. E. J. Degen, USA; and Lt. Col. David Tohn, USA, *On Point: The United States Army in Operation Iraqi Freedom* (Annapolis, Md.: Naval Institute Press, 2005), 178. This impressive study is unswervingly joint-minded in its appreciative treatment of the air component's contribution to CENTCOM's campaign to topple Hussein and should be mandatory reading for all those interested in understanding what the air war was supporting on the ground throughout the three weeks of major combat. With regard to the early transition in focus of the air offensive from independent strategic operations to direct support of the land advance, Colonel Fontenot later recalled that "to me, the best thing about [General] Moseley [the campaign's air commander] was that he was able to anticipate when to shift effort and did so very well" (comments on an earlier draft by Col. Gregory Fontenot, USA [Ret.], October 22, 2010).

16. Iraqi Freedom also offered a base of experience from which to identify lessons that were *not* duly heeded by Washington and CENTCOM, suggesting areas that continue to need remedial work.

17. Gen. Tommy Franks, USA (Ret.), with Malcolm McConnell, *American Soldier* (New York: Regan Books, 2004), 411–412.

18. See, among numerous others, Jon Lee Anderson, *The Fall of Baghdad* (New York: Penguin Press, 2004); Rick Atkinson, *In the Company of Soldiers: A Chronicle of Combat* (New York: Henry Holt, 2004); John Koopman, *McCoy's Marines: Darkside to Baghdad* (St. Paul, Minn.: Zenith Press, 2004); Tim Pritchard, *Ambush Alley: The Most Extraordinary Battle of the Iraq War* (New York: Random House, 2005); Bing West and Maj. Gen. Ray L. Smith, USMC (Ret.), *The March Up: Taking Baghdad with the United States Marines* (New York: Bantam Dell, 2003); Evan Wright, *Generation Kill: Devil Dogs, Iceman, Captain America, and the New Face of American War* (New York: G. P. Putnam's Sons, 2004); Karl Zinnmeister, *Boots on the Ground: A Month with the 82nd Airborne in the Battle for Iraq* (New York: St. Martin's Press, 2003); and David Zucchino, *Thunder Run: The Armored Strike to Capture Baghdad* (New York: Atlantic Monthly Press, 2004). Of those books that have appeared on the war more broadly defined, Thomas Donnelly, *Operation Iraqi Freedom: A Strategic Assessment* (Washington, D.C.: AEI Press, July 2004), and John Keegan, *The Iraq War* (New York: Alfred A. Knopf, 2004), do not address air operations at all; and Purdum, *A Time of Our Choosing*, and Williamson Murray and Maj. Gen. Robert H. Scales Jr., USA (Ret.), *The Iraq War: A Military History* (Cambridge, Mass.: Belknap Press of Harvard University

Press, 2003), do so only cursorily. Franks' memoir, *American Soldier*, likewise discusses allied air operations only briefly and superficially. A more detailed treatment of the air war is offered in Walter Boyne, *Operation Iraqi Freedom: What Went Right, What Went Wrong, and Why* (New York: Tom Doherty Associates, 2003). By far the most richly informed account of allied air and space operations thus far is Michael Knights, *Cradle of Conflict: Iraq and the Birth of the Modern U.S. Military* (Annapolis, Md.: Naval Institute Press, 2005), 235–327. At a more general policy and strategy level, see also Keith L. Shimko, *The Iraq Wars and America's Military Revolution* (New York: Cambridge University Press, 2010), 142–172.

19. I am grateful to my RAND colleague Karl Mueller for drawing my attention to this important point.

20. Amy Butler, "Lack of Embedded Reporters a Hurdle for Air Force Media Ops," *Inside the Air Force*, April 4, 2003, 5–6.

21. *Joint Lessons Learned: Operation Iraqi Freedom Major Combat Operations*, coordinating draft, U.S. Joint Forces Command, Norfolk, Va., March 1, 2004, 33.

22. Anthony H. Cordesman, "The 'Instant Lessons' of the Iraq War: Main Report," third working draft, Center for Strategic and International Studies, Washington, D.C., April 14, 2003, 8.

23. Murray and Scales, *The Iraq War*, 73.

Chapter 1. The Road to War

1. Murray and Scales, *The Iraq War*, 13.

2. Bush and his national security adviser stated succinctly in their joint memoirs published seven years later: "Had we gone the invasion route, the United States could still be an occupying power in a bitterly hostile land" (George Bush and Brent Scowcroft, *A World Transformed* [New York: Alfred A. Knopf, 1998], 489).

3. Donald Rumsfeld, *Known and Unknown: A Memoir* (New York: Sentinel, 2011), 415.

4. Quoted in Charles Krauthammer, "What Ever Happened to the Powell Doctrine?" *Washington Post*, April 20, 2001. An informed assessment of Hussein's risk calculus eight years after Operation Desert Storm ended suggested that the Iraqi dictator's ultimate decision to withdraw his occupying forces from Kuwait "stemmed from his fear of losing both the war and his entire army. . . . The destruction of the Iraqi army would have stripped Baghdad of its ability to defend itself. . . . It also would have meant the destruction of the Republican Guard. . . . Finally, such a crushing defeat would have been such

a humiliation that he would have had to expect an immediate challenge from within his power base" (Daniel Byman, Kenneth Pollack, and Matthew Waxman, "Coercing Saddam Hussein: Lessons from the Past," *Survival*, autumn 1998, 134).

5. Bush, *Decision Points*, 228; Rumsfeld, *Known and Unknown*, 418.

6. This prolonged pattern of behavior on Hussein's part is chronicled in detail in Kenneth M. Pollack, *The Threatening Storm: The Case for Invading Iraq* (New York: Random House, 2002), 55–108.

7. Rumsfeld, *Known and Unknown*, 414.

8. Purdum, *A Time of Our Choosing*, 20.

9. Woodward, *Plan of Attack*, 25.

10. Ibid.

11. Ibid., 1.

12. Ibid., 34.

13. Michael R. Gordon, "Pointing Finger, Bush Broadens His 'Doctrine,'" *New York Times*, January 30, 2002.

14. Charles Krauthammer, "Redefining the War," *Washington Post*, February 1, 2002.

15. Woodward, *Plan of Attack*, 108–109.

16. Ibid., 116.

17. Ibid., 119–120.

18. Mike Allen and Karen De Young, "Bush: U.S. Will Strike First at Enemies," *Washington Post*, June 2, 2002. In fact, according to one of CENTAF's key air operations planners, the first steps toward developing a concept of operations for the air war were taken in early February 2002 when, "upon returning from Tampa to Shaw, under General Moseley's direction, CENTAF planners put together the first draft of a three-day MAAP using a force structure that General Moseley had passed to Shaw from the CAOC in Saudi Arabia. This three-day MAAP would be continuously refined over the next 13 months, but it formed the foundation of the air campaign" (comments on an earlier draft by Lt. Col. Mark Cline, USAF, January 11, 2008; Cline headed the MAAP cell in the CAOC during the final preparations for and execution of the major combat phase of Operation Iraqi Freedom).

19. Allen and De Young, "Bush: U.S. Will Strike First at Enemies." Secretary Rumsfeld chose to characterize the emergent Bush doctrine of preemption as "anticipatory self-defense" (Rumsfeld, *Known and Unknown*, 423).

20. Woodward, *Plan of Attack*, 112.

21. Ibid., 169.

22. Ibid., 161.

23. Karen DeYoung, "Bush Cites Urgent Iraqi Threat," *Washington Post*, October 8, 2002.

24. Alison Mitchell and Carl Hulse, "Senate, in 77–23 Vote, Passes Iraq Resolution," *New York Times*, October 11, 2002.

25. "Mr. Bush's UN Mandate," *Wall Street Journal*, November 11, 2002.

26. "The State of the Union Message," *New York Times*, January 29, 2003.

27. For amplification on this assertion in an unclassified extract of the estimate in question, see *Iraq's Weapons of Mass Destruction Programs* (Washington, D.C.: Director of Central Intelligence, October 2002), 1.

28. Woodward, *Plan of Attack*, 23.

29. Ibid., 2.

30. Ibid., 9.

31. Ibid., 34.

32. Ibid., 71.

33. Evan Thomas and Martha Brant, "The Education of Tommy Franks," *Time*, May 19, 2003.

34. Franks with McConnell, *American Soldier*, 315, 331.

35. Woodward, *Plan of Attack*, 8.

36. Rumsfeld, *Known and Unknown*, 427.

37. Gordon and Trainor, *Cobra II*, 28.

38. Franks with McConnell, *American Soldier*, 337.

39. Ibid., 334.

40. Ibid., 335.

41. Woodward, *Plan of Attack*, 60–61.

42. Before becoming CENTCOM's director of operations, Renuart commanded Joint Task Force Southwest Asia, which enforced the southern no-fly zone over Iraq through Operation Southern Watch.

43. Thomas and Brant, "The Education of Tommy Franks."

44. Franks with McConnell, *American Soldier*, 361.

45. Vice Adm. David C. Nichols, USN, "Operation Iraqi Freedom: CFACC/CAOC/NALE [Naval Air Liaison Element]," briefing by the then deputy combined force air component commander, Operation Iraqi Freedom, no date given.

46. Woodward, *Plan of Attack*, 96.

47. Col. Mason Carpenter, USAF, "Rapid, Deliberate, Disciplined, Proportional, and Precise: Operation Iraqi Freedom Air and Space Operations—Initial Assessment," unpublished paper, 3–4. Colonel Carpenter headed the CAOC's strategy division during the three-week major combat phase of Operation Iraqi Freedom.

48. Lt. Gen. T. Michael Moseley, USAF, "Operation Iraqi Freedom: Initial CFACC Roll-up," briefing given at a CENTAF-sponsored symposium to assess and document allied air operations during the three weeks of major combat in Operation Iraqi Freedom, Nellis AFB, Nev., July 18, 2003.

49. Amy Butler, "Data Links a Solid Weapon against Scuds, Friendly Fire, Jumper Says," *Inside the Air Force*, April 11, 2003, 1. As General Moseley later put it, "*no* Scuds" was the rule for the western desert (conversation with Gen. T. Michael Moseley, USAF, chief of staff, Headquarters U.S. Air Force, Washington, D.C., August 2, 2006).

50. The National Intelligence Estimate on Iraq that had been provided to Congress by the CIA in October 2002 indicated that Iraq possessed as many as several dozen Scud missiles with ranges of 400 to 550 miles. Yet in the years since Desert Storm, U.S. reconnaissance efforts had not succeeded in capturing a single image of an Iraqi Scud. Gordon and Trainor, *Cobra II*, 335–336.

51. Woodward, *Plan of Attack*, 98–99.

52. Ibid., 110.

53. Conversation with General Moseley, August 2, 2006.

54. With respect to his burglar reference, Franks later explained that it meant that "you didn't roll over and go back to sleep when there was an intruder downstairs with a gun" (Franks with McConnell, *American Soldier*, 383).

55. Woodward, *Plan of Attack*, 113–114.

56. Franks with McConnell, *American Soldier*, 383.

57. Gordon and Trainor, *Cobra II*, 44–45.

58. Franks with McConnell, *American Soldier*, 352.

59. For a concise synopsis of effects-based targeting that was published more than a decade ago, see Col. David A. Deptula, USAF, *Firing for Effect: Change in the Nature of Warfare* (Arlington, Va.: Aerospace Education Foundation, 1995; updated in 2001 under the new title *Effects-Based Operations*).

60. In addition, CENTAF staffers worked closely with the 32nd Air Operations Group, a similar planning entity attached to CENTAF's counterpart, U.S. Air Forces in Europe (USAFE) headquartered at Ramstein, in building a working relationship with that organization's staff that would endure throughout the major combat phase of Iraqi Freedom. Conversations with Col. Douglas Erlenbusch, USAF, CENTAF director of operations; Maj. Anthony Roberson, USAF, chief of the CENTAF commander's action group; and other CENTAF staff during a visit to CENTAF headquarters, Shaw AFB, S.C., January 29, 2007.

61. Woodward, *Plan of Attack*, 114.

62. Nichols, "Operation Iraqi Freedom: CFACC/CAOC/NALE."

63. Ibid.

64. Conversations with Colonel Erlenbusch, Major Roberson, and other CEN-TAF staff, January 29, 2007.

65. Ibid.

66. The White Plan covered a duration of between seventy-two hours and seven days, sufficient time for the 509th Bomb Wing to get its B-2 stealth bombers into the fight. The Red Plan, also known as Running Start, covered seven days. A CENTAF planner recalled that CENTAF "developed three different Blue Plans and three different White Plans, with one focused on Iraq's air forces, one on the Republican Guard, and one on suspected facilities associated with WMD production" (comments by Lieutenant Colonel Cline, January 11, 2008).

67. Comments on an earlier draft by Lt. Col. David Hathaway, USAF, February 19, 2007.

68. Conversations with Colonel Erlenbusch, Major Roberson, and other CEN-TAF staff, January 29, 2007.

69. Woodward, *Plan of Attack*, 126.

70. Gordon and Trainor, *Cobra II*, 51.

71. Purdum, *A Time of Our Choosing*, 97–98.

72. Ibid., 102.

73. Woodward, *Plan of Attack*, 124–125.

74. Ibid., 146.

75. Franks with McConnell, *American Soldier*, 352. Another unplanned-for contingency, which Franks had taken to calling "catastrophic success," was the outside chance that Iraqi resistance would crumble both quickly and unexpectedly (ibid., 392). That possibility raised the obvious question of what CENTCOM should do next.

76. A similar arrangement between the Air Force and the Navy involving the sharing of satellite-aided JDAMs had been brokered earlier during Operation Enduring Freedom by the Air Force chief of staff at the time, Gen. John Jumper, and the chief of naval operations, Adm. Vern Clark. Conversations with Colonel Erlenbusch, Major Roberson, and other CENTAF staff, January 29, 2007.

77. Earlier in June, General Moseley had approached Air Combat Command for help in developing new concepts of operations for the counter-Scud mission. The team of experts that Air Combat Command supplied in response to his request became an integral part of the broader CENTAF planning process.

78. Conversations with Colonel Erlenbusch, Major Roberson, and other CEN-TAF staff, January 29, 2007.

79. Woodward, *Plan of Attack*, 154–155.

80. Elaine M. Grossman, "Coalition Will Calibrate Force to Limit Casualties in Baghdad Attacks," *Inside the Air Force*, April 4, 2003, 4.

81. *Lessons of Iraq: Third Report of Session 2003–04*, vol. 2 (London: House of Commons, Defence Committee, HC 57-II, March 16, 2004), Ev 51 (hereinafter cited as *Lessons of Iraq*, vol. 2).

82. Woodward, *Plan of Attack*, 157–159.

83. Ibid., 207.

84. Conversations with Colonel Erlenbusch, Major Roberson, and other CEN-TAF staff, January 29, 2007.

85. Thomas E. Ricks, "War Plan for Iraq Is Ready, Say Officials," *Washington Post*, November 10, 2002.

86. Tom Squitieri and Dave Moniz, "U.S. War Plans: Blast Away Saddam's Support," *USA Today*, November 11, 2002.

87. Woodward, *Plan of Attack*, 327.

88. In military parlance, a Red Team is a group of skilled military professionals convened to detect and assess identifiable weaknesses in a plan's or unit's capability and readiness for combat.

89. CENTAF staffers also met about this time with their counterpart planners at CENTCOM headquarters to clarify the emerging war plan's various operational objectives and anticipated "supported" and "supporting" command relationships to ensure synchronization across the involved warfighting components. Conversations with Colonel Erlenbusch, Major Roberson, and other CENTAF staff, January 29, 2007.

90. Comments on an earlier draft by Col. Matt Neuenswander, USAF (Ret.), October 22, 2010.

91. Comments by Lieutenant Colonel Cline, January 11, 2008.

92. Carpenter, "Rapid, Deliberate, Disciplined, Proportional, and Precise," 9.

93. Tim Ripley, "Planning for Iraqi Freedom," *Jane's Intelligence Review*, July 2003, 10.

94. Comments by Lieutenant Colonel Cline, January 11, 2008.

95. Conversations with Colonel Erlenbusch, Major Roberson, and other CEN-TAF staff, January 29, 2007.

96. Comments by Lieutenant Colonel Cline, January 11, 2008.

97. Michael R. Gordon, "The U.S. Battle Plan: Make Friends and War," *New York Times*, March 11, 2003.

98. Carpenter, "Rapid, Deliberate, Disciplined, Proportional, and Precise," 5.

99. Comments by Lieutenant Colonel Hathaway, February 19, 2007.

100. Nichols, "Operation Iraqi Freedom: CFACC/CAOC/NALE."

101. Mark Thompson, "Opening with a Bang," *Time*, March 17, 2003.

102. Gordon and Trainor, *Cobra II*, 35. For the work in question, see Harlan K. Ullman and James P. Wade, *Shock and Awe: Achieving Rapid Dominance* (Washington, D.C.: National Defense University Press, December 1996). "Shock and awe" was never used, let alone promoted, by CENTCOM's air component. It was entirely a construct that emanated from and was popularized by the Office of the Secretary of Defense with a view toward shaping the tone and focus of Secretary Rumsfeld's desired battle plan for Operation Iraqi Freedom and reflecting his personal determination to see the plan embody less "massive build-up and overwhelming force" and more "light, lean, speed, and agility." Colonel Hathaway later recalled that the construct did affect the evolution of OPLAN 1003V as CENTCOM moved toward a more operationally risky simultaneous execution of major air and land operations, but "none of the planners actually expected the visually awe-inspiring orgy of air-delivered fire and destruction that the press had begun to envision. My goal was to build a plan that would deliver a blow to the Ba'athist regime on Day One and never allow it to recover or regroup. To this extent, we *did* have 'shock and awe'" (comments by Lieutenant Colonel Hathaway, February 19, 2007).

103. Woodward, *Plan of Attack*, 311. In his memoirs President Bush freely acknowledged that "later, many of the assertions in Colin's speech would prove inaccurate. But at the time, his words reflected the considered judgment of intelligence agencies at home and around the world" (Bush, *Decision Points*, 245).

104. Woodward, *Plan of Attack*, 150.

105. Ibid., 233.

106. CENTAF staffers strongly preferred the long-established time-phased force and deployment data (TPFDD, pronounced "tip-fid") procedures rather than the multiple individual ad hoc deployment orders that Secretary Rumsfeld insisted on. CENTAF planners did, however, press for an early flow of forces in order to meet the growing demands that CENTCOM's emerging war plan was placing on the air component. These mission support needs included forces for strategic attack, counterair, SOF support, and now earlier-than-anticipated support to the land component. Conversations with Colonel Erlenbusch, Major Roberson, and other CENTAF staff, January 29, 2007. Army planners were likewise unhappy with Rumsfeld's insistence on piecemeal deployment orders in lieu of the time-tested TPFDD

approach. A postcampaign assessment from the Army's perspective candidly noted that deviating from the detailed TPFDD "had unintended consequences as logistics units fell farther back in the force flow. This affected not only Army units but also those from sister services that depended on Army supporters. . . . As the campaign progressed, the force flow never caught up with the operational requirements; the approach ultimately failed to provide either the flexibility or responsiveness anticipated" (Fontenot, Degen, and Tohn, *On Point*, 74).

107. Scott C. Truver, "The U.S. Navy in Review," *Proceedings*, May 2003, 94.

108. Vice Adm. Timothy J. Keating, USN, "Naval Aviation Key to Iraqi Freedom Victory," *The Hook*, winter 2003, 4.

109. Kerry Gildea, "Ammunition Stocks Ready for War, Navy, Marine Corps Leaders Report," *Defense Daily*, February 27, 2003, 4.

110. Hampton Stephens, "Deployments Force Cancellation of January Red Flag," *Inside the Air Force*, January 17, 2003, 5.

111. Hampton Stephens, "USAF Cancels Second Red Flag in a Row, Citing Lack of Available Assets," *Inside the Air Force*, March 14, 2003, 2.

112. Hampton Stephens, "At Rhein-Main, Activity Increases as U.S. Prepares for Iraq War," *Inside the Air Force*, February 28, 2003, 4–5.

113. Gen. John W. Handy, USAF, *Operation Iraqi Freedom—Air Mobility by the Numbers* (Scott AFB, Ill.: Headquarters Air Mobility Command, October 1, 2003), 3.

114. Ibid., 5.

115. Ibid., 18.

116. Gordon and Trainor, *Cobra II*, 48.

117. Franks with McConnell, *American Soldier*, 342. These "spikes" in force deployment and use were directly connected to Operation Southern Focus, CENTCOM's concurrent expanded use of reactive air attacks in response to Iraqi provocations against coalition aircraft operating in the southern no-fly zone (see Chapter 2). Lieutenant Colonel Hathaway later explained, "We didn't want to trip them [the Iraqis] into any action that would trigger the start of major hostilities until we were ready. During the final weeks before the actual execution of OPLAN 1003V, General Franks directed that we terminate the 'spikes' to ensure that we wouldn't inadvertently do anything that might force a premature execution of the plan, as well as to allow the President's last-chance diplomatic effort to play out unimpeded" (comments, February 19, 2007).

118. Not only was General Leaf an experienced fighter pilot, he also was intimately familiar with U.S. Army operations, having been an honor graduate

of the Army's Command and General Staff Officer Course and a graduate of the Army's pre-command course. Fontenot, Degen, and Tohn, *On Point*, 31.

119. For detailed discussion, see Benjamin S. Lambeth, *Air Power against Terror: America's Conduct of Operation Enduring Freedom* (Santa Monica, Calif.: RAND Corporation, MG-166–1-CENTAF, 2005), 163–231.

120. Col. Matthew D. Neuenswander, USAF, "JCAS in Operation Anaconda— It's Not All Bad News," *Field Artillery*, May–June 2003, 2.

121. General Moseley created the first ACCE organization in May 2002, shortly after Anaconda. It was established with the SOF community's Combined Joint Task Force (CJTF) 180 in Afghanistan to provide senior air-component representation to other fighting elements of CENTCOM, much as those elements provided representation to the CAOC. This was a new idea that paid off impressively in improved intercomponent operations. The arrangement became the template for the ACCE that was subsequently established with the land component for Operation Iraqi Freedom. CENTAF staffers later called the concept "new doctrinal territory" and an initiative that "paid huge dividends by improving communications and staff relationships" (conversations with Colonel Erlenbusch, Major Roberson, and other CENTAF staff, January 29, 2007).

122. Amy Butler, "As A-10 Shines in Iraq War, Officials Look to JSF [Joint Strike Fighter] for Future CAS Role," *Inside the Air Force*, May 23, 2003, 13.

123. Elaine M. Grossman, "Iraq War Could Feature Unprecedented Air-Land Collaboration," *Inside the Pentagon*, February 13, 2003, 1, 16–18. The fact that an ACCE was needed at all for Iraqi Freedom reflects the widespread geographical distribution of CENTCOM's subordinate warfighting components, requiring a ponderous CAOC that, in the case of Afghanistan, had been located thousands of miles to the rear of the fight. There was no ACCE arrangement in Operation Desert Storm because joint theater headquarters were all collocated in Saudi Arabia. In the case of current counterinsurgency operations in Iraq and Afghanistan, with the air component commander and the CAOC both far removed from the center of action, one has begun to hear increasingly compelling arguments that what is really needed is not just an ACCE, but even more a pushing of some CAOC tactical-level functions down to the Air Force air support operations centers in Baghdad and Kabul that are collocated with U.S. ground commanders to ensure that the air component's potential contributions are fully engaged in the joint fight. For an insightful recent commentary along these lines, see Lt. Col. Jeffrey Hukill, USAF (Ret.), and Daniel R. Mortensen, "Developing Flexible Command and Control of Air Power," *Air and Space Power Journal*, spring 2011, 53–63.

124. This willingness bore out an observation later put forward in the U.S. Marine Corps' official postmortem on I MEF's role in the campaign that General McKiernan "was not afraid of new ideas and wanted to find the best organization for the fight—as opposed to doing things the way they always had been done." The same account also noted that McKiernan "had what *Newsweek* was to call 'a temperament as . . . even as the desert,' which also made it easy for him to work with other services" (Col. Nicholas E. Reynolds, USMC [Ret.], *Basrah, Baghdad, and Beyond: The U.S. Marine Corps in the Second Iraq War* [Annapolis, Md.: Naval Institute Press, 2005], 13). Before the campaign kicked off, General McKiernan made it a special point to stress that "there will never be a Third Army fight. We will always be in a combined [and] joint contest" (interview by Maj. John Aarson with Lt. Gen. David McKiernan, November 17, 2002, as quoted in Fontenot, Degen, and Tohn, *On Point*, 31).

125. Comments by Lieutenant Colonel Cline, January 11, 2008.

126. Robert Wall, "Rescue Enhancements: U.S. Air Force Helicopters Employ Longer-Range Guns and New Threat-Avoidance Technology," *Aviation Week and Space Technology*, June 16, 2003, 168.

127. Franks with McConnell, *American Soldier*, 398.

128. General Moseley played a major role in negotiating many of these forward basing arrangements. The senior Australian air planner in the CAOC later remembered "Moseley complaining at one stage that he was dispatched again to the Middle East to talk to the minister of defense in Saudi or wherever and saying, 'I'm supposed to be planning the air war. Why the heck am I doing all this?' But the reality was that Moseley had a very good working relationship with all the defense organizations in the area, had a very good network. He was well known to a lot of the politicians, the ministers of defense and the governments in that area, and he became the front man. Without his efforts, the State Department would have had a lot of problems" (official interview with Group Captain Otto Halupka, RAAF, Operation Falconer Air Planner, May 14, 2008, provided to the author by the RAAF Air Power Development Centre, Canberra, Australia).

129. By the account of one key planner, CENTAF's logistics personnel were heroic in working munitions issues, getting the munitions into the theater, and setting up all the bases. British and Australian logisticians were also fully engaged in this planning activity at Shaw AFB. "I don't know who said it," he added, "but it's true—amateurs do strategy, professionals do logistics" (comments by Lieutenant Colonel Cline, January 11, 2008). See Kristin F. Lynch, John G. Drew, Robert S. Tripp, and Charles Robert Roll Jr., *Sup-

porting Air and Space Expeditionary Forces: Lessons from Operation Iraqi Freedom (Santa Monica, Calif.: RAND Corporation, MG-193-AF, 2005).

130. Esther Schrader and Richard Boudreaux, "U.S. Seeks Overflights in Turkey," *Los Angeles Times*, March 12, 2003.

131. Ibid.

132. Elaine Grossman, "U.S. Air Force Spent Millions on Turkish Bases Unused in Iraq War," *Inside the Pentagon*, August 14, 2003, 1, 12–13.

133. Franks with McConnell, *American Soldier*, 428.

134. Woodward, *Plan of Attack*, 330–331.

135. Robert Burns, "U.S. Gulf Force Nears 300,000 as Commander, Bush Consult," *Philadelphia Inquirer*, March 5, 2003.

136. *Nimitz*, with her embarked air wing and crew, had sustained a record-setting nine-and-a-half-month deployment more than two decades before in 1979 and 1980 when the Soviets invaded Afghanistan and the Iranian hostage crisis first kicked off.

137. Eric Schmitt, "Pentagon Ready to Strike Iraq within Days if Bush Gives the Word, Officials Say," *New York Times,* March 6, 2003.

138. David E. Sanger with Warren Hoge, "U.S. May Abandon UN Vote on Iraq, Powell Testifies," *New York Times*, March 14, 2003.

139. Reynolds, *Basrah, Baghdad, and Beyond*, 50.

140. Jay A. Stout, *Hammer from Above: Marine Air Combat over Iraq* (New York: Presidio Press, 2009), 27–28.

141. Lt. Gen. T. Michael Moseley, USAF, *Operation Iraqi Freedom—by the Numbers* (Shaw AFB, S.C.: Headquarters U.S. Central Command Air Forces, Assessment and Analysis Division, April 30, 2003), 6–10.

142. Christopher Cooper and Greg Jaffe, "U.S. Use of Saudi Air Base Shows Kingdom's Quiet Commitment," *Wall Street Journal*, March 12, 2003.

143. David Lynch and John Diamond, "U.S., British Forces Are 'Ready Today' for Invasion," *USA Today*, March 17, 2003.

144. Moseley, "Operation Iraqi Freedom: Initial CFACC Roll-up."

145. Ibid.

146. Elaine M. Grossman, "U.S. Forces to Take Close Battlefield Approach into Baghdad Fight," *Inside the Pentagon*, March 20, 2003, 2–3.

147. Ripley, "Planning for Iraqi Freedom," 9.

148. Conversations with Colonel Erlenbusch, Major Roberson, and other CENTAF staff, January 29, 2007.

149. Hunter Keeter, "Next Internal Look to Spotlight Deployable Command and Control," *Defense Daily*, October 31, 2002, 6.

150. "XC4I" stands for experimental command, control, communications, computers, and intelligence.

151. Hunter Keeter, "Exercise Internal Look to Evaluate Joint Task Force Command Capability," *Defense Daily*, December 5, 2002, 4.

152. Gordon and Trainor, *Cobra II*, 89.

153. Woodward, *Plan of Attack*, 237.

154. Franks with McConnell, *American Soldier*, 414.

155. Jeremy Feiler, "Iraqi Campaign Lessons Show Shift to 'Overmatching Power' Doctrine," *Inside the Pentagon*, October 9, 2003, 13.

156. One might add here, as a fourth consideration, the important fact that allied air superiority had already been established over Iraq's northern and southern no-fly zones. Comments by Lieutenant Colonel Cline, January 11, 2008.

157. *Lessons of Iraq: Third Report of Session 2003–04*, vol. 1 (London: House of Commons, Defence Committee, HC 57-I/II/III, March 16, 2004), 35 (hereinafter cited as *Lessons of Iraq*, vol. 1).

158. Comments by Lieutenant Colonel Hathaway, February 19, 2007.

159. Woodward, *Plan of Attack*, 257.

160. Conversations with Colonel Erlenbusch, Major Roberson, and other CENTAF staff, January 29, 2007.

161. Woodward, *Plan of Attack*, 264–265.

162. Conversations with Colonel Erlenbusch, Major Roberson, and other CENTAF staff, January 29, 2007.

163. Ibid.

164. Ibid. U.S. air-launched cruise missiles delivered by B-52s were mainly used during the first days of the air war against preplanned targets but also were employed as an alert response capability and in reactive targeting.

165. Ibid.

166. Ibid.

167. Ibid.

168. Eric Schmitt and Elisabeth Bumiller, "Top General Sees Plan to Shock Iraq into Surrender," *New York Times*, March 5, 2003.

169. Woodward, *Plan of Attack*, 217–218.

170. Franks with McConnell, *American Soldier*, 440.

171. Woodward, *Plan of Attack*, 365.

172. Dana Milbank and Mike Allen, "President Tells Hussein to Leave Iraq within 48 Hours or Face Invasion," *Washington Post*, March 18, 2003.

173. Richard W. Stevenson, "As Diplomatic Effort Ends, President Vows to Act," *New York Times*, March 18, 2003.

174. Woodward, *Plan of Attack*, 335.

175. Ibid., 352.

176. Betsy Pisik, "Human Shields Take a Powder," *Washington Times*, March 5, 2003.

177. Tom Bowman, "U.S. Aims to Curtail Civilian Casualties," *Baltimore Sun*, March 5, 2003.

178. Rowan Scarborough, "Bush Convenes War Cabinet," *Washington Times*, March 6, 2003.

179. Elaine M. Grossman, "Decision to Hasten Ground Attack into Iraq Presented New Risks," *Inside the Pentagon*, March 18, 2004, 1, 14–17.

180. Comments by Lieutenant Colonel Hathaway, February 19, 2007.

181. Ibid.

182. Ibid.

183. Prior to Operation Desert Storm, Iraq was Turkey's second-largest trading partner, with $3 billion in exchange each year. See Jeremy Feiler, "Turkey Could Move Forces into Northern Iraq to Thwart Refugee Crisis," *Inside the Pentagon*, March 13, 2003, 11–12.

184. Thom Shanker and Eric Schmitt, "Rumsfeld Seeks Consensus through Jousting," *New York Times*, March 19, 2003; and Eric Schmitt with Dexter Filkins, "Erdogan to Form New Turkish Government as U.S. Presses for Use of Military Bases," *New York Times*, March 12, 2003.

185. Rowan Scarborough, "Lightning Air Strikes, Then March to Baghdad," *Washington Times*, March 18, 2003.

186. Greg Jaffe, "U.S. Rushes to Upgrade Base for Attack Aircraft," *Wall Street Journal*, March 14, 2003.

187. Peter Baker, "Marine Predicts Brief Bombing, Then Land Assault," *Washington Post*, March 17, 2003.

188. Thomas E. Ricks, "Myers Depicts War on Two Fronts," *Washington Post*, March 5, 2003.

189. Squadron Leader Sophy Gardner, RAF, "Operation Iraqi Freedom: Coalition Operations," *Air and Space Power Journal*, winter 2004, 88. At the outset, CENTAF had not anticipated this prospective complication. Eventually, it enlisted the help of two airmen from the Air Force Doctrine Center at Maxwell AFB, Ala., to assist in working through the associated command and control issues. Comments by Lieutenant Colonel Cline, January 11, 2008.

190. B-1Bs carrying twenty-four JDAMs were used extensively in the counter-Scud effort in the western desert. CAOC planners understood that if those munitions were not required to support that mission during any given air-

craft time on station, the B-1s would undertake dynamic or time-sensitive targeting elsewhere in the war zone.

191. Franks with McConnell, *American Soldier*, 434.

192. In a sidebar comment titled "Sometimes Even a Nonlethal Attack Can Be Lethal," Lt. Col. Carl Ayers, commander of the Army's 9th PSYOP (Psychological Operations) Battalion, described the unusual death of an Iraqi border guard in the western desert: "The cause of death was a box of leaflets that fell out of a [C-130] Combat Talon aircraft when the static line broke. The box impacted on the Iraqi guard's head, and 9th PSYOP Battalion may have achieved the first enemy KIA [killed in action] of Operation Iraqi Freedom" (Fontenot, Degen, and Tohn, *On Point*, 108).

193. Comments by Lieutenant Colonel Hathaway, February 19, 2007.

194. There is no evidence that any Air Force leader at any time in the planning for Iraqi Freedom insisted on the Air Force being the first in "for matters of pride," as was later alleged by CENTCOM's deputy commander in his memoirs. See Lt. Gen. Michael DeLong, USMC (Ret.), *Inside CentCom: The Unvarnished Truth about the Wars in Afghanistan and Iraq* (Washington, D.C.: Regnery, 2004), 86.

195. Franks with McConnell, *American Soldier*, 439.

196. Steve Davies and Doug Dildy, *F-16 Fighting Falcon Units of Operation Iraqi Freedom*, Osprey Combat Aircraft No. 61 (Oxford, England: Osprey Publishing, 2006), 16. The rules of engagement for Iraqi Freedom were substantially simplified compared with those that had prevailed throughout Operations Northern Watch and Southern Watch. During those operations, aircrews were prohibited from attacking a target unless it could be confirmed to lie within fifty feet of the geographic coordinates that had been provided for the target by the CAOC. Once Iraqi Freedom was under way, any target inside a kill box assigned to be attacked could be struck so long as positive identification could be made and collateral damage estimates were satisfactorily met, and there were no friendly ground forces in the area. Conversations with Colonel Erlenbusch, Major Roberson, and other CENTAF staff, January 29, 2007.

197. The SPINs document itself was divided into eight sections: commander's guidance, flight planning, communications and data links, airspace, rules of engagement, operations, personnel recovery, and air defense. CENTAF staffers continually updated and refined this document as the air operations plan evolved. For the sake of continuity, General Moseley determined that the format of the daily SPINs for the war against Iraq would be essentially the same as the earlier SPINs documents for Operations Northern Watch,

Southern Watch, and Enduring Freedom. During the actual campaign, the daily document averaged more than 350 pages in length and contained a variety of matrices, graphs, diagrams, and illustrations. Conversations with Colonel Erlenbusch, Major Roberson, and other CENTAF staff, January 29, 2007.

Chapter 2. CENTCOM's Air Offensive

1. Franks with McConnell, *American Soldier*, 348–349.
2. Nichols, "Operation Iraqi Freedom: CFACC/CAOC/NALE."
3. *Lessons of Iraq: Third Report of Session 2003–04*, vol. 3 (London: House of Commons, Defence Committee, HC 57-III, March 16, 2004), Ev 414 (hereinafter cited as *Lessons of Iraq*, vol. 3).
4. Woodward, *Plan of Attack*, 102.
5. A sortie is one mission flown by one aircraft.
6. Conversation with General Moseley, August 2, 2006.
7. Actually, as early as November 2001, on assuming command at CENTAF, General Moseley had already begun to refocus no-fly zone operations over southern Iraq expressly toward what he called "increased air defense threat mitigation" (Moseley, "Operation Iraqi Freedom: Initial CFACC Roll-up").
8. Steve Davies, *F-15C/E Eagle Units of Operation Iraqi Freedom*, Osprey Combat Aircraft No. 47 (Oxford, England: Osprey Publishing, 2004), 19.
9. Woodward, *Plan of Attack*, 10–11.
10. Rumsfeld, *Known and Unknown*, 418–419.
11. Woodward, *Plan of Attack*, 14.
12. Knights, *Cradle of Conflict*, 258.
13. Ibid., 235.
14. Comments by Lieutenant Colonel Hathaway, February 19, 2007.
15. Carlo Kopp, "Iraqi Freedom—the Hammer and Anvil," *Australian Aviation*, May 2003, 26.
16. For further details, see Knights, *Cradle of Conflict*, 236–238.
17. Thomas Ricks and Alan Sipress, "Cuts Urged in Patrols over Iraq," *Washington Post*, May 9, 2001, quoted in Knights, *Cradle of Conflict*, 239.
18. The CAOC later determined that the E-2C pilot had reacted to self-defense flares fired from a flight of fighters that was conducting a flare check above him. The reported missile shot was never validated, and Iraq's IADS did not have SA-3s positioned that far south at the time the alleged incident was reported. Comments by Colonel Neuenswander, March 6, 2007.
19. Knights, *Cradle of Conflict*, 256–257.
20. Quoted in ibid., 257.

21. Ibid., 257.

22. Ibid., 258.

23. Neil Tweedie and Michael Smith, "Britain 'To Play Full Role in Iraq Invasion,'" *London Daily Telegraph*, March 13, 2003.

24. Lt. Col. Rob Givens, USAF, "'Let Slip the Dogs of War': Leadership in the Air War over Iraq," student term paper, National War College, Washington, D.C., 2005, 11.

25. Franks with McConnell, *American Soldier*, 388.

26. Davies and Dildy, *F-16 Fighting Falcon Units of Operation Iraqi Freedom*, 55.

27. Knights, *Cradle of Conflict*, 241–242.

28. This escalated effort in no way entailed a purposeful misuse by CENTCOM of its no-fly-zone mandate from the UN. The CAOC always worked within the established Southern Watch rules of engagement, the subtle difference being that rather than being constrained to respond only against the specific system that had threatened a coalition aircraft, allied aircrews were now authorized to respond against related targets, so long as such targets were expressly associated with the Iraqi IADS and command and control networks. E-mail communication to the author by Air Chief Marshal Sir Glenn Torpy, chief of the air staff, RAF, March 17, 2007. General Moseley later explained that Southern Focus operations "never expanded attacks beyond what [were] necessary, proportional, and authorized . . . in self-defense" (quoted in SSgt Jason L. Haag, USAF, "OIF Veterans Discuss Lessons," *Air Force Print News*, USAF Air Warfare Center Public Affairs, Nellis AFB, Nev., July 31, 2003).

29. Knights, *Cradle of Conflict*, 258–259.

30. Carpenter, "Rapid, Deliberate, Disciplined, Proportional, and Precise," 4.

31. The targets that were attacked included Ababil 100, FROG 7, and other missile launchers.

32. Knights, *Cradle of Conflict*, 263.

33. Ibid., 259.

34. Davies and Dildy, *F-16 Fighting Falcon Units of Operation Iraqi Freedom*, 13.

35. Ibid., 14. There also was a significant concurrent nontraditional ISR effort over western Iraq involving F-16C+s of the Alabama Air National Guard (ANG) (F-16C+ is an unofficial designation given to ANG aircraft equipped with the AN/AAQ-28 Litening II target pod). In addition to gathering intelligence on possible Iraqi Scud-related activities, this effort contributed to clearing the way for SOF team operations on the ground once the campaign began in earnest.

36. Robert Wall, "Time Runs Short: Final War Preparations Continue Even as Controversy Keeps a Start Date Uncertain," *Aviation Week and Space Technology*, March 17, 2003, 28. The E-8 uses advanced synthetic aperture radar (SAR) and ground moving-target indicator (GMTI) radar to find and monitor fixed and moving vehicles and other objects on the ground. It allows commanders and mission planners to detect, locate, classify, track, and target hostile ground movements irrespective of weather or smoke obscuration.

37. Karen DeYoung and Colum Lynch, "Three Countries Vow to Block U.S. on Iraq," *Washington Post*, March 6, 2003.

38. Mike Allen and Bradley Graham, "Franks Briefs Bush on War Plans, Says Military Is Ready," *Washington Post*, March 6, 2003. See also "U.S., Britain Double Daily Flights over Southern Iraq," *Baltimore Sun*, March 6, 2003.

39. Davies and Dildy, *F-16 Fighting Falcon Units of Operation Iraqi Freedom*, 16.

40. Michael R. Gordon with John F. Burns, "Iraq's Air Defense Is Concentrated around Baghdad," *New York Times*, March 17, 2003.

41. Tom Squitieri, "What Could Go Wrong in War," *USA Today*, March 13, 2003. For more on Serb tactics, see Benjamin S. Lambeth, *NATO's Air War for Kosovo: A Strategic and Operational Assessment* (Santa Monica, Calif.: RAND Corporation, MR-1365-AF, 2001), 102–120.

42. David A. Fulghum, "Frustrations and Backlogs," *Aviation Week and Space Technology*, March 10, 2003, 33.

43. Carpenter, "Rapid, Deliberate, Disciplined, Proportional, and Precise," 24.

44. Jim Krane, "Pilotless Warriors Soar to Success," CBS News, April 25, 2003.

45. Conversation with General Moseley, August 2, 2006.

46. "Moseley Details 'The War before the War,'" *Air Force Magazine*, October 2003, 14.

47. Carpenter, "Rapid, Deliberate, Disciplined, Proportional, and Precise," 11.

48. Moseley, "Operation Iraqi Freedom: Initial CFACC Roll-up."

49. Elaine Grossman, "Critics Decry 2002 Air Attacks on Iraq That Predated Key U.S., UN Votes," *Inside the Pentagon*, July 24, 2003, 19–20.

50. Suzann Chapman, "The 'War' before the War," *Air Force Magazine*, February 2004, 53.

51. Merrill A. McPeak, "Leave the Flying to Us," *Washington Post*, June 5, 2003.

52. Linda Robinson, "The Men in the Shadows," *U.S. News and World Report*, May 19, 2003.

53. Comments by Lieutenant Colonel Cline, January 11, 2008.

54. Woodward, *Plan of Attack*, 108–109.

55. Ibid., 301.

56. Ibid., 304.

57. Ibid., 42.

58. As a further hedge against that eventuality, CENTCOM had sent a small team to Israel headed by Maj. Gen. Charles Simpson, director of air and space operations at USAFE headquarters, and Peter Flory, the principal deputy assistant secretary of defense for international security affairs, to help ensure Israel's noninvolvement by providing daily campaign progress briefings to the Israeli military leadership.

59. Carpenter, "Rapid, Deliberate, Disciplined, Proportional, and Precise," 9.

60. Col. Robert B. Green, USAR, "Joint Fires Support, the Joint Fires Element and the CGRS [Common Grid Reference System]: Keys to Success for CJSOTF West," *Special Warfare*, April 2005, 12.

61. Jack Kelly, "Covert Troops Fight Shadow War Off-Camera," *USA Today*, April 7, 2003.

62. Andrew F. Krepinevich, *Operation Iraqi Freedom: A First-Blush Assessment* (Washington, D.C.: Center for Strategic and Budgetary Assessments, 2003), 18.

63. The GBU-31 JDAM's 2,000-lb Mk 84 bomb core contains 945 pounds of tritonal, which consists of solid TNT laced with aluminum for stability. The bomb's 14-inch-wide steel casing expands to almost twice its normal size before the steel shears, at which point 1,000 pounds of white-hot steel fragments fly out at 6,000 feet per second with an initial overpressure of several thousand pounds per square inch and a fireball 8,500 °F. The bomb can produce a 20-foot crater and throw off as much as 10,000 pounds of dirt and rocks at supersonic speed. David Wood, "New Workhorse of U.S. Military: A Bomb with Devastating Effects," Newhouse.com, March 13, 2003.

64. Nick Cook, "Shock and Awe?" *Jane's Defence Weekly*, April 2, 2003, 21.

65. Lorenzo Cortes, "B-1 Crews Moved Quickly with JDAM Loads during Iraqi Freedom, Pilot Says," *Defense Daily*, April 22, 2003, 1.

66. Carpenter, "Rapid, Deliberate, Disciplined, Proportional, and Precise," 10.

67. Vago Muradian, "Allied Special Forces Took Western Iraq," *Defense News*, May 19, 2003, 1.

68. General Moseley later conceded his personal doubt at that time that Saddam Hussein still maintained a viable Scud launch capability in Iraq's western desert. Yet because of the clear precedent of Desert Storm in 1991, when Iraq fired eighty-eight Scuds into Israel, Saudi Arabia, and Bahrain from western-desert launch sites, the possibility had to be taken seriously. Accordingly, using known Desert Storm launch information as a starting point, CENTAF conducted a massive precampaign ISR effort to map out and

subsequently plan and rehearse attacks against every potential Scud hide site and key transportation node while minimizing to the fullest extent possible unnecessary damage to Iraqi infrastructure. The joint air and SOF attacks that were ultimately executed in the western desert against the assessed Scud threat included the immediate seizure of the H-1 and H-3 airfields and precision air attacks against some eighty plausible Scud transportation nodes, including thirteen or fourteen bridges to prevent the crossing of any possible Scud transporters and launch vehicles. Conversation with General Moseley, August 2, 2006.

69. Ibid.

70. Tony Holmes, *U.S. Navy Hornet Units of Operation Iraqi Freedom*, pt. 2, Osprey Combat Aircraft No. 58 (Oxford, England: Osprey Publishing, 2005), 46.

71. The FSCL is a procedural device for controlling and managing standoff fire support to ground combat operations that is established by the land component commander and adjusted by him as deemed necessary, but at intervals of no less than twelve hours.

72. Holmes, *U.S. Navy Hornet Units of Operation Iraqi Freedom*, pt. 2, 59.

73. Carpenter, "Rapid, Deliberate, Disciplined, Proportional, and Precise," 15–16.

74. The senior CAOC director during the three-week campaign recalled that allied SOF teams operating in northern Iraq confronted a large contingent of Iraqi conventional and paramilitary forces and later provided "overwhelming" feedback to the air component in enabling them to neutralize those superior numbers of enemy forces in short order. He added that the SOF land warfare community now "gets" air power and its potential for contributing to joint operations. Conversation with Maj. Gen. Daniel J. Darnell, USAF, director of legislative liaison, Headquarters U.S. Air Force, Washington, D.C., August 2, 2006.

75. Barton Gellman and Dana Priest, "CIA Had Fix on Hussein," *Washington Post*, March 20, 2003.

76. Franks with McConnell, *American Soldier*, 378–379.

77. Maj. S. Clinton Hinote, USAF, "More than Bombing Saddam: Attacking the Leadership in Operation Iraqi Freedom," master's thesis, School of Advanced Air and Space Studies, Air University, Maxwell AFB, Ala., June 2006, 114.

78. Ibid., 188.

79. Ibid., 136–137.

80. Gordon and Trainor, *Cobra II*, 177. Hussein's personal secretary, Abd Hamid, was apprehended after the regime's collapse and told U.S. interrogators that Hussein had not been to Dora Farms since 1995 and was nowhere near the site on the night of the attack (ibid.).

81. Davies, *F-15C/E Eagle Units of Operation Iraqi Freedom*, 40.

82. All of the TLAMs fired were Block IIIC variants, which featured not only the inertial navigation system and terrain contour–matching and digital scene-matching area-correlation systems of earlier versions, but also a GPS receiver that made the missile much easier to update with target information, increasing its accuracy. Only one failed on launch. With the addition of GPS and other guidance system improvements, the Navy had shortened the length of time required to detect, classify, and attack targets with TLAMs from days to hours. Hunter Keeter, "Navy Fire Control, Targeting Capability Improvements Shorten Strike Timeline," *Defense Daily*, March 21, 2003, 7. On the night of this first decapitation attempt, the reported position accuracy of GPS was 2.2 meters, thanks to careful system refinement by Air Force Space Command. The average reported GPS accuracy for targeting between March 19 and April 18 was 3.08 meters, with a 95 percent confidence level. William B. Scott, "'Sweetening' GPS: Squadron Boosted GPS Accuracy 'Window' to Support Iraq Air Campaign," *Aviation Week and Space Technology*, June 9, 2003, 49. Of the more than five hundred TLAMs that were fired during the three-week campaign, there were reportedly only six or seven failures—duds that either never left the launch tube or else fell into the sea before getting successfully airborne. Cordesman, "The 'Instant Lessons' of the Iraq War," 27.

83. Lorenzo Cortes, "Air Force F-117s Open Coalition Air Strikes with EGBU-27s," *Defense Daily*, March 21, 2003, 1.

84. Purdum, *A Time of Our Choosing*, 110.

85. Davies and Dildy, *F-16 Fighting Falcon Units of Operation Iraqi Freedom*, 25.

86. Ibid., 25–26.

87. Purdum, *A Time of Our Choosing*, 111.

88. Franks with McConnell, *American Soldier*, 459.

89. John Liang, "Myers: Saddam Hussein Is a Legitimate Target," *Inside the Air Force*, March 21, 2003, 15.

90. Five days after the abortive attack, the CIA officer who was running the Rockstars operation personally visited the Dora Farms complex and found no sign that a bunker had been there. Likewise, a U.S. Army colonel in charge of inspecting targeted sites in Baghdad reported that giant holes had been created but "no underground facilities, no bodies" were found. See "No Bunker Found under Bomb Site," *New York Times*, May 29, 2003.

91. The Army's theater air and missile defense (TAMD) was fielded to protect not only coalition forces in CENTCOM's area of operations but also the nearby friendly countries of Kuwait, Turkey, Qatar, Bahrain, Saudi

Arabia, and Israel. Improvements to the Patriot advanced capabilities version 2 (PAC 2) that was deployed to the region included software upgrades and hardware changes that enabled better target acquisition and tracking, with the PAC 3 version putatively offering even greater capability and reliability. Fontenot, Degen, and Tohn, *On Point*, 65.

92. Franks with McConnell, *American Soldier*, 65.

93. Elaine M. Grossman, "First Attacks on Coalition Were Iraqi Missiles Aimed at Kuwait," *Inside the Air Force*, March 21, 2003, 1, 13–14.

94. Lorenzo Cortes, "Patriots Intercept Eight Iraqi Ballistic Missiles, Involved in Two Friendly Fire Incidents," *Defense Daily*, March 28, 2003, 3.

95. Franks with McConnell, *American Soldier*, 468.

96. Walter Pincus, Bob Woodward, and Dana Priest, "Hussein's Fate Still Uncertain," *Washington Post*, March 21, 2003.

97. Fontenot, Degen, and Tohn, *On Point*, 88, 99.

98. Gordon and Trainor, *Cobra II*, 331–332.

99. "Flexibility: Rumsfeld Tactical Signature Writ Large," *London Daily Telegraph*, March 21, 2003.

100. Thomas E. Ricks, "Calibrated War Makes Comeback," *Washington Post*, March 21, 2003.

101. Darren Lake, "How Different It All Is from the Last Gulf War," *Jane's Defence Weekly*, March 26, 2003, 3.

102. Comments by Lieutenant Colonel Hathaway, February 19, 2007.

103. Nichols, "Operation Iraqi Freedom: CFACC/CAOC/NALE."

104. Knights, *Cradle of Conflict*, 265.

105. Bradley Graham and Vernon Loeb, "An Air War of Might, Coordination, and Risks," *Washington Post*, April 27, 2003.

106. Capt. Mark I. Fox, USN, "Air Wing of Destiny," *Foundation* (published by the Naval Aviation Museum Foundation), fall 2004, 75, 77.

107. Lorenzo Cortes, "B-2 Drops Pair of 4,700-Pound GBU-37 GAMs [GPS-Aided Munitions] on Iraqi Communications Tower," *Defense Daily*, March 31, 2003, 5.

108. Carpenter, "Rapid, Deliberate, Disciplined, Proportional, and Precise," 6.

109. As for actual SAMs themselves, those would be struck by TLAMs only if the CAOC had a confirmed location for them. Had an Iraqi SAM operator activated his radar long enough to detect a target and fire and guide a SAM, he would have been instantly attacked by a HARM or an ALARM [RAF air-launched antiradiation missile.] Comments by Lieutenant Colonel Cline, January 11, 2008.

110. Davies, *F-15C/E Eagle Units of Operation Iraqi Freedom*, 48.

111. Davies and Dildy, *F-16 Fighting Falcon Units of Operation Iraqi Freedom*, 28.

112. Comments by Lieutenant Colonel Cline, January 11, 2008.

113. Conversations with Colonel Erlenbusch, Major Roberson, and other CEN-TAF staff, January 29, 2007.

114. Hampton Stephens, "B-1 Bomber Being Used in a Variety of Missions during Iraq War," *Inside the Air Force*, March 28, 2003, 1, 8–9.

115. A well-informed account explained: "Taking the standard Block 50D/52D F-16C and upgrading it to perform the SEAD role involved the addition of two main pieces of mission-specific equipment. The most obvious of these is the addition of the AN/ASQ-213 HTS—the HARM targeting system. HTS is a small pod carried on the right side of the [aircraft's air] intake cheek that is used to find, classify, range, and display threat-emitter systems to the pilot. In doing so, it allows the pilot to cue the . . . HARM to specific threat systems. Supplementing the HTS is the AN/ALR-56M advanced radar warning receiver, AN/ALQ-131(V)14 electronic counter-measures pod, and the addition of under wing-mounted chaff dispensers to complement those already mounted on the lower rear fuselage adjacent to the horizontal stabilizers. The second key component . . . is the avionics launcher interface computer (ALICS), which resides in the . . . HARM launcher pylon and acts as the conduit between the HTS, the central computer, and the missile itself. Pronounced 'A-licks', the ALICS is essential for successful handoff of radar threats from the jet to the HARM" (Davies and Dildy, *F-16 Fighting Falcon Units of Operation Iraqi Freedom*, 7–8).

116. Ibid., 27. The HARM's most effective operating mode against SAM threats is its "range-known" mode, in which the missile has accurate azimuth and ranging information against potential enemy IADS targets. "This is the mode that offers the best probability of kill, and known emitter locations can be programmed into the missile's seeker head prior to flight, or passed dynamically via the ALICS during flight as the HTS sniffs the air for electrons. However, for much of Operation Iraqi Freedom, HARMs were launched using the preemptive mode, which allows the AGM-88 to be fired toward suspected or known sites in an arcing trajectory that maximizes the weapon's time of flight. In this mode, the missile seeker activates as it heads toward earth and then waits to see if its assigned target [begins to emit]." The F-16CJ's ability to react so swiftly to pop-up SAM threats is due almost entirely to intelligent software programming and the integration of hands-on-throttle-and-stick switchology in the cockpit. A pilot explained: "The jet's smart enough that if we see something in the HTS pod, all we do is put our cursors over the threat and get a pretty accurate idea of its position,

which will be good enough to launch a missile at it. At that point, we designate the target and let the HARM go" (ibid., 48).

117. Ibid., 42.

118. Lieutenant Colonel Hathaway explained that "the problem was that the SAM operators in the Super MEZ refused to turn their radars on. We didn't know whether it was out of their fear of the coalition's SEAD assets or . . . reflective of a determination to preserve their capabilities for a later ambush of coalition nonstealth aircraft. To support the land component's imminent movement into the Baghdad area, we needed to get nonstealthy aircraft into the Super MEZ as quickly as possible so we could gain air supremacy and prepare the battlespace on the ground. After three days of not being able to draw down Iraq's densest concentration of SAM radars with HARMs, we switched to a DEAD [destruction of enemy air defenses] campaign to track down and physically destroy the SAM sites" (comments by Lieutenant Colonel Hathaway, February 19, 2007).

119. Comments by Lieutenant Colonel Cline, January 11, 2008.

120. Knights, *Cradle of Conflict*, 18.

121. Elizabeth Rees, "363rd AEW [Air Expeditionary Wing] Weighs In on Ops Tempo, Force Strain, Enemy Air Defenses in War," *Inside the Air Force*, March 28, 2003, 9. The SEAD campaign was also rendered relatively manageable because the Iraqi IADS in the Super MEZ surrounding Baghdad and Tikrit, while dense, was also both known and antiquated, consisting of such threat systems as SA-2s, SA-3s, SA-6s, and some Rolands that CENTAF's aircrews had faced many times before. It did not include any advanced SAM systems like the SA-10 or SA-20. Lorenzo Cortes, "Leaf: Iraq Air Defenses Were Dense, Antiquated in OIF; Stealth Needed in Future," *Defense Daily*, June 9, 2003, 6.

122. Fox, "Air Wing of Destiny," 78.

123. Davies and Dildy, *F-16 Fighting Falcon Units of Operation Iraqi Freedom*, 40–41.

124. Elizabeth Rees, "Old Predators Used as Decoys to Provoke Iraqi Air Defenses," *Inside the Air Force*, April 11, 2003, 7.

125. An Australian analyst pointed to "perhaps the most bizarre happening in this phase of the air campaign," namely, "the repeated gathering of Baghdadis on the opposite bank of the Tigris River—watching the mesmerizing sound and light show through the night" while standing mere hundreds of meters away from where allied munitions were detonating (Kopp, "Iraqi Freedom—the Hammer and Anvil," 32).

126. Knights, *Cradle of Conflict*, 18.

127. Philip P. Pan, "Turkey Lets U.S. Use Airspace," *Washington Post*, March 21, 2003.

128. Philip P. Pan, "Turkish Leader Makes Request on Airspace," *Washington Post*, March 20, 2003. See also Richard Boudreaux, "Two Errant Missiles Fall in Turkey," *Los Angeles Times*, March 24, 2003.

129. Although the 3rd ID would eventually take in some 2,600 enemy prisoners of war, there was never any massive capitulation of entire units as occurred during Operation Desert Storm. Fontenot, Degen, and Tohn, *On Point*, 109.

130. Carpenter, "Rapid, Deliberate, Disciplined, Proportional, and Precise," 12.

131. *Lessons of Iraq*, vol. 2, Ev 204.

132. Quoted in Murray and Scales, *The Iraq War*, 88.

133. Michael R. Gordon, "The Goal Is Baghdad, but at What Cost?" *New York Times*, March 25, 2003. A CENTAF planner later noted that another reason for this last-minute removal of multiple targets from the initial strike list was General McKiernan's determination to avoid potential fratricide as his troops continued their high-speed advance north toward Baghdad. "Regrettably," said this planner, "a lot of those targets were the local security offices in towns in southern Iraq" (comments by Lieutenant Colonel Cline, January 11, 2008).

134. Nichols, "Operation Iraqi Freedom: CFACC/CAOC/NALE."

135. Knights, *Cradle of Conflict*, 279.

136. Ibid., 275.

137. Ibid.

138. Ibid., 274.

139. Ibid.

140. Ibid., 273.

141. Ibid., 275.

142. Comments by Lieutenant Colonel Hathaway, February 19, 2007.

143. Knights, *Cradle of Conflict*, 275–276. Another senior CAOC planner later recalled, "this was disappointing, because every town from Mosul to Basra had a Directorate of General Security, Iraqi Intelligence Service, and Special Security Organization building or prison and torture chamber, and we wanted ... to kill the bad guys inside as a symbol to the people who lived in those towns that the security forces were no longer in control" (comments by Lieutenant Colonel Cline, January 11, 2008).

144. Conversation with General Moseley, August 2, 2006.

145. Knights, *Cradle of Conflict*, 276. On the other hand, a senior CAOC planner later pointed out, "I don't think I would have wanted to be the one sitting in

Kuwait waiting to uncoil as Iraqi artillery and FROG rockets started raining down" (comments by Lieutenant Colonel Cline, January 11, 2008).

146. Davies, *F-15C/E Eagle Units of Operation Iraqi Freedom*, 44.

147. Elaine Grossman, "Air Chief Won Ability to Hit Iraqi Bridges to Prevent Scud Launch," *Inside the Pentagon*, June 12, 2003, 1, 10–11.

148. *Lessons from Iraq*, vol. 2, Ev 48.

149. On this point, during his briefing to media representatives as the campaign entered its last week, General Moseley commented: "The term 'shock and awe' has never been a term I've used. . . . We withheld some targets based on the initiation conditions and based on where the surface forces were. But that [was the] right thing to do anyway" ("Coalition Forces Air Component Command Briefing," Washington, D.C.: Department of Defense, April 5, 2003).

150. Greg Jaffe, "Plan Is to Cut Off Top Officers while Allies Strike Air Defenses," *Wall Street Journal*, March 20, 2003.

151. Anthony H. Cordesman, "Understanding the New 'Effects-Based' Air War in Iraq," Center for Strategic and International Studies, Washington, D.C., March 15, 2003, 3.

152. Nichols, "Operation Iraqi Freedom: CFACC/CAOC/NALE."

153. Ripley, "Planning for Iraqi Freedom," 11.

154. Knights, *Cradle of Conflict*, 278.

155. Bush, *Decision Points*, 255.

156. Carpenter, "Rapid, Deliberate, Disciplined, Proportional, and Precise," 13.

157. Thomas E. Ricks, "Unfolding Battle Will Determine Length of War," *Washington Post*, March 25, 2003.

158. As the focus of the air war shifted from attacking preplanned fixed targets to supporting coalition ground units on the move, the air component's target development planners unexpectedly found themselves obliged to create "bomber boxes." Their initial attempt to create such bomber holding areas, according to CENTAF staff, "failed to meet operator requirements." Ultimately, the B-52 liaison element in the CAOC provided three essential requirements for a bomber operating box: the geographic coordinates of the box's center, the length and width of the box measured in feet, and the magnetic heading (in degrees) of the bomber box's major axis. Conversations with Colonel Erlenbusch, Major Roberson, and other CENTAF staff, January 29, 2007.

159. Ibid.

160. Ibid.

161. Ibid. In March 2003 the SCAR mission was not a formally recognized Air Force combat mission. CAOC planners adopted it from the Navy and Marine Corps for kill-box interdiction because of the mission's assessed value. The same planners strongly recommended afterward that the Air Force formally include the mission in its operating repertoire and continue to perform it in any future engagements in which it might provide value to the land component.

162. Carpenter, "Rapid, Deliberate, Disciplined, Proportional, and Precise," 25.

163. The "push-CAS" arrangement entailed maintaining an even flow of interdiction sorties into the Kuwaiti theater of operations around the clock, with a proviso that any of those sorties could be diverted as necessary to service CAS requests made by the Army's corps commanders. Its point was to assure the corps commanders that they had on-call CAS should it ever be needed without tying up coalition aircraft.

164. As used in this context, a minute is a unit of angular measure equal to one-sixtieth of a degree.

165. For a detailed explanation, see Green, "Joint Fires Support, the Joint Fires Element and the CGRS," 15–17. A later effort was initiated in the joint arena to develop and implement a "global area reference system" (GARS) that would align all regional combatant commanders using the same methodology to enable standardization of software and training for warfighters who might end up fighting in any of several theaters around the world. Now in joint use, GARS is essentially the same as CGRS but provides a single, globally referenced set of boxes, quadrants, and keypads.

166. Comments by Colonel Neuenswander, March 6, 2007.

167. Stout, *Hammer from Above*, 270.

168. Davies, *F-15C/E Eagle Units of Operation Iraqi Freedom*, 44.

169. Tim Ripley, "Closing the Gap," *Jane's Defence Weekly*, July 2, 2003, 26.

170. Conversations with Colonel Erlenbusch, Major Roberson, and other CENTAF staff, January 29, 2007.

171. Fontenot, Degen, and Tohn, *On Point*, 89.

172. Murray and Scales, *The Iraq War*, 109.

173. Ibid., 172.

174. Conversations with Colonel Erlenbusch, Major Roberson, and other CENTAF staff, January 29, 2007.

175. Fontenot, Degen, and Tohn, *On Point*, 90.

176. Rajiv Chandrasekaran and Peter Baker, "Sandstorm Delays Army's Advance; Units Set to Hit Guard near Capital," *Washington Post*, March 26, 2003.

177. Quoted in Capt. John W. Anderson, USAF, "An Analysis of a Dust Storm Impacting Operation Iraqi Freedom, 25–27 March 2003," master's thesis, U.S. Naval Postgraduate School, Monterey, Calif., December 2004, 2.

178. Throughout the buildup for and subsequent execution of OPLAN 1003V, the CAOC received twice-daily briefings on current and anticipated future weather conditions in CENTCOM's area of responsibility. Five-day fore-casts kept ATO planners informed of prospective future conditions at major bases and in key target areas. During the three-week major combat phase of Iraqi Freedom, more than 75 percent of the daily ATOs were adversely affected by weather, with 20 percent suffering from "major" weather effects and more than 6 percent of their scheduled sorties having been either can-celed or declared noneffective. Ibid., 84.

179. Fontenot, Degen, and Tohn, *On Point*, 142.

180. Davies and Dildy, *F-16 Fighting Falcon Units of Operation Iraqi Freedom*, 33.

181. Ibid.

182. Ibid.

183. For a graphic account of these harassment operations written by a Marine reconnaissance platoon commander whose unit was caught in the midst of them for several days, see Nathaniel Fick, *One Bullet Away: The Making of a Marine Officer* (New York: Houghton Mifflin, 2005), 205–290.

184. Andrew Koch, "Did Washington Underestimate Iraqi Resolve?" *Jane's Defence Weekly*, April 2, 2003, 2.

185. Kevin M. Woods, with Michael R. Pease, Mark E. Stout, Williamson Murray, and James G. Lacey, *Iraqi Perspectives Project: A View of Operation Iraqi Freedom from Saddam's Senior Leadership* (Norfolk, Va.: Joint Center for Operational Analysis, U.S. Joint Forces Command, March 2006), 55. A summary of the main findings of this landmark assessment may be found in Kevin Woods, James Lacey, and Williamson Murray, "Saddam's Delusions: The View from Inside," *Foreign Affairs*, May–June 2006. Saddam Hussein established the Fedayeen in October 1994 in response to the Shiite and Kurdish uprisings of March 1991 that immediately followed Operation Desert Storm.

186. Carpenter, "Rapid, Deliberate, Disciplined, Proportional, and Precise," 13.

187. Peter Baker and Rajiv Chandrasekaran, "Republican Guard Units Move South from Baghdad, Hit by U.S. Forces," *Washington Post*, March 27, 2003.

188. Elaine M. Grossman, "Key Generals: Response to 'Fedayeen' a Vital Mile-stone in Iraq War," *Inside the Pentagon*, May 8, 2003, 1.

189. Quoted in Knights, *Cradle of Conflict*, 304.

190. See Chapter 4 for more on the Blue Force Tracker system. The system also reduced fratricide because an allied tank equipped with it could be identi-fied at a distance. Fontenot, Degen, and Tohn, *On Point*, 63.

191. Knights, *Cradle of Conflict*, 305.

192. Ibid., 314.

193. Elaine M. Grossman, "Marine General: Iraq War Pause 'Could Not Have Come at Worse Time,'" *Inside the Pentagon*, October 2, 2003, 1.

194. Lorenzo Cortes, "Leaf Says Severe Weather Accelerated Iraqi Forces' Defeat," *Defense Daily*, June 5, 2003, 1.

195. TSgt. Michael Keehan, USAF, "15th EASOS [Expeditionary Air Support Operations Squadron] Operation Iraqi Freedom TACP Stories," briefing by TACP team assigned to the 3rd Squadron, 7th Cavalry, 3rd Infantry Division, no date given, provided to the author by Col. Matt Neuenswander, head of the Air Force element, U.S. Army Command and General Staff College, Fort Leavenworth, Kansas.

196. Ibid.

197. Ibid.

198. James Kitfield, "Attack Always," *National Journal*, April 26, 2003, 1292–1296.

199. Keehan, "15th EASOS Operation Iraqi Freedom TACP Stories."

200. Ibid.

201. The others were, respectively, SSgt. Thomas Case, SSgt. Travis Crosby, SSgt. Joshua Swartz, TSgt. Eric Brandenberg, and TSgt. Jason Quesenberry.

202. "Citation to Accompany the Award of the Silver Star Medal to Michael L. Keehan III," document provided to the author by AFCENT/A9, Shaw AFB, S.C., April 17, 2009.

203. "Citation to Accompany the Award of the Silver Star Medal to Michael S. Shropshire," document provided to the author by AFCENT/A9, Shaw AFB, S.C., April 17, 2009.

204. An assessment of the land offensive noted that "the sandstorm actually improved the coalition's logistical situation, as it slowed the fast-moving spearheads enough to allow resupply convoys to reach them and replenish food and ammunition that had dwindled during the long, rapid advance. When the sandstorm lifted on March 27, the advance thus continued afresh with no meaningful long-term effect from the delay" (Biddle and others, *Toppling Saddam*, 18).

205. Stout, *Hammer from Above*, 209.

206. Max Boot, *War Made New: Technology, Warfare, and the Course of History, 1500 to Today* (New York: Gotham Books, 2006), 395. Of such air support, however, Col. William Grimsley, commander of the 3rd ID's 1st Brigade, later noted that there is a "host of Marine Corps, Navy, Air Force, and Royal Air Force pilots I would love to meet some day" (Fontenot, Degen, and Tohn, *On Point*, 167).

207. Although the three-day sandstorm did not materially hinder the air compo-
     nent's contribution to the campaign effort, between March 25 and March
     27, 817 scheduled ATO sorties were either canceled or declared nonef-
     fective due to the weather. See Anderson, "An Analysis of a Dust Storm
     Impacting Operation Iraqi Freedom," 88, 50.

208. Dave Moniz and John Diamond, "Attack on Guard May Be Days Away,"
     USA Today, March 31, 2003.

209. Stout, *Hammer from Above*, 260.

210. Kim Murphy and Alan C. Miller, "The Team That Picks the Targets," *Los
     Angeles Times*, March 25, 2003.

211. Rajiv Chandrasekaran and Peter Baker, "As Marines Resume Advance,
     Army Fights Baghdad Defenders," *Washington Post*, April 2, 2003.

212. Fontenot, Degen, and Tohn, *On Point*, 227.

213. Handy, *Operation Iraqi Freedom—Air Mobility by the Numbers*, 11.

214. Anthony Shadid, "In Shift, War Targets Communications Facilities," *Wash-
     ington Post*, April 1, 2003.

215. Quoted in Knights, *Cradle of Conflict*, 322. "Comical Ali" was a play on the
     epithet "Chemical Ali," which referred to Ali Hassan Abd Al Majid Al Tikriti,
     the former Iraqi minister of defense, interior minister, and chief of the intel-
     ligence service who gained notoriety during the 1980s and 1990s for the
     role he played in Saddam Hussein's campaigns against domestic opposition
     forces. Dubbed "Chemical Ali" by Iraqi Kurds for his use of chemical weap-
     ons against them (in one instance killing more than five thousand civilians),
     Al Majid was captured by allied forces after the three-week campaign in
     2003 and was tried, convicted, and sentenced to death in 2007 for crimes
     committed during the Al Anfal campaign against Kurdish resistance forces
     in the 1980s.

216. Conversation with Major General Darnell, August 6, 2006. General Mose-
     ley's chief of strategy later amplified: "While the primary target was indeed
     the ministry of information, intelligence reporting told us that many West-
     ern journalists were being held there as 'guests.' In the end, we decided to
     go against the antennas on the roof as the best way to achieve the desired
     effect" (comments by Lieutenant Colonel Hathaway, February 19, 2007).

217. Hinote, "More Than Bombing Saddam," 152. See also Kim Burger, Nick
     Cook, Andrew Koch, and Michael Sirak, "What Went Right?" *Jane's Defence
     Weekly*, April 30, 2003, 21.

218. Davies, *F-15C/E Eagle Units of Operation Iraqi Freedom*, 65.

219. Rajiv Chandrasekaran and Peter Baker, "Baghdad Hit Hard from Air as
     Ground Forces Regroup," *Washington Post*, March 28, 2003.

220. Evan Thomas and John Barry, "A Plan Under Attack," *Time*, April 7, 2003.

221. Murray and Scales, *The Iraq War*, 165.

222. Eric Schmitt, "Rumsfeld Says Important Targets Have Been Avoided," *New York Times*, March 24, 2003.

223. Michael R. Gordon, "Allied Plan Would Encourage Iraqis Not to Fight," *New York Times*, March 11, 2003.

224. Although triple-redundant, the communications nodes were in principle easy to target. The difficulty stemmed from the fact that destroying the main switches in Baghdad entailed high collateral damage potential. In addition, there were the uncertainties that attended damaging something that the coalition intended to rebuild later and destroying an enemy equity that could provide intelligence value if left intact. Comments by Lieutenant Colonel Cline, January 11, 2008.

225. Bradley Graham, "U.S. Air Attacks Turn More Aggressive," *Washington Post*, April 2, 2003.

226. David J. Lynch, "Marines Prevail in 'Toughest Day' of Combat," *USA Today*, March 24, 2003. See also Vernon Loeb, "Patriot Downs RAF Fighter," *Washington Post*, March 24, 2003.

227. "Patriot Under Fire for Second Error," *Flight International*, April 8–14, 2003, 10.

228. Atkinson, *In the Company of Soldiers*, 133.

229. Col. Darrel D. Whitcomb, USAFR (Ret.), "Rescue Operations in the Second Gulf War," *Air and Space Power Journal*, spring 2005, 97.

230. Gordon and Trainor, *Cobra II*, 354.

231. Ibid.

232. Jonathan Weisman, "Patriot Missiles Seemingly Falter for Second Time," *Washington Post*, March 26, 2003. It was not correct, as Rick Atkinson reported regarding this incident, that a HARM had been "mistakenly" fired by a "confused F/A-18 pilot" (*In the Company of Soldiers*, 154).

233. Davies and Dildy, *F-16 Fighting Falcon Units of Operation Iraqi Freedom*, 52.

234. Comments on an earlier draft by Lt. Col. John Hunerwadel, USAF (Ret.), Air Force Doctrine Center, Maxwell AFB, Ala., May 23, 2007. In Israeli military practice, anything that flies (short of artillery and surface-to-surface rockets), from fixed-wing and rotary-wing combat and combat support aircraft to such surface-to-air weapons as Patriots, Hawks, and even AAA, is owned and operated by the Israeli Air Force, in part precisely to prevent such possibilities for fratricide.

235. Patrick E. Tyler, "Attack from Two Sides Shatters the Iraqi Republican Guard," *New York Times*, April 3, 2003; and Bradley Graham, "Patriot System Likely Downed U.S. Jet," *Washington Post*, April 4, 2003.

236. Or, he might have added, Australian, as the RAAF contributed fourteen F/A-18s to the overall campaign effort. Charles Piller, "Vaunted Patriot Missile Has a 'Friendly Fire' Failing," *Los Angeles Times*, April 21, 2003.

237. Comments by Lieutenant Colonel Hathaway, February 19, 2007.

238. Gordon and Trainor, *Cobra II*, 354–355.

239. Thom Shanker, "Risk of Being Killed by Own Side Increases," *New York Times*, April 8, 2003. There also were a number of fratricidal air-to-ground engagements, including one involving an Air Force A-10 that was providing CAS to Marines approaching An Nasiriyah. The A-10 strafed the wrong side of a bridge on which friendly and enemy vehicles were commingled and shot up a Marine amphibious assault vehicle, killing six Marines (see Chapter 5). Murray and Scales, *The Iraq War*, 122.

240. Davies and Dildy, *F-16 Fighting Falcon Units of Operation Iraqi Freedom*, 50.

241. Ibid., 51.

242. Ibid.

243. Carpenter, "Rapid, Deliberate, Disciplined, Proportional, and Precise," 11.

244. ATO M followed the previous day's ATO L, which was the last ATO executed in the context of Operation Southern Watch before the start of OPLAN 1003V and major combat operations.

245. David A. Fulghum, "New Bag of Tricks: As Stealth Aircraft and Northern Watch Units Head Home, Details of the Coalition's Use of Air Power Are Revealed," *Aviation Week and Space Technology*, April 21, 2003, 22.

246. Davies and Dildy, *F-16 Fighting Falcon Units of Operation Iraqi Freedom*, 29.

247. "Coalition Forces Air Component Command Briefing."

248. David A. Fulghum, "Fast Forward," *Aviation Week and Space Technology*, April 28, 2003, 34–35.

249. Davies and Dildy, *F-16 Fighting Falcon Units of Operation Iraqi Freedom*, 30.

250. Ibid., 31.

251. Conversation with General Moseley, August 2, 2006.

252. Ibid.

253. Ibid.

254. Carpenter, "Rapid, Deliberate, Disciplined, Proportional, and Precise," 11.

255. Woods, Lacey, and Murray, "Saddam's Delusions," 5.

256. On the failure of the Iraqi air force to fly, Air Marshal Torpy later noted: "They had obviously been watching the way we had been operating in the no-fly zones for 12 years, so they had good knowledge of our capability and they inevitably also knew what we had brought into the theater as well" (*Lessons of Iraq*, vol. 1, 96).

257. Rajiv Chandrasekaran and Peter Baker, "U.S. Takes Battle to Baghdad Airport," *Washington Post*, April 4, 2003.

258. Davies and Dildy, *F-16 Fighting Falcon Units of Operation Iraqi Freedom*, 60.

259. Major Roberson later remarked that although delivering leaflets was not initially accepted in the squadrons as a legitimate "combat mission," the pilots eventually came to understand that "it was one of those necessary evils, in that the psyops part of Operation Iraqi Freedom was as important as the . . . kinetic effects of the war. You don't get any feedback when you [dispense the leaflets], but I think everybody in the squadron accepted the fact that it was something that needed to be done" (ibid., 59).

260. Carpenter, "Rapid, Deliberate, Disciplined, Proportional, and Precise," 23.

261. Hampton Stephens, "Compass Call Was Key to Special Operations in Iraq, Afghanistan," *Inside the Air Force*, April 2, 2004, 1, 4.

262. I am grateful to Col. Gregory Fontenot, USA (Ret.), for bringing this important consideration to my attention.

263. Paul Richter, "Risky Fight for Baghdad Nears," *Los Angeles Times*, March 24, 2003.

264. "Coalition Forces Air Component Command Briefing."

265. Kopp, "Iraqi Freedom—the Hammer and Anvil," 29.

266. Butler, "As A-10 Shines in Iraq War, Officials Look to JSF for Future CAS Role," 1.

267. Ripley, "Planning for Iraqi Freedom," 11.

268. Cordesman, "The 'Instant Lessons' of the Iraq War: Main Report," 40.

269. This composite portrait of events was assembled from the citations accompanying the award of the Silver Star to Kenneth E. Ray, Bruce R. Taylor, and James Winsmann, provided to the author by AFCENT/A9, Shaw AFB, S.C., April 17, 2009. In addition to the eleven Silver Stars awarded to Air Force airmen, the majority of them JTACs, fifty-eight Distinguished Flying Crosses with special citations for heroism were also awarded to Air Force airmen for similar acts during the same period. Information provided to the author by AFCENT/A9, Shaw AFB, S.C., April 17, 2009.

270. Lt. Col. Michael W. Kometer, USAF, *Command in Air War: Centralized versus Decentralized Control of Combat Air Power* (Maxwell AFB, Ala.: Air University Press, June 2007), 142. An earlier version of this study was submitted as the author's doctoral dissertation in security studies at the Massachusetts Institute of Technology.

271. Reynolds, *Basrah, Baghdad, and Beyond*, 24.

272. Ibid., 23. The above-noted after-action assessment added: "Amos's personal style was, by Marine Corps standards, laid back; he was unusually approachable and looked for the common-sense solution as opposed to asserting his status or rank. That said, he was nothing if not results-oriented" (ibid., 49).

273. Gordon and Trainor, *Cobra II*, 534. The core issue has to do with the extent of situational awareness on the part of the CAS controller in differing circumstances. In Type I CAS (the most exacting variant), the JTAC or FAC-A must have visual contact with both the target and the attacking aircraft. Type II requires visual contact with either the aircraft or the target. Type III does not require visual contact with either, but the JTAC or FAC-A must be in communication with the attacking pilot and approve the release of weapons. All of the attendees at the warfighter conference convened by General Moseley at Nellis AFB in August 2002 during CENTCOM's initial planning workups agreed that draft Joint Publication 3-09.3 for joint CAS offered a serviceable basis on which to ground the emerging KI/CAS concept. They specifically pulled from the draft publication the new types of specified joint CAS control (Types I, II, and III), as well as its definition of a JTAC. The challenge proved to be getting all component players to implement the three types consistently. Conversations with Colonel Erlenbusch, Major Roberson, and other CENTAF staff, January 29, 2007.

274. Murray and Scales, *The Iraq War*, 11.

275. Jonathan Finer, "For Marines, a Fight with a Foe That Never Arrived," *Washington Post*, April 4, 2003.

276. Rajiv Chandrasekaran and Peter Baker, "Baghdad-Bound Forces Pass Outer Defenses," *Washington Post*, April 3, 2003.

277. Evan Thomas and Martha Brandt, "The Secret War," *Time*, April 21, 2003.

278. Michael R. Gordon, "Tightening a Noose," *New York Times*, April 4, 2003.

279. Rajiv Chandrasekaran and Alan Sipress, "Army Has First Close Fighting with Republican Guard Units," *Washington Post*, April 1, 2003.

280. Patrick E. Tyler, "Two U.S. Columns Are Advancing on Baghdad," *New York Times*, April 1, 2003.

281. Kopp, "Iraqi Freedom—the Hammer and Anvil," 30.

282. Carpenter, "Rapid, Deliberate, Disciplined, Proportional, and Precise," 14.

283. Michael R. Gordon, "Battle for Baghdad Begins in Area Surrounding Iraqi Capital," *New York Times*, April 2, 2003.

284. Ibid., 120.

285. Michael Sirak, "Interview with James Roche: Secretary of the U.S. Air Force," *Jane's Defence Weekly*, May 14, 2003.

286. Maj. Gen. Franklin Blaisdell, the Air Force's director of space operations, similarly said that "any enemy that would depend on GPS jammers for their livelihood is in grave trouble" (quoted in "Iraq Is Expected to Try Jamming U.S. Signals," *Baltimore Sun*, March 13, 2003).

287. "DoD Says Russian Sale of GPS Jammers to Iraq Not Affecting Air Campaign," *Inside the Pentagon*, March 27, 2003, 19.

288. "CENTCOM, Pentagon Confirm Destruction of GPS Jamming Equipment," *Defense Daily*, March 26, 2003, 1. The Air Force announced plans in early 2003 to allocate $40 million toward countering the effects of potential jamming of GPS-aided air-delivered munitions. Elaine M. Grossman, "Air Force Aims to Redirect $40 Million in FY03 to Counter GPS Jamming," *Inside the Pentagon*, January 30, 2003, 1, 14.

289. Murray and Scales, *The Iraq War*, 115.

290. Carpenter, "Rapid, Deliberate, Disciplined, Proportional, and Precise," 14.

291. Kopp, "Iraqi Freedom—the Hammer and Anvil," 32.

292. Sean Boyne, "Iraqi Tactics Attempted to Employ Guerilla Forces," *Jane's Intelligence Review*, July 2003, 16–17.

293. Mark Mazetti and Richard J. Newman, "The Seeds of Victory," *U.S. News and World Report*, April 21, 2003.

294. Purdum, *A Time of Our Choosing*, 3.

295. Merrill A. McPeak, "Shock and Pause," *New York Times*, April 2, 2003.

296. Gordon and Trainor, *Cobra II*, 360.

297. Ibid., 373.

298. Ibid., 412, 426.

299. This technique was first employed on a trial basis during the late 1990s by the commander of Operation Northern Watch, then Brig. Gen. David Deptula. It offered an effective measure for mitigating collateral damage, although the technique required a steep weapon impact angle in order to prevent the munition from ricocheting off hard surfaces, with unpredictable consequences.

300. For a more detailed discussion of the carrier air contribution to the three weeks of major combat in Iraqi Freedom, see Benjamin S. Lambeth, *American Carrier Air Power at the Dawn of a New Century* (Santa Monica, Calif.: RAND Corporation, MG-404-NAVY, 2005), 39–58.

301. Nichols, "Operation Iraqi Freedom: CFACC/CAOC/NALE."

302. A "bolter" is an unplanned touch-and-go landing on the carrier deck that occurs when the aircraft's tailhook fails to engage an arresting cable.

303. This discussion has been informed by the description of carrier cyclic operations contained in Peter Hunt, *Angles of Attack: An A-6 Intruder Pilot's War* (New York: Ballantine Books, 2002), 53–55.

304. Robert Wall, "E-War Ramps Up: EA-6B Prowler to Resume Traditional Radar-Jamming Role if Iraqi Conflict Escalates," *Aviation Week and Space Technology*, March 17, 2003, 49.

305. Holmes, *U.S. Navy Hornet Units of Operation Iraqi Freedom*, pt. 2, 17.

306. Lyndsey Layton, "Building Bombs aboard the *Abraham Lincoln*," *Washington Post*, March 14, 2003.

307. "Bring-back" capability refers to the total weight of ordnance that a Navy or Marine Corps combat aircraft can recover with. It depends on the carrier's landing weight limitations and other operating factors. Munitions in excess of the bring-back weight must be jettisoned before the aircraft can land.

308. Whitcomb, "Rescue Operations in the Second Gulf War," 97.

309. Patrick E. Tyler, "Iraq Is Planning Protracted War," *New York Times*, April 2, 2003.

310. Carol J. Williams, "Navy Does Battle with Sandstorms on the Sea," *Los Angeles Times*, March 27, 2003.

311. "Defense Watch," *Defense Daily*, November 12, 2002, 1. GBU-35 was the initial Navy designation for its 1,000-pound JDAM based on its Mk 83 general-purpose bomb. The Navy has since adopted the same GBU-32 designation used by the Air Force.

312. Carol J. Williams, "Super Hornet Creates a Buzz in the Gulf," *Los Angeles Times*, April 1, 2003.

313. Robert Wall, "Super Hornets at Sea: U.S. Navy's New F/A-18Es Are Showing Surprising Reliability and Added Endurance," *Aviation Week and Space Technology*, March 17, 2003, 46–47.

314. Lt. Cdr. Richard K. Harrison, USN, "TacAir Trumps UAVs in Iraq," *Proceedings*, November 2003, 58–59.

315. Michael J. Gething, Mark Hewish, and Joris Janssen Lok, "New Pods Aid Air Reconnaissance," *Jane's International Defence Review*, October 2003, 59.

316. Robert Wall, "Weather or Not: The F-14D Strike Fighter Can Now Drop Precision Weapons Even on Cloud-Shrouded Targets," *Aviation Week and Space Technology*, March 17, 2003, 48.

317. Holmes, *U.S. Navy Hornet Units of Operation Iraqi Freedom*, pt. 2, 17.

318. "Coalition Forces Air Component Command Briefing."

319. Conversation with Major General Darnell, August 2, 2006.

320. Holmes, *U.S. Navy Hornet Units of Operation Iraqi Freedom*, 14.

321. Sandra I. Irwin, "Naval Aviators Experience Success in Iraq, but Worry about the Future," *The Hook,* fall 2003, 69. For a fuller discussion of the development of this close working relationship since the 1991 Persian Gulf War, see Benjamin S. Lambeth, *Combat Pair: The Evolution of Air Force–Navy Integration in Strike Warfare* (Santa Monica, Calif.: RAND Corporation, MG-655-AF, 2007); Benjamin S. Lambeth, "Air Force–Navy Integration in Strike Warfare: A Role Model for Seamless Joint-Service Operations," *Naval War College Review*, winter 2008; and Benjamin S. Lambeth, "Aerial Partners in Arms," *Joint Force Quarterly*, second quarter, 2008.

322. Vice Adm. Michael Malone, USN, "They Made a Difference," *The Hook*, summer 2003, 26.

323. Moseley, *Operation Iraqi Freedom—by the Numbers*, 10.

324. Murray and Scales, *The Iraq War*, 174.

325. "Coalition Forces Air Component Command Briefing."

326. John M. Broder, "Allies Fan Out in Iraq—Resistance Outside City Is Light," *New York Times,* April 9, 2003.

327. "Citation to Accompany the Award of the Silver Star Medal to Raymond T. Strasburger," document provided to the author by AFCENT/A9, Shaw AFB, S.C., April 17, 2009. In yet another indication that allied control of the air over Iraq was still not absolute, an Air Force A-10 was shot down two days later near the Baghdad International Airport, evidently by an optically guided Roland SAM. The pilot ejected safely and was recovered. John F. Burns, "Key Section of City Is Taken in a Street-by-Street Fight," *New York Times*, April 9, 2003.

328. Carla Anne Robbins, Greg Jaffe, and Dan Morse, "U.S. Aims at Psychological Front, Hoping Show of Force Ends War," *Wall Street Journal*, April 7, 2003.

329. Michael Knights, "USA Learns Lessons in Time-Critical Targeting," *Jane's Intelligence Review*, July 2003, 33. The GBU-31 penetrates ten to twenty feet below the surface of its target before being detonated, with the depth depending on the type of material the weapon must go through.

330. "Baghdad Raid Takes 12 Minutes from Targeting to Attack," *Flight International*, April 15–21, 2003, 8. See also "Speed Kills," *Inside the Pentagon*, April 10, 2003, 13.

331. Murray and Scales, *The Iraq War*, 176.

332. Giles Ebbutt, "UK Command and Control during Iraqi Freedom," *Jane's Intelligence Review*, July 2003, 42.

333. Fontenot, Degen, and Tohn, *On Point*, 118, 130.

334. Stout, *Hammer from Above*, 200.

335. Ibid., 269.

336. David E. Johnson, *Learning Large Lessons: The Evolving Roles of Ground Power and Air Power in the Post–Cold War Era* (Santa Monica, Calif.: RAND Corporation, MG-405-AF, 2006), 115.

337. Fontenot, Degen, and Tohn, *On Point*, 214.

338. Anthony Shadid, "Hussein's Baghdad Falls," *Washington Post*, April 10, 2003.

339. On July 22, 2003, Hussein's two sons Uday and Qusay were killed when a detachment of troops from the 101st Airborne Division and a joint SOF and CIA team raided a house where their presence had been detected; see

Kevin Sullivan and Rajiv Chandrasekaran, "Hussein's Two Sons Killed in Firefight with U.S. Troops," *Washington Post*, July 22, 2003. Saddam Hussein himself was finally captured by U.S. forces on December 13, 2003, in a farmhouse near Tikrit. He was subsequently tried and executed by the elected Iraqi government that replaced him.

340. Nichols, "Operation Iraqi Freedom: CFACC/CAOC/NALE."

341. Rowan Scarborough, "White House: 'We've Won,'" *Washington Times*, April 15, 2003.

342. David E. Sanger and Thom Shanker, "Bush Says Regime in Iraq Is No More: Victory 'Certain,'" *New York Times*, April 16, 2003.

343. Michael R. Gordon, "American Forces Adapted to Friend and Foe," *New York Times*, April 10, 2003.

344. Greg Jaffe, "Rumsfeld's Vindication Promises a Change in Tactics, Deployment," *Wall Street Journal,* April 10, 2003.

345. Stephen J. Hedges, "Air War Credited in Baghdad's Fall," *Chicago Tribune*, April 22, 2003.

346. Neil Tweedie, "U.S. Fighter 'Shot Down with Missile Left by SBS,'" *London Daily Telegraph*, June 6, 2003.

347. Once the major fighting was over, the commander of the wing to which the F-15E had been assigned took a recovery team to the crash site. He reported: "After I briefed General Moseley on what I found there, he declared the jet and crew combat losses—end of story" (comments on an earlier draft by Maj. Gen. Eric Rosborg, USAF, March 19, 2007).

348. Moseley, "Operation Iraqi Freedom: Initial CFACC Roll-up."

349. Nichols, "Operation Iraqi Freedom: CFACC/CAOC/NALE."

350. General Myers, the JCS chairman, dismissed that criticism as "bogus," adding that it came from people who "either weren't there, don't know, or they're working another agenda" (Jonathan Weisman, "Rumsfeld and Myers Defend War Plan," *Washington Post*, April 2, 2003). A far more compelling criticism would have faulted the Bush administration and its subordinate Rumsfeld Pentagon for having entered into a regime-change campaign with a ground force grossly insufficient to consolidate the military victory with postcampaign stabilization and restoration of public order. See Chapter 6.

351. Gen. Charles A. Horner, USAF (Ret.), "Operation Iraqi Freedom and the Transformation of War," *Aviation Week and Space Technology*, May 5, 2003, 66.

352. Former Air Force chief of staff Gen. Ronald Fogleman, in criticizing a common American war-gaming practice that persists to this day, complained in a memorandum to the chairman of the Joint Chiefs of Staff in 1996 that

"these legacy models are most relevant when considering . . . an employment strategy of attrition and annihilation. Models assessing force-on-force engagements, based on force ratios and territory gained or lost, lack the capability to fully and accurately portray the significant effects of operations . . . directly attacking the enemy's strategic and tactical centers of gravity." A standard campaign model still widely used by the Department of Defense and Joint Staff, called TACWAR (for "tactical warfare"), for example, does not model anything approaching the application of air power to achieve decisive functional effects as was demonstrated in both Desert Storm and Iraqi Freedom. For further discussion of this important point, see Lt. Col. Steve McNamara, USAF, "Assessing Air Power's Importance: Will the QDR [Quadrennial Defense Review] Debate Falter for Lack of Proper Analytic Tools?" *Armed Forces Journal International*, March 1997, 37.

353. Dennis Cauchon, "Why U.S. Casualties Were Low," *USA Today*, April 21, 2003.

354. *Lessons of Iraq*, vol. 1, 37.

355. Terry McCarthy, "What Ever Happened to the Republican Guard?" *Time*, May 12, 2003, 38.

356. Ibid.

357. Quoted in Lt. Col. Mark Simpson, USAF, "Air Power Lessons from Operation Iraqi Freedom," Headquarters Air Combat Command, ACC/XPSX, Langley AFB, Va., November 25, 2003.

358. McCarthy, "What Ever Happened to the Republican Guard?"

359. DeLong, *Inside CentCom*, 114.

360. *Lessons from Iraq*, vol. 2, Ev 50.

361. Fontenot, Degen, and Tohn, *On Point*, 374.

362. Ibid.

363. Rear Adm. David C. Nichols Jr., USN, "Reflections on Iraqi Freedom," *The Hook*, fall 2003, 3.

364. Fontenot, Degen, and Tohn, *On Point*, 273, 329.

365. Gordon and Trainor, *Cobra II*, 56.

Chapter 3. The Allies' Contribution

1. For official commentary on the United Kingdom's contribution to Operation Desert Storm, which the British code-named Operation Granby, see Michael Mates, *Preliminary Lessons of Operation Granby: House of Commons Papers 1990–91* (London: Stationery Office Books, 1991); and Nicholas Bonsor, *Implementation of Lessons Learned from Operation Granby: House of Commons Papers 1993–94* (London: Stationery Office Books, 1994).

2. For more on that contribution by the United Kingdom, see Lambeth, *Air Power against Terror*, 116–119. See also Nora Bensahel, *The Counterterror Coalition: Cooperation with Europe, NATO, and the European Union* (Santa Monica, Calif.: RAND Corporation, MR-1746-AF, 2003), 55–63.

3. As but one indicator that British involvement in the prospective war against Iraq was anything but assured at that point, RAF aircraft were proscribed from taking part in some elements of Operation Southern Focus. Conversation with senior staff officers at RAF Strike Command, RAF High Wycombe, UK, October 28, 2004.

4. Keegan, *The Iraq War*, 125.

5. As the United Kingdom's forward deployment for the campaign began, that effort enjoyed only 32 percent public support—about the same level that prevailed in 1956 when British forces deployed for the Suez campaign. That support rose to 85 percent by the time combat operations commenced, then dropped to 50 percent before the campaign had ended and to a considerably lower level thereafter. Air Chief Marshal Sir Brian Burridge, RAF, "Iraq 2003—Air Power Pointers for the Future," *Royal Air Force Air Power Review*, autumn 2004, 7–8.

6. *Operations in Iraq: First Reflections* (London: Ministry of Defence, July 2003), 3, hereinafter cited as *First Reflections*.

7. *Operation Telic: United Kingdom Military Operations in Iraq* (London: Report by the Comptroller and Auditor General, HC 60 Session 2003–2004, December 11, 2003), 1.

8. Ibid., 1.

9. *Ministry of Defence: Operation Telic—United Kingdom Military Operations in Iraq* (London: House of Commons, Committee of Public Accounts, 39th Report of Session 2003–04, July 21, 2004), 3–4.

10. David Willis, "Operation Iraqi Freedom," *International Air Power Review*, summer 2003, 16–18.

11. Information provided by Group Captain Richard Keir, RAAF, director, RAAF Air Power Development Centre, Canberra, Australia, July 2, 2009.

12. In connection with Operation Slipper, the Australian government dispatched an Australian national commander to Kuwait in October 2001. It also concurrently deployed a SOF task group to Afghanistan, four F/A-18 Hornet fighters for the local air defense of Diego Garcia, two Boeing 707 tankers to support allied air operations against the Taliban and Al Qaeda in Afghanistan operating out of Manas, Kyrgyzstan, and in early 2003 sent two P-3 Orion maritime patrol aircraft to the Persian Gulf region.

13. Press interview with Senator the Honorable Robert Hill, Minister for Defence, RAAF Base Richmond, New South Wales, Australia, February 7, 2003.

14. The first RAAF officer, Wing Commander Otto Halupka, joined CEN-TAF's initial planning deliberations at Shaw AFB, S.C., as early as August 2002 after having deployed shortly before for initial in-briefs at CENT-COM's headquarters at MacDill AFB with the designated Australian national commander, Army Brigadier Maurie McNarn, and the designated Australian air contingent commander, Group Captain Geoff Brown. Official interview with Group Captain Geoff Brown, RAAF, Operation Falconer air component commander, April 9, 2008, provided to the author by the RAAF Air Power Development Centre, Canberra, Australia.

15. Tony Holmes, "RAAF Hornets at War," *Australian Aviation*, January–February 2006, 38.

16. *Australia's National Security: A Defence Update 2003* (Canberra, Australia: Department of Defence, 2003), 15.

17. The Honorable John Howard, address to the House of Representatives, Parliament House, Canberra, Australia, March 18, 2003.

18. *Lessons of Iraq*, vol. 1, 33.

19. The MoD assigned a three-star RAF representative, then Air Marshal Jock Stirrup, to CENTCOM headquarters in Florida at the start of Operation Enduring Freedom. Stirrup was later replaced by a two-star successor as the Afghan air war ramped down, but the position was again upgraded to a three-star billet for Operation Iraqi Freedom with the assignment of Air Marshal Burridge as national contingent commander.

20. Conversation with Air Chief Marshal Sir Brian Burridge, RAF, commander-in-chief, RAF Strike Command, on board a 32 Squadron HS 125 en route from RAF Northolt to RAF Lossiemouth, UK, October 27, 2004.

21. At the time, Air Vice-Marshal Torpy was serving as the air officer commanding of No. 1 Group within RAF Strike Command, who oversaw all RAF strike fighter operations.

22. *Lessons of Iraq*, vol. 2, Ev 42.

23. *Lessons of Iraq*, vol. 1, 52.

24. Ibid., 53.

25. *Lessons of Iraq*, vol. 2, Ev 42.

26. Ibid., Ev 44.

27. Ibid., Ev 43.

28. Claire Bannon, Media Liaison Officer, "Op Bastille/Falconer Timeline," Canberra, Australia, Government of Australia, no date.

29. *The War in Iraq: ADF Operations in the Middle East in 2003* (Canberra, Australia: Department of Defence, 2004), 13.
30. *Lessons of Iraq*, vol. 1, 32.
31. *Lessons of Iraq*, vol. 2, Ev 198.
32. *Operations In Iraq: Lessons for the Future* (London: Ministry of Defence, December 2003), 6–7, hereinafter cited as *Lessons for the Future*.
33. *Lessons of Iraq*, vol. 3, Ev 416.
34. *First Reflections*, 4.
35. Conversation with senior staff officers at Headquarters Strike Command, October 28, 2004.
36. "RAF Contribution to Operation Iraqi Freedom," briefing given to the author by 23 Squadron, RAF Waddington, UK, October 29, 2004.
37. *Lessons of Iraq*, vol. 2, Ev 44.
38. *The War in Iraq: ADF Operations in the Middle East in 2003*, 8.
39. The Honorable John Howard, Address to the Committee for Economic Development of Australia, Canberra, Australia, November 20, 2002.
40. *Darwin* and *ANZAC*, along with the RAAF's AP-3s, were already deployed in CENTCOM's AOR in support of Operation Slipper, the ADF's contribution to Operation Enduring Freedom against the Taliban and Al Qaeda in Afghanistan.
41. Once regional air defense was no longer a serious concern, the F3s were pulled out to free up more ramp space for other aircraft. Although ramp space was at a premium throughout the campaign, sufficient strike aircraft were always present to satisfy the commitments levied on the British contingent by the daily ATO. Conversation with Air Vice-Marshal Andy White, RAF, air officer commanding, No. 3 Group, Headquarters RAF Strike Command, RAF High Wycombe, UK, October 28, 2004.
42. *First Reflections*, 43–48.
43. *Ark Royal* carried Royal Navy Sea King and RAF Chinook helicopters.
44. *First Reflections*, 43–48.
45. Conversation with Air Vice-Marshal White, October 28, 2004.
46. Holmes, "RAAF Hornets at War," 38.
47. A fourth F/A-18 squadron, and the first to have been stood up at Williamtown in 1986 after the RAAF acquired the Hornet to replace its aging Mirage fighters, is 2 Operational Conversion Unit, the RAAF's transition squadron that consists mainly of dual-control F/A-18B trainer versions of the aircraft.
48. Official interview with Group Captain Bill Henman, RAAF, Operation Falconer commander of the air combat wing, April 9, 2007, provided

to the author by the RAAF Air Power Development Centre, Canberra, Australia.

49. Ibid.

50. Conversation with Air Marshal Glenn Torpy, RAF, commander, Permanent Joint Headquarters, Northwood, London, UK, October 26, 2004.

51. *Lessons of Iraq*, vol. 2, Ev 52.

52. *Lessons of Iraq*, vol. 1, 59.

53. Ibid.

54. Torpy further volunteered that experience from previous operations had demonstrated the need for delegated targeting responsibility in order to maintain a sufficiently high tempo during Operation Telic. He also noted that the British defence minister, Geoffrey Hoon, fully understood those needs and was pivotal in securing the needed streamlining of the approval process. Conversation with Air Marshal Torpy, October 26, 2004.

55. Gardner, "Operation Iraqi Freedom: Coalition Operations," 94.

56. *Lessons of Iraq*, vol. 1, 59.

57. *Lessons for the Future*, 27.

58. "Op Bastille/Falconer Timeline."

59. On this point, ADF legal officers vetted targets "in concert with RAAF intelligence personnel to produce what was called a 'legal target apprecia-tion' for each target to be hit by RAAF aircraft. Also, each target was briefed to Group Captain Brown for his approval. This was done in parallel with the U.S. process, not sequentially, so as to not hold up the CAOC process. Any-thing outside Group Captain Brown's approval level was either not accepted as a target or, if there was time, referred back to Australia for a decision. If there was an issue with a target, we were always able to pull it from the U.S. allocation to us and have it replaced with something more suitable. For this level of involvement, we relied heavily on RAAF planners within the GAT [guidance, apportionment, and targeting] and MAAP cells" (comments on an earlier draft by Group Captain Richard Keir, RAAF, chief of intelligence and targeting for the RAAF under Group Captain Brown, director, RAAF Air Power Development Centre, Canberra, Australia, July 2, 2009).

60. Official interview with Group Captain Brown, April 9, 2008. Later, Group Captain Brown recalled that one of his most memorable moments in the CAOC occurred when General Moseley invited him to join him, alongside General Franks and RAF Air Vice-Marshal Torpy, in a video teleconference with President Bush, a former Texas Air National Guard F-102 pilot, who said to Franks: "Well, lucky you're surrounded by three fighter pilots to keep you under control there, Tommy!" (Ibid.).

61. Official interview with Wing Commander Melvin Hupfeld, RAAF, Operation Falconer commanding officer, No. 75 Squadron, September 16, 2003, provided to the author by the RAAF Air Power Development Centre, Canberra, Australia.

62. A parachute recovered by Iraqis that they claimed was that of a downed coalition airman was actually an ALARM parachute under which the missile descends slowly as it searches for its target. Conversations with senior staff officers at Headquarters Strike Command, October 28, 2004.

63. *Operation Telic: United Kingdom Military Operations in Iraq*, 7.

64. *First Reflections*, 14.

65. *Lessons of Iraq*, vol. 2, Ev 200.

66. "Storm Shadow Appears ahead of Official Entry into Service Date," *Flight International*, April 1–7, 2003, 6.

67. *First Reflections*, 23. The munition includes an initial penetrator charge followed by the main explosive charge in order to breach reinforced structures. Neil Baumgardner, "RAF Spokesman: Enhanced Paveway 'Outstanding' in Operation Iraqi Freedom," *Defense Daily*, April 2, 2003, 7–8.

68. The loss of the use of Turkish bases for conducting combat operations into Iraq created a major ripple effect as the RAF's Tornado GR4 Storm Shadow shooters were forced to strike critical hard targets in northern Iraq that had originally been scheduled to be attacked by F-15Es configured with GBU-28 5,000-pound bunker busters. The GR4 was able to range farther north into Iraq than was the F-15E from the latter's southern base at Al Jaber, Kuwait. Conversations with Colonel Erlenbusch, Major Roberson, and other CENTAF staff, January 29, 2007.

69. Flight Lieutenant Andy Wright, RAF, "GR4 Reconnaissance: Operation Telic," *RAF 2004*, Ministry of Defence, Directorate of Corporate Communication (RAF), Ministry of Defence, London, 2004, 24–25. Just before the start of combat operations the RAF modified some of its Tornado F3 counterair fighters to carry ALARM missiles for use in defense suppression but determined that the modification was not sufficiently robust to warrant introducing it into combat. Air Chief Marshal Sir John Day, RAF, "Air Power and Combat Operations—the Recent War in Iraq," *RUSI Journal*, June 2003, 35.

70. Comments by Lieutenant Colonel Cline, January 11, 2008.

71. "RAF Contribution to Operation Iraqi Freedom."

72. Flight Lieutenant Roz Rushmere, RAF, "E-3D Sentry: Operation Telic," *RAF 2004*, Ministry of Defence, Directorate of Corporate Communication (RAF), London, 2004, 20–22.

73. Squadron Leader Hugh Davis, "VC-10 Tanker: Operation Telic," *RAF 2004*, Ministry of Defence, Directorate of Corporate Communication (RAF), London, 2004, 44, 49.

74. Conversation with then Wing Commander Stuart Atha, RAF, Ministry of Defence, Whitehall, London, October 26, 2004.

75. *Operation Telic—United Kingdom Military Operations in Iraq*, 8.

76. *Lessons of Iraq*, vol. 2, Ev 47.

77. Gardner, "Operation Iraqi Freedom: Coalition Operations," 98.

78. Ibid., 47. This niche expertise in tactical reconnaissance was valuable because the U.S. Air Force had withdrawn its dedicated RF-4C tactical reconnaissance aircraft from service after the conclusion of Operation Desert Storm in 1991. The use of a reconnaissance pod on the Harrier GR7 and the RAPTOR system on the Tornado GR4A represented the culmination of a process for upgrading the RAF's tactical reconnaissance capability that began in 1991 with the acquisition of six early-generation improved low-level reconnaissance pods to supplement the original pods carried by the RAF's single dedicated Jaguar reconnaissance unit, 41 Squadron, based at RAF Coltishall. Gething, Hewish, and Lok, "New Pods Aid Air Reconnaissance," 52.

79. Gardner, "Operation Iraqi Freedom: Coalition Operations," 92.

80. *Lessons of Iraq*, vol. 1, 62.

81. Conversation with Air Marshal Torpy, October 26, 2004.

82. Holmes, "RAAF Hornets at War," 39. Nevertheless, as the commanding officer of 75 Squadron later recounted, the RAAF's deployed Hornet pilots did get some useful in-theater acclimation short of participating in Southern Focus operations before the campaign formally kicked off: "We did some missions where we flew up the North Arabian Gulf along the administrative route that would take us into the Iraqi theater. We flew up over Kuwait as well and did some training over there. While they were massing the army forces in Kuwait, we used that for our own training benefit to look at what a tank would look like on the ground, how we could see it on the radar or our other sensors, and so we experienced the communications process, the operation and coordination with our command and control agencies. We did all that and practiced that prior to actually deploying across the line, so we became quite familiar with what was there. We just hadn't experienced going across the border into a combat area" (official interview with Wing Commander Hupfeld, September 16, 2003).

83. Comments on an earlier draft by Air Vice-Marshal Geoff Brown, RAAF, deputy chief of air force, RAAF, July 2, 2009.

84. Holmes, "RAAF Hornets at War," 40.

85. Official interview with Wing Commander Hupfeld, September 16, 2003.

86. In his later recollection of this precedent-setting event for the Australian defense establishment, the RAAF's chief targeting adviser to CENTCOM characterized the final decision-making process: "The target was an Iraqi leadership target. . . . It just so happened that at the particular time that the target was detected and went through the approval chain, our aircraft were the closest ones to it. So after a quick national validation, I remember standing next to Geoff Brown with the lawyer in the CAOC, and I can't remember the exact words, but it was really: 'Are you happy, are you happy, are you happy' sort of thing, and we sort of said: 'Yep, it all appears good to us, your decision now, Boss.' So he said, 'Do it'" (official interview with Wing Commander Keir, February 19, 2007, provided to the author by the RAAF Air Power Development Centre, Canberra, Australia).

87. Air Marshal A. G. Houston, RAAF, "Message from Chief of Air Force: Operation Falconer," Canberra, Australia, March 24, 2003.

88. Air Commodore Geoff Brown, RAAF, "Iraq: Operations Bastille and Falconer—2003," in *Air Expeditionary Operations from World War II until Today*, ed. Commander Keith Brent, RAAF (Canberra: Proceedings of the 2008 RAAF History Conference, April 1, 2008).

89. Ibid.

90. *The War in Iraq: ADF Operations in the Middle East in 2003*, 26–28.

91. Brown, "Iraq: Operations Bastille and Falconer—2003."

92. *The War in Iraq: ADF Operations in the Middle East in 2003*, 29.

93. "Op Bastille/Falconer Timeline."

94. Air Marshal A. G. Houston, RAAF, "Message from Chief of Air Force: Operation Falconer," Canberra, Australia, April 4, 2003.

95. "Operation Falconer Honors List," Canberra, Department of Defence, November 28, 2003.

96. Brown, "Iraq: Operations Bastille and Falconer—2003."

97. The RAAF also is acquiring the AGM-158 JASSM and twenty-four F/A-18F Super Hornets to replace its aging F-111Cs and has taken on four C-17s and will acquire five KC-30B tankers and six Wedgetail AWACS aircraft. The RAAF's capability in the second decade of the twenty-first century will be significantly greater than that of the 2003 force. Comments by Group Captain Keir, July 2, 2009.

98. Ibid.

99. Holmes, "RAAF Hornets at War," 39.

100. Ibid., 42.

101. *First Reflections*, 19.
102. *Lessons of Iraq*, vol. 2, Ev 43.
103. *Lessons of Iraq*, vol. 1, 32.
104. Group Captain Chris Finn, RAF, "Air Aspects of Operation Iraqi Freedom," *Royal Air Force Air Power Review*, winter 2003, 19.
105. On this point, Air Chief Marshal Burridge stressed the criticality of joint air-ground training being conducted "end to end" in such a manner that it "exercises the entire kill chain" (conversation with Air Chief Marshal Burridge, October 27, 2004).
106. Conversation with General Moseley, August 2, 2006.
107. Conversations with Colonel Erlenbusch, Major Roberson, and other CENTAF staff, January 29, 2007.
108. Conversation with Air Chief Marshal Sir Glenn Torpy, RAF, chief of the air staff, London, UK, May 19, 2009.

Chapter 4. Key Accomplishments

1. During the third week of the major combat phase, General Moseley asked rhetorically on this point: "Did we get 30 days of [prior air] preparation like in the first desert war? No. But I don't think we needed 30 days of preparation. . . . While we didn't have 30 days of preparation, we've certainly had more preparation pre-hostilities than perhaps some people realize" ("Coalition Forces Air Component Command Briefing").
2. These statistics were drawn from Moseley, *Operation Iraqi Freedom—by the Numbers*; Maj. Gen. Daniel J. Darnell, USAF, "Operation Iraqi Freedom," undated briefing charts; and Nichols, "Operation Iraqi Freedom: CFACC/ CAOC/NALE," undated briefing charts.
3. An experienced A-10 pilot and combat commander offered the insightful observation that "in most cases, the A-10 gun is considered a precision munition. Given that an average burst in combat is around 50 rounds and that our A-10s shot 311,597 rounds in all, I would suggest that the Air Force actually did in the neighborhood of another 6,230 precision attacks (311,597 total rounds divided by 50 per burst), or, perhaps more correctly, at least 5,000-plus, a number that is not insignificant, since only two other precision munitions, the GBU-12 LGB and GBU-31 JDAM, exceeded that number" (comments by Colonel Neuenswander, March 6, 2007).
4. Knights, *Cradle of Conflict*, 327. A *Los Angeles Times* survey of records from 27 hospitals in Baghdad and outlying areas indicated that at least 1,700 Iraqi civilians were killed and more than 8,000 were injured in the Baghdad area alone during the campaign and in the initial weeks thereafter. The great-

est obstacle impeding the establishment of a more accurate count was the problem of distinguishing between Iraqi soldiers and civilians. Many soldiers continued to man their positions as the campaign unfolded, but dressed in civilian clothing and without ID tags. Laura King, "Baghdad's Death Toll Assessed," *Los Angeles Times*, May 18, 2003.

5. Knights, *Cradle of Conflict*, 14–15.

6. Willis, "Operation Iraqi Freedom," 19.

7. Ibid., 11.

8. Ibid., 40.

9. Another F-16 pilot added: "When you're dropping JDAM, we call it 'O-6 bombing,' because even the colonels can hit the target" (Davies and Dildy, *F-16 Fighting Falcon Units of Operation Iraqi Freedom*, 44, 88).

10. Hampton Stephens, "Wind-Corrected Anti-armor Weapon Used for First Time in Iraq," *Inside the Air Force*, April 4, 2003, 9.

11. Stephen Trimble, "Air Force's AMC Tallies Massive Airlift Effort for OIF," *Aerospace Daily*, May 29, 2003.

12. See Martin Streetly, "Airborne Surveillance Assets Hit the Spot in Iraq," *Jane's Intelligence Review*, July 2003, 34–37.

13. Trimble, "Air Force's AMC Tallies Massive Airlift Effort for OIF."

14. Cynthia Di Pasquale, "Russian Planes Expand U.S. Airlift Capability Strained during OIF, OEF," *Inside the Air Force*, April 2, 2004, 9.

15. Trimble, "Air Force's AMC Tallies Massive Airlift Effort for OIF."

16. *Lessons of Iraq*, vol. 2, Ev 50.

17. Ibid., Ev 59. An RAF logistics officer at Strike Command headquarters similarly proposed that slack in logistical support is essential not merely as insurance but also as a potential force multiplier by virtue of the overinsurance that it provides. He added, in a thoughtful cautionary note, that "just in time" logistics can all too often end up meaning "just too late."

18. Rowan Scarborough, "Myers Says 'Annihilation' of Iraqi Army Wasn't Goal," *Washington Times*, June 30, 2003.

19. Thom Shanker, "Assessment of Iraq War Will Emphasize Joint Operations," *Washington Post*, May 1, 2003.

20. Ibid. JFCOM's commander, Adm. Edmund Giambastiani, added in this regard that General Franks "doesn't care where he gets capability to go kill a target, to accomplish a mission, or take an objective. So whether we do it with air power, artillery, naval gunfire, naval aircraft—it doesn't make a difference. He just cares about taking care of a target."

21. Capt. David A. Rogers, USN, "From the President: The Health of Your Tailhook Association," *The Hook*, fall 2003, 4. In January and February 2003,

with CENTCOM's complete cooperation and support, JFCOM established a joint "lessons-learned" team of subject matter experts to observe, assess, and document joint combat operations while they were still under way. JFCOM subsequently deployed more than thirty of its team members to CENTCOM's area of responsibility just before the campaign's start. Admiral Giambastiani later remarked, "We were there before operations started and followed the entire campaign in real time. We had complete access to all commanders and their staffs for all operations at all levels. General Franks set the tone and welcomed this team with open arms." In a synopsis of the team's initial findings seven months later, Giambastiani offered as the effort's ultimate key judgment that "our traditional military planning and perhaps our entire approach to warfare have shifted . . . away from employing service-centric forces that must be deconflicted on the battlefield to achieve victories of attrition to a well trained, integrated joint force that can enter the battlespace quickly and conduct decisive operations with both operational and strategic effects" (statement by Adm. Edmund P. Giambastiani Jr., commander, U.S. Joint Forces Command, before the House Armed Services Committee, U.S. House of Representatives, Washington, D.C., October 2, 2003).

22. Moseley, "Operation Iraqi Freedom: Initial CFACC Roll-up."

23. Feiler, "Iraqi Campaign Lessons Show Shift to 'Overmatching Power' Doctrine," 1, 12–13.

24. For a thorough account of that experience, see Lambeth, *Air Power against Terror*, 163–231.

25. Elaine M. Grossman, "General: War-Tested Air-Land Coordination Cell Has Staying Power," *Inside the Air Force*, March 12, 2004, 13–14.

26. Elizabeth Rees, "Standup of 484th AEW Proved Vital to Army, Air Force Ops Integration," *Inside the Air Force*, September 5, 2003, 3.

27. The primary ASOC supporting V Corps remained collocated at the latter's principal command post in Kuwait. A tactical ASOC advanced with the V Corps tactical command post and allowed for a long-range communications relay from the main ASOC. The E-2, E-3, and E-8 aerial and ground surveillance aircraft also fulfilled as-needed communications relay functions, but there was no command and control aircraft that was dedicated exclusively to support ASOC employment.

28. Maj. Alexander L. Koven, USAF, "Improvements in Joint Forces: How Missteps during Operation Anaconda Readied USCENTCOM for Operation Iraqi Freedom," research report, Air University, Air Command and Staff College, Maxwell AFB, Ala., April 2005, 20–21, emphasis added. The author

was a command and control duty officer in the CAOC's time-sensitive targeting cell during the major combat phase of Iraqi Freedom.

29. Earlier in January 2003, during CENTCOM's final precampaign workups, V Corps planners had met with their CENTAF counterparts at Shaw AFB to discuss the ASOC's concept of operations for urban CAS. Out of that exchange emerged the foundation for the ultimate arrangements for conducting that mission that were finalized in March 2003. Conversations with Colonel Erlenbusch, Major Roberson, and other CENTAF staff, January 29, 2007.

30. In this important distinction, "operational control" entails "organizing and employing forces, sustaining them, and assigning [them] general tasks," whereas "tactical control" is "the specific direction and control of forces, especially in combat" (Reynolds, *Basrah, Baghdad, and Beyond*, 10).

31. The first priority of Marine Corps aviation is to support Marines on the ground. Accordingly, the Marines look at their combat air assets first and foremost as integral components of their combined arms team, or MAGTF.

32. Stout, *Hammer from Above*, 16–17.

33. Conversations with Colonel Erlenbusch, Major Roberson, and other CENTAF staff, January 29, 2007.

34. Ibid.

35. Although the V Corps shaping effort was called "Corps CAS" and was conducted inside the FSCL using Type III CAS procedures, that effort really represented air interdiction, which does not require the terminal attack control that the V Corps commander nonetheless demanded for the battlespace that he controlled (see Chapter 5).

36. Stout, *Hammer from Above*, xiv–xv.

37. Ibid., 14.

38. "Air Support Operations Center (ASOC) Employment," briefing presented at the Air Force Doctrine Summit IV sponsored by the Air Force Doctrine Center, Maxwell AFB, Ala., November 17, 2003.

39. Fontenot, Degen, and Tohn, *On Point*, 428.

40. Ibid.

41. *Third Infantry Division (Mechanized) After Action Report: Operation Iraqi Freedom* (Fort Stewart, Ga.: U.S. Army 3rd Infantry Division, 2003), 29. The concurrent after-action assessment of 3rd ID's Division Artillery called the conduct of CAS both a "winner" in Iraqi Freedom and a welcome testament that the Air Force had finally become "rededicated to CAS." See *Fires in the Close Fight: OIF Lessons Learned* (Fort Stewart, Ga.: 3rd Infantry Division DIVARTY [Division Artillery], November 2003).

42. Ibid., 137.

43. Ibid., 138.

44. Holmes, *U.S. Navy Hornet Units of Operation Iraqi Freedom*, pt. 2, 68–69.

45. Expanding on this, the commanding officer of VFA-15, Cdr. Andy Lewis, recalled that "communication with the FAC was usually via our KY-58 secure radio, which is akin to talking with your head in a trash can" (ibid., 70).

46. "Coalition Forces Air Component Command Briefing."

47. Ibid.

48. Koven, "Improvements in Joint Fires," 25.

49. Krepinevich, *Operation Iraqi Freedom: A First-Blush Assessment*, 20–21.

50. Charles E. Kirkpatrick, *Joint Fires as They Were Meant to Be: V Corps and the 4th Air Support Operations Group during Operation Iraqi Freedom*, Land Warfare Papers no. 48 (Arlington, Va.: Association of the U.S. Army, Institute of Land Warfare, October 2004), 1.

51. *Third Infantry Division (Mechanized) After Action Report*, 86, 137.

52. John Liang, "JFCOM Commander Outlines 'Good' and 'Ugly' in Iraq Lessons Learned," *Inside the Pentagon*, March 25, 2004, 15.

53. Knights, *Cradle of Conflict*, 285. By one report, PowerPoint briefings consumed as much as 80 percent of the bandwidth used during the major combat phase of Iraqi Freedom.

54. The assessment added that the resultant common operating picture "worked only within the CFLCC zone. Other forces operating on the ground in other components' areas of operations were not included in the CFLCC picture and had to devise their own workarounds" (*Joint Lessons Learned*, 55).

55. Ripley, "Closing the Gap," 26.

56. Tony Capaccio, "U.S. Commanders Wore General Dynamics Transmitters," Bloomberg.com, April 30, 2003. After the campaign ended, the Air Force considered ways to improve the Blue Force Tracker system to ensure that pilots could talk ground forces onto targets and to enable life-or-death decisions involving, for example, the presence of friendly forces. "That could be deadly if we are being spoofed or if the display is not proper," General Leaf noted. "Or it could be a reverse decision . . . to employ weapons based on the absence of Blue Force Tracking" (Elaine M. Grossman, "Air Force May Expand Significantly on Army Battlefield Tracking System," *Inside the Pentagon*, November 6, 2003, 3).

57. Franks with McConnell, *American Soldier*, 447.

58. For a concise synopsis of the main technical and performance features of these aircraft, see Carlo Kopp, "Intelligence, Surveillance and Reconnaissance in Operation Iraqi Freedom," *Defence Today* magazine, June 2004, 1–6.

59. "Global Hawk Feats in Iraq Could Lead to ISR Fleet Lessons," *Inside the Pentagon*, May 29, 2003, 8.

60. Loren B. Thompson, "ISR Lessons of Iraq," briefing prepared for the *Defense News* ISR Integration Conference, Washington, D.C., November 18, 2003.

61. Ibid.

62. The only reason why the Air Force's F-22 Raptor fifth-generation air dominance fighter, the most data-linked combat aircraft in the world by far, was not used in the offensive and defensive counterair roles and for precision ground attack missions in which stealth would have been required for survival in Iraq's most challenging threat envelopes was that the aircraft was not yet ready for combat employment when the campaign began. It only achieved initial operational capability two years later with the 1st Fighter Wing at Langley AFB, Virginia.

63. Davies, *F-15C/E Eagle Units of Operation Iraqi Freedom*, 21.

64. They also pointed up some clear limitations on the use of electro-optical and infrared targeting pods for positive target identification. Most pods of that sort used during Iraqi Freedom required that their aircraft operate at altitudes between 5,000 and 10,000 feet in order to provide sufficient resolution to enable such identification. That operating limitation highlighted a major unsatisfied need for combat aircraft to be able to identify positively such tactical-sized targets as tanks and other armored vehicles while maintaining sufficient standoff to survive in a medium and high surface-to-air threat environment.

65. Lorenzo Cortes, "Air Force Offered Improved Networking Capabilities during OIF," *Defense Daily*, June 4, 2003, 5.

66. Ibid., 46.

67. Capt. David C. Hardesty, USN, "Fix Net Centric for the Operators," *Proceedings*, September 2003, 69.

68. Sandra I. Irwin, "Iraqi Freedom Tests Naval Aviation's Flexibility," *The Hook*, summer 2003, 65.

69. Knights, *Cradle of Conflict*, 286–287.

70. Gordon and Trainor, *Cobra II*, 352.

71. John Gordon IV and Bruce Pirnie, "'Everybody Wanted Tanks': Heavy Forces in Operation Iraqi Freedom," *Joint Force Quarterly*, 4th quarter, 2005, 86, 89.

72. In particular, as an Air Force space officer who served on the ACCE staff with Major General Leaf recalled four years later, "there was a big problem getting enough satellite communications so that all the mission reports could get through in a timely fashion. This created major difficulties for making timely assessments of targets to attack for the next [ATO] cycle,

especially as the ground forces approached to contact. We were able to work additional communications, but the problem was never completely resolved before we departed" (comments on an earlier draft by Lt. Col. Chris Crawford, USAF, National Security Fellows Program, Kennedy School of Government, Harvard University, Cambridge, Mass., March 4, 2007).

73. John T. Bennett, "Smaller Bombs among Needs Revealed In Iraq, Navy Officers Say," *Inside the Pentagon*, August 7, 2003, 4.

74. Joris Janssen Lok, "Communication Weaknesses Endanger Allied Integration in U.S.-Led Air Campaigns," *Jane's International Defence Review*, March 2004, 4.

75. For a thorough assessment of this important development in U.S. joint force interoperability, see Lambeth, *Combat Pair*.

76. For a full discussion of the earlier complications in the relationship between CENTCOM and its air component principals in the CAOC that had necessitated General Moseley's intervention, see Lambeth, *Air Power against Terror*, 295–311.

77. There were, however, numerous instances within a given ATO cycle in which targets on the joint target list (JTL) that had been approved by General Moseley for inclusion on the JIPTL were subsequently moved by CENTCOM to either the restricted target list (RTL) or the no-strike target list (NSTL). The head of the CAOC's combat plans division later recalled in this regard, "We had a problem with CENTCOM moving targets onto and off of the JTL to the RTL and the NSTL inside the ATO cycle. That required a manual scrub of the ATO to ensure that we were not hitting targets on restricted and no-strike lists. The MAAP cycle, accordingly, had to run for twenty-four hours rather than the normal twelve to fourteen hours due to the rapid pace of land component movement and the need to continually adjust each ATO right up to its moment of execution" (comments on an earlier draft by Col. Douglas Erlenbusch, USAF, CENTAF director of operations, February 4, 2007). Throughout the three weeks of major combat, CENTCOM updated the JTL, RTL, and NSTL every twelve hours. That meant that there were three changes to those three lists between the approval of the JIPTL and the execution of each ATO. On several occasions aircraft in the midst of conducting scheduled attacks had those attacks aborted at the last minute because their target had been moved from the JTL to the RTL. In a few instances targets were struck after they had been moved to the RTL. As CAOC planners later recounted, neither the MAAP toolkit nor TBMCS had the ability to take an updated RTL and NSTL and reconcile them against an already approved JIPTL. Fortunately, none of

these residual limitations on the CAOC's freedom of action turned out to have been serious complicating factors affecting the conduct of the air war to the latter's detriment.

78. Kometer, *Command in Air War*, 140, 169.

79. Amy Butler, "Moseley: Time-Sensitive Targeting Improved from Afghanistan to Iraq," *Inside the Air Force*, June 20, 2003, 1.

80. A "time-sensitive target" is any target identified within an ATO cycle that is deemed to be of such importance to the combined force commander that it must be struck as soon as possible with any available asset, regardless of that asset's prior tasking. During Operation Iraqi Freedom, CENTCOM determined which target sets would be designated time-sensitive. A "dynamic target" is any target identified within an ATO cycle that is deemed of sufficient importance to all components that it should be struck within the ATO with any assets available. During Iraqi Freedom, those targets were determined by the chief of the guidance, apportionment, and targeting (GAT) cell in the CAOC.

81. Butler, "Moseley: Time-Sensitive Targeting Improved from Afghanistan to Iraq," 10. The highly disciplined rules of engagement of Southern Watch that had generated the "Mother may I?" attitude among allied strike pilots persisted well into the first week of the Iraqi Freedom campaign. Such initial hesitancy did *not* inhibit those Air Force A-10 pilots who were working in support of I MEF ground operations, because they had never played a part in Southern Watch. Conversation with Major General Darnell, August 2, 2006.

82. Comments by Lieutenant Colonel Hathaway, February 19, 2007.

83. Conversations with Colonel Erlenbusch, Major Roberson, and other CEN-TAF staff, January 29, 2007.

84. Maj. Gen. Daniel J. Darnell, e-mail communication to the author, January 11, 2006.

85. Keith J. Costa, "Draft JFCOM 'Lessons Learned' Study Examines Early Iraq War Moves," *Inside the Pentagon*, March 18, 2004, 1, 12–13.

86. Conversation with Gen. Charles F. Wald, USAF (Ret.), Washington, D.C., August 1, 2006.

87. *Lessons of Iraq*, vol. 2, Ev 52.

88. The entire "process" narrative that follows below was informed by conversations with Colonel Erlenbusch, Major Roberson, and other CENTAF staff, January 29, 2007.

89. Lt. Col. David C. Hathaway, USAF, "Operational Assessment during Operation Iraqi Freedom—Assessment or Assumption?" research report, Air War College, Maxwell AFB, Ala., May 25, 2005, 5–6.

90. The mechanism that had been established within the land component for providing CAS to Army ground forces was the Air Force's TACS, which in turn was closely aligned with the counterpart Army air-ground system (AGS). Within that arrangement, the air component's ground command and control elements were the ASOC, collocated with V Corps at its rear headquarters, and the ASOC's subordinate tactical air control party (TACP) staffed by air liaison officers (ALOs) and joint terminal attack controllers (JTACs) assigned directly to and in direct support of forward fighting elements at the division level and below. The primary mission of TACPs from corps level down to brigade level was to advise their supported ground commanders on the capabilities and limitations of air power and to help those commanders in planning, requesting, and coordinating CAS. The TACP also provided the principal means for the terminal control of CAS in support of friendly ground troops. The CAOC served as the senior element of the TACS and thus as the direct overseer of both the ASOC and the latter's TACPs. The TACPs processed and executed both preplanned and immediate CAS requests, although the majority of those requests were for immediate CAS. Only about 6 percent of those immediate air support requests entailed direct troops-in-contact situations, unless one considers such broader categories as "troops taking mortar or artillery fire." I am grateful to my RAND colleague Jody Jacobs for helping me to better understand this process and its complex inner workings.

91. Conversations with Colonel Erlenbusch, Major Roberson, and other CENTAF staff, January 29, 2007.

92. Ibid.

93. E-mail message to the author from Col. Douglas Erlenbusch, USAF, former CENTAF director of operations, then serving as commander of Air Force ROTC Detachment 40, Loyola Marymount University, Los Angeles, Calif., April 21, 2009. With respect to concerns over the timeliness of the AOD, Colonel Erlenbusch added, "The strategy division also tried to flex with the speed of operations by publishing multiple AODs for a single ATO (for example, 'Change 1, Change 2,' and so on). This was a bit cumbersome for the planners to get their hands around and to merge into the ATO cycle, but it at least provided some up-to-date guidance. Target sets that were proposed by CENTCOM and then inserted into the ATO outside the cycle also made it necessary for us to have qualified MAAP staff available around the clock."

94. Mark Hewish, "Out of CAOCs Comes Order," *Jane's International Defence Review*, May 2003, 23–24.

95. Conversations with Colonel Erlenbusch, Major Roberson, and other CEN-TAF staff, January 29, 2007.

96. Kerry Gildea, "Air Force Says TBMCS Played Critical Role in Air War Execution," *Defense Daily*, May 6, 2003, 1–2.

97. Comments by Colonel Erlenbusch, February 4, 2007.

98. The combat air forces and military airlift forces use different systems to plan and conduct their respective missions. The combat air forces use TBMCS, and the airlift community uses C2IPS (for command and control information processing system). An interface between C2IPS and TBMCS was developed to integrate airlift mission data in the daily ATO, but it was cumbersome and unreliable. Conversations with Colonel Erlenbusch, Major Roberson, and other CENTAF staff, January 29, 2007.

99. Ibid.

100. Ibid.

101. As yet another example of the assorted minor frictions the CAOC staff encountered from time to time, the air component's target development team was located in a separate and extra-secure ISR division building, whereas the key combat plans cells were located in the CAOC proper. This physical separation of the two groups often complicated communications and the synchronization of target information. Numerous occasions arose when ISR division target development team members were processing target candidates to be nominated for the ATO, only to learn later that combat plans staffers had already nominated those targets for previous ATOs, making for a needless duplication of effort. Ibid.

102. Ibid.

103. Ibid.

104. Ibid.

105. *Lessons for the Future*, 27.

106. Conversation with Air Chief Marshal Burridge, October 27, 2004.

107. Amy Butler, "Iraq War Underscores Need for Improved and Standardized AOCs," *Inside the Air Force*, May 16, 2003, 3.

108. Carpenter, "Rapid, Deliberate, Disciplined, Proportional, and Precise," 20–21.

109. Ibid.

110. Murphy and Miller, "The Team That Picks the Targets."

111. Nichols, "Operation Iraqi Freedom: CFACC/CAOC/NALE."

112. Paul Dolson, "Expeditionary Airborne Battlefield Command and Control," *Joint Force Quarterly*, 4th quarter, 2005, 68–75.

113. Crews of AWACS and JSTARS aircraft operating in an ABCCC capacity were sometimes so overtasked that they could not receive and forward

higher-priority assignments to available strike aircraft in the target's vicinity. In at least two instances, B-1B missions took on 140,000 pounds of fuel from tankers and still ran out of fuel while awaiting CAOC tasking from airborne AWACS or JSTARS aircraft whose crews were preoccupied with ABCCC tasking. Conversations with Colonel Erlenbusch, Major Roberson, and other CENTAF staff, January 29, 2007.

114. Quoted in Maj. Joseph G. Matthews, USA, "The E-8 Joint Surveillance Target Attack Radar System Support to Counterinsurgency Operations," research report, Air University, Air Command and Staff College, Maxwell AFB, Ala., April 11, 2006, vii.

115. Dolson, "Expeditionary Airborne Battlefield Command and Control."

116. Matthews, "The E-8 Joint Surveillance Target Attack Radar System Support to Counterinsurgency Operations," 22.

117. Ripley, "Closing the Gap," 27. The Marine Corps employed its palletized direct air support center (DASC) in a KC-130 tanker aircraft to overcome such problems in I MEF's sector.

118. Butler, "Iraq War Underscores Need for Improved and Standardized AOCs," 3.

119. Conversations with Colonel Erlenbusch, Major Roberson, and other CENTAF staff, January 29, 2007.

120. Comments by Lieutenant Colonel Hathaway, February 19, 2007.

121. Ibid.

122. Comments by Colonel Neuenswander, March 6, 2007. The former commander of the 4th Fighter Wing, one of the two Air Force F-15E Strike Eagle wings that took part in the air war, aptly noted four years later: "One of the great weaknesses of all the post–Iraqi Freedom literature [on the air contribution] is that it generally does not capture the 'color' of combat operations at the wing level. It only focuses on the CAOC and higher. Although the CAOC in this instance indeed represented the supreme evolution to date of air and space power command and control, there was still a lot going on in the trenches" (comments by Major General Rosborg, March 16, 2007).

123. Thompson, "ISR Lessons of Iraq."

124. Jeremy Feiler, "CSIS Report: U.S. Victory in Iraq Showed 'Flexibility' of U.S. Planning," *Inside the Pentagon*, May 1, 2003, 19.

125. Lorenzo Cortes, "Coalition Forces Have Fired 15,000 Guided Munitions during Iraqi Freedom," *Defense Daily*, April 11, 2003, 7. See also Carpenter, "Rapid, Deliberate, Disciplined, Proportional, and Precise," 22. This assured navigation accuracy was crucial for the effective delivery of more than 5,600 satellite-aided JDAMs that relied on GPS signals for achieving

pinpoint accuracy. As the campaign unfolded, space operators in the CAOC provided daily assessments of the GPS constellation's predicted geometry and accuracy. During the three-day *shamal*, coalition aircraft destroyed entire divisions of the Iraqi Republican Guard using GPS-aided munitions against targeted positions that had been detected and geolocated by space-based synthetic aperture radar.

126. Gen. Lance W. Lord, USAF, commander, Air Force Space Command, address to the 2005 Air Force Defense Strategy and Transformation Seminar Series sponsored by DFI International, Washington, D.C., March 9, 2005.

127. Kerry Gildea, "Next-Generation Imaging Satellite Team Formed with News of Bush Policy Shift," *Defense Daily*, May 14, 2003, 7.

128. James Hackett, "Tracking Targets from Space," *Washington Times*, July 8, 2003.

129. Carpenter, "Rapid, Deliberate, Disciplined, Proportional, and Precise," 22.

130. Conversations with Colonel Erlenbusch, Major Roberson, and other CEN-TAF staff, January 29, 2007.

131. Elizabeth Rees, "USAF Moves Space Forces Director Back into Iraq Air Ops Center," *Inside the Air Force*, June 4, 2004, 4.

132. One notable downside of space support to combat operations had to do with repeated shortfalls in satellite communications capacity. "With demand already high due to operations in Afghanistan, CENTCOM struggled to find enough UHF [ultra-high frequency] tactical satellite channels and was just able to address the critical operational needs for [the campaign]. To complicate matters [was] the fact that many [satellite communications] systems did not support mobile communications at the data rates needed" (*Joint Lessons Learned*, 31).

133. William B. Scott and Craig Covault, "High Ground over Iraq," *Aviation Week and Space Technology*, June 9, 2003, 44, as cited in Kometer, *Command in Air War*, 170.

134. Jeremy Feiler, "Pentagon Officials Examine UAV 'Lessons Learned' in Iraq," *Inside the Pentagon*, December 11, 2003, 15.

135. Willis, "Operation Iraqi Freedom," 22.

136. Cook, "Shock and Awe?" 21.

137. Eric Schmitt, "In the Skies over Iraq, Silent Observers Become Futuristic Weapons," *New York Times*, April 18, 2003. Operating out of a base in the United Arab Emirates, the RQ-4 flew combat support missions every day of the war, in the process imaging some two hundred to three hundred sites of interest to CENTCOM during sorties that lasted up to twenty-six hours.

138. "Unmanned Systems: UAV Shows Effectiveness as a Targeting Platform," *Flight International*, April 22–28, 2003, 9.

139. The ground stations required to support such UAV operations include nearly thirty interconnected trailers that require seventeen C-5 sorties to be deployed forward. For that reason, it makes more sense to leave those facilities at their home bases in the United States whenever possible. Technical panel presentation, 2003 Tailhook Association annual symposium, Reno, Nev., September 20, 2003; Jeremy Feiler, "Officials: UAV Lessons among Most Vital Gleaned in Iraq War," *Inside the Pentagon*, July 17, 2003, 1, 10.

140. Rowan Scarborough, "Hovering Spy Plane Helps Rout Iraqis," *Washington Times*, April 3, 2003.

141. Richard J. Newman, "The Joystick War," *U.S. News and World Report*, May 19, 2003.

142. Lorenzo Cortes, "Operation Iraqi Freedom Required Unique Wartime Use of E-8C Joint STARS," *Defense Daily*, June 11, 2003, 5.

143. Amy Butler, "JSTARS Faced 'Learning Curve' for CAOC Officials Unfamiliar with System," *Inside the Air Force*, May 30, 2003, 9.

144. Cortes, "Operation Iraqi Freedom Required Unique Wartime Use of E-8C Joint STARS," 5.

145. William M. Arkin, "Fliers Rose to Occasion: In Iraq, a Pause Refreshed Ground Troops and Let Planes Inflict Major Damage," *Los Angeles Times*, June 1, 2003.

146. Richard J. Dunn III, Price T. Bingham, and Charles A. Fowler, *Ground Moving Target Indicator Radar and the Transformation of U.S. Warfighting* (Arlington, Va.: Northrop Grumman Analysis Center, February 2004), 25.

147. Butler, "JSTARS Faced 'Learning Curve' for CAOC Officials Unfamiliar with System," 8.

148. "Coalition Forces Air Component Command Briefing."

149. Adam J. Hebert, "Building Battlespace Awareness," *Air Force Magazine*, October 2003, 66–67.

150. U.S. commanders experienced difficulty keeping track of Iraqi force positions once the Iraqis began dispersing to avoid allied air strikes. Costa, "Draft JFCOM 'Lessons Learned' Study Examines Early Iraq War Moves," 1, 12–13.

151. Dunn, Bingham, and Fowler, *Ground Moving Target Indicator Radar and the Transformation of U.S. Warfighting*, 16–17.

152. Ibid., 19.

153. Andrew Koch, "Information War Played Major Role in Iraq," *Jane's Defence Weekly*, July 23, 2003, 5.

154. CENTCOM's SOF teams also used money freely as a part of the psychological warfare campaign. As one senior planner put it: "How much does a cruise missile cost? Between one and two and a half million dollars. Well, a

bribe ... achieves the aim, but it's bloodless and there's zero collateral damage" (Vago Muradian, "Payoffs Aided U.S. War Plan," *Defense News*, May 19, 2003, 1).

155. Koch, "Information War Played Major Role in Iraq," 5.

156. Elaine Grossman, "Coalition Drops 'Capitulation Leaflets' over Iraqi Troops," *Inside the Pentagon*, March 20, 2003, 16.

157. Elaine Grossman, "Land, Air Commands Struggled on Iraq Leaflet Timing, Coordination," *Inside the Pentagon*, June 26, 2003, 4–6. A member of General Leaf's staff recalled that "when we arrived, there was no organized method within the land component organization to nominate types of leaflets against specific targets. Two things happened before the war to fix that. First, there was a memorandum of agreement that established the types of information that would be provided to the CAOC. We even developed a form that was used. . . . Second, the information operations working group under the land component commander began to play a bigger role in shaping the various messages, timing, targeted groups, and so on. I watched this overall process closely for General Leaf, and most of the major problems were fixed by the time the war started" (comments by Lieutenant Colonel Crawford, March 4, 2007).

158. Elaine Grossman, "Evolving Threats May Offer Air Force 'Unlearned Lessons' in Iraq," *Inside the Pentagon*, July 17, 2003, 17.

159. Andrew Koch, "Information Warfare Tools Rolled Out in Iraq," *Jane's Defence Weekly*, August 6, 2003, 7.

160. Carpenter, "Rapid, Deliberate, Disciplined, Proportional, and Precise," 24.

161. Koch, "Information War Played Major Role in Iraq," 5.

162. Holmes, *U.S. Navy Hornet Units of Operation Iraqi Freedom*, pt. 2, 24.

163. Hunter Keeter, "Cartwright: Threat Location, Prediction Capability Should Be Priorities," *Defense Daily*, April 30, 2003, 4.

164. Willis, "Operation Iraqi Freedom," 19.

165. Lorenzo Cortes, "Air Force Integrated Litening Pods for Block 40 and Block 50 F-16s before OIF," *Defense Daily*, June 20, 2003, 5. The more capable Sniper targeting pod was not used during the campaign because qualification testing on it had not been completed.

166. "WCMD-Equipped Sensor Fuzed Weapons Dropped on Iraqi Vehicle Column," *Defense Daily*, April 3, 2003, 1; Kopp, "Iraqi Freedom—the Hammer and Anvil," 26.

167. Holmes, *U.S. Navy Hornet Units of Operation Iraqi Freedom*, pt. 2, 32.

168. Michael Sirak, "U.S. Air Force Reveals New Strike Munition," *Jane's Defence Weekly*, May 14, 2003.

169. "USAF Offers Details of Weapon Tailored for Iraq War," *Aerospace Daily*, May 5, 2003.
170. Gordon and Trainor, *Cobra II*, 432.
171. Ibid., 432–433.
172. Hinote, "More Than Bombing Saddam," vi.
173. Ibid., 116.
174. Ibid., 165.
175. Kitfield, "Attack Always," 1292–1296.
176. Krepinevich, *Operation Iraqi Freedom: A First-Blush Assessment*, 8.
177. Woods and others, *Iraqi Perspectives Project*, x. For a subsequent RAND report that exploited much of the same source material and arrived at roughly the same conclusions, see also Stephen T. Hosmer, *Why the Iraqi Resistance to the Coalition Invasion Was So Weak* (Santa Monica, Calif.: RAND Corporation, MG-544-AF, 2007).
178. Woods and others, *Iraqi Perspectives Project*, 27–28.
179. Hinote, "More Than Bombing Saddam," 12.
180. Ibid.
181. Woods and others, *Iraqi Perspectives Project*, 125.
182. Ibid., 125.
183. Ibid., 126.
184. Ibid., 147.
185. Ibid., 128.
186. Ibid., 128.
187. Biddle and others, *Toppling Saddam*, 7.
188. Ibid., 24.
189. Krepinevich, *Operation Iraqi Freedom: A First-Blush Assessment*, 10.
190. Comments by Colonel Neuenswander, March 6, 2007.
191. Kopp, "Iraqi Freedom—the Hammer and Anvil," 30. On this point, the above-noted assessment implied that the coalition's defeat of Iraq's ground forces was essentially due to "the M1 tank's ability to fire on the move, hit targets on the first shot at ranges of multiple kilometers, and penetrate both sand berms and T-72 frontal armor at the same distances," disregarding CENTAF's relentless kill-box interdiction attacks independent of ground action that accounted for the vast majority of Iraqi tanks destroyed during the campaign (Biddle and others, *Toppling Saddam*, 30). A less unabashedly parochial treatment of that capability concurred that "the combination of protection and firepower on the American M1A1 [Abrams main battle tank] played a critical role in ensuring that Iraqi forces could not brings tanks to bear at ranges that allowed them to be effective." The latter study

added, however, that "questions arise . . . about what would have happened if Iraq had large numbers of more modern antitank guided weapons like the Russian-designed Kornet" (Cordesman, "The 'Instant Lessons' of the Iraq War," 13). Notably, Hezbollah's well-disciplined militia units used such weapons against the Israel Defense Forces in southern Lebanon during the thirty-four-day war there in 2006, with significant costs to Israel's Merkava main battle tank.

192. Krepinevich, *Operation Iraqi Freedom: A First-Blush Assessment*, 14.

193. Gen. Richard Myers, USAF, Department of Defense briefing, Washington, D.C., April 7, 2003.

194. Krepinevich, *Operation Iraqi Freedom: A First-Blush Assessment*, 21.

195. Benjamin S. Lambeth, *The Transformation of American Air Power* (Ithaca, N.Y.: Cornell University Press, 2000), 320–321, emphasis in the original.

196. Jody Jacobs, David E. Johnson, Katherine Comanor, Lewis Jamison, Leland Joe, and David Vaughn, *Enhancing Fires and Maneuver through Greater Air-Ground Joint Interdependence* (Santa Monica, Calif.: RAND Corporation, MG-793-AF, 2009), 6.

197. Johnson, *Learning Large Lessons*, 115, 140.

198. Jacobs and others, *Enhancing Fires and Maneuver through Greater Air-Ground Joint Interdependence*, 6.

Chapter 5. Problems Encountered

1. James R. Schlesinger and others, *Final Report of the Independent Panel to Review DoD Detention Operations* (Washington, D.C.: Department of Defense, 2004).

2. Thomas E. Ricks, *Fiasco: The American Military Adventure in Iraq* (New York: Penguin Press, 2006), 116.

3. Powell further remarked that he had counseled the president beforehand at a private dinner in August 2002, well before the war was initiated: "My caution was that you need to understand that the difficult bit will come afterwards—the military piece will be easy. This place [Iraq] will crack like a crystal goblet, and it'll be a problem to pick up the bits" (Charles Moore, "Colin Powell: 'I'm Very Sore,'" *London Daily Telegraph*, February 26, 2005).

4. "Top Navy Aviation Officials Predict Few Major Lessons from Iraq," *Inside the Pentagon*, May 22, 2003, 10.

5. Ibid.

6. Grossman, "Evolving Threats May Offer Air Force 'Unlearned Lessons' in Iraq," 1. The twofold intent of that symposium, whose participants included many key players in the planning and execution of air and space operations during the three-week campaign, was, first, to produce an exhaustive

overview report aimed at providing a solid foundation for improving CEN-TAF's ability to plan and execute major air operations in a future joint and combined setting, and, second, to document the essential facts of the three-week air war to facilitate subsequent efforts to develop and apply tactical lessons learned; update platform-specific tactics, techniques, and procedures; and improve joint and service doctrine. Working groups at the symposium explored such specific subjects as strategy; target development; guidance, apportionment, and targeting; the master air attack plan; ATO production; command and control arrangements; SPINs development; combat operations; time-sensitive targeting; counter-Scud operations; ISR; combat assessments; the tactical air control system; space operations; information operations; KI/CAS; defensive counterair; SEAD and DEAD operations; tanker issues; and combat search and rescue. Although the final report is not available to the general public, the present book has been informed throughout by extensive inputs from numerous CENTAF personnel, from General Moseley on down, who took part in the symposium and in the many events that it addressed.

7. Elaine M. Grossman, "Giambastiani Flags Battle Damage, Friendly Fire 'Lessons Learned,'" *Inside the Pentagon*, March 11, 2004, 3.

8. Moseley, "Operation Iraqi Freedom: Initial CFACC Roll-up."

9. Another issue lies in recognizing the difference between operations that went well because allied forces were good at them and those that succeeded because the Iraqis were weak or inept; the latter should counsel caution not to be excessively complacent as we look ahead. I wish to thank my RAND colleague Karl Mueller for bringing this important point to my attention.

10. Tim Ripley, "Iraq Friendly Fire Was Worse Than Reported," *Jane's Defence Weekly*, July 16, 2003, 3.

11. The PAC-3, which, unlike the PAC-2, can reach higher and is a hit-to-kill weapon, saw its first operational use in Iraqi Freedom.

12. Bradley Graham, "Radar Probed in Patriot Incidents," *Washington Post*, May 8, 2003. In a campaign history published by General Bromberg's organization five months after the major combat phase ended, the 32nd AAMDC spoke frankly of "cluttered cyberspace" in the area of operations around Karbala where the F/A-18 was downed by one of the unit's Patriot batteries: "Patriot and field artillery FireFinder acquisition radars radiated on the area. Helicopter and fixed-wing aircraft moved throughout the area . . . employing various radio and radar systems and filling cyberspace along other portions of the electromagnetic spectrum. Overhead, JSTARS and AWACS aircraft added to the clutter carrying multiple emitters on board.

Simultaneously, EA-6B electronic warfare aircraft conducted jamming and support missions for various air packages. In the midst of this electronic clutter, an F-18 was mistakenly engaged and destroyed by Patriot missiles.... While not the proximate cause, ... it is possible that [this] electronic clutter contributed to [the F/A-18's inadvertent downing]," suggesting that "deliberate examination must be made of the operational impact of cluttered cyberspace and [that] joint approaches to cyberspace management must be undertaken" ("Operation Iraqi Freedom: Theater Air and Missile Defense History" [Fort Bliss, Tex.: 32nd Army Air and Missile Defense Command, September 2003], 94).

13. Michael Smith, "U.S. 'Clears' Crew Who Shot Down Tornado," *London Daily Telegram*, July 16, 2003.

14. Ibid.

15. Theodore A. Postol," An Informed Guess about Why Patriot Fired upon Friendly Aircraft and Saw Numerous False Missile Targets during Operation Iraqi Freedom," briefing charts, Security Studies Program, Massachusetts Institute of Technology, April 20, 2004. Lending strong credence to this independent analysis, the Army briefing that it addressed candidly conceded that there was "no voice link between [the Patriot] battalion headquarters and higher authority [with respect to identification and engagement]; that there was a "different air picture at different levels of command"; that there were "varying degrees of standards [across the Patriot force]"; that Patriot operators focused "solely on TBMs [and] did not work identification of unknown aircraft on [their] scope"; and that those operators "lost situational awareness of air tracks," indicating a clear need to "train [for] scope awareness [regarding] *all* air platforms" (emphasis added). "Operation Iraqi Freedom," briefing charts, 32nd Army Air and Missile Defense Command, Fort Bliss, Tex., September 2003, 54, 56–57.

16. Robert Riggs, "Blue on Blue: How Did an Army Patriot Battery Shoot Down a Navy F-18?" *CBS 11 News* (Dallas/Fort Worth, Tex.), February 4, 2004, at http//:www.globalsecurity.org/news/2004/040505-patriot-shootdown.htm

17. Givens, "'Let Slip the Dogs of War,'" 25.

18. Davies, *F-15C/E Eagle Units of Operation Iraqi Freedom*, 45.

19. *Report of the Defense Science Board Task Force on Patriot System Performance: Report Summary* (Washington, D.C.: Office of the Under Secretary of Defense for Acquisition, Technology, and Logistics, January 2005), 1.

20. Ibid., 2.

21. Ibid., 3.

22. Conversation with General Moseley, August 2, 2006.

23. "Army Announces Patriot Missile System's Performance in Operation Iraqi Freedom," U.S. Army News Release, December 10, 2004.

24. Reynolds, *Bashar, Baghdad, and Beyond*, 78.

25. Lt. Gen. T. Michael Moseley, USAF, "USCENTAF Friendly Fire Investigation Board: A-10—USMC Friendly Fire Incident (near An Nasiriyah, Iraq, 23 March 2003)," memorandum for commander, U.S. Central Command, Shaw AFB, S.C., May 23, 2003.

26. Executive summary attached to Gen. John P. Abizaid, USA, "Investigation of Suspected Friendly Fire Incident near An Nasiriyah, Iraq, 23 March 2003," memorandum for commanders, USCENTAF, USARCENT, USNAV-CENT, USMARCENT, SOCCENT, and Joint Forces Command, U.S. Central Command, MacDill AFB, Fla., March 6, 2004.

27. Ibid.

28. Ibid.

29. Peter Pae, "'Friendly Fire' Still a Problem," *Los Angeles Times*, May 16, 2003.

30. Rod Andrew, *U.S. Marines in Battle, An Nasiriyah, 23 March–2 April 2003* (Washington, D.C.: Headquarters U.S. Marine Corps, 2009), 20. Type III CAS does not require the FAC to have visual contact with either the designated target or the supporting aircraft.

31. Pae, "'Friendly Fire' Still a Problem."

32. Stout, *Hammer from Above*, 270.

33. *Operation Telic: United Kingdom Military Operations in Iraq*, 25.

34. *Third Infantry Division (Mechanized) After Action Report: Operation Iraqi Freedom*, 141.

35. Ripley, "Iraq Friendly Fire Was Worse Than Reported," 3. Many of the fratricide incidents were ground-to-ground in nature, despite the land component's extensive use of CENTCOM's Blue Force Tracker capability.

36. *Lessons of Iraq*, vol. 1, 108.

37. Quoted in Gardner, "Operation Iraqi Freedom: Coalition Operations," 93.

38. Fontenot, Degen, and Tohn, *On Point*, 110.

39. Atkinson, *In the Company of Soldiers*, 148.

40. Ibid.

41. Ibid., 151.

42. Robert Hewson, "Apache Operations over Karbala," *Jane's Intelligence Review*, July 2003, 27. Not long after the Apache went down, CENTAF geolocated it with overhead imagery and destroyed it with four well-placed 2,000-pound LGBs. Conversation with Major General Darnell, August 2, 2006.

43. Neil Baumgardner, "V Corps Commander: Army 'Altered Use' of Apaches following Failed Attack," *Defense Daily*, May 8, 2003, 3.

44. Rowan Scarborough, "General Tells How Cell Phone Foiled U.S. Attack in Iraq," *Washington Times*, May 8, 2003; Atkinson, *In the Company of Soldiers*, 148–154.

45. Neil Baumgardner, "101st Airborne Division Packaged Apaches, ATACMS during OIF," *Defense Daily*, May 14, 2003, 2.

46. Fontenot, Degen, and Tohn, *On Point*, 192.

47. Ibid., 193.

48. "Army to Reevaluate Apache Tactics," *Air Force Magazine*, October 2003, 15.

49. Scarborough, "General Tells How Cell Phone Foiled U.S. Attack in Iraq."

50. Fontenot, Degen, and Tohn, *On Point*, 160.

51. Ibid., 179.

52. Ibid., 192. The 3rd ID's after-action assessment likewise observed candidly that current Army attack helicopter doctrine "is still oriented on deep attack operations [which are] not the best use for the division attack helicopter battalion. The heavy division attack helicopter battalion is best employed in conducting shaping operations between the division coordinated fire line (CFL) and the division forward boundary (DFB)." The assessment recommended "readdressing attack aviation doctrine to discuss the employment of the attack helicopter battalion in the heavy division to support shaping operations as opposed to deep attack operations" (*Third Infantry Division (Mechanized) After Action Report: Operation Iraqi Freedom*, 36–37).

53. Richard J. Newman, "Ambush at Najaf," *Air Force Magazine*, October 2003, 60.

54. Johnson, *Learning Large Lessons*, 129–131.

55. Knights, *Cradle of Conflict*, 295.

56. Rebecca Grant, "Saddam's Elite in the Meat Grinder," *Air Force Magazine*, September 2003, 43.

57. General Merrill A. McPeak, USAF, *Presentation to the Commission on Roles and Missions of the Armed Forces* (Washington, D.C.: Headquarters United States Air Force, September 14, 1994), 35.

58. Maj. John M. Fawcett Jr., USAF, "Which Way to the FEBA (and FSCL, FLOT, Troops in Contact, Etc.)?" *USAF Weapons Review*, fall 1992, 26 (emphasis added).

59. Knights, *Cradle of Conflict*, 297.

60. Regarding the nature of these responsibilities, a postcampaign report issued by the USAF Air Ground Operations School described the ASOC as "the principal air control agency of the theater air control system responsible for

the direction and control of air operations directly supporting the ground combat element. It processes and coordinates requests for immediate air support and coordinates air missions requiring integration with other supporting arms and ground forces. It normally collocates with the Army tactical headquarters senior fire support coordination center within the ground combat element." The ASOC "manages [CAS] assets within the ground force AOR, processes CAS requests and controls the flow of CAS aircraft, deconflicts airspace control measures and aircraft, assigns aircraft to [TACP] terminal attack controllers, and manages the joint air request net (JARN) and the tactical air direction net (TAD)." Its subordinate TACPs attached to deployed Army troop formations "advise ground forces on aircraft employment and capabilities, coordinate and control aerospace operations, participate in battle planning, request air assets to support ground force requirements, and direct air strikes against enemy targets in close proximity to friendly forces" (Curt Neal, "JAGO [Joint Air Ground Office of Air Combat Command] ASOC Tiger Team: ASOC/TACP Reorganization to Support UEx [Unit of Employment 'X']," briefing slides, USAF Air Ground Operations School, Nellis AFB, Nev., 2005). This report summarizes key findings of a conference convened by ACC's JAGO at the USAF Air Ground Operations School at Nellis AFB on January 25–27, 2005, aimed at developing a "new ASOC construct" with the goal of providing "the most air power on target with the least amount of [command and control]."

61. Conversations with Colonel Erlenbusch, Major Roberson, and other CENTAF staff, January 29, 2007.

62. Ibid.

63. Davies and Dildy, *F-16 Fighting Falcon Units of Operation Iraqi Freedom*, 52.

64. Most of the requests from V Corps for both preplanned and immediate CAS were fulfilled by allied strike aircraft that were either pushed to or pulled from the airborne CAS stack nearest to the requesting ground unit. CAS stacks were typically maintained at altitudes between 10,000 and 20,000 feet. Because of the total air dominance enjoyed by the coalition, these CAS stacks were able to operate very close to the land battle and were accordingly moved forward as the ground offensive advanced northward, such that they were able essentially to provide almost constant overhead coverage. As a rule, the ASOC supporting V Corps typically had at least four available aircraft in the CAS stack for immediate on-call response to air support requests. CENTAF planners later recalled that the synergistic combination of numerous forward-positioned orbiting CAS stacks and the more than ample supply of appropriately armed aircraft populating those stacks were

major reasons not only for the effectiveness but also for the responsiveness of the CAS that the CAOC provided V Corps throughout the campaign. Conversations with Colonel Erlenbusch, Major Roberson, and other CENTAF staff, January 29, 2007.

65. The Afghan and Iraq air war experiences showcased the ability of today's air assets to exhaust even a substantial fixed target list in a very short time. In contrast, the inherently more difficult challenges of conducting the mobile target attacks that often distinguish counterland operations inevitably lead to weapons bring-back by strike aircraft. CENTAF planners concluded in this respect that "future mission planners should be prepared for this" and, "when it occurs, not react emotionally but rather view it as a predictable occurrence. In this manner, CAOC operators and aircrews can 'stick with the plan' instead of creating more confusion by 'trying to make something happen'" (conversations with Colonel Erlenbusch, Major Roberson, and other CENTAF staff, January 29, 2007).

66. Conversation with Major General Darnell, August 2, 2006.

67. Comments by Lieutenant Colonel Hunerwadel, May 23, 2007.

68. Comments by Colonel Neuenswander, October 26, 2010.

69. A knowledgeable former U.S. Army officer affirmed that the coalition's war plan "emphasized nonlinear ground operations," the result of which was "a battlefield with no clear front and rear areas" (Krepinevich, *Operation Iraqi Freedom: A First-Blush Assessment*, 14).

70. Maj. Kenneth A. Smith, USAF, "Joint Transformation of Aerial Interdiction by Enhancing Kill-Box Operations," research report, Air Command and Staff College, Air University, Maxwell AFB, Ala., April 2006, 22.

71. Joint Chiefs of Staff, *Doctrine for Joint Operations*, Joint Publication 3-0 (Washington, D.C.: Department of Defense, September 10, 2001), III-44.

72. Joint Chiefs of Staff, *Joint Fire Support*, Joint Publication 3-09 (Washington, D.C.: Department of Defense, November 13, 2006), A-4.

73. Secretary of the Air Force, *Counterland Operations*, Air Force Doctrine Document 2–1.3 (Maxwell AFB, Ala.: Air Force Doctrine Center, September 11, 2006), 69.

74. Kometer, *Command in Air War*, 175.

75. Ibid.

76. Ibid., 206, citing Lt. Gen. William S. Wallace, USA, "Joint Fires in OIF: What Worked for the V (U.S.) Corps," briefing slides, U.S. Army Combined Arms Center, Fort Leavenworth, Kans., no date. "The problem with this claim," the assessment citing it added, "is that there was no good way to keep track of the damage done by KI" (ibid.).

77. Patrecia Slayden Hollis, "Trained, Adaptable, Flexible Forces = Victory in Iraq," interview with Lt. Gen. W. Scott Wallace, *Field Artillery*, September–October 2003, 5–9.

78. Wallace, "Joint Fires in OIF."

79. Ibid.

80. Comments on an earlier draft by Col. Gregory Fontenot, USA (Ret.), October 25, 2010.

81. Lt. Col. Michael B. McGee Jr., USAF, "Air-Ground Operations during Operation Iraqi Freedom: Successes, Failures, and Lessons of Air Force and Army Integration," research report, Air War College, Maxwell AFB, Ala., February 25, 2005, 55–56. Among the 660 missions that did not drop ordnance, 126 of their aircrews could not find the target, 177 could not positively identify the target, 188 were unable to drop because of weather considerations, 130 had to depart the area because of low fuel, and 39 were noneffective for assorted other reasons.

82. Lt. Gen. William S. Wallace, USA, "Joint Effects in OIF [Operation Iraqi Freedom]: A V Corps Perspective," briefing slides, U.S. Army Combined Arms Center, Fort Leavenworth, Kans., no date, slide 21.

83. Further testifying to his satisfaction, General Wallace quoted Lt. Col. J. R. Sanderson, the commander of Task Force 2-69 in the fight for Objective Titans north of Baghdad: "The F-15s and F-16s were good. The A-10s were absolutely fantastic. It is my favorite airplane. I love those people. If I had enough coins, I would send one to every A-10 driver in the Air Force just to tell them how much I appreciate them, because when those guys come down and they start those strafing runs, it is flat awesome. It is just flat awesome" (ibid.).

84. Stout, *Hammer from Above*, 114.

85. Comments on an earlier draft by Col. Scott Walker, USAF, Air Force Studies and Analysis Agency (AF/A9L), Washington, D.C., February 16, 2007.

86. Carpenter, "Rapid, Deliberate, Disciplined, Proportional, and Precise," 14; Grant, "Saddam's Elite in the Meat Grinder," 43.

87. Ibid.

88. *Lessons of Iraq*, vol. 1, 60.

89. Jacobs and others, *Enhancing Fires and Maneuver through Greater Air-Ground Joint Interdependence*, 10. This experience highlighted for General Moseley the need for air component commanders to insist on more—and more realistic—air-ground integration in routine peacetime large-force joint training as well as more realistic joint force training. For decades, the joint Air Warrior training program has placed artificial constraints on air power so that

the Army captain can see the tank-on-tank battle from the opening round of a training engagement, resulting in a misleading and negative impression of air power's true effectiveness. If properly employed in actual joint and combined warfare, allied air power would never allow that tank-on-tank battle to occur. I am indebted to Lt. Col. Mark Cline for bringing this important point to my attention.

90. Kometer, *Command in Air War*, 143–144.

91. *Third Infantry Division (Mechanized) After Action Report: Operation Iraqi Freedom*, 108–109.

92. Knights, *Cradle of Conflict*, 303. In the MAGTF construct, the BCL was the main measure of fire support control, roughly analogous to the FSCL in Army–Air Force practice, but the BCL was extended only to the maximum range of the MAGTF's organic artillery. Every kill box inside the BCL was closed to air attack unless expressly declared otherwise by prior arrangement. Kill boxes on the far side of the BCL but still inside the FSCL, however, were open to the MAGTF's organic fixed- and rotary-wing strike assets unless declared otherwise.

93. McGee, "Air-Ground Operations during Operation Iraqi Freedom," 2, 4, 7. This outspokenly argumentative yet also scrupulously professional assessment is the most comprehensive account available of the ASOC's perspective with respect to the relative merits of ASOC-controlled "corps shaping" versus CAOC-controlled KI/CAS in V Corps' area of operations. Although many CAOC principals would emphatically disagree, the lead author of the best study to date of U.S. Army operations during the campaign commented that "McGee has it pretty close to right," bearing strong testimony to the abiding axiom of organizational life that where you stand depends on where you sit (comments by Colonel Fontenot, October 22, 2010).

94. Conversations with Colonel Erlenbusch, Major Roberson, and other CENTAF staff, January 29, 2007.

95. *Third Infantry Division (Mechanized) After Action Report: Operation Iraqi Freedom*, 108.

96. Ibid.

97. "Lapses in Coordinating Missile Launches in Iraq Pinned on V Corps," *Inside the Pentagon*, June 19, 2003, 1.

98. Comments on an earlier draft by Col. Richard Turner, USAF, commander, 479th Flying Training Group, Moody AFB, Georgia, April 24, 2007.

99. Ripley, "Closing the Gap," 25–26.

100. Conversations with Colonel Erlenbusch, Major Roberson, and other CENTAF staff, January 29, 2007.

101. Quoted in "Air Support Operations Center (ASOC) Employment."
102. Ibid.
103. Bill Kaczor, "Air Force Chief Says Military Must Cooperate," *Miami Herald*, October 22, 2003.
104. This was decidedly *not* the case, however, when it came to joint and combined air component and SOF training for the impending counter-Scud effort in Iraq's western desert. On the contrary, the air and land components of the counter-Scud team, allied as well as American, enjoyed ample opportunities to work together in realistic large-force training exercises in the Nellis range complex in 2002 and early 2003 aimed at developing, validating, and refining tactics, techniques, and procedures for nonlinear CAS and SOF support. Conversations with Colonel Erlenbusch, Major Roberson, and other CENTAF staff, January 29, 2007.
105. *Joint Lessons Learned*, 22.
106. Conversation with Air Vice-Marshal Andy White, RAF, October 28, 2004; comments on an earlier draft by Air Chief Marshal Sir Brian Burridge, RAF.
107. *Lessons for the Future*, 9.
108. Ibid., 29.
109. In the view of a former CAOC planner, since the ASOC is really an extension of the CAOC, this ultimately represents a problem that demands the attention of both the air and land component commanders. CAS is inherently inefficient because it is impossible to predict what kind of support will be needed and when and where it will be needed. When one adds to that the fact that none of the players (other than perhaps the Marines) had done CAS operations on such a large and sustained scale, the air and land components arguably need to address this problem from the top down. Comments by Lieutenant Colonel Cline, January 11, 2008.
110. *Lessons of Iraq*, vol. 1, 61. Reflecting further on this point, the same former CAOC planner remarked: "I'm not so sure we were great at CAS [even] in 1989 when I started flying F-16s. But I will say that after Desert Storm, there seemed to be a move away from CAS in a lot of F-16 wings as LANTIRN came on board and as many F-16s transitioned to SEAD. In addition, the F-15E was viewed almost as a 'strategic' asset that was too good for CAS because of its precision strike capability. (Ironically, they were the only aircraft that could not employ JDAMs at the beginning of Operation Iraqi Freedom.) Also, the focus of exercises like Red Flag tended to be more 'strategic attack' strike-package-oriented, since that was what occurred in Desert Storm. Air Warrior became the only major CAS training and [as noted above] was actually negative training for Air Force aircrews and ground

maneuver commanders. Finally, we failed to evolve our joint doctrine to keep up with technology. After the initial stages of Operation Enduring Freedom, we tried to catch up rapidly in January 2002 as we rewrote [joint manual] 3-09.3 to come up with Types I, II, and III CAS. . . . [T]oo many still think of CAS as the air marshal described" (comments by Lieutenant Colonel Cline, January 11, 2008).

111. *Lessons of Iraq*, vol. 2, Ev 62.

112. *Lessons of Iraq: Government Response to the Committee's Third Report of Session, 2003–2004* (London: House of Commons, Defence Committee, HC 635, June 8, 2004), 7; and "UK Multiplying Close Air Support Capability," *Jane's International Defence Review*, October 1, 2005. By the same token, members of the Australian national contingent noted similar shortfalls within their own force contingent, as a result of which notable improvements were subsequently made in JTAC training and standardization in air-land integration within the ADF. Comments by Group Captain Keir, July 2, 2009.

113. Hathaway, "Operational Assessment during Operation Iraqi Freedom," 12.

114. Ibid., 2.

115. "Task Force Enduring Look Lessons Learned," briefing, as quoted in Kometer, *Command in Air War*, 177.

116. Kometer, *Command in Air War*, 177.

117. Johnson, *Learning Large Lessons*, 126.

118. Conversations with Colonel Erlenbusch, Major Roberson, and other CENTAF staff, January 29, 2007.

119. Commanding General, 1st Marine Division, "Operation Iraqi Freedom (OIF): Lessons Learned," MEF-FRAGO 279–03, May 29, 2003, quoted in Johnson, *Learning Large Lessons*, 196.

120. Hathaway, "Operational Assessment during Operation Iraqi Freedom," 15–16.

121. Ibid., 18.

122. Conversations with Colonel Erlenbusch, Major Roberson, and other CENTAF staff, January 29, 2007.

123. Simpson, "Air Power Lessons from Operation Iraqi Freedom."

124. The same could be said for equally accurate inertially aided munitions. An F-16 pilot recalled that on arriving in their assigned area of operations, he and his wingman received immediate tasking to drop CBU-103s on a SAM site south of Baghdad: "There was an undercast, but the CBU-103 is fairly accurate and has its own inertial guidance system. When I released the bombs, I watched them fall toward the white clouds below. The dark green contrast against the sunlit clouds was a picture that is hard to describe, but

as they fell, I knew that they were going to hit their assigned targets, which would soon cease to exist" (Davies and Dildy, *F-16 Fighting Falcon Units of Operation Iraqi Freedom*, 31).

125. Conversations with Colonel Erlenbusch, Major Roberson, and other CEN-TAF staff, January 29, 2007.

126. Ibid.

127. The lack of adequate situation awareness that ensued from the CAOC's inability to track accurately the status of potential targets throughout the three-week campaign proved highly detrimental to the target development process. CAOC staffers noted that "the JIPTL tracker was responsible for reporting which targets on each JIPTL were actually struck. Unfortunately, this process failed to account for the many strikes performed against targets that were not on the JIPTL for any given ATO day. CAOC leadership accordingly identified a requirement for tracking the history of every target aim point in existence for Iraq, to include (1) what JIPTL, if any, the aim point had been placed on; (2) if the aim point had been MAAPed; (3) if the aim point was struck; and (4) if it was struck, what were the results of that strike" (ibid.).

128. Conversation with Major General Darnell, August 2, 2006.

129. Hathaway, "Operational Assessment during Operation Iraqi Freedom," 20. Colonel Hathaway further observed that "improvements in air and space technology have greatly enhanced our ability to find, fix, and target. Consequently, we have greater demands to assess the resulting effects. This, in turn, requires a greater demand on the same technology used to find, fix, and target. It is a self-perpetuating cycle that the CAOC must balance to ensure that execution does not get blindly in front of assessment" (p. 21).

130. Elaine M. Grossman, "JFCOM Draft Report Finds U.S. Forces Reverted to Attrition in Iraq," *Inside the Air Force*, March 26, 2004, 14–15. Another after-action inquiry that bears mention here was the CENTAF-led analysis done by the combined weapons effectiveness assessment team (CWEAT) that sent nearly one hundred experts in targeting, weapons, engineering, and intelligence throughout Iraq, starting on June 8, 2003, to more than five hundred weapon impact points targeted by the CAOC to assess the performance of air component weapons. The team consisted of civilian and military members from all branches of the U.S. armed services, U.S. Department of Defense agencies, the Royal Navy, the British Army, and the RAAF. As this investigation entered its second week, the CENTAF team chief, Col. Tom Entwhistle, said that its "ultimate goal . . . [was] to learn [from the campaign experience] so that in the future we can operate with increased

precision" ("Team Assessing OIF Air Component Effectiveness," Camp As Sayliyah, Qatar: AFPN [Air Force Print News] news story, June 13, 2003).

131. Elaine Grossman, "Battle Damage Assessment Process Found Unwieldy in Iraq Combat," *Inside the Pentagon*, June 19, 2003, 10.

132. Ibid., 11.

133. Simpson, "Air Power Lessons from Operation Iraqi Freedom."

134. Anne Barnard, "Death Lurks in Unspent U.S. 'Bomblets,'" *Boston Globe*, May 1, 2003.

135. A former senior CAOC planner noted emphatically that "we as a CAOC staff did not help the BDA effort. . . . Even against non-KI/CAS targets, we were hard-pressed to accurately track what munitions went against what set of coordinates. If we could not give the raw data to CENTCOM, we were not helping the assessment efforts" (comments by Lieutenant Colonel Cline, January 11, 2008).

136. Conversation with General Moseley, August 2, 2006.

137. Holmes, *U.S. Navy Hornet Units of Operation Iraqi Freedom*, pt. 2, 36.

138. Carpenter, "Rapid, Deliberate, Disciplined, Proportional, and Precise," 18.

139. Comments by Lieutenant Colonel Cline, January 11, 2008.

140. Remarks at a flag panel presentation during the Tailhook Association's 2003 annual symposium, Reno, Nev., September 20, 2003.

141. David A. Fulghum, "Tanker Puzzle: Aggressive Tactics, Shrinking Tanker Force Challenge Both Planners and Aircrews," *Aviation Week and Space Technology*, April 14, 2003, 23–26.

142. Ibid.

143. Carpenter, "Rapid, Deliberate, Disciplined, Proportional, and Precise," 18.

144. Lorenzo Cortes, "Seizure of Tallil Base Improved A-10's Effectiveness in Iraqi Freedom, Commander Says," *Defense Daily*, April 18, 2003, 8.

145. General Moseley personally flew on one of those early tanker sorties inside Iraqi airspace to demonstrate his confidence in their tactical soundness from an aircrew safety point of view.

146. So-called flex-deck operations, a more frenetically paced activity than normal cyclic operations involving waves of launches and recoveries at carefully selected intervals, typically have at least one of the carrier's two bow catapults firing continually while the two waist catapults in the landing area are kept clear to accommodate a steady stream of recovering aircraft.

147. Cdr. James Paulsen, USN, "Naval Aviation Delivered in Iraq," *Proceedings*, June 2003, 35.

148. Davies and Dildy, *F-16 Fighting Falcon Units of Operation Iraqi Freedom*, 52.

149. On this point, the commander of one F-15E wing that participated in the war recalled: "We did some creative things to ensure that our jets had significant loiter time and the ability to penetrate deep into Iraq, given the loss of Incirlik. For example, we dumped gas all the way up the Persian Gulf to be light enough to land at Al Jaber with a full load of nine GBU-12s, hot-pitted at Al Jaber, then went deep and long. Our guys did the Al Jaber hot-pits twice and sometimes three times before returning to Al Udeid. The average Strike Eagle mission was six to nine hours during the surge period. We also flew the jets [more than twice a day each] the entire time—unprecedented" (comments by Major General Rosborg, March 16, 2007).

150. Conversations with Colonel Erlenbusch, Major Roberson, and other CEN-TAF staff, January 29, 2007. The doctrine referred to here presumes that intratheater tankers are inherent parts of a global aerial refueling mobility scheme that requires direct control by the CAOC's air mobility division (AMD), which is also subordinated to the Air Force's Air Mobility Command. Yet as CAOC planners later noted, "in reality, once major combat operations commence, virtually 100 percent of all intratheater tankers, which are operationally controlled by the air component commander, are used for direct combat support missions within CENTCOM's area of responsibility. These missions do not require any special global AMD coordination. Current doctrinal guidance usurps planning control of combat assets from the CAOC, negatively affecting the air component commander's ability to perform his missions" (ibid.).

151. Ibid.

152. Gardner, "Operation Iraqi Freedom: Coalition Operations," 95.

153. SIPRNet "is a classified Defense Department network that is functionally equivalent to the civilian World Wide Web." In the ten years prior to Iraqi Freedom it had become "ubiquitous, with units at every echelon having access to a secure network where classified plans, discussions, and information could be shared free." Obviating the need to mail classified data or to talk over a secure telephone, it made for "a quantum leap in efficiency and effectiveness. In addition to desktop access to the latest plans and intelligence information, the secure e-mail and chat rooms fostered crosstalk at all levels. Planners and home stations could follow current operations and conduct parallel planning to anticipate requirements" (Fontenot, Degen, and Tohn, *On Point*, 11).

154. Ibid., 95.

155. Conversations with Colonel Erlenbusch, Major Roberson, and other CEN-TAF staff, January 29, 2007.

156. This point was driven home emphatically during a conversation with Air Commodore Chris Nickols, RAF, commander, Air Warfare Center, RAF Waddington, UK, October 29, 2004. Air Commodore Nickols served as one of CENTAF's three rotating CAOC directors during Operation Iraqi Freedom and was uniquely well placed to appreciate the real-time opportunity costs of the NOFORN caveat in intracoalition relations during an ongoing multilateral campaign.

157. *Lessons of Iraq*, vol. 2, Ev 44.

158. Ibid.

159. For further discussion of that earlier dual-ATO arrangement and the strain that it placed on the cohesion and ease of execution of the joint and combined air operation, see Lambeth, *NATO's Air War for Kosovo*, 188–189.

160. Conversations with Colonel Erlenbusch, Major Roberson, and other CEN-TAF staff, January 29, 2007.

161. *Review of Operational-Level Interoperability between the Military Forces of Australia and the United States of America* (Camp H. M. Smith, Hawaii: U.S. Pacific Command; and Canberra, Australia: Department of Defence, October 2004), 15, 17. The other two identified categories entailed issues relating to security cooperation arrangements and the management of the relationship and separate issues of a more technical nature involving capability development and force transformation.

162. Official interview with Group Captain Henman, April 9, 2007.

163. Official interview with Wing Commander Keir, February 19, 2007.

164. *Review of Operational-Level Interoperability between the Military Forces of Australia and the United States of America*, 15.

165. Official interview with Group Captain Halupka, May 14, 2008.

166. *Review of Operational-Level Interoperability between the Military Forces of Australia and the United States of America*, 27.

167. Ibid., 48–51.

168. Ibid.

Chapter 6. Toward a New Era of Warfare

1. Susan Page, "War May Realign World and Define a Presidency," *USA Today*, March 17, 2003.

2. Ibid. The intellectual foundation for such a change was laid down in the administration's new national security strategy released in September 2002, which stated the logic of a strategy of preemption: "We must be prepared to stop rogue states and their terrorist clients before they are able to threaten

or use weapons of mass destruction against the United States and our allies and friends" (ibid.).

3. Carla Anne Robbins, "U.S. Nears War in Embrace of Strategy of Preemption," *Wall Street Journal,* March 18, 2003.

4. Woodward, *Plan of Attack*, 428. Box-cutters were the weapon of choice for the September 11 terrorist hijackers.

5. Peter Spiegel, "Thinking ahead with the Pentagon's Planners," *London Financial Times,* April 16, 2003.

6. Fontenot, Degen, and Tohn, *On Point*, xvi.

7. Ibid., 249–250.

8. Cordesman, "The 'Instant Lessons' of the Iraq War," 5.

9. Fontenot, Degen, and Tohn, *On Point*, 102.

10. Vernon Loeb, "Sniping at the 'Plan' Strikes Some Nerves," *Washington Post*, April 2, 2003.

11. Conversation with Major General Darnell, August 2, 2006.

12. Conversations with Colonel Erlenbusch, Major Roberson, and other CEN-TAF staff, January 29, 2007. A CENTAF planner who served in key CAOC positions in both Enduring Freedom and Iraqi Freedom stressed the indispensable role played by General Moseley in setting the right tone at all levels in building those close trust relationships, noting emphatically how "his attitude pervaded our staff as we worked with our lower-level component counterparts" (comments by Lieutenant Colonel Cline, January 11, 2008).

13. Moseley, "Operation Iraqi Freedom: Initial CFACC Roll-up."

14. Conversation with General Moseley, August 2, 2006. Indeed, as General Moseley went on to observe, Enduring Freedom was a "microcosm" of the subsequent joint and combined campaign against Iraq when it came to such crucial functions as the buildup of forces, the establishment of air superiority, the extensive use of GPS- and inertially aided munitions, cruise missile operations, and the introduction and support of SOF teams and conventional ground forces. A senior CENTAF planner pointed out that "many of the successes enjoyed during [Iraqi Freedom] were a direct result of the 'smart' application of the successes [achieved earlier in Afghanistan] and the determination not to repeat the mistakes" (conversations with Colonel Erlenbusch, Major Roberson, and other CENTAF staff, January 29, 2007).

15. Conversations with Colonel Erlenbusch, Major Roberson, and other CEN-TAF staff, January 29, 2007.

16. Ibid.

17. Koven, "Improvements in Joint Forces," 8. As an example of the sort of joint counterland training that is arguably required to exercise and validate new

concepts of operations, CENTAF planners pointed to the notable success of the counter-Scud concept of operations that was repeatedly tested and ultimately validated in the Nellis range complex by joint and combined forces before being actually executed in Iraq's western desert. Conversations with Colonel Erlenbusch, Major Roberson, and other CENTAF staff, January 29, 2007.

18. Simpson, "Air Power Lessons from Operation Iraqi Freedom."
19. *Lessons for the Future*, 9.
20. Simpson, "Air Power Lessons from Operation Iraqi Freedom."
21. Ibid.
22. Ibid.
23. Knights, *Cradle of Conflict*, 304.
24. DeLong, *Inside CentCom*, 129.
25. Michael Knights, "Iraqi Freedom Displays the Transformation of U.S. Air Power," *Jane's Intelligence Review*, May 2003, 19.
26. Comments by Lieutenant Colonel Cline, January 11, 2008.
27. Carpenter, "Rapid, Deliberate, Disciplined, Proportional, and Precise," 25.
28. Ibid., 2.
29. *Lessons of Iraq*, vol. 2, Ev 60.
30. Woods and others, *Iraqi Perspectives Project*, passim.
31. Dunn, Bingham, and Fowler, *Ground Moving Target Indicator Radar and the Transformation of U.S. Warfighting*, 5.
32. Carpenter, "Rapid, Deliberate, Disciplined, Proportional, and Precise," 2.
33. Fick, *One Bullet Away*, 289.
34. Comments by Lieutenant Colonel Hunerwadel, May 23, 2007.
35. Thomas E. Ricks, "What Counted: People, Plan, Inept Enemy," *Washington Post*, April 10, 2003.
36. Woodward, *Plan of Attack*, 118. Despite his avowed emphasis on "jointness," however, Franks clearly brought a pronounced land-centric bias to his war planning, routinely characterizing allied ground forces as "*supported* [emphasis added] by overwhelming air power" and portraying the overall concept of operations as one in which slow-reacting Iraqi ground formations would be fixed and ultimately destroyed by the combined effects of artillery, air "support," and attack helicopters (Franks with McConnell, *American Soldier*, 415).
37. Fontenot, Degen, and Tohn, *On Point*, xv, xvii. The landmark Goldwater-Nichols Defense Reorganization Act of 1986, among other things, reduced the uniformed services from fighting forces in and of themselves to being simply force providers to joint force combatant commanders who reported

directly to the secretary of defense and who, at least in theory, were expected to plan and conduct military operations in their respective regional areas of responsibility around the world in a manifestly integrated and joint way. For a good overview of the origins, nature, and intent of this game-changing legislation regarding the way in which the United States has conducted its defense enterprise ever since, see Vincent Davis, "Organization and Management," in *American Defense Annual, 1987–1988*, ed. Joseph Kruzel (Lexington, Mass.: D. C. Heath, 1987).

38. Cordesman, "The 'Instant Lessons' of the Iraq War," 23.

39. Quoted in Amy Svitak, "Force of the Future," *Army Times*, November 25, 2002.

40. Cordesman, "The 'Instant Lessons' of the Iraq War," 8.

41. Murray and Scales, *The Iraq War*, 163.

42. DeLong, *Inside CentCom*, 110.

43. Carpenter, "Rapid, Deliberate, Disciplined, Proportional, and Precise," 1.

44. Stephen Trimble, "Cebrowski: Iraq War Offers Clues for Transformation Agenda," *Aerospace Daily*, April 23, 2003.

45. Hunter Keeter, "Cebrowski: Iraq Shows Network-Centric Warfare Implementation," *Defense Daily*, April 23, 2003, 4.

46. Knights, "Iraqi Freedom Displays the Transformation of U.S. Air Power," 16.

47. Elaine M. Grossman, "Key Generals: Response to 'Fedayeen' a Vital Milestone in Iraq War," *Inside the Pentagon*, May 8, 2003, 14.

48. Ripley, "Closing the Gap," 27.

49. Vernon Loeb, "Pentagon Credits Success in Iraq War to Joint Operations," *Washington Post*, October 3, 2003.

50. Thom Shanker, "Pentagon Criticizes High Rate of Allied Deaths by Allied Fire," *New York Times*, October 3, 2003. A substantially larger allied ground presence from the outset almost certainly would have been the preferred alternative for either heading off or better containing the postcampaign insurgency, sectarian violence, and rampant civil disorder that persisted in Iraq for nearly six years after Hussein's regime was driven from power.

51. Statement of Brig. Gen. Marc Rogers, USAF, director for joint requirements and integration, U.S. Joint Forces Command, before the House Armed Services Committee, Subcommittee on Terrorism and Unconventional Threats, House of Representatives, 108th Congress, Washington, D.C., October 21, 2003.

52. Scarborough, "Myers Says 'Annihilation' of Iraqi Army Wasn't Goal."

53. Jeremy Feiler, "Speed, Unpredictability Led to Victory in Iraq, Defense Officials Say," *Inside the Pentagon*, March 4, 2004, 1, 14.

54. Conversation with then Wing Commander Stuart Atha, RAF, Ministry of Defence, London, October 27, 2004.

55. Davies and Dildy, *F-16 Fighting Falcon Units of Operation Iraqi Freedom*, 68–69.

56. Carpenter, "Rapid, Deliberate, Disciplined, Proportional, and Precise," 1.

57. Robert A. Pape, "The True Worth of Air Power," *Foreign Affairs*, March–April 2004, 127.

58. Murray and Scales, *The Iraq War*, 114.

59. Interview with Lt. Gen. David D. McKiernan, USA, U.S. Army Center of Military History, Washington, D.C., June 30, 2003, cited in Reynolds, *Basrah, Baghdad, and Beyond*, 12.

60. Elaine M. Grossman, "A-10 Aircraft Took Heavy Fire while Performing Unusual Mission," *Inside the Air Force*, April 11, 2003, 10.

61. John M. Broder, "General Franks Makes First Visit to Troops in the Battle Zone," *New York Times*, April 8, 2003. The "pot" mentioned by Franks referred to a reporter's earlier allusion to the Ba'athist regime as a large clay pot against which allied forces were constantly tapping in different ways and at different times.

62. Vince Crawley, "Less Is More," *Army Times*, April 21, 2003.

63. Jeremy Feiler, "Goldwater-Nichols Changes Key to U.S. Success in Iraq, Pace Says," *Inside the Pentagon*, September 25, 2003, 2.

64. Interview with Vice Adm. Timothy J. Keating, USN, "This Was a Different War," *Proceedings*, June 2003, 30.

65. *Joint Lessons Learned*, 14, 21.

66. For amplification on this point, see Lambeth, *Combat Pair.*

67. Johnson, *Learning Large Lessons*, 195, 197.

68. Ibid., 199–200, 206–207. Writing a year later, the USAF's Lt. Gen. David Deptula similarly observed that as the American defense establishment has evolved since the end of the Cold War, "Goldwater-Nichols has created unintended consequences. It has resulted in a focus on military integration, but failing to develop a corresponding focus on incorporating all the elements of national power has delayed us from achieving true integration of all the pillars of national security. It has also led to an unsophisticated interpretation of jointness that drives some to seek homogeneity among the services, while others use 'jointness' as an excuse to participate in every mission. This has led some services to seek self-sufficiency rather than synergy—and to the degree that they have been allowed to do so has actually resulted in divergence from the tenets of Goldwater-Nichols by some as they replicate other services' core competencies" ("Toward Restructuring National Security," *Strategic Studies Quarterly*, winter 2007, 16).

69. Comments by Colonel Fontenot, October 13, 2010. Colonel Fontenot hastened to add that "despite that, the [fact remains] that the V Corps troops truly appreciated the role that fixed-wing air played. CAS played a decisive role in more than one fight."

70. Whether it also was a lesson "learned" and duly assimilated remains to be determined, given the continued inefficiencies in air-land interaction that predominated in the nation's subsequent counterinsurgency operations in Iraq through 2010 and that persist to this day in CENTCOM's continuing counterinsurgency effort against the Taliban in Afghanistan.

71. Conversations with Colonel Erlenbusch, Major Roberson, and other CENTAF staff, January 29, 2007.

72. Knights, "Iraqi Freedom Displays the Transformation of U.S. Air Power," 19.

73. Commenting on the bottom-line meaning of the above, a Russian defense analyst, Yevgeny Pashentsev, said immediately after the campaign ended: "The Americans have rewritten the textbook, and every country had better take note." Likewise, a former Soviet Strategic Rocket Forces general and later head of the Russian military's official research organization, Vladimir Dvorkin, remarked that "the gap between our capabilities and those of the Americans has been revealed, and it is vast" (quoted in Fred Weir, "Iraqi Defeat Jolts Russian Military," *Christian Science Monitor*, April 16, 2003).

74. Comments by Colonel Fontenot, October 22, 2010.

75. Among the many books that have been written on the American postcampaign experience in Iraq since April 2003, particularly notable are Fouad Ajami, *The Foreigner's Gift: The Americans, the Arabs, and the Iraqis in Iraq* (New York: Free Press, 2006); Ali A. Allawi, *The Occupation of Iraq: Winning the War, Losing the Peace* (New Haven, Conn.: Yale University Press, 2007); Nora Bensahel et al., *After Saddam: Prewar Planning and the Occupation of Iraq* (Santa Monica, Calif.: RAND Corporation, MG-642-A, 2008); Larry Diamond, *Squandered Victory: The American Occupation and Bungled Effort to Bring Democracy to Iraq* (New York: Times Books, 2005); James Dobbins et al., *Occupying Iraq: A History of the Coalition Provisional Authority* (Santa Monica, Calif.: RAND Corporation, MG-847-CC, 2009); Michael R. Gordon and Bernard E. Trainor, *The Endgame: The Inside Story of the Struggle for Iraq from George W. Bush to Barack Obama* (New York: Random House, 2012); Peter R. Mansoor, *Baghdad at Sunrise: A Brigade Commander's War in Iraq* (New Haven, Conn.: Yale University Press, 2008); Thomas E. Ricks, *Fiasco: The American Military Adventure in Iraq* (New York: Penguin Press, 2006); Thomas E. Ricks, *The Gamble: General David Petraeus and the American Military Adventure in Iraq, 2006–2008* (New York: Penguin Press, 2009); Linda Robinson, *Tell Me How*

This Ends: General David Petraeus and the Search for a Way out of Iraq (New York: Public Affairs, 2008); Bing West, *The Strongest Tribe: War, Politics, and the Endgame in Iraq* (New York: Random House, 2008); Bob Woodward, *State of Denial: Bush at War, Part III* (New York: Simon and Schuster, 2006); and Bob Woodward, *The War Within: A Secret White House History, 2006–2008* (New York: Simon and Schuster, 2008). For the personal recollections of the Bush administration's proconsul to Iraq, who headed the Coalition Provisional Authority and oversaw the badly flawed allied occupation of Iraq from May 2003 to June 2004, see L. Paul Bremer III, *My Year in Iraq: The Struggle to Build a Future of Hope* (New York: Simon and Schuster, 2006).

76. Melvin R. Laird, "Iraq: Learning the Lessons of Vietnam," *Foreign Affairs*, November–December 2005, 22.

77. James Dobbins, "Iraq: Winning the Unwinnable War," *Foreign Affairs*, January–February 2005, 16. CENTCOM's target priorities for the opening days of the campaign may have been partly culpable for this ensuing downside consequence of the allied invasion, if only indirectly. A knowledgeable commentator later suggested in this regard: "Unfortunately, leadership attack may have contributed to the difficulty in establishing a lasting peace after the major combat operations ended. . . . [The approach chosen] enabled an overall strategy using a relatively small invasion force. This force was sufficient for the drive to Baghdad, but it proved insufficient for establishing security after the regime's collapse. . . . [That said], the chaos that engulfed Iraq in the opening days of coalition rule was not an indictment of leadership attack, but rather a consequence of incorrect assumptions made by coalition leaders about the nature of postwar Iraq" (Hinote, "More Than Bombing Saddam," 168, 175).

78. Grossman, "Evolving Threats May Offer Air Force 'Unlearned Lessons' in Iraq," 16.

79. For perhaps the most thorough survey of the many individuals both in and out of government who urged the Bush administration to anticipate and duly hedge against the likely needs of postcampaign stabilization, see Bensahel et al., *After Saddam*.

80. Atkinson, *In the Company of Soldiers*, 187.

81. "Prepared Testimony by U.S. Secretary of Defense Donald H. Rumsfeld to the Senate Armed Services Committee," U.S. Senate, Washington, D.C., July 9, 2003.

82. This theme was first developed in depth more than four decades ago in the widely acclaimed study by the late Samuel P. Huntington, *Political Order in Changing Societies* (New Haven, Conn.: Yale University Press, 1968).

83. Thomas L. Friedman, "If I Had One Wish," *New York Times*, October 4, 2006.

84. Ricks, *Fiasco*, 127–128.

85. Eliot Cohen, "No Way to Win a War," *Wall Street Journal*, December 7, 2006.

86. Frederick W. Kagan, *Finding the Target: The Transformation of American Military Policy* (New York: Encounter Books, 2006), 358–359, 369–370. The 3rd ID's after-action assessment of its campaign experience candidly noted that the division "did not have a dedicated plan to transition quickly from combat operations to SASO [stability and support operations]. . . . As the division transitioned to SASO, it did not have sufficient forces or effective rules of engagement (ROE) to control civilian looting and rioting throughout the city." The assessment concluded regarding this point that "we must be ready for rapid success. Follow-on SASO plans must be developed in advance and the necessary resources readily available for commitment," with arrangements in place "to conduct SASO concurrently with combat operations or immediately after the completion of combat operations" (*Third Infantry Division [Mechanized] After Action Report: Operation Iraqi Freedom*, 13, 18).

87. Krepinevich, *Operation Iraqi Freedom: A First-Blush Assessment*, 7–8.

88. Ibid., 11.

89. This characterization of fourth-generation warfare was put forward by Vice Adm. David Nichols, USN, deputy commander of U.S. Central Command, during a flag presentation at the 2004 annual symposium of the Tailhook Association, Reno, Nev., September 11, 2004.

90. Col. Thomas X. Hammes, USMC (Ret.), *The Sling and the Stone: On War in the 21st Century* (St. Paul, Minn.: Zenith Press, 2006), 2.

91. Stout, *Hammer from Above*, 378.

92. Colin S. Gray, *The Air Power Advantage in Future Warfare: The Need for Strategy* (Maxwell AFB, Ala.: Air Power Research Institute, Air University, 2007), 15, 18, 20.

SELECTED BIBLIOGRAPHY

Government Documents

Abizaid, Gen. John P., USA. "Investigation of Suspected Friendly Fire Incident near An Nasiriyah, Iraq, 23 March 2003." Memorandum for commanders, USCENTAF, USARCENT, USNAVCENT, USMAR-CENT, SOCCENT, and Joint Forces Command. U.S. Central Command, MacDill AFB, Fla., March 6, 2004.

Andrew, Rod. *U.S. Marines in Battle, An Nasiriyah, 23 March–2 April 2003.* Washington, D.C.: Headquarters U.S. Marine Corps, 2009.

"Army Announces Patriot Missile System's Performance in Operation Iraqi Freedom." U.S. Army news release. Department of the Army, Washington, D.C., December 10, 2004.

Australia's National Security: A Defence Update 2003. Canberra, Australia: Department of Defence, 2003.

Bannon, Claire. "Op Bastille/Falconer Timeline." Canberra, Australia, no date.

"Coalition Forces Air Component Command Briefing." Department of Defense, Washington, D.C., April 5, 2003.

Duelfer, Charles, and others. *Comprehensive Report of the Special Adviser to the DCI on Iraq's WMD.* Washington, D.C.: Iraq Survey Group for the Central Intelligence Agency, September 30, 2004.

Fires in the Close Fight: OIF Lessons Learned. Fort Stewart, Ga.: 3rd Infantry Division DIVARTY [Division Artillery], November 2003.

Haag, SSgt. Jason L., USAF. "OIF Veterans Discuss Lessons." *Air Force Print News.* USAF Air Warfare Center Public Affairs, Nellis AFB, Nev., July 31, 2003.

Handy, Gen. John W., USAF. *Operation Iraqi Freedom—Air Mobility by the Numbers.* Scott AFB, Ill.: Headquarters Air Mobility Command, October 1, 2003.

Houston, Air Marshal A. G., RAAF. "Message from Chief of Air Force: Operation Falconer." Canberra, Australia, March 24, 2003.

———. "Message from Chief of Air Force: Operation Falconer." Canberra, Australia, April 4, 2003.

Howard, Hon. John. Address to the Committee for Economic Development of Australia, Canberra, Australia, November 20, 2002.

———. Address to the House of Representatives, Parliament House, Canberra, Australia, March 18, 2003.

Iraq's Weapons of Mass Destruction Programs. Washington, D.C.: Director of Central Intelligence, October 2002.

Joint Chiefs of Staff. *Doctrine for Joint Operations.* Joint Publication 3-0. Washington, D.C.: Department of Defense, September 10, 2001.

———. *Joint Fire Support.* Joint Publication 3-09. Washington, D.C.: Department of Defense, November 13, 2006.

Joint Lessons Learned: Operation Iraqi Freedom Major Combat Operations. Coordinating draft. Norfolk, Va.: U.S. Joint Forces Command, March 1, 2004.

Lessons of Iraq: Government Response to the Committee's Third Report of Session, 2003–2004. London: House of Commons, Defence Committee, HC 635, June 8, 2004.

Lessons of Iraq: Third Report of Session 2003–04. Vols. 1–3. London: House of Commons, Defence Committee, HC 57-I/II/III, March 16, 2004.

Moseley, Lt. Gen. T. Michael, USAF. *Operation Iraqi Freedom—by the Numbers.* Shaw AFB, S.C.: Assessment and Analysis Division, Headquarters U.S. Central Command Air Forces, April 30, 2003.

———. "USCENTAF Friendly Fire Investigation Board: A-10–USMC Friendly Fire Incident (near An Nasiriyah, Iraq, 23 March 2003)." Memorandum for commander, U.S. Central Command, May 23, 2003. U.S. Central Command Air Forces, Shaw AFB, S.C.

"Operation Falconer Honors List." Canberra, Australia, Department of Defence, November 28, 2003.

"Operation Iraqi Freedom: Theater Air and Missile Defense History." 32nd Army Air and Missile Defense Command, Fort Bliss, Tex., September 2003.

Operations in Iraq: First Reflections. London: Ministry of Defence, July 2003.

Operations in Iraq: Lessons for the Future. London: Ministry of Defence, December 2003.

"Prepared Testimony by U.S. Secretary of Defense Donald H. Rumsfeld to the Senate Armed Services Committee." U.S. Senate, Washington, D.C., July 9, 2003.

Report of the Defense Science Board Task Force on Patriot System Performance: Report Summary. Washington, D.C.: Office of the Under Secretary of Defense for Acquisition, Technology, and Logistics, January 2005.

Review of Operational-Level Interoperability between the Military Forces of Australia and the United States of America. Camp H. M. Smith, Hawaii: U.S.

Pacific Command; and Canberra, Australia: Department of Defence, October 2004.

Schlesinger, James R., and others. *Final Report of the Independent Panel to Review DoD Detention Operations.* Washington, D.C.: Department of Defense, 2004.

Secretary of the Air Force. *Counterland Operations.* Air Force Doctrine Document 2-1.3. Maxwell AFB, Ala.: Air Force Doctrine Center, September 11, 2006.

"Statement by Admiral Edmund P. Giambastiani Jr., Commander, U.S. Joint Forces Command, before the House Armed Services Committee." Washington, D.C.: U.S. House of Representatives, October 2, 2003.

"Statement of Brigadier General Marc Rogers, USAF, Director for Joint Requirements and Integration (J8), U.S. Joint Forces Command, before the 108th Congress, House Armed Services Committee, Subcommittee on Terrorism and Unconventional Threats." Washington, D.C.: U.S. House of Representatives, October 21, 2003.

"Team Assessing OIF Air Component Effectiveness." AFPN [Air Force Print News] news story, Camp As Sayliyah, Qatar, June 13, 2003.

Third Infantry Division (Mechanized) After Action Report: Operation Iraqi Freedom. Fort Stewart, Ga.: U.S. Army 3rd Infantry Division, 2003.

The War in Iraq: ADF Operations in the Middle East in 2003. Canberra, Australia: Department of Defence, 2004.

Books

Ajami, Fouad. *The Foreigner's Gift: The Americans, the Arabs, and the Iraqis in Iraq.* New York: Free Press, 2006.

Allawi, Ali A. *The Occupation of Iraq: Winning the War, Losing the Peace.* New Haven, Conn.: Yale University Press, 2007.

Anderson, Jon Lee. *The Fall of Baghdad.* New York: Penguin Press, 2004.

Atkinson, Rick. *In the Company of Soldiers: A Chronicle of Combat.* New York: Henry Holt, 2004.

Boot, Max. *War Made New: Technology, Warfare, and the Course of History, 1500 to Today.* New York: Gotham Books, 2006.

Boyne, Walter. *Operation Iraqi Freedom: What Went Right, What Went Wrong, and Why.* New York: Tom Doherty Associates, 2003.

Bremer, L. Paul III. *My Year in Iraq: The Struggle to Build a Future of Hope.* New York: Simon and Schuster, 2006.

Bush, George [H.W.], and Brent Scowcroft. *A World Transformed.* New York: Alfred A. Knopf, 1998.

Bush, George W. *Decision Points*. New York: Crown Publishers, 2010.

Davies, Steve. *F-15C/E Eagle Units of Operation Iraqi Freedom*. Osprey Combat Aircraft No. 47. Oxford, England: Osprey Publishing, 2004.

Davies, Steve, and Doug Dildy. *F-16 Fighting Falcon Units of Operation Iraqi Freedom*. Osprey Combat Aircraft No. 61. Oxford, England: Osprey Publishing, 2006.

Davis, Vincent. "Organization and Management." In *American Defense Annual, 1987–1988*, ed. Joseph Kruzel. Lexington, Mass.: D. C. Heath, 1987.

DeLong, Lt. Gen. Michael, USMC (Ret.). *Inside CentCom: The Unvarnished Truth about the Wars in Afghanistan and Iraq*. Washington, D.C.: Regnery, 2004.

Diamond, Larry. *Squandered Victory: The American Occupation and Bungled Effort to Bring Democracy to Iraq*. New York: Times Books, 2005.

Fick, Nathaniel. *One Bullet Away: The Making of a Marine Officer*. New York: Houghton Mifflin, 2005.

Fontenot, Col. Gregory, USA (Ret.); Lt. Col. E. J. Degen, USA; and Lt. Col. David Tohn, USA. *On Point: The United States Army in Operation Iraqi Freedom*. Fort Leavenworth, Kans.: Combat Studies Institute Press, 2004.

———. *On Point: The United States Army in Operation Iraqi Freedom*. Annapolis, Md.: Naval Institute Press, 2005.

Franks, Gen. Tommy, USA (Ret.), with Malcolm McConnell. *American Soldier*. New York: Regan Books, 2004.

Gordon, Michael R., and Bernard E. Trainor. *Cobra II: The Inside Story of the Invasion and Occupation of Iraq*. New York: Pantheon Books, 2006.

———. *The Endgame: The Inside Story of the Struggle for Iraq, from George W. Bush to Barack Obama*. New York: Pantheon Books, 2012.

Haass, Richard N. *War of Necessity, War of Choice: A Memoir of Two Iraq Wars*. New York: Simon and Schuster, 2009.

Hammes, Col. Thomas X., USMC (Ret.). *The Sling and the Stone: On War in the 21st Century*. St. Paul, Minn.: Zenith Press, 2006.

Holmes, Tony. *U.S. Navy Hornet Units of Operation Iraqi Freedom*. Part 2. Osprey Combat Aircraft No. 58. Oxford, England: Osprey Publishing, 2005.

Hunt, Peter. *Angles of Attack: An A-6 Intruder Pilot's War*. New York: Ballantine Books, 2002.

Huntington, Samuel P. *Political Order in Changing Societies*. New Haven, Conn.: Yale University Press, 1968.

Keegan, John. *The Iraq War*. New York: Alfred A. Knopf, 2004.

Knights, Michael. *Cradle of Conflict: Iraq and the Birth of the Modern U.S. Military*. Annapolis, Md.: Naval Institute Press, 2005.

Kometer, Lt. Col. Michael W., USAF. *Command in Air War: Centralized versus Decentralized Control of Combat Air Power*. Maxwell AFB, Ala.: Air University Press, June 2007.

Koopman, John. *McCoy's Marines: Darkside to Baghdad*. St. Paul, Minn.: Zenith Press, 2004.

Lambeth, Benjamin S. *The Transformation of American Air Power*. Ithaca, N.Y.: Cornell University Press, 2000.

Mansoor, Peter R. *Baghdad at Sunrise: A Brigade Commander's War in Iraq*. New Haven, Conn.: Yale University Press, 2008.

Murray, Williamson, and Maj. General Robert H. Scales Jr., USA (Ret.). *The Iraq War: A Military History*. Cambridge, Mass.: Belknap Press of Harvard University Press, 2003.

Purdum, Todd S. *A Time of Our Choosing: America's War in Iraq*. New York: Henry Holt, 2003.

Reynolds, Col. Nicholas E., USMC (Ret.). *Basrah, Baghdad, and Beyond: The U.S. Marine Corps in the Second Iraq War*. Annapolis, Md.: Naval Institute Press, 2005.

Ricks, Thomas E. *Fiasco: The American Military Adventure in Iraq*. New York: Penguin Press, 2006.

———. *The Gamble: General David Petraeus and the American Military Adventure in Iraq, 2006–2008*. New York: Penguin Press, 2009.

Robinson, Linda. *Tell Me How This Ends: General David Petraeus and the Search for a Way Out of Iraq*. New York: Public Affairs, 2008.

Rove, Karl. *Courage and Consequence: My Life as a Conservative in the Fight*. New York: Simon and Schuster, 2010.

Rumsfeld, Donald. *Known and Unknown: A Memoir*. New York: Sentinel, 2011.

Shimko, Keith L. *The Iraq Wars and America's Military Revolution*. New York: Cambridge University Press, 2010.

Stout, Jay A. *Hammer from Above: Marine Air Combat over Iraq*. New York: Presidio Press, 2005.

West, Bing. *The Strongest Tribe: War, Politics, and the Endgame in Iraq*. New York: Random House, 2008.

West, Bing, and Maj. Gen. Ray L. Smith, USMC (Ret.). *The March Up: Taking Baghdad with the United States Marines*. New York: Bantam Dell, 2003.

Willis, Clint. *Boots on the Ground: Stories of American Soldiers from Iraq and Afghanistan*. New York: Thunder's Mouth Press, 2004.

Woodward, Bob. *Plan of Attack*. New York: Simon and Schuster, 2004.

———. *The War Within: A Secret White House History, 2006–2008*. New York: Simon and Schuster, 2008.

Wright, Evan. *Generation Kill: Devil Dogs, Iceman, Captain America, and the New Face of American War*. New York: G. P. Putnam's Sons, 2004.

Zinnmeister, Karl. *Boots on the Ground: A Month with the 82nd Airborne in the Battle for Iraq*. New York: St. Martin's Press, 2003.

Zucchino, David. *Thunder Run: The Armored Strike to Capture Baghdad*. New York: Atlantic Monthly Press, 2004.

Monographs

Bensahel, Nora, et al. *After Saddam: Prewar Planning and the Occupation of Iraq*. Santa Monica, Calif.: RAND Corporation, MG–642-A, 2008.

Biddle, Stephen, and others. *Toppling Saddam: Iraq and American Military Transformation*. Carlisle, Pa.: Strategic Studies Institute, U.S. Army War College, April 2004.

Deptula, Col. David A., USAF. *Firing for Effect: Change in the Nature of Warfare*. Arlington, Va.: Aerospace Education Foundation, 1995.

Dobbins, James, et al. *Occupying Iraq: A History of the Coalition Provisional Authority*. Santa Monica, Calif.: RAND Corporation, MG–847-CC, 2009.

Donnelly, Thomas. *Operation Iraqi Freedom: A Strategic Assessment*. Washington, D.C.: AEI Press, 2000.

Dunn, Richard J. III, Price T. Bingham, and Charles A. Fowler. *Ground Moving Target Indicator Radar and the Transformation of U.S. Warfighting*. Arlington, Va.: Northrop Grumman Analysis Center, February 2004.

Gray, Colin S. *The Air Power Advantage in Future Warfare: The Need for Strategy*. Maxwell AFB, Ala.: Air Power Research Institute, Air University, 2007.

Hosmer, Stephen T. *Why the Iraqi Resistance to the Coalition Invasion Was So Weak*. Santa Monica, Calif.: RAND Corporation, MG–544-AF, 2007.

Jacobs, Jody, David E. Johnson, Katherine Comanor, Lewis Jamison, Leland Joe, and David Vaughn. *Enhancing Fires and Maneuver through Greater Air-Ground Joint Interdependence*. Santa Monica, Calif.: RAND Corporation, MG–793-AF, 2009.

Johnson, David E. *Learning Large Lessons: The Evolving Roles of Ground Power and Air Power in the Post–Cold War Era*. Santa Monica, Calif.: RAND Corporation, MG–405-AF, 2005.

Kirkpatrick, Charles E. *Joint Fires as They Were Meant to Be: V Corps and the 4th Air Support Operations Group during Operation Iraqi Freedom*. Land Warfare Papers No. 48. Arlington, Va.: Institute of Land Warfare, Association of the U.S. Army, October 2004.

Krepinevich, Andrew F. *Operation Iraqi Freedom: A First-Blush Assessment*. Washington, D.C.: Center for Strategic and Budgetary Assessments, 2003.

Lambeth, Benjamin S. *Air Power against Terror: America's Conduct of Operation Enduring Freedom*. Santa Monica, Calif.: RAND Corporation, MG-166-1-CENTAF, 2005.

———. *American Carrier Air Power at the Dawn of a New Century*. Santa Monica, Calif.: RAND Corporation, MG-404-NAVY, 2005.

———. *Combat Pair: The Evolution of Air Force–Navy Integration in Strike Warfare*. Santa Monica, Calif.: RAND Corporation, MG-655-AF, 2007.

———. *NATO's Air War for Kosovo: A Strategic and Operational Assessment*. Santa Monica, Calif.: RAND Corporation, MR-1365-AF, 2001.

Lynch, Kristin F., John G. Drew, Robert S. Tripp, and Charles Robert Roll Jr. *Supporting Air and Space Expeditionary Forces: Lessons from Operation Iraqi Freedom*. Santa Monica, Calif.: RAND Corporation, MG-193-AF, 2005.

Mueller, Karl P., and others. *Striking First: Preemptive and Preventive Attack in U.S. National Security Policy*. Santa Monica, Calif.: RAND Corporation, MG-403-AF, 2006.

Ullman, Harlan K., and James P. Wade. *Shock and Awe: Achieving Rapid Dominance*. Washington, D.C.: National Defense University Press, December 1996.

Woods, Kevin M., with Michael R. Pease, Mark E. Stout, Williamson Murray, and James G. Lacey. *Iraqi Perspectives Project: A View of Operation Iraqi Freedom from Saddam's Senior Leadership*. Norfolk, Va.: Joint Center for Operational Analysis, U.S. Joint Forces Command, March 2006.

Articles, Reports, and Theses

Anderson, Capt. John W., USAF. "An Analysis of a Dust Storm Impacting Operation Iraqi Freedom, 25–27 March 2003." Master's thesis, U.S. Naval Postgraduate School, Monterey, Calif., December 2004.

"Army to Reevaluate Apache Tactics." *Air Force Magazine*, October 2003.

"Baghdad Raid Takes 12 Minutes from Targeting to Attack." *Flight International*, April 15–21, 2003.

Baumgardner, Neil. "101st Airborne Division Packaged Apaches, ATACMS during OIF." *Defense Daily*, May 14, 2003.

———. "RAF Spokesman: Enhanced Paveway 'Outstanding' in Operation Iraqi Freedom." *Defense Daily*, April 2, 2003.

———. "V Corps Commander: Army 'Altered Use' of Apaches Following Failed Attack." *Defense Daily*, May 8, 2003.

Bennett, John T. "Smaller Bombs among Needs Revealed In Iraq, Navy Officers Say." *Inside the Pentagon*, August 7, 2003.

———. "USAF Constellation, Navy FORCENet Step Up Interoperability Efforts." *Inside the Pentagon,* July 31, 2003.

Biddle, Stephen. "Speed Kills? Reassessing the Role of Speed, Precision, and Situation Awareness in the Fall of Saddam." *Journal of Strategic Studies,* February 2007.

Boyne, Sean. "Iraqi Tactics Attempted to Employ Guerilla Forces." *Jane's Intelligence Review,* July 2003.

Brown, Air Commodore Geoff, RAAF. "Iraq: Operations Bastille and Falconer —2003." In *Air Expeditionary Operations from World War II until Today,* ed. Commander Keith Brent, RAAF. Canberra, Australia: Proceedings of the 2008 RAAF History Conference, April 1, 2008.

Burger, Kim, Nick Cook, Andrew Koch, and Michael Sirak. "What Went Right?" *Jane's Defence Weekly,* April 30, 2003.

Butler, Amy. "As A-10 Shines in Iraq War, Officials Look to JSF for Future CAS Role." *Inside the Air Force,* May 23, 2003.

———. "Data Links a Solid Weapon against Scuds, Friendly Fire, Jumper Says." *Inside the Air Force,* April 11, 2003.

———. "Iraq War Underscores Need for Improved and Standardized AOCs." *Inside the Air Force,* May 16, 2003.

———. "JSTARS Faced 'Learning Curve' for CAOC Officials Unfamiliar with System." *Inside the Air Force,* May 30, 2003.

———. "Lack of Embedded Reporters a Hurdle for Air Force Media Ops." *Inside the Air Force,* April 4, 2003.

———. "Moseley: Time-Sensitive Targeting Improved from Afghanistan to Iraq." *Inside the Air Force,* June 20, 2003.

Byman, Daniel, Kenneth Pollack, and Matthew Waxman. "Coercing Saddam Hussein: Lessons from the Past." *Survival,* autumn 1998.

Capaccio, Tony. "U.S. Commanders Wore General Dynamics Transmitters." Bloomberg.com, April 30, 2003.

Carpenter, Col. Mason, USAF. "Rapid, Deliberate, Disciplined, Proportional, and Precise: Operation Iraqi Freedom Air and Space Operations—Initial Assessment." Unpublished paper.

"CENTCOM, Pentagon Confirm Destruction of GPS Jamming Equipment." *Defense Daily,* March 26, 2003.

Chapman, Suzann. "The 'War' before the War." *Air Force Magazine,* February 2004.

Cook, Nick. "Shock and Awe?" *Jane's Defence Weekly,* April 2, 2003.

Cordesman, Anthony H. "The 'Instant Lessons' of the Iraq War: Main Report." Third working draft. Center for Strategic and International Studies, Washington, D.C., April 14, 2003.

———. "Understanding the New 'Effects-Based' Air War in Iraq." Center for Strategic and International Studies, Washington, D.C., March 15, 2003.

Cortes, Lorenzo. "Air Force F-117s Open Coalition Air Strikes with EGBU-27s." *Defense Daily*, March 21, 2003.

———. "Air Force Integrated Litening Pods for Block 40 and Block 50 F-16s Before OIF." *Defense Daily*, June 20, 2003.

———. "Air Force Offered Improved Networking Capabilities during OIF." *Defense Daily*, June 4, 2003.

———. "B-1 Crews Moved Quickly with JDAM Loads during Iraqi Freedom, Pilot Says." *Defense Daily*, April 22, 2003.

———. "B-2 Drops Pair of 4,700-Pound GBH-37 GAMs on Iraqi Communications Tower." *Defense Daily*, March 31, 2003.

———. "Coalition Forces Have Fired 15,000 Guided Munitions during Iraqi Freedom." *Defense Daily*, April 11, 2003.

———. "Combined Air Operations Center Crews Credit TBMCS and IWS for OIF Success." *Defense Daily*, June 3, 2003.

———. "Leaf: Iraq Air Defenses Were Dense, Antiquated in OIF; Stealth Needed in Future." *Defense Daily*, June 9, 2003.

———. "Leaf Says Severe Weather Accelerated Iraqi Forces' Defeat." *Defense Daily*, June 5, 2003.

———. "Operation Iraqi Freedom Required Unique Wartime Use of E-8C Joint STARS." *Defense Daily*, June 11, 2003.

———. "Patriots Intercept Eight Iraqi Ballistic Missiles, Involved in Two Friendly Fire Incidents." *Defense Daily*, March 28, 2003.

———. "Seizure of Tallil Base Improved A-10's Effectiveness in Iraqi Freedom, Commander Says." *Defense Daily*, April 18, 2003.

Costa, Keith J. "Draft JFCOM 'Lessons Learned' Study Examines Early Iraq War Moves." *Inside the Pentagon*, March 18, 2004.

"Defense Watch." *Defense Daily*, November 12, 2002.

Deptula, Lt. Gen. David A., USAF. "Toward Restructuring National Security." *Strategic Studies Quarterly*, winter 2007.

Di Pasquale, Cynthia. "Russian Planes Expand U.S. Airlift Capability Strained during OIF, OEF." *Inside the Air Force*, April 2, 2004.

Dobbins, James. "Iraq: Winning the Unwinnable War." *Foreign Affairs*, January–February 2005.

"DoD Says Russian Sale of GPS Jammers to Iraq Not Affecting Air Campaign." *Inside the Pentagon*, March 27, 2003.

Dolson, Paul. "Expeditionary Airborne Battlefield Command and Control." *Joint Force Quarterly*, no. 38, fourth quarter, 2005.

Ebbutt, Giles. "UK Command and Control during Iraqi Freedom." *Jane's Intelligence Review*, July 2003.

Feiler, Jeremy. "CSIS Report: U.S. Victory in Iraq Showed 'Flexibility' of U.S. Planning." *Inside the Pentagon*, May 1, 2003.

———. "Draft Study Says Technology, Iraqi 'Ineptitude' Key to Victory." *Inside the Pentagon*, October 2, 2003.

———. "Goldwater-Nichols Changes Key to U.S. Success in Iraq, Pace Says." *Inside the Pentagon*, September 25, 2003.

———. "Iraqi Campaign Lessons Show Shift to 'Overmatching Power' Doctrine." *Inside the Pentagon*, October 9, 2003.

———. "Officials: UAV Lessons among Most Vital Gleaned in Iraq War." *Inside the Pentagon*, July 17, 2003.

———. "Pentagon Officials Examine UAV 'Lessons Learned' in Iraq." *Inside the Pentagon*, December 11, 2003.

———. "Speed, Unpredictability Led to Victory in Iraq, Defense Officials Say." *Inside the Pentagon*, March 4, 2004.

Flibbert, Andrew. "The Road to Baghdad: Ideas and Intellectuals in Explanations of the Iraq War." *Security Studies*, April–June 2006.

Fox, Capt. Mark I., USN. "Air Wing of Destiny." *Foundation* (published by the Naval Aviation Museum Foundation), fall 2004.

Fulghum, David A. "Fast Forward." *Aviation Week and Space Technology*, April 28, 2003.

———. "Frustrations and Backlogs." *Aviation Week and Space Technology*, March 10, 2003.

———. "New Bag of Tricks: As Stealth Aircraft and Northern Watch Units Head Home, Details of the Coalition's Use of Air Power Are Revealed." *Aviation Week and Space Technology*, April 21, 2003.

———. "Tanker Puzzle: Aggressive Tactics, Shrinking Tanker Force Challenge Both Planners and Aircrews." *Aviation Week and Space Technology*, April 14, 2003.

Gething, Michael J., Mark Hewish, and Joris Hanssen Lok. "New Pods Aid Air Reconnaissance." *Jane's International Defence Review*, October 2003.

Gildea, Kerry. "Air Force Says TBMCS Played Critical Role in Air War Execution." *Defense Daily*, May 6, 2003.

———. "Ammunition Stocks Ready for War, Navy, Marine Corps Leaders Report." *Defense Daily*, February 27, 2003.

———. "Next-Generation Imaging Satellite Team Formed with News of Bush Policy Shift." *Defense Daily*, May 14, 2003.

Givens, Lt. Col. Rob, USAF. "'Let Slip the Dogs of War': Leadership in the Air War over Iraq." Term paper, National War College, Washington, D.C., 2005.

"Global Hawk Feats in Iraq Could Lead to ISR Fleet Lessons." *Inside the Pentagon*, May 29, 2003.

Gordon, John IV, and Bruce Pirnie. "'Everybody Wanted Tanks': Heavy Forces in Operation Iraqi Freedom." *Joint Force Quarterly*, October 2005.

Grant, Rebecca. "Saddam's Elite in the Meat Grinder." *Air Force Magazine*, September 2003.

Green, Col. Robert B., USAR. "Joint Fires Support, the Joint Fires Element and the CGRS: Keys to Success for CJSOTF West." *Special Warfare*, April 2005.

Grossman, Elaine M. "A-10 Aircraft Took Heavy Fire while Performing Unusual Mission." *Inside the Air Force*, April 11, 2003.

———. "Air Chief Won Ability to Hit Iraqi Bridges to Prevent Scud Launch." *Inside the Pentagon*, June 12, 2003.

———. "Air Force Aims to Redirect $40 Million in FY03 to Counter GPS Jamming." *Inside the Pentagon*, January 30, 2003.

———. "Air Force May Expand Significantly on Army Battlefield Tracking System." *Inside the Pentagon*, November 6, 2003.

———. "Battle Damage Assessment Process Found Unwieldy in Iraq Combat." *Inside the Pentagon*, June 19, 2003.

———. "Coalition Drops 'Capitulation Leaflets' over Iraqi Troops." *Inside the Pentagon*, March 20, 2003.

———. "Coalition Will Calibrate Force to Limit Casualties in Baghdad Attacks." *Inside the Air Force*, April 4, 2003.

———. "Critics Decry 2002 Air Attacks on Iraq That Predated Key U.S., UN Votes." *Inside the Pentagon*, July 24, 2003.

———. "Decision to Hasten Ground Attack into Iraq Presented New Risks." *Inside the Pentagon*, March 18, 2004.

———. "Evolving Threats May Offer Air Force 'Unlearned Lessons' in Iraq." *Inside the Pentagon*, July 17, 2003.

———. "First Attacks on Coalition Were Iraqi Missiles Aimed at Kuwait." *Inside the Air Force*, March 21, 2003.

———. "General: War-Tested Air-Land Coordination Cell Has Staying Power." *Inside the Air Force*, March 12, 2004.

———. "Giambastiani Flags Battle Damage, Friendly Fire 'Lessons Learned.'" *Inside the Pentagon*, March 11, 2004.

————. "Iraq War Could Feature Unprecedented Air-Land Collaboration." *Inside the Pentagon*, February 13, 2003.

————. "JFCOM Draft Report Finds U.S. Forces Reverted to Attrition in Iraq." *Inside the Air Force*, March 26, 2004.

————. "Key Generals: Response to 'Fedayeen' a Vital Milestone in Iraq War." *Inside the Pentagon*, May 8, 2003.

————. "Land, Air Commands Struggled on Iraq Leaflet Timing, Coordination." *Inside the Pentagon*, June 26, 2003.

————. "Marine General: Iraq War Pause 'Could Not Have Come at Worse Time.'" *Inside the Pentagon*, October 2, 2003.

————. "U.S. Air Force Spent Millions on Turkish Bases Unused in Iraq War." *Inside the Pentagon*, August 14, 2003.

————. "U.S. Forces to Take Close Battlefield Approach into Baghdad Fight." *Inside the Pentagon*, March 20, 2003.

Hardesty, Capt. David C., USN. "Fix Net Centric for the Operators." *Proceedings*, September 2003.

Harrison, Lt. Cdr. Richard K., USN. "TacAir Trumps UAVs in Iraq." *Proceedings*, November 2003.

Hathaway, Lt. Col. David C., USAF. "Operational Assessment during Operation Iraqi Freedom—Assessment or Assumption?" Research report, Air War College, Maxwell AFB, Ala., May 25, 2005.

Hebert, Adam J. "Building Battlespace Awareness." *Air Force Magazine*, October 2003.

Hewish, Mark. "Out of CAOCs Comes Order." *Jane's International Defence Review*, May 2003.

Hewson, Robert. "Apache Operations over Karbala." *Jane's Intelligence Review*, July 2003.

Hinote, Maj. S. Clinton, USAF. "More Than Bombing Saddam: Attacking the Leadership in Operation Iraqi Freedom." Master's thesis, School of Advanced Air and Space Studies, Air University, Maxwell AFB, Ala., June 2006.

Hollis, Patrecia Slayden. "Trained, Adaptable, Flexible Forces = Victory in Iraq." Interview with Lt. Gen. W. Scott Wallace. *Field Artillery*, September–October 2003.

Holmes, Tony. "RAAF Hornets at War." *Australian Aviation*, January–February 2006.

Horner, Gen. Charles A., USAF (Ret.). "Operation Iraqi Freedom and the Transformation of War." *Aviation Week and Space Technology*, May 5, 2003.

Hukill, Lt. Col. Jeffrey, USAF (Ret.), and Daniel R. Mortensen. "Developing Flexible Command and Control of Air Power." *Air and Space Power Journal*, spring 2011.

Iraq Body Count Project. At http://www.iraqbodycount.org

Irwin, Sandra I. "Iraqi Freedom Tests Naval Aviation's Flexibility." *The Hook*, summer 2003.

———. "Naval Aviators Experience Success in Iraq, but Worry about the Future." *The Hook,* fall 2003.

Keating, Vice Adm. Timothy J., USN. "Naval Aviation Key to Iraqi Freedom Victory." *The Hook*, winter 2003.

———. "This Was a Different War." Interview in *Proceedings*, June 2003.

Keeter, Hunter. "B-1 Drops 2000-Pound JDAMs in 'Iraqi Leadership' Strike." *Defense Daily*, April 9, 2003.

———. "Cartwright: Threat Location, Prediction Capability Should Be Priorities." *Defense Daily*, April 30, 2003.

———. "Cebrowski: Iraq Shows Network-Centric Warfare Implementation." *Defense Daily*, April 23, 2003.

———. "Exercise Internal Look to Evaluate Joint Task Force Command Capability." *Defense Daily*, December 5, 2002.

———. "Navy Fire Control, Targeting Capability Improvements Shorten Strike Timeline." *Defense Daily*, March 21, 2003.

———. "Next Internal Look to Spotlight Deployable Command and Control." *Defense Daily*, October 31, 2002.

Kitfield, James. "Attack Always." *National Journal*, April 26, 2003.

Knights, Michael. "Iraqi Freedom Displays the Transformation of U.S. Air Power." *Jane's Intelligence Review*, May 2003.

———. "USA Learns Lessons in Time-Critical Targeting." *Jane's Intelligence Review*, July 2003.

Koch, Andrew. "Did Washington Underestimate Iraqi Resolve?" *Jane's Defence Weekly*, April 2, 2003.

———. "Information War Played Major Role in Iraq." *Jane's Defence Weekly*, July 23, 2003.

———. "Information Warfare Tools Rolled Out in Iraq." *Jane's Defence Weekly*, August 6, 2003.

Kopp, Carlo. "Intelligence, Surveillance and Reconnaissance in Operation Iraqi Freedom." *Defence Today*, June 2004.

———. "Iraqi Freedom—the Hammer and Anvil." *Australian Aviation*, May 2003.

Koven, Maj. Alexander L., USAF. "Improvements in Joint Forces: How Missteps during Operation Anaconda Readied USCENTCOM for Operation Iraqi Freedom." Research report, Air Command and Staff College, Maxwell AFB, Ala., April 2005.

Krane, Jim. "Pilotless Warriors Soar to Success." CBS News, April 25, 2003.

Laird, Melvin R. "Iraq: Learning the Lessons of Vietnam." *Foreign Affairs*, November–December 2005.

Lake, Darren. "How Different It All Is from the Last Gulf War." *Jane's Defence Weekly*, March 26, 2003.

Lambeth, Benjamin S. "Aerial Partners in Arms." *Joint Force Quarterly*, 2nd quarter 2008.

———. "Air Force–Navy Integration in Strike Warfare: A Role Model for Seamless Joint-Service Operations." *Naval War College Review*, winter 2008.

Liang, John. "JFCOM Commander Outlines 'Good' and 'Ugly' in Iraq Lessons Learned." *Inside the Pentagon*, March 25, 2004.

———. "Myers: Saddam Hussein Is a Legitimate Target." *Inside the Air Force*, March 21, 2003.

Lok, Joris Janssen. "Communication Weaknesses Endanger Allied Integration in U.S.-Led Air Campaigns." *Jane's International Defence Review*, March 2004.

Malone, Vice Adm. Michael, USN. "They Made a Difference." *The Hook*, summer 2003.

Matthews, Maj. Joseph G., USA. "The E-8 Joint Surveillance Target Attack Radar System Support to Counterinsurgency Operations." Research report, Air Command and Staff College, Maxwell AFB, Ala., April 11, 2006.

Mazetti, Mark, and Richard J. Newman. "The Seeds of Victory." *U.S. News and World Report*, April 21, 2003.

McCarthy, Terry. "What Ever Happened to the Republican Guard?" *Time*, May 12, 2003.

McGee, Lt. Col. Michael B. Jr., USAF. "Air-Ground Operations during Operation Iraqi Freedom: Successes, Failures and Lessons of Air Force–Army Integration." Research report, Air War College, Maxwell AFB, Ala., February 25, 2005.

McNamara, Lt. Col. Steve, USAF. "Assessing Air Power's Importance: Will the QDR [Quadrennial Defense Review] Debate Falter for Lack of Proper Analytic Tools?" *Armed Forces Journal International*, March 1997.

"Moseley Details 'The War before the War.'" *Air Force*, October 2003.

Muradian, Vago. "Allied Special Forces Took Western Iraq." *Defense News*, May 19, 2003.

———. "Payoffs Aided U.S. War Plan." *Defense News*, May 19, 2003.

Neuenswander, Col. Matthew D., USAF. "JCAS in Operation Anaconda—It's Not All Bad News." *Field Artillery*, May–June 2003.

Newman, Richard J. "Ambush at Najaf." *Air Force Magazine*, October 2003.

———. "The Joystick War." *U.S. News and World Report*, May 19, 2003.

Nichols, Rear Adm. David C. Jr., USN. "Reflections on Iraqi Freedom." *The Hook*, fall 2003.

"No Satisfaction, No Resignation." *The Economist* (London), October 29, 2011.

Pape, Robert A. "The True Worth of Air Power." *Foreign Affairs*, March–April 2004.

"Patriot Under Fire for Second Error." *Flight International*, April 8–14, 2003.

Paulsen, Cdr. James, USN. "Naval Aviation Delivered in Iraq." *Proceedings*, June 2003.

Rees, Elizabeth. "Old Predators Used as Decoys to Provoke Iraqi Air Defenses." *Inside the Air Force*, April 11, 2003.

———. "Standup of 484th AEW Proved Vital to Army, Air Force Ops Integration." *Inside the Air Force*, September 5, 2003.

———. "363rd AEW Weighs In on Ops Tempo, Force Strain, Enemy Air Defenses in War." *Inside the Air Force*, March 28, 2003.

———. "USAF Moves Space Forces Director back into Iraq Air Ops Center." *Inside the Air Force*, June 4, 2004.

Riggs, Robert. "Blue on Blue: How Did an Army Patriot Battery Shoot Down a Navy F-18?" *CBS 11 News* (Dallas–Fort Worth, Tex.), February 4, 2004. At http//:www.globalsecurity.org/news/2004/040505-patriot-shootdown.htm

Ripley, Tim. "Closing the Gap." *Jane's Defence Weekly*, July 2, 2003.

———. "Iraq Friendly Fire Was Worse Than Reported." *Jane's Defence Weekly*, July 16, 2003.

———. "Planning for Iraqi Freedom." *Jane's Intelligence Review*, July 2003.

Robinson, Linda. "The Men in the Shadows." *U.S. News and World Report*, May 19, 2003.

Rogers, Capt. David A., USN. "From the President: The Health of Your Tailhook Association." *The Hook*, fall 2003.

Scott, William B. "'Sweetening' GPS: Squadron Boosted GPS Accuracy 'Window' to Support Iraq Air Campaign." *Aviation Week and Space Technology*, June 9, 2003.

Scott, William B., and Craig Covault. "High Ground over Iraq." *Aviation Week and Space Technology*, June 9, 2003.

Sirak, Michael. "Interview with James Roche: Secretary of the U.S. Air Force." *Jane's Defence Weekly*, May 14, 2003.

———. "U.S. Air Force Reveals New Strike Munition." *Jane's Defence Weekly*, May 14, 2003.

Smith, Maj. Kenneth A., USAF. "Joint Transformation of Aerial Interdiction by Enhancing Kill-Box Operations." Research report, Air Command and Staff College, Air University, Maxwell AFB, Ala., April 2006.

"Speed Kills." *Inside the Pentagon*, April 10, 2003.

Stephens, Hampton. "At Rhein-Main, Activity Increases as U.S. Prepares for Iraq War." *Inside the Air Force*, February 28, 2003.

———. "B-1 Bomber Being Used in a Variety of Missions during Iraq War." *Inside the Air Force*, March 28, 2003.

———. "Deployments Force Cancellation of January Red Flag." *Inside the Air Force*, January 17, 2003.

———. "USAF Cancels Second Red Flag in a Row, Citing Lack of Available Assets." *Inside the Air Force*, March 14, 2003.

———. "Wind-Corrected Anti-armor Weapon Used for First Time in Iraq." *Inside the Air Force*, April 4, 2003.

"Storm Shadow Appears ahead of Official Entry into Service Date." *Flight International*, April 1–7, 2003.

Streetly, Martin. "Airborne Surveillance Assets Hit the Spot in Iraq." *Jane's Intelligence Review*, July 2003.

Thomas, Evan, and John Barry. "A Plan Under Attack." *Time*, April 7, 2003.

Thomas, Evan, and Martha Brandt. "The Education of Tommy Franks." *Time*, May 19, 2003.

———. "The Secret War." *Time*, April 21, 2003.

Thompson, Mark. "Opening with a Bang." *Time*, March 17, 2003.

Tirpak, John A. "The Blended Wing Goes to War." *Air Force Magazine*, October 2003.

"Top Navy Aviation Officials Predict Few Major Lessons from Iraq." *Inside the Pentagon*, May 22, 2003.

Trimble, Stephen. "Air Force's AMC Tallies Massive Airlift Effort for OIF." *Aerospace Daily*, May 29, 2003.

———. "Cebrowski: Iraq War Offers Clues for Transformation Agenda." *Aerospace Daily*, April 23, 2003.

Truver, Scott C. "The U.S. Navy in Review." *Proceedings*, May 2003, p. 94.

"Unmanned Systems: UAV Shows Effectiveness as a Targeting Platform." *Flight International*, April 22–28, 2003.

"U.S. Casualties in Iraq." At http://www.globalsecurity.org/military/ops/iraq_casualties.htm

"USAF Offers Details of Weapon Tailored for Iraq War." *Aerospace Daily*, May 5, 2003.

Wall, Robert. "E-War Ramps Up: EA-6B Prowler to Resume Traditional Radar-Jamming Role If Iraqi Conflict Escalates." *Aviation Week and Space Technology*, March 17, 2003.

———. "Rescue Enhancements: U.S. Air Force Helicopters Employ Longer-Range Guns and New Threat-Avoidance Technology." *Aviation Week and Space Technology*, June 16, 2003.

———. "Super Hornets at Sea: U.S. Navy's New F/A-18Es Are Showing Surprising Reliability and Added Endurance." *Aviation Week and Space Technology*, March 17, 2003.

———. "Time Runs Short: Final War Preparations Continue Even as Controversy Keeps a Start Date Uncertain." *Aviation Week and Space Technology*, March 17, 2003.

———. "Weather or Not: The F-14D Strike Fighter Can Now Drop Precision Weapons Even on Cloud-Shrouded Targets." *Aviation Week and Space Technology*, March 17, 2003.

"WCMD-Equipped Sensor Fuzed Weapons Dropped on Iraqi Vehicle Column." *Defense Daily*, April 3, 2003.

Whitcomb, Col. Darrel D., USAFR (Ret.). "Rescue Operations in the Second Gulf War." *Air and Space Power Journal*, spring 2005.

Willis, David. "Operation Iraqi Freedom." *International Air Power Review*, summer 2003.

Wood, David. "New Workhorse of U.S. Military: A Bomb with Devastating Effects." Newhouse.com, March 13, 2003.

Woods, Kevin, James Lacey, and Williamson Murray. "Saddam's Delusions: The View from the Inside." *Foreign Affairs*, May–June 2006.

Newspaper Articles

Allen, Mike, and Karen DeYoung. "Bush: U.S. Will Strike First at Enemies." *Washington Post*, June 2, 2002.

Allen, Mike, and Bradley Graham. "Franks Briefs Bush on War Plans, Says Military Is Ready." *Washington Post*, March 6, 2003.

Arkin, William M. "Fliers Rose to Occasion: In Iraq, a Pause Refreshed Ground Troops and Let Planes Inflict Major Damage." *Los Angeles Times*, June 1, 2003.

Baker, Peter. "Marine Predicts Brief Bombing, Then Land Assault." *Washington Post*, March 17, 2003.

Baker, Peter, and Rajiv Chandrasekaran. "Republican Guard Units Move South from Baghdad, Hit by U.S. Forces." *Washington Post*, March 27, 2003.

Barnard, Anne. "Death Lurks in Unspent U.S. 'Bomblets.'" *Boston Globe*, May 1, 2003.

Boudreaux, Richard. "Two Errant Missiles Fall in Turkey." *Los Angeles Times*, March 24, 2003.

Bowman, Tom. "U.S. Aims to Curtail Civilian Casualties." *Baltimore Sun*, March 5, 2003.

Broder, John M. "Allies Fan Out in Iraq—Resistance outside City Is Light." *New York Times,* April 9, 2003.

———. "General Franks Makes First Visit to Troops in the Battle Zone." *New York Times*, April 8, 2003.

Burns, Robert. "Key Section of City Is Taken in a Street-by-Street Fight." *New York Times*, April 9, 2003.

———. "U.S. Gulf Force Nears 300,000 as Commander, Bush Consult." *Philadelphia Inquirer*, March 5, 2003.

Cauchon, Dennis. "Why U.S. Casualties Were Low." *USA Today*, April 21, 2003.

Chandrasekaran, Rajiv, and Peter Baker. "As Marines Resume Advance, Army Fights Baghdad Defenders." *Washington Post*, April 2, 2003.

———. "Baghdad Hit Hard from Air as Ground Forces Regroup." *Washington Post*, March 28, 2003.

———. "Sandstorm Delays Army's Advance; Units Set to Hit Guard Near Capital." *Washington Post*, March 26, 2003.

Chandrasekaran, Rajiv, and Thomas E. Ricks. "U.S. Opens War with Strikes on Baghdad Aimed at Hussein." *Washington Post*, March 20, 2003.

Chandrasekaran, Rajiv, and Alan Sipress. "Army Has First Close Fighting with Republican Guard Units." *Washington Post*, April 1, 2003.

Cohen, Eliot. "No Way to Win a War." *Wall Street Journal*, December 7, 2006.

Cooper, Christopher, and Greg Jaffe. "U.S. Use of Saudi Air Base Shows Kingdom's Quiet Commitment." *Wall Street Journal*, March 12, 2003.

Crawley, Vince. "Less Is More." *Army Times*, April 21, 2003.

De Young, Karen. "Bush Cites Urgent Iraqi Threat." *Washington Post*, October 8, 2002.

De Young, Karen, and Colum Lynch. "Three Countries Vow to Block U.S. on Iraq." *Washington Post*, March 6, 2003.

"Flexibility: Rumsfeld Tactical Signature Writ Large." *London Daily Telegraph*, March 21, 2003.

Friedman, Thomas L. "If I Had One Wish." *New York Times*, October 4, 2006.

Gellman, Barton, and Dana Priest. "CIA Had Fix on Hussein." *Washington Post*, March 20, 2003.

Gordon, Michael R. "Allied Plan Would Encourage Iraqis Not to Fight." *New York Times*, March 11, 2003.

———. "American Forces Adapted to Friend and Foe." *New York Times*, April 10, 2003.

———. "Battle for Baghdad Begins in Area Surrounding Iraqi Capital." *New York Times*, April 2, 2003.

———. "The Goal Is Baghdad, but at What Cost?" *New York Times*, March 25, 2003.

———. "Pointing Finger, Bush Broadens His 'Doctrine.'" *New York Times*, January 30, 2002.

———. "Tightening a Noose." *New York Times*, April 4, 2003.

———. "The U.S. Battle Plan: Make Friends and War." *New York Times*, March 11, 2003.

Gordon, Michael R., with John F. Burns. "Iraq's Air Defense Is Concentrated around Baghdad." *New York Times*, March 17, 2003.

Graham, Bradley. "Air War Targets Enemy Troops." *Washington Post*, March 25, 2003.

———. "Patriot System Likely Downed U.S. Jet." *Washington Post*, April 4, 2003.

———. "Radar Probed in Patriot Incidents." *Washington Post*, May 8, 2003.

———. "U.S. Air Attacks Turn More Aggressive." *Washington Post*, April 2, 2003.

Graham, Bradley, and Vernon Loeb. "An Air War of Might, Coordination, and Risks, *Washington Post*, April 27, 2003.

Hackett, James. "Tracking Targets from Space." *Washington Times*, July 8, 2003.

Hedges, Stephen J. "Air War Credited in Baghdad's Fall." *Chicago Tribune*, April 22, 2003.

"Iraq Is Expected to Try Jamming U.S. Signals." *Baltimore Sun*, March 13, 2003.

Jaffe, Greg. "Plan Is to Cut Off Top Officers while Allies Strike Air Defenses." *Wall Street Journal*, March 20, 2003.

———. "Rumsfeld's Vindication Promises a Change in Tactics, Deployment." *Wall Street Journal,* April 10, 2003.

———. "U.S. Rushes to Upgrade Base for Attack Aircraft." *Wall Street Journal,* March 14, 2003.

Kaczor, Bill. "Air Force Chief Says Military Must Cooperate." *Miami Herald*, October 22, 2003.

Kelly, Jack. "Covert Troops Fight Shadow War Off-Camera." *USA Today*, April 7, 2003.

King, Laura. "Baghdad's Death Toll Assessed." *Los Angeles Times*, May 18, 2003.

Krauthammer, Charles. "Redefining the War." *Washington Post*, February 1, 2002.

————. "What Ever Happened to the Powell Doctrine?" *Washington Post*, April 20, 2001.

Layton, Lyndsey. "Building Bombs aboard the *Abraham Lincoln*." *Washington Post*, March 14, 2003.

"Letter Is Purported to Be from Saddam." *St. Louis Post-Dispatch*, May 11, 2003.

Loeb, Vernon. "Patriot Downs RAF Fighter." *Washington Post*, March 24, 2003.

————. "Pentagon Credits Success in Iraq War to Joint Operations." *Washington Post*, October 3, 2003.

————. "Sniping at the 'Plan' Strikes Some Nerves." *Washington Post*, April 2, 2003.

Lynch, David, and John Diamond. "U.S., British Forces Are 'Ready Today' for Invasion." *USA Today*, March 17, 2003.

Lynch, David J. "Marines Prevail in 'Toughest Day' of Combat." *USA Today*, March 24, 2003.

McManus, Doyle, and Esther Schrader. "Rumsfeld Support Is in High Places." *Los Angeles Times*, April 2, 2003.

McPeak, Merrill A. "Leave the Flying to Us." *Washington Post*, June 5, 2003.

————. "Shock and Pause." *New York Times*, April 2, 2003.

Milbank, Dana, and Mike Allen. "President Tells Hussein to Leave Iraq within 48 Hours or Face Invasion." *Washington Post*, March 18, 2003.

Moniz, Dave, and John Diamond. "Attack on Guard May Be Days Away." *USA Today*, March 31, 2003.

Moore, Charles. "Colin Powell: 'I'm Very Sore.'" *London Daily Telegraph*, February 26, 2005.

"Mr. Bush's UN Mandate." *Wall Street Journal*, November 11, 2002.

Murphy, Kim, and Alan C. Miller. "The Team That Picks the Targets." *Los Angeles Times*, March 25, 2003.

"No Bunker Found under Bomb Site." *New York Times*, May 29, 2003.

Pae, Peter. "'Friendly Fire' Still a Problem." *Los Angeles Times*, May 16, 2003.

Page, Susan. "War May Realign World and Define a Presidency." *USA Today*, March 17, 2003.

Pan, Philip P. "Turkey Lets U.S. Use Airspace." *Washington Post*, March 21, 2003.

————. "Turkish Leader Makes Request on Airspace." *Washington Post*, March 20, 2003.

"Persian Gulf Skies Crowded with Jets." *New York Times,* March 6, 2006.

Piller, Charles. "Vaunted Patriot Missile Has a 'Friendly Fire' Failing." *Los Angeles Times*, April 21, 2003.

Pincus, Walter, Bob Woodward, and Dana Priest. "Hussein's Fate Still Uncertain." *Washington Post*, March 21, 2003.

Pisik, Betsy. "Human Shields Take a Powder." *Washington Times*, March 5, 2003.

Richter, Paul. "Risky Fight for Baghdad Nears." *Los Angeles Times*, March 24, 2003.

Ricks, Thomas, and Alan Sipress. "Cuts Urged in Patrols over Iraq." *Washington Post*, May 9, 2001.

Ricks, Thomas E. "Calibrated War Makes Comeback." *Washington Post*, March 21, 2003.

———. "Myers Depicts War on Two Fronts." *Washington Post*, March 5, 2003.

———. "Unfolding Battle Will Determine Length of War." *Washington Post*, March 25, 2003.

———. "War Plan for Iraq Is Ready, Say Officials." *Washington Post*, November 10, 2002.

———. "What Counted: People, Plan, Inept Enemy." *Washington Post*, April 10, 2003.

Robbins, Carla Anne. "U.S. Nears War in Embrace of Strategy of Preemption." *Wall Street Journal,* March 18, 2003.

Robbins, Carla Anne, Greg Jaffe, and Dan Morse. "U.S. Aims at Psychological Front, Hoping Show of Force Ends War." *Wall Street Journal*, April 7, 2003.

Sanger, David E., with John F. Burns. "Bush Orders an Assault and Says America Will Disarm Foe." *New York Times*, March 20, 2003.

Sanger, David E., with Warren Hoge. "U.S. May Abandon UN Vote on Iraq, Powell Testifies." *New York Times*, March 14, 2003.

Sanger, David E., and Thom Shanker. "Bush Says Regime in Iraq Is No More: Victory 'Certain.'" *New York Times*, April 16, 2003.

Scarborough, Rowan. "Bush Convenes War Cabinet." *Washington Times*, March 6, 2003.

———. "General Tells How Cell Phone Foiled U.S. Attack in Iraq." *Washington Times*, May 8, 2003.

———. "Hovering Spy Plane Helps Rout Iraqis." *Washington Times*, April 3, 2003.

———. "Lightning Air Strikes, Then March to Baghdad." *Washington Times*, March 18, 2003.

———. "Myers Says 'Annihilation' of Iraqi Army Wasn't Goal." *Washington Times*, June 30, 2003.

————. "White House: 'We've Won.'" *Washington Times*, April 15, 2003.

Schmitt, Eric. "In the Skies over Iraq, Silent Observers Become Futuristic Weapons." *New York Times*, April 18, 2003.

————. "Pentagon Ready to Strike Iraq within Days If Bush Gives the Word, Officials Say." *New York Times,* March 6, 2003.

————. "Rumsfeld Says Important Targets Have Been Avoided." *New York Times*, March 24, 2003.

Schmitt, Eric, and Elisabeth Bumiller. "Top General Sees Plan to Shock Iraq into Surrender." *New York Times*, March 5, 2003.

Schmitt, Eric, with Dexter Filkins. "Erdogan to Form New Turkish Government as U.S. Presses for Use of Military Bases." *New York Times*, March 12, 2003.

Schrader, Esther, and Richard Boudreaux. "U.S. Seeks Overflights in Turkey." *Los Angeles Times*, March 12, 2003.

Shadid, Anthony. "Hussein's Baghdad Falls." *Washington Post*, April 10, 2003.

————. "In Shift, War Targets Communications Facilities." *Washington Post*, April 1, 2003.

Shanker, Thom. "Assessment of Iraq War Will Emphasize Joint Operations." *Washington Post*, May 1, 2003.

————. "Pentagon Criticizes High Rate of Allied Deaths by Allied Fire." *New York Times*, October 3, 2003.

————. "Risk of Being Killed by Own Side Increases." *New York Times*, April 8, 2003.

Shanker, Thom, and Eric Schmitt. "Rumsfeld Seeks Consensus through Jousting." *New York Times*, March 19, 2003.

Smith, Michael. "U.S. 'Clears' Crew Who Shot Down Tornado." *London Daily Telegram*, July 16, 2003.

Spiegel, Peter. "Thinking Ahead with the Pentagon's Planners." *London Financial Times*, April 16, 2003.

Squitieri, Tom. "What Could Go Wrong in War." *USA Today*, March 13, 2003.

Squitieri, Tom, and Dave Moniz. "U.S. War Plans: Blast Away Saddam's Support." *USA Today*, November 11, 2002.

Stevenson, Richard W. "As Diplomatic Effort Ends, President Vows to Act." *New York Times*, March 18, 2003.

Sullivan, Kevin, and Rajiv Chandrasekaran. "Hussein's Two Sons Killed in Firefight with U.S. Troops." *Washington Post*, July 22, 2003.

Svitak, Amy. "Force of the Future." *Army Times*, November 25, 2002.

Tweedie, Neil. "U.S. Fighter 'Shot Down with Missile Left by SBS.'" *London Daily Telegraph*, June 6, 2003.

Tweedie, Neil, and Michael Smith. "Britain 'To Play Full Role in Iraq Invasion.'" *London Daily Telegraph*, March 13, 2003.

Tyler, Patrick E. "Attack from Two Sides Shatters the Iraqi Republican Guard." *New York Times*, April 3, 2003.

———. "Iraq Is Planning Protracted War." *New York Times*, April 2, 2003.

———. "Two U.S. Columns Are Advancing on Baghdad." *New York Times*, April 1, 2003.

"U.S., Britain Double Daily Flights over Southern Iraq." *Baltimore Sun*, March 6, 2003.

Weir, Fred. "Iraqi Defeat Jolts Russian Military." *Christian Science Monitor*, April 16, 2003.

Weisman, Jonathan. "Patriot Missiles Seemingly Falter for Second Time." *Washington Post*, March 26, 2003.

———. "Rumsfeld and Myers Defend War Plan." *Washington Post*, April 2, 2003.

Williams, Carol J. "Navy Does Battle with Sandstorms on the Sea." *Los Angeles Times*, March 27, 2003.

———. "Super Hornet Creates a Buzz in the Gulf." *Los Angeles Times*, April 1, 2003.

Briefings

"Air Support Operations Center (ASOC) Employment." Briefing presented at the Air Force Doctrine Summit IV, sponsored by the Air Force Doctrine Center, Maxwell AFB, Ala., November 17, 2003.

Darnell, Maj. Gen. Daniel J., USAF. "Operation Iraqi Freedom." Undated briefing.

Moseley, Lt. Gen. T. Michael, USAF. "Operation Iraqi Freedom: Initial CFACC Roll-up." Briefing given at a CENTAF-sponsored symposium to assess and document allied air operations during the three weeks of major combat in Operation Iraqi Freedom, Nellis AFB, Nev., July 18, 2003.

Neal, Curt. "JAGO [Joint Air Ground Office of Air Combat Command] ASOC Tiger Team: ASOC/TACP Reorganization to Support UEx [Unit of Employment 'X']." Briefing slides, USAF Air Ground Operations School, Nellis AFB, Nev., 2005.

Nichols, Vice Adm. David C., USN. "Operation Iraqi Freedom: CFACC/CAOC/NALE." Briefing by the then deputy combined force air component commander, Operation Iraqi Freedom, no date.

"Operation Iraqi Freedom." Briefing charts, 32nd Army Air and Missile Defense Command, Fort Bliss, Tex., September 2003.

"RAF Contribution to Operation Iraqi Freedom." Briefing by 23 Squadron, RAF Waddington, October 29, 2004.

Simpson, Lt. Col. Mark, USAF. "Air Power Lessons from Operation Iraqi Freedom." ACC/XPSX, Headquarters Air Combat Command, Langley AFB, Va., November 25, 2003.

Thompson, Loren B. "ISR Lessons of Iraq." Briefing prepared for the *Defense News* ISR Integration Conference, Washington, D.C., November 18, 2003.

Wallace, Lt. Gen. William S., USA. "Joint Effects in OIF [Operation Iraqi Freedom]: A V Corps Perspective." Briefing slides, U.S. Army Combined Arms Center, Fort Leavenworth, Kans., no date.

————. "Joint Fires in OIF [Operation Iraqi Freedom]: What Worked for the V (U.S.) Corps." Briefing slides, U.S. Army Combined Arms Center, Fort Leavenworth, Kans., no date.

Interviews

Brown, Group Captain Geoff, RAAF, Operation Falconer air component commander, April 9, 2008. Official interview provided to the author by the RAAF Air Power Development Center, Canberra, Australia.

Halupka, Group Captain Otto, RAAF, Operation Falconer air planner, May 14, 2008. Official interview provided to the author by the RAAF Air Power Development Center, Canberra, Australia.

Henman, Group Captain Bill, RAAF, Operation Falconer commander of the air combat wing, April 9, 2007. Official interview provided to the author by the RAAF Air Power Studies Center, Canberra, Australia.

Hill, Senator the Honorable Robert, Minister for Defense. Press interview, RAAF Base Richmond, New South Wales, Australia, February 7, 2003.

Hupfeld, Wing Commander Melvin, RAAF, Operation Falconer commanding officer No. 75 Squadron, September 16, 2003. Official interview provided to the author by the RAAF Air Power Development Center, Canberra, Australia.

Keir, Wing Commander Richard, RAAF, Operation Falconer air element headquarters chief of intelligence and targeting, February 19, 2007. Official interview provided to the author by the RAAF Air Power Development Center, Canberra, Australia.

McKiernan, Lt. Gen. David D., USA. Interview, U.S. Army Center of Military History, Washington, D.C., June 30, 2003.

INDEX

Afghanistan: Anaconda operation, 39–40, 187, 189, 297, 324n121; collateral damage and casualties in, 276; Iraqi Freedom plans and concurrent war in, 31; study of war in, xiii; terrorist attacks and offensive against Taliban, 11–12. *See also* Enduring Freedom, Operation

Air Combat Command, 29, 32–33, 274, 276, 293–94, 320n77

air component coordination element (ACCE), 39–40, 187–88, 191–92, 324n121, 324n123

Air Force, U.S.: adaptability of, ix; ASOC operations, 266–69, 384n93; deployment orders and flow of forces, 38–39; Iraqi Freedom role of, 1–2, 4; munitions requirements and interservice trading, 320n76; no-fly zones, enforcement of, 1, 147, 313n1; professionalism of, ix; reporters embedded with units, 6; traditional roles of land and air power, 239–41; training exercises and air-ground integration training, 38, 147, 176–77, 361n105; Turkey airspace and operations of, 55; working relationship between Navy and, 137, 350n321

Air Forces Central (AFCENT), xiii. *See also* Central Command Air Forces (CENTAF)

Air Forces in Europe, U.S. (USAFE), 32, 319n60

air offensive: accounts of and writings about, 6–7, 315–16n18, 371n122; achievements and success of, 51, 123–29, 137–46, 236, 242–43, 289–92, 310–11; A-day and ATOs, 41, 48–49, 50, 51, 82–84, 90–95, 339n133, 339n143; air assets, coordination between and integration of, x–xi; air strikes and fighting capacity of enemy, 4, 5, 7, 295–97, 304;

air-only operations, 22, 23–24, 48–49, 53–55, 75, 82–84, 289–90, 327n156; concurrent air-ground operations, x, 1–2, 18, 19–20, 74, 95–111, 299–300; effects on Iraqi ground forces, 4, 5, 7, 127–29, 137–46, 236, 295–97, 304; effects-based operations, 23, 33, 295–97; embedded journalist restrictions, 6–7; force improvements for, ix; ground offensive liaison, 40–41; ground-air power integration and coordination, x, 1–2, 4–5, 18, 20, 27–28, 33, 48–49, 53–55, 187–97, 315nn15–16, 321n89; kinetic operations, 16, 36; management organization and structure, 33; merge meeting about, 24; multiple mission demands, x; munitions requirements, 24, 29, 31, 320n76; objectives for, 20, 34, 53–54; objectives for, success in securing, xiii; on-call strike operations, 35; planning and execution concerns, 44, 46; planning and preparations for, 24–25, 31–36, 43–44, 317n18, 321nn88–89, 322n102; quality-control checks on plans, 49; sorties flown, 81, 137, 178–80, 199, 212, 241, 295; speed and tempo of operations, 102–11, 145–46, 178, 344n207; SPINs release to aircrews, 57–58, 329–30n197; strategic air operations, 5, 35, 315n15; strategic role of, ix; tactical objectives and tasks, 34; timing of and timeline for, 28–30, 35–36, 46, 53–55, 57–58, 75, 93, 329n194; training for, ix; trust relationships and cross-service harmony, x, 28, 29, 290–91, 292, 302–4, 319n60, 391n12. *See also* fuel supplies and refueling operations

air power: achievements during campaign, 178–87; air asset advances and, 304–5, 395n73; air-ground integration training, 269, 292–93, 383–84n89, 385n104,

Royal Air Force (RAF): achievements and performance during campaign, 163–69, 175–77, 358nn68–69, 359n78; air offensive planning, 28; air-ground power integration and coordination, 270–71; command and control structure, 151–54, 175–76; force strength, 157–59, 356n41; information sharing and force interoperability, 282–87, 389n153, 390n156, 390n161; Iraqi Freedom role of, ix, xiii, 1–2, 4–5; no-fly zones, enforcement of, 1, 147, 313n1; planning, participation in, 155–56; planning and preparations for campaign, 32; relationships among coalition forces, 28, 29, 147–48, 168, 176–77; target identification and selection, 161–62; training exercises and air-ground integration training, 147, 176–77, 361n105; warfighter conference, 29

Royal Australian Air Force (RAAF): achievements and performance during campaign, 163, 169–75, 359n82, 360n86, 360n97; aircraft from, 346n236; force strength, 159–60, 356n47; Iraqi Freedom role of, ix, xiii, 1–2, 4–5; planning and preparations for campaign, 31, 32; relationships among coalition forces, 149, 163; target identification and selection, 162–63, 357n59; training exercises and air-ground integration training, 176–77, 361n105

Rumsfeld, Donald: air defense responses, 62, 66, 331n28; combat operations planning and briefing sessions, 49; commitment of U.S. to regime change in Iraq, 11; CRAF activation, 39; decapitation opportunity, 75; deployment orders, 36–37, 322–23n106; Desert Storm outcome, 9–10; Enduring Freedom leadership role, 5; force strength for peace and nation-building, 306–7; groundwork for war, 12, 15, 317n19; initiation of war, 42–43; Iraqi Freedom leadership role, 5; OPLAN 1003V acceptance, 28; planning and preparations for campaign, 12, 15–16, 18–19, 26–28, 31; postwar Iraq, planning for, 352n350; prewar briefing, 52; shock and awe campaign, 36, 322n102; ultimatum to Hussein, 43

sandstorms, 2, 29, 100–110, 132–33, 260, 289, 342n178, 343n204, 344n207

satellite communications systems, 221, 366–67n72, 372n132

Saudi Arabia: airspace use and overflight approval, 56, 135–36; bases in and combat and combat-support operations conducted from, 17, 35, 41, 43, 44, 45, 277; combined air operations center in, 6, 18, 33, 50–51, 207, 210–11, 218, 221; Scud missile attacks on, 333–34n68; visual observation posts near, 56

Scud missiles: control of missile sites, 20–21, 43, 56, 319nn49–50; counter-Scud operations, x, 71–73, 94, 227–28, 333–34n68; counter-Scud operations, planning for, 29, 320n77; counter-Scud operations, training for, 385n104, 391–92n17; Desert Storm use of, 20–21, 72, 333–34n68; location and destruction of, x; number and range of, 319n50; targeting of, 35, 44, 328–29n190

September 11, 2001, terrorist attacks, xiii, 2, 11, 15, 44, 47, 288, 391n4

shock and awe campaign, 36, 90, 93, 94, 141, 322n102, 340n149

SIPRNet (secure Internet protocol router network), 185, 198, 215, 282–83, 285–87, 389n153

Slipper, Operation, 149, 156, 285, 354n12, 356n40

Southern Focus, Operation, 26, 51, 54, 61–66, 69–71, 80, 82, 118, 207, 290, 323n117, 331n28, 354n3, 359n82

Southern Watch, Operation, 1, 18, 24, 25, 26, 37, 39, 50, 57, 58, 61–71, 142, 178, 285, 313n1, 318n42, 329n196, 329n197, 368n81

Special Operations Forces (SOF): air offensive to support, x, 20, 24, 71–74, 123–24; air-ground power integration and, 28, 301; force strength, 72; goals and objectives of operations, 56–57; missions and operations, 16, 17, 26, 27, 56–57, 70, 71–74, 81, 334n74; planning operations, 25; psychological warfare campaign, 373–74n154; reconnaissance operations, 41; timing of and timeline for operations, 21, 28–30, 56–57, 75; training of, 301, 385n104

About the Author

Benjamin S. Lambeth is a Senior Fellow with the Center for Strategic and Budgetary Assessments, a position he assumed in 2011 following a thirty-seven-year career at the RAND Corporation. A long-time specialist in international security affairs and air warfare, he has extensive flight experience in more than forty different combat aircraft types worldwide. He is the author of *The Transformation of American Air Power*.

The Naval Institute Press is the book-publishing arm of the U.S. Naval Institute, a private, nonprofit, membership society for sea service professionals and others who share an interest in naval and maritime affairs. Established in 1873 at the U.S. Naval Academy in Annapolis, Maryland, where its offices remain today, the Naval Institute has members worldwide.

Members of the Naval Institute support the education programs of the society and receive the influential monthly magazine *Proceedings* or the colorful bimonthly magazine *Naval History* and discounts on fine nautical prints and on ship and aircraft photos. They also have access to the transcripts of the Institute's Oral History Program and get discounted admission to any of the Institute-sponsored seminars offered around the country.

The Naval Institute's book-publishing program, begun in 1898 with basic guides to naval practices, has broadened its scope to include books of more general interest. Now the Naval Institute Press publishes about seventy titles each year, ranging from how-to books on boating and navigation to battle histories, biographies, ship and aircraft guides, and novels. Institute members receive significant discounts on the Press's more than eight hundred books in print.

Full-time students are eligible for special half-price membership rates. Life memberships are also available.

For a free catalog describing Naval Institute Press books currently available, and for further information about joining the U.S. Naval Institute, please write to:

Member Services
U.S. Naval Institute
291 Wood Road
Annapolis, MD 21402-5034
Telephone: (800) 233-8764
Fax: (410) 571-1703
Web address: www.usni.org